SHADE HOUSE CONVERSATIONS

SHADE HOUSE CONVERSATIONS

The Story of an American Family

Colette Waddell

Published by Topcat Press

This book is dedicated to the Yazzie family and their kin.
Thank you for allowing me to be part of your lives.
Coco - Woman Who Asks Many Questions

Special thanks to my dear friend and book shepherd, Lori Krein. This book would never have become a reality without your help.

Shade House
ISBN-13: 978-0-9791518-1-1

Cover art by Kee Yazzie

Contents

AUTHOR'S PREFACE

"We will be known forever by the tracks we leave." — Lakota

OFF THE BEATEN PATH

Effie Yazzie and I drove deep into the heart of Monument Valley in my rented four-wheel Explorer. I maneuvered the wiggling steering wheel as we bounced along on the Arizona portion of the Navajo Indian Reservation. This certainly wasn't like any of the 'real' roads I knew back in my world, but I wasn't home anymore. Out here we were definitely off the beaten path, heading toward a destination most folks could barely imagine, let alone locate without difficulty. Would we become mired in the loose bits of gravel that threatened to bring our excursion to a halt? I sent out my usual silent prayers to the Travel Gods, and asked them to please keep us safe while we rolled toward the massive stone formation ahead.

The sand grew deep, but Effie maintained her usual cool. This part of the valley was virtually her back yard, and I relied on her confidence and innate sense of direction to get us through the open sea of red-orange dirt that surrounded us and licked at our tires. We fishtailed through a little canyon until my companion slowly pointed to a clearing along the monolith known as Little Dragon. "It's right over there." She directed us to the spot where her brother, Lonnie, waited.

Lonnie Yazzie and I had become quite close after hours upon hours in deep conversation, covering topics both great and small. We eventually became dear comrades in the shared quest to record his family's history. The task began at Lonnie's request in 1997, two years after my husband and I met him on a horseback riding excursion in 1995. Although we were from completely different worlds, we somehow managed to find a connection. Over the course of some twelve years our friendship grew. That friendship led to Lonnie, along with five of his family, sharing their stories with me. Initially I focused on recording Lonnie's mother, Suzie Yazzie, and her recollection of family history and legend. She was the matriarch, vibrant and active even at the time of our meeting when she was in her eighties. My small plan of recording only Suzie quickly grew much more ambitious, and in no time most of the family of six and their relations was involved in the project. I grew especially close to Lonnie's sister Effie, his wife Emily, and Effie's daughter, Elvina. Suzie spoke only her native Navajo tongue, and every time one of the Yazzies translated the old woman's words, some personal anecdote inevitably slipped out. These diversions were to become a rich source of still more stories that make up the Yazzie history.

I learned about life in the reservation from the early 19th century to the present, about the harsh treatment of all the Navajo, but especially to the children stuck inside oppressive Indian boarding schools. Most importantly, I recorded the Yazzie's vast dreams, numerous disappointments, and their commitment to keeping the Navajo traditions alive over the years. We spent many long days in conversation, and I eventually became a sort of adopted sister and honored to be given my own Navajo name "asdzani' na'idishkid lai' na'idikid," which means "Woman Who Asks Many Questions." Perfect. Over a ten year period, from 1997 to 2005 I hung out, collected stories, and worked with the family whenever I could make my way to the reservation. By 2006 their story grew from a collection of anecdotes into a full scale manuscript.

THE PHONE CALL, MAY 2006
"The rain falls on the just and the unjust." – Hopi

I was sitting in my bedroom that beautiful spring day in California. I kept wondering – should I write, or go outside and enjoy the fine weather? That's when the phone rang. Startled, I ran to pick it up and heard a distraught Effie. There had been "a terrible automobile accident." She told me her family needed me. I was touched and concerned and considered flying out immediately. But I took a moment and wondered how best to help. I decided to send the money I would have spent on a fast flight directly to the Yazzies. I knew they were now desperate for cash. I felt awful about not being there personally for the family I had grown to love. But I had to be pragmatic. This was one of many lessons they had taught me. I sent money to help out, vowing to travel out to see them as soon as possible. Sadly, life and circumstances didn't allow me to make it back to the valley until that fall.

Some months later…

Effie and I sat quite still after I parked the car, until by some unspoken agreement we simultaneously stepped onto the soft and welcoming red earth. The desert stillness was shattered only by the sound of our metal doors slamming shut, and the movement caused a layer of dirt to slide off my filthy rental car. The sand moved in a little wave, reminding me of a dog shaking hard after his bath. Effie stepped quickly ahead of me toward something in the distance. I trudged behind her through ankle deep soil. My eyes hadn't adjusted to the bright desert sun. Eventually I could make out a raised bit of earth surrounded by a crude wire fence partially covered with the relentless sand of Monument Valley. Effie stopped at a locked gate on one side, and motioned to a small placard within the modest memorial. We stood side by side and gazed at the lonesome mound. The rusting metal of the knee-high enclosure was meant more to mark the perimeter of this now sacred place rather than to secure it from unlikely human invasion. A light breeze tickled the silk petals of faded fake lilies someone had thrust into the dirt long ago. Flowers like that certainly did not grow on the reservation. They must have been purchased last spring from a craft store, possibly from as far away as Flagstaff, Arizona. The rocks jutting up on either side of the mound regarded us in reverent silence, the sun burned our shoulders, and we stood perfectly still…remembering.

INTRODUCTION

"Walk on a rainbow trail; walk on a trail of song, and all about you will be beauty. There is a way of every dark mist, over a rainbow trail." – Edward A. Navajo

MEET THE YAZZIES

Suzie Yazzie was born into the Cly family, probably around 1920. She was raised in Monument Valley. She became well-known in the area, not only for her beautiful weaving, but also for appearing in the John Ford movies; films like "Cheyenne Autumn," "The Searchers," and many others that eventually made the valley a tourist attraction and also typecast the Navajo as the generic "Red Man," so popular in the early twentieth century. Suzie also successfully raised five children; Harvey, Leonard, Lonnie, Effie and Kee.

I spent many hours listening to Suzie spin her stories, and any time my husband Ross decided to join me on my expedition, Lonnie would find a way to kidnap him. Lonnie was Suzie's middle child. He was one of the sons who spent time in the Valley caring for the old woman, and he loved to whisk Ross away on the premise of "finding wood" or "collecting water." But I knew they were headed to mysterious destinations within Lonnie's beloved homeland. After disappearing for hours the "boys" would then storm Suzie's little home, interrupting our work to relay some adventure they'd shared. When we weren't working in the Shade House or the hogan Suzie and I were in "Tully's house." Built sometime in the late 1950s by her deceased husband, Tully had drawn upon the carpentry skills acquired over the years and provided his wife with a dwelling that was more spacious than the nearby hogan made of juniper logs and dried earth.

The more conventional home had a main room that doubled as a sort of kitchen with a crude stovetop flanked by shelves of canned food and sacks of dry goods. There was a proper wood stove in the center of the room, and it was here where Suzie slept and kept most of her belongings. An extra wing off the side of the house provided extra storage and held two bunk beds maintained for family visits. There was no electricity, no running water, and the only "bathroom" was the ramshackle outhouse many steps outside in back of the house.

Suzie and I logged hundreds of hours huddled around that wood stove and deep in female conversation. Suzie's daughter or daughter-in-law would patiently translate some story about the past that drew me deeper and deeper into the Navajo world. So involved were we in our project that the commotion of Lonnie and Ross bursting into the little house broke us abruptly out of one world and into the present one. The boys paid no mind to our disapproving looks. They only stomped the sand or snow off their feet, depending on the season. Every time I asked where they had been I received the same answer, often in unison: *"You don't want to know!"* The two men kept a pact of silence about these adventures, and their private escapades where only a few Navajo ventured remained a secret. And so, whenever I telephoned Lonnie from California saying Ross would be joining me on my next visit I heard a deep, knowing chuckle. *"Better rent a four-wheel drive,"* was his typical reply.

I AM NOT NAVAJO

"...I have seen full-bloods who have virtually no idea of the great legacy entrusted to their care. Yet, I have seen people with as little as 1/500th blood quantum who inspire the spirits of their ancestors because they make being Cherokee a proud part of their everyday life." — Jim Pell, Principal Chief of the North Alabama Cherokee Tribe

I am not Navajo, but an Anglo-Saxon. Yes, a blue-eyed white woman born and raised in a number of states throughout America. As a Navy Brat I learned to make friends very quickly because, after all I might not be in any particular town for very long. A series of dismal jobs and one failed marriage brought me back to college and eventual success in obtaining my degree in history and anthropology. I had also found my soul mate, Ross while working at a major U.S. corporation, and instantly acquired a family of four children.

Writing down my thoughts and experiences was a habit instilled by my mother, who is also a writer. I think I must have enjoyed writing all of my life, but I did not truly begin to embrace this skill until I met the Yazzies on a trip between school semesters to the southwest. By chance, intention, great luck, and circumstance, I have had the rare opportunity to spend precious time with the Yazzies, an extended Navajo family. In the process of gathering their stories, I kept a personal diary as well. After I reviewed my hours of transcriptions from a long day of 'story' I began the ritual of taking a break to review my own daily journal entries. I realized it made sense to integrate the personal into the collective as a way of building a manuscript that could engage a reader on multiple dimensions. Not only could I provide the essential facts of the Yazzie's story; I also had the opportunity to reveal the personalities of each family member and how they felt as human beings, and processed their unique experience as individuals inside an extended family.

It wasn't easy to know exactly when the Yazzie story was complete, but when I had recorded three generation's worth of history I sensed I had plenty to work with. By that time I realized the Yazzie family had become an integral part of my own story as well. I could see that my interaction with this loving and multifaceted group of people was best revealed if I presented my personal diary along with it. As their story unfolded my diary somehow revealed another side of the personalities of each family member. My relations with them could be described in a way that went beyond the study of an ethnographer with his subject. My hope is that these entries, in conjunction with the interview and research information, will illustrate the magic and wonder of Monument Valley and the people who live there.

STRADDLING THE FENCE
"If we wonder often, the gift of knowledge will come." - Arapaho

I struggled over how to begin this story, and more importantly how to meld my own perceptions of the Yazzies with what they truly are. The observer always affects the observed. Most of the time we don't think about this dynamic, but when I collected this history I had to be sensitive to the overlaps, assumptions and how I might color what I heard in a different tone than it was shared. These are the challenges of oral histories. Certainly I wanted to focus on the Yazzie family and their story, but I could not deny that spending time with them had permanently touched me, and I them. When I first thought about recording their family history it all seemed straightforward enough. But from the very first day I showed up at Suzie's hogan with tape recorder in hand, my assumptions, my sense of self, well…everything changed. Life and the mystery of the terrain loomed large. The magic of Monument Valley and the people who have called it home for centuries became a complex revelation. The experience and the essence of this place was a reflection of something inhabiting the earth in a way that had been distant from me. The connection between land and people was truly awesome to observe. Unfortunately, that connection has become lost to so many of us. But I'm jumping ahead.

I assumed that I could collect and organize the Yazzie history in a way that was logical to me. I had done it before and my plan seemed thorough. Having recorded the story for my first book, "Through the Eyes of a Survivor" about a woman who had survived the Holocaust – I followed suit and naturally planned to set up a series of regular interviews that would become increasingly intimate as the family felt more comfortable with me. With this information I integrated my journal entries when they added value or insight. I didn't question the process. Why wouldn't my interviews with Suzie Yazzie work using the same protocol?

I began my interviews with Suzie at the same time I completed my undergraduate work in history and anthropology at the University of California Santa Barbara in 2000, with the intention of using Suzie's story as the subject of my undergraduate honors thesis. I entered into the project with grand visions and saw myself immersed in Navajo life where all would be revealed to me in perfect sequential order. I had in mind the rather cliché image of the objective anthropologist recording a native's story. Although working with the Yazzies was indeed an adventure, it became a much different experience than I imagined. I soon discovered that it could never work as a chronological collection encased in what I saw as a logical form.

The work turned out to be more complicated and surprising. I became part of an intricate dance that involved gathering the big story while living inside the real nuts and bolts of surviving in the Valley. Life is never easy on the reservation, and the Yazzies constantly struggled to make ends meet. I soon came to realize that my presence was an interesting diversion to them, so long as I never interfered with their work. Schedules went undisturbed regardless of my need to interview. Suzie, so accustomed to acting as the head of the family, accomplished her many tasks in her own time, and she was not keen on any change of daily routine that might hinder the Yazzie's going concerns. This meant that family and hogan business, and the constant turnaround of tourists, took priority over our conversations. In time I understood that, although the Yazzies wanted their story told, they preferred to keep the rhythm and flow of daily life alive and well.

I went along with whatever pace the family set on any particular day, discovering the intricacies of *Dine'* life more by accident than by design. In the Navajo language "Dine'" means The People, and living in traditional Dine' fashion seemed to come naturally to the Yazzies. They all worked together to maintain their herd of sheep, to weave rugs and create jewelry to sell, and to honor the Dine' faith whenever possible. My lofty ideals of recording an American Indian history was gradually replaced by the more realistic goal of allowing the Yazzie's to reveal their stories when it was the right time and place for them. It required that I shift my focus and perception in ways that were unimaginable when this project was first conceived. I had to let go of my academic training and settle into the reality of a totally different lifestyle. Yes, a bit of information would be delivered in response to my interview questions, but I was just as likely to learn something "on the fly." I heard Yazzie history while walking through the desert, or on the back of a horse splashing through a creek. The Yazzies might divulge a clever anecdote during one of our long drives into the Valley, or whisper an important lesson in protocol during a Navajo ceremony. I never knew when a story was going to plop inadvertently into my lap, and I always had to be ready for this possibility.

As I collected these tales I also reviewed my diary entries. This forced me to confront myself on many levels, and at first it shook my confidence as a writer. It seemed awfully unsophisticated of me, for instance, to have assumed that the Dine' way of life as seen by the Yazzies was a universal concept shared by all Navajo. Before

I was even into my second year of visiting the reservation I came to understand that there were many facets of Dine' existence, and they included many of the same problems that plagued other American communities. Poverty, addiction, loss of faith and the separation of families; all of the challenges plaguing our society also existed on the reservation. I soon abandoned my plan to write about what I perceived as traditional Native American life, and focused more on the way the Yazzie family lived. I also became more flexible in how I viewed each individual on the reservation beyond the family system itself. As in any culture, Dine' society has been in flux for centuries, so all I could really hope to accomplish was to present a point of view held by one particular Navajo family. Would it be enough, I wondered, to show how the Yazzies negotiate the intricacies of reservation life? Or would this present only a narrow picture of Navajo culture? I had to resign myself to the fact that I was only one person observing one particular family. I would simply do the best I could to witness and interpret the experience.

Although my original concept of working with the Yazzies was naïve, I never felt disappointment over what our interviews ultimately revealed. I found their reactions and answers to my questions to be refreshingly authentic. Perhaps this was because they were accustomed to the constant scrutiny of tourists that ran in and out of their lives in Monument Valley. Though I would never completely grasp what it meant to grow up as Dine,' the Yazzies' candor and acceptance of my presence allowed me to get an intellectual and even a visceral sense of what it means to live in Navajo skin. Time went on and I worked when I could, sat around and watched when necessary, and no doubt made a general nuisance of myself over the course of several years. Before long the people I interviewed became important to me, not only as a writing project, but as real friends. They in turn treated me like family.

I suspect that, at first, the experience of a white woman, or *Bilaga'ana* nosing around was strange, intrusive and a bit unnerving to the Yazzies. They must have wondered who this Anglo was, and why she was asking questions about things with such obvious answers. Thankfully they tolerated me, and I learned that the occasional trip to a reservation does not a native make. I could only visit the Valley once or twice a year for a week at a time, and this transient nature kept my status as outsider or "visitor" for some time. My relationship with Suzie, Lonnie, Emily, Effie and Elvina Yazzie became stronger when I began to have a stake in their lives. Suzie's son, daughter-in-law, daughter and granddaughter spent hours with me beyond the interview process. This social interaction caused our association to evolve into something more meaningful.

COLLECTING THE STORIES: THE LANGUAGE BARRIER AND OTHER CHALLENGES
"Listen or your tongue will keep you deaf."- Cree

Working with the Yazzies went beyond a mere history lesson. We shared the desire to record their story as accurately as possible, but in the process we also came to see how much our families had in common. Lonnie, Emily, Effie and I were around the same age, so we found it easy to empathize over the topics of childhood dreams, marriage and raising a family. Over time these people became as curious about my life as I was about theirs. When my husband and children began to occasionally join me on trips to the reservation, our families began to entwine. In a strange way we came to rely on each other.

It was wonderful to watch Suzie's son, Lonnie bond with my husband Ross. Both men found they held many of the same values and beliefs regarding family, work, and a love for horses. They also shared an independent nature. Ross and Lonnie knew how satisfying a good day's work could be, and they were not shy about rewarding themselves for it with the occasional pleasure of a ride around the Valley. Similarly Effie, Emily and I shared the joy and heartache of motherhood, the trials and comfort of married life, and the unique challenge of maintaining an identity beyond that which our families had given us. Our friendships evolved into something unique and intimate, and to this day we refer to each other as *shah kis*, or "sister"

Collecting the Yazzie story was a fascinating project on so many levels. Because Suzie Yazzie speaks no English, and I speak only a few words of Navajo, I conducted my interviews with her through family members who acted as interpreters. The family then completed transcripts of these translations which were later sent to me for review. I searched for subtleties throughout our English/Navajo sessions, and for nuances within Suzie's stories, looking at not only what was said, but also defining the importance of what was left unsaid. I learned to be respectful of Suzie's occasional silences, often brought about after stumbling upon a topic that was sensitive or considered sacred. At times Suzie would reveal portions of stories that she normally kept to herself or shared only with family. On other occasions she diplomatically changed the subject, politely signaling me to move on to another. I avoided questions that might involve any information that might be considered taboo to Suzie. Intricate details concerning ceremonies, prayers, and certain songs were never mentioned, and I often asked Suzie for permission to write about a subject we were discussing as a safeguard against printing any data considered religiously sacred.

I asked family members in charge of translating interviews to take special care in recording every word verbatim, and I believe we have presented Suzie's dialogue as accurately as possible. I added brackets or parenthesis to provide explanation where dialogue was vague, and I noted where family members completed translation from Navajo to English since the two languages differ in grammar and form. Whenever I could, I maintained Suzie's speaking style. For example, by including the "s" that some Navajos add to words where an Anglo would not, we hear that one has "gone looking for the sheeps." Like other Navajo speakers, Suzie also tended to end a narrative with the phrase "I was told," or "they say." Anthropologists attribute this speaking style to issues of authority that have long been important among the Navajo.[1] I believe that Suzie's speaking style indicated a connection to ancestors. The act of retelling a story must therefore be accompanied by respect for her elders and reverence for their memory.

In spite of my efforts to make Suzie's narrative accessible to readers, there arose some unexpected obstacles. Her very delivery may at first come across as somewhat choppy. Unlike the western style of chatter and inflection, Suzie's halting manner of speaking can be awkward to read until one settles into it. I discovered that even when her relatives translated Suzie's Navajo dialogue to English, her communication seemed 'foreign' to me. I also had to admit to myself that I liked the difference of it, and over time I became comfortable with this distinct speaking style.

A certain amount of caution had to be used in analyzing the Yazzie oral history. My narrator's memory contained elements of both the temporal and spiritual world. I found it fascinating, for example, to see how the Dine' cyclical view of time caused Suzie to speak of the past and present as parallel to one another. Although the basic storyline of these oral histories appear to have changed little over time, it is important to remember that they have been shaped and reshaped by the generations repeating them.

Initially my goal in collecting this oral history was to reveal Navajo strategies of cultural survival, historical memory, gender, and the life course, as well as the impact of tourism on Navajo life from the mid-nineteenth century to the present. I wished to learn how the Anglo world affected a Navajo woman and her family from the period of relocation, known as the Long Walk of 1864, to the present. By closely analyzing my interviews with the Yazzies I could better understand the role of narrative in this family. It was an ethnographic project that allowed me to work closely with Suzie and her family within the beauty of Monument Valley Navajo Tribal Park. The people and the setting opened my eyes to new ideas concerning cultural survival. I thought, for example, that the Navajo maintained much of their pre-contact lifestyle by adapting quickly to Anglo intrusion. While investigating this theory, I discovered a unique method used by Navajo like the Yazzies, wherein they embraced or discarded various aspects of Anglo culture, depending on how well it allowed them to maintain their own.

Again, my preconceived notions of what defined a person as truly Dine' initially impeded a true understanding of the Yazzies. Only by spending time with a variety of Yazzie family and friends did I ultimately come to recognize what should have been obvious to me from the beginning; that Navajo society reflects the choices of many individuals continuously adjusting their views regarding family roles, religion, economy and education. Similarities did exist among the Navajo as they developed strategies for the survival of their culture. Yet, their personal perceptions of what it meant to be Navajo varied depending on the individual's experience. A number of the Yazzies

---

[1] Kluckhohn, Clyde and Dorthea Leighton. <u>Children of the People.</u> Cambridge: Harvard University Press, 1948, 107.

adopted as many Navajo traditions as possible. Other family members would pick and choose those traditions that suited their own lifestyle. It seemed there was no concrete way to be Dine'; yet, within the Yazzie family at least, I saw no judgment regarding the choices any individual made regarding their culture.

With this in mind, I became fascinated by the manner in which the Yazzies adapted through each generation, and it was in the process of studying their culture that I was drawn into their lives. A transformation occurred over time in which I ceased looking at the Yazzies from an Anglo perspective, and instead began to see the world through their eyes. Consequently, what began as an academic work is now a story of how two very different cultures may learn from one another. I must confess that "Shade House Conversations" has become personal, and I hope those who read about the Yazzies come away with a sense of the love that grew between us in creating this work.

GETTING STARTED: DIARY OF A MAD WHITE WOMAN
"Tell me and I'll forget. Show me, and I may not remember. Involve me, and I'll understand."
Tribe Unknown

Like other families living "on the rez," the Yazzies were committed to honoring and maintaining some form of traditional Navajo life. How did they manage it, I wondered, and how different was this life from that of their own fathers, grandfathers and distant ancestors? I believed that the answers would emerge within the Yazzie story, and I thoroughly enjoyed discovering those answers. From my very first meeting with Lonnie and his family, I was struck by how the Yazzies were more prone to laughter rather than to complaints over the hardships that went with living on the reservation. I was also impressed with the tenacity they showed in making Navajo traditions the foundation, if not always the center, of their lives. I saw how, like many of their friends and neighbors, they had been forced to adapt to pressures from a white culture that became more and more prevalent with each passing year.

I began the project of recording Suzie Yazzie's life impetuously, with very little preparation. It was only after my first trip out to the Valley that I began to read literature written by anthropologists and historians who had studied the Navajo. Initially, there simply had not been time for any formal research of Navajo history and culture, and perhaps this was a good thing. Other than the brief encounters I had with the Navajo artisans selling blankets and jewelry in Monument Valley, I had not spent much time with these people, and so I had no real understanding about Navajo culture. I was also sadly lacking in any previous experience documenting other societies, and only a limited knowledge regarding how such research had already been done on Navajo life. Undaunted, I blindly pushed on, telling myself I would learn as I went along. I wished to approach the Yazzie's story with an open-mind; to begin with a sort of blank canvas on which they could paint with the colors of their lives as I came to know them. Driven by a compelling urge to connect with these people I became attracted to the way they regarded themselves and the world around them. There seemed no alternative to them but to appreciate their surroundings and each other in a very deep and personal way.

In spite of my best efforts, the first solo trip out to Monument Valley was ill-planned and far too complicated. Although Suzie still had an exceptional memory, she was in her early eighties, and I was always in a hurry to collect my interviews. I flew out of Santa Barbara, where I lived and, after a series of nearly missed connections, I eventually found myself in the airport parking lot of Albuquerque, New Mexico. I would later find shorter routes to Monument Valley, but this first trip was an initiation of sorts. It was a kind of a mythological beginning out of one familiar door across a threshold into another world.

Looking back, I'm not surprised that the journey proved both convoluted and magical. I was a good driver and figured I needed something sturdy and reliable in case I got stuck in the sand or encountered a flash flood. So I rented a four-wheel drive SUV. I was a little nervous about the long ride into such an isolated place, and remembered a trick my sister taught me about driving as a single female. I propped up my duffel bag on the passenger side, wrapped it in a sweater, and topped off my faux "companion" with my oil skin wide-brimmed hat. It was a silly idea, but it made me feel safe. I mean I was out there literally, and out of my element for sure. Tuning into a country music station I made my way out of the city and tried to relax.

The landscape surrounding me seemed empty and desolate, and my cell phone lost its signal almost as soon as I headed west. Fortunately the scenery became quite stunning as I drew closer to the reservation. Time passed pleasantly while I marveled at the stark and vast beauty of the Southwest. I wondered how Suzie would respond to a white woman, let alone one who could not speak Navajo. I knew Lonnie and his wife well enough from our previous horseback riding excursion in the Valley, but I doubted Suzie would remember our brief encounter. I recalled the first day we met, when she ventured into the camp erected behind a bluff by her home. She came to sell jewelry, silently displaying her wares to our curious bunch of riders. At that time I lusted after a set of hair clips adorned with beads, but the price I offered was politely rebuked. "Suzie doesn't barter," was the only explanation I received, and I felt stupid for having tried. Now as I made my way to Suzie's home once more, I sort of hoped she wouldn't remember me after all.

I planned to stay at Goulding's, a lodge and camping area popular with tourists visiting the Valley. I traveled light, only my bag with three day's worth of clothes, a flashlight, and a new tape recorder accompanied by cassette tapes for my interviews. Not wishing to risk losing any time I took a backup recorder in case of mishap. The nearest town was some twenty or thirty minutes away, (depending on whether you became stuck behind a slow vehicle), and so I was basically a one-woman interview/recording studio. Keyenta, the town nearest Monument Valley, had a school, a good grocery store and other conveniences that served the native populace, but most of the locals drove three hours north to Flagstaff for larger purchases.

My route was highlighted in yellow on my map, my wallet was full of twenties, and I carried plenty of water. I was prepared, albeit in a rather paranoid fashion that made me laugh years later after making the trip dozens of times. I looked forward to meeting Lonnie and Emily for breakfast the next day. The Goulding's restaurant was our rendezvous point so that we might get a good amount of coffee in our bellies for the day's work. Over the phone, Lonnie had explained to me that his mother would be busy receiving tourists at the family hogan during much of my visit. Although I knew the importance of Suzie selling her rugs through weaving demonstrations, I secretly cringed over the idea of cramming all of my prepared questions into a fixed amount of limited time. I soon learned that flexibility with any and all plans was a must when visiting the Yazzies. They wanted to accommodate me, but Valley life marched on. I thought of working with Suzie at night after the tourists left; however this would hinder my plan of using my evenings to write up the day's experiences. Looking on the positive side, Native Americans were known to reserve the evenings for telling legends and discussing ancestors. It would be nice to be a part of such a tradition. Looking back now, I am struck by the realization that I never once conducted an interview with the Yazzies in the evening.

For the final night of my stay in the Valley I planned on treating the Yazzies to dinner. I had asked my friend Don Donnelly what to expect when socializing with the Navajo. He knew more than most white folks since he ran the outfit that provided horses to ride in the Valley. He also knew the Yazzies well and had a good relationship with the family. He considered them reliable employees and a pleasure to be around. "Don't be surprised to see the entire family show up for dinner," he warned. "They don't get an opportunity to eat out too often."

The long trek to Monument Valley turned out to be the exact opposite of the tedium I expected it to be. Looking at my map, my trip appeared to take a complicated route. However, as I transferred from one highway to the next the journey began to make sense to me; every connection becoming less crowded with vehicles. I anticipated, and then left behind each little town from Gallup to Chinle. My very first visit to this area was during the dry season, when the desert foliage was a dismal and uninspiring gray. According to Lonnie's last telephone call, the rains blissfully arrived in June and had squelched the latest drought. The "rez" had been transformed into a place of life and color. Traveling deeper onto the reservation I took a mental inventory of memorable sights. At the end of five hours of driving I had seen four dogs, (two of them sadly dead on the road), three cows, (only one of these dead, on its back with four hooves sticking straight up), and a number of hogans, the traditional Navajo home constructed of Juniper branches and covered with dried, packed earth.

By the time I got to the little town of Many Farms the desert grass held a green tint enhanced by thickening clouds heralding an approaching storm. Lightning flashed across the late afternoon sky and huge raindrops hit my windshield, washing away hours of dust and bug juice. My fear of encountering flash floods quickly faded. The storm ceased as suddenly as it had begun, leaving a beautiful sky as its only memory. Surrounding me were hills, sage-green and gently rolling. No other vehicles were in sight, and I felt as if Mother Nature was presenting this show exclusively for me. Tired from driving I cranked up the radio and, since there was no audience to critique me, sang at the top of my lungs. I opened my window and breathed in the clean air, letting the warm, wet breeze hit my face. The clouds hovering above were still billowy and threatening, but the sun shone through in halo-white streaks that met the desert floor. It looked like the hand of God was reaching down to touch the highway. Enjoying my desert reverie I drove on in bliss until…thwap! Something hit me hard on the cheek.

"Hmm", I mused, "pretty big raindrops." Two more pelts of the mysterious stuff hit my chin and forehead until I realized I was under assault. Checking my mirror I found to my horror the remnants of three huge, black bugs decorating my face. I screamed and wiped the carnage with a coffee stained paper napkin. Whack! Another hit me by the ear and dragged the remainder of its body up to my nose like a soldier dying on some war-torn field. I screamed again, whisked the insect from my face and shut the window in a panic. After carefully searching every inch of my exposed body for any other unwelcome passengers I tried to compose myself. Gripping the wheel and managing an involuntary shudder I told myself to get over it…so much for my idyllic desert moment.

I made Goulding's Lodge in pretty decent time; a little over five hours. Nevertheless, I felt done in from a day's worth of travel. I dragged myself to the lodge office, collected my keys and dropped my bags into a room that, like all rooms at the lodge, offered a stunning view of the Valley. I would have appreciated it more had I not been starving. I made the short walk to the lodge restaurant and inhaled a "Navajo Taco" wrapped in sinful Indian bread that had been fried, in shortening no less! I then decided to investigate the indoor pool. Floating on my back in the cool water I thanked the heavens above for Harry Goulding and his wife "Mike." Though such accommodations would be expected anywhere else, in the Valley they were an absolute luxury.

Bobbing in the pool and staring at the ceiling I thought back to the tents where my husband and I spent our time riding with Don Donnelly. That first trip had us battling the dust storms that occasionally kick up in the Valley. Some of the tents blew away, and a fine grit covered every piece of clothing and some of the food. It was fine roughing it when horseback riding was involved, but not ideal for conducting interviews. I had a strong suspicion that Goulding's would be welcome at the end of my long days. I returned to my room, turned off the light and snuggled into bed, silently congratulating myself for successfully enduring the first leg of my journey. I then remembered my mother's stories about how she traveled as a Navy wife across the U.S. and back again. All alone she had hauled along me, my three siblings and a dog or two to the next base where dad was stationed. Falling into a humbled sleep I wondered if I'd inherited her moxie. I would need it if I were to have any success speaking with another very strong woman, Suzie Yazzie.

I awoke the next morning with last night's dream still fresh in my mind. In my sleep I saw myself in the rental car, waiting on an abandoned highway for a herd of cattle to step aside. A beast stood directly in my path, gazing at me with big cow eyes. Implying that she had all the time in the world she chewed on some brush, indicating she had no intention of moving for a non-bovine. Just as I was coming to terms with the fact that livestock had the right of way on the rez, my dream morphed to another scene in which I was pumping gas at a station in Chinle. Next to me was a truck with

Navajo children sitting in the back, what would come to be a familiar sight whenever I visited the reservation. The dark-eyed kids stared as I stood by my brand new rental truck, their look neither rude nor welcoming. They simply stared with a "what the hell is she doing here" expression. The alarm clock in my room pulled me out of this uncomfortable situation, and I prepared for the day ahead.

I carefully organized the gear that I'd set out the night before, and I crammed it all into my backpack with anticipation of what the day might bring. I was excited to begin. The idea of sitting privately with Suzie as she allowed her memories tumble out to me gave a delicious feeling of anticipation. I locked the door to my room and headed up the long, steep stairway that led to the restaurant. The high desert elevation made my heart race as I breathlessly asked the hostess for a table with a view; rather a redundant request. Just like every room at the lodge, each table had a spectacular view of the Valley. No matter how many times I visited the Valley, I could never stop admiring the panorama of buttes and mesas. Sitting quietly at my table, waiting for the Yazzies, the breathtaking view held me captive.

As I finished my third cup of coffee I began to wonder if the Yazzies were coming to meet me after all. I turned my attention to the menu, when suddenly I heard a "shiip shiip" noise; a soft whistle I would come to know so well. It sounded as if someone was calling to a horse, but it was for me and it came out of Lonnie's grinning mouth. He'd been standing in front of me for some time. I had been so distracted by the view I didn't notice the two Navajo standing in front of me, watching, waiting and giggling. I invited them to join me, and treated all of us to a hearty breakfast while we talked about anything and everything "Navajo."

We devoured our meals and gazed out the window. Our coffee cups were never more than half-empty before our server, a local girl the Yazzies knew and greeted, appeared with a refill. I soon learned that coffee accompanied just about every conversation with those on the rez'. I drank gallons of it during my interviews with the Yazzies. Sometimes I brought a gift of tea to Suzie. She loved the packs of herbal varieties. But most of the time we sipped the strong, black brew that sat perpetually perking on the old wood-burning stove positioned in the middle of her home. I truly cannot recall ever arriving at Suzie's to find the coffeepot empty or cold, no matter what the time.

With our stomachs full we soaked in the vista, and Emily took on the role of storyteller. Suzie, she informed me, was the oldest original inhabitant of the Valley. The sole "owner" of a large tract of land by way of a grazing permit granted to her family long ago, it was she who gave permission for entry to "MV" as most of the family referred to the Valley. Film crews seeking permission to tape car commercials, or the occasional western, always spoke to Suzie first through one of the family interpreters. She and her family had been extras in movies produced in the Valley from the 1940s to the present. Suzie also granted right of way through the Valley for horseback riding excursions, and members of her family were usually the guides required for these endeavors. It tickled me to learn that, for such a diminutive lady, Suzie wielded quite a bit of power.

Lonnie excused himself, and asked if Emily could ride with me to his mother's place. He had the unenviable errand of the day; waiting in line at the well for water. In the back of the family truck perched a container the size of a bathtub, constructed of heavy-duty plastic. When filled, the 325 gallon tank could provide enough water for Suzie and her livestock lasting up to a week. "The horses sometimes try to sneak up and steal the sheep's portion of water," Emily informed me, "but I can usually scare 'em away with a slingshot. I'm pretty good with it," she giggled. One can spot these huge containers in the back of trucks all over the Valley, either completely empty, (on the way to the well), or completely full, (on their way back). The lines are long and boring, so most of the locals bring a friend or a book to pass the time.

We drove into the park, stopping at the ticket window only long enough for the Navajo park employee to recognize Emily and wave us in. Over time I learned of the side road into the park. Even on my own I could have taken that route, but it seemed unfair to avoid the paltry three dollars fee charged for entry. Judging by the condition of the washboard and pitted roads I figured park management could certainly use the funds. In the beginning I felt a sense of privilege to be waved in as if I were a member of some secret Navajo club. Over the twelve or so years I visited I have often tried to imagine what it would be like to live full time in such a beautiful place. I'd have to be Navajo to actually live in the park, so the idea remained a dream.

The two bags of groceries I'd purchased at the Goulding's market bounced around in the back of my rental. I did not wish to impose on Suzie and her family, so I brought supplies to make my own lunch. As it turned out I could never polish off an entire loaf of bread and a package of cold cuts, and I ended up leaving most of it along with the extra snacks, water and fruit at the family hogan. This gifting of food became a ritual of sorts between Suzie and me. Over the years I made certain to arrive with a bag of oranges, potato chips, or her favorite Hostess treat of coconut covered "snowballs." It made me feel more connected to Suzie when I left her some food to enjoy for a few days after my departure. I knew that Suzie was perfectly capable of caring for herself and her needs, and she had family that checked in on her. But she became my own special and favorite grandmother, and I knew she appreciated the extra food in her cupboard.

Along with the food, I'd usually indulge in purchasing a couple of glossy magazines. Whenever Suzie was occupied with tourists Emily and I couldn't resist pouring over the pages of celebrities in fancy clothes. It felt strange to read about the indulgence so prevalent in that world, while immersed so comfortably in Suzie's modest digs. Most of the time however, Suzie and I spoke in her "Shade House."

AT THE SHADE HOUSE:
I DON'T SPEAK DINE.'
'The Great Spirit gave you two ears and only one mouth, so you can talk half as much as listen." — Unknown Tribe

Emily and I chattered away in the car, past "The Mitten" and "Three Sisters" monuments, until finally we turned the bend to Suzie's place. She was in the hogan demonstrating her weaving skills to tourists. The "visitors," as Suzie called them, paid her a dollar for photos of her sitting at a large wooden loom, and sometimes purchased the rugs or jewelry made by the Yazzies. Emily and I decided to wait inside her regular living quarters; the weather-beaten house built by her husband years ago. Emily helped me gather my things and we made our way to the house. There were a few relatives to meet, so I offered the traditional loose handshake and sat down, unsuccessfully attempting to melt into the background. The people who came to Suzie's house had known each other all their lives. Oftentimes I would try to become invisible while the family talked to one another. Even though I could not understand the conversations going on in Dine,' I still felt as if I were eavesdropping. I felt like an alien and wished only to sink into the walls. Every time I was introduced to a Yazzie I underwent a kind of baptism by fire. The long looks and unreadable faces made me wonder if I would ever truly know any of them. The Navajo I met were as gentle as their handshakes, and the Yazzies were always incredibly kind and gracious. I knew, however, that unless I actually resided with them in the Valley I could never expect this family to be completely comfortable with me. How could I blame them? I certainly could not speak freely with a stranger hanging around only two or three times out of the year? How does anyone trust a cipher on the wall?

I sat with Emily for only a short time in the room crammed with relatives, and then wandered off to set up shop in the "Shade House." This was a structure made in the same shape as the hogan, but without the dirt packed around the juniper branches. It stood to the side of Suzie's house and served as a general meeting place for family and friends during the warmer months. The branches and sticks arranged around the Shade House provided shelter while allowing the occasional breeze in to cool the occupants. In the middle of the house, folding chairs and upturned boxes surrounded the ever-reliable wood burning stove. An old sofa was positioned at the back of the Shade House, and it was here the children generally snuggled and giggled throughout the day. At the side, by the east-facing door stood a somewhat shaky, wooden table that was used for preparing food. All in all, it was a very comfortable place to sit and talk. Serving as my office and sanctuary, the Shade House would eventually become one of my favorite places for our interviews. The only problem was that over time our chairs would sink into the soft sand; forcing us to reposition ourselves from time to time.

Before long Emily joined me and explained Suzie's continued absence. She assured me that other family members could run the hogan business if Suzie ever needed a break, but her mother-in-law preferred doing the weaving demonstration. She enjoyed seeing new people, and liked to be in charge of things. Even before the older members of her family had passed away, Suzie was placed in charge of the hogan operation. Her business thrived due to her natural ability to charm the tourists. Suzie was also a good manager of people. In her younger days, it was she who had made certain the sheep and other livestock were well cared for, and she encouraged other family members to contribute their arts and crafts to the business for sale.

Unwilling to remain idle until Suzie appeared; I abandoned my plan to focus all of my preliminary interviews on her. Why should I stubbornly stick to some self-imposed rule that I must learn the Yazzie's story from the eldest family member up to the youngest? I could not count on a particular family member to be present whenever I needed them, so instead I would interview whoever was willing to sit with me and talk into the recorder. In the Valley, things did not work according to my schedule. Any job was difficult to come by. If a position became available outside of the park then off the Yazzies would go for that reliable paycheck. The uncertainty of employment meant that the family had to maintain irregular work schedules at Suzie's compound. In an attempt to remain flexible I decided that afternoon to interview Emily. I enjoyed speaking with this woman, who over the years would become an ally and dear friend, sympathetic with my own struggles to be a good stepmother and wife. We built an intimate trust and an easy willingness to confide in one another about the things that mattered most in our lives.

In our first interview Emily began to tell me about her relationship with Suzie. As she spoke, a little summer rainstorm began to creep into the Valley, rebelling against a full and shining sun. I could hear the hard pat-pat-pat of big drops hitting the branches of the Shade House, and enjoyed a little shiver. Emily ignored the rain, carefully choosing her words to describe Suzie to me. She cared very much for her second family because relations with her own had been turbulent in the past. Emily had a great respect for her mother-in-law, and she was pleased to list for me the woman's many qualities. Emily spoke eloquently and I saw in her a natural ability to tell stories. Each word was measured and carefully chosen. Listening back to the tape later that night, I could sense that Emily was very thoughtful about the things she said and how she said them. "How do I tell you about Suzie…" she began, and continued to describe the matriarch in lovely detail.

Not long into this first interview the tape recorder clicked off for no apparent reason. It was a rocky first start, and as I fumbled and clicked the annoying little box Emily waited with a patient smile. When I finally got the machine to work properly again she began just where she had left off, speaking in exactly the same manner as if she had memorized her words long before our interview. "How do I tell you about Suzie? She is firm, but she's quiet about it. My husband says she has a power that goes beyond words." She continued to describe her mother-in-law, and the life she and the other Yazzies lived within the Valley.

Every time we sat down to work Emily approached our project with a fresh attitude. She always seemed to know which way I wanted the conversation to go, and she tended to look at the past in a way that was neither judgmental nor an exaggeration. She turned out to be a very accomplished interpreter, and seemed to enjoy acting as translator during my interviews with Suzie. Unlike direct relations who often took it for granted that I would understand the subtleties of each tale, Emily had not grown up hearing Suzie's stories. She knew when to nudge her mother-in-law for more detail. I discovered that each family interpreter had their own style, ignoring some portions of a story that seemed obvious to them, while highlighting others they personally favored. This caused me some trouble in recording an accurate and detailed account of the family history.

Suzie's daughter Effie, for example, would at first give a scaled-down version of her mother's stories, focusing on the humorous aspects of the tale. Both Lonnie and his sister tended to translate their mother's words in a condensed manner, and I sometimes had to request an explanation of remarks that had left me baffled due to some cultural confusion. Effie once related a story about how her parents met. Apparently, Suzie's intended, who went by the name of Tully, rode up to Suzie and her young sister on a donkey, asking if either of them were married and generally trying to get their attention with teasing.

Effie translated back to me that Suzie once told her sister that "she had no time for a man who rode a donkey." After this remark, she and her mother began to laugh with gusto as if it had all been a big joke. I wondered, did this mean that Suzie truly held her future husband in contempt for riding a donkey, as opposed to a horse? Had she been ambiguous about her courtier's affections? Emily later straightened me out with the real meaning behind her mother-in-law's statement. Suzie had actually used the tactic of teasing to show her appreciation of Tully. I came to understand that the Navajo engage in teasing as a way of lightening a situation that would otherwise be awkward or uncomfortable. This allows them to express themselves in a subtle way that is acknowledged throughout their community. Suzie was, in fact, very interested in Tully, and she was counting on her sister to help her enlist this teasing as an indication that further inquiries should be made about his intentions.

Emily's husband, Lonnie had an altogether different style of translating from that of his wife's. Lonnie enjoyed listening to his mother's tales and, upon hearing the entire saga would consider what parts of the story were best relayed back to me. He would drink in his mother's words, taking pleasure in their familiarity. Long moments of time passed before he began to translate back to me, and naturally some intricate details were left out. After hearing all the discussion going on in front of me I was sometimes disappointed with the limited amount of story I eventually received. I knew that I was missing large portions of dialogue that might be important.

I took to breaking into the conversations between mother and son in order to catch anything Lonnie might leave out. This served as a frustration to Suzie, as it interrupted her flow when telling a story. She was a good sport about the intrusion however, and learned to tell her stories in portions, taking periodic breaks to allow for translation. I, in turn, tried to sense the rhythm of her tale, secure in the fact that the details were captured on tape for later examination. I only followed the general point of each story so that I could pose appropriately leading questions. I also learned that Lonnie needed time to search his mind for the English word which might best resemble a term spoken in the Navajo language or *Dine' bizaad*. I appreciated his efforts and again, tried my best to be patient.

At times he seemed to forget that I could not speak Navajo. I had to watch his face for signs of the direction each story was taking. If he laughed at something his mother said, but gave me a strictly factual translation I would have to ask what had been so funny. The entire process gave me the feeling that I was never quite in on the joke. In spite of these little challenges, I enjoyed watching Lonnie and his mother whenever they were deep in conversation. The two of them had the same demeaner. Both were a little shy, yet they also shared a wicked sense of humor. They clearly took pleasure in each other's company, and it was nice to see a mother and son so engaged.

In some ways, it was a good thing that I could not speak the language of my new friends. It gave me an opportunity to study the facial expressions and mannerisms unique to each family member, as well as to observe the different ways in which they interacted with Suzie as well as with one another. After awhile they became more comfortable in my presence. They even managed to ignore my tape recorder and relax into daily life. While I waited for translations, I made notes and formed questions that came to mind. I scribbled a reminder, for instance, to ask about each family member's responsibilities in caring for Suzie, and if any particular hierarchy existed among them. I read that in Navajo society it is customarily the eldest daughter who inherits her mother's property. Was this still practiced? If so, did it mean that Effie was the primary caregiver to her mother, or did her brothers take turns helping Suzie manage her sheep and the hogan business? It seemed that the women were involved in taking Suzie's place in the hogan during her breaks, while the men and children were more focused in caring for the livestock.

Was there any rhyme or reason to these chores, or did everybody just pitch in where needed and according to his or her talents? If Suzie's only daughter stood to inherit the family property, would that mean that it was up to Effie to continue the hogan business as well? Effie once told me that she preferred working at Goulding's and was never much interested in weaving, though she has produced very nice work in this art form. It seemed as if Emily was more suited to the working in the hogan, particularly since she enjoyed weaving, and kept up a routine of creating rugs for sale.

One of her favorite designs was that of the *yeibechi*.[2] Blankets representing this winter spirit were woven with great care, and some weavers simply were not up to the challenge of making them. "They are afraid of doing it wrong. It could mean bad luck for them," Emily informed me. She and her mother-in-law were quite skilled in creating these designs however, and made this type of rug their personal specialty. While we were in the Shade House I asked Emily if she would like to run the hogan for Effie. She was unsure if she could take the long hours of sitting in the dark hogan waiting for the occasional visitor. It remains to be seen whether or not the hogan business will continue once Suzie retires or passes away.

Emily and I moved onto other topics. I asked my friend what qualities her peers admired most. Emily responded that the women she respected were those who had weathered some calamity with perseverance and a sense of calm. "Strength" was a word that often came up in our conversations when discussing women. There were

---

[2] Per my discussion with Ron Maldonado, (Head of the Navajo Nation Historic Preservation Department), Yeibechi refers to the Night Way Ceremony and not to a specific rain deity. However, one of the masked dancers is known as "water sprinkler." Yeibechi's are held only in the winter when the thunder is sleeping after the first snow fall.

stories Emily told about female ancestors that inevitably ended with the phrase, "she was a real strong woman."

What then, I wondered, did the Navajo think of women who might be described as weak? The Yazzies rarely spoke of others in a negative fashion, a trait that I found particularly pleasing. Yet this made it difficult for me to discover what it was they deemed undesirable in a person. Navigating this kind of conversation could be tricky. It was not as if I were speaking to one of my fellow Californian suburbanites who might readily proclaim they disliked people who smoked or who were not vegetarians. The Yazzies considered it bad form to criticize anyone in such a blunt way, and I had read that most Navajo would avoid negative confrontations because they are considered impolite.

This was reflected in their language as well. I once asked Emily how one would day "I am sorry" in her native language. I wanted to be prepared for the inevitable occasion when I would unintentionally insult Suzie with an insensitive question or remark. "Oh we don't have a real translation for that," Emily informed me, "the closest you could come is to say *doo t'ah a koh shnay go' esh t'ee da*. This translates to "I did not mean to do that." I would have to be careful to avoid any cultural blunders, because I was pretty certain that I would never remember this phrase.

Emily taught me some additional phrases that might also prove useful when conversing with Suzie. I wrote the Navajo way of saying "please" and "thank you" in a phonetic manner so that I could study them on my own. I learned that the word *che* meant "grandfather," but could also refer to certain animals. This is because the Dine' believe that an ancestor might return as anything from a lizard to an owl. Because of this belief children are discouraged from harming any desert creature. Lonnie later told me that he and his brothers would brush off snakes or lizards when they were young saying, *no wot ah non naah che*, or "outta my way gramps!" The last phrases I was able to learn in the Shade House were also useful; one of them being *ben den le hish ne'* meaning "do you remember?" It was a difficult phrase to pronounce. The "den le" portion must be formed by placing the tongue on top of the bottom teeth which produced a nasal sound. The slashed "L" sound in many Navajo words was also a challenge for my Anglo mouth. It involved laying one's tongue in a lazy fashion against the roof of the mouth, then blowing through the space to make a noise that sounded like a drunken snake. My favorite phrase was "please", or *ah shon dee*. One could emphasize this phrase in a pleading fashion by drawing out the end, saying "*ah shon deeeee*". Children often used this as a way of saying "pretty please." Over the years I would hear this phrase quite a bit from Suzie's grandchildren.

CHAPTER 1 - THE STORY BEGINS

"Each bird loves to hear himself sing." - *Arapaho*

THE STORY BEGINS

My language lesson drew to an abrupt halt when Suzie sauntered into the Shade House. The tourists had gone on their way, and I would finally have the opportunity to interview this respected matriarch. Suzie now seemed ready to sit with us. Initially I was concerned that I would not gather enough to call this endeavor a serious project, but after one hour of interviewing I realized there was an abundance of information, anecdotes, insights; far more than I could imagine. Her children and grandchildren also had experiences to share that I thought would be of interest to people outside the reservation. Emily, Suzie and I sat around the wood stove in our folding chairs, and worked diligently. As Emily explained the interview process to her mother-in-law I carefully clipped the microphone onto her blouse. It felt odd to be this close to Suzie, and I hoped that it was not uncomfortable for her to have a virtual stranger approaching her in this way. We started slowly, and as they conversed I studied Suzie closely for the first time.

Her brown face was smooth for her age, but the lines around her eyes revealed many years spent in the sun. Her white hair was combed back in traditional Dine' style with the roll of thinning snowy hair wrapped neatly in yellow yarn. She wore clipped beaded barrettes on either side of her temples, and the turquoise jewelry around her collar matched the rings she wore on every finger. On anyone else it would have been too much, but Suzie could pull off this bold ensemble with natural elegance and beauty. As she spoke, her hands danced about her lap like two delicate birds playing in the air. Her long fingers betrayed evidence of arthritis, but they looked beautiful and strong from weaving. Suzie's nails were impeccably clean and polished. The only anachronism she displayed that hinted at the invasion of modern life were a pair of stylish, very thick, purple-rimmed eyeglasses and a black fanny pack, worn in front of her skirt. She had a habit of shifting the bag from side to side as we worked. I later asked Lonnie what it was that she kept in her bag. "Lots of credit cards," he said with a very straight face. I wondered what on earth Suzie might purchase with so many credit cards, until Lonnie burst out laughing. "I have no idea what she keeps in there," Lonnie confessed, "It's a mystery to me."

In Western society the written word has reigned supreme as a way to record history, and has helped to legitimize states and nations. Yet the power of oral narrative has remained essential to many Native American communities, as it has for many cultures misrepresented in so-called "legitimate" history books. Native Americans continue to challenge the written Anglo record. What causes members of a society to proclaim "It didn't happen that way"? How do narratives define societies, communities and families as they pass their stories from generation to generation? What role do such narratives play in cultural preservation? These questions came to mind during the time I spent with Suzie and her family. I was especially intrigued by Suzie, the oldest and key storyteller of the family. I wanted to show how her use of narrative both illuminates the past of her people, and serves as an important strategy of cultural survival. This oral history also speaks to Suzie Yazzie's experiences as a Navajo woman coming of age in the twentieth century who faced challenges that ranged from economic survival to the rising importance of tourism in Navajo life.

Suzie has lived her entire life in the Valley, adhering to a lifestyle that many Navajo would consider "traditional." Because of her mother's untimely death, Suzie became responsible for her siblings during her own adolescence. In the years that followed, she cared for the family livestock, traded her woven rugs to provide for her siblings, and ventured so far into Western culture as to participate in John Ford's film productions. She has gained status within the Navajo community because of her business savvy and her generosity toward those in need. Suzie also has a reputation as a reliable midwife and "hand trembler" (a Navajo who uses traditional and inherited skills to diagnose illness). She is dedicated to her family and to Dine' life, preserving her culture by relating a rich personal history through stories told in the oral tradition. I was fortunate to have the Yazzie's blessings and encouragement in recording their history. In this way an important part of Native American history may be passed on, and we gain a unique Navajo perspective on white-Indian contact since the nineteenth century.

Many of the Yazzies do their best to remain true to a lifestyle that is rich in Navajo culture. Suzie continues to raise sheep on property that her family has inhabited since the late 1800s. The family hogan, or *hooghan* in the Dine' language, is a windowless, nine-sided structure made of juniper wood and packed soil and is often the center of activity for the Yazzies. As with many conservative Navajo families Suzie's hogan has a dirt floor and a wood-burning stove in the center. The door faces east and all that enter the hogan move in a clockwise fashion, circling from left to right as a symbolic gesture honoring the sun's journey through the sky. The women of the family are famous for their beautifully woven blankets that are sold to tourists who frequent the Valley. Other family members produce jewelry and crafts that contribute to the hogan business.

The entire family works together to maintain the property in Monument Valley that once supported crops of corn, melons and peach trees. Sadly, the early twentieth century ushered in climate conditions that reduced the land's fertility. Only by maintaining her sheep herds and redirecting her efforts toward the tourist business has Suzie managed to continue living in her homeland as a traditional Navajo woman. There is no indoor plumbing anywhere on the Yazzie compound, and water must be transported by truck into the area of Monument Valley Tribal Park where Suzie resides. Yet, she is content to remain and enjoy a simple and relatively independent existence amidst the awe-inspiring monoliths and buttes of the Monument Valley Tribal Park. Suzie and a number of the family also continue to adhere to traditional Navajo religious practices. Similar to other Native American religions, the Dine' practice a faith that interacts with nature and recognizes the individual as well as one's role in the community or "clan." Religious ceremonies often take place within the hogan, and customs are respectfully maintained whenever possible. Most family members speak the Dine' language and Suzie's grandchildren are exposed to Navajo culture whenever possible.

Through Lonnie I learned that the Yazzies are one of the last surviving families to have continuously inhabited Monument Valley since the 1800s. As the oldest woman of her family, (a distinction of note in a society that still respects matrilineal descent), Suzie has earned an important place within that family and in her community. However, the Anglo[3] world has also influenced her role as matriarch. By assaying how she reacted to ever-increasing contact with Anglos, I hoped to better understand Suzie and her people.

With these ideas in mind, I set about the task of interviewing Suzie. The first obstacle involved communication. Emily offered not only to do the translating during our interviews, but also to transcribe the finished tapes for my use in the book that was to tell the Yazzie story. She proved to be an indispensable facet in my work. Her translating abilities and natural feel for the project were beyond compare. At this early point, however, I was simply elated to have a family member willing to assist me. While Suzie regarded me with some suspicion, I explained through Emily our ambitious project. I then dove headlong in with questions, and prayed Suzie would not see me as I felt at the time; impudent and pushy.

I felt out of place and out of my element. My questions seemed as awkward as sitting cross-legged on the dirt floor of her hogan. I later realized that it was my own notion of "comfort" that caused me to perceive Suzie's living conditions as both challenging and foreign. In addition to a lack of water or electricity, rooms that offered any opportunity for privacy was virtually nonexistent in Suzie's home. Until I became

---

[3] I chose to refer to non-natives as EuroAmericans, Anglos or "white." These terms include Mexicans and Europeans and, although it may not have been how settlers, traders, soldiers, missionaries and others identified themselves, I use these terms for simplicity's sake. The term "Indian" is used in conjunction with "Native American" because current native attitudes suggest that both terms are considered acceptable.

used to it, the little government house seemed cramped and crowded. Most of the floor was given up to weaving space and supplies. Every corner served as storage for Suzie's possessions, which included boxes of fabric, pots and pans, dry goods, and tools. Family memorabilia competed for space on the walls. Photos of relatives were pressed side by side against children's school artwork and hand-crafted Navajo gifts. I eventually became accustomed to these surroundings, even finding comfort in them. However I preferred conducting interviews in the family hogan or Shade House. The hogan was an energy-efficient structure that could be cool in the summer as well as warm in the winter, offering an almost cocoon-like security within. In any case, I learned that spatial needs vary depending on the individual. Suzie appeared to be satisfied with the organized clutter of her home, perhaps because of the vast areas of open space available outside. For her first interview, I was fortunate to sit with Suzie in her Shade House, or "The Shade" as the family sometimes called it.

SuzieSuzie

CHAPTER 2 - THE ANCESTOR LIVES

"The one who tells the stories rules the world." Hopi

INTRODUCTION TO FOUR-HORNED WOMAN

My very first questions to Suzie were about what the Navajo call "The Long Walk." This forced exodus of the Navajo, supervised by Kit Carson and sanctioned by the United States government in the 1860s, is considered by the Dine' as one of the darkest events in their history. The survival story of Suzie's ancestor, Four-Horned Woman is a crucial part of Yazzie family legend. It is also the story that inspired my efforts to chronicle their lives.

I happened across her story during the very first horseback excursion I took into Monument Valley. Suzie Yazzie's son, Lonnie was employed by the riding outfit to act as a guide. He and wife Emily also provided a demonstration of Navajo traditions with fireside singing, dancing and Dine' legends. We rode through the Valley, and all the while Lonnie called out the Navajo names for the local vegetation, and explained how certain sites held significance for his people. He recounted family stories that had been told over generations, pointing out former camps and landmarks in which his family played a role in Navajo history.

The day I learned about Four-Horned Woman, (or "Lady Four-Horn" as she is sometimes called), Don Donnelly had taken us on a brisk morning ride. By noon most were taking the lunch hour break to rest aching bones and bodies sore from riding. Seeking out some privacy I found a juniper tree somewhat removed from the others, and lay down in its shade for what I hoped would be a refreshing nap. This was not to be. Lonnie sauntered up, dusty from the ride, and stood in the bow-legged manner that would come to define him in my memory. "Want some company?" he asked. Not waiting for an answer he plopped down beside me and, after gazing off to some unknown point on the horizon, asked if I'd like to hear a story. He then told me about Suzie's revered ancestor.

The tale revolved around Suzie's great-grandmother, Four-Horned Woman, a survivor of the 1864 Navajo relocation to Bosque Redondo, New Mexico. Four-Horned Woman's odyssey began with a debilitating four-hundred mile trek known among the Navajo as "The Long Walk." Her tale of survival is the foundation of the

Yazzie family history. It was a fascinating story, and it left me wanting more. The historian in me could not suppress my big question to Lonnie; "Has anyone ever written down this legend?"

"Nah," Lonnie casually replied, "I think maybe you should do it." His response surprised me. It was as if he had expected me to take on the job all along. But why would he want a white woman to write his family's history? I pushed aside my doubt and insecurities, deciding to trust Lonnie's decision. After all, how could I pass up the opportunity to engage in historical research that seemed so alive? Even better was the idea of conducting interviews with the Yazzies. This would allow me to delve into my second love, cultural anthropology and gain ethnological experience at the same time. As these thoughts raced through my head Lonnie continued to smile at me, already knowing I would agree to become the family historian. This was the pivotal moment that began the Yazzie project and sealed our friendship.

The earliest history books that chronicled the forced relocation of the Navajo only grazed the tragic fact that many Dine' died during the four-hundred mile march to the Bosque Redondo internment camp. More recent history revised the story of the Navajo roundup, exposing how hundreds had died on the way to, and within the camp. Four years of starvation among the Navajo people took place until the United States government finally realized their farming settlement was a failure. As Suzie told the story of Four-Horned Woman's survival in this camp I realized how much work lay ahead. I wanted to confirm dates and places of which she spoke, and I would need to research cultural aspects of her story as well. I also had to investigate whether certain subjects were considered taboo, and therefore should not be brought up during our discussions. I did not want to insult the family because of my own ignorance. I made a mental list of all the work to be done, took a deep breath, and plowed ahead with the vigor of a neophyte.

RELOCATION: The First Long Walk
"They are not dead who live in the hearts they leave behind." Tuscarora Tribe

Suzie's recollection of her family's history begins with The Long Walk of 1864. When questioned about other relatives who lived prior to the 1860s, she indicated that most of the details concerning ancestors before relocation had been largely forgotten over the years. The Long Walk, however, gained a foothold in her memory, and is considered the foundation of the past by other family members. Because relocation is, for Suzie, the logical starting point of her family history, the statement, "I don't remember them…I just don't remember" tends to meet all other inquiries regarding any pre-relocation history involving her ancestors. She recalled only hearing that relatives once lived in Gallup and Nachitti, New Mexico. When asked where her great-grandmother lived before her capture for the Long Walk, Suzie gestured beyond her hogan and explained that the family lived "Over there. What was the place called?

Where we were told we live before…at Gallup? In Gallup, someplace over there we use to live."

Suzie recalled the legend of the Long Walk as one of the first she inherited from her elders. Before the later part of the twentieth century Navajo accounts were given little historical credence, and historians tended to overlook the extent to which relocation affected Dine' life. The story of Navajo encounters with whites remained incomplete when compared with other Native American historical accounts.[4] The forced march of the Navajo from their homelands was, in fact, a disastrous event for that nation. Suzie's grandmother, Four-Horned Woman, was captured while herding her family's sheep. She became the unfortunate victim of a round-up operation that began with Colonel Edwin Vose Sumner's campaign in 1851, and culminated in the Long Walk to Bosque Redondo in 1864.[5]

The Navajo exodus and incarceration is part of Dine' collective memory, and for the Yazzies this event symbolizes Navajo strength. By telling this story Suzie provided her family with a lesson in how one might face life's challenges the Navajo way. Additionally, she benefited from the prestige gained from imparting important genealogical information to those in her clan. Suzie enjoyed her role as storyteller and became quite animated whenever she spoke of her ancestors. Four-Horned Woman was a young adult during the time of Kit Carson's campaign involving the capture of Navajo and forcing them into a life of Anglo-style farming.

Suzie estimated the age of Four-Horned Woman at the time of capture as "around twenty." It was difficult to determine the exact age of this woman because the family used a non-Western style of narrative. While out riding in the Valley Lonnie once spoke of Four-Horned Woman as Suzie's "great, great, great, great, great-grandmother." When I attempted to correct him by pointing out this would indicate Four-Horned Woman was long dead by the 1800s, he countered, "She was a great woman." I would come to understand this type of remark as typical Navajo humor, and in his quiet way Suzie's son was teasing me. However I was forced to recognize the subtle reminder that, to the Yazzies, Four-Horned Woman's age was simply not a crucial element to the story. I never ascertained if this loose interpretation of time was a characteristic unique to Suzie's son, or if it was a Navajo trait suggesting time remained somewhat relative in their culture. Through my relationship with the Yazzies I did learn that in Dine' storytelling, events and seasons function as more reasonable

---

[4] In her collection of narrative concerning the Long Walk, Navajo historian Ruth Roessel described Native American history as incomplete when only Anglo sources are recognized as historically legitimate. She wrote that the Navajo version and interpretation of events such as the relocation of 1864 are important primary accounts that must be studied in order to gain a full understanding of historical events that affected them. Roessel, Ruth. Navajo Stories of the Long Walk Period. Tsaile, (Navajo Nation): Navajo Community College Press, 1973, ix, x-xi.

[5] Trafzer, Clifford E. The Kit Carson Campaign. Norman: University of Oklahoma Press, 1982, 37.

gauges of time than do actual calendar years or specific dates, and this concept of keeping time remained in Navajo consciousness.

I have heard Suzie's son and other family members make reference to time in a similarly ambiguous manner. Years were given as a succession of possibilities. Thus, a relative may have experienced an important event "...ten- fifteen-twenty years ago." Quite simply, a person's date of birth might be given as "in the late summer." Once again, it is the event or the person that retains importance to a Dine' storyteller, and exact figures matter less, so long as one is given a general idea of time. As a white student of history trained to record events in as factual a manner as possible this could prove maddening. I had to adjust my way of thinking to that of the Navajo, and accept that in their oral tradition the meaning or lesson behind an ancestor's story took precedence over precise dates, time, or other facts I might feel were important.

Anthropologists Clyde Kluckhohn and Dorothea Leighton recognized that this way of regarding time was "a hallmark of most rural peoples." These scholars who studied the Navajo in the mid-twentieth century came to realize that the Dine' also slight metric measurements in conceptualizing physical space. They observed that; "Navajo conceptions of space and time are hopelessly fluid from the white point of view. When a Navajo says a place is a mile off it may be 500 yards or ten miles away."[6] After obtaining this information I suddenly understood why asking Lonnie the distance to a particular location led to the answer of it being, "...around five-ten- maybe fifteen miles up the road."

These anthropologists hastened to point out, however, that the Navajo way of judging time had served the people well over the years. The white way of telling time was deemed arbitrary for the Dine',:

"Because it is not geared to observable natural phenomena. Navahos (sic) remember seasons of the year and sequences of events rather accurately – in fact, the correctness of their memories over many years in these respects often astonishes white people. It is on absolute dates that they err. Most white men...have been trained to be clock-watchers since they were infants fed on a schedule. The experience of the Navahos has been quite different. To be sure, they distinguish about eight positions of the sun during the day and about four points of time at night, (using the moon and stars), but these bear a varying relationship to an absolute time system in accord with the seasons of the year."[7]

It is important to understand that these anthropologists made this observation some fifty years ago. Today's Navajo may feel that he is as much a slave to the clock as any Anglo. Nevertheless, the fact that Suzie's son continued to view time in the Navajo way when discussing his ancestors indicates that this custom lives on.

Suzie's youngest son, Kee, recalled very clearly the stories his mother told, and he prides himself on keeping the family history intact. "I was the youngest," Kee explained, "so I guess I was really paying attention when my mom talked about our ancestors." He later confirmed that Four-Horned Woman would have been born

---

[6] Kluckhohn and Leighton, *Children of People*, 108.

[7] Ibid., 108-109.

around 1845, and that she was first captured by Mexicans intent on acquiring the Navajo to work as slaves on Mexican owned farms and ranches. This first abduction occurred about one year before the Long Walk of 1864, and resulted in Four-Horned Woman being carried away as far as Texas. "She got away though," Kee informed me, "because back then our people were used to traveling long distances on foot. They were pretty tough!" According to Suzie, Four-Horned Woman was indeed a strong young woman when abducted. She revealed the story of her ancestor's kidnapping, and the tactics enlisted by the Mexicans, who she claimed were "soldiers" while rounding up the Navajo:

"She was just picked up; stolen from her home. I was told people were sitting around in the hogan. They [Navajo ancestors] said soldiers surrounded them. There were a bunch of them on horseback going around. At each home they would surround the hogan, . And they would move in closer together towards the hogan. Some use to live in Forked Stick hogans, and soldiers would on horseback rope the sticks on top of the hogan and drag the hogan down. Our ancestors would be running this way and that way, and some got away. Gladly some escaped, but Four-Horned Woman…she was caught."

For many Navajo at this time, dying in an attempt to escape was preferable to a life of slavery. The Mexican soldiers must have realized their captives were motivated to flee, because they did all they could to deter the Navajo from doing so. Suzie spoke of her great-grandmother's fortune of having been placed on a horse for the journey. This saved her the misery of treading the long distance to Texas on foot; however this transportation was not without certain indignities. Suzie explained that those Navajo on horseback were bound and blindfolded. If any opportunity did present itself for escape the captives would have no way of remembering their way back home.

"They were wrapped up," Suzie explained, "because they were young and strong their hands were tied and they were thrown onto the horse, and then tied onto the horse again. Yes, my ancestor was wrapped up and tied onto a horse while dangling over the back of it. Her face was covered up too." To further discourage escape soldiers were careful to monitor the Navajo as they rested. Suzie described how this was done, saying, "Whenever they slept they were covered up with canvas tents and soldiers would be sleeping on each end of the canvas." The soldiers continued to maintain control of their captives, even when the Navajo needed to venture into the brush to relieve themselves. "They went out with ropes tied to them," Suzie explained, "while the soldiers kept an eye out."

According to Yazzie legend, Four-Horned Woman immediately began to devise a scheme that would allow for her eventual escape. The plan involved memorizing the landscape that she was able to glimpse from time to time, and continuously recounting the scenes in her head. During breaks to take water and rest the horses, the young woman was temporarily relinquished of the stifling hood forced upon her head:

"At the place where they were camping the soldiers would give the Navajo a bit of food or a sip of water. My ancestor looked around and surveyed or studied the land where they were at, where mountains are, and she would think to herself, 'I must remember this is the way we came.' Yes, she wanted to run away, but first she studied every detail of her long trip. Then she was blindfolded again and wrapped and tied onto a horse. Even when they slept, she still would recreate the scenery in her mind where they were situated."

Such a fine memory would serve Four-Horned Woman well, as she seized upon her one chance for escape.

BREAKING AWAY
"Force, no matter how concealed, begets resistance." Lakota

Escaping from the Mexican slave traders was no simple feat, since captives were kept under very close scrutiny at all times. Nevertheless, a resourceful Four-Horned Woman eyed a line of scrub-covered hills some miles away. She set her mind on getting out, and bided her time. Suzie spoke of her great-grandmother's restricted conditions while awaiting an opportunity to escape:

"When they were traveling they were just living in canvas tents. The people were kept inside and the soldiers were sleeping on both ends of the canvas in the tent. That's the way our ancestors slept. There were dogs outside barking all the time. Yeah, big like mountain lions and these animals were tied up on each sides of the tents at the doorway."

In spite of these intimidating methods the Mexicans enlisted to watch over the Navajo, Suzie's great-grandmother began to recognize that less energy was devoted to guarding as more distance was placed between the captives and their home. Eventually, patrols began to leave in search of more Navajo, leaving Four-Horned Woman's group to travel further south. Suzie explained:

"They sort of forgot about us. The soldiers would go hunting. Time went by when they didn't pay much attention to our people. The soldiers would leave to find more Navajos, and so they forgot my great-grandmother a little, maybe because she had been with them so long. This made the Mexican men lazy."

One rather odd decision made by the Mexicans was to place an elderly blind woman in charge of guarding the Navajo girls. Finding humor in such an arrangement, Suzie giggled as she further revealed how Four-Horned Woman thought of a way to escape:

"I guess that's when the soldiers left her with an old lady…that's when she decided to run away. This blind woman was taking care of them, guarded them and she slept near them. She was a Mexican lady. This blind woman would feel her way around for the presence of our ancestors. When she felt them all around her she went back to sleep, and that's when Four-Horned Woman got up to leave."

The irony of a blind woman placed in charge of guarding her people tickled Suzie every time she told this story. I admit that it was a bizarre picture Suzie painted of a blind Mexican lady stumbling through a tent full of Navajo women, trusting the count of her charges by her own touch. I was intrigued to discover a similar story about an ineffective matron guard in a book entitled *Navajo Sacred Places*. This narrative, recorded in 1988, came from Sylvia Manygoats, who remembered her maternal grandmother mentioning: "An old white lady guarded the young girls. She would sit at the door, watch the girls, and even sleep there."[8] As with the case of Four-Horned Woman, escape was on the mind of this Navajo girl. Mrs. Manygoats explained that, "Even as they got there, she had already made up her mind she was going to go home."[9]

A cold, frightened, and starving Four-Horned Woman made up her mind to escape. Suzie told of her great-grandmother's apprehensive and cautious approach to the journey home she was determined to make:

"She decided to only travel at night, while the daylight hours she would spend sitting around and hiding, and that way she could see the soldiers from up on top of the hills."

Suzie never revealed whether Four-Horned Woman decided the time was right for escape, or whether she left during a moment of extreme desperation. She only stressed that her great-grandmother left in the dead of night with no shoes on her feet and wrapped only in a light wool blanket. The Mexicans customarily collected each Navajo's shoes at nightfall to discourage any escape attempts. Moccasins were tied in bundles on the tent poles just out of reach. This provided a frustrating temptation to Four-Horned Woman. As Suzie related:

"Yeah, they were without their shoes. There were beaded shoes hanging nearby, but she thought she might wake someone so she did not grab them. She just took off without any shoes and grabbed a thin blanket, I was told, probably around midnight. She was scared of the guard dogs, so she slowly tiptoed out through the other side of the tent where the dogs weren't sleeping and they didn't hear her."

Four-Horned Woman did everything possible to obscure her scent from the dogs that she knew would eventually be set on her trail. Suzie explained:

"There was a river nearby, (Kee later suggested that his mother was referring to the Pecos River), and she ran into the water and started upstream heading this way, toward Monument Valley. She ran a long time in the water, I was told. Finally she got out and ran into a lot of weeds and bushes. She just kept running on it and she got a lot of thorns under her feet (giggles). She wanted to stay in the brush to hide her tracks, but the thorns tore up her feet. She was in a big hurry and didn't notice it until later."

It was Suzie's application of humor when telling her great-grandmother's story that surprised me most. Before I asked Emily for clarification about this kind of reaction, I had a hard time understanding why something so sad and frightening caused Suzie to laugh. In her book, *Translated Woman*, Ruth Behar noted how her own subject, a Mexican-Indian woman named Esperanza, erupted into peals of laughter after describing the hardships of her life.[10] Suzie likewise found reason to break into her trademark giggling as she told of the challenges that she and her ancestors experienced. I tried to hide my confusion when questions about Four-Horned Woman's internment

---

[8] Kelly & Francis. Navajo Sacred Places. Bloomington: Indiana University Press, 1994, 31.

[9] Ibid., 31.

[10]Behar, Ruth. Translated Woman. Boston: Beacon Press, 1993, 27.

and escape resulted in deep chuckles from those family present with me and listening to her tale. How could her ancestor's suffering be considered humorous?

Was there an explanation to the Yazzies reaction to the tale of Four-Horned Woman? Was this laughter a reaction characteristic of the Navajo, or could it be seen as a Native American trait in general? Certainly there have been instances when many non-native cultures resorted to a sort of black humor in times of stress. But to express humor continuously throughout her narrative as Suzie did struck me as rather unique. I found parts of Four-Horned Woman's story to be harrowing, and I came to regard Suzie's great-grandmother as something of a hero. I understood eventually that, while Suzie and her family agreed that Four-Horned Woman's actions were heroic, they also regarded the insanity of her barefoot escape over a thorny desert worth a laugh. Adding to their delight was the way in which, destitute yet resourceful, a young Navajo woman managed to make fools of her well-equipped Mexican captors.[11] The daring Four-Horned Woman had successfully escaped without the benefit of shoes or supplies. Perhaps by laughing at tragedy the Yazzies had discovered a way to heal their family of a sense of loss so often associated with the Long Walk. It could be that Four-Horned Woman stands as a symbol to the family; a sort of emblem against the cruelty and duplicity of whites.

After her giggling subsided Suzie settled into her tale once more:

"She kept running, and I was told she would look at the mountains to get her bearing, but it was still far away...a gray speck of a mountain. She found her way by memory, saying to herself 'that one there is the mountain we passed during our travels', and she ran off to whatever mountain she remembered."

Regardless of the exact distance, it is clear that Four-Horned Woman must have run until dawn in order to reach safety and escape the soldiers pursing her. Suzie further explained her great-grandmother's fearful journey:

"She ran through the heavy weeds and cactus and didn't leave any footprints, but by early dawn she heard the dogs still barking behind her trying to find her tracks. She quickly ran up the mountain while it was still dark. She was young and could run fast for a long time. She then lay on top of the mountain and noticed her feet hurting her real bad. She was relieved and finally was thinking about sleeping some by this time. She rested when she realized she could not walk on her feet anymore."

Recognizing her injuries prevented further travel, Four-Horned Woman hid in a tree far from the Mexican's sight, and tended to her wounds:

"She broke off some juniper branches and collected them to make a bed for herself (giggles). She took the thorns from under her feet and covered all the bottom of them with tree sap. Tree sap was an important Dine' medicine and made things heal faster. She got some tree barks and wrapped it around her feet, and this way she could shuffle around."

---

[11] It is possible that Suzie may also be masking feelings of sadness or embarrassment with her giggling. I do not feel this is the case, however, and family members have confirmed that Suzie's laughter is due to her sense of wonder that Four-Horned Woman was able to survive under such severe conditions.

According to Suzie's family, the soft, pliable bark of juniper produces a sap containing a natural healing compound, one that draws impurities from the skin. The sap protected wounds and prevented infection. I found other first-hand accounts from escapees that suffered wounds while escaping who used a similar treatment. A woman by the name of Mary Juan told such a story involving her paternal grandmother. After being enslaved by a Mexican family, this ancestor managed one night to escape. Juan's grandmother suffered terrible blisters from her journey, yet the sap proved an effective medicine. Ms. Juan's grandmother told her, "When my feet blistered I put some *tsin'bi'jeeh*, (spruce pitch), on them to keep from getting too sore. Then I wrapped them with wide leaves."[12] In my search for survival accounts that mirrored Suzie's, I would discover still more similarities between Four-Horned Woman's experience and that of her contemporaries.

SURVIVAL
"A danger foreseen is half avoided." — *Cheyenne*

Four-Horned Woman spent her first two weeks of freedom in the mountains, crawling from her treetop hideaway to the surrounding brush. Each day she moved further from her hiding place in search of food and water. Suzie claimed that until these essentials could be found her ancestor made do with what nature provided:

"She ate juniper berries, and she also found some red berries, (The Yazzies assume these were chokeberries; small, hard berries from a tree that grows in the Four Corners region and has a slight chocolate taste when ripe.) She started collecting these and hauled them back up to her camp. It was her only source of food. The blanket she slept with would have Jack Frost (ice crystals) on it at night, and she would lick it off the blanket for her thirst. That was her only water for awhile."

Eventually Four-Horned Woman found a source of water, and her feet continued to heal:

"She went further up the mountain and found water. She came upon a stream where water seeped out, and she made her bedding right there. She spent many days there while her sore feet were peeling (giggles). Her feets were raw and red, but after about two weeks they felt better and she began to walk normally."

With her feet exposed and tender, Four-Horned Woman made protective shoes in order to hunt for food more efficiently:

"She started making a sandal out of yucca thorns, (I believe Suzie means the leaves of the Yucca plant which are long, narrow and sharply pointed), and she would be weaving the thorns all the time. She just ate berries and drank water and made the shoes. It was good that the mountain had a lot of berries, and sometimes she could catch a squirrel, because she spent a long time in that mountain."

---

[12] Chee, Patty et al.,(Staff of Lake Valley Title Project). Oral Stories of the Long Walk. Crownpoint, New Mexico: Lake Valley Navajo School, 1994, 82. I would later learn of other instances in which juniper sap aided healing

Four-Horned Woman finally decided to begin the dangerous journey home using the landmarks she had memorized during the Long Walk to navigate her way:

"When my ancestor took off from where she was resting she looked at each mountains and went by them like stars. The only time she traveled was after sunset. She went beside the path, not on the exact trail where the Mexicans might be looking for her."

As Four-Horned Woman made her way back home, her fellow Navajo began to hide from Kit Carson and his men. This army had been sent to round up Four-Horned Woman's people for the "Long Walk" to Bosque Redondo. While Suzie's great-grandmother struggled to return home, her family fought to remain alive and free.

RESISTANCE
"The weakness of the enemy makes our strength." — Cherokee

Suzie's great-grandmother traveled some three hundred miles to find her family. There were, however, no guarantees that the relatives she sought had successfully evaded capture. If they had managed to escape, Four-Horned Woman's people may then succumb to starvation. Records show that a number of Navajo did manage to avoid internment throughout the period of Carson's roundup. Paul Begay, a resident of that area, recalled oral history about this time. "The land around here belongs to the Navajos [because] about five families hid out here and never went to Fort Sumner."[13] Unfortunately, evading the soldiers cost these families much needed supplies. Those in hiding were intentionally denied government distributions of rations and other essentials that were later granted to those Dine' interred. Begay explained, "after Fort Sumner, sheep were given to the Navajos at Fort Defiance, but [my clan] around here didn't get any. That's because they were hiding out."[14] For those Dine' who were able to avoid Carson's soldiers it soon became clear that they would have to struggle in an effort to feed themselves and their families.

Running throughout Navajo legend are many individual stories that tell of survival and the evasion of Carson's soldiers. Themes of the Dine' underdog tricking the white man is popular among native storytellers. It is well known that a number of Navajo evaded capture by fleeing to the safety of Canyon de Chelly. This traditional sanctuary was accessible only to those who were skilled in traversing the precarious hand and toeholds. Carved by the Anasazi centuries before, the Navajo had intricate knowledge of obscure routes leading to the safety of the mountain tops. These natives quietly survived atop places such as Fortress Rock, where water could be collected from depressions that filled with rainwater during the occasional storm. One story in particular illustrates Navajo ingenuity. Natives stationed on these mesas were, at one point, directly above Carson's men. During the night they lowered containers on yucca ropes to a water hole in the soldiers' camp. This clandestine collection of water

---

13 Ibid.
14 Ibid.

continued until daybreak. All the while ropes slid back and forth only steps away from the sleeping soldiers. The soldiers awoke in the morning to continue their search for the renegade natives, oblivious to the previous night's activities.[15] Navajo elder Teddy Drapper, Sr. recalled his own great-grandmother's story of deception:

"All mothers, children, older people and younger people were instructed to stay quiet until the soldiers passed us...From where I was they looked very small, but they were well armed and had good horses. They camped below us at the junction. Our men didn't try to attack them. The next day they moved down the canyon and disappeared."[16]

Rebels such as Manuelito, Delgadito and Barbancito, the last of whom made his base in the customary Navajo sanctum of Canyon De Chelly, led other resistance efforts, and many narratives tell of how the Dine' fought Carson's soldiers. One of Suzie's favorite stories involves a small Navajo victory:

"For Dine' that were slow or disabled was built a fork-stick hogan. When the soldiers would come, the ones that could, ran away, but other Dine' stayed in the hogan with knives in their hands, (giggles). The soldiers on horseback crawled on top of the hogan, but their legs broke through a hole in the top. The Dine' cut them as the soldiers' legs came through. Those inside would hang on to the soldiers legs and cut them here and there. They knew that if one soldier got hurt the rest of them would retreat. The Dine' that were disabled were the ones doing the cutting, while their family came back and used arrows on the soldiers circling the hogan. This made the soldiers eventually run off."

While she recognized that her ancestors were reacting to a desperate situation, Suzie once again could not contain her laughter. The vision of Carson's men, flailing atop the hogan while besieged by invalids, struck her as ridiculous. In a potentially tragic story, Suzie used her narrative to demonstrate how even the weakest Navajo could muster enough strength and intelligence to ward off the very soldiers sent to destroy them. It occurred to me that Suzie's stories conveyed the power and force behind Navajo survival. When relayed by elders to a modern Dine' audience, that generation gains a greater sense of Navajo identity and allows them to glean something positive from the Long Walk event.

While renegade family members survived on sparse supplies and avoided capture, Four-Horned Woman struggled to rejoin her own clan. The journey left her hungry and weak, as she picked her way through brush and along hills running parallel to the path traveled by the Mexican slave-traders. Suzie claimed that the long trek all the way from Texas back to her home in the territory of New Mexico left Four-Horned Woman unable to speak. I assumed this was caused by the trauma and loneliness brought on by her ancestor's escape. At this stage of the legend an entity appears in the form of an owl. The creature was to act as Four-Horned Woman's guide and protector.

---

[15] Roberts, John. Three Navajo Households: A comparative study in small group culture. Cambridge: Peabody Museum Publishers, 1951, 57.

[16] Ibid., 58.

Suzie suggested that, while the owl was ultimately responsible for delivering her ancestor safely home, the strong magic needed to do so might actually have been the cause of her mute condition. It was at this point in the story that Suzie's daughter Effie appeared at the door of the Shade House. Sitting down to join us she confirmed the story of this legendary owl:

"Yes, Four-Horned Woman was protected by the owl all the way back, and we were told that when she got home she had feathers growing out here and there, from the ears and nose, because of her closeness to it."

Suzie nodded in agreement:

"It happened when she was on her way back. There was an owl sitting near her one night when she woke up to go walking, and that's probably why she lost her speech. She just wasn't speaking anymore."

The details concerning Four-Horned Woman's protector differ depending on which family member repeats the story. Some individuals believe that the owl successfully guided their ancestor by flying in the direction of her home and steering her clear of the soldiers. Others remember hearing that the owl kept Four-Horned Woman warm and safe by spreading its wings over the exhausted girl as she slept. Suzie's son, Lonnie voiced his own belief that his ancestor stopped talking because of "the fright she went through, because she had no one to talk to." All would agree, however, that the owl made it possible for their ancestor to survive the elements and to return home.

The owl as protector is a recurring symbol among the Navajo in their tales of the Long Walk. In the Lake Valley School collection of oral history pertaining to Navajo relocation, a woman named Mayla Benally passed on a story told to her "by word of mouth" among the people in her clan:

"In some places they had to cross rivers, and the owl would give a warning signal to the people to tell them how deep the water was and where they should cross. The owl would fly in a direction where it was safe to cross."[17]

The story I found most similar to Suzie's came from Hoskie Juan regarding his great-grandmother. Placed in charge of her family's remaining sheep, this ancestor wandered too far from Carson's encampment at Bosque Redondo and became lost in a snow storm:

"She heard an owl in the distance. The sound came closer, and then the owl sat on a tree branch that she was standing under. She said to the owl, 'Please Grandfather, help me. I am freezing.' She spread her saddle blanket in the snow and sat on it. Then she heard tree branches breaking off a tree, and she listened to the sound. She went to sleep and slept all night. When she woke up at dawn the next day, she noticed that her blanket, buckskin dress, and moccasins were dry. The snow had melted and dried around her, and the horse was eating grass. The owl was sitting on the tree branch looking at her. She said to the owl, 'Thank you, Grandfather, for helping me survive

---

[17] Chee, *Oral Stories of Long Walk*, 35.

the snow storm.' There were no clouds or snow, and she could see her way to the sheep camp. The owl flew off in that direction and she followed it." [18]

In an effort to understand how the owl might symbolize both "grandfather" and protector, I researched scientific literature and information that might confirm the owl as a protective entity. I found that some Anglo scholars painted the creature in a somewhat negative light. The owl in these stories came as a symbol of foreboding or evidence of some dark magic. My investigation led me to anthropologist Clyde Kluckhohn's study of the imitation owls made of plastic he and his team observed hanging among the more rural hogans. He noted that "at night one can easily get the illusion that the owl is real, and the child is warned that it will take them off. This threat is the more sinister because of the association of owls with ghosts and witches." [19]

Maintaining a healthy suspicion of owls was also recommended in a more recent book by Ernie Bulow, in which Navajo taboos are explained. "Don't go where you hear owls hoot in the daylight," the author wrote. He learned from his Navajo sources that, "Owls are spies for the evil spirits." [20] Bulow also stated that horned toads and other creatures could be considered re-incarnates of "grandfathers," and should be left unharmed. [21] The mystery of the owl and its purpose in Navajo lore remains, but certainly in Four-Horned Woman's case this entity served as protector and guide for Suzie's ancestor, and provided a similar service to escapees making their way back home from Bosque Redondo.

REDEMPTION: Home and healing
"If a man is to do something more than human, he must have more than human powers." – Unknown Tribe

After months of solitude and fear, Four-Horned Woman found her way home. Bone thin, ragged, and unrecognizable to neighbors, her family remained ignorant of her return for some days. Unable to speak, Four-Horned Woman received care from neighboring families until they could determine her identity and she was returned to her own clan. Suzie described the experience of her great-grandmother's return in detail:

"I heard she came back very thin, no meat on her at all (giggles). While she was heading home someone was herding sheep right around the spot where she use to live. She went to the sheepherder, but she couldn't talk. The person herding sheep thought 'Who the heck is this skinny lady?' A lot of her clan was still in hiding, but eventually they got her back where some of Four-Horned Woman's family still lived. Once they

---

[18] Ibid., 78.

[19] Kluckhohn & Leighton, *Children of People,* 52.

[20] Bulow, Ernie. Navajo Taboos. Gallup: Buffalo Medicine Books, 1991, 199.

[21] Ibid., 79.

realized who she was they were happy, but because of the magic done on her she was told to sit outside while they figured something out for her."

Whether she lost the power of speech through contact with the owl spirit or because of her months of isolation, it became clear to Four-Horned Woman's family that she was in need of healing. Traditional Dine' belief holds that one may be spiritually contaminated by non-natives harboring ill will. Because this harmful essence may be transmitted to others, a period of seclusion is needed until ceremonies can be performed to cleanse those exposed to this negative energy. Suzie explained how the services of a Medicine Man were sought before her great-grandmother could interact among others or enter the family hogan:

"She was told that she couldn't go back into her home just like that. There was a lot of traditional faith back then, and they felt that because she had been taken away and held prisoner she should be cleansed of the bad days and thoughts. So she just sat outside the hogan for awhile, and they looked for someone to heal her. They found a Medicine Man and brought him back. He preformed prayer on my ancestor and there was chanting and singing when she was led back in the hogan.

Then there was a ceremony for the people who lived there. There were about ten of her family including her mother, and after the prayers they could really recognize her as her old self. Her mother was saying the prayers for her because Four-Horned Woman was unable to utter the prayers herself. That's when she spoke again. Yes, it was during the ceremony and prayers when she finally spoke. From the blessing-prayers and ceremony she was cleansed, washed. They knew a lot about the Blessing Way Ceremony back then, and we still have it today on some people."

The Blessing Way and the Navajo Enemy Way are both healing ceremonies carried out for the purpose of maintaining harmony among clans and within individuals as well and are still performed among Dine' today. The Navajo soldiers who fought in World War II, Korea and Vietnam still attend Enemy Way ceremonies in an effort to rid themselves of enemy spirits. Some Navajo believed that these spirits might continue to pursue a victim even beyond their death. At some point the Navajo adopted the term Squaw Dance, used by non-natives as a way of identifying the ceremony. However, the Dine' term for this occasion is *'Anaa' ji' nda'a'* or in its shortened form *Nda*. There is a belief among the Navajo that the taking of a life will continue to affect a person such as a soldier of war until an "Enemy Way" ceremony is performed often enough to drive away any angry and confused spirits. In his account of one Navajo man's life, Vincent Crapanzano quoted his subject who spoke of the link between this ceremony and negative encounters with enemies:

"You have a Squaw Dance if you have killed a white man or if you've killed someone in war. This bothers you when you come back. You have bad dreams. You can't sleep. This is one way to have a Squaw Dance." [22]

Cleansing ceremonies remain popular among the Navajo whenever contact with non-natives caused distress. The Squaw Dance is still requested by some Dine' women

---

[22]Crapanzano, Vincent. The Fifth World of Forster Bennett. New York: The Viking Press, 1972, 215.

as a way of counteracting intimate relations with white men they feel have caused negative feelings. Suzie's daughter-in-law discussed this practice with me on one occasion after she had attended a *Nda*. "It's not that it's necessarily a bad thing for a Navajo woman to be with a white man, it's just that he's not Dine,' and for some of us who are more conservative it's a healing thing. It's traditional and it makes these Navajo feel more at peace."

Anthropologist Gladys Richard, who worked extensively with the Navajo, confirms the necessity of these ceremonies. She claims that "if a woman sees a dead person or the bones of one other than a Navajo while carrying a child, the child when it grows up may have bad luck in the form of disease which could only be cured by *anadji*, or War Dance, (another name for the Enemy Way ceremony)."[23] Another ceremony known as "Blessingway" may be used to guarantee good health that might have been adversely affected from witnessing a fatal accident, exposure to an eclipse, or encountering any number of acts deemed unhealthy.[24] These healing ceremonies have held an important place in Navajo culture throughout their history, and have been proven to be powerful and effective enough to withstand the test of time as well as the introduction of modern, white medicine.

A Blessingway ceremony provided comfort to Four-Horned Woman after her ordeal, and her family believed that this rite cleared her spirit of negative forces she acquired while held captive by the Mexicans and during her long journey home. Soon afterwards she began to contribute as a family member and was once more assigned to herding the family's sheep.

RECAPTURE: The second Long Walk
"Not every sweet root gives birth to sweet grass." – Unknown Tribe

Suzie continued the story of her ancestor and how she actually suffered recapture just before a treaty was signed that allowed for the release of the Navajo internees. Forced to withstand yet another long journey, Four-Horned Woman's own mother died as a result of this capture:

"Yes, I remember she was captured twice, and that was when her mom died. They were using wagons for hauling everyone, I was told. Her mom was an elder lady, and the soldiers just threw kids on top of her and she was crushed along with some others. They just threw them into the wagon one on top of each other...even babies, and suffocation killed her."

---

[23] Richard., Gladys. <u>Dezba, Woman of the Desert</u>. Glorieta: The Rio Grande Press, 1971, 125, 127-128.

[24] Schwartz, Maureen Trudelle. <u>Molded in the Image of Changing Woman: Navajo views of the human body and personhood</u>. Tucson: University of Arizona Press, 1997, 127.

Suzie paused in her story, playing with the yarn she used for weaving in a distracted manner. This gave me a moment to reflect on the horrendous scene she had just painted of Navajo children and grandparents perishing in terror and confusion. I had experienced this sick feeling in my stomach before, while chronicling the life of a Holocaust survivor, and I was reminded of how hatred, racism and ignorance play a part in the human drama. It may be difficult for the modern reader to understand the atmosphere of indifference of Carson's soldiers that prompted such a cavalier attitude toward suffering, even when women and children were involved.

Nineteenth century notions of white superiority forged attitudes toward Native Americans, and fostered a mentality of America's "manifest destiny." It was their duty, even a higher calling, to clear Western lands of Indians and therefore make way for the white settlement. A good number of white soldiers who worked at relocating the Navajo no doubt believed that Indians were savages in need of direction and instruction in 'superior' white ways. Still others may have believed the natives were nothing more than a nuisance to be dealt with quickly and severely. In this connection, Raymond Lock's book on the Navajo provided useful material on one method of transport employed by the army. Wagons carried "the aged and the crippled," but were ultimately put to other uses during the Long Walk.[25] In his book about the Bosque Redondo incident, William Moore wrote of the conditions under which the Navajo captives traveled:

"Parties of Navajos, escorted by troops, traveled to Bosque Redondo. This 'Long Walk' became notorious among the Navajos. They would tell tales of a forced march wherein stragglers were gunned down to hurry along the caravan. Food supplies and transportation were limited, resulting in hunger and fatigue. The Navajos felt horror, and their subsequent oral histories would naturally blame the army."[26]

By the beginning of winter in 1864, roughly the same period of time when Four-Horned Woman was captured, the first groups of Navajo (led by Delgadito) had already surrendered and were living in captivity at Bosque Redondo. Impatient soldiers engaged in Carson's second campaign were less willing to exert the time and energy needed to control and care for captives destined for their own Long Walk. Made up of small patrols, these soldiers were known to shoot on sight any Navajo they discovered in hiding. In the Navajo's haste to evade the soldiers some elderly, lame, or pregnant family members were left behind.[27] Portions of oral history reveal ancestors who withstood great calamity at this time. According to research, "Mothers were sometimes forced to suffocate their hungry, crying babies to keep the family from being discovered and butchered by an army patrol or taken captive by slave raiders."[28] Those

---

[25] Locke, Raymond Friday. The Book of the Navajo. Los Angeles: Mankind Publishing Company, 1992, 363.

[26] Moore, William Haas. Chiefs, Agents and Soldiers. Albuquerque: University of New Mexico Press, 1994, 2-3.

[27] Locke, The Book of the Navajo, 358.

[28] Ibid.

who were captured and forced to walk the three hundred miles to Bosque Redondo suffered still more hardships on the way:

"Many of the elderly and those too weak to keep up the march, were left behind and watched hopelessly as the column passed out of sight. Their relatives gave them a little food and marched on with tears in their eyes. Those that a jeering soldier wasted a bullet on were fortunate. When that group straggled into Fort Sumner (the initial holding area for captured Navajo) 197 had been left behind, dead or dying on the trail."[29]

Four-Horned Woman would eventually find her way home once more. Until then, the painful process of learning the soldiers' rules within the internment camp awaited the intrepid young captive.

---

[29] Locke, 363.

INTERNMENT
"A rocky vineyard does not need a prayer, but a pick ax." – Navajo

Designated by the U.S. government in 1864 for the Navajo Indian reservation, Bosque Redondo was initially believed an ideal location to introduce white methods of agriculture to the Dine' people. General Carlton believed the absence of a nearby mountain range where escapees could hide would also deter escape. With no nearby mountains where internees could flee and hide, military surveillance of the Navajo was easily maintained.[30] Situated in eastern New Mexico and providing vast expanses of open land, Bosque Redondo eventually held up to eight thousand natives. Both in written white history and in Navajo memory this location was later viewed as virtually uninhabitable. Author William Moore wrote: "The water was brackish and so unfit for human consumption that the Indians complained that it made them sick. Housing was poor and firewood was nearly nonexistent. The soil was infertile."[31] Suzie told of how Four-Horned Woman was put to work along with the other Navajo growing food that might provide for the reservation population:

"They hoed cornfields and she would hoe weeds and the soldiers would be watching. That was her chore or job, the only thing she did while the bosses (soldiers) guarded her. All during the day our ancestors were told to hoe weeds in the field, and one of the guards would always watch over them while they worked in the field.."

Unfortunately, it was not immediately determined that the soil or conditions at Bosque Redondo were impervious to farming. The Navajo who had arrived the summer before Four-Horned Woman dug irrigation canals and cleared mesquite roots with either poor equipment or their bare hands. By the time Four-Horned Woman arrived winter had begun to set in, and she worked amidst crops that were doomed to fail. Internees were often forced to travel by foot as long as twenty miles searching for wood they desperately needed for fuel. At that isolated distance from camp the Navajo were threatened by Apache and Comanche enemies as well as the ever-present Mexican patrols eager to snatch unprotected women and children to use as slaves.[32]

In the midst of these unfavorable conditions the Navajo were supplied with unfamiliar tools and instructed to use white farming techniques that were impractical for the land and climate. The internees were expected to embrace the concept of becoming independent farmers in the Anglo style. The successful Navajo pattern of pastoral life supplemented by the growing of corn and melons was replaced by a completely agricultural subsistence based on the Anglo-American ideal; sedentary farming by nuclear families. The Navajo had been successful in growing corn, melon, peaches and other foods with their own native methods. These methods were largely ignored by the soldiers in favor of those familiar to white farmers. Since their efforts

---

[30] Gwyther, G. "Navajo Indian Reservation." *Overland Monthly* 10 (1873), 123 & 127.

[31] Moore, William Haas. *Chiefs, Agents & Soldiers*, 3.

[32] Locke, 368 & 372.

were meant to support food for the entire Dine' community, the Navajo had no choice but to implement the new farming methods.

Soon they relented to altering their diet and accepted the only food offered, army rations distributed by the reservation soldiers. The captives refused, however, to completely discard their own traditions and replace them with the trappings of white culture. They resisted learning the English language, and kept their children away from tents offering white schooling. They also became experts at forging ration tickets when the meager supply allotted by the soldiers failed to meet the needs of their families.[33] This only caused friction between the soldiers and internees and frustrated the government officials placed in charge of converting the Indians to an Anglo way of life.

Descendants of the Bosque Redondo inhabitants spoke of the reservation as was more than an agricultural challenge for the Dine.' Their ancestors were also vulnerable to attacks from within the camp itself at the hands of the very men charged with protecting them. The possibility of rape was one very real danger Native American women had to consider. In one twentieth century account regarding the camp, Navajo Dave Wilson revealed the dubious legacy wrought upon generations of his family due to his ancestors' internment. Proof that his ancestor was molested by one of Carson's men came when she gave birth to a child that was clearly part Anglo. Wilson explained, "Everybody in my family has this curly hair. When my great-great grandmother was released from Bosque Redondo she was already pregnant, at age fourteen or fifteen. She was probably raped there."[34]

Yet the first reports trickling back from the camp to Washington D.C. were optimistic. Contemporary observer G. Gwyther, writing for the widely read *Overland Monthly*, expressed an Anglo perspective on Navajo relocation. This journalist claimed that, "Ultimately, the Navajoes [sic] arrived at their destination in safety, and at once proceeded to accustom themselves to the mode of life--principally agriculture--designed for them by General Carlton".[35] Gwyther went on to write of the favorable conditions awaiting the Navajo at Bosque Redondo once they arrived. The attitudes of those whites placed in charge of initiating the reservation project could be seen in the journalist's account: "It was argued by experienced persons that here all the essential conditions of a successful reservation appropriate to a people with the antecedents of the Navajoes, would be found." Gwyther claimed that these conditions included "plenty of agricultural, grazing, and hunting lands; fuel, water, distance from White settlements, and an absence of mountains."[36]

According to revised histories, the reality of Bosque Redondo was quite different. Those who could not escape the camp became victims of the unforgiving Southwestern Plains climate, enduring extreme temperatures in both summer and

---

[33] Moore, 5.

[34] Roberts, David. "The Long Walk to Bosque Redondo." *Smithsonian* 28, no. 9 (December 1997): 46.

[35] Gwyther, 127.

[36] Ibid.

winter months. Arid conditions meant that little water was available to the Navajo who were accustomed to locating rain caches in their ancestral lands. Food resources also became increasingly limited. Internees suffered from a constant shortage of rations owing to graft by Army suppliers and mismanagement by the Army itself. [37] The situation turned disastrous by harvest time, and records revealed that:

"Alkaline water brought about intestinal and stomach problems, a twelve to twenty mile walk was required to obtain fuel, and the corn crop failed for two consecutive summers. In addition to the threat of starvation, cramped living conditions led to outbreaks of dysentery and measles, while sexually transmitted diseases further diminished the number of Navajo. Almost two hundred miles east of the easternmost frontier of the people's ancestral heartland, the Bosque was a virtual concentration camp."[38]

Four-Horned Woman faced sickness and possibly death if she remained in the failing camp.

LIFE AND DEATH IN BOSQUE REDONDO
"A starving man will eat with the wolf." – Oklahoma

Conditions worsened on the reservation, and hungry Navajos began to look beyond its boundaries to feed themselves and their families. Some Navajo men resorted to rustling livestock from local white farms. New Mexicans became increasingly nervous as local newspapers printed stories about Navajo raids. This created an alarmist atmosphere amongst the Anglos living near Bosque Redondo. The *Santa Fe Daily New Mexican* ran a piece that proclaimed:

"The whole county swarms with Indians hostile and bloodthirsty. On the eastern side of the Rio Grande, the country is overrun by Indians from the Bosque Redondo Reservation, who have already destroyed stock and property to the amount of many thousands of dollars, and slain many of the best citizens... Unless something is soon done to protect the people, they will take the matter into their own hands and avenge their massacred friends and relatives by killing every Navajo found outside the reservation—passport or no passport. Let this idea be carried out and we will guarantee that in short time the Navajos that are left will be content to remain inside the limits of the reservation."[39]

According to contemporary publications, Bosque Redondo supervisor General Carlton designed his crackdown in response to public concern. One historian notes that, "With the New Mexican newspapers running stories of depredations supposedly

---

[37] Trafzer, *Carson Campaign*, 179, 189, 227.
[38] Roberts, 51.
[39] Moore, 5-6.

committed by Navajos from the Bosque Redondo, Carlton decided to take stringent measures against any Indian found off the reservation without a passport."[40]

Those struggling within the camp continued to work the infertile land and survived on meager rations. When food did become available to the internees it was often a source of confusion for the Navajo and the cause of illness. Unaccustomed to the provisions supplied by white soldiers, many Dine' became sick after ingesting improperly prepared food. Suzie's oral history serves as confirmation that communication was lacking between white soldiers and their captives regarding supplies:

"Yes, when they returned to the camp they were given flour (as opposed to the corn the Navajo were accustomed to preparing). They were given coffee and I heard they ate it like that (laughter). I heard they cooked it just like dry bread over a flame in a pan, and ate it just like they would eat beans. They got constipated because of it."

A number of Navajo narratives relate stories regarding the mishandling of food foreign to the Navajo. A woman by the name of Helen Begay recalled her grandmother's story of food distributed at Fort Defiance as part of a treaty agreement allowing the Dine' to return to their homeland. Supplies distributed for the long trek home proved inadequate because no instruction was given regarding how the food might be consumed. Helen Begay stated:

"Some of the food included flour, bacon, and coffee. The people did not know how to prepare these foods. Some people ate the bacon raw and the flour without mixing it, and they chewed the coffee beans without boiling them. Many Navajos got sick from the improper preparation of this foreign food."[41]

I found an account of this cultural confusion and the accompanying problems presented through miscommunication with the Navajo in the testimony of Agent Henry B. Bristol. The man in charge of distributing food among the Navajo reported directly to his superior General Carlton that his charges were becoming sick from the flour given them at Fort Sumner. Bristol, however, believed it was the flour itself, and not its misuse, that was causing illness among the Indians. Carlton disagreed, claiming the Indians were eating the flour raw, and were making matters worse by under-cooking their food.

Eventually the Navajo were given cornmeal and wheat meal as a healthier substitute to the white man's flour, but other complications arose when the soldiers began to provide temporary housing for the Navajo. The white custom of constructing dwellings side by side proved problematic whenever a death occurred among the natives. Dine' belief called for bereaved families to abandon or burn down any structure where death had occurred. The only possible compromise General Carlton could arrange was for the displaced family to erect a new hogan at the end of the orderly row of their neighbor's homes.[42]

---

[40] Thompson, Gerald. The Army and the Navajo. Tucson: The University of Arizona Press, 1986, 76.

[41] Chee, 13.

[42] Thompson, The Army and the Navajo, 32-33.

Contemporary attitudes toward Native Americans caused those whites residing in the Navajo region to dismiss both the Indians and the Bosque Redondo experiment as a nuisance and a hindrance to the advancement of white settlement. An article appearing in one local paper, the Santa Fe *New Mexican*, expressed the impatience local whites exhibited toward their Navajo neighbors. The article stated that the current administration:

"...favors the benefit of the lazy thieving Indian at the expense of the honest and industrious white man. We are for the white man. We hold that the people, the farmers and stock growers, should not be crowded off their lands for the benefit of a pack of thieving redskins.... should the white man be deprived of his rights and property that the Indian may enjoy them? Should the white man hunger that the Indian may rejoice in a full belly?" [43]

The same article commended Lieutenant Bristol:

"...for his untiring zeal and energy in controlling the Navajo tribe of Indians at the Bosque Redondo, and for his praiseworthy efforts in advancing their condition from that of savages to that of civilized men."[44]

The Anglo press either ignored or remained ignorant of the fact that the natives themselves had been taken from their land, and crowded onto a reservation where starvation was rapidly decreasing their numbers.

Not all whites saw the Navajo as an impediment to Western civilization. Nevertheless, a condescending view toward the Indians often prevailed among nineteenth century Anglos. A traveling journalist by the name of J.H. Beadle wrote in 1871 about the Navajo he encountered during his journey:

"Both men and women work and are quite industrious until they have accumulated a fair share of property; then they seem content to take things easy. In short, they are as much unlike the Stage Indian and as much like a tribe of dark Caucasians as it is possible to conceive...More interesting to me than any of their handicrafts is the unwearying patience they display in all of their work and their zeal and quickness to learn in everything which may improve their condition. Surely such people are capable of civilization."[45]

At this time Anglos with such an attitude operated under the assumption that 'civilizing' the Navajo by assimilating them into white culture, would be beneficial to the Indians while, not incidentally, making them less troublesome to their white neighbors and the U.S. government. Although Beadle's observations suggest a relatively sympathetic view of the Navajo, he hardly contemplates the question of whether the Indians desired the white version of civilization. The Navajo had in fact enjoyed their own civilization for some time before the appearance of whites. Recent carbon dating points to Navajo settlements that existed as early as 1300 A.D. What this contemporary writer failed to realize was that Dine' had little choice but to have, "a

---

[43] Ibid., 68.

[44] Ibid.

[45] Young, Robert W. "The Role of the Navajo in the Southwestern Drams." Gallup: *The Gallup Independent*, 1968, 46.

quickness to learn everything that may improve their condition." Clearly this was the one path to Dine' survival.

The events that U.S. officials labeled the Bosque Redondo experiment resulted in the deaths of almost one-fourth of the Navajo population of around twenty-thousand. Two thousand died in the camp itself while hundreds perished during the Long Walk of over two hundred miles. Such loss of life was a sadly typical experience of many other Native American tribes during westward U.S. expansion.[46] Because the Navajo were able to engage in evasive maneuvers, and avoid capture by Carson's soldiers, they suffered a more limited encounter than did other Native Americans who fiercely resisted the white soldiers. Escape and evasion were accepted tactics within the flexible Navajo culture, and they ultimately proved to be more effective than those methods employed by Geronimo of the Apache tribe, or even by the more confrontational Sioux Indians who defeated Custer. The Navajo would continue this form of resistance much as the Cherokee had before them, preserving their identity as Dine', at times quietly pursuing their Navajo ways under the guise of assimilation into white culture.

Most of the Navajo warriors and their families, weak from starvation, eventually surrendered to Carson and his men. Sharing their misery was the smaller tribe of Mescalero natives. These long-time enemies of the Navajo were forced to live amidst their rivals within the same confines of the internment camp. The tension and intermittent violence this situation created, along with occasional raids led by members of the Comanche tribe, caused American officials in Washington D.C. to judge the relocation of the Navajo to Bosque Redondo a complete failure. The U.S. government negotiated a treaty with the Navajo, and General Carlton received instructions allowing the natives to return to their homeland in 1868. [47] The Long Walk had finally ended, but at an immense cost to the Navajo people.

THE LEGACY OF RELOCATION

"It is no longer good enough to cry peace, we must act peace, live peace and live in peace."
— Shenandoah

Oral history has played an important role in the lives of the Navajo family members whose ancestors experienced relocation. In the introduction of *Navajo Stories of the Long Walk Period*, Navajo scholar Ruth Roessel wrote how her people's history has been unfairly placed in the hands of white historians. She pointed out that...

"No American ever would allow all his history books to be written by residents of Germany, the Soviet Union or any other foreign country. And yet, for more than a hundred years, this is exactly what transpired with regard to the Navajos. They had a history – and they had no history. They had a history in the sense that they had traditions and stories and events that took place in the past; in another sense, they had

---

[46] Locke, 380.

[47] Kelly, Lawrence C. Navajo Roundup: Selected correspondence of Kit Carson's expedition against the Navajo, 1863-1865.Boulder: The Pruett Publishing Company, 1970, 168.

no history because it was never interpreted, presented nor published by the Navajos – only by white historians and anthropologists."[48]

In the midst of recounting the atrocities that took place during the Long Walk Suzie's storytelling would, at times, abruptly cease. Clearly some details were left out, no doubt because they were too painful to recall. It was in these moments that I held my tongue and my curiosity. Pushing Suzie on such matters would have been insensitive. I did ask on several occasions whether she felt that the blame for Navajo relocation and the consequence of the Long Walk should be placed on the U.S. government and the prevailing attitude that whites had toward Indians in the nineteenth century. Her response was that the abuses suffered by her people must remain in Dine' collective memory and the whites that committed those crimes should be recognized as having done the Navajo harm. Actual blame served no real purpose to Suzie, who implied that she prefers to live in the present.

And so, remembering the event of the Long Walk has been key to Suzie and her family as part of their legacy as Dine.' The role that Suzie's ancestors played in this event has inhabited a lasting place in their hearts that gives them strength and pride. I suggested to Suzie that we travel to Bosque Redondo along the same route that her great-grandmother took during her escape. Perhaps we could honor Four-Horned Woman's memory by recreating the Long Walk. Suzie expressed a desire to take this memorial journey to see with her own eyes the place where her great-grandmother had been incarcerated. "I think about that sometimes," Suzie responded. "It's best to go during the winter, that's when there's no visitors, (tourists who visit her hogan). I just think about that, going to Bosque Redondo, just to look."

Maintaining knowledge of the female line seemed to be crucial to Navajo genealogy. Suzie explained her feelings about the legacy of her great-grandmother's escape. "My late great-grandmother used to say 'If I was killed by Carson's soldiers you guys would not have been around.' She used to say this a lot." When I asked what had become of Four-Horned Woman Suzie told me that her ancestor lived to enjoy many children and grandchildren, and that these generations settled deeper into Monument Valley. Suzie believed that, because her own mother had been ill most of her life, she found neither the time nor the strength to divulge much of the family history to her eldest daughter. Consequently, the story of Four-Horned Woman took on an even greater importance to Suzie, and she saw to it that the legend became deeply rooted in Yazzie family history. This story of survival not only provided Suzie with a proud heritage, but is also presented to the Yazzie children as a lesson about diligence and courage.

The key to the story's importance lies in Four-Horned Woman herself, who has served as a role model and heroine. Driven by her loyalty to family and longing for home, the young woman made an escape that Suzie herself described as "crazy." Yet, Four-Horned Woman is admired for the resourceful ways she managed to survive. Finally Four-Horned Woman is recognized by the Yazzie family as a Navajo woman

---

[48] Johnson, Broderick H., ed. Navajo Stories of the Long Walk Period. Tsaile: Navajo Community College Press, 1973, xii-xiii.

who persevered and remained strong in spite of encountering obstacles that should have caused her to turn back and give up hope of regaining the life she knew and loved. The Yazzies truly view this ancestor as an example of Navajo strength and consider her story part of their identity as Dine.'

Suzie finished her story about the Long Walk then stood up to leave. Upon some silent signal known only to the Yazzies, it had been decided that the day's interview was over. The gracious old lady smiled at me and shook my hand. More questions bumped around in my head, but she was making her way back to the hogan in a manner that was both casual and determined. Effie gave me a smile and followed her mother out. I glanced at my watch and was astonished to see that a little over five hours had passed. Suddenly I was exhausted. Standing to gather my things I felt an ache in my back and soreness in my hand where I had griped my pen.

The good-byes between Emily and me were brief. Rain clouds were forming overhead, and I wanted to get back to my room before a storm made the roads too muddy. Navigating the road and washes back to Goulding's, I saw another bus full of tourists zip by me heading toward the compound. I imagined the eldest Yazzie ducking once more into her hogan to greet them. The day was not quite over for Suzie, and I sensed that she would be pleased to perform yet another demonstration of her weaving and possibly sell some of the Yazzie's rugs or jewelry. I pulled into Goulding's just as a light rain began to fall, quenching the thirsty red soil.

A CHANGE OF PLACE
"May the Great Spirit's blessings always be with you." — Cherokee

The next day I was to leave the Valley, and I planned to break my journey back to Albuquerque into two days. I thought it would be nice to sleep in a little before the long trip home. Emily met me in the Goulding's parking lot, and forgoing breakfast for a change we made the drive into the park to say goodbye to Suzie. A tourist bus stood empty in front of the hogan when we arrived. Lonnie worked at a steady pace chopping wood for his mother's stove. He looked up from his task when he saw us, and motioned toward the hogan indicating there were many visitors inside. "You can poke your head in if you want to say so long," Lonnie suggested, "but she'll be pretty busy." I looked at Emily for guidance. "Oh well," my friend said with a giggle, "we're not too big on goodbyes around here anyway." I tried not to show my disappointment, but reasoned that my friends were probably right. Suzie loved spending time with her visitors, and I didn't want to break her stride.

Emily asked if she could accompany me to Chinle where she and Lonnie lived. She wanted to check on her kids, and Lonnie would be busy at his mother's for most of the day. "You two girls go ahead," Emily's husband advised, "I'll see you back in the big city." Emily shook her head with a smile, and then took my arm to lead me back to the car. She explained that she and Lonnie had two teen-aged sons together. Emily's niece also lived with the family in a small, two-bedroom condo within the Indian Housing complex. Another family member residing in Chinle was Emily's nineteen-year-old daughter from a previous marriage. Nina and her boyfriend lived in a separate housing unit with their baby son.

I thought that it would be interesting to see how differently Emily and Lonnie lived from Suzie, so we departed from the compound with little fanfare and were soon bumping along the dirt road that led out of the park. Before long we were on the open highway and heading for Keyenta. From that little town we turned onto the road leading to Chinle. This drive took another forty-five minutes, past the tiny town of Rough Rock where a school teaching Navajo culture had been established. It was an institution founded by Ruth Roessel, the author of many books regarding the Navajo that I was in the process of reading. I would have liked to stop there, but Emily was anxious to see her kids, so we pressed on.

As we pulled into Chinle I began to understand why Emily had laughed at her husband's description of this "big city." As the gateway to Canyon de Chelly it was certainly an important town, but other than this distinction there didn't seem to be much more to it. I followed Emily's instructions into her neighborhood while she told me a little about the life on the reservation. "A lot of families here have problems that need solving, and sometimes it takes time because everybody is busy just trying to survive," Emily informed me. Limited job opportunities, teen pregnancy and alcoholism were only a few of the challenges Emily said the Navajo faced within their communities.

The comment regarding alcohol surprised me. I told Emily that I always believed drinking would be less of a problem for the Navajo since alcohol is banned from the reservation. "Well, any time there's unemployment, or not enough programs for kids, there's the possibility that people will drink because there's nothing better to do," she informed me. "I think there's a little bootlegging here and there and people can also smuggle in alcohol through places like Cortez, although there are checkpoints in Gallup and other areas." She went on to say, "I understand the reasoning behind restricting liquor on the reservation, but I think there are better solutions."

As we pulled into Emily's complex I could see that life was indeed difficult for the families living there. The government housing seemed adequate enough; however the area around these homes were a little depressing with their sparse vegetation. I had a strong feeling that there were very few conveniences available with this sort of lifestyle. Emily and Lonnie had made their little apartment comfortable and clean, but with Emily's daughter visiting and two teenage boys the space was somewhat crowded, and it seemed to me that the desert was doing its best to invade their home. The constant wind had pushed under the door the familiar fine red dust and it lightly covered the linoleum floor. The family had a washing machine that occasionally worked, but no clothes dryer. For a family of four, (not including visiting relatives), they managed well, but I believed there were many things that would have made life easier for them; everyday items that I took for granted.

Emily introduced her boys and her daughter, each of them politely shaking my hand. We sat for a while and talked about Emily's trip out to the Valley and how Suzie was doing. It grew dark and I was hungry. Lonnie called to say that he was on his way home in the couple's only car, so I asked if he would like to meet us at my hotel for dinner. He happily agreed and we shared a nice meal and conversation at the Holiday Inn. We ate and talked until our stomachs were full and our tongues were tired. By nine o'clock I was accompanying the couple out to the hotel parking lot where we paused to gaze at the beautiful desert sky. It was jam-packed with stars, and I stood there feeling small and a little homesick. After a sigh I gave both of my friends a big Anglo hug. We had all had a wonderful time together, and I was leaving them with a heavy heart. Although it seemed as if the trip was ending too soon, I had to admit to myself that I still felt out of place there on the reservation.

As the Yazzies drove off I wondered how many more visits it would take to gather their family history. There were so many questions I had yet to ask Suzie. How would I ever record her entire story when I only visited once or twice a year for only a few days at a time? In spite of the questions swirling around my head I fell asleep as soon as my head hit the pillow.

I awoke the next day devoid of the enthusiasm I experienced every morning since I'd arrived. Throwing my things into the rental car I came to terms with the fact that I had a long drive ahead of me. Navigating the long and empty highways seemed more familiar and less threatening than when I'd made the trip out. I concluded that in spite of its isolation, the reservation was actually much safer than many places in California. As I drove along I enjoyed the scenery more and took note of places I would like to visit during my next trip. "Visit St. Michael's," one billboard suggested, "see historical site, botanical garden, zoo and museum on highway 264." Every so often I saw an abandoned structure and wondered at its hidden history. I even passed a deserted trading post that looked as if it had once done a pretty brisk business. What had caused its demise?

As a way of passing time I made mental notes of things I had promised the Yazzies before I left. Suzie would love to have some of the varieties of tea I brought from home. Emily and Lonnie hinted that they wouldn't mind a copy of the traditional Navajo music I found at the visitor's center at the park's entrance. I was surprised that they had not already purchased the tape, since they drove in and out of the park all the time. As a parting gift I gave Emily a framed sand painting of some yeibechi. She seemed to like it, but I now knew that most of what the family needed was of a practical nature. The kids were always short of decent clothes because the dry dessert was hard on jeans and shirts. The red soil stained and the rocks the kids played on wore holes into just about everything.

I was still imagining Suzie's austere little house as I pulled into Albuquerque. I had reserved a room at a comfortable hotel, and the late afternoon heat made me want nothing more but to nap. Unfortunately, my room was next to the pool where a wedding party was celebrating. I learned from the man at the front desk that the bride was a former Miss Navajo, and as I looked out my balcony door I could see the happy couple dancing to the latest pop tune. The boom-boom-boom of the bass made it impossible to sleep, so I watched the festivities until things quieted down. That night I dreamt I'd walked down to the wedding reception and told the revelers, "There's a perfectly good Squaw Dance going on just outside of town...why don't you party there instead and you can dance all night!" This place was really starting to get to me.

CHAPTER 3 – SUZIE'S STORY

"A hungry stomach makes a short prayer." – Paiute

EARLY RESERVATION LIFE

My second visit to the Valley went more smoothly because I learned I could fly from Phoenix to Farmington, a small town bordering the reservation. This cut down on my driving time to Goulding's. "Smooth" was hardly the word for our landing however. I clutched my seat in the rocking little plane and prayed to God for a safe landing. After several alarming bumps from turbulence I began praying to the Yazzies' gods as well. First, I pleaded with Changing Woman. Then I moved on to White Shell Woman, and finally I threw in a request to Coyote the Trickster, for good measure. I detest flying. To me it has always felt unsafe and very uncomfortable. When we finally touched down I swore that someday I would investigate a more civilized mode of travel. I mean…to my bones, this raggedy experience isn't too different from the rough and tumble stagecoach days.

I made good time to the lodge, and immediately called to Emily and Lonnie at their home in Chinle. Emily answered, and it was great to hear her voice. We arranged a time to meet up the next morning. I spent the rest of the day organizing my work for the weekend and jotted down questions I wished to ask Suzie and took another look into my reference material. I had one book on Navajo culture written by Ruth Roessel that I found especially interesting. I learned that Ms. Roessel lived and worked with the Navajo in the 1940s and spent years getting to know the people and their culture. I envisioned a much smaller project with the Yazzies. Now that I had recorded the legend of Four-Horned Woman I planned to record Suzie's story, and perhaps obtain some testimony from one or two of her adult children. However, the more I read about Navajo life, the more questions came to mind. There was so much that wasn't covered in the literature I'd read thus far. My goal for this particular trip was to correlate Suzie's accounts with historical references of the same period. My plan stemmed on augmenting her stories with those of her contemporaries so that I could better illustrate what life was like in the Valley years ago.

During the winter break I had visited the university library and compiled three pages of information regarding the Navajo. Sadly, what I read seemed quite limited and skewed, particularly in older books that clearly did not represent Navajo life today. I found plenty of dated literature that spewed the tired history and old rhetoric about how the Navajo were "relocated" by Kit Carson, and how much better off they are with the proper Anglo education. It simply did not satisfy, and I was excited about compiling a contemporary piece of work based on listening and recording a real story from the words of someone who truly knew, on so many levels, the plight, fight, dreams and successes of these people.

My primary questions revolved around how much the Navajo people have changed over time and whether there have been, as I suspected, a revival of Dine' traditions among them. Most of my queries centered on cultural issues. In my search for the Dine' version of their history I realized very few primary sources were quoted or even referenced. I began to wonder if this sort of material ever existed. Maybe I was not looking in the right place. I read late into the night and hoped to discover more from Suzie the next day.

The next morning Emily and Lonnie sauntered into Goulding's restaurant with their usual nonchalance. After heartfelt greetings and a hearty breakfast I followed Lonnie's car into the park, with Emily at my side for company. We caught up on each other's news and I realized I had missed my friend as much as the Valley itself. When we drove into Suzie's compound I was delighted to see it devoid of "visitors." I went to gather my things but was halted by Emily's gentle hand. "Don't pop out just yet," she advised, "let Suzie see you from her window and then we'll come in slowly. That's how it's done." I could see Suzie peering from the cracked and dusty window her home, and sat quietly as I was told. I wondered to myself if Suzie preferred this dwelling over the hogan where she usually received guests. Did coming to the house mean I was no longer myself a "visitor"? The idea of being on more intimate terms with the old woman gave me a strange feeling of satisfaction. Something was already shifting in my assumptions about being an outsider.

After a few minutes Emily indicated enough time had passed, and we ventured into Suzie's home. My friend made the appropriate introductions and I offered the customary weak handshake to Suzie in the manner I had seen other family members greet one another. I still felt awkward however, and I realized how much I needed to study Dine' protocol. Suzie took a seat on her bed and I on a creaky chair beside her. I gently clipped a microphone to her collar and unpacked my tape recorder while Emily translated that her mother-in-law remembered me from my last trip out. The old woman smiled at me with ease, and began to answer my questions while her hands danced in the manner they always did when we spoke together; like two birds playing in flight.

I began to work with Suzie as I had on my previous visit; adjusting my speedy off-reservation sense of timing to the slower pace of the Valley. When in doubt of where

Suzie's story was going I waited instead of pressing on. Time did not stand completely still here, but neither was it in any hurry. While working with Suzie I learned a new way of being, and a different kind of rhythm. This applied not only to my listening skills, but also to my way of speaking, walking, and even dreaming. Originally I was impatient with the Navajo sense of time, but it didn't take long to understand and trust that Suzie's stories would unfold without much prodding. This tactic turned into a kind of internal knowing, and it served both me and Suzie well during what would become years of interviews together. My real concern revolved around how the heck I would tie all the information together into some kind of book. I had a muse of sorts who I could call upon when necessary and I eventually trusted the idea that I was working with the Yazzies for a reason. Everything would work out somehow. I think, however, that my muse must also have been Navajo, because she took her sweet time to kick in! Fumbling for my list of prepared questions I tried to keep Suzie engaged and interested.

As she spoke, I thought of how arrogant I must be in my attempts to structure and analyze the life of others, particularly of a people so different from me. I approached this task with the same mantra I used toward every new thing I had attempted in the past; "might as well give it a try. The worst that could happen is I'd embarrass myself." I had stumbled and fallen a lot in life, but it never permanently damaged me. The only problem with this new endeavor seemed to be that I might show the Yazzies in a bad light by incorrectly telling their story. The nagging thought of somehow failing them tormented me while I worked.

As Suzie's life history began to unreel I could see the interaction that grew between Dine' and Anglo peoples throughout the twentieth century. Her stories exposed the details of two cultures often colliding, but also working in a kind of harmony. I heard how the Navajo dealt with white trade, tourism, and eventually the motion picture industry. The Yazzie view of history went beyond those dated textbooks I had back in my room at the lodge. As for religion, both Christian missionary evangelism and the introduction of the Native American Church (a movement originating among the Plains Indians) affected the Yazzies and other Navajo. Why did some Navajo like Suzie continue traditional religious practices, while later Yazzie generations came to accept new doctrines? This was a question I hoped to explore. It wanted to investigate the Yazzies' personal experiences with enforced Anglo education and Christian missionary work.

During our time together I also learned how Suzie's life was altered by the avid uranium mining that took place in the Monument Valley region and throughout the Four Corners area of New Mexico from the 1940s up to the 1970s. I was interested in how Suzie coped with the challenges brought on by her husband's work in mining. Perhaps I could compare her experience with that of other Navajo families who challenged the mining companies. I had heard that some Navajo sought restitution by proving that these companies were negligent. Sadly, many of the natives were forced to deal with the physiological and environmental damage brought on by uranium contamination.

THINKING LIKE A NAVAJO
"Do not judge your neighbor until you walk two moons in his moccasins." — Cheyenne

Obviously white interests have affected the Yazzies in big ways. How did the Navajo respond to these changes, and in what way did they manage to keep their culture alive? It is my belief that Navajos such as the Yazzies have been largely successful in resisting complete assimilation because of an acquired flexibility they came to rely upon when dealing with cultures other than their own. Though they seemingly adopted a non-confrontational stance, a steadfast commitment to Navajo culture has remained among the Dine.' One may arguably say that methods used to subdue other Indian nations ultimately failed in forcing the Dine' to completely assimilate into white society. This style of indirect resistance appeared within the Yazzie family, and it seems to have allowed them the ability to maintain their traditions.

I learned early on that Suzie divulged her life story in her own way and in her own time. I found that I could not force her to describe her life, from birth to her more recent experiences, in the linear or chronological fashion so familiar to Anglos. Nor did time have the same meaning to Suzie as it had come to have for me, a white woman living in what she would have viewed as luxury. In my world, time was viewed as a commodity that could be bought and sold. Not so for Suzie. She answered my questions about her childhood until deciding another period of her life was more important to discuss. Suzie did not worry about keeping things 'straight,' and instead went from one story to the next depending on how much it amused her.

It was not as if Suzie were not doing her best to answer my questions. She was very courteous about trying to do so. But the old woman kept her answers brief, sometimes refusing to explain certain events in more than a cursory manner. Suzie's personal history was not contained as a neat package in her mind. Like any woman her age, my subject's life was multi-faceted. Conflicts arose as she learned to live as both a Native American and a modern American woman. In writing her story I tried to give Suzie a very strong and coherent voice. Although her thoughts have been placed in hard print, I hoped Suzie's personality would shine through. I also hoped to make her world view more accessible to those interested in the life of a Navajo woman.

After hearing Suzie's story it occurred to me that she possessed a sharp mind and a quiet strength. Her character was undeniably shaped by the legend of Four-Horned Woman. The story of this colorful and remarkable ancestor provided an excellent example of Navajo cultural resilience to Suzie at a very young age. She learned how the desire to pursue a Dine' way of life compelled her own great-grandmother to escape Bosque Redondo at huge risk to herself. Like many of her contemporaries, the decisions she made while resisting assimilation were often spontaneous, and her agility in adapting to the pressures surrounding her allowed for her very survival. The telling and re-telling of Four-Horned Woman's struggle became more than a good fireside story to Suzie. It actually shaped what Suzie was to become, and she passed on her ancestor's lessons to her family. This helped the Yazzies to challenge attempts made by outside forces to alter or exterminate their way of life.

In a way, the Yazzies quiet preservation of their ancestor's culture may be the ultimate revenge for the suffering endured by Four-Horned Woman. Throughout Suzie's own life she and her family managed to negotiate within the boundaries set by whites who attempted to control them. While a Western brand of education, economy and religion was introduced into the "subordinate" Navajo culture, the Yazzies and many other Navajo resisted their influences. The Yazzie's methods may have been unique to their own experience, but there is a record of how other Navajo maintained a sense of cultural identity in much the same manner. In his work on domination and resistance Author James C. Scott compared the kind of compliance demanded by Anglos of the Navajo, and the actual beliefs held by the natives:

"Two general findings from a variety of experiments are of interest. First, they indicate that forced compliance not only fails to produce attitudes that would sustain that compliance in the absence of domination, *but produces a reaction against such attitudes*.[49] Second, they show that individual beliefs and attitudes are likely to reinforce compliance with power holders' wishes if, and only if, that compliance is perceived as freely chosen – as voluntary. Coercion, it would seem, can produce compliance but it virtually inoculates the complier against willing compliance." [50]

Coercion did not work among the Navajo at Bosque Redondo, nor was it entirely successful in areas of education, economy, or religion. The power of individual choice and the influence of Dine' culture proved stronger in many instances among native families like the Yazzies.

LISTEN AND HEAR
"All things share the same breath – the beast, the tree, the man, the air shares its spirit with all the life it supports." – Chief Seattle

Native American women and Suzie's self-view
I learned so much from listening to the legend of Four-Horned Woman, but now I was curious about the role of Suzie's narrative. Why did the Yazzie's show such enthusiasm in retelling their family stories, particularly to a non-Navajo like me? What was my place as a white woman recording their family stories? Would compiling these stories in written form attract young people who were now less inclined to spend evenings listening to their elders? Certainly there was less opportunity now for children to spend time with their grandparents. I felt this was a shame, because there seemed to be important ritual aspects behind the passing on of Navajo ceremonies, legends, songs, and family history. I could never hope to be present while sacred stories or

---

[49] Author's italics.
[50] Scott, James C. Domination and the Arts of Resistance, Hidden Transcripts. London: Yale University Press, 1990, 109.

songs were passed on. The Navajo community restricts such knowledge so that it may remain exclusively within Dine' consciousness. However, to the best of my knowledge, recording a family's history has never been considered a subject among the Navajo that may not be shared with a non-native. Was it then unusual to entrust this sort of native cultural property to an Anglo? My work with the Yazzies was likely perceived by them as a kind of insurance in preserving the family's past; it constitutes backup to an oral tradition that may or may not be continued by future Yazzie generations.

Of course, it was possible that the Yazzies had no set motive for sharing family and cultural information with me. I was inclined to believe, however, that storytelling was more than an idle distraction among the Yazzies, nor is the practice exclusive amongst their family members. The legend of Four-Horned Woman has been told around the campfire to countless tourists as part of the Monument Valley excursion offered by the Yazzies. What did matter to the family was my treatment of their stories, and the Yazzies took great care to direct and guide me in my efforts. They examined each new section of my project for error, patiently correcting any questionable segment. They took pains to ensure clarity be given to their family legends, knowing they would be revealed to non-natives. As one who frequently stepped in and out of their world I suppose I was the appropriate conduit for this task. The Yazzies believed that respect for another's culture comes about from understanding it, and that was their ultimate goal when sharing family traditions and narrative.

I hoped that by recording Suzie's life from a female Dine' perspective, I might challenge previous constructs of Native American women accepted by earlier historians. In the past, anthropologists diligently researched Navajo life by focusing on what others in their field deemed important. Questions were formulated to reveal details concerning the usual matrix of subjects investigated in anthropological study. Researching Dine' women often meant devoting a great deal of attention to female puberty rites, marriage and child rearing. This type of study took place from the 1940s to the 1960s; the heyday of anthropological research on the Navajo. Though the information gathered during this time was a necessary starting point in understanding Native American life, women's roles and their place in society was often overlooked or misinterpreted.

During my early school years in the 1960s, Native Americans seemed to always appear in our history books as a people who either helped or hindered the white man's "Manifest Destiny" to settle the North American continent. A myriad of different tribes was presented as one people. Indians were one-dimensional characters who altered between the role of "noble savage," or a friend and foe of the pilgrim. The subject of Native American women was rarely touched upon, and when Indian women were discussed the history books regarded them as either exotic creatures or submissive wives and daughters to warrior males. By the 1970s instructors were beginning to present more revisionist histories, and I learned of the Sand Creek Massacre and Native American memory of the Battle of Little Big Horn. However, any real history regarding Native American women continued to elude me.

When Suzie expressed her willingness to relate to me her life story, a different sort of history emerged that spoke of a woman's power and independence within her tribe.

I learned how a Navajo woman experienced both the hardships and the benefits of Navajo life during the transition from a centuries-old tradition to twentieth century life. Throughout our relationship this woman revealed a sometimes tragic life story. Yet, she never once presented herself as a victim. On the contrary, Suzie appeared to regard the difficulties and challenges she experienced as part of a normal life that prepared her for the role of family matriarch and respected elder.

In her essay entitled "Native American Women," published in 1980, anthropologist Rayna Green lamented the way in which others in her field had depicted Indian women. These subjects remained elusive foreign figures in the vein of either the pure Pocahontas or the lusty earth-goddess tending the fires in the family wigwam.[51] Green challenged future historians and anthropologists to look beyond the Indian woman presented by white scholars, and to discover the rich history Indian women offer as members of very complex societies in which they have traditionally enjoyed a great deal of status and responsibility. "Now scholars," wrote Green, "native and non-Native American, must consult Native American women in determining where to go." [52]

My ultimate goal was to move beyond the practical facts regarding Navajo life, and discover how Suzie viewed herself as a Navajo woman. What made her decide, for example, to maintain Dine' culture in her home? How did she experience love? What situations in her life brought fear or elation? Allowing Suzie to determine the flow of our interviews helped to bring about the answers I craved. I presented questions based on a loose, linear outline that ranged from her family history to her own adulthood, then waited for Suzie to guide her stories to those subjects most important to her. I believed this method was best for both of us. We enjoyed the process, and I was able to move somewhat beyond what had already been written about Navajo women because I had access to the reflections of a woman who had experienced a great deal of change over the years within her culture.

I was also interested in Suzie's memory of reservation life in the early twentieth century. Like all of us, her early experiences formed her personality, and I suspected there was much to her than the image she portrayed to Anglos passing through the Valley. As a wise businesswoman she played the role of Navajo weaver to those early groups of tourists who entered Monument Valley with very distinct ideas of what an Indian should be. Hollywood portrayed Indian women in a very particular way at that time, and Suzie did not disappoint. She was able to take advantage of an opportunity that early western films presented and used their image of native women to augment her income. The additional resources obtained from this white/native relationship allowed Suzie to remain in her homeland; however she saw herself as a very different individual than the one-dimensional "squaw" Anglos expected to encounter.

---

[51] Green, Rayna. "Native American Women." Chicago: The University of Chicago, *Journal of Women in Culture and Society*, 1980, vol. 6, no. 21, 249-250.

[52] Ibid., 267.

Scholars have predicted the demise of Native American life since Indians first appeared in historical writing.[53] Many whites believed that unless an Indian lived a purely Native American life as it functioned at the time of Anglo contact, the Indian could not survive and would eventually die out or become so thoroughly assimilated into white culture that he would effectively "disappear." Yet the Navajo people have provided one example of how cultures need not necessarily remain stagnant in order to be considered viable or pure in form. Like many Native American societies, the Navajo had been adapting to changes even before white contact. By shedding images of the Indian that developed from the past, and the negative feelings those images provoke, Native Americans like Suzie have managed to hold on to those aspects of their culture that sustain them and give their lives meaning.

Far from disappearing, the American Indian has survived. Though still grappling with the challenges of living in both the modern and traditional world, the Navajo in particular have proven that maintaining one's culture can be a conscious choice, one that individuals within a community have the power to exercise. Not all Native American groups have had this option, and perhaps the modern Navajo have benefitted from the harsh environment in which they have lived. Enduring a hardscrabble life may have been the key to Suzie finding a place for herself within the largest Indian nation in the U.S. Most importantly, through Suzie's story I learned how both Navajo and twentieth century woman could exist as compatible identities.

---

[53] In their *Cambridge History of the Native Peoples of the Americas*, historians Bruce Trigger and Wilcomb Washburn discussed the manner in which Native Americans were treated in historical literature during the late nineteenth and early twentieth centuries. The authors noted that, "to the extent that they [Indians] were mentioned at all, their negative image as a primitive people that was doomed to disappear persisted, even if this image was expressed in more neutral language than it had been previously." Trigger & Washburn, The Cambridge History of the Native Peoples of the Americas. Cambridge: Cambridge University Press, 1989, 97.

A SHORT CHILDHOOD

"Grown men can learn from very little children for the hearts of the little children are pure. Therefore, the Great Spirit may show to them many things which older people miss." —
Black Elk

Suzie appeared enthusiastic about speaking to me of her childhood that began in the early 1920s. This period in Navajo history saw an increase in contact with Anglos. Exposure to the white world brought the Navajo some economic security, yet it also threatened to alter Navajo culture, forcing upon the Dine' western ideas about education and religion, as well as introducing new challenges such as Anglo standards of material wealth that would appeal to Navajo youth.

Once again I had to alter my concept of time to match Suzie's more cyclical version. An event that happened "a while ago" may well have occurred a decade or more past. Suzie saw events as patterns woven throughout life that everyone she knew experienced. This led to some difficulty in convincing her that certain portions of her life story were useful to me in understanding her choices and how they shaped her view of Dine' culture. Suzie's sense of what was truly significant caused her to omit details that, to me, were noteworthy. Because her childhood was typical of her contemporaries living in Monument Valley, she found no reason to explain every facet of it. Suzie particularly enjoyed telling stories about her family. She took great pride in her children and the home she made for them, and she spoke freely of her life as both wife and mother. When we broached these subjects she became quite animated and happily launched into a colorful description of family life.

Suzie spent her youth on the Navajo reservation, isolated from much of the outside world and Anglo influences. The Four Corners region, with its limited resources and arid climate, appealed to very few whites except for the occasional trader, government worker, or adventurous tourist. In many ways Suzie and her family lived as their ancestors had. Herding and trade served as the major source of income with agriculture providing food such as corn, squash, melon and peaches. Living in such a far-flung location as Monument Valley allowed Navajo like the Yazzies to resist acculturation for some time. In his study of the Black Mesa, Arizona Navajo anthropologist James Downs made note of this resistance as late as 1964. He wrote that:

"The unwillingness of the Navajo to participate in the institutions of American society or to adopt cultural elements that would threaten his autonomy is notorious and has resulted in the Navajo being rated as the most 'unacculturated' people in America. This separateness, manifested among the Puebloan people in a mental reservation about certain types of behavior that excludes foreign elements, is expressed by the Navajo by maintaining actual physical and social distance between himself and foreigners. He stubbornly retains his language and his notorious unresponsiveness to conversion." [54]

---

[54] Downs, James F. Animal Husbandry in Navajo Society and Culture. Berkeley and Los Angeles: University of California Press, 1964, 96.

Downs viewed the disinterest that the Navajo expressed in white society as a conscious action. Yet, the fact that families such as Suzie's were also very physically removed from the Anglo world certainly must have helped them to retain a traditional Navajo life. An anthropologist conducting research on the reservation during Suzie's childhood also saw that it was the Navajos' isolation that allowed them to retain their native lifestyle. He recognized this in the behavior of a Navajo man involved in his study:

"There is little evidence of acculturation. While he displays white manners when eating with a white family, he uses Navaho table manners at home. He points with his lips...and buys groceries in the Navajo way – paying for each item separately and pausing some time before making the next purchase. [His] knowledge of what is going on in the outside world is extremely limited. He has no idea of world geography nor of world events other than what might be told him by another Navaho." [55]

During her childhood the major source of transportation for Suzie and her people remained the horse and wagon. Technological advances trickled into the area very slowly, and John Roberts noted that even by 1946 very few Navajo had used a telephone or a camera. According to the anthropologist, one Navajo man had, "taken some photographs, and he knew how to operate the small borrowed Brownie box camera which was kept hanging in his hogan." However, no other clan member was familiar with this object, one that, by the time of Robert's research, was commonly owned and used throughout the United States. [56] Roberts went on to say, however, that some technological advances were slowly making their way onto the reservation in minor ways. By the late 1940s the Navajo were becoming familiar with phonographic records, motion pictures, and radios. Telephones existed at trading posts, but few Navajo had actually used one. Roberts stated that "all of the Navajo informants had shouted in communicating at a distance."[57] Suzie recalled this type of communication during a number of our interviews, telling me of friends and relatives who yelled information from the surrounding hills or from the huge monuments surrounding their home:

"When someone was sick or needed something we just ran from home to home, or on horseback. That's why horses were always tied up. I saw my first telephone just recently, ("recently" being the 1960s), when my kids started school. Before this there were no phones. I saw my first television just recently too. They would tell me that you could see lots of things on it and then I saw one. It showed nice and true."

Suzie's limited exposure to Anglos that allowed for such isolation created within the young girl a very different outlook on life. Growing up as a Navajo meant that Suzie had a sense of time that was distinctly Dine.' I recorded the birth dates of family members with the understanding that most of these dates had been randomly chosen. Suzie could only recall the time of season in which she and her loved ones were born.

---

[55] Vogt, Evon Zartman. Navajo Veterans; A study of changing values. Cambridge: Peabody Museum Publishers, 1951, 76-B.

[56] Roberts, *Three Navajo Households*, 28-B.

[57] Ibid., 27-B.

It simply had not been crucial during Suzie's youth to record birth dates and in fact, no one is really certain of Suzie's own exact age or birth date. Her children eventually gave Suzie the date of April 15th to serve as her day of birth, with 1920 as a reasonable estimate of her birth year. Because Dine' regarded time in a seasonal or cyclical sense, most Navajo were acutely aware of the environmental changes that indicated time to them. When I asked Suzie about her birth date she explained how seasons and the movement of the sun and moon were her guidelines:

"I knew what time of the season or month it was when I was born. I was told that we go by the moon, starting with a quarter moon and going forth from there. We could also tell by the stars and where they were located at the time. Also we could tell by where the sun rises and the sunset is, depending on where the sun lights or hits your hogan inside, you go by that."

Suzie's earliest memories concerned her mother, her paternal grandparents, and the daily challenges of growing up on the reservation. She remembered how the area of Monument Valley where she now resides appealed to her at a very early age:

"I like the rocks formation, the rocks surrounding me, [the] different shapes of rocks. I got use to this a long time ago. There is nothing I don't like about it. Since I was a child I liked it here. My late father's father use to live here, my paternal grandfather and [also my] grandmother. So I liked it here very much."

Suzie's parents practiced the customary roles of a Navajo man and wife. Their chores involved tasks such as, "Mom weaving...and father would be hauling woods with a wagon and horse." One aspect of Navajo life that differed from that of Suzie's ancestors was the absence of her father as he sought wage work outside the reservation. A study conducted by Kluckhohn and Leighton determined:

"Navahos have for years worked for white ranchers on a seasonal basis or during the seasons of heavy work. In ever increasing numbers they have been going as seasonal laborers to the best fields of Colorado. To Arizona mines, and to ranches as far away as Texas. The increase from all categories of wage work was 2.133 per cent, for the period between 1940 and 1958." [58]

Suzie recalled that her father was often away while her mother minded the children, her weaving, and the family sheep. The rugs her mother produced were exchanged at the local trading post for basic supplies. "Yes, she weaved a lot," recalled Suzie, "Mostly for food. That was all she had time to do." It became clear that Suzie had been a helpmate of extreme importance to her mother, who went by the name of Sunshine. Their relationship was a reflection of how the eldest girl could become essential to Navajo family economy. Suzie helped with household chores and cared for her siblings while her mother worked. Weaving done by Suzie's mother successfully augmented the family's diet to include food items other than mutton and goat's milk. Consistently trading rugs for these foodstuffs allowed for the family's survival for some time.

Suzie had fond memories of her mother. Sunshine seemed to have a special bond with her eldest daughter. "I was called 'My Daughter' by my late mom," Suzie laughed.

---

[58] Kluckhohn, Clyde and Dorthea Leighton. The Navajo . Garden City: Anchor Books, 1962, 61.

Giggling softly she went on to say, "That's the only name she had for me, and then later it just became my name for a long time. When my mom had another daughter she was "My *Little* Daughter." Suzie's close relationship with her mother might be considered overwhelming if compared to the mother-daughter associations in white families. However, it was considered quite normal among Navajos at this time for mothers to rely upon their daughters in this way.

Because the first born girl in a Navajo family customarily held a position of greater responsibility, mother and daughter then naturally formed an alliance. Under the tutelage of her mother this daughter was expected to quickly learn the skills allowing her to effectively maintain the household as well as the family's property. The mother, as the owner of that property, had to instill in her daughter a sense of value for the family holdings. A young girl interviewed by anthropologists Kluckhohn and Leighton in the 1940s spoke of her mother's influence in a way that mirrored the relationship between Suzie and her mother:

"Father is the one who taught me to do the right thing, but my mother taught me how to boil coffee, tea, and how to fry bread, meat, teach me how to milk the goat. In winter she teaches me how to do things, and how to feed the baby sheep. My mother has to go out and call me in. There was a pile of wool all ready to card. So I got to work and carded all day. It was hard work. It was hot in the hogan. When we had done this we put our work away until morning, when we start to work again. When we got tired we rest for a while. If I card my fingers too, they get sore and hurt."[59]

So it was that in most conservative Dine' families the eldest daughter ultimately acquired her mother's land. Yet the role of eldest daughter also brought with it the underlying burden for the care and financial well-being of her immediate family. Suzie's daughter-in-law confirmed this tradition when I questioned her about the eldest daughter's role. "The oldest girl is usually given a lot of responsibility," she explained. "Suzie's younger sister was taught by Suzie to help out. She was Suzie's right-hand man." Research on Navajo family dynamics point to the eldest girl's elevated role and unique position. The overall care for sheep and other property rests on the daughter with the assumption that any sons will leave their maternal homes in order to live with their wife's family. Anthropologists studying the Navajo learned that the eldest daughter "is concerned to see that as much of [family property] as possible stays there or is used for family ceremonials and that eventually her children should inherit the bulk of it."[60] The role of younger sisters was that of helpmate to her siblings until the eldest eventually married and had children of her own. According to the authors, "the sisters of the mother are secondary and substitute mothers throughout childhood, and this relationship prevails throughout life."[61]

During Suzie's childhood the tradition of placing family property in the care of the oldest daughter may have seemed unusual to whites, whose culture favored the oldest male as the ultimate successor. However Navajo custom prevailed and continues on

---

[59] Kluckhohn & Leighton, *Children*, 54.
[60] Kluckhohn & Leighton, *Children*, 99-100.
[61] Ibid., 102.

some levels to this day. Even so, the Navajo do not appear to be rigid when dealing with distribution of family property and certainly some Dine' families have encountered situations that might have called for a child other than the eldest daughter to inherit. When Suzie was growing up in the 1920s, however, it was expected that she take her rightful place as provider when her mother was no longer physically able to perform these duties.

HOW THE FAMILY WORKED
"One finger cannot lift a pebble – Hopi

Suzie and her siblings were brought up to respect and obey their elders and to work hard for the good of the family. Suzie informed me that her parents maintained a strict household, but that "they weren't that bad." She felt loved and cared for by her mother and father in her early childhood. It was her parents that taught Suzie to be proficient in basic mathematical skills. "I learned to count sheep and money from my late mom, and dad too," Suzie told me, "that's who I learned it from so I could count our sheep and trade my rugs." Of her father she said, "He didn't whip us." The only exception to her father's leniency occurred when Suzie's brother received a sound spanking any time he neglected the family sheep:

"Yeah, just my late older brother kept an eye on the animals at first. He was a little more mature so he would always herd the sheep. We had some nice sheep. My late dad use to just whip him for that one thing (giggles). When he use not to take care of the sheep, he would be whipped for that."

Authors Kluckhohn and Leighton confirm that failure to care for livestock was one of the few infractions that could result in corporal punishment for Navajo children. During their study in the 1940s they noticed that young herders were chastised for putting their own comforts first at the expense of a family's herd:

"Children are severely rebuked and even whipped if they take shelter during a storm while out herding and lose track of sheep. Neglect or abuse of livestock is the least forgivable of childhood misdemeanors. When children first begin to help with the herding at six or seven, they tend to ride and chase the sheep and goats and otherwise disturb and distract them from feeding. Harsh scoldings break them of these habits quite quickly, but a young herder will go to sleep or play with other children so that animals wander off or get killed by coyotes. When their loss is discovered, the culprit is dressed down properly, and an effort is made to shame him into more responsible conduct."[62]

Although non-Natives might have considered caring for an entire flock of sheep and goats too difficult for children as young as six years old, it was essential to a Navajo child's upbringing that they learn sheep and other livestock were important for their family's survival. These animals served as a valuable source of protein as well as a major element of the trade economy so important on the reservation. In his study of

---

[62] Kluckhohn & Leighton, *Children*, 57-58.

the Navajo James Downs commented on the importance of sheep to the families whose lives he researched:

"The relationship between the family and the herd is one tinged with rather deep emotion and a great deal of symbolism. Sheep are not only wealth in an objective sense but serve as a measure of family well-being on a more abstract level of discourse. One is quickly impressed with the identification between "the family" and "the sheep."[63]

Downs went on to note how, in spite of the herd's value, it was acceptable for the youngest Navajo to care for their family's livestock. So long as a child was reared to respect his animals and their behavior, the task remained relatively simple. The anthropologist explained how caring for the herd became a skill that the Navajo learned as children and maintained as adults:

"The fact that sheep are so easily handled and only have to be directed rather than driven makes it possible for anyone – man, woman, or child older than seven or eight – to assume the duties of herder. In short, a Navajo child may begin his life as a herder of sheep before he is ten and continue as a herder into very old age, stopping only when he or she is no longer able to walk. Sheep, then, require a maximum of care but are easily controllable, so that a great variety of people can take part in this care."[64]

Suzie admitted that pastoral life was not easy, and there were times when the task of caring for the herds was given to an older relative. One of her girlhood memories was when she saw her maternal aunt herding sheep on especially warm days, her face painted red with clay to protect her from the sun. This was a habit her aunt maintained into old age. Suzie explained, "my late mom's sister, she was the youngest, the last one born. She use to always say putting the clay on doesn't dry up your face." Suzie's granddaughter who was sitting with us laughed in agreement. "Even when I was a kid my great auntie would always be coming here with her face red." Suzie remembered the conditions she endured as a young sheepherder, and how she sought shelter on very hot days:

"Long ago, we use to live just under some brushes or under trees, and that's how we grew up. Just a log in the ground slanting upward [served as shelter]. Logs are put upward and piled weeds, or tree branches were put around it. That's the way it was, the way we (the children when herding) use to live."

Suzie's son confirmed that long after the young herders had grown up these protective structures continued to stand. "When we are on horseback," he explained, "we see some of that along the trail, some long ago homes." Suzie took on the responsibility of herding sheep along with the other youngsters in her family. Most children during Suzie's youth were relatively successful in caring for their herds, and they accepted the task as part of their role as family members. In their study of the Navajo in 1948, Dorothea Leighton and Clyde Kluckhohn noted that children were indeed herding at a young age:

"The young herder feels…he is also looking after his own property. His own interests become involved in his learning to care properly for the flocks. The child

---

[63] Downs *Animal Husbandry*, 89.
[64] Ibid., 58.

learns that he cannot indefinitely continue to have his own way, so between five and eight he has to acquire a sense of responsibility."[65]

The authors went on to describe how tasks became gender-specific, as the Navajo child grew older:

"From about the age of eight on, the children of the two sexes tend to be separated a good deal of the time. Each group is trained in certain skills by their elders of the same sex...Girls learn to cook and tend children under the supervision of their mothers and other women relatives. They begin to card and spin at about ten and to weave a little later."[66]

In her book *Women in Navajo Society*, author Ruth Roessel explained a Navajo woman's role as the center of her home and mentor to her daughters:

"The role played by the women in the life of the Navajos' homes was one of primary importance. They were the center of the home, and around them revolved the lie of each family. As a small child a daughter would learn from her mother about the important and central role that women played in Navajo life. The mother would instruct carefully each of her girl children about their role in the home and what they, as they grew up and became mothers themselves, must learn and be able to teach their own children."[67]

Roessel went on to explain the importance of religion, food, water and plants in Navajo households. A woman taught her daughter how to build the family fire, and cook, and where to gather water as well as plants. Even obtaining water might only be achieved through a Navajo girl's expenditure of enormous energy. Roessel explained that girls as young as eight years old would, "have to go some distance to a spring or a well to get water, not only for that meal but for use throughout the day."[68] Girls of this age would learn the value, both symbolic and utilitarian, of household items. Even the family sheepskins were to be placed in such a way that would symbolically protect family members. With so much responsibility placed upon her shoulders at a young age, it is understandable why Suzie would become comfortable with her independence and confident in the decisions she made regarding her culture.

The significance of corn to the Navajo, and to a Dine' woman in particular, took on a symbolic purpose. According to Roessel, a typical morning for a young girl of Suzie's age was full of this symbolism:

"After building a fire, the Navajo woman would begin to grind the corn and prepare breakfast for her family. It would be perhaps cornbread, with mush or some other food...Often, a young daughter would grind the corn and prepare the cornmeal for use at breakfast or at some other time. Grinding corn was an important function in the life of Navajo women, and girls would learn at an early age how to grind it properly. The Navajos believed that corn in the morning would make a person strong

---

[65] Kluckhohn & Leighton, *Children,* 58.

[66] Ibid., 59.

[67] Roessel, Ruth. <u>Women in Navajo Society</u>. Rough Rock: Navajo Resource Center, 1981, 71.

[68] Roessel, *Women in Navajo Society*, 73.

and help a girl grow into ideal womanhood as exemplified by Changing Woman (an important female deity in the Navajo faith)."[69]

Similarly, Suzie described a childhood in which fire and food preparation was entirely her responsibilities:

"I use to be pretty good at chopping wood. We use to hunt for firewood in a wagon near the mesa, which was sandy then. Way over there we would be chopping and hauling wood back in for ourselves and my late paternal grandmother. We use to split the firewood between us. Back then I use to always grind corn because that was our main source of food. It seems like that was all we ate, food made out of corn. I use to just do a lot of grinding, when I was small. It was cornmeal. I use to make hot cornmeal cereal. Then I started to weave and sometimes I would herd sheep. My chore then was taking care of the sheep when they were lambing too."

When I asked Suzie what chores she preferred, she cited herding sheep. She enjoyed the opportunities that herding presented for her to play alone with toys that she had fashioned from the desert environment:

"Herding sheep you would be playing around (giggles). You would see my toys scattered where I used to herd sheep, [I made] mud animals…anything, straws made into women with skirts and with shade houses. Pebbles would be sheep (more laughter)."

I learned that this sort of entertainment was quite popular among Navajo children at the time. In her record of a Navajo woman, anthropologist Gladys Reichard wrote of a child engaged in similar activities. Her subject, an elderly woman by the name of Dezba whom she was interviewing in the late 1930s, had a granddaughter named Alaba. Reichard explained how little Alaba amused herself while out herding with her young cousin:

"She meant to model a little flock, a pastime in which she frequently engaged especially when she went toward the water with the sheep. Not far from the water there was a bank of clay which was just right for fashioning sheep, goats, horses or dogs. Alaba had already prepared quite a herd of sheep from the clay. They were small and well shaped. Some were ewes with suckling lambs. She had also made goats, kids and a dog. She had just started to build the corral by laying small sticks one upon another…"[70]

Because these clay toys were so prevalent among children throughout the reservation, evidence of their use could still be found in some areas. When I described these earthen figurines to a Hispanic friend, he informed me that his children had found similar objects discarded around his home in Window Rock, Arizona.[71] I remarked to Suzie that fashioning these toys seemed like a very clever way for a young herder to pass the time.

---

[69] Roessel, *Women*, 72.

[70] Reichard, *Dezba*, 35.

[71] Telephone conversation with Ron Maldonado, Navajo Nation Department of Historic Preservation, Windowrock, AZ. 15 February 2001.

I became intrigued with the vision of Suzie as a little girl, playing with her tiny "herd" of clay while standing guard over the family livestock. What sort of life would this be for a young girl? Keeping the herd from harm must have been a constant thought, and the boredom that accompanies such a task might have affected Suzie as it would any active child. Yet, the beautiful and peaceful surroundings of the Valley could also have provided a very pleasant environment in which a child might play. My curiosity about her early life led me to ask Suzie about the type of clothing the Dine' were wearing when she was a young girl. Suzie remembered the old style of clothing before it ultimately morphed into the costume we so readily associate with the Navajo, which became the full-length skirt and velveteen blouse:

"Long ago the people wore rugs (woven blankets). That was way back before when my great-grandmother was around. Back then they use to have clothes like that. The rugs were their clothes. Even moccasins with the leg wrappings were worn. But when I was young we dressed like I dress now. We use to dress like this, even my late mom and my grandmother, her too. That was the way back then, except blouses were velveteen, not velour as they are now. Yes, they were real thick."

Suzie could now easily acquire the jeans and T-shirts that many of the younger Yazzies wear. There was no reason for her to dress in the traditional style of clothing, particularly if there were no tourists about. She seemed to prefer the type of skirts and blouses that she had worn as a child and all through adulthood however. Throughout the reservation I saw many women of Suzie's age dressed in a similar fashion, and so I assumed that the decision to sport the traditional skirt and blouse was a common one among her peers. Younger Navajos might consider the outfit somewhat old-fashioned. It seemed to me that because it was primarily worn by the older women this uniform commanded respect. In traditional costume these women were revered not only as elders, but as representatives of their community. For Suzie, the traditional clothing she wore symbolized her decision to present herself as a Navajo with many of the same standards and beliefs she held dear as a child.

My last tape ran out, and as the recorder automatically clicked off I sensed that it was just as well. I could hear visitors approaching in one of the trucks used to ferry tourists throughout the Valley, and with their arrival Suzie would be keen on entertaining them. I promised Emily and Lonnie I would return in a few month's time to continue working with Suzie and reluctantly packed up my things. It was becoming difficult to leave the Valley. The beauty and serenity of the place was starting to pull at my soul, and the people were beginning to feel like family. Driving out from the lodge I turned on the only station available on the radio. The announcer spoke primarily in Navajo, and though I could not understand one word of it, I listened to her all the way back to the airport.

49

CHAPTER 4 - FAIR-SKINNED WOMAN

"There are many good moccasin tracks along the trail of a straight arrow." - *Lakota*

The task of pulling together all of my work with Suzie continued at a healthy pace back home in Santa Barbara. I also began to look over my diary entries. The scribbled notes looked like some sort of jagged and unreadable code. I remembered then how exhausted I had been during my trips to the Valley. After spending so much energy interacting with and observing the Yazzies, it had been all I could do just to jot down anything. I resolve to make sense of it all later when I had time to focus.

Another opportunity to conduct interviews in the Valley came later that year. I had a break in my studies and my mentor, Ann Plane's blessing to forge ahead with a focus on both the historical and anthropological aspects of the Yazzie's story. I also benefitted from consulting my professor of cultural anthropology, Michael Glasgow. Having two of my favorite instructors as a resource I felt more confident and excited to start again. I made it to the lodge just as a storm rumbled behind me, letting loose a deluge of water that the dry and greedy desert soil did its best to suck in. I slept poorly that night in spite my fatigue and the soothing patter of rain. I was staying on the first floor, and the family occupying the quarters above me spent their evening thumping from one end of their room to the other. Throwing the pillow over my head at eleven p.m., I cursed Mr. and Mrs. Bigfoot and their three hundred-pound children, and eventually fell into a fitful sleep.

I awoke the next day with a head that felt as if it were stuffed with marshmallows. Nevertheless, I had a day with the Yazzies to look forward to, and the morning felt promising. The previous night's rain left behind a freshly washed landscape, and behind the restaurant where a huge monolith towered a waterfall flowed, created by last night's sudden downfall. The smell of wet rock surrounded me, and I imagined how wonderful it must have been for Harry and his wife, "Mike," Goulding to make a home here in the trading post's heyday. What a unique adventure it must have been living in such a beautiful and isolated spot and dealing with the Navajo on a daily basis.

I imagined they were a resourceful and unusual couple to have even thought up the idea of constructing a trading post, accessible only via poorly maintained dirt roads hundreds of miles into the reservation.

The restaurant was nearly empty. I found a table by the window and settled in once more to wait for Lonnie and Emily. I was beginning to learn, however, that my idea of punctuality was very different compared to "Navajo time." I repeated the ritual of inhaling gallons of coffee and made a promise to myself to switch to juice or water tomorrow to keep my insides from cramping. My friends showed up a mere half-hour late, and we had only a light breakfast before heading to Suzie's for full day's work. When we arrived at the hogan I followed the now familiar routine of waiting a bit in the car, and then entered the hogan where Suzie sat weaving a colorful blanket on a huge loom made of juniper branches.

After she gave me a shy smile and an approving glance we settled in to work as if no time at all had passed since my first visit to her home. Suzie demurely lowered herself onto a little stool in front of the loom. Emily found a place to sit next to her mother-in-law, all the while explaining to me the necessity of working in the hogan. It appeared that last night's rain had completely soaked all of the chairs in the Shade House. We three women were all happy to be within the cool cocoon of the hogan, and began work in earnest taking very few breaks.

I must confess that there were periods of time during the interview process when I experienced a lack of ambition. Listening to Emily and Suzie chatter away made me a little homesick for my own family. Adding to this challenge was the awkward way I sat cross-legged on the floor at Suzie's feet. Emily had done many hours of weaving in the hogan, and so was accustomed to the seating arrangement. But after an hour or so of working this way my knees began to ache. By then I was pining for the rickety folding chairs of the Shade House.

Still, the hogan certainly had its charm. It was quiet except for the sound of Suzie carding wool as she spoke. Never one to be idle, she kept the two plaques of wire held in each hand sliding one over the other in a peaceful rhythm, pulling the coarse wool into a fine thread. I loved the way dappled sunlight streamed in through the smoke pipe hole in the ceiling. By the late morning I had settled into a routine of questioning that felt more natural and effortless. If Suzie was on a roll with a story I let her go on, making notes of things to ask later. After she gave up one memory, we then dealt with those questions that her story had generated in my mind. These follow-up questions cleared up details and often caused Suzie to launch into still more stories that stemmed from the original. Her courtship with Tully, the man who would become her husband, led to tales about her son, Lonnie's childhood. When Suzie recalled portions of her youth this brought about legends about her mother's upbringing, and so on. The breaks we did take were mostly for my benefit. Suzie patiently waited, giggling at each effort I made to stretch my weary muscles.

Of course, there were those moments when we needed to use the latrine; this structure being just a ramshackle little shed positioned to the left of Suzie's horse corral. I eventually grew used to using the old clapboard closet surrounding a shallow hole with only a barbed wire tacked on to fasten the door closed. It faced the northernmost rock formations, and its isolation provided an opportunity to sit and admire the view while attending to business. Over time I found that the old outhouse was preferable to those port-a-potties that I'd been forced to visit at various campsites and concerts throughout my life. I joked with Effie that the family latrine was "the best seat in the house." On other occasions we would call it "a room with a view" or…my favorite nickname, "The Library." It could be quite peaceful just sitting there, admiring the scenic wonders framed by the door less structure…a wisp of breeze occasionally stirring the toilet paper roll left hanging on a nail to the right. This latrine wasn't terribly secure however, and was rumored to blow away, end over end, in the strong wind storms so famous in the Valley. On really hot days I discreetly slipped away to a cluster of rocks that provided a comparable view and privacy without the aroma. But for now my focus was on learning all I could about Suzie's childhood. The tape recorder hummed, and as Suzie pulled at a soft lump of grey wool she began to speak.

GROWING UP NAVAJO: Family dynamics and an introduction to ritual and ceremony
"The Great Spirit Chief who rules above all will smile upon this land…and this time the Indian race is waiting and praying." – Chief Joseph

Emily slowly began to translate my questions concerning Suzie's adolescent life. I learned that Suzie's time for play was abruptly cut short. As she neared her teenage years her mother fell ill. Complications following the birth of a younger brother caused her mother to grow weak, and because she was the eldest daughter, many of the domestic chores became Suzie's responsibility. By the age of fifteen, Four-Horned Woman's great granddaughter was quickly becoming the female head of the household. Sunshine's care required frequent visits to the hospital some three hundred miles away. Suzie became the surrogate mother to her five brothers and sisters in her mother's absence. "My late mom was always sick and I use to take care of her," Suzie remembered. It was at this time that Suzie began to grow closer to her paternal grandparents, who often provided care and emotional support. When it was possible to do so she avoided her maternal grandmother, whom she disliked. Suzie felt that this relative was neglectful of her grandchildren:
"I remember how it was when I was a child. My late mom lived for awhile in Dennehotso. My late grandma use to live out there in Little Monument Valley, and my mom use to always want to be there with her mom. But when we visited her I use to not like it. At my late grandma's place there was a lack of food. When you'd go visit her she would just boil corn. She would get a cup, take some out and offer it to you and say "Eat this, with that you go herd sheep." Over here in Monument Valley was my late father's mother's place. This grandmother's name was Lightweight Woman, and she took better care of us. We ate a lot when over there. She would feed us lots and was always cooking. She would sprawl out a thin blanket and put food down there for us; always a lot of different foods, never a few. There would be a variety and lots of it. Because we were hungry that's what we wanted. My mom was mostly sick and at the

hospital, and so she would put us with her mom, but we would always run away to Lightweight Woman's place" (giggles).

Suzie's paternal grandmother became her favorite relative. One can understand this preference when considering the fact that Suzie not only had to think of her own hunger, but also about filling the stomachs of her siblings. Her grandmother, known as Lightweight Woman, demonstrated her feelings for her grandchildren by attending to their most basic needs:

"My dad's mother was not like my maternal grandmother. Lightweight Woman made good fry bread that she use to feed us, and food was always on our minds, (giggles). We barely knew our other relatives at this time."

Suzie explained how family dynamics deviated from normal Navajo structure because of her relatives' conflicting methods of caring for their grandchildren:

"The man is supposed to live with the new bride's family. Some are like that, but some go to their husband's home too. We even did that. We use to live way over there, (on the outskirts of Monument Valley), with my late father's family. They use to live here and at the arches and behind this rock and all the way down the Valley, Behind Flat Wide Rocks and Meridian Rock. We use to move with Lightweight Woman. She use to plant near the valley ridges and so there would be lots of corn. There would be a harvest of watermelons, even squash. When it was harvest time we use to all be there. Even though my maternal grandma was also close enough to visit we didn't like to go there very much. She had a lot of sheep, but she was not very generous. We preferred Lightweight Woman and we felt more looked after with her. We use to run away from home just to visit her near the Arches."

THE LAST GREAT JOURNEY
"In death I am born." – Hopi

Suzie attributed her mother's failing health to the difficult birth of her second child. As with many Navajo families living on the reservation at that time, the death of a loved one was not an unusual occurrence, and young children were particularly vulnerable to illness and death. The high infant mortality was partly due to infection acquired during childbirth. Unsanitary conditions and the lack of nearby medical facilities contributed to the problem. Statistics compiled as late as 1962 indicated a high incidence of infants who died during childbirth, reporting that:

"There are many deaths among young children (three times the national average) and maternal mortality is high.[72] The Navaho infant mortality rate far exceeds that for the rest of the country – in spite of tremendous decrease in recent years. In 1952, the Navajo infant mortality rate was 110.2 per 1,000 live births, that for the United States

---

[72] Kluckhohn & Leighton, *The Navajo*, 153.

28.4; provisional figures for 1957 show a Navaho rate of 74.7 as opposed to a United States rate of 26.3."[73]

Suzie's earliest memory of a death in the family was that of her younger sister. According to Suzie, her mother's experience of giving birth to this child caused Sunshine to grow increasingly weak and unable to continue domestic tasks. Although Sunshine survived this birth, the child grew increasingly weak and eventually perished at the age of four. Suzie was quite young at the time, probably around two years of age. However the memory of her sister's death left an impression. She spoke of the method of burial practiced by her people:

"My mom lost her third child, my younger sister. She first had my brother, George, then me. After that my sister died. Ella was borned next, and then my brother John. Kee Tso was my next brother, and then my sister Jean. Kee Yazzie was the youngest. He was the last one borned before my mom passed away. That was the one I raised, with help from my sister Ella."

"They buried my younger sister past the Flat Wide Rocks. I was about four or so when she just got sick. Back then, there was no hospital nearby. There were just medicine men saying prayers. They tried it, (traditional medicine), on my sister but failed. When people died they use to just put them near the rocks, under rock ridges, and just stack rocks around it; just wrap the body. Some use to put the body in the ground, and some just buried the body a little beneath the surface. They would just throw a little bit of dirt on the body somewhere far from the hogan. These were the different ways. I had bad dreams about losing that sister. I would wake up crying and tell my mom that my sister wasn't gone, that she was waiting for me in the rocks."

I learned over time that burial methods during Suzie's youth varied depending on family preference. There is, however, a great deal of literature confirming Suzie's statements regarding burial practices among her people, one source stating:

"Navahos who are no kindred of the deceased are hired by the family to dispose of the body. If the relatives must themselves carry out the work...four (or two) mourners are selected. One of these is a near relative or clansman of the deceased; another is commonly taken from the clan of the father, the wife, or the husband of the dead person. The body and grave offerings are often placed in a rock niche in and out-of-the-way place and the opening is sealed with rocks against the intrusion of coyotes and other animals."[74]

In her book *Navajo Religion* anthropologist Gladys Reichard explained in detail the meaning of burial procedures practiced by the Navajo communities of the late 1940s:

"The Navajo look upon death as failure to grow, and upon the land of the dead as static, although they do not emphasize stagnation...The Navajo destroy or bury property so the dead may "cut a swell" in the underground world. My informants say,

---

[73] Ibid, 52.
[74] Kluckhohn & Leighton, *Children* 91-92.

"We give to the dead to show respect, to indicate that they were loved by those who survive."[75]

Another author wrote of the fear many Navajo harbored when dealing with the dead:

"Death and everything connected with it is repulsive to the *Dineh* and dead humans are buried as quickly as possible. The shell, or body, of the deceased is buried with elaborate precautions by relatives. The dead, if proper precautions are not taken, are believed to be capable of returning to earth as ghosts to plague the living."[76]

The Yazzies spoke of these precautions when Suzie revealed to me information regarding the death of her sibling. Suzie's daughter Effie had joined us in the hogan, and she asked if what she heard about the old way of burial was true. "You did once say they use to set aside a couple of men to do this, and they would be separate of other members of the family. Wasn't that right?" Effie asked. "Yes, it was like that," Suzie confirmed:

"Sometimes women, if a man wouldn't do it, even women [would perform the burial]. The ones that are related to the deceased decide who will help. The decision-makers are the ones that holds the family together, leaders. They could be mothers, sisters or older ones. Just two people were chosen to take away and bury the deceased. They would just wash the hair of the deceased and dress them. People would volunteer or sometimes just get picked. They would sit around separately after the burial. They would just sit over in an entirely different spot, separate from everyone else. They were served their meals, but they didn't eat with the rest of the family, and they were not allowed to do anything but to sit...all by themselves. The people who helped with the burial stayed apart from everyone else for two or four days. After that time everybody would wash their hair. You also had to start a fire, maybe by burning some leaves, and walk around in the smoke. By burning some plant leaves you put the smoke onto you. I don't know why the people who did the burying were set aside; probably to keep it sacred."

"They use to sometimes dig holes for the body, or they would be buried in their own homes when they died. A hole was dug inside the hogan and the body was put in there. Usually you buried some of their possessions with them. Only families were around for that; the people that lived right here. There weren't very many people getting together for it. Now there is usually a bunch of people at the burials, and they come from all over. We still use the red powder to bury people, like we did in the past. But people also use to dress the deceased backwards. A necklace would be put on backwards, and the shoes on the wrong side. I don't know when this kind of traditional burial stopped, probably when *bilaga'ana* (white people) started doing it for us. I think that's why it changed."

Kluckhohn and Leighton wrote of the type of ritual described by Suzie when the Navajo dealt with the dead:

---

[75] Reichard, Gladys. <u>Navajo Religion</u>. New York: Bollingen Foundation, 1950, 42-43.

[76] Locke, 29-30.

"The mourners unfasten their hair and strip to the breechcloth. Then they bathe the corpse and dress it in fine garments, placing the left moccasin on the right foot and the right moccasin on the left foot, in the manner prescribed by the origin myth."[77]

The Yazzies told me that the custom of family placing clothes on the body of a deceased relative in a backward fashion evolved only later. Shoes were also put on the wrong feet as well as backwards. The Dine' believed that this would confuse the deceased, thus hindering any chance of his return to harass the living. I was assured that even today the Dine' prefer to distance themselves from the dead and that their attitudes toward death remain very different from those of whites.

I learned over time that not all Navajo placed rocks over the crevices where the dead were hidden. Suzie once explained that when her little sister was buried in a rock shelter the body had been intentionally left exposed. In this way animals would take the body away, thus returning it to the nature from which it had come. I realized at this point that I had been no more acute than the early anthropologists who had studied the Navajo before me. Rituals such as burial rites could be quite diverse, and were carried out depending on each individual family's wishes and beliefs. Like Anglos, not all Navajo reacted to things in a similar way. Every family had its own traditions along with those passed on by Dine' over the years.

I found other evidence that death brought on by difficulty in childbirth was fairly common among the Dine' in the early 1900s. In her narrative, Navajo Irene Stewart told of events that affected her childhood in a way similar to Suzie. "In the year of 1910 my mother died after giving birth to a boy," wrote Mrs. Stewart, "The baby lived only two days. Father was away, working on the railroad; he got home after Mother was buried."[78] Still more examples of infant mortality on the Navajo reservation could be found in a 1948 study done by Kluckhohn and Leighton stated in their 1948 study in which they state that "during the early years the Navajo child has been much less sheltered from the fact of death than are most white children."[79] Because the incidence of death in infancy was high during the early twentieth century, one can be relatively certain that Suzie's early exposure to it was sadly not uncommon.

Suzie and her family had little time to mourn the death of a small child. As Sunshine grew weaker, Suzie's father began to travel more under the pretense of finding work. It was later discovered that her father was selling the rugs made by Suzie and her mother in order to obtain cash for gambling:

"My late father use to always run around after card games. We would finally finish a rug, and before we could sell it he would take it off with him. We found out he would just gamble the whole thing away. He didn't know much about gambling but he did it anyway. He wasn't like my late husband. That man was a pro. My late husband was even called "Handsome Gambler," and he always won. My late dad never did. He would take a rug to the store to sell and then he would go to Monument Pass. He

---

[77] Kluckhohn & Leighton, *Children*, 92.

[78] Stewart, Irene. A Voice In Her Tribe: A Navajo woman's own story. Socorro: Bellena Press, 1980, 12.

[79] Kluckhohn & Leighton, *Children*, 39.

would just disappear over there, but we heard about what he was doing from others. When he did these things we wouldn't have any food for a while. My late father would lose all the money we made from our rugs, many times even when he was gambling with family. The women over there where he gambled were related to him. But it didn't matter. Their men use to beated him all the time. And still my late father kept doing this. He was crazy a little." (giggles)

Navajo during this time did not view gambling with the same negative connotations as it holds among whites. Author Raymond Locke pointed out in his *Book of the Navajo* that "the Navajos' innate sense of humor also manifests itself in their games, and particularly in gambling." He went on to say:

"The People love to gamble but they do not put the emphasis on winning that white Americans do. They have adopted American card games and are particularly fond of poker. The Navajos deal from the bottom of the deck and double-dealing, or hiding or marking cards, are not considered cheating – as long as one doesn't get caught. If a player is caught doing tricks with the cards he merely loses the pot and everyone has a good laugh at his expense. Navajos still play their ancient games, stick dice, the arrow game and the moccasin game, and informal foot and horse races are very popular."[80]

Although gaming was an acceptable aspect of Dine' culture, an unsuccessful gambler who lost control of his finances did lose respect within the Navajo community. It was not that gaming was "morally" wrong, but the lack of control an individual exhibited that was frowned upon. As Kluckhohn and Leighton noted:

"Control of the individual is achieved in Navajo society primarily by 'lateral sanctions' rather than by sanctions from above. That is, the Navajo from childhood on is brought into line more by the reactions of all the people around him rather than by orders and threats of punishment from someone who stands above him in a hierarchy."[81]

Suzie's mother may not have complained about her husband's unsuccessful gambling habits, yet disapproval was surely felt among family members and perhaps within her community. I asked Suzie whether she had been closer to her mother or father. I wondered about the relationship that she had with her father in particular, since I knew that he had not been a good provider to the family, putting more pressure on his eldest daughter to care for their home:

"I wanted him to stop gambling. I wished him to make nice hogans like the one I have now. His brother use to be married to my mom's sister, and that man could make nice hogans with doors. We didn't have a door to ours, and I didn't like that. I use to wish he could these things to take care of us…I was a child then."

In all of our conversations this was the one instance in which Suzie actually seemed to verbally resent her father's gambling and the effect it had on her family. This came across more as a sense of pity for her father, however, and for the things he might have

---

[80] Locke, *Book of the Navajo*, 28-29.
[81] Kluckhohn & Leighton, *Children*, 105-106.

done to help himself and his family. I had a rather poignant picture of Suzie's childhood, working in the family hogan and dreaming of a simple door for their home.

Suzie told me that she was quite close to both of her parents, and that she actually had loved her father very much. The only real flaw Suzie saw in his character was how his penchant for gambling consistently proved unsuccessful and taxed the family's resources. Like many children, Suzie forgave her father his weaknesses and loved him in spite of them. Unfortunately, while Sunshine's health deteriorated, Suzie's father left his eldest daughter to care for her siblings with greater frequency. As her father's absences increased, Suzie was forced to become more independent and decisive in matters concerning her own life and the lives of her siblings.

LEARNING TO TRADE
"A man must make his own arrows." – *Winnebago*

Suzie was forced to deal with her father's abandonment at a very tender age. As her mother's illness advanced, her father spent less and less time at home. Left alone to care for her mother as well as her siblings, Suzie struggled to provide for all of them. "My late mom was always sick," Suzie explained, "and I use to take care of her because my father was not working then." During this time Suzie began to travel with her mother to the health clinic as well as to the trading post. Before long she realized the necessity of learning how to trade her own rugs as a way of providing for her hungry siblings. This meant overcoming her inherent shyness and learning how to barter the best price for her work. She was a young girl of ten before she came into contact with any Anglo, however over time her confidence grew, and she began to acquire the bartering skills and financial savvy that continues to serve her today. Suzie explained in detail the process of learning to trade with the Anglos:

"That's why I weave, because I started when I was very young. I was about seven when I learned to weave, and not much later I learned to sell my rugs use to bring back supplies. All we had to take us to the store was one horse. My late mom and I would both hop on horseback, and sometimes we spend the night there at Goulding's. I was spending a lot of time with my mom then, and I always did the cooking for the kids. My late mom was always laying down. The weaving really helped out, and that's why I'm an excellent weaver now. My mom would set up the loom for me, but then she would have to rest. She was always at the clinic, but staying over there didn't get her better with it. Us kids were down there at the hogan by ourselves a lot, and we were usually hungry. It was hard with just with my younger sister Ella and me staying up all night weaving. Pretty soon we didn't give the rugs to my dad anymore. We told the oldest kid to take care of the younger ones, and my sister and I would take off to sell our rugs and buy food. This was earlier when Mr. Goulding just had a tent, before he built the store up there by the rocks. We could get about twenty dollar's worth of food for a medium size rug."

In fact, Suzie always traded her rugs for staples and did not begin to receive cash for her work until the 1970s. I asked her when she began to request cash payment for her work, and she could only guess. "I'm not sure. Not for a long time, maybe about twenty years ago." I was unsure if she meant "twenty years" as I knew time, or if she meant the Navajo version of twenty years. She turned to her grandchild who was translating and, in an attempt to calculate the time that had passed she asked, "How old are you?" "About 100" her granddaughter answered, and the matter of time was once again put to rest amid fits of laughter from the two women.

Suzie spoke of the hard life she shared with her siblings in a pragmatic way. "Yes," she admitted, "We were all small when she passed away, my late mom. We were by ourselves with only my dad, but he use to run off all the time. That's why we followed around our paternal grandmother so much." I made certain to ask Suzie whether some statements pertaining to her father might be too personal to print. As with many topics that I might otherwise have skirted or handled with great caution, Suzie appeared quite determined to let her feelings be known. "It is okay to be put on paper," she assured me, "let the kids read it." Suzie went on to say, "My kid's grandfather was like this long ago, and people who knew him would say the same thing, so you should tell it right."

Even though Suzie expressed no concern over the confidentiality of our conversations, I continued to explain to her the nature or our project. After all, my professors and peers would eventually read what I believed to be intimate details about Suzie's life, and I felt that protecting Suzie as a respected friend was crucial. I tried my very best to make her understand not only the extent to which her story would be broadcast, but also how it could be useful to other students such as myself.

Suzie's exposure to trade arose from her dealings with a man who became one of the best known and respected whites to enter the Monument Valley region. Harry Goulding and his wife Leone began a trading business in the 1920s that benefited families like Suzie's in many ways. A smaller post called Oljeto was situated some ten miles behind the Goulding site and had been operating since 1910 on a smaller scale. Eventually the Goulding's went from trading out of their tent to building a number of stucco structures. They forged a strong business relationship with their Indian neighbors, and the Navajo gave Harry Goulding the name of "Tall Sheep", or *Dibe' Neez*. His wife became known by her nickname, "Mike". In an effort to conduct business more efficiently, and to adjust to the new culture surrounding them, the couple learned the Navajo language. Their narrative, compiled in a book by Samuel Moon, detailed many of their experiences. From this I learned that it was common for women and children like the Yazzies to stay overnight at the white trading post after completing their transactions. Harry Goulding recalled:

"We were busy all the time. It didn't make any difference to the Navajos. They didn't know what Sunday was until they got into the trading post. We had a hogan for them to stay overnight, just down off the hill, between the corral and the trading post. They stayed around the camp there, fixed a campfire, and we'd usually give them a coffeepot. The mother if she came, she'd bring her littlest one, or maybe the two littlest ones, and the rest would stay home."

Suzie recalled that the first white people she met were the Goulding's and their Anglo guests who stayed at the trading post. She remembered Harry Goulding quite well and claimed that his influence was clearly felt throughout the Valley:

"I was told "he is a *bilaga'ana* (a white man). He was the first one I ever saw. He use to come to walk upon (among) our people. I was small when he came here, about seven or eight years old, but I remember he use to help us a lot. Back then he was the only one who gave us food. Then he started to drive the first tourists I saw to the Valley. This helped us out too because they came asking us to cook for them. We made fry bread for them and Mr. Goulding would boil coffee or just help cook. The tourists looked somewhat strange to me at first, but I wasn't afraid because they were staying with the Goulding's."

Suzie began to enjoy her increased contact with whites, as they provided the occasional distraction and a welcome supplement to the Yazzie's income.

A CHANGE IN THE WEATHER
"One rain does not make crop, but crop makes rain." — Creole

Lonnie entered the hogan, wiping his hands from the morning chores just completed. He took his place next to Effie and listened intently to the exchange that passed between his wife, his mother, and me. I learned that as Suzie entered adolescence she began to experience different condition in her homeland that would require her people to further adjust. They were now obliged to adapt not only to an increased Anglo presence, but to a change in their environment as well. Suzie slowly became aware of the alterations in her environment:

"I noticed things around the time when my late mom had already passed away, and a little before then. We use to plant way over here by where I live now. But we no longer planted once my mother died, because things were not growing well."

Lonnie, recalled similar changes in field fertility as he was growing up:

"Yeah, even when I was a kid I noticed that there was still a lot of cornfield in the backcountry. Here we use to try and plant at least a little corn. We also use to plant way over beyond the rocks, and we even had groves with peaches. But after a while things really started to dry up. The wind blew hard, and it really started storming. This lasted for some years. Afterwards we tried planting again, but nothing came up. Even when we put water directly onto the corn it would only grow about three feet. Before those wind storms our corn use to grow pretty big, but with short corn we couldn't get much food."

By the mid-1920s environmental conditions within the Valley worsened. Crops that had thrived in the past became less hardy, and the once fertile topsoil began to blow away in ever more frequent windstorms. Suzie and her son spoke of plants and animals that had once flourished in their homeland. "A lot of birds were here, even eagles" Suzie claimed, "Now we hardly ever see a larger bird." Her son corrected her: "there are still a few larger birds at Flat Wide Rocks." (This area is also known as Meridian

Rock). "Yes," Suzie agreed, "or at your Uncle's house too. There are some at the home of my eldest brother. There are just a few there, but not larger animals. Bobcats use to live around here, and also desert antelopes. But as you grew up we didn't even see them anymore." Suzie's son recalled hearing stories of the desert antelope. "Maybe it was during the Anasazi period when there were plenty of antelope," he speculated, "over by *Dennehotso*; I heard there were a few at one time even there. Remember they call that area "Antelope Lookout"? "Yeah," Suzie agreed, "there use to be antelope there, but now there are only porcupines"

I had discovered within some of my Navajo literature a legend concerning a bear, so I asked Suzie if she recalled ever seeing such an animal. She answered that she had never seen a bear, but she remembered hearing of them as a child:

"I never saw a bear; just talking about it in oral history is what I remember. One bear was a monster that use to eat Navajo people I've been told. We use to live in poorly constructed homes that the bears could get into. I was told The People had to gather big logs criss-cross for bonfires. I guess when one of these monsters use to catch you, you would grab the big logs and hang on (giggles). Yes, you hang onto the lighted logs because the bears were afraid of fire. If it was kids he grabbed, he would run off with them. Kids didn't have a chance."

I stifled my own giggle. This sounded very much like a spooky campfire story told to scare children. But Lonnie confirmed that, in spite of the fact that they no longer lived in the area, bears did figure prominently in their culture. He asked his mother if she remembered, "in some ceremonies… those bear claws or bear toenails, weren't they used for protection?" "Yes," Suzie answered, "that's the way it's been told. We had one of those claws around here somewhere, passed on by my parents. I don't know where it is now. Maybe your uncle took it and lost it." Suzie also recalled hearing of an eagle that was found by her sons. This was very interesting to me because the only bird of prey I had seen in the region was one hawk in Farmington, miles away from the Valley, and I had never heard of an eagle sighting. Suzie assured me that one had been found however:

"I guess that one couldn't fly anymore, it was wounded somehow. So when they found it, my son and his boy watched that eagle die right here. It was strange, because we had not seen one for many years. People were asking for feathers when they heard one had been found, so they took feathers off the bird and were going to give them away. But I told them "No", because you can't sell those…the real stuff. It would be an improper thing to do."

Apparently Suzie wielded enough authority to deter the men from distributing the eagle feathers that most certainly would have been highly valued for ceremonial use. I had the distinct impression that the matriarch felt the rare appearance of this bird was a sort of magic, and good or bad, that magic and the message it sent was to be quietly respected. Some years later I would receive my own message from an eagle within the Valley. But while Lonnie and his mother conversed, I could only try and imagine what a different world their home had been, and wonder at the meaning of it all.

Suzie continued to describe the days when planting took place in the Valley:

61

"My paternal grandfather use to say that long ago there was a lot of corn. Even we use to go into the cornfield all the time when I was younger. There was even lots of water here, coming out all the time, because there was a lot of rain then. There was peaches like my son said, and watermelons and squash too. We even had honeydew melons. Over near the ridges we use to plant a lot with my late paternal grandfather. We had our fields near the overhangs where the water drops. We put fences around our groves in the canyon, and hardly had to wait at all for it to rain."

Lonnie claimed he was still a small boy when the climate changed even more drastically within the Valley:

"Yes, that's when it started with windstorms for about thirty years in a row. People were sort of getting by with less and less crops starting with when my mom was a girl. But as I grew up it got worse. When we tried planting the corn, it just wouldn't grow anywhere. I think the fertile sand blew away with the windstorms. It was still sand, but had a darker color and that stuff grows good crops, that's the way it is. When the fertile sand blows away it will not grow anything. It just becomes regular sand. All of this happened because of the windstorms."

Suzie spoke of the hardship and hunger that accompanied the passing of a life that was once tied to the soil. "Even as a young girl I noticed that we began to live in real hunger then," she remembered, "that was when I first met the Goulding's because my late mom use to make bread for them, when they use to come over. It was also when we use to begin making more rugs; not so much for ourselves anymore, but for trading with the Goulding's."

As the fertility of the region declined, the need among Navajo families like Suzie's became more intense, and alternative methods of obtaining food were desperately sought. It was fortuitous that tourists began to visit the Valley more frequently during this period of want. They presented an opportunity for Navajos living in the scenic area to charge the occasional fee for services. These services included guiding tourists through the Valley, cooking for them, and demonstrating Navajo weaving techniques. With this income along with the money made from selling blankets, many Dine' families were able to purchase food and household goods from the trading post and compensate for decreasing crop yields. The climate in the Valley has remained arid, yet both Suzie and her son expect the environment to return to its more fertile condition. "Probably in another fifty or hundred years it'll change back again," Lonnie explained. "Yes," agreed Suzie, "Probably the rain will start again someday." The conversation about the Valley's declining fertility had made all of us rather sad, and so it seemed a good time to stop the interview. I had a lot to work with, and I was anxious to put all my notes in order back in my room. We said our goodbyes to Suzie and Effie, and I followed Emily and Lonnie out of the park. They pulled off on the road toward Chinle, while I headed for the lodge and an early dinner.

SUZIE MEETS SPIDER WOMAN

"All dreams spin out from the same web." Hopi

I ate a hasty breakfast the next morning and met Emily and Lonnie at the park's entrance. We arrived at Suzie's house by nine. There would be plenty of time to work this day. I had purchased a book from the souvenir shop at Goulding's that contained photographs of old weaving styles. I proudly it to Suzie, and she sat mesmerized with it for several minutes. Motioning for me to sit beside her on the old bed she pointed out the patterns that were familiar to her. Emily translated what her mother-in-law remembered from her early instruction in the Navajo art of weaving, and how it was used to entertain white tourists:

"At first I had a hard time learning to weave. My late grandmother taught me to do the double weave. You count every other strings, and skip here and there, using each rod going up as you weave, and then down. My late grandmother use to come here a lot on a mule, and she use to bring a rug rolled up and re-set up a loom outside. That's when Goulding use to bring the tourist over. I guess that's why she came over here with her work. She would demonstrate her weaving, and once she did a rug just like this one in the book. I remember her riding in with it on her back when she came. When my sisters and I started to do weaving on our own things became more accessible, like food. Before trading the only time you would eat was when you could grind some corn. There was no money."

As her family made the transition from a pastoral/horticultural subsistence to one that involved trade, Suzie began to recognize her situation as different from that of her peers. Between her mother's frequent stays at the clinic, and an increasingly absent father, the young Suzie felt the burden of her situation as the eldest daughter. It was a lonely and difficult existence, and she longed for her favorite granny. It became very clear to Suzie that her life at her grandmother's home was far more secure:

"Other children had fathers and they were taken care of. My sister, Ella, and I were different. My dad's brother and grandmother lived over at Meridian Rock, and I could see that man took good care of his kids. They had a real nice home, and my sister and I use to always say "He takes good care of his family." We wished our dad was like that. My sister Ella was just a little girl then, but even though my grandmother's home was a long walk we would both go over there for food or just to be with family. I would carry my sister piggyback every now and then. This was when my late mom was always at the hospital. One time we traveled as far as from here to Sand Springs, just walking and piggyback for over ten miles.

Over there at grandma's house, I guess they were herding sheep over behind the rock. We found their tracks, but we were barely keeping up as they herded the sheep over the dunes. My sister wasn't as fast as I was, so that was when I would pick her up again and again on piggyback. I was kind of scrawny too, but I carried her anyway. We finally caught up. From the time I was around five years old I had been left alone a lot, and my paternal grandmother would always say, "Why are you guys staying over there by yourself?" I never knew what to tell her, so she would just feed us and take care of us for a while."

Although Sunshine's visits to the clinic increased, she received only limited care at the facility. At this time most Navajo continued to rely primarily on the skills of their local Medicine Man. It was only the willingness of trader Harry Goulding to provide transportation to the hospital in Tuba City that encouraged Navajo like Sunshine to seek more intensive medical care offered at the government-run hospital in Tuba City, some fifty miles away. In addition to the many logistical difficulties involved with obtaining professional medical care, some Navajo continued to have more faith in their own traditional healing methods. In her narrative written in 1982, Irene Stewart, a Navajo woman from Chinle, spoke about her initial reactions to both white trading posts and hospitals. Very close in age to Suzie, Mrs. Stewart explained how her contemporaries regarded both structures with suspicion in her youth:

"At Chinle, I saw for the first time a trading post. I didn't want to go inside because I was afraid of strange people, especially white people, so we sat and rested under a cottonwood tree near the store. I never went to the hospital when I was sick, because I was afraid of the doctors. Also, I had been told that many people died there, and that there must be a lot of children-ghosts."[82]

Suzie and her family began to rely more and more on both the Anglo trading business and the medical care provided by the government. Suzie encountered more whites with every visit to the trading post or hospital, and her sense of independence grew along with her responsibilities. As we spoke of her experiences she reflected on the irony of depending on her children now that she has reached old age. She seemed impatient with her dependency on her children's automobiles, when she had been so willing to ride by horseback in her youth. While driving her back from Goulding's one morning, Suzie spoke with her daughter-in-law about a time when she was hungry but independent.

By conducting business at the trading post as a very young child, she had learned to become self-reliant in spite of her young age. "Remember yesterday?" her daughter-in-law, Emily, reminded Suzie the next day during an interview, "yesterday you're in a rush to get back to the hogan," she giggled, "and you told me that when you were young you wouldn't wait around for anybody! You would just grab a horse or hook one up to a wagon, and ride into Goulding's? You, by yourself, would travel to this place, even though you were just a kid!"

Unfortunately, Suzie's new found independence would not allow her to pursue other ventures that were becoming available to children her age. The option of attending school was one of the advantages offered to her peers in which she could not take part, though she expressed an interest in the new learning offered by Anglos. At a period in life when school would have been a priority for most children, Suzie abandoned any hope of attending in order to continue working for her family's survival and caring for her mother. She carried on in her role as surrogate mother throughout her childhood and into adolescence. Yet, sending the Navajo children to school was the policy of a U.S. government determined to assimilate the Navajo into white culture.

---

[82] Stewart *A Voice in her Tribe*, 13 & 21.

By the time Suzie had children of her own children would have no choice but to board at the government schools far from their homes.

Suzie's son Lonnie had been sitting nearby, quietly sipping coffee and listening to us women chatter away. Before long he became restless however, and alluding to the chore of "finding the sheeps," he went clomping out of the warm little house. His wife, Emily, and I looked out the cracked window just in time to see him hop upon his horse "Beano" and take off across the desert sand toward a distant butte. "He'll have to fill the water tank today too," Suzie said through Emily. She did not bother looking out the window, but seemed to know exactly what was on her son's mind. She was also adept at hearing a tourist bus pull up. Emily and I hadn't even noticed, but somehow Suzie had deciphered the sound of truck wheels crunching the hard dirt by her hogan. She stood and smoothed her skirt, then left to do business with the visitors without another word.

It was these moments when Suzie stepped away that I heard snippets of Emily's story as well. Our dialogue centered on the usual topics of husbands and children, but there were also times when we compared our childhoods, our dreams and our disappointments. All too often our discussions would begin with a joke from Emily. "Most white guys look pretty bad with their shirts off," she would proclaim out of the blue. Once we finished giggling over this latest revelation she would launch into the details of her first marriage, or her first experience giving birth, or what it had been like to have Lonnie courting her. Our conversations ranged from racism, to self-awareness, then to chauvinism and around and around until we began to feel as if we had known each other for ages.

Mostly we talked about what it was to be Dine.' It seemed to me at that time that the "Navajo way" of doing things was preferable to my complicated Anglo lifestyle, and Emily was inclined to agree. She had been through a lot in her forty some years living on the reservation. Through good times and bad she had managed to come through it all a stronger person. Her approach to most things was practical, seasoned with a healthy sense of humor. Like Suzie, Emily did not take herself too seriously, nor did she lament over past hardships.

I took advantage of days like these to interview other family members. Sometimes I found myself alone with Emily, and other times Lonnie and I would sit in the little government house where he began to tell me a bit about his own life. And so the day flowed along with me grabbing chunks of stories until the sun cast shadows on the rocks that surrounded Suzie's compound, indicating it was time for me to go. I repeated the exercise of packing up my car with the minimum of fuss, and after a few brief good-byes, bumped back to my hotel room to shower off the day's sand. Mercifully, the family of Big Foots had blissfully checked out, and I fell immediately to sleep, barely remembering to turn off the light.

CONVERSATION, CULTURE AND CONFUSION

"Thoughts are like arrows: once released, they strike their mark. Guard them well or one day you may be your own victim." - Navajo

I now faced another end to a reservation visit. There was so much more I wished to accomplish during this particular trip, and I jumped out of my bed at the lodge eager to get an early start. I met with Emily and Lonnie for a brief meal, and soon left for another day of capturing stories. Lonnie followed behind in his car, while Emily and I took the lead in my rental. The breakfast of oatmeal I'd gulped down now flopped around in my belly as we rumbled down the washboard road to Suzie's place. Emily and I drove along in comfortable companionship while she spoke of her childhood. She felt her early years on the rez were very different from her own children's experience. "Things are changing," she cautioned, "there's not as much respect for elders and lots of kids aren't being taught the traditional ways." I shared with her my belief that this seemed to be a common occurrence throughout America, and we both giggled over how we sounded; two grumpy old women complaining about the younger generation. We were lost in conversation, and the half-hour drive to Suzie's compound flew by.

I took my usual parking spot in front of the little dirt-brown house and unpacked my things. Emily grabbed the few groceries we'd purchased for her mother-in-law, and I followed her into the house. Light was streaming through the dirty, cracked window over Suzie's bed and the faithful coffeepot perked away. Effie had spent the night with her mother, and she helped to unpack my supplies while her mother smiled a hello. Familiar now with the preparation of our meetings, Suzie sat on the bed and arranged her velveteen skirt around her. Effie, Emily and I settled into folding chairs by the woodstove to chat; all of us equipped with steaming cups of strong coffee. The woody smell of cedar burning in the wood stove filled the room. It created a memory that I hold dear to this day. We soon heard Lonnie's car pulling up next to mine, and in minutes he had joined our little reunion. The gossip continued as the family shared private jokes and teased one another. Even the occasional ribbing seemed gentle when Suzie was involved. As Lonnie later told me, there were never any real arguments with his mother, only "strong opinions."

The conversation meandered to the days when everybody was younger. The women spoke of Suzie's older son, Leonard. There were five surviving children in the Yazzie family. From the eldest to the youngest were Harvey, Leonard, Lonnie, Effie and Kee, with a number of nieces and nephews coming and going through their households at any given time. I had read that it was not uncommon for Navajo children to live with various female family members while their fathers left home in search of work. These "aunties" worked together in raising their young relatives, pooling their time and resources until the parent's return. While listening to the ladies' stories I learned that back in the seventies Effie and her mother were helping to raise Leonard's daughter, Lucille. They all lived in a hogan by the Three Sisters monument. This had been an area popular among Suzie's family in which to set up house.

Throughout the course of their young lives they returned to the spot time and again. It was also an ideal location for doing business with spring and summer visitors, and the girls often drove their sheep out to the Arch monument to pose for photographs. Charmed tourists gave them change for halting their horses amidst the beautiful scenery. I have seen some of these photos, resurrected in glossy guidebooks sold at Goulding's or the Tourist Center. The young ladies held striking poses, even coming off as casually defiant. It seemed odd to view staged photographs of these women that I now knew so personally. In the tourist books they appeared mysterious and one-dimensional. Yet these same ladies had become, to me, complex personalities. The "pictures of Indians" were presented as part of the scenery of Monument Valley. But I knew they were individuals with a distinct past and dreams for a better future. They had become "family."

Effie spoke of the manner in which Suzie kept her eye on her young charges back in the 1960s and 70s. She insisted the children accompany her every day while she cared for the family herd. In doing so she was able to pass on her knowledge of shepherding. "We got good at herding, just like Four-Horned Woman," proclaimed Effie. She went on to explain her ancestor's name. Animals that possessed rare traits were considered a blessing to the Navajo. Owning a paint horse or a four-horned ram presumably brought good fortune to the owner of such livestock. Four-Horned Woman was so named because of the unique sheep born to her flock. What her name had been before this anomaly occurred I have yet to discover.

With the end of her story Effie excused herself from our group to check on the sheep. A strong wind caused the door to slam loudly behind her, and we all jumped at the sound. This was followed by a round of giggles, and when things settled down Emily began to tell me how much she respected her sister-in-law "for her strength." A strong woman was one who commanded respect in this community and most certainly among the Yazzies. I learned from Emily that Effie was currently holding a job as a nursing assistant at the clinic still situated behind Goulding's. This was the same clinic where Sunshine had received care. According to Emily, Effie had the ability to master any job that might present itself. Having married in her teens, the young Effie found it necessary to remain flexible and open to employment opportunities. She separated from her husband while still quite young, and she was literally on her own in caring for her four children. Effie's eldest boy, Thomas, was twenty-nine at the time of this interview, (1999). She also had a daughter, Elvina, who was twenty-four and another, Erlene, who was twenty-two. Finally, there is the youngest son, Timmy, who was twenty. At the age of forty-five Effie was only four years older than I, yet so much more experienced, and her children nearly grown. "My sister was too young to know what love was back then," Lonnie said of Effie, "in those days marriages were still arranged a lot of the time. You married for survival."

Emily agreed, stating "I remember hearing about my grandparents' marriage. My grandpa was thirty and my grandma was only fourteen. But he was well-off and secure, so she was happy to have him!" "Now you marry who you're happy or comfortable with," Lonnie interjected, "but I don't know about this modern romance. Sometimes I wonder if the old way is better." Emily cast him a knowing look and he grinned. I was observing a happily married couple whom, after many years together, still enjoyed teasing each other. "I remember the day I met him," laughed Emily, "I saw him at a dance from clear across the room." "My husband is a singer of traditional Navajo songs, and he was singing even then, and I just wanted to grab him," she giggled. "Well, if you're just going to make fun of me I'm going to go herd my sheep," grumbled Lonnie, feigning disgust. He walked out to the continued giggles of the remaining women gathered around the stove. "Oh he likes to think of himself as a sheepherder," Emily laughed, "but everybody knows his clan is drawn to teaching." From what I have seen this is relatively true, because even now both Lonnie and Emily continue to take on work as substitute teachers for the grammar school in Chinle.

We also felt the need to escape the toasty little house, so we adjourned with Suzie to the Shade House and began making lunch. Emily recited to me the recipe for Navajo Fry Bread, talking me through the ingredients and how to mix them as she went along. She combined two and a half cups of flour with two and a half tablespoons of baking powder. She then added one and a half cups, (more or less), of lukewarm water to the mixture, stirring it until the dough no longer stuck to her fingers. I watched her strong brown fingers knead the dough until the proper puffy texture had been achieved. Throwing a flour sack cloth over the mixture Emily then left the concoction to rise for about fifteen minutes. She headed back to the house to scout out some lard. Returning with a huge tub of Crisco, she peered under the cloth and perceived the dough as ready for action. She threw a glob of shortening into a frying pan that was heating on the wood stove that stood in the center of the Shade House.

The individual cakes of bread were patted out like tortillas until they flattened to the size of a medium sized plate. Emily demonstrated how to turn the bread in a clockwise motion. Just as the Navajo enter a hogan, or dance in a circle, the clockwise motion is meant to reflect the rising sun and promotes harmony. My harmony, unfortunately, was slightly skewed. Every time I attempted to flatten my own supply of little cakes I managed only to drop them into the dust of the Shade House, one after the other. After the resounding "plop" of my third cake reduced the Yazzies to uncontrollable giggles I gave up and watched the others finish shaping the dough. It would not have been so humiliating if Lonnie hadn't captured my failures with the camera I'd brought along. Lured by the smell of bread frying he had snuck into the Shade House and snapped the unflattering photo. Not to be outdone by the ladies, he fashioned his own cakes. These were done with great skill, much to my despair. Emily tried to soothe me with stories of her dreadful first attempts, but I continued to pout until a tasty cake was cooked for me, and my humility gave way to hunger.

As I tore away at my bread I scanned the compound. I could see that nothing went to waste here in the Valley. Cast off pieces of machinery, rusty nails and car parts were discreetly tucked away into makeshift storage sheds. Even food scraps were spared, thrown out to the sheep dogs who eyed every bite. Other than the Navajo themselves these animals were the primary protectors over the herd. Consequently, they were considered more employees than pets, and they ate according to the success or failure of the sheep they so closely guarded. The herd was safely tucked away, and so we threw bits of our fry bread to the hungry dogs while Suzie settled once again into a chair to talk. She had removed the microphone from her blouse, so I scrambled for my notepad and pen to take down any interesting information.

Suzie and Lonnie shared stories while Emily translated for me. Mother and son began to chuckle, and I asked Emily what had been so funny. She told me that they were discussing the death of Suzie's mother, Sunshine. Still a young woman, Sunshine became ill after giving birth to Suzie, her second child, and she continued to struggle with illness with every following pregnancy. "But," I wondered, "why the laughter?" Seeing my puzzled expression Emily tried to explain, "Hardship is funny. If you don't laugh at it sometimes, it can hurt you." I pondered this while munching on the remainder of my bread. Lonnie and his mother continued to giggle and I began to feel slightly left out of things. I couldn't grasp the concept of using humor as a shield against sadness. I also sensed that I was missing more of the conversation than Emily let on.

We somehow meandered onto the subject of Navajo names. Suzie's daughter had returned from her chores, and grabbing her own piece of fry bread she told me that most Navajo have an Anglo name they use officially and in public. What one might call the true name, or the name they are given as Dine,' is entirely different and rarely spoken. Effie explained that this name comes from the family and identifies the person as a Navajo in ways that are still unclear to me. I did learn that one's Navajo name is kept private from most of the world and used only under specific circumstances, for instance in a healing ceremony. Suzie's daughter did not wish to tell me her name in Navajo for fear of bad luck. "Some people believe that if you say your Dine' name out loud you will turn into that name," warned Effie. "If you are named after a particular animal, for example, you'll become that animal." I did eventually learn the Navajo title of Suzie's daughter. It is a lovely name, but out of respect for her I will not mention it here.

Lonnie then asked me about the different route I took to get to the Valley that weekend. He and Emily had been expecting my usual call that I always made to them once I reached the reservation. Unfortunately, I had been too tired to make any calls that evening. I apologized to my friends for falling asleep without contacting them first. What had I been thinking? When the Yazzies did not hear from me they figured the best thing to do was to wait, a familiar tactic among the family. After a few trips out to the reservation I felt comfortable and safe. I could usually spot a trailer or hogan every ten or so miles, so I knew there was always assistance if I needed it. Still, it had been rude not to call Lonnie and Emily. They knew I was apprehensive about the long drive, so as a favor to me they wanted to make certain that I reached my destination safely.

I let Lonnie in on the fact that I had been driving blissfully into his homeland at a brisk speed ten miles beyond the already gracious sixty-five mph limit. Because of this, and the fact that I had the road practically to myself, I had made very good time. He just giggled and shook his head. "Better watch it," he warned, "it's the writers and journalists who always get thrown in jail around here. The tribal police will pull you over for going seventy miles per hour, and sometimes they even throw you in jail just to prove a point."

On the off-chance he wasn't kidding, I filed Lonnie's piece of information away in my mind for future reference. Since then always made sure I was going no more than sixty-five miles per hour while on the Rez, even on the long straight-aways with nobody else in sight. I have noticed that most of the Navajo do the same, and they sometimes drive even slower. Why take chances? Emily began wiping out the frying pan. "Stop trying to scare her," she scolded her husband, and Lonnie reassured me with a devilish smile. "It wouldn't matter if you got thrown in the slammer," he laughed, "we'd come looking for you and bail you out."

The talk of road trips allowed Emily to muse out loud about her desire to travel. It amazed me to hear that many of the older family members hardly ever ventured beyond the extensive boundaries of the rez. They traveled long distances by car to reach each other's homes, or to acquire goods that were unavailable in their region. Yet many of those to whom I spoke simply had neither the time nor the money to go much further. Emily, however, dreamed of a chance to see a world that existed beyond her homeland. "We went to Phoenix once," she quietly explained, "but I'd really like to see more of the states; maybe even go to another country."

Suzie was left out of conversation when we spoke in English, and she started to look a little bored. I had been plaguing her with so many questions, and I now wondered if she had any for me. I had Emily translate this to Suzie, and found that all of her curiosity revolved around how many children I have, their ages, and why my husband put up with my long absences to visit the Valley. I tried to explain that from where I came things were different, but I could tell by the expression on her face that Suzie was not satisfied with this answer. I sat squirming under her gaze, then noticed with unusual relief that a tourist bus was pulling up to the hogan. I wouldn't have to defend my way of life to Suzie if she were busy tending to the visitors. No such luck. Emily offered to meet with the tourists in the hogan so Lonnie and I could continue to work with Suzie.

I needn't have worried. Lonnie and his mother had already gone off on another subject. I asked my friend what they were talking about, and he said they were comparing how life had changed on the reservation. Lonnie expressed concern over the next generation of Navajo and what their world could possibly offer them. He felt that many Dine' youth were "not on the right track." He attributed their lack of direction to limited opportunities. Very few after-school programs were available, and most young people had difficulty finding summer employment. With little else to occupy their time, teens could easily slip into a pattern of boredom relieved only by looking for trouble and drinking. I explained to Lonnie that this was a problem for teenagers nation-wide, but he felt his children were more at risk because of the intermittent poverty his family experienced during the off season. Jobs tended to disappear when tourist activity slowed in the winter months. How could young people save up for college tuition, Lonnie asked, when employment was so unreliable?

I didn't have an answer for him, and we sat in the cool quiet of the Shade House wondering to ourselves if this way of life could continue for much longer. While we sat, a group of the tourists began to creep from the hogan. I thought Emily must be wrapping up her weaving demonstration, and this inquisitive group meandered closer to the Shade House. Judging by their accents I surmised they were part of the European group staying at Goulding'. We sat watching them as they peered in between the branches of the shade, curious over what sort of attraction waited inside. Finally, one brave visitor came to the door of the structure. Lonnie then stood and quietly informed the tourist that he had ventured into a private area. The visitor towered over Lonnie; his fair skin and blond hair a striking contrast against my friend's dark and compact appearance. Patiently but firmly Lonnie directed the hapless stranger back to the parking area by the hogan. I marveled at the way the Yazzies handled situations such as these, and over the years I spent with them I witnessed many occasions when visitors crossed the vague boundaries of privacy that existed within the compound. Each and every time the family addressed intruders in a very polite manner. As for me…well, I secretly yearned for the winter months when visitors stopped coming altogether, and I could have Suzie all to myself.

As the guests slowly filed back onto the tour bus, I asked Lonnie if it ever bothered the family when tourists became intrusive. Later this struck me as a rather hypocritical question, since for some time I too had been invading their privacy. Lonnie told me that, even though having visitors on the property could be disruptive, he had become used to them, and he tried to remember that they provided the family with much-needed income. What about Suzie, I asked. Didn't she wish the tourists would remain in the hogan where the demonstrations took place and where jewelry manufactured by the family was for sale? If she and her family could not relax in the Shade House during breaks, when could they ever escape the scrutiny of strangers? "Oh it bothers her plenty," Lonnie assured me, "but she just sits and doesn't show it." Overall, Suzie seems to enjoy the tourists, and she looks forward to their unexpected forays to the hogan. Lonnie told me that she has learned about people of different nationalities through these visits. In a way the tourists are her window to a world beyond the reservation.

Our conversation now wandered to various topics. We continued to discuss the way many Navajo informally adopt their relatives' children when times are hard. Suzie has taken in her grandchildren whenever her sons were between jobs or experiencing marital problems. Emily and Lonnie cared for a niece and ended up formally adopting her. This custom of informal adoption allows families to stay relatively intact in spite of divorces, financial difficulties or personal problems. It limits the necessity of foster parents and provides children with some sense of security in the midst of upheaval. The idea of caring for each other seemed to come so naturally to the Yazzies, and the focus on family was refreshing. It was not as if my own siblings would not come to my aid if I found myself in dire straits. We too were a tight-knit family. However I think the idea of "adopting" my children would not automatically be considered any kind of solution. Our concept of families has always been very nuclear, with each group fending for themselves whenever possible; only seeking assistance from relatives as a last and temporary resort. I wondered if this practice of caring for each other's children would eventually die out among the Navajo. For now it remains a popular solution to family problems. Additionally, it allows those relatives who have no children some youthful company and help with household chores.

The discussion shifted to livestock and their value. "In the old days people would walk long distances all the time," Lonnie told me, "but my mom had it good when she was a kid because her family had horses as well as sheep." Suzie told how she and her sister, Ella, were able to contain their horses while traveling throughout the Valley. As young girls they frequently went out together to visit friends, track down the family herd, or do business at Goulding's. The trick, Lonnie translated, was to tie the horse to something so that it would not wander off as the girls attended to other things, or even camped out for the night. In a place with few trees this could be a challenge. The solution was to tie the horses' two front feet together in a loose fashion that allowed them to graze, but not to walk away. This "hobbling" worked very well when the girls found themselves in the middle of the desert with no trees in sight.

As I continued the interview I could tell that Suzie was finished with any particular story by the way she paused in her speaking. I became accustomed to these subtle lulls in conversation and the way we randomly went from one subject to another, depending on what Suzie could recall, and in this manner we suddenly began to speak of certain Dine' beliefs. I was fascinated to learn that animals are viewed as sacred and related in some way to humans. I was reminded again that one had to use caution with every desert creature because an animal as small as a lizard might very well turn out to be your *che*, or "grandfather." Lonnie told me that the Navajo did not take the killing an animal lightly. If one intended to hunt for deer, for example, a sweat lodge ceremony was first required. It was during the sweat when prayers were said and songs offered as appreciation for the opportunity to take the animal's life. After killing and butchering the animal, an additional cleansing ceremony would have to take place as a way of thanking the creature for giving up its life. This also prevented the animal's spirit from haunting the hunter in the future.

"Taking a life is a very serious thing to us," Lonnie explained, "that's why so many guys who came back from wars have to attend ceremonies. They have broken the natural law, so they go to these ceremonies to get rid of the flashbacks and nightmares. The spirits of those they killed will keep returning if they don't do this. It helps to put a person's thinking back in their right mind."

The idea of praying for forgiveness was not new to me, but the Navajo seemed to take the act of killing even an animal much more to heart than in my Anglo world. In Dine' culture there was a way to atone for killing and to me this seemed proper and very healing. But how many ceremonies were required before one felt cleansed from an act as serious as killing another human? If a Navajo went to war then chances are many men might be killed in the course of fighting. I thought that this must weigh very heavily on a Navajo soldier's mind if he had been raised in the traditional way.

I did not have much time to mull over this, because some visitors of a different type pulled up to pay a visit. These Navajo women came in dusty old cars, or "chiddies" as the clunkers were called. The ladies had known Suzie for years, and as everyone loosely clasped hands in greeting they threw curious glances my way. Lonnie suggested we go into the house and leave the ladies to "talk business." The women were relatives who had contributed goods to be sold at the hogan. Suzie was responsible for seeing that they were compensated for any crafts that had been sold, however this was often a rather loose arrangement. Family members were sometimes loaned additional money depending on need, and at times this reduced the amount available for others. The entire procedure was a mystery to me. However, I never asked Suzie how she managed it. The topic seemed a little too personal for our project.

While waiting for these business dealings to end I looked over my notes on the Navajo language. Lonnie assisted me and tried not to laugh as I struggled with minute differences in certain words. He scribbled out words for me as they are read by the Dine,' but I would then have to rewrite them phonetically just to see how they were actually spoken. The words felt clumsy upon my tongue, and I looked with some relief to see that Suzie had completed her business and was coming to join us in her house. She found my struggle to speak her language extremely amusing. After the fry bread debacle I'd had enough humiliation. So I decided to regain some of my pride and call it a day. I had little energy for a language lesson anyway.

Emily helped me carry my things to the rental car, and we paused to look out over the beautiful landscape together. "I have to drive out tomorrow morning, but I don't feel like leaving," I sighed. "Yeah," Emily said in her quiet way, "we don't really want you to go either. When do you suppose you'll be coming back?" I thought of what the coming months would bring me. An endless schedule of classes jammed with assignments loomed ahead. I imagined what my step-children would be going through while getting used to the new school where we'd recently signed them up. Then there was my busy husband's travel plans. He would be sent as far away as Japan next month, to negotiate business with a huge company there. I thought to myself how much Emily would like to go in his place. Pushing the busy itinerary from my mind I listened to the wind whistle through the massive rocks. The gentle warmth of desert air caressed my face and brushed loose bangs of hair in front of my eyes. When would I be coming back here? "Soon," I finally answered Emily, "very soon."

CHAPTER 5- LIFE AND DEATH IN MONUMENT VALLEY

"Everything the power does, it does in a circle." - *Lakota*

BACK TO THE REZ

On my next visit to the Valley I brought along a new laptop computer so that I could work in the evenings with any material collected during the day. The notes I had scribbled during my last interview with Suzie had waited patiently to come to life in complete sentences. For too long the details of this trip to the Valley lingered in my head, and when I finally sat down to commit the memories to paper they perched on the end of my brain; vague and fuzzy like some dream I couldn't shake. Now I was determined to capture every nuance of my Valley experiences by typing out my notes each and every evening. I could type much faster and clearer than with handwriting, but deep down I knew I would miss my beloved longhand. It seemed that my thoughts flowed more easily in sloppy cursive. Yet the time had come to jump into the twenty-first century and become acquainted with a laptop like the rest of the modern world. The ritual of typing out my diary entries at the end of the day began!

When I arrived at Goulding's I attacked my writing with vigor. This time I had reserved one of the little condominiums offered as an alternative to a room at the lodge. One could choose from three separate buildings, each complete with a balcony and a kitchenette. There was also a little house situated on the rocky mounds behind the lodge. I discovered this "Hill House" while driving around with Emily, and was curious. Emily told me it had housed the Valley's only doctor years ago; since then it stood empty but for the occasional tourist family in need of roomier accommodations. Thinking it would be a wonderful place to have the Yazzies over for dinner in a more comfortable social environment, I planned to inquire about its availability for my next visit.

Other than looking a bit weathered, my little condo offered a much better work place than the customary lodge room. I had plenty of space to set up my computer and materials, and lots of light coming through a window looking out to the balcony. I went straight to work. The purpose of this trip was to pose additional questions to Suzie allowing me to fill in some of the gaps that remained throughout her story. Some aspects of her life continued to elude me, and of course this may have been intentional on her part. At the risk of coming across as too pushy I decided to make one last attempt at getting to the heart of Suzie's feelings about certain events. I settled upon a strategy of re-wording previous questions, presenting them in a broader format. Only if I continued to receive evasive answers from Suzie would I then let these subjects alone. After the candor Suzie had shown thus far I could hardly complain about full disclosure of every aspect of her life.

My undergraduate thesis had now reached the length of ninety-five pages. This last installment centering on Suzie's early life, marriage and her exposure to white culture, covered over forty pages alone. I was excited to complete this work on my new computer, a Valentine's present from my husband. The gift came as quite a surprise since it was from a man who swore he would never be coerced into recognizing February 14th. During our earlier years of dating I had made an attempt at encouraging romance on this particular date. I gave my guy a card or make a special dinner date, but eventually abandoned the idea of celebrating what Ross called a "Hallmark Holiday." Until one day, my husband finally presented me with the object I longed for since beginning the Yazzie project. This was nothing short of a miracle. Now I could escape my noisy home that crawled with loud teenagers and interruptions, and set up in a quiet place where I could work in peace. I now looked forward to working within the delicious solitude of Monument Valley.

I rushed to organize the dialogue that had taken place between Suzie and me so far. I put aside my usual routine of cross-referencing Navajo history with her narrative. I even dispensed with inserting anthropological information that backed up her experiences. In this way I could see the pesky holes left in Suzie's stories, and prepare for what would be my last trip out to the Valley before completion of my thesis. It never occurred to me that there would be many more visits to the Valley after I graduated from UCSB. On the advice of my mentor, Professor Ann Plane, I applied for the graduate program in the History department. She pointed out that, since my project would eventually be of book length, I should present it as my doctoral thesis. Seeing the sense of this I applied, however I was worried about the lackluster scores I had received on the GRE test for which I had no time to study. At least the score for my English skills was high, and on the recommendations of professors who knew my work, I was eventually accepted. This would mean at least three more years of school, but I truly loved studying at the university, and I sincerely believed at the time that I wished to continue.

I looked forward to returning to the quiet of the place Emily abbreviated "M.V." and I packed light with the idea that fewer encumbrances would keep me focused on work. I had the usual adventures, saving one-hundred dollars by flying out of Oxnard at the very severe cost of waking up at 5:15 a.m. to do so. I didn't even have time to kiss my kids goodbye, and for all this trouble my flight was left in a holding pattern due to heavy air traffic in Los Angeles. Sprinting to make the connection to Denver I huffed up two hallways that seemed to grow longer with every step, never mind the sight I made; backpack and laptop case flopping around my body like so many broken limbs. I dodged like a linebacker through the crowds of travelers leisurely walking through the terminal, and arrived wheezing to my gate just before they began to board. Too many people bother with dieting and the gym; traveling is the ideal weight loss plan. Ironically enough, I ended up waiting an hour for the flight to arrive that would take me on the last leg of my trip. This delay had something to do with a missing flight plan, which I still believe was a diversionary tactic they used while scotch-taping the wings back on to our plane.

I had decided to fly into Farmington. This saved me some driving time. I was alarmed to discover, however, that the flight was a great deal bumpier than the one into Albuquerque. Some might see the little town of Farmington as a desolate place, but I found the sparse surroundings refreshing. It took only minutes to gather my bag and plop into my rental car. For one as logistically challenged as I was, the nearly deserted streets came as a relief. I weaved effortlessly through the town and made the interstate in minutes. What a difference from my last driving odyssey. Unfortunately, at least a half-hour of driving time I hoped to save was surrendered to a pickup truck filled with Navajo in no particular rush to get anywhere. As the weather turned bad I decided I wasn't in a hurry either, and I happily stayed behind the truck operated by a local who obviously knew the area better than I did. His battered truck shielded me from a rain that pummeled my little rental so badly I had trouble seeing the road. Admittedly, the drive from Farmington is not as pretty as the Albuquerque route. I was blissfully shorter however, and it eventually brought into view the striking landscape I had come to expect from the reservation. I tuned into the only radio station that came in clearly and let the country music blare. Normally I would have taken advantage of the long drive by listening to my Navajo language instruction tapes, or perhaps played the Native American tunes that always got me into the mood of the work ahead. Today the high desert cast its spell over me without all of that, and I was already keyed up for work. I kept reminding myself to keep expectations low and that all things concerning the Yazzies' history would come in their time. When would the family tire of my presence I wondered. Could it be that the very differences between us made my constant questioning tolerable? Though I would never be Dine,' it seemed that I had become an accepted nuisance.

FINDING FAMILY IN MY HOME AWAY FROM HOME

"I have been to the end of the earth, I have been to the end of the waters, I have been to the end of the sky, I have been to the end of the mountains, I have found none that are not my friends." – Navajo

I made it to Goulding's just before dusk, and just as huge raindrops turned to snow. Good timing. I pulled into the lodge parking lot with my headlights reflecting the little flakes coming straight at me, the car heater blasting, and A.M country music blaring. At last, I arrived safe and sound at my home away from home. By next morning the weather had cleared. Looking out the wide balcony window I wondered if I had imagined last night's snow. 'Just as well,' I thought. Maybe today my car and other possessions would not be covered with the invasive, red dirt surrounding Suzie's home. I grabbed my backpack and hurried out the door. As I made my way to the lodge restaurant to meet Lonnie and Emily I noted the time. We were to meet at ten, but "Navajo time," meant there was no telling when my friends would show up.

Settling into my usual window seat I realized I actually welcomed a long wait. It allowed me to enjoy the spectacular view and clear my head. I gazed outside and sipped coffee until I sensed somebody standing next to my table. There was Effie wearing a wide grin, a white chef's hat and a once-white jacket now stained with a tapestry of grease and what looked like some kind of sauce. Apparently, my friend had secured a job on the seasonal tourist cookout. She was on her way back to work but wanted to introduce me to one of the few Yazzies I had not met. Effie's brother, Kee looked so much like Lonnie I had to do a double take. He had heard of my work through his siblings, but I don't think he realized the extent to which we hoped to carry the project, and I was struck by the fact that while learning so much about Suzie, her family knew very little about me.

Suzie had spent last night in Effie's little house just beyond the Oljeto trading post, and she was placed in Kee's care until Lonnie and Emily arrived and could drive her back to her home in the park. "Oh and where is your mother?' I asked. Effie pointed out the window where Suzie stood fidgeting in the parking lot below. She stood in the snow-covered parking lot wearing her usual purple petticoat accompanied by a maroon velveteen blouse, the neck of it framed with turquoise. Her head was adorned with a thin purple headscarf I learned was popular with the older women on the rez. The entire ensemble was topped off with enormous, black framed eyeglasses that made dwarfed her face. Catching sight of a pair of old running shoes peeking out from beneath her skirt, I had to smile. Suzie had missed this modern anachronism, but she didn't seem to mind just one glitch within her presentation of traditional Navaho grandma. She wandered aimlessly around the lot, and I felt a twinge of protectiveness. Once happy to ride a horse to and from the trading post, Suzie was now required to hitch a ride with any family member who happened to have a working vehicle. Here she was patiently waiting to see who would take her home, and I thought how frustrating getting older must be when it meant depending so much on others.

Effie left for work, and since Emily and Lonnie were late, Kee fetched Suzie to join me for breakfast. Much like his brother, Kee turned out to be an exceptional storyteller. He was comfortable with discussing life with me, and our conversation followed an easy rhythm. He commented on the snow that fell in the Valley the week before, and recalled one winter in the 1980s when an unusual two feet fell in a single day. On that afternoon Kee drove out to check on his mother, but his car died at the Three Sisters monument forcing him to set out on foot. He eventually found his mother out in the snow, looking for her sheep. Kee told me she actually had a pair of binoculars for the task, and it tickled me to envision the matriarch with them, scanning the horizon for her livestock like some park ranger.

Kee told me about the increasingly dry winters that were occurring in the Valley. He claimed that everyone was concerned about water levels in the natural springs. If water resources became scarce it could affect tourism, and many Navajo would be forced to move from the area in search of work. So far Kee had a job as a schoolteacher, and he liked the work very much. The Yazzies were proud of the teaching tradition in their family, and even Lonnie and his wife took positions as substitute teachers whenever possible. Kee said that they all enjoyed working with the young people of their tribe, and so teaching was as an agreeable way of making extra money. According to Kee, the locals associated the name, "Yazzie," with a loose translation of the Dine' word meaning, "teacher." He believed a number of his family naturally gravitated to the profession, and he fondly recalled teaching in his younger days at a grammar school that used to operate in an old building just behind Goulding's. There a small community continues to exist, complete with a trailer that operates as a post office, and a small building housing a health clinic. Kee worked as a teacher in the little oasis for twenty-nine years, then switched to the tour guide business for seventeen more. I found it difficult to believe this man was some fifty years old, but then all of the Yazzies look young for their age.

Kee was optimistic that the rains would someday increase in the Valley, but I had my doubts. We both agreed that the tourist economy was a blessing now that agriculture was no longer a viable prospect in the area. He enjoyed his work as a guide, answering the tourists' questions and teaching about Navajo life. Yet, he expressed a longing to use the skills he learned as a boy in cultivating corn and other crops. He liked the idea of staying connected to the land and living in a traditional way, and to that aim many of the family continued to rely on Navajo ceremonies. After breakfast he planned to run some errands that would prepare his family for just such a ceremony taking place that week. There were a number of items he needed to obtain for the Medicine Man that would allow the family to take part in this ceremony promoting mental health.

As Kee gave a litany of items needed for the event his mother fidgeted in her seat. She had been sitting next to her son, quietly sipping her coffee and occasionally glancing around the restaurant. But now she focused on the busloads of tourists leaving the lodge. She lightly tapped Kee's arm and pointed at them with pursed lips. Her son explained that many of those tourists were preparing to visit his mother's hogan for a weaving demonstration. This meant the possibility of selling some of the family crafts, and Suzie wanted to arrive home in time to welcome them. I offered to take Suzie to her compound; bravely even offering to feed the animals there. But Kee instead opted to put off his errands until later, and rose to help his mother out of the booth and drive her into the park. It probably saved both Suzie and I a lot of uncomfortable and confusing grunts and gestures, but I thought it would be nice to someday spend time alone with her. Soon after Kee and Suzie said their goodbyes a waitress announced to a room empty but for me that there was "a call for Coco."

Over the phone Emily informed me that she and Lonnie had spent the night in Shiprock to obtain some kind of permit, but were now well on their way. I nursed my coffee until their old car limped into view. Paying for my coffee I scurried out to tell the couple that Kee and Suzie had left for the Valley a half hour ago, so Lonnie left Emily in my care for a little "girl talk" and followed his brother out to the park. With a twinkle in her eye Emily said she'd never been in one of the condos at Goulding's. Clearly she was curious to see my new digs, and as we headed back to my room I thought to myself that nothing ever went precisely according to plan in the Valley.

My friend and I climbed the stairs up to my place, and when we reached the door I followed Emily's lead and stomped my feet to remove the snow now tarnished by red dirt. She marveled at my cozy dwelling and marveled over the convenience of a kitchenette. "Now you can spend money at the Goulding's grocery instead of the restaurant," she giggled. I showed her all the books I'd unearthed at the university library. Emily was especially interested in the book "Navajo Women" by Ruth Roessel. She said she knew some of the families pictured in this book, and she had spent time with Ms. Roessel's daughter, Faith. Faith's pictures in the book showed her as a cherub-faced baby sitting with her grandmother. Another photo appeared in a later chapter, taken later when she was a young girl sitting proudly on her horse. Emily had attended the same school as Faith who later became an advisor for President Clinton in the Indian Affairs department. Emily remembered the Roessel children as very kind and intelligent. Two of the Roessel boys attended college, and this information prompted me to ask if it was difficult for Navajo families to raise money for their children's higher education. She remarked that, although some scholarships were available to the Navajo, many parents could not afford to send their young people to college.

Emily said that for many Dine' it was difficult to make a living on the reservation. Those family members who could not afford school often moved to the larger cities seeking employment where they remained to start families of their own. She mentioned that this could lead to relationships with people outside the Navajo tribe, and I asked if there was any stigma amongst the Navajo over marrying outside their own people. Emily felt that most Dine' were open to any kind of relationship that resulted in a happy union. She recalled hearing stories about the early 1900s when some Navajo parents encouraged their daughters to marry a white man, because he might be more financially secure than the native men living on the reservation. This did not appear to be a popular choice among women at that time however, and most were content to live closer to home even if it meant a more frugal existence. I found no mention of the subject in the literature available to me, and it would be difficult for me to truly gauge the hearts and minds of young people on the reservation without directly asking them. But this was the sort of subject I wished to explore, and Emily promised to assist me in presenting the subject to Suzie and we packed up our things and finally made our way to the Yazzie compound.

EDUCATING THE NAVAJO

"When the white man discovered this country Indians were running it. No taxes, no debt, women did all the work. White man thought he could improve on a system like this." – Old Cherokee Saying.

We reached Suzie's place just as a tourist bus was pulling away. "Perfect timing again," I thought to myself. What a relief not to have to pull Suzie away from her hogan business. It seemed that the Valley was especially quiet on cooler days. Unless the weather was fine visitors tended to shy away from an adventure in the open-air buses. The air this day had a bite to it, and the sky was a threatening gray. If my luck held this day with the Yazzies would be uninterrupted and fruitful. I felt a little guilty over this selfish thought. I knew that Suzie and her family counted on the tourists for their income. "How," I wondered, "could I help this family out financially?" The thought occurred to me that while interviewing the Yazzie's their stories always played out in my mind like a movie. I could envision Four-Horned Woman wandering the desert in the night in search of her home. I saw Suzie as a little girl making the long trek to Goulding's to trade her rugs. My mind's eye concocted a bug-eyed Suzie encountering her first White man. Perhaps someday I could create a non-fiction book that brought the Yazzie's experiences to others. I found their stories fascinating. Maybe students interested in Native American history would want to purchase a book about Navajo life. This was the first time such a thought crossed my mind, and while it seemed unlikely I could ever obtain enough stories for an entire book about the Yazzies, once the idea came to me it never completely went away.

I entered the warmth of Suzie's home and basked in the familiar smell of cedar wood and coffee. Suzie, Lonnie, Emily and I took our perspective places. No one mentioned whether or not Kee was still on the premises, but I had not seen his car parked in front of the house and assumed he had left on his errands. As I delicately placed the microphone on Suzie's blouse I wondered how Emily and I had missed seeing him drive past us on his way out of the Valley. Lonnie pulled me from my reverie with a question about my schooling. "How did you manage to get into college so late?" he wanted to know. It was true that I was older than the typical university student. I was acutely aware of this from the very first day I attended UCSB. I never quite fit in with the other kids with their fresh faces and Abercrombie and Fitch clothing. It must have seemed twice as strange to Lonnie that a woman my age was taking university courses instead of raising the four young children now in her care. He must have sensed my discomfort, because he followed up his question with an explanation. "It's just that in our family we value a good education. It can cost a lot of money to get into college, and even though us older folks would like to continue our education we have to save up to send the kids first," he said quietly. "It wasn't always that way," Lonnie continued, "a lot of us kids didn't want to go away to school when the government came looking for us."

The U.S. government's belief that Indians must be exposed to Western education was based on the concept that Native Americans could only survive in the Anglo world through assimilation. In the early twentieth century a plan to educate Navajo children was pursued in spite of the racially-fueled assumption that an Indian's capacity to learn was limited. Many government officials felt that, although it was their duty to make an attempt in imparting EuroAmerican knowledge upon the natives, the Indian might inherently be incapable of grasping western intellectual thought. Nevertheless, after the obvious failure of Navajo relocation the government deemed it essential that the Indians obtain a basic education in arithmetic, the English language, and even certain trade skills in order to operate within the White world. While reporting on the conditions at Bosque Redondo, journalist G. Gwyther divulged the basic consensus among his peers concerning the Anglo's initial attempts to "educate" the Navajo. His statements reveal a considerable lack of objectivity in regard to the Navajo and what he took to be their obstinate refusal to educate their children. The nineteenth century journalist wrote:

"Schools for the young were established, and some excellent and zealous young men of the Catholic priesthood, sent by the Bishop of New Mexico, undertook to instruct them in the rudiments of the (English) language. I do not think the juvenile savages showed either love of or aptitude for the alphabet, nor rightly appreciated the treasure to which it was the key; insomuch as they often stipulated for additional bread rations as a condition of longer attendance at school. The mothers, too, were equally obtuse, arguing that the long-gowned men ought to pay for the amusement they evidently found in teaching children."[83]

While Anglos at the time saw education as a way of "saving" the Red Man, there was little sensitivity about whether the Navajo felt any need to embrace this foreign Anglo culture. It is no wonder to us now that the Navajo resisted education in an effort to save their own threatened way of life. After reading this article I found it interesting how the Navajo managed to subtly turn the tables on their white instructors. Perhaps to the Dine' it made perfect sense to benefit from the Anglos' desire to force Anglo education upon them. It seemed fair enough for their children to provide amusement to the white man in exchange for food. However the game ceased to be acceptable once the children were needed to help with herding sheep or attending to other necessary chores.

A Navajo interviewed by anthropologist Edward Sapir in the early twentieth century told of the way in which the Dine' struggled over a condition in their treaty with the government that involved their children's Anglo education. While languishing at Bosque Redondo, a group of leaders came to Sapir's subject, Charlie Mitchell, and told him and his father how exercising the freedom to return to their homeland would involve a change of lifestyle for all Navajo children:

"You will walk again on your country...When you get back to your country, your children will learn paper (taught to read). Your children will understand, they will understand the American (language), they will know paper. What do you think of this? In your country schools will be placed for you...At the place called Fort Sumner over there it was spoken of, it is so. In your country to which you have returned your children shall go to school...you must consent to [this]. As time goes on, as soon as

---

[83] Gwyther, *Navajo Indian Reservation*, 127-128.

they are born, a date is set aside for school for every one of them...you must promise! Some are boys, some are girls; you who have them promise them! Otherwise, after some time, we shall be put in prison."[84]

From the beginning of its implementation the program met with resistance. Mr. Mitchell recalled his uncle telling him that such an important decision as relinquishing their children could not be made on behalf of all Dine.' He admonished those who were encouraging the acceptance of this program:

"Without our knowing about it, you promised all of our children. What were you thinking about to speak in that fashion? One who is my son, one who is my daughter; it seems you have promised them. But I am stingy with them. They will not go to school, I think."[85]

So it came to pass that many Navajo children were essentially rounded up against their parents' will, and taken to schools where they were boarded for the better part of a year. White officials believed that by removing the Navajo child from his traditional environment he might better adjust to white standards of schooling. Examples of misconceptions regarding the conditions of Indian schools can be found in documents such as the Twenty-second Annual Report of the Board of Indian Commissioners. This document, printed in 1890, reported that the children schooled by the Roman Catholic sisters at Fort Yuma had become "decent" and "modest." Members of the Lake Mohawk Indian Conference stated that "the children in the school were neatly clad in civilized garments, including good shoes and stockings and head-gear. In a few instances the pride or vanity of a boy would not allow him to sacrifice his abundant locks of black hair...but in most cases the barber had done his work." The writer went on to congratulate himself and his fellow reformers on their efforts to assimilate the natives, stating that these Indian students "recognized the superiority of the white race," and that the sight of the docile children eliminated the "whole lump of savagery" that formerly existed within them.[86]

The Dine' continued to resist by refusing to relinquish all of their children to Anglo educators. By the beginning of the twentieth century it appeared that Navajo families had complied with the government's demands. However, it was often one child out of many within a family who was given up to the agents of the "BIA," or Bureau of Indian Affairs. These children dutifully enrolled in the boarding schools or "Indian Schools," as they came to be known amongst the natives. Apparently the Navajo had read the fine print within the treaty of 1868, in which it was agreed that the Dine' need only agree to send "at least" one child to the government-run schools in order for the young people of their tribe to obtain education of Anglo design. Anthropologists

---

[84] Sapir, Edward. Navajo Texts. New York, Iowa City: AMS Press, 1942, 365 & 375.

[85] Sapir, Navajo Texts, 377 & 389.

[86] Lake Mohonk Indian Conference, First Session Oct 8, 1890. Twenty-Second Annual Report of the Board of Indian Commissioners for the Year 1890. Washington, D.C.: GPO, 1891, 69.

Kluckhohn and Leighton observed that even by the 1940s school attendance continued to remain flexible among the Navajo:

"By no means do all Navajo children go to school. But most families where there are a number of children see to it that at least one attends school. Definite policies of selectivity are followed. In some families those who have better memories and are quicker to learn are chosen. But in at least the poorer families the prevailing tendency has been to send the more delicate or crippled children who are less useful in the home economy. In the early 1900s, persuasion after took the form of literally kidnapping scholars for the boarding schools. In addition, Indians who had been to school were sometimes sent around the Reservation to hold out promises of good food, free clothes, and comfortable buildings to lure reluctant pupils. Parents retaliated by hiding their children when the school people came in view. Prior to 1930, government schools for the Indians were most often characterized by bleak barracks-like buildings and a lock-step life. Homesick children were intimidated from running away by stern measures."[87]

Gladwell Richardson wrote of an educated Navajo man with whom he traded, by the name of Maxwell Yazzie, (no relation to Suzie), who confirmed that the methods used by Indian agents to round up pupils were harsh. Mr. Yazzie was herded along with other crying Navajo children and loaded into a trailer "like canned sardines" for the transport to Tuba City. At what I believe was the same boarding school eventually attended by Suzie's son Lonnie, Maxwell was relieved of his clothing by the "Whipper;" a name given to the school disciplinarian by native students because of the stick he carried to coerce the children to mind. The young Maxwell then had his head shaved and deloused in scalding water.[88]

By the time Suzie became eligible for schooling most Dine' families were willing to relinquish at least some of their brood in order to attend white boarding schools. Suzie's contribution to the family economy was far too crucial at the time however, and so school did not appear to be an option for her or even for her siblings. When questioned, Suzie told me that she had entertained the idea of attending school, but her mother's illness kept her at home and out of sight from government officials:

"Yes, I wanted to go to school. I don't know why I never learned English. I think it was because my mother's family used to hide us. We were told to go out and herd sheep clear to the next little Valley. There's no other place like the Valley to hide when you are with the sheep. They were hiding us when our parents got a visit from the school people. I think my mother needed a lot of help with the house chores. My father was gone a lot then, and it was just me to do all the weaving and to get the younger ones to help with the sheep."

In fact, Suzie could recall only one uncle within her family who had attended school while she was young. She described him as being an older relative and not one of her peers. "Locally, maybe my father's sibling was the only one [to attend school],"

---

[87] Kluckhohn & Leighton, *Children of People*, 64.

[88] Richardson, Gladwell. Navajo Trader. Tucson: The University of Arizona Press, 1986, 142.

Suzie remarked, "except for the schooling in English that my little sister had when she was in the hospital. That's the only way even one of us got some schooling." For Navajo like Suzie's parents, an education involving Anglo culture served no real purpose. According to Suzie, there were many within her community at the time who even wished to communicate in English. She remembered that only her uncle bothered to utter a word of the white man's language. "He was the only one that went to school and could communicate in English," Suzie confirmed "other than that, there was no one. Others did not even try to understand English." It would appear, then, that the inconsistent school attendance that Kluckhohn and Leighton reported among the children on the reservation could be attributed to the reluctance among the Navajo to give up the children they so loved and needed for a successful home life

Even so, like many other tribes before them, the Navajo increasingly felt the effect of Anglo education, religion, and white influence in the twentieth century. Although a significant number of Navajo children in the Monument Valley managed to evade white education during Suzie's girlhood, her children would be affected by it in later years.

Lonnie told me that he had managed to temporarily evade the government agents who came looking to send him to school, but was finally forced to attend by the age of eight. His sister Effie claimed that she initially thought it "would be fun" to go to school, yet education for many females at this time was of secondary importance to maintaining the family home. Suzie's daughter commented during our interview session that, as a girl, she was expected to pursue traditional tasks such as sheep herding and weaving. Although methods of educating Indians improved over time, white educators were rarely self- critical regarding their mission to introduce Western culture to a people whom they saw as 'backward.' During Suzie's years as a young adult, Anglos felt justified in educating Native Americans to become functional Christian citizens, and they strongly believed that their methods were entirely appropriate and helpful.

HOW TO WEAVE A LIFE

"When a man does a piece of work which is admired by all we say that it is wonderful; but when we see the changes of day and night, the sun, the moon, and the stars in the sky, and the changing seasons upon the earth, with their ripening fruits, anyone must realize that it is the work of someone more powerful than man." — Chased-by-Bears (1843-1915) Santee-Yanktonai Sioux

As a young woman Suzie continued the tradition begun by her mother of weaving blankets meant exclusively for trade with the trading post erected by Harry Goulding and his wife. When we spoke of this period of time she reported that once tourists began to appear things changed significantly in the Valley. "At times it was one white person coming after another," she marveled, "when my late mom was alive they would come by more often for fry bread, but now they were coming mostly to buy our blankets." Although exchange rates for staples were considered fair at the time, the blankets, as well as any jewelry crafted by Suzie's family, fetched a considerable price outside the reservation. The price of blankets and jewelry produced by the Navajo were then marked up; providing a healthy profit to white traders during this period. The trading post system emerged in the Southwest territory beginning in the 1870s, and the exchange of blankets, hides, and wool brought in products and supplies formerly unknown to the Navajo.[89] Because the trading post acted as an artery to larger populations outside the reservation, a market emerged for Indian arts and crafts, and manufacturing these items became a valuable source of income for the Navajo.

The completion of the Santa Fe Railroad also provided an important method of exchange to the tribe. As federal policy shifted to encourage native self-sufficiency, the support of the Indian Arts and Crafts Board offered an incentive to the Navajo and other Southwest tribes to produce traditional artwork.[90] The early twentieth century saw a revival of trading post activity as interest in the area grew. Historic literature printed in the 1950s described the white traders as friends of the Navajo, as well as visionaries who introduced tourism into an area badly in need of economic development, stating that:

"So great was the vision and faith of Harry Goulding...that [he] built ultra-modern tourist accommodations long before a surfaced highway was even completed. [Traders were] interested as businessmen in a reasonable return on their investment, but equally interested in the welfare of their friend and partners, the Navajo people."[91]

Trade in Navajo-fashioned crafts became more crucial in supplementing the Yazzie economy, yet trade among Anglos and Navajos had been part of the Four Corners economy for over a century. The written history of Navajo crafts is first noted with Spanish and later European contact in the 1700s. Navajo author LeNora Begay Trahant wrote of the early fame her people acquired through the trading of handmade goods. "The Navajos have been noted for their unique artistic talents," she wrote, "in fact, the word *Navajo* often appears in connection with various artworks: Navaho rugs, Navajo necklaces, and even a Navajo design."[92] This early trade evolved into an ongoing business relationship between whites and Navahos. Trahant described how Navajos in the early twentieth century recognized the opportunity to augment their income through trade, pointing out that: "The trading of Navajo crafts was started by white traders who came to the reservation after 1900. They came for the rare jewelry and rugs (then called Navajo blankets) that many people in the East were interested in buying."[93] Anthropologist James Downs noted how the white trader became

---

[89] Young, Robert W. The Role of the Navajo in the Southwestern Drama. Gallup: The Gallup Independent, 1968, 48.

[90] Hoxie, Frederick E. Indians in American History: An Introduction. Illinois: Harlan Davidson, Inc., 1998, 259.

[91] Young, *Role of Navajo*, 85.

[92] Trahant, LeNora Begay. The Success of the Navajo Arts and Crafts Enterprise. New York: Walker and Company, 1996, 3.

[93] Ibid., 7.

established very early on: "As low as the price might be, Navajo wool did have a value, as did Navajo rugs, sheep pelts, cattle hides, and jewelry. To make a profit on these items the traders began to appear in the Navajo country even before the time of military defeat and incarceration."[94]

The rugs that Suzie learned to weave at such an early age were created using time-honored techniques. These began with appropriating quality material, including wool from the family sheep. Natural dyes gathered from the surrounding desert provided the traditional color for their rugs. Mrs. Trahant explained that:

"Before starting to weave a rug, a Navajo weaver seeks out plants and herbs that will dye the wool into many colors. She then prepares the wool by washing, dyeing, and drying out the bundles; brushing and carding out the wool into small fluffy rolls; and finally spinning the wool into thin strings of yarn. A loom is set up with warps strung lengthwise from top to bottom. The weaver begins at the bottom by stringing the yarn through each warp thread. Each row of weaving is threaded across the loom from left to right. A design begins to change the colors of the yarn. Sometimes a design is not apparent until she finishes a border about two or three inches from the bottom of the rug…Yei-bi-chai rugs are more colorful, portraying several yeis, or Navajo deities, dancing or standing."[95]

Suzie commented on the old way of weaving she learned as a child while leafing through a book I purchased at the Lodge that showed early rug designs:

"Yes, I like the way we use to do it a little better. Some of the weaving in this book is from old days long ago. Yei (deities representing forces of nature), their heads are connected together. Snakeweed and mahogany were collected to make the greenish-yellow dye. Now we buy our yarn already colored. Well…not all of it. Sometimes we do use some vegetable dye. You can see it in the design, the yellow kind of dye. The old way of doing Yei skirts are in this book, I do know how to do this. You have to count the warp strings to set your loom. My grandmother would also weave for tourists, and she showed me the way to do things. She would bring a rug that wasn't done. It was only woven up to half way. Then I set up near hers, just the warpstring, and I followed her way of weaving according to her loom. I counted my strings just like hers. That's how I learned. You count the strings; different counts for each design. I did one rug real fast watching her that way, then I set up another, and I don't know how many more. When you finish the rug, you trim the yarns that are still out, and clean it all up that way. Then you have to take the trimmings, and get some hot embers from the stove to make smoke from it. You are suppose to put the embers on top of the wool scraps to burn them. Then you use the smoke to put on you. The ash you rub onto you. You massage yourself with it. In this way you will feel good, with no soreness in the arms, hands and back."

Although girls were encouraged to weave, boys could also learn the craft without fear of ridicule. A male weaver is still considered quite rare, however. I asked Suzie if she had known any male weavers, and how she felt about them. "It's okay," she mused,

[94] Downs, James F. The Navajo. New York: Holt, Rinehart & Winston, 1972, 115.
[95] Trahant, *Navajo Arts & Enterprise*, 40-41.

"I never seen one yet, but I heard that a male had done certain ones which are displayed at trading posts." For Suzie, weaving was more than a way to earn income; it has become part of her identity. Weaving gave Suzie an immense feeling of pride and self-worth as an artisan as well as a successful businesswoman.

Early literature tends to present the white trader as a hero to the Navajo when, in fact, not all traders were completely innocent of conducting transactions that could be unfair to their Indian business partners. However, during our interviews Suzie always spoke highly of Mr. Goulding, stating that she never once felt she had been cheated during her trading relationship with him. Indeed, Suzie confirmed that Mr. Goulding acted as a vital link between the isolated reservation and the outside Anglo world where provisions and health care might be obtained. I expected to hear the usual accounts of unfair business transactions instigated by whites that took advantage of Native American need, yet Suzie confirmed that such exploitation apparently not the rule in the Monument Valley region.

In his memoirs, trader Gladwell Richardson spoke highly of his Navajo associates. He did not, however, always trust the white tourists who frequented his store. "The arrival of tourists always called for increased watchfulness," lamented Richardson. He complained that the tourist crowds often included children, and inevitably goods "managed to disappear." Richardson went on to say that, "sometimes even small children, without restraint from parents, would pick up 'souvenirs.' No Navajo child ever stole anything in a trading post or anywhere that I ever heard of."[96] But I was interested in knowing how Suzie's business relationship with Harry and Mike Goulding formed her younger years. Suzie always spoke with affection about this couple that operated the local trading post. She recalled how the Goulding's provided assistance to the local Navajo in ways other than trade. Suzie especially admired Harry Goulding's kind offers to drive ailing Navajo such as her mother to the hospital. Anthropologist recognized this type of assistance Adams who studied the Navajo in the 1950s:

"It is the trader who tries to obtain jobs or relief for individuals, not because they are formally qualified but because in his opinion they need them. It is he who does favors and performs services for his clientele not because he gets paid for it but for more indirect benefits and in the interest of personal friendship and community goodwill."[97]

According to interviews conducted by Samuel Moon, who wrote a biography about Harry Goulding, the trader and his wife "Mike" enjoyed doing business with the Navajo, and they spoke fondly of the experience. In the biography entitled *Tall Sheep*, Harry remarked, "Oh, it was lots of fun to trade with [the Navajo]. That's why I never had any time on my hands, because I enjoyed those people, they were always fun."[98] Goulding also respected the business sense exhibited by his native neighbors, never

---

[96] Richardson, *Navajo Trader*, 191.

[97] Adams, William Yewdale. Shonto: a study of the role of the trader in a modern Navajo community . Washington, U.S.: Government Printing Office, 1963, 22

[98] Moon, Samuel. Tall Sheep Harry Goulding Monument Valley Trader. Norman: University of Oklahoma Press, 1992, 50.

taking for granted the quality of their wares: "When you started to buy that rug, it was business then, you always knew that was their business."[99] Relations between trader and Navajo before Goulding's time were not always respectable on the reservation. As even Goulding testified:

"The traders have been a good influence, but there have been some rotten eggs among the traders too, and nobody to cull them out. There's not many of them that are not a proper character, darned few on the reservation today, but it used to be that's all you found out here. When we first came out, there was quite a number of traders around over the reservation that their thought was in the pocketbook…and I could see a lot of stuff going on that the traders was pulling on them."[100]

Goulding gave credit to the Navajo themselves for demanding better treatment in business dealings when they felt that certain whites were abusing the trading relationship:

"A Navajo himself, you're not going to tread too hard on him. Listen, them old Navajos, just when you start selling them short, why they're going to get you. You've got to think a little bit like they do. There's no question in my mind at all but what there's a lot of talk all along about this trader or that one. They do a lot of visiting in that direction. And they've been successful, I think, in cleaning up the traders. Some of the real early traders that had a proper mind, they thought the Navajo, really, what a good trader could do, how he could be of help. It started with those early traders that were real human beings. They had to make a profit to stay in business too, but they at the same time had a feeling for the Navajo, could see a lot of good in him. It was honesty and friendliness; your thought was with them."[101]

Reading this caused me to remember my introduction to Suzie. During my first riding trip in the Valley she came very quietly to our encampment to sell some jewelry, and I longed for two colorfully beaded hair clips. My husband tried to barter with Suzie through a family interpreter, but Suzie held firm on her price. Ultimately, we both left empty-handed, and I learned a hard lesson in just how much the old woman valued her work. I did unearth a few stories concerning dishonest transactions performed by Navajos in the early days of trade. Perhaps these were in retaliation for the unfair practices some Navajo experienced when trading with whites in the early twentieth century, as suggested by Harry Goulding. Perhaps the Indians simply discovered a way in which they might gain an edge in the trading of blankets. What may have provided the Navajo with an incentive to take advantage of the trading situation was the way that a blanket's worth was determined in the early twentieth century. For a brief time the quality of craftsmanship or aesthetic appeal of a blanket mattered less than its weight. Consequently the quality of weaving suffered as some Navajo struggled to produce a greater volume of blankets for tourists hungry to obtain Indian crafts. Author Raymond Locke described the methods some weavers employed to increase the weight of their blankets:

---

[99] Moon, *Tall Sheep*, 50.
[100] Ibid.
[101] Ibid., 50-51.

"The traders, who found a ready market for the heavier Navajo rugs in the East, paid the Navajo weavers for their work by the pound. As a result the women worked quickly; yarn was poorly cleaned and the spinning and dying was carelessly done. Soon Navajo women quit washing the wool to remove grease and dirt and some went so far as to pound sand into the yarn to make the blankets heavier. The fine weavers were also paid by the pound – at the same rate – for their product."[102]

Locke also noted, however, that by the 1930s, when Suzie was consistently trading her rugs, the craft had experienced a revival. "Navajo women gradually returned to the old techniques and designs," he noted, "and began using native dyes again." He went on to state that "today many of the good weavers refuse to use any dyes that they, or a member of their family, have not prepared themselves."[103] In her book *Wide Ruins* Trader Sallie Wagner also recalled a decline in the quality of Navajo rugs when she and her husband began to run the post at Wide Ruins, Arizona. She noticed that weight and customer demand played a role in price. Mrs. Wagner recalled:

"When my husband and I bought the trading post the Navajos in the area were making very poor rugs, the kinds that were sold from knocked-together stands along Highway 66. The wool was not well cleaned or well spun. The bordered designs were the kind that had originated in Oriental rugs or were crossed arrows and swastikas, and the colors were red, black, and white – the designs and colors usually thought of as 'Indian.'"[104]

Over time the Wagners were able to encourage the Navajo in their area to produce a higher quality of rug: "We had seen the very beautiful rugs that the weavers at Canyon de Chelly produced, and we hoped to guide the Wide Ruins weavers into the production of beautiful rugs too. We knew they were capable of such work."[105]

I asked Suzie about the days when rugs were purchased by weight. "Yeah," she remembered, "traders use to weigh rugs, but I never knew people who put sand in them." As a young woman she had only heard rumors about the scheme. When I questioned her about the motives of these weavers Suzie laughed and shook her head. "Yeah, I was told they use to put in the wet sand from the ground. They did nutty things like that and we heard about it." Yazzie memory indicates that the family has always enjoyed pleasant relations with the whites with whom they traded. Suzie recalled her visits to the trading post very fondly, and she spoke of the old trading days when she received the occasional treat when accompanying her mother to the post. "Candy was my favorite," she confessed, "just candy and sometimes soda pop." "There wasn't a chance to get too much pop then," she lamented, "it sold pretty fast."

Once the Navajo learned how much economic opportunity their goods provided, they also discovered how to refashion these goods to appeal more to white customers. This sometimes meant a change in traditional styles that had prevailed since before

---

[102] Locke, 37-38.

[103] Ibid., 38.

[104] Wagner, Sallie. Wide Ruins. Albuquerque: University of New Mexico Press, 1997, 50.

[105] Wagner, *Wide Ruins*, 50.

Navajo memory. The Navajo believe that Spider Woman, the entity who introduced the art of weaving to their people, must be granted an outlet out of respect for her knowledge. Before the twentieth century trade business, Dine' weavers always completed their blankets with a hole at the center of the blanket as a way for Spider Woman to escape the divinely inspired design. A blanket sporting a hole at its center, however, was not aesthetically pleasing to most whites. Possibly unaware of the significance the mark held, Anglo customers expressed their preference for "unflawed" crafts. According to author Raymond Locke:

"In acknowledgment of their debt to Spider Woman, one of the Holy People of Navajo mythology, Navajo weavers left a hole in the center of each blanket, like that of a spider's web, until the traders in the early part of the twentieth century refused to buy such blankets."[106]

Locke went on to explain how the Dine' altered their crafts while maintaining the religious connotations within their products: "Most Navajo weavers still acknowledge the debt by leaving a "spirit outlet" in the design. The spirit outlet usually takes the form of a thin line made from the center of the blanket to the edge, and also serves, Navajo weavers believe, to prevent 'blanket sickness.'"[107]

Anthropologist and ethnologist Maureen Trudelle Schwarz also took note of the continued, if somewhat adapted, Navajo practice of weaving a spirit outlet into their rugs. In her study of Dine' personhood she cited both early twentieth century and more modern sources in her explanation of the outlet's purpose:

"Weavers are cautioned to include a "way out," from the center to the right selvage – toward the south – in the design of textiles (Bennett 1974: 7-8; Atonilth 1990). Such openings enable a waver's energies to move on to future undertakings. If a weaver concentrates all of her creative and physical energies on the manufacture of any one textile without including a way out, she risks losing her vision and even her mind (Franciscan Fathers 1910: 294)."[108]

When I asked Suzie about the "spirit outlet," she could recall only very early instances in which it involved a center hole. By the time she began to weave the practice had already been adapted to its present use. "Yes," she remembered, "my late mom use to do it that way. I use to try weaving my blankets like that for awhile, but I never understood it like my late mom did." By the time Suzie increased her trading practice, the less obvious symbol of a discrete line following the very edge of a blanket borders had become the norm. I questioned Suzie about whether weavers throughout the reservation now practice this style of weaving.

"I don't know," she answered with a shrug, "that's just the way I do it." I have since discovered that not all modern Navajo weavers make use of the spirit line. It appeared to be a trademark of the Two Grey Hills style and is only present in rugs surrounded by a border. I often had the opportunity to watch Suzie weave during our interviews. I loved the care with which the wool was spun and later woven into a rug

---

[106] Locke, 34.
[107] Ibid.
[108] Schwarz, 48.

of beautiful design. Clearly Suzie's elders had taught her well in the craft. The Yazzies have a reputation of producing fine rugs, with patrons commissioning work from as far away as Europe. In this way Suzie maintained a cultural tie with her past and preserved an art for non-natives to appreciate and enjoy.

SUZIE ON HER OWN

"I have seen that in any great understanding it is not enough for a man to simply depend upon himself." – Lone Man, (Isna-k-wica) Teton Sioux

Approaching her teen years Suzie witnessed more change within her family and clan. As in the case of her father, who left the family for long periods of time, Suzie saw other family relationships falter. Her maternal grandparents separated while she was still young. Although she was not so close to her mother's parents, this event clearly left an impression. Suzie recalled, "Grandma, I remember her. My grandpa, I don't know him well." I asked my translator Emily if I had heard her correctly. It struck me as odd that Suzie was using the present tense while referring to a relative that certainly must have passed away by now. "No," Emily assured me, "she said it that way because she is thinking of him now, so even though he has passed away, in her memory right now he is existing." I struggled to understand this Navajo way of seeing time as fluid and flexible. Suzie simply smiled and continued on.

"My grandma split up with my grandpa when I was a young woman," she explained, "so he use to visit us on his own. He was from Red Bluff or Red Mesa. It's over there near Farmington. I don't know what the place was called then. I think maybe they called it *Tiee nos pos* or *Tse' li chee das kidi*. My grandpa was from that vicinity, but he preferred to come visit here. Now it seems so long ago, but it was sad when he split up with my grandma. They had three kids who were young ladies by then. Those were the only kids she borned. Not many people split up permanently at that time. Back then people mostly thought of home life. People still separated, but not as bad as now."

Younger members of the Yazzie family have divorced from their marriage partners, but there is no stigma placed upon these couples any more than there is on couples in Anglo communities outside the reservation. But I wanted to know Suzie's thoughts regarding marriage. When I asked her views on the subject I received the usual even-handed response. "Marriage isn't the only way," she commented, "it's up to the woman. If she wants to be married or be by herself, that's okay." Her thoughts regarding divorce indicated again that this was a rarity among her people when she was young. "When couples separated," she explained, "they probably just got pouty at each other. The men would just leave for a little while, I think. Nobody hardly ever did that very much, but it was done at times, I was told, to make things better." Suzie's daughter-in-law told me that in the past if a woman grew displeased with her husband she indicated her wish to separate by placing his saddle and other belongings outside the family hogan. Tradition dictated that the woman keep all livestock, including horses, as well as all other property. Children tended to stay with the mother and her side of the family, and this is more or less true today. Nowhere in the literature available to me did I find confirmation of the divorce custom that involved placing the husband's saddle outside the hogan. Yet Kluckhohn and Leighton wrote that historically, divorce among Navajo was a simple matter that consisted of the partner's merely moving back in with relatives. [109] Although Suzie remembered divorce as a rare occurrence in her youth, Kluckhohn and Leighton's study of the 1940s found that the concept of marriage was somewhat flexible among the Navajo. According to the two anthropologists:

"Only about one woman out of three and one man out of four reach old age with the same spouse, and men who have had six or seven different wives in succession are frequently encountered. Some of these changes are the result of deaths, but the majority is consequent upon desertion. "Divorce" is simple, consisting ordinarily in the return of one partner or the other to his or her own people."[110]

The fact that divorce was once a less complicated procedure among the Navajo than among whites does not mean that it occurred frequently. When I questioned Suzie further on the subject she stated again that when she was a girl divorce was very rare among the Navajo in her community.

---

[109] Kluckhohn & Leighton *Children*, 83.
[110] Ibid.

KINAALDA'

"Children were encouraged to develop strict discipline and a high regard for sharing. When a girl picked her first berries and dug her first roots, they were given away to an elder so she would share her future success...The child was encouraged not to be lazy and to grow straight like a sapling." – Mourning Dove [Christine Quintasket] (1888-1936) Salish

Our conversation turned to the puberty ritual as it existed in Suzie's time. As I have previously stated, my intention was to step off the path of research done by those who studied the Navajo, so it would seem that such a ceremony should be left to those who have written at length of Navajo ritual. However, it didn't feel right to ignore an event in Suzie's life that carried so much importance to herself and her family. Around the age of fourteen Suzie experienced her first menstruation, an event of great significance for a young woman, according to Navajo tradition. The *Kinaalda'* ceremony, a type of puberty ritual, was immediately planned. According to anthropologist Maureen Schwarz this ceremony is "the next step to Navajo personhood" after childhood. The Kinaalda' ceremony is an invitation for the spirit of Changing Woman to enter into a young woman's body. The spirit then acts as both a comfort and a guide to the young girl in her new role as a full grown woman. Young men had a ceremony of their own that involved spending time in a sweat lodge. Schwarz wrote that:

"...During puberty ceremonies young men and women may be dressed in specific attire, painted with various substances, and expected to run, to participate in sweat bathing, or to grind corn...a fundamental theme of the female puberty ceremony is rejuvenation through a transfer of reproductive powers from the Kinaalda' to Mother Earth."[111]

I asked Suzie about her impression of the ceremony that was meant to hold such reverence in her young life. I wondered how she felt about the ritual, and also whether she could make the decision to forego it. Did she anticipate the ceremony with eagerness, or was she ambivalent or even embarrassed over it? A response to my questions came with Suzie's usual economy of words. Suzie claimed to have participated in the ceremony, but only because all of the young girls in her community did so as a matter of course. This explanation did not come across as a tautology, but more of an acceptance of the traditional was a way of life Suzie and her family embraced in a very natural manner.

Suzie gave me the details of her Kinaalda in a manner that implied the love she felt for her family's traditions:

"It was always done like this, the Kinaalda. It was mandatory, and you never said you didn't want it. When it was their time, girls never thought of saying "no" to the ceremony. Yes, (giggles) I remember it pretty well. When I had the ceremony on me I did my running over there to the edge of the mesa. We lived near the Jackson's residence at that time. And so I had the puberty ceremony, at Rain God Mesa, and I ran toward Sand Springs. My late paternal grandmother helped me prepare for it. Even though my late mom was still alive then, it was mostly this grandmother who helped

---

[111] Schwarz, 155.

me. I had a successful cake (giggles), and my late paternal grandmother helped me with the corn. Her uncle's wife helped too. We used the stones for grinding then, and there was so much corn. I grinded the corn the old way, with mano and metate. They use to say you would walk through life in harmony by having the ceremony, so my hair was tied with a slab of hide cut from a deer. Back then you used a deer's hide that was not killed with a gunshot. An arrow was used if possible. Anyway back then that's all they hunted with."

"Your hair was tied in a ponytail," Suzie continued, now deep in the memory of her ceremony, "and the top of your hair would be loose. Then you paint your face, just using water with the red sand. You just paint your face below the eyes, and also use white clay; just a dab here and there. When the singing is in process you wash your hair."

The woman Suzie's family selected to assist in creating the corn cake, as well as to participate in other preparations, was called "The Ideal Woman" in Dine.' Due to her important place in the ceremony, Suzie's paternal grandmother must have exhibited characteristics that were much revered among the Navajo. Schwarz interviewed a woman who explained the importance of this role:

"[The Ideal Woman] knows how to weave, she moves fast, she does things fast, she knows how to prepare cornmeal, she can herd sheep, she can shear, you know, she's swift at everything. That's the kind of person that's ideal [for the family]. You don't just select anyone to tie your hair and do that exercise for you. She guides you all the way."[112]

In Suzie's day the Kinaalda ceremony was performed on two separate occasions, once at the initial onset of a girl's menstruation, and again six months afterward. Today, young girls may choose whether or not to have the puberty ceremony at all, and few follow the tradition of performing the ritual twice.[113] This decision may reflect either the decrease of available medicine men, or the significant expense in carrying out the ceremony twice in one year. Suzie did, in fact, participate in the second ceremony according to tradition:

"I went through it twice in the customary way. They tied my hair again. I heard it works pretty good on you when you do it twice in the proper way. The prayers are stronger. Back then there was not much to eat and things were tough, so the need for harmony was strong. There was struggle and a shortage of things. I ran two miles one way and two miles back, maybe more, just the way you're supposed to. I think it worked pretty good on me."

Suzie's children enjoyed bragging about their mother and the strength she showed during her Kinaalda. Her son proudly explained, "She was a great runner. She ran many miles out there by the Three Sisters monument where they use to live." He grinned at his mother, saying, "She ran all the way to Sand Springs and back. Suzie's daughter-in-law remembered stories from her mother and aunts about their own ceremonies. She told me about the difficulties of running in the traditional outfit. "You

---

[112] Schwarz, 176.

[113] Yazzie family member, 20 March 2001.

would have your jewelries on and run with all of that stuff," she marveled. "Yes," confirmed Suzie, "They would dress you all up. You would run just like that and even sleep like that (giggles)…all dressed up." This coming of age must have had some impact on Suzie, because she frequently recounted the event to her children. As with any landmark in one's life Suzie, naturally wished to share the moment with her family, particularly the female family members.

Suzie's Kinaalda' officially marked her transition in status from that of child to an adult member of her community. However, the responsibilities placed upon her at an early age to care for her siblings had introduced the adult world to this young Navajo girl long before the Dine' puberty ceremony. Although Suzie was not the only Navajo child compelled to shoulder the burdens of a family, she recognized her situation as unique among her peers within the Valley community. While the role of surrogate mother and provider called for a premature entry into adulthood for Suzie, she embraced her new post as a matter of course. On several occasions I asked her if she was ever angry or sad that she had such a brief childhood due to her parent's physical and emotional limitations. At no time did she express the feelings I expected would come from one who had been forced to grow up so quickly. Suzie's personality and strength of character may have provided her with the resolve to do what was necessary for her family's survival. Perhaps her cultural upbringing encouraged acts of selflessness as well as an independent spirit. Whatever it was within Suzie that allowed her to weather these years of hardship, it would resurface in her adult life when she again met with the challenges of reservation life.

A PASSING
"Coyote is always out there waiting, and Coyote is always hungry." – Navajo

Suzie would later come to rely on her paternal grandparents when her mother became increasingly ill. Until that time, Sunshine visited her own mother as much as possible, the bond between them pulling her back to her place of birth, and Suzie did her best to deal with her grandmother's difficult personality. She spent her time caring for both of her grandparents' extensive herds and continuing to act as a substitute mother to her siblings. It became clear shortly after her Kinaalda that her mother's illness had reached a critical stage. She spoke to me of the period of time in her life that was to be one of her saddest:

"I remember my late mother as always being sick, but she was about in her thirties when she first got really ill. It was childbirth that did it. Every time she had a baby, she gets sick. She kept saying that she didn't want to have any more babies, but back then they didn't have any birth control method. When she had my little brother…that was the worse time. She had gotten into her older age. She gave birth to my youngest brother after all her other babies…some who lived and some who passed on. But from the last baby she had she died. She had the last baby at home past Little Monument Valley at Meridian Rock. He was borned there."

95

"Yeah, it was a tough delivery. They were gathering old people; I think medicine men, to see her to help. She always had ceremonies done on her, and different types of medicine men. When my little brother was finally borned my mom couldn't get up, and she just got worse. Back then there were no vehicles around, so she couldn't make it to the clinic. My dad just rode a horse around for transportation, so he rode his horse to the trading post to see Harry Goulding. He knew this man always helped the Navajo. My dad left his horse at the post and Harry Goulding took him to Keyenta. They got an ambulance from there and it followed him back to my mom. They stopped at the post for my dad's horses, and then they just followed my dad who rode ahead of them. There was no hospital, just a little place clinic at Chinle (an hour's drive from the Valley). So I guess they took my mom to the hospital in Tuba City. They just carried her in that vehicle all the way to the hospital."

With their mother recuperating in a hospital miles away, care for the new baby rested on Suzie and her sister, Ella.

"My siblings were all small. There were six of us and I was the maturist. My sister and I were carrying this little baby around wherever we went now. He was just a little baby, and my sister and I cared for him as best as we could. I was about sixteen, and my sister was around seven then. We just stayed down there at the hogan and waited. We didn't know what to do because he wouldn't eat anything. We tried to feed him food we got from the trading post store (giggles). Then my sister and I would squeeze the goat's milk for him, and that's finally all he drank. We would be at the sheep pen late at night, squeezing the milk for him. Every time he use to cry we would milk the goats (giggles). We knew to boil it first, and we used a spoon to put milk in his mouth. After a few days we got a bottle for him. Sometimes the goats ran out of milk, and then we just gave him cornmeal."

The two girls were left with their new baby brother for some weeks. There was no communication concerning their mother's condition during this time:

"My late dad was the only one that went over there to the hospital in Tuba City. When my mom woke up she was told that she had surgery. It was probably in her stomach or somewhere. I don't know, probably in her uterus, where she had her birth. Then she was okay for awhile, but all of a sudden she got critically ill again, I was told. We had been on our own for about a month, I think, when we were told she had passed away. She died at the hospital at Tuba City. My dad came home one last time to tell us. My mom's sister, *Adzaa Tse' nit aal*, the older one that use to come to her a lot, she went over to Tuba City with my sister, and they buried her over there, because we had nothing to put her away in."

It was at this time that Suzie officially became the head of her household in her father's absence. She spoke of the way she and her sibling shared responsibility for caring for their infant brother:

"My sister and I took care of the baby. He was wrapped up in a sheepskin when we took him to herd sheep and milk the goats. Underneath he was in a gunnysack, wrapped up with the sheepskin on top just plopping around (giggles). We would sometimes have to go out at night, and leave the others sleeping. All of our siblings were small then too. *Tsosie* was six years old, Jean was four, and she was my youngest sister. John was seven...no, eight years old. He died later as a man, we think of uranium exposure (in the 1970s). My older brother George was twenty then, but he had a woman. A year later she was pregnant and they were living in *Dennehotso* with his father-in-law where he planted corn. He was the son-in-law over there, but he was married to one of our own clan. He married my aunt's daughter.[114] So in this way we ended up alone, but it didn't faze us. We felt there was nothing wrong about it."

During our conversations Suzie never once complained about looking after her baby brother. However, the work involved in caring for an infant must have been exhausting, particularly for girls as young as Suzie and her sister. One of Suzie's favorite stories involved the manner in which the two girls struggled with instant motherhood:

"We use to sleep where we wouldn't hear him cry so much, way over on the other side of the hogan. He once crawled out of the sheepskin and was on the hogan floor, crying. My sister got up and started to rock the sheepskin, only he wasn't there! I looked up and saw her half-asleep, rocking the sheepskin. But my brother was way over there on the floor...kicking and screaming (giggles). That boy is still alive today and has a son of his own."

Suzie was reluctant to say more regarding her mother's illness and subsequent death; however I read that reservation children were often forced to deal with the death of their mother. I learned from one anthropological study of this period that "the proportion of the children of The People who have been wholly or partially reared by grandparents, sisters of the mother, or other relatives is, to white people, surprisingly high.[115]" If the incidence of mothers dying while giving birth, (or shortly afterward), was a reality for most Navajo children during the early and mid twentieth century, then Suzie's experience might be seen as somewhat common for any Dine' child growing up during this period. Thankfully, Suzie could rely on her favorite grandparents during this difficult time. She remembered their participation in her life quite fondly:

"Where the Three Sisters rocks is (one of the rock formations in the Valley), on the East Side, there we had our hogans, where we were growing corn too. It was probably my late dad that planted all the corn then. He left some time after that, I think to work in Bluff someplace. Maybe he went there to see a woman (giggles). Anyway, he never came back after that. He just drifted away from us..."

"We were struggling then, but our family had two hogans, one after another. Even where I live now, where that tree is, we had some corn there too, and another hogan. Back then there use to be two hogans here and there all around the Valley where we herded. There was always a male and a female hogan built together. My grandparents stayed in one, and we stayed in the other, so there was privacy. There were some near the Jackson place and another place by the rock behind my house now, near the ridges,

---

[114] This relationship was probably distant enough so as not to be considered taboo. Possibly the connection is with Suzie's father's clan. The "aunt" of which Suzie speaks may be (according to family members) a relation from the third or forth clan, because relations of first and second clans never marry.

[115] Kluckhohn & Leighton, *Children*, 46.

so we were really spread out depending on what work had to be done and what season it was."

"When my dad was still a boy his family built a lot of those hogans. That family was all boys, and my grandfather hauled wood around with them all the time. He was a good chopper and could cut down whatever wood they needed to build with. We moved all together to one of these places depending on the season. We moved for grass. You would herd sheep here, and then move on to other areas for more grass, each time moving into a different hogan. We moved all over the Valley. The grass grew best around March, and it was yellowish-greenish like it is now. We moved again when it started getting cold, at the start of winter. My paternal grandfather finally died when I was older, but we lived happily with our paternal grandmother. There were lots of cornfields for food, and we just stayed there to herd sheep on horseback."

As a very young woman Suzie had to face her father's abandonment of the family. However, a father's continual absence was not necessarily unusual within Navajo families at this time. Kluckhohn and Leighton noticed that, among the families of Dine' living on the reservation in the early twentieth century, the father was often away in search of work. Although Navajo children remained attached to the absent parent, this did bring about more of an emotional dependence on the mother. The anthropologists wrote that:

"A Navaho father's role may be compared in some ways with that of the white father who is a sailor or who commutes early in the morning and late at night and is at home with the child only on some weekends. Most Navaho fathers habitually spend much time away from the residence of their wives. Sheepherding, hunting and trading trips, and journeys for salt all take the father away from the home for short or long periods. In addition, increasing numbers of Navahos in young adult life and early middle age work for white men on the railroad, on various jobs for the government, and even in distant cities..."[116]

Suzie's relationship with her father was unique in that it placed undue stress upon her at a very young age. She and her siblings eventually became aware of the fact that his absences rarely benefited the family. Ultimately his long excursions failed to produce any wages or provisions that might have given his children the sense that he was an active participant in their lives. However, living with her grandparents assured Suzie of a relatively normal life for the remainder of her youth. Although there were some lean periods of struggle, Suzie remembered the years with her grandparents as primarily a time of plenty. She enjoyed a home life surrounded by siblings who shared in the family responsibilities, while her elders provided the love and security she craved.

Suzie grew silent, indicating it was the end of her story. Once more the timing was perfect. My hand ached from furiously taking notes on everything from instructions on weaving to Suzie's mother's death. I had also run out of both questions and energy. Lonnie, Emily, Suzie and I made small talk and sipped the last of the coffee, now lukewarm in our cups. I glanced out the cracked window, and was moved as usual.

---

[116] Kluckhohn & Leighton, *Children*, 47-48.

Even clouded with years of sand I could see a spectacular sun set. Had we been working all day? Looking at the pages of notes in my lap I realized the day had been dedicated to capturing the entire childhood of Suzie Yazzie. I felt a mixture of satisfaction and uncertainty. Should I continue to press Suzie for more details of her younger days, or push on to her memories of marriage, childbirth and more? I was too tired to even consider my next step, and Suzie seemed ready to stop our session and check on her sheep. With a silent and mutual decision we all rose and left the little house. Suzie followed her son and daughter-in-law to my car. Lonnie and Emily would be spending the night in the Valley, and they embraced me with a light hug one after the other to bid goodnight. "Are you sure you know the way out by yourself," Emily giggled, "we don't want to find your dry old bones somewhere along the road tomorrow."

"Of course," I laughed along nervously, "how hard can it be to get lost." This brought on loud guffaws from both Lonnie and Emily, and a wondering smile from Suzie. I took the old woman's cool long fingers in a light hand shake. "Ah heh-heh" I said in Dine,' meaning "thank you." "Ahoe" she answered back, "yes." Her eyes crinkled warmly behind the huge glasses, and she smiled patiently. I started up my dusty car and drove off waving to the little group surrounded now by barking sheepdogs. They disappeared from view when I turned the corner past the first big monolith. My only worry now was to decide if I was to take a left at the coming fork in the road, or continue straight to what I hoped was the main sightseeing route. I hoped the Yazzies would give my dry old bones a decent burial.

CHAPTER 6 – DOUBT AND REVELATION

"Everyone who is successful must have dreamed of something." Maricopa

DOUBT AND REVELATION

My next trip out to visit the Yazzies was in November, and I looked forward to spending time with Suzie without having to work around the many visitors that took up so much of her time during the tourist season. I flew from Santa Barbara without incident, then got stuck waiting two hours at the Phoenix airport until my plane would leave for Flagstaff. I settled into the boarding area with a book on Navajo culture that lay open and unread on my lap.

I had completed all required classes for both of my degrees, and had only to complete the honors thesis in order to graduate. With this rather unnerving low maintenance kick-off to the school year, I spent most of my time that September and October alone in the library, writing out my thesis. No assignments or deadlines plagued me. I finally had time to do what I enjoyed the most, writing about the Yazzies. But sitting in my favorite spot on the fourth floor, (the section devoted to the study of history), I found myself staring out of the big windows and watching the light change long stacks of volumes lining the walls. My plan of finishing up my courses early so that I could concentrate more on the thesis project had backfired. I now felt uninspired and more out of place than I ever had on the rez.

Amidst all of the activity at school I could not help but feel like an imposter, especially when questioned about my project and its status. Those who cared to listen to the by now well-rehearsed description of my work were supportive. "How fascinating," they would tell me, "to follow the history of a Native American family and spend so much time with them in such a beautiful setting." But the truth was, after all my time and study I really didn't have a handle on what it meant to "be Navajo." How could I even know if this family would be considered "typical" as a depiction of Navajo life? Was there such a thing? I could only compare and contrast their life if I studied several more families in various locations on the reservation, and I certainly didn't have the resources to do that. I also believed that I could never spend a sufficient amount of time with the Yazzies. How could I study the evolution of this family without living among them? My flight was called over the intercom. I closed my book and gathered my things to prepare for boarding, pushing aside the crazy idea of living with Suzie. Even if the Yazzies were willing to tolerate me for any length of time, it was an impossible notion while I attended school.

STUMBLING FORWARD
"He who would do great things should not attempt them all alone." — Seneca

The Yazzies and other Navajo I had met were undeniably part of white society in the way they worked at making a living, educated their children, and went about their daily routines. The differences I found were more subtle and best revealed in a setting such as that of Monument Valley where a traditional Dine' life was still practiced by elders and passed on only when younger family members were open to it. Of course, I never expected to find every Navajo I encountered to be adorned in silver, turquoise and velveteen. Nor did I expect them all to be herding sheep and weaving rungs. But I suppose I secretly hoped to see that style of life making a comeback.

I couldn't really complain. Many of the Yazzie family members expressed a deep interest in keeping to their roots. And I was thankful to gain insight into the minds of people who lived in a way that seemed to promote balance and harmony. The Dine' word for this is *hozone*, and I felt that this harmony was the main point behind Navajo philosophy. Sitting in the airport however, I felt very little "hozone." I was reconsidering the idea of graduate work. I could only envision hours of redundant study that might turn me into the jaded professionals I sometimes encountered on campus. Some professors actually discouraged undergraduates from graduate work because their field had been reduced to over-specialized muck awash in university bureaucracy and politics. The idea that I was "in love" with my subjects, as one professor put it, made me second guess my work even more. Were the Yazzies like any other American family with no unique experience to relate? Was the study of other cultures in America an obsolete endeavor because the differences were so minute and the populace so homogenous? I chalked this blue period up to a symptom of the university environment and tried to work around it.

I continued to see the Dine' as unique in a number of ways. I admired their tenacity and their willingness to teach non-natives about their culture. There were, however, some topics the Yazzies refused to discuss with anyone who was not Navajo. These topics dealt primarily with issues considered sacred to their people. Information was carefully guarded whenever we discussed religious practices, because the Dine' believe that revealing too much lessens the power and effectiveness of prayers and ceremonies. Throughout the interview process I sensed that details about Navajo religion were being carefully withheld, and I tried to understand why this was necessary. All I could hope for was that the family would provide enough information to produce a coherent thesis.

Meanwhile, I continued to dream of the opportunity to actually live with Suzie for a week or two. I felt that this would expose me to the nuances of life on the reservation. Maybe the Navajo had managed to preserve so many of their cultural practices because most Whites were interested in settling in other, less forbidding environments. Even now this area of the southwest is not an easy place to build a home. There are few employment opportunities. Farming is no longer practical without a reliable source of water, and access to goods and materials often involves driving long distances. At any rate, I felt that spending time at Suzie's compound would help me to get a feel for what her life had been like growing up. Perhaps I could convince her and the family to someday allow me to stay overnight.

As I boarded the plane I thought about the wisdom of making Suzie's story public. I had to respect that she was, in a way, giving up her right to be the sole proprietor of her life stories. Even with all the information she had given me I had still more questions. She had wanted to attend school, but had the lack of a formal education really affected her? Did she wish could speak English now? Our "conversations" could never flow as well as they did when I spoke to her daughter-in-law Emily, (the easiest interview I conducted), or her children, who were also somewhat restrained but at least willing to explain their feelings on any matter. Most of the time I got the sense that Suzie didn't necessarily feel the need to explain anything. Perhaps it was her age, or maybe she had always been shy about expressing her feelings. No matter what the reasons, my wily friend and I often danced around the particulars of her stories. I patiently reworded the same questions whenever I received a dead-end answer. This was a method I had nearly perfected by the time I made my plans to visit Suzie for another interview. However, as I began the fall quarter I encountered a number of glitches that had the potential of blocking my research.

Lost in the memory of this I didn't even notice the plane taking off. I could only review the beginning of that school year and wonder how I had survived it. That September I learned from my anthropology mentor, Dr. Michal Glassow that a form would have to be submitted in order to gain approval from the university to conduct interviews with my "human subjects." It seemed ominous and constricting as I read through the required procedures that would allow me to continue the project that was already nearing completion. I was dismayed over the number of questions I needed to answer pertaining to every aspect of my interview process. Would I be asking questions that could infringe on my subject's privacy? Well, of course this being her life story she was clearly opening her private life to me, or to anyone who was willing to read my thesis. Would I inform my subject or subjects of the intent of our work and their right to cease the interview at any time? The Yazzies had already approved the idea behind our work together and anyway, I didn't believe they would reveal anything they did not want made public. They were always sensitive about keeping family history to themselves that might do harm. Now I was required to remind them as if they were guileless children.

102

I felt as if I were being too careful and politically correct, but I forced myself to remember that others had not taken these precautions in the past. The result had often meant that a culture became over-exposed and exploited. The Navajo themselves had inadvertently revealed too much sacred information to anthropologists who ventured onto the reservation in the early twentieth century. With the university's guidelines I was now required to make it very clear to the Yazzies what we could and could not discuss in our interviews. I grudgingly completed all forms, mailed and received back consent papers from the Yazzies, and contacted the Navajo Nation Historic Preservation, Cultural Resources Compliance Section. This agency had still more forms for me to complete, and only after gaining permission from the local chapter head of Monument Valley could I obtain the necessary permit to continue my interviews. Once I came to know my contact person, Ron Maldonado, a supervisor in the compliance department, I became familiar with their real concerns and the necessity of permits. The same issues of sacred and sensitive information were discussed, but Ron felt that my purposes for collecting a family history were fairly benign compared to an archaeologist's request to dig up bones or artifacts. I liked Ron's easy-going nature, and over the years he became a valuable resource and a good friend; all because of those nasty forms required by the university, the Navajo nation and, it seemed, God himself.

The whole process made me acutely aware of the notion that my work might affect the Yazzie's family relationships and their standing in the Navajo community. I was fairly certain that my work wouldn't do any harm, but with every assurance I gave to the Human Subjects Committee at the university I felt my previous research ideas slowly wither away. I wondered now if it should ask the Yazzies about the family hogan business or about their personal relationships. Of course, now any questions concerning alcoholism or abuse were completely out. I would also have to be cautious about any questions I planned to present to the younger Yazzie children.

COMING "HOME"
"Sharing and giving are the ways of God." - Sauk

The intercom announcing our preparation for landing yanked me back into the present. At last I would be on my way out of Flagstaff, or "Flag" as the folks on the Rez' preferred to call this pretty college town. After all of the problems I experienced trying to make connections, and the usual bumpy ride in the small plane, I promised myself that the next trip to the Valley would be by train. No way was I going to suffer the white knuckle descent in another shaky puddle-jumper. As I pulled into Goulding's once again I resolved to look at the Amtrak schedule and find a more civilized method of travel.

I arrived before dark, and this time my room was a trailer located some distance from the main building. It was a little isolated, but it would offer lots of privacy to work. I planned on saving some money again by making most of my own meals in the little trailer's kitchen. The double-wide itself was quite roomy; almost luxurious. Better still, the price was reasonable. It even had a big bathtub in which I could soak away my work of the day! It would also feel good after one of my runs. I enjoyed going for a little jog at the end of a long day of interviews, and now looked forward to it as part of my Valley experience. For now I was content to settle in and work. As usual there was a nice view of the buttes and mesas, and I set my laptop on the table closest to the window for inspiration. I stepped out onto the porch and felt the strain of air travel ebb from my body. The crisp November air and enveloping silence of the Valley made me wonder how I ever allowed myself to doubt my project. The Valley had a way of affecting me, and with the rock formations towering over me like so many friends I once again became confident that the people who called this place home were special.

I was especially decadent the next day and slept until nine-thirty. I later went to the market for food and met Joe, the check-in lady's husband. They were the new managers of Goulding's and they were both a little curious as to why a woman would be staying alone in the trailer off to hotel's side. We chatted while packing up the usual groceries I purchased for the Yazzies and myself. I had Suzie's favorite fruit and some candy for the grandkids along with everything I needed to make sack lunches to eat at the hogan while I worked. Emily and Lonnie had already called to say they were held up in Chinle with car trouble. I couldn't reach Effie, so I returned to my trailer and sat down to study for the rest of the day. Unlike my struggles in the university library, I worked effortlessly until four that afternoon. By then I needed to stretch my legs with a run. As I took off down the road toward the high school I wondered what people driving by might think of the crazy lady sprinting down the road to nowhere. I had never seen anyone else run around the lodge, and I always caught curious glances from the Navajo going by. Whenever I ran in the Valley I was reminded of the Navajo ritual of Kinaalda. What was it like to celebrate your puberty by dashing off in the four directions over the course of a few days? Occasionally a truck would pass me, and the Navajo kids back stared; no doubt asking themselves what a woman my age was doing preparing for her Kinaalda!

After returning to my trailer I prepared my questions for the next day's interview. I was going to meet Lonnie and Emily for breakfast. Effie was going to try and join us. She was usually off working during our interviews, and she felt as if she was "missing out on the fun." I showered after my run and then I drove up to the restaurant to order food "to-go." While waiting for my order I asked the waitress if anyone was staying in the old Goulding's trading post building. I had seen the lights on that evening, but she assured me that nobody would ever stay the night there. "You might run into John Wayne's ghost!" she teased. I really didn't believe a Navajo would want to stay in that old building and I was pretty sure I wouldn't either. Still, given the chance....

Dawn broke over the rocks around me in vibrant reds and oranges. Monument Valley in the fall is especially quiet and peaceful, with far less tourist activity. The road stretched out devoid of the usual buses and R.V.s. The entire Valley was encapsulated with the silence of fresh, cool desert air, and the wind lightly blew at grass that had sprung up from the rains of August. The quiet was overwhelming. I held my breath and let it wash over me in a way that left me feeling peaceful and content. Emily called to say that she and Lonnie were running late, so we agreed that I would meet Effie, her daughter Elvina, and Suzie for breakfast. Emily and Lonnie would meet us "back at the ranch" where we could work. Emily guessed they would arrive at the hogan "around noon," (which in Navajo time turned out to be two o'clock.)

I mistakenly went to breakfast at the restaurant an hour early, motivated by some time zone that was neither California's nor Arizona's. The Navajo waitresses giggled en masse when they learned that I was waiting for people who wouldn't show for another hour. For the first time ever they remembered me from previous visits, which was kind of nice. Another pleasant surprise came when Effie and her family showed up. After a short conversation with her mother Effie claimed Suzie actually recognized me! This was a first, and it made me feel almost like family. We all sat down to a big breakfast, and I was glad that I ate my fill because that day we would end up working through lunch, never even stopping to make fry bread. Suzie dug lustily into her eggs, oatmeal, ham and hash browns. She let out a contented belch at the table, then again as we walked out to the truck, then once more in the hogan! Effie excused her mother every time, but I really didn't mind. At least I knew she had enjoyed the meal.

DRIVING WITH GHOSTS

"If a man is to succeed on the hunt or the warpath, he must not be governed by his inclination, but by an understanding of the ways of animals and of his natural surroundings, gained through close observation. The earth is large, and on it live many animals. The earth is under the protection of something which at times becomes visible to the eye." – Lone Man [Isna la-wica] (late 19th Century) Sioux

Effie's daughter Elvina accompanied me to the hogan in the rental SUV, while Effie took her mother in her own car, or *chiddy* as she called it. Elvina and I had a wonderful time listening to my cassette; the soundtrack from "Smoke Signals." This was an independent film made by and about Native Americans, and we both loved the music from this movie. We talked about whatever came to mind. Elvina had taken a job as a substitute teacher at the local high school; not a bad opportunity for a woman of twenty-four living on the Rez.' Her aunt Emily was suggesting she go back to school for her teaching credentials, and I agreed this was a good idea. Elvina would have more opportunities on the reservation as a schoolteacher, and after all, the Yazzies had a tradition of teaching in their family.

We drove deeper into the Valley, and I asked Elvina if Suzie had ever claimed to be frightened about staying alone at the hogan. Elvina's grandmother was rarely left alone anymore, but surely there had been times when the old woman felt vulnerable, particularly at night. I had read that some of the older Navajo were more apt to believe in lost spirits of the dead that roamed the earth. Legend had it that these spirits could do harm and cause misfortune to the living, and I wondered if this belief still held true for any Navajo today. Dirt falling from a hogan ceiling, for example, might not be attributed to the wind, but could be a "skin walker" or "wareperson" traveling over one's home. Tradition would then dictate that a corn pollen blessing be done immediately to counteract the effect of the Skinwalker's curse.

I was surprised to learn that even some younger Navajo like Elvina respected the power of certain supernatural forces said to exist on the reservation. Apparently, Skinwalkers and other powerful entities continue to be very real to some natives. I was uncertain as to how influential and widespread these beliefs were, and thought it might be a belief based on a particular region, such as the more remote areas of Monument Valley. Perhaps it was an unspoken consensus among the Navajo that certain supernatural beings exist. Elvina stated quite sincerely that, although she had never encountered such a creature "up close," she knew enough to be careful of them. She recounted to me the story of a girl she remembered during her high school years who was rumored to be a Skinwalker. Most of her peers avoided this girl because to anger her could mean a period of bad fortune.

As an Anglo, my first instinct was to dismiss the idea that these fearsome beings even existed. After some thought, however, I wondered what it was in my culture that assured me that supernatural forces of this type did *not* roam the earth? I had an unsettling experience the day of my father's funeral that convinced me some remnant of his spirit was making itself known to the tangible world. How was my belief that he was attempting to contact me any different from the belief some Navajo had in Skinwalkers?

Elvina and I were so engrossed in our conversation that we took a wrong turn on the way to Suzie's place. We only realized our error as we headed out to the open range where Effie's auntie lived! I had made this wrong turn before, and I told Elvina that one day I would certainly end up there and be forced to introduce myself. As we turned back to the proper road we saw a pretty, little gray-blue bird that even Elvina didn't recognize, and she asked me what sort of wildlife I'd glimpsed in the Valley so far. During this trip I was to spot both a coyote, (what the Dine' refer to as "the trickster"), and a desert fox. Keeping to the spiritual frame of mind I took all of these sightings as signs of good fortune, though I wasn't sure how a Navajo might interpret them.

I asked Elvina not to tell her mom how we I had gotten us lost. I knew Effie would tease me mercilessly about it. Lonnie and Emily had already laughed at the number of times I had become confused and lost in the Valley. Unfortunately, we ran into Effie and Suzie as we drove out of Auntie's road, so my reputation of being directionally challenged remained. When we at last settled into the hogan I prepared for my interview in the usual manner. This time, however, I asked Suzie for her permission to tape our conversation, and I informed her of her "rights" as in interview subject. She replied that she had no objections or questions regarding the process, stating that she actually enjoyed our sessions.

It was at this time that Effie mentioned to me that Suzie had begun to ask who I was and what my purpose was every time I came to the hogan. According to Effie, her mother wanted to know why I plagued her with so many questions, and why I never dropped a contribution into her tip box. She had, after all, spent a considerable amount of time with me, and so she assumed I was just another tourist looking for a rug and a weaving demonstration. I had never thought to pay Suzie for her time, and I felt badly that none of us had ever really explained my purpose to her.

Effie revealed that her mother had worked with an anthropologist before. It was only for a brief period, perhaps one visit to tell stories. However that person had not paid either, and so naturally Suzie was checking on our status. Through Effie it would become necessary to re-explain the purpose of my visits to Suzie, who could not figure out why anyone other than a Navajo would be interested in her old tales. With her usual shy smile she began to tell me through her daughter's interpretation, about her life as a young woman in the Valley.

MEETING TULLY

"Do not walk behind me; I may not lead. Don't walk in front of me; I may not follow. Walk beside me that we may be as one." — Ute

After the untimely death of her mother Suzie began to consider marriage. She clearly recalled the first wedding that she ever attended. "I was small then," she explained, "only about five or six years old. It was my paternal aunt who was getting married, and they had the ceremony where she lived with her mom near Mitchell Mesa. The wedding was at Little Monument Valley, and I watch them herd the horses in." Once again Suzie used the present and the past tense interchangeably when describing events. I found it fascinating how she would slip into the present tense as if the scene were happening before her eyes:

"The boys hold the ropes and they try to push the horses into the box canyon. My paternal uncle, the bride's brother, and other men that were just born into that family, roped some horses and brought them back. Then my paternal uncle just hit one over the head and killed it (giggles), because they should always kill one horse as part of the marriage ritual. He killed the one that was held by the other men. The horses actually belonged to the bride's immediate family. Back then horses were eaten as part of the ceremony, but they only ate horsemeat because times were hard. Sometimes people didn't have a lot of sheep."

I did my best to conceal the horror I felt over the practice of killing and eating a horse. The horses I rode back home in California were considered practically part of the family. I could not imagine killing, let alone eating, one of my beloved pets. Of course, I had also not experienced the feeling of hunger that would give a starving Navajo the gumption to eat whatever was available. Suddenly curious, I asked Suzie about the taste of horsemeat. She wrinkled up her nose and remarked, "It's not for me. It really TASTES like horse!" Amid the laughter that followed Effie clarified that horses were not considered a culinary treat in the Valley. They were only eaten in times of scarcity.

At this point my two wayward friends, Lonnie and Emily appeared at Suzie's door. They stomped the dust off their feet; each then giving me a hug and pouring themselves a cup of strong coffee. *"Yah tah hey* White Lady," Lonnie teased while Emily giggled, "what 'er we talkin' about today?" I filled the two newcomers in on our discussion and Lonnie beamed. "Oh, this is a good story," he laughed. While he and Emily settled into the last available chairs I asked Suzie if all courtship and marriages followed Dine' custom while she was a young woman. "Yes," she nodded, "some just got together, but most had traditional marriages." Suzie and her son discussed in detail how marriages were customarily carried out, and Lonnie described how a person could never marry anyone affiliated with his or her clan. He then asked Suzie whether the decision regarding whom a man would court was up to certain elders in the clan. "It was up to the parents," Suzie replied, "the mother and father. They made the choice and the arrangement."

Lonnie then asked "If the groom's family had horses and a home they were well off back then, right?" "Yes," his mother answered, "the bride's family would look around the groom's family home and make a study in their minds about how those people take care of their homes and family." Suzie was in a rather unique position for a young woman in her day because she was acquainted with her fiancée before the wedding ceremony. "Yes," she explained, "I met him before the wedding ceremony. But even though I did, we had a traditional marriage. He was of the Red House Clan, and close in ties to my clan of Many Goats. But that was okay, because they live quite a distance from us. It's not the same as marrying a clan member."

Because her husband's relation to her clan was distant by blood as well as geographically, marriage between Tully and Suzie would be acceptable among members of their community. Research described in their book *The Navajo* Kluckhohn and Leighton pointed to similar situations concerning clan taboos. Over time it appeared that clan relations had become more flexible in terms of who might be a prospective marriage partner. By 1962 the authors discovered that:

"All the prohibitions and obligations, which apply to clansmen, apply in strict theory, to all members of linked clans, but, today at least, these must be thought of as binding only in a very mild form. Marriages into linked clans, especially those of the father, are not very infrequent. There are disagreements even among older Navajos as to whether or not certain clans should be considered linked, while many younger Navajos are almost completely ignorant of such associations."[117]

I learned that, for the most part, inter-clan marriages have always been avoided among the Dine' in their region. Although it was eventually deemed acceptable, the courtship between Suzie and Tully was closely examined among fellow clansman before the match was officially approved.

Emily asked her mother-in-law what sort of woman an eligible man sought in those days. "A woman that makes things," Suzie responded. She further explained:

"A hard-working woman of strong will was wanted. A weaver, back then it was the main thing. A man wanted a lady that thinks of a home. Some ladies, they are going every places like dances, singing, gambling and such. Men did not want a wandering woman like that. Women also preferred men a certain way. Some men are crooks and some are crazy. A woman doesn't want these kinds of people. They don't help a woman with her family."

Kluckhohn and Leighton reveal similar characteristics that were considered desirable during Suzie's courtship years:

"In terms of the traditional conceptions of men and of women, The People are promoting the economic security of the society when they place a large share of the property and its control in the hands of women. Women are thought of as more stable. They do not go around gambling and wasting money in drink and other ways to as large an extent as the men. Their interests are centered on family and children so that they can be expected to use the resources placed in their hands to promote the stability of the family and the welfare of their children. There is a compensation for men in that

---

[117] Kluckhohn & Leighton, *The Navajo*, 113-114.

they maintain control of the horses, which provides them with independence from a too constraining family life."[118]

The authors went on to list the qualities that a Navajo man might seek in a wife. In the mid-1940s these qualities were good health, competence, and diligence. Just as Suzie claimed, it was stated that, "Girls who are known as good weavers are more in demand. Some value is placed on youth and virginity...Otherwise there are few physical or psychological qualifications for marriage, and the majority of marriages are still arranged by the parents or other primary adults."[119]

By all accounts Suzie and her future husband both appeared to possess the qualities admired in Navajo men and women of marriageable age. Suzie went on to describe how her introduction to her future husband did not quite follow in the traditional Navajo manner:

"Normally a couple wouldn't know each other. Only the mom would finally agree to who is a couple and you as a daughter wouldn't know about it. They would just herd the horses over. You would still be playing around, and then all of a sudden they would tell you the horses are coming (giggles). The paternal grandparents would make the agreement with your father and mother too. But it was just them. My late husband's uncle comes over and talks to my paternal grandparent, and they were just sitting and discussing it for a little while. He would see my grandfather from *Dennehotso* and hang out with him just over there. I guess my future husband sent his grandfather to us. Yes Lonnie, he was your late father's grandfather. LightWeight Face Man was his name. He came to see my family, and he use to ride his horse over. He was an older, elder man, and he was married into Folding Arm Clan. That man said to me and my sister, "Are you guys married?" We thought it was funny that he would just bother us like that, so we use to lie to him and say, 'You betcha, we do have some husbands that comes over to stay with us.' We always knew he goes around looking for women for his grandson, and we didn't want to get married at that time."

Suzie reiterated how she and her sister teased this man about their eligibility, going so far as to question his relationship with their grandmother:

"We always knew Tully's grandfather would go around matching couples up to marry. So every time we kept telling him, 'We do have some husbands already.' After a while he got suspicious and asked us 'How come I haven't seen one of those husbands around?' (giggles). We just laughed and told him, 'Oh, they come sneakingly because they don't want to be seen.'

We thought it was fun to tease him. He was actually our grandfather in a way. Even though he had a woman, a wife, he courted my paternal grandmother. He would ride his horse this way and we would tell him, 'Our husbands run around looking for other women just like you!' (giggles) We would say, 'You too, you have a wife and you come and see our paternal grandmother.' (giggles). This would never make him give up though, and he use to always just laugh about it."

---

[118] Kluckhohn & Leighton, *Children*, 83.
[119] Ibid, 79.

I wanted to ask Suzie more about her husband, Tully, but she was very shy when discussing their relationship. Effie offered to translate this particular story, and this seemed to make the topic more comfortable for Suzie. The tale was sweet and their courtship very innocent, however Suzie implied that she kept her new beau on his toes. Soon we were all laughing our heads off over her description of the couple's romantic escapades. I learned through Effie that Suzie teased Tully constantly during their period of "dating." I came to understand that teasing was a typical way of expressing affection among family members. Many questions came to mind as Suzie spoke, but like the rest of her family Effie liked to listen, and so she wouldn't often interrupt her mother's tales to interpret them back to me. Because of this whenever I heard Suzie's stories I was always a beat behind on the laughter, and a little in the dark concerning details. I thought that if only I could learn the Dine' language then Suzie's stories would be greatly enhanced. However, I had already tried to memorize a few Navajo phrases, and found the language complex and some of the words awkward in my Anglo mouth.

Emily watched me from her seat at Suzie's kitchen table. By now she knew me well enough to pick up on my frustrations, in spite of my efforts to hide them. She did her best to explain why Suzie and her daughter were giggling over this latest story. Apparently, the young Suzie appeared to initially snub Tully's advances. When Suzie and her sister Ella were out with the sheep, Tully suddenly appeared alongside them, riding on a donkey. Doing his best to catch Suzie's attention, she ignored the persistent suitor. Instead the object of his attention turned to her sister, giggling and saying, "Why would I want to get together with a man who only has a donkey to ride?"

Upon hearing this translation from Emily, Effie and her mother broke into peals of laughter once more. I remained as confused as ever. "But Suzie," I chided, "how could you be so mean? Didn't this discourage your future husband from courting you further?" The old woman gave me a sly smile while Emily went on to explain that Suzie's disinterest was an act, and actually contributed to Tully's determination to pursue courting her. "This was a way of teasing that's common among the Dine,'" Emily explained, "Suzie really did like her future husband, but she was very shy. So she let him know that she liked him by teasing him." This made much more sense to me, and also brought a feeling of relief. If teasing is any indication of how much a Navajo likes you, then I was definitely in with the Yazzies.

Although divorce was rare in her community, Effie told me that Suzie suspected her husband was divorced when she met him:

"I don't know…I think he had a wife before and I guess he didn't want her anymore…so he just left her. He once told me he use to herd sheep for a white man somewhere, and he sometimes teased me about just leaving her there because she didn't like him anymore (giggles)."

I once heard from Lonnie that a new bride could leave her husband should their union be an unhappy one. All a woman need do to indicate her displeasure with her husband was to place his saddle outside the family hogan. She would then take ownership of all livestock and care for the children. Suzie claimed that such a thing was possible, but she had never witnessed it firsthand. "I never wanted to do that," she laughed, "I liked my husband most of the time."

Suzie claimed to be "around twenty years old" when her future husband came to the Valley looking for a bride:

"I guess my husband visited his grandfather a lot at *Dennehotso* where he lived. And they were headed back when he asked his grandfather about me. That's how he came over to my house. We use to live at the Arches, and he came looking for me. He said, 'I'm going back to *Dennehotso* with my grandfather, but to see you first." He told me he wanted to stay there at the Arches with me and that he wanted to be with my family. His grandfather said that his grandson wanted me to be asked about this, and I said that would be alright with me."

I eventually learned that, although Suzie's feelings regarding any prospective beau would ultimately be respected, permission to begin the actual courtship was granted by her family only after parents from both families conferred. This traditional method of courtship resulted in marriage if all parties concerned, the young couple and their parents, agreed to the match. Although Suzie's marriage was arranged in the sense that her husband gained permission to initiate a courtship, a true romance did occur between them. According to the Yazzies this sort of courtship would have been considered unusual at the time. Anthropologists investigating Dine' customs in the 1940s also claimed that, "Though the Navahos have been introduced to the white concept of romantic love in schools, it is still not widely held, and almost no emphasis is placed on psychological compatibility as a prerequisite for marriage."[120] In a more current study, writer Raymond Locke stated that, "It is still not unusual for the prospective groom and bride to be strangers; in rare cases they may not have ever seen each other…The prospective bride is usually consulted in the matter today but she seldom was in the past."[121]

That Suzie not only had genuine feelings of affection for her beau, but also made it clear that she reserved the right to accept or reject his marriage offer, indicate once more that she possessed rather an independent spirit. While speaking to her daughter and me, Suzie shyly revealed how she felt about the courtship between herself and her husband:

"My sister and I use to talk about marriage. We used to pretend what our husband's names would be and we would say, 'his name is…' this and that. We talked about how many kids we would have, but my sister ended up never having any."

"When I met my children's dad through his grandfather he was handsome. That was his name, Handsome Gambler. He used to gamble a lot, and he was good at it. When his grandfather said, 'My grandson wants to stay with this family' I was kind of surprised. We had a cornfield near one of the grandfather's homes, and we would be hauling corn back with the wagon. Effie, I thought it was funny how your dad use to follow me and my sister around on his mule. He would follow us on this donkey and say things to get our attention until we would hate it. Every time he tried to get our

---

[120] Kluckhohn & Leighton, *Children*, 79.
[121] Locke, 21.

attention we use to say, 'Who wants anyone that rides a mule!' (giggles). Your dad use to tease me about that remark after we were married. He would say, 'I guess you like mules after all!'"

According to her children, Suzie secretly enjoyed the attention of her handsome suitor and began to look forward to his visits. This was something she would never admit in my presence, however. Whenever Suzie told the story of her first meetings with her husband she gave the impression that she scorned his advances and was uninterested in his romantic gestures. "I sort of hated him," she said, "When we had something going the house he use to be there all the time and just sit there at the ceremony. It use to make me angry," she would laughingly claim. Still, no matter how much Suzie claimed to be was annoyed at Tully's constant presence at her home, her daughter assured me the match had been securely made. Effie told me that it was "just her way" for her mother to laugh off the idea of romance. I thought that requesting to spend time with Suzie's family was a wise move for any prospective husband. In this way Tully would have the opportunity to become familiar with Suzie and to ingratiate himself into her family.

In spite of her professed dislike of him, Suzie told of how her future husband persevered with an argument that convinced the coy girl to take his advances seriously:

"He was saying what was real and true. He said, 'Remember, your father is not looking after you. There is no one taking care of everyone but you, and your dad is wandering around someplace.' He said, 'You are just staying with your paternal grandmother now, but when you have a man around things are better because for once someone will take care of you.' Even his grandfather said, 'My grandson is telling you all this because he really plans to take care of you.' My sister was younger than me. So I said to the grandfather, 'You must mean you are going to give your grandson to my sister.' But he said I got it all wrong. He said, 'No, I mean you, of course!'

My sister wanted to make sure this man meant business, so she said 'What are you to us? Men must pay for women, remember? You don't just come over here and get married for free.' She was sticking up for me, and my sister was clear about this saying, 'you have to have certain things done; there are horses involved. You are responsible for it, so what are you to going to give us?' The grandfather thought this over and said, 'I'll just tell my grandson you're available, and it will be up to him what he will pay. He's probably sitting around over the hill thinking things over.' And just like that he rode off and told my future husband everything was set."

Suzie then described how her beau delivered the proper gifts to her family as a marriage offer:

"His grandfather told my husband, 'go ahead and get what you need for us to finish this, and quickly.' He came back over and told my sister, 'Okay, we can handle this on our own and my grandson will probably chase a horse over. We have horses over there somewhere. My grandson will send one of them, and maybe a necklace or something.' That's all he said, and that was the way I was given to his grandson. I got married at about twenty, but a lot of women got married at an earlier age back then."

Gifts continue to be important in some Navajo marriage arrangements. As late as 1992 Raymond Locke wrote that " In the old days a boy's family would offer up to

113

twelve horses and several sheep…Nowadays it is more usual for jewelry or other goods, which may include livestock, to be offered."[122] I asked Suzie if she had ever heard of a family returning bridal price if it quickly became apparent that the union was an unhappy one. I was attempting to confirm something I had read in an old book about the Navajo stating that bridal gifts could be returned if the new couple proved to be incompatible. I thought that because this might result in economic hardship on both sides, families would have an incentive to encourage newlyweds to work through their differences unless they were truly irreconcilable.[123] Suzie laughed at the suggestion of returned bridal gifts, however, and said she had never heard of such a practice. This may be an indication that such an occurrence was rare in her youth.

With the decision made to unite the young Suzie with Handsome Gambler, the wedding day drew near, and a traditional ceremony was planned. Suzie claimed to have been like any bride nervous about starting a new life:

"My late husband came back again after the gifts were brought here. And then all of a sudden it was time for the wedding. We had it at my paternal grandparents' place and my grandma made the corn mush. My husband came only with his grandfather and a couple other family members. I felt two ways about marriage. I use to think, 'Gee, I really hate him, this man I have to marry. But it is also okay because we *are* by ourselves.' It was true that my dad wasn't taking care of us, so I just figured marrying this handsome gambler will be okay."

Suzie went on to describe the actual wedding ceremony:

"We sat in the hogan and ate corn mush. There was a Fork stick hogan, a male hogan (giggles) and we had the ceremony in there. It was during summer, and there was a lot of corn in the fields. We were living in the shade house because it was so warm. I guess I didn't dress up much, just the traditional skirt and blouse. We didn't have very much nice clothing back then, but my grandma had necklaces and bracelets. She loaned me that and a belt. I wore combs in my hair that had turquoise, and even some rings and bracelets that my paternal uncle loaned to me. My grandma had a lot of Pendleton blankets, and she gave me one of those. You wrapped it around you while you take in the corn mush. My husband wore Dine' clothing too; a red shirt and a bandana. The only thing not traditional was that his hair was short."

"The ceremony took a while. I walked in and sat by my husband. Then we washed with the water the Medicine Man brought. We poured it on our hands. First my husband did it, and then I did the same. You pour water on each other's hands. Then corn pollen was sprinkled by my uncle on the corn mush in a crisscross way. It's in the wedding basket and you get some from the east, west…all four directions. You put it in each other's mouth. First the bride eats just a little bit and then the groom eats it. After that it's given to his relatives, but for my husband it was only his paternal grandmother and another man they came with. The groom's family has to eat all the

---

[122] Locke, 21.

[123] Among other texts there was extensive information regarding the "bridal gift" and the possible conditions of its return in Kluckhohn and Leighton's *Children of the People*, pages 78-80 in particular.

corn meal, and they keep the Navajo wedding basket (giggles). Then come the talks. Lectures come from all family members, and they talk to you about the way of life and how to stay happy and married to each other. They eat while the talk is going on. Then you are married. The food is packed and you give it all to your husband's family."

Suzie claimed that her marriage was a happy one that lasted for many years. Whenever I asked about her husband she always spoke of him with great affection. According to her family they lived a full life and worked together to support their family. However, to this day Suzie teases about how ambivalent she was regarding his marriage proposal and how he so diligently pursued her hand. "Yeah, he probably did want me," she laughed, "as for me, I didn't want him, but he was a young man, and he use to tell me how great it would be to be with him (giggles)." And so, in her way, Suzie made the decision as to who should court her, as well as whom she would marry, and a new Yazzie family was formed.

AN EXTRA WIFE: Polygamy among the Navajo
"The bird who has eaten cannot fly with the bird that is hungry." – Omaha

According to Suzie, one custom with which she had personal experience was that of "plural marriage." This practice involved a Navajo man taking two wives. After learning that Suzie's grandmother received her husband's married grandfather as a suitor, I began inquiring about these plural marriages. I was able to confirm that the man in search of a bride for his grandson was, indeed, very close to Suzie's paternal grandmother. Suzie's grandmother was by this time a widow. I was told that, although her grandmother's lover was married, these somewhat polygamous arrangements were acceptable under certain conditions. If a man's wife was ill or lived some distance from the other woman, then he might be permitted to pursue this sort of arrangement.

Although this sort of arrangement was accepted in the past, it could also be temporary. The first wife's health might improve, for example, prompting the husband to return. The primary wife could also eventually object to her husband's other relationship. The history of how polygamy began amidst the Navajo remained unclear to me, though there is mention of it in nineteenth century white records. At any rate, it is important to note that not all Navajo families engaged in plural marriages, and the practice was often contingent upon the approval of a man's first wife. Suzie explained how her husband's grandfather, like other Dine' men, kept two wives for economic and personal reasons:

"We all knew my husband's grandfather had a wife way over there, some distance from my grandmother's home. He would come on horseback and to see my paternal grandmother anyway. There was another man named Grey Whiskers who had two wives also. They were sisters. Then another relative, one who lived at *Dennehotso*, he had two wives also. He was a Bitterwater Clan one and lived at Monument Pass. His second wife took care of the sheep, but he would live with the woman at *Dennehotso* where they had a cornfield. From there he would take his horse and go visit the other one."

Suzie joked about how she and her sister feared that they would become wives of their grandmother's lover as well. "We were afraid of him," she admitted, "people would warn us not to herd sheep for him because his wife was sick and he was looking for help from young women," (giggles). According to Suzie, the plural marriage arrangement did not always run smoothly:

"The lady from *Dennehotso*, she would be hauling her blankets over for sale when the sun set. We use to live a little ways from her when my mom was still alive. She would say to my mom, 'I'm here now taking care of things because my husband ran off again!' She would say her husband had gone to see her older sister who was living elsewhere, (giggles), and here she was hauling her blankets over. She would even tease my mom, saying 'I think there is a woman with your husband too.' They were the Folding Arm Clan, and my late dad was of that Clan, so I guess she thought she could tease that way. We never liked that lady."

With respect to the observance Suzie made her own decisions, and she made it quite clear that she would not tolerate her husband associating with another woman. I once asked Suzie her feelings about polygamy, and her daughter answered for her, since they had spoken of the matter before. "She probably couldn't stand it," she stated, "once my dad started running around with a woman she didn't approve of, and she became angry that he was with another woman." Suzie's daughter went on to describe Suzie's reaction to her husband's infidelity:

"My mom found out that some woman was following my dad around when he was herding the sheep. She asked my dad about her and he said, 'I'm not interested in this woman, but if she's gonna keep coming around I might just take her up on it because she keeps flirting with me.' My mom decided she didn't like this woman, and the next time she saw her hanging around my dad she came after her," (giggles all around)."

"My mother went over to where the woman was living nearby. She was mad and took a rope to that lady! That woman was running from my mom who was on the horse with a rope whip. She ran that lady off, and after that nobody saw her around our place anymore."

The only plural marriage that Suzie accepted for a short time was that between her husband and her younger sister. This was the sister who was present when Suzie met her husband, and her daughter confirmed that Suzie felt that this was a privileged connection that she and her sister shared. When I asked to hear this story Suzie explained that, "back then men could have two wives," and frankly described the situation:

"Yes, my husband was going with my sister. Even after I married my sister and I were always together, so my husband saw a lot of her. There was nothing wrong in it because I was always sick then. He use to always look for work, far away, and my sister helped out. Sometimes he would stay there at my sister's because that was where the work was. Whenever I would have a child I would get sick. That's probably why he sometimes spent time with my sister."

"My sister would ride the horse to Goulding's to get paid for rugs, and that's how she met the man she's with now. But before that she was around here more. She still lives near here and we are still close sisters."

Seeing my look of bewilderment, Emily explained that living in isolation had sheltered Suzie from some of the doubts that other Navajos began to eventually have about plural marriages. She believed that because her mother had not been subjected to such "outside influences" as Anglo Christian missionaries, it never occurred to Suzie to become jealous over the relationship between her husband and her sister. Suzie did not object to her husband seeking the companionship of her sister because illness made it impossible for her to meet her husband's physical needs. She could trust her sister to care for her husband until she recuperated. When another woman from outside her clan made advances, however, she then felt it necessary to assert her position as first wife.

Kluckhohn and Leighton also observed a strong bond between sisters among the Dine.' This included the custom of sharing a husband in certain circumstances. According to the study:

"The relationship of sisters is usually one of solidarity. Occasionally there is rivalry between adult sisters, and where matrilocal residence prevails this usually arises from jealousy over a common husband. Even this is very much less frequent than might be expected. Otherwise the interests of adult sisters tend to be merged, except where one or more have gone off to live in separate locations. Generally speaking, one sister is equivalent to another among The People; it is "one for all and all for one." This means that they help each other out in any crisis."[124]

Although many non-Navajos may find it difficult to understand the relationship they shared, for Suzie the experience of plural marriage, when her sister was involved, was something that evolved naturally and caused no harm to her marriage. Only when an outsider was introduced did Suzie feel it was necessary to preserve her union with Tully.

MAKING A HOME
"A man can't get rich if he takes proper care of his family."- Navajo

As Suzie and her husband began their life together they took on responsibilities according to what their culture dictated appropriate for their gender. Suzie told me that her husband was responsible for "making sheep and horse corrals, and shade houses too." A shade house could often be larger than the family hogan and somewhat more temporary. Tully constructed a fine "Shade" made of juniper branches and other odd available pieces. This structure was essential to the family during the warmer months. Even today it provides a place to weave, prepare food and spend time escaping the afternoon heat. Wood is vertically stacked into a dome-like shape so thick that a

---

[124] Kluckhohn & Leighton, *Children*, 98-99.

majority of the sun's rays are blocked. Extra chairs and tables are used as furnishings, and the familiar wood burning stove occupies the center. The stove is used for cooking coffee, mutton, and bread. Overall, the shade house is quite a pleasant place to pass the time, and it serves as an intimate place where the family can gather.

Early married life consisted of a definite schedule for Suzie and her mate. "Sometimes my husband use to herd sheep," Suzie stated, pointing out that this was more often done by the females or children of the group. "There was a lot of sheep," she went on, "We use to herd sheep with my daughter. She was small, but she use to ride a horse real good." Suzie revealed how her husband, like many Navajo men during this time, contributed to the family income by seeking work off the reservation. "For him," Suzie said in describing her husband, "it was always time to go look for work. Way far away, my daughter's dad, he would go looking. At Salt Lake, he use to spend all winter there, and he always sent us money. He looked for work ever since we met. Even now most men travel to earn money, because around here there is no work."

Her husband's tenacity in supporting his family meant a great deal to Suzie. Her own father's absence during her youth had brought about a desire within Suzie to provide a more secure existence for her children. She admired how her new husband sought work, even if this meant long periods of time spent apart. I asked Suzie if she ever felt lonely when her husband traveled in search of employment. "No," she laughed, "I never felt loneliness. It didn't cross my mind. There was always too much to do, and I wasn't like that." Suzie's independent spirit drove her to work diligently at home, and she remained confident that her husband would eventually return. The young bride focused on her family, her weaving and her sheep and looked forward to the cards and notes Tully sent regularly through mail.

According to the study conducted by William Adams in the mid-1950s, this was a typical way for Navajo wives to keep in touch with husbands working outside the reservation. Williams discovered that "…during one month (8 mail deliveries) when records were made, 88 Shonto individuals in 61 households received a total of 191 letters and packages – largely from absent schoolchildren (who are required to write home every 2 weeks) and from husbands working on the railroad."[125]

Unfortunately, few Navajo could read or write in either English or the Dine' language at this time. Adams went on to note that, "Less than a quarter of the recipients were able to read and answer their mail themselves. Not all letters are faithfully answered, but the volume of outgoing mail is about half of that incoming."[126] Suzie was fortunate to have a relative who could read her husband's letters to her and provide the emotional contact so important in a young marriage:

"My paternal uncle, he could understand a little reading and writing in both English and Navajo. He learned it while he was in the hospital. He hurt himself once. He poked a knife in his eyes, and that's how he ended up in the hospital. He picked up reading and writing there, and I would give him my husband's letters all the time to read back to me. He was the only one in our community that understood these things.

---

[125] Adams, *Shonto*, 223.
[126] Ibid.

My husband also knew some English. I think he went to school at some time, because he knew how to read and write a little. But he didn't write too good (giggles)."

I asked Effie why her mother never learned English, and she answered that without attending school, learning English was simply out of the question for Suzie. Even though she was now married, as the eldest girl and substitute mother, Suzie's siblings continued to rely on her to provide care and income. The long absence needed to attend the government-run boarding schools would have created great hardship for the struggling family. According to Effie, there was another reason why Suzie had been denied the opportunity to go away to school. "Suzie said that she wanted to go to school," Effie explained:

"Eventually, her sister, Ella went, but even she became sick at school. I don't remember why, but for some reason Ella had to stay at the clinic. They kept her there for a while, and I think her mom felt that the school was an unhealthy place, so Sunshine wouldn't let Suzie go. It was too bad, because my mom said she'd like to have learned English. She always told me, 'before I had kids I thought it would be a good thing to learn how to speak to the Whites better.' I think after we came along, and she got grandkids, then she learned a little more English. She always says to me, 'I pick out little things in English that I needed from you kids.' I think she does understand some of it. Sometimes the tour guides are talking and she can figure out what they're saying."

Effie went on to explain her mother's desire to attend Indian boarding school:

"As she got older she was kind of scared to stay at home, because she thought once she grew up they'd marry her off to an old man or something like that. She said the thought of that made her want to get away and go to school. Anyway, that all worked out okay, and now my mom gets by with the few English words she need. I think she likes hearing it. But my mom wants her kids and grandkids to talk and learn Navajo too."

Suzie and Tully worked hard to build a home for themselves and for the family they planned on creating. It was during this period that she received her English name from her husband. Until that time she had always been called by her mother's pet name for her, "Fair-Skinned Daughter." Suzie's husband had difficulty with the Navajo term, however, and wished to give his new wife an English name to use around Anglos. Suzie explained, "When he married me my husband said, 'I don't like your name. It doesn't sound right to me.' I think he just wasn't used to it. My mom had given me my name from birth because I was very light. A lot of Navajo are not like that and have darker skin. Anyway, my husband called me 'Suzie' because he liked the name."

As she grew older Suzie became a respected member of the community. At some point in her adult life she began to be referred to more often by the name her mother initially gave her; one that described her physical appearance. This was the name she maintained as a mother and a married woman. Suzie was her Anglo name, but to her people she was known as "Fair Skin Woman," and like their mother the Yazzie children have the same fair skin. Suzie told me that she maintained the name "Daughter" up until the time of her mother's death. She remembered that "no one named me anything but 'Daughter' until then. It was only afterwards they kept the other part of my name of, "Fair Skin" or "Light Skin Woman."

MAKING A FAMILY
"Remember that your children are not your own, but are lent to you by the Creator."
Mohawk

In time Suzie and her husband made the decision to start a family of their own. Because her husband was often away looking for employment, Suzie depended on family members to assist with her numerous births. Throughout each pregnancy however, Suzie worked hard at maintaining the hogan, the sheep, and a growing family. Although Tully was often away working when his children come into the world, Suzie was comforted to have a Medicine Man present for every birth. She recalled the ceremony that took place with the arrival of each child:

"If there is a Medicine Man nearby that knew that kind of ceremony, the Blessingway, you would always want to get them involved. All of my kids were born in this way. The late Medicine Man Leon chased out my first boy when he was being born. He was my dad's brother. For My next son a guy from *Dennehotso*, one of our own clan, did it. He was also my uncle. My other boy was done by Grey Whiskers."

Suzie explained the traditional birth process and what it had been like for her:

"Yep, it was very painful and the labor was always long. I never had a short one, and so I had a hard time. Singing was done during the birth while I was hanging onto a sash belt. You put a hole about two feet west of the hogan's center, where the stove usually is. You dig a small hole, and then you string the sash through so you can lean into it when you have pain (contractions) and when it's time to push. You have to help out too, before they set up the pole. You would be moving around, helping out, looking for sheepskin to lie on. Then they put the pole in and then the sash belt. While the singing prayer is done the sash is wrapped around the pole up there. As the Medicine Man is singing he puts the sash belt around you and you hold onto it. You just roll around over there anywhere, and sometimes lean against the roof too (the upper sides of the hogan). You do it sitting up in a squatting position, just like sitting on a chair. They put a pillow on each side of you and when you want to lie down, you lay on either side. I had difficult deliveries. That's why I always didn't feel good after giving birth. It use to always get me sick, and I would sometimes end up in the hospital. Having a baby would keep me sick for a while."

According to anthropologist Maureen Schwarz, in addition to serving as a birthing aid, the sash belt has great religious significance. Talking God instructed First Man and First Woman (all important Navajo deities) how to use the first sash belt:

"A red sash (*sis lichi' I*) was wound sunwise and suspended from a ceiling beam or a supplementary support pole on the west side of the hooghan, between the fire and the back wall. The sash was for the woman to grip while in labor. To offer greater support, a knot was tied in a sunwise direction near the lower end of the sash. Corn pollen was placed along the sash from the top to the bottom after it was suspended (Bailey 1950:56)."[127]

---

[127] Schwarz, 129.

The birth ritual is done to ensure the health of the baby and to comfort the mother. Schwarz stated that Changing Woman, another Dine' deity of extreme importance to women, "established precedents for the Navajo birthing process."[128] She added that this process was followed in nearly every Navajo home "up to the late 1930s and early 1940s."[129] I asked Suzie what sort of material was used for swaddling the baby after it was born. "Regular cloth," Suzie's son answered for her, "not very much of it either, anything that was available was used." Suzie spoke of the Medicine Man's importance during the birth. "They use an eagle feather and pat you with it," she explained, "and this helps the baby to come. Schwarz' description of this process was very similar to Suzie's. "A ceremonial practitioner may 'chase the baby out,'" wrote Ms. Schwarz, "by means of 'singing-the-baby-out' songs from the Blessing Way and an eagle feather fan."[130] Suzie slowly regained her health after each pregnancy. Two of her babies succumbed to illness soon after they were born. However, Suzie recalled naming every child with pleasure:

"I gave them all Dine' names when they were born. They only got English names when they went to school. This was not true for my only daughter's English name. I gave her that name because I wanted to do it instead of the school people. I heard of another Navajo girl who had it. There were some students at Keyenta. They were getting treated at the hospital when I was there. There was a girl there with that name, and I thought it was nice. That is how my only daughter was given the name of Effie."

I asked Suzie how a Navajo name was created for a child, and with her answer I learned more about Suzie's own name and how it related to her physical appearance:

"It all depends on how a person looks; that's how names were made. My daughter had light skin like me. She was like that, but not anymore, because she likes to be outside so much (giggles). When she was younger people would say to her, 'are you born from a white man?' They even say this to her daughters now! I remember how they use to say that to me too, but I'd say, 'No, I'm born into a Navajo.' People were always saying how nice that skin looks. That's why I gave my daughter a name in Dine' that tells how her skin is like mine. Her name means 'Crystal Girl,' and that's how I describe how she is light. Even though she is tan now, she is still the same girl."

The actual birth date of Suzie's children remains elusive. The custom at that time called for relating a child's birth to the season in which he or she was born. Suzie's daughter laughed when I first asked whether her mother could remember the year in which each child was born. "Oh, the exact year is unknown for all of us. My dad only said, 'you were born in the summer,' or this and that. He didn't make up a date until the government officials asked him to. We're pretty sure that each kid is younger that

---

[128] Space and time do not permit me to describe the entire birthing process and its religious importance. The procedure is steeped in symbolism and meaning to the Dine.' Their legends are rich with explanations as to why certain rituals are followed, however these rites also serve many practical purposes in aiding childbirth.

[129] Schwarz, 128.

[130] Ibid., 134. (Information cited by Ms. Schwarz as Knoki-Wilson, 8/10/92; McCabe, 8/19/92).

what is legally recorded." This information prompted the usual bevy of giggles from all present. "But my mom, she had her kids in the Blessing Way," Effie continued with pride, "and we always liked that she made an effort to do that." Suzie's children always expressed a certain reference for their mother, and the way she insisted on giving birth to them in a traditional way. They were especially fond of the special Navajo names she gave each one of them; all of which remain to this day, unknown to me.

Suzie enjoyed recounting stories about her children and their lives on the reservation. Tales about her youngest son provided hours of entertainment to me and for those family members present during our conversations. As a boy, this particular child of Suzie's seemed to have a gift for getting himself into difficult situations. Suzie recalled the early days of her son's childhood:

"We had nothing while he was growing up. We were playing it all by ears. We use to go by wagon to pick pinions near the mountain by Keyenta. This was when my son was just starting to try and walk (giggles). He was just learning to stand, around eight months, but while I was working he was still in the cradleboard some of the time. But he liked standing better, and he would stand up in that wagon then flop back down on the seat. That's all he did for the entire trip there and back. He flopped down so much he got sores on his rare, bare butt!"

While interpreting this story, Suzie's daughter-in-law remarked that her husband still had difficulty sitting still.

"His dad saw Lonnie's butt," Suzie continued amidst the now uncontrollable laughter of her audience:

"...And he said, 'Oh just put tree sap on it.' He meant the sap that is on the pinon tree, just like my ancestor Four-Horned Woman used. Back then, in that place, that was our only medicine. So we smeared his butt with sap and tied him up in the cradleboard. He wailed because he didn't like that, but he got better!"

I asked Suzie whether she believed that the cradleboard used by her people was an efficient method of carrying a child compared to more modern methods. While translating this question her son assured me that the Navajo style of a cradleboard was still in use. "Nowadays kids are still using it," he informed me, "a lot of young parents like them." Suzie agreed that nothing was better for keeping a child safe and secure, stating that, "Most Dine' put babies in it for a little while. Even if the baby falls over, the board in front of their heads protects them. It's good also because the baby is wrapped up tight, and feels as if it is being held."

Lonnie nodded and described how, "you hold a baby in a cradleboard, and you tie them like this, and the baby feels comfortable and happy." He went on to explain that "the cradleboard forbids the baby from falling, and even when the board is standing upright the baby will fall asleep." Suzie recalled that her paternal grandfather was known for his expertise in fashioning cradleboards as well as saddles. "My real paternal grandfather, my father's father, he use to run around on top of those mesas to find the type of wood needed to make a good cradleboard. He would chop it and haul it back down. He only used pinon trees, and he would make saddles out of that too. He carved them out really well. He carved different shapes for men and women."

Suzie continued to speak of her son's earliest mishaps:

"After we put sap all over his butt he got well real quick. That sore butt…it was fine, and we had no more problems with him as he grew. He was about five when he started doing chores. He learned how to chop wood, and he was chopping wood real good. We took our wagon to my paternal grandmother's place when they told us she was very sick. She use to live by Red Rock. We were told that she was having a ceremony on her because she was very sick, and I hadn't seen her for awhile. It was very serious, and at the ceremony there was a man chopping woods. Well, my young son went over and started to also chop (giggles), and he was only five. Later on the man came in with my son by his side. The family told him thanks for the wood and that he should sit down to eat. But he just laughed and told them to feed my son. He said, Wow, this man really can chop wood, he did more than me!"

The pride and affection Suzie felt for all of her children were most apparent when she spoke of the experiences they had shared. The family matriarch never seemed to grow tired of telling these stories again and again, particularly in her children's presence. Since family members often visited Suzie at her hogan, there was usually a good crowd who appreciated her offer to reminisce and giggle over past foibles. Like any family, these stories of adventure and mishap brought the individual back into a collective time, allowing for a shared experience and a sense of unity. For the Yazzies, and perhaps for many Navajo living on the reservation, storytelling provided an opportunity to reconvene as a supportive social unit. This could be essential for families who lived great distances apart, but wished to periodically reconnect.

Having learned of the important bond that existed between a mother and daughter in Dine' culture, I asked Suzie about her only daughter. Had Effie been raised with the same values and customs that Suzie learned as a girl? Suzie smiled and said, "My daughter was Clear Girl or Light Complexion Girl. She grew up nicely. She herded sheep a lot, and I use to herd sheep with her. That's all we did sometimes, just taking care of the sheep. She rode a horse on her own when she was five."

I was also curious to know if Suzie's daughter had the Kinaalda ceremony when she reached adolescence. I wanted to determine whether this tradition was followed from each generation to the next, and whether it had continued to be important in the Yazzie family. At first Effie claimed not to have participated in a Kinaalda ceremony of her own. This surprised me because I understood that Suzie's was firm about raising her children according to the Navajo traditions. I wondered whether financial hardship was the cause of Suzie's daughter's decision not to take part in a ceremony otherwise considered so important.

When I broached the subject again Effie shifted a bit under her mother's questioning gaze. Only then did her only daughter admit that she had, in fact, experienced this puberty rite. However her ceremony took place in a small and more private manner than had her mother's. Suzie had not been in an economic position at the time that would enable her to fully pay for many of the materials. Even the Medicine Man's compensation, which was negotiable, could have imposed an economic strain on the family. Suzie regretted that a larger ceremony had not been possible. "We had no resources," she said with just a hint of a wistful sigh, "We were by ourselves most of the time. I wanted my daughter's ceremony to be bigger, but I had no help then. That's maybe why it just passed unnoticed at first. It seemed like we were always by ourselves, the kids and I. The Kinaalda – it's a lot of work. That's what my daughter said at the time too. There were a lot of things to gather. Who would help us out?"

In her book *Navajo Religion* Gladys Reichard noted that among the Navajo, "Prayers, formulas, songs, song series, rites, and ceremonies all have material values that must be recognized as an element of ethical control." Reichard added that:

"Comparable with the offering to deity is the advance payment made to the chanter. Having decided upon a ceremony, a person customarily sends an intermediary to the singer chosen, offering him an unstipulated, preferably large, amount – horses, sheep, silver, money, buckskin, buffalo robe, or other goods. The chanter will not necessarily refuse to sing if the payment is small. Like some of our doctors, he considers the patient's circumstances, accepting the best a poor man can offer. The arrangement is not, as might appear at first glance, purely economic, for both chanter and patient believe that the ceremony could not possibly be efficacious if nothing were paid. Kinship may be a substitute for property in a transaction of this kind. Yet the patient believes he should pay something to validate the ceremony, even if the chanter is a close relative."[131]

As I began to spend more time with Suzie and her daughter, I learned that discussing her Kinaalda caused Effie discomfort. Suzie explained that a smaller version of the puberty ritual took place for more than just financial reasons:

"My daughter did have the ceremony. Her dad was looking for work at that time, and I was by myself again. All of her brothers were at school. They (BIA officials) came all the time then, and they always dragged the kids back to school. I didn't want my daughter to go, but they took her anyway. She didn't tell about her menstruation because she had started it at school, and she was embarrassed. She just didn't say anything. It was not until she was about fourteen years old when I saw blood on her and asked her about it. She explained to me then that she had it long ago (giggles). I could not understand why she hid it. I told her we should have some kind of the ceremony, so we grinded corn and cooked it in the ground by ourselves. Back then you use to have cornhusks all the time, and we put the mush in them. We wrapped it and put it in the ground to cook. That was all. My paternal grandmother was the only other one there. My daughter did run in the four directions, and she had the Blessingway with the prayers, so I guess it was okay."

When I asked Suzie's daughter why she had kept such a significant event to herself, she said that by the time she returned home it had ceased to have the same meaning to her until her mother suggested the ceremony take place retroactively. This seemed to me a real shame, and an obvious example of how one culture can slowly infiltrate a family. Because the BIA officials insisted that Suzie's daughter attend boarding school, a ceremony that was considered vital to a young girl's initiation into womanhood had been forfeited. What should have been a joyful and memorable experience instead became a source of embarrassment for Suzie's daughter. It seemed so sad to me that a

---

[131] Reichard, *Navajo Religion*, 126-127.

ceremony that held such importance to Suzie and her ancestors became diminished in her daughter's eyes. Although Suzie's daughter still remembers her ceremony, it remained awkward for her to reveal the details to me. I could not get the picture out of my head of a forlorn little girl, struggling alone to understand a moment so private. How could it be fair to isolate a young girl in such a way at a time when she must have needed her mother both as a parent and as a woman?

Suzie and I then discussed her feelings about sending her children to school. By the time they were ages ten through six all had been spirited away by school officials who swept through the reservation looking for truant Navajo children. During this time the Bureau of Indian Affairs was making every attempt to ensure that all Navajo children were attending one of the boarding schools situated throughout the reservation. Suzie stated that she did, in her way, encourage the children to obtain some education at the Indian schools:

"I guess I wanted them to go to school just for a little while. I don't know much about white culture because I didn't go to school. That probably would have helped me. I really didn't know any English until my kids learned it. When my daughter finally went to school she came home for breaks and would read to me. She told me, "This is what it means, and what it is, and what it says." And from there I learned some English, but I don't like to try it out on people (giggles)."

With the arrival of the BIA officials Suzie faced a turning point. For the first time in her life, a decision as important as her children's education did not rest on her shoulders. No matter how accustomed Suzie had become in taking responsibility for her family's welfare, whether or not her children went to school depended on Anglo strangers. Her son informed me that at time a parent was not given the choice regarding their child's schooling; the BIA simply insisted upon attendance. I learned that a few of Suzie's children had managed to keep their attendance sporadic. "I didn't really want to go to school," Lonnie explained, "and my mom didn't want Effie to go at all. She was 'Mama's girl.'"

Suzie's reluctance to send her daughter to school is also indicative of the family's gendered division of labor. As the only daughter it was imperative for Effie to learn how to care for the family business and attend to other tasks traditionally passed on from mother to daughter. Effie eventually followed her brothers' school schedule on a more consistent basis, but only after she decided she liked school after all. This was around 1956 according to Yazzie family memory. The only daughter periodically returned to her home in Monument Valley, however, in order to assist her mother in running the family outfit. Suzie's thoughts were never far from her children living at schools many miles away. "I would worry and think about them." She softly said when asked about that period of her life. "It was like that," she remembered, "I was use to having my kids around me, and when they were gone I would wonder if they were okay...." Suzie trailed off in thought.

This conflict that arose between Navajo families and the BIA existed throughout the reservation at this time, and it was duly noted by anthropologists studying white influences on Dine' culture. Kluckhohn and Leighton observed that:

"When finally the school course is completed and there is a permanent return to the family, the adjustment is often painful on both sides. The boy or girl has become accustomed to white food, white clothing, and white standards of cleanliness. He is torn between his abiding affection for his family and his drive to live up to what he has been taught are higher standards. Their impulsion conditioned in early childhood, to participate reverently in the native ceremonials conflicts with what they hear in school about "ignorant superstitions." Generally the "ignorant superstitions" win out in the end, but only after a deal of discomfort."[132]

Suzie's children appeared to have successfully balanced Navajo and Anglo culture. The family members I interviewed seemed to prefer most aspects of traditional Navajo life. The exposure to white culture seems to have left them relatively unaffected. However, there must have been some discomfort involved in the transition from their mother's hogan, to white boarding school, and then back again to traditional Dine' life again.

I eventually asked Suzie how she felt children should be raised. "Just calmly, that's all," she answered, "I didn't yell at them and I didn't physically abuse them." Again, this style of child rearing, in which proper behavior is suggested but in which the child is left ultimately responsible, was not noted by Kluckhohn and Leighton:

"Never have the writers known a Navaho parent to demand socially acceptable behavior as the condition of parental love and protection...There are occasionally conditional statements "If you act like this we won't take you to the trading store this afternoon." Physical punishment is rare, slight, and usually spontaneous...One seldom hears threats of physical punishment."[133]

Suzie's style of parenting suited her personality and benefited her children. With independence and responsibility promoted and physical discipline kept to a minimum, the Yazzie family managed to work together as a cohesive unit of equals. Although Suzie always maintained her position as the head of the family while her husband was away, each child earned respect when he or she contributed as expected. Of course, because I was an outsider, I may not have been told any stories of unrest within the family. Yet, when I witnessed how the Yazzies treated each other in my presence, I was left with the impression that their relations were generally harmonious.

Between pregnancies Suzie kept her eye out for extra work in order to supplement her husband's income. One industry that frequently provided work to Navajos was the railroad. Suzie informed me that her husband, "always worked there... the railroad, especially in Salt Lake. That's where he always went." Once she had the good fortune to accompany her husband on one of his many jobs working for the railroad. She began this particular story with her usual teasing:

"I worked on the railroad too, like my husband (giggles). I use to haul rails around (laughter). I am just kidding (more laughter). I use to cook for the railroad workers. My middle son was small then, he was about three. My oldest son was here with his aunt herding sheep, taking care of the sheep. My husband always went to the railroad

---

[132] Kluckhohn & Leighton *Children*, 68-69.
[133] Ibid., 52-53.

looking for work, and he probably wrote most of his letters over there. One time he was told they needed a cook for the laborers."

"I had to go to Mexican Hat, (a very small town about twenty miles outside Monument Valley), and the horses we rode there were then brought back to our place by family. We had to do it that way, because the bus didn't go through here. From here we took the horses up to the Mexican Hat Bridge. My little sister that now lives in Keyenta was still a young girl then. She was younger than my sister Elly. But she brought the horses back from the Mexican Hat Bridge all by herself. From Mexican Hat we just hitched a ride, my husband, small son, and I. My younger sister Elly took care of our sheep. We were living around my two sisters all the time and they really helped out. We hitched rides all the way up to Montecello. It was there, I think the bus could finally pick us up. We went from there on the bus, and we worked for a while. I didn't mind because it was a nice change, and it was nice to have the extra money."

Suzie spoke of the conditions under which she and her husband worked. "Housing was not as good as our hogan when we were working for the railroad, but there were houses where we use to sleep, and we just use to cook in there too. It was just like this. And there weren't many supplies. Anything I could come up with for me to cook, I would cook it (giggles). The workers, they worked on the railroad all day, so they would eat whatever you put in front of them."

The work provided by companies off the reservation helped many Navajos such as the Yazzies through difficult times. This earning power could never have been possible on the reservation, where opportunity was scarce. Hardship and struggle were understood as the price the Dine' paid to live on their ancestor's homeland. However, most Navajos worked close to home and their loved ones whenever possible. The chance to do this came for Tully during one of the most economically difficult periods in recent Navajo history, the Great Depression.

The Valley outside was growing dark. Though none of the Yazzies seemed the worse for wear, I was tired and hungry. Elvina, who had been sitting quietly for most of the day, offered to drive back to the lodge with me. From there she could hitch a ride with one of her brothers back to Effie's place in Oljeto. Lonnie and Emily would be spending the night with Effie and the compound, but they promised to meet me the next morning at Goulding's restaurant. "We don't want to miss out on another good meal!" Emily giggled. I said my good-byes and followed Elvina out the door. "Put that tape in again," Elvina instructed me, "I really like it!" We drove back to the lodge learning every word on that tape, and I ended up giving it to Elvina as a gift. When I dropped her off at the restaurant parking lot she gave me an unexpected hug. "Thanks for everything," the pretty girl beamed, "I learned a lot." She got out of my rental and walked away into the darkness, and as I drove down to my little trailer I wondered if she would be afraid of encountering any Skinwalkers that might be about.

CHAPTER 7 – LEARNING THE WAY

"Before me peaceful, behind me peaceful, under me peaceful, over me peaceful, all around me peaceful." - Navajo

NO MORE FRIENDLY SKIES

I was fully ready to leave the stress of flying out to the Valley behind me, and booked a sleeping berth on the train, specifically the "Southwestern Chief." I assumed the name was a nod to the native population in the region, but it rang a little suspect. From my little beach town of Carpinteria, just south of Santa Barbara, I made the two hour train trip connecting me to Union Station in downtown Los Angeles. I lingered for an hour at Union Station, settling deep into one of the soft leather chairs in the main waiting area. I loved the high ceilings and stained glass so beautifully restored to their 1930's Art Deco luster. When the "Chief" arrived I found my little sleeping compartment and set up my laptop. The privacy and comfort were so luxurious compared to the flying experience. Two meals were included, and I was scheduled to arrive in Flagstaff around six the next morning…fully rested. Why on earth had I not thought of going by train earlier?

Staring out my compartment window I watched the Los Angeles "river" trickle through its concrete culvert and thought about how to structure my work schedule with Suzie and her family. It was early spring, and I had a full nine days off from school, two of which would be spent traveling out and back. I felt that I made up for the extended time it took to reach the Rez' by train by eliminating missed connections of flights. I would be able to work on the train, and I wouldn't have to worry about the dreaded turbulence so prevalent when flying into "Flag." I was overjoyed to know I could nod off fully reclined while the train gently rocked me to sleep.

I arrived in Flagstaff around eight the next morning. It didn't take long to realize that Amtrak time was similar to Navajo time. It was nice to sleep in however, and after a sunrise breakfast and a tidy little shower I gathered my things and hopped off with anticipation. The air was brisk, but there was no threat of snow, and I drove leisurely to the Valley for a change, feeling once more as if I was returning home. The Hill House welcomed me like an old friend, and I unpacked a little radio cassette player I brought along to play classical tapes while working. True to my routine I took my afternoon run to the high school and back, and then purchased my groceries at the little market. After a simple dinner I hit the bed hard and slept a dreamless sleep. I expected to hear from Emily and Lonnie the next day and looked forward to having my friends join me for breakfast.

I awoke early to prepare for the interviews I expected to conduct with Emily, (who I'd recently begun calling "Em"), and Lonnie. I went through my routine of cleaning up and making certain that my tape recorder was in working order. I made a point of drinking my tea out in the fenced yard in front of Hill House where the buttes rise up on either side of me. I loved the way the sun hit the walls of rock around the house, revealing a burnished red that made me feel warm and safe. The management of Goulding's listed Hill House as having "no view," yet I have discovered that it offers a startling landscape of the monuments just as good as the gift shop postcards depicting Monument Valley. It is not quite the scene that guests enjoy from their hotel balconies, but it is enough for me, and the silence is healing. I stood there drinking it in, my reverie interrupted only by the occasional little bird chirping, or by a wind whistling down the pass. How I had grown to love this place!

After my morning meditation I gathered up my questions for Suzie. With time to spare I turned to learning some Navajo, or as the book called it *"Dine' bizaad."* I was determined to speak with Suzie in her own tongue someday, but the structure of the language was difficult for me to grasp, and the instructional tapes I purchased were hard to follow. I soon gave up on the project, and instead listened to the local Navajo radio station. Lying on my stomach in the sun by a big picture window I worked at writing Navajo words from the notebook on flash cards. Traditional songs played on the radio and gave me a pleasant background for study. It was Sunday, and I thought that a good number of *Dine'*, or "The People," must be practicing Christians, since a fair amount of songs mentioned God or Jesus in between the Navajo phrases. After a very pretty tune, the announcer mentioned its title in Navajo. I could make out the word "sodizin," meaning "prayer," and this was exciting to me. It was the first word in Navajo I ever recognized!

I spent the remainder of the morning writing and practicing, making a list of words and phrases that might come in handy around Suzie. In my own language I wrote out "Should I go looking for the sheep?" and "How do you say this in Navajo?" The family had agreed that I should someday stay with Suzie, perhaps an entire season, just to learn how things were done out in the Valley and to get to know her better. I considered this invitation quite an honor and the thought of having a real one-on-one conversation with the matriarch made me attack the *Dine' bizaad* with renewed vigor.

The minutes ticked by with still no word from Em and Lonnie. This was frustrating since I was sure they knew that I was in M.V. waiting for them. I couldn't stay angry when Emily called at noon apologizing all over the place. I was a mother of four, and so I understood how things had gotten hectic. When she took care of her two boys that morning she had lost track of time. We agreed to meet the next day instead, and I called Effie's house to see if she would be available to serve as a translator. She picked up her phone whenever I had called her before, and it seemed there was always somebody at Effie's place. I hoped this time I wouldn't reach a relative, some niece or nephew, who had no idea who I was. Sure enough, a young man answered the phone and I felt so awkward. I explained why I needed to speak with Effie, and the stranger told me that Effie had already taken her mother to the Valley. I thanked him, and made the brave decision to go in search of the ladies myself, if even just to say hello.

I drove up to the park entrance and paid my three dollars at the booth. The man stationed there informed me that the price would be going up to five dollars that summer. I told him it was about time and that I couldn't believe they had been squeaking by with three measly dollars all this time. He introduced himself as Lawrence, and he asked if I'd been to the Valley much. The conversation felt easy and he seemed trustworthy, so I revealed to him that I was helping to write the Yazzie family history. He verified that Effie came in that morning, so I continued on my journey, driving past the monuments standing vigil over the Valley. I passed each sentry with awe and respect; the "Mittens" that were so recognizable on post cards, and my favorite "Three Sisters" standing beyond "Two Elephants." I took a right away from "The Hub" onto the private road that sported a sign proclaiming it off limits to everyone but guides. I always felt a sense of privilege driving to Suzie's.

I imagined that all of the tourists that I passed along the way had no idea how much this land and its people offered; how special the whole place was. I felt fortunate to know the place so well. The landscape continued to impress me, but it was different for me now. It was familiar, and for the first time since I began coming to Suzie's I drove to her hogan with confidence, never hesitating about which dirt road to take.

I arrived at the compound and saw that a jeep was parked in front. Certainly somebody must be inside entertaining the "visitor?" I drove around back and parked by the residence as a local would, then waited in the car for a spell to give whoever might be in the little home a chance to look out the window. As I sat, I imagined the conversation inside; "Hmm, Coco's here," Effie would comment in an even tone, as if I'd just been by last week. Smiling to myself I made my way to the earth-colored house, and following protocol, knocked softly on the weathered door. If the house was empty I would wait there while they finished with the visitor. Much to my surprise it was Suzie who opened the door! This was my second awkward moment of the day. She was alone, which meant that I would have to struggle to communicate with her. For a moment I was terror-stricken, and then she smiled. With some relief I realized that the matriarch once again had some memory of who I was. Perhaps Effie had told her that I was coming. Of course, there was always the chance she only saw me as some lost tourist asking for directions back to the main road. So much time passed between each of my visits, and I wondered if I would have to reintroduce myself to my old friend.

I made some lame attempt at a Navajo greeting; "Yah-ta hey....Effie?" I asked. Suzie gave a broad smile and nodded, "Ahoe" she said and pointed to the hogan. Luckily for both of us Effie appeared at the hogan's door just at that moment. We were saved! "Hey stranger!" she called out, and throwing a wave back to the tourists

131

getting into their jeep, walked stiffly toward us. "I was sittin' at the loom for my mom for once. I'm not used to it and I got sore. How long have you been here? Did mom get who you were? Did you have trouble finding us?" I stared stupidly as her rapid-fire questions morphed into Navajo dialogue with Suzie. All the while Effie ushered me into the house. She sat her mother down on the bed, and proceeded to get me a cup of coffee. I couldn't be sure that Effie was successful in explaining to her mother who I was. A light of recognition only appeared in the old woman's eyes when I began to clip the microphone onto her velveteen blouse. At least she seemed pleased to see me.

I lightly clasped her hand and told her I was "Coco," making a mental note to learn how to introduce myself in Navajo. Suzie nodded, saying something in her own tongue, assuming that I would understand it. I showed Suzie the bag of goodies that I always brought as a sign of my gratitude. There were the usual things she and her family enjoyed snacking on; string cheese and sunflower seeds. Sucking the salt off the seed, then cracking it open for the meaty part inside, was a pastime I'd adopted from the Yazzies. It kept us all amused during the long interviews, and we settled in as usual to begin working. Just as we three women were getting comfortable we heard a car drive up outside, and it wasn't long before my wayfaring friends Em and Lonnie came to the door.

The Navajo I have met have always been polite and quiet. They have a subtle way of moving about in an inconspicuous way. So I could not say that Emily and Lonnie "burst" into the room, but their appearance did surprise me. I assumed it would be some time before they could meet me at Suzie's. How wonderful to see them here at Suzie's little home. "We knew you'd be missing us," Emily laughed as she shuffled into the warm little room.

"Yeah," Lonnie agreed, "we figured you'd get pretty lost without us showin' you around. It's a good thing Effie found you, or you may have become food for the coyotes." This brought about hoots of laughter from everyone but me. Even Suzie giggled as if she were in on the joke. "As a matter of fact, I found your Mama just fine," I informed the laughing Yazzies, "I just didn't know what to say to her once I did." This caused even more laughter, and my moment of pride was dashed like the fry bread I'd dropped in the dirt last summer.

Lonnie dusted off his black cowboy hat and reached for the coffee, "Aw, we're just giving you a hard time. We knew you'd be okay, but we got out here fast cos' we don't like to miss anything good." Both he and Em found a place to sit and filled their hands with sunflower seeds. As frustrating as this day had begun, it was turning out to be a good start to what I hoped would be hours of pleasant conversation. The five of us settled in for our typical question-and-answer repartee. I had been very curious about the Navajo faith system and how Suzie related to it, so this is where my questions began.

NAVAJO RELIGION IN EVERYDAY LIFE

"Brother, you say there is but one way to worship and serve the Great Spirit. If there is but one religion, why do you white people differ so much about it? Why not all agreed, as you can all read the Book?" — Sogoyewapha, "Red Jacket" : Seneca

Suzie and some members of her family still practice what may be considered "traditional" Navajo religion; one that focuses on maintaining harmony both among themselves and with the natural forces around them. Suzie's son explained how his mother and her family adhere to the Dine' religion:

"We still take the corn pollen, we all do; when you use the corn pollen you go out early in the morning and take just a little of it in your mouth. You lick it off your thumb and then you say 'Nizhooniigo naashadoo.' That means, 'I will walk in happiness and safety.' My mother says that doing this means nothing will faze you physically or mentally. We never forget about that. And we don't forget about things that you don't do…things like…you don't bother your siblings (in any sexual way), because if you do you'll go nuts. That's still what you call 'taboo.' My mom asked me once if whites have taboos. I told her that all of the white taboos are probably forgotten. Our taboos involve many things; like Coyote shouldn't cross your path. We still abide by this, all of us. My mom said when you run into a taboo, immediately you do something about it. Maybe when we mention these things white people will think and learn about it also."

Lonnie felt that the Dine' religion was still a very strong belief system. He went so far as to suggest that a Navajo ritual could be helpful to non-Navajos in times of fear or stress. I once mentioned to him my fear of flying, explaining how I endured every flight with the nagging concern that I might at any time plummet to my death in the fiery remnants of a flimsy aircraft. He advised me to follow the corn pollen ritual to ensure my safety during all journeys:

"I know you're afraid of flying in airplanes, when it suddenly jerks down or sideways. I spoke to my mom about it. I told her you should do just like us and go out early in the morning and take your corn pollen. That should work for you too if it works for us. Maybe when you get up early in the morning and say those prayers it will make your flight safer. I think this is true because it's always worked for me. My day goes right as it should when I say my prayers first thing."

I thought it very considerate of my friend to offer his faith as a way to comfort me. I vowed to give the corn pollen prayer a try, and I hoped that its power was as effective when uttered by an Anglo.

Beginning each day or journey with a prayer has always been an important part of Suzie's life. For many years she spoke the same prayers, enlisting the corn pollen that many Navajo believe to be a powerful and sacred substance that provides harmony and protection. Suzie told me that these prayers were still in use by traditional Dine,' and were helpful for every aspect of life. "We pray for sheep and horses," she explained, "we even pray for me (ourselves), also for our home." Lonnie went on to say, "We pray for cats, dogs everything…every living being. Songs are also important. When he was alive, my dad learned many of them, and he wrote them down on paper for me." In my research I came across information that confirmed that by the 1970s many

Navajo were hard at work passing on sacred information to their children. This provided the details of ceremonies and served as an instructional aid for novice medicine men. One anthropologist noted that using written notes allowed a young Navajo:

"...to use some learning aids so that the student can bring "lessons" home and study them alone without the constant presence of his teacher. One such aid is to take "notes" of ceremonial songs to help in remembering them. Though still not a popular practice, this method has been used by some singers in recent times."[134]

Unfortunately, the act of writing down this sacred information did not always serve as a way of preserving it, as important details could easily be lost by a careless student. Suzie told me how one of her relatives lost or destroyed many of the ceremonial notes he had gathered:

"He took off with them because he felt jealousy. I don't know if this family member wanted to learn the songs, and he was just careless, or if he hid them away for his own medicine. I don't know where he took the songs, but he probably did put them away somewhere secret because he didn't believe in them. I think this must be true, because he talks now as if he doesn't want anyone else to believe in the songs either."

Lonnie recalled this incident as well. "Yeah," he shook his head sadly, "this family member was talking about how the songs should be stopped, and maybe that's why he left boiling and mad. For me, I know he talks against the songs, and I don't like it."

Conflicts regarding religion have come between the Yazzies before. Even today there are occasional discussions among some relatives regarding the validity of the Dine' religion compared to others that are practiced on the reservation. Some family members practice the Native American church ceremonies that involve peyote. Others younger family [135]members consider themselves Christians. It saddened me to hear that exposure to alternative native religions along with Christian beliefs introduced by whites has caused tension and confusion among some Navajo. Emily recalled a younger family member asking why she refused to be "saved" by accepting salvation through Christ. Like Lonnie and Suzie, Emily holds fast to her Navajo faith and continues to find comfort in it.

MEDICINE BASKET

"Trouble no one about their religion; respect others in their view and demand that they respect yours." — Tecumseh

---

[134] Chiao, Chien. Continuation of Tradition in Navajo society. Nankang, Taiwan: Acandemia Sciica, Institute of Ethnology, 1971, 93.

[135]

We paused in conversation, and refilled our coffee cups. Glancing up to a shelf in the upper right-hand corner of the house, I noticed a basket covered with a worn cloth. I asked Emily what it was, and she told me it was her mother-in-law's "medicine basket." This basket held Suzie's medicine bundle, or *Jish*, which is generally kept in a discreet place that is easily accessible. The bundle contains items that promote harmony as well and provide protection for its owner and his or her household. The *Jish* is only brought down for the purpose of making a specific blessing. A number of medicine baskets have been investigated in the past by anthropologists who misunderstood their importance. The earliest accounts I found referring to the basket stated that:

"Each family had its "bag of keepsakes," usually containing a few small pouches of pollen, pieces of flint, and some feathers. This item, for most local Navajos, had more sentimental meaning than medicinal or spiritual value."[136]

Clyde Kluckhohn presented a more detailed description in *Navajo Material Culture*. He wrote that the bundles within family baskets were made of buckskin and contained "precious stones and rock crystal" or "feathers...stones, pollens...and additional paraphernalia for specific chants..."[137] A more complete description of the type of basket and bag Suzie kept is in Schwarz' study of Navajo views of personhood. Schwarz noted that the medicine bundle kept at home symbolized motherhood. Elements significant to mother figures within the Navajo religion are included in the bundle. White shell, for example, symbolizes Changing Woman, also known as White Shell Woman. Earth from sacred mountains located throughout Navajoland, as well as turquoise and abalone, would also be secured to represent the four directions of the earth. According to Schwarz, these materials found in the family medicine basket are very personal and are believed to possess significant power. Ms. Schwarz recounted the Navajo creation story, describing how the objects in a *Jish* symbolized important aspects belief.

"The Holy People had with them the four sacred minerals. With the seed of white shell, turquoise, abalone shell and black jet, the human body was made...We are a seed, a plant, in the eyes of the Holy People. We are the flesh and the seed of the Holy People."[138]

When asked, Suzie described the various items within the basket and their use better than any of the scholarly studies on the subject. She stopped short of showing me the separate, smaller bundle made of deer hide, explaining it must only be brought out for a specific and special need. This portion of the basket was not to be shown or explained to anyone outside the Yazzie family. There were a total of four bundles in Suzie's basket; each one containing items of significance that promoted the well being of those living in her home. Suzie explained through her son the ways in which her *Jish*

---

[136] Blanchard, Kendall A. The Economics of Sainthood; Religious change among the Rimrock Navajos. Rutherford, N.J.: Fairleigh Dickinson University Press, 1977, 77.

[137] Kluckhohn, Clyde, W.W. Hill and Lucy Wales Kluckhohn. Navajo Material Culture. Cambridge: Harvard University Press, 1971, 336.

[138] Schwarz, 27, 21 and 63.

represented important aspects of Navajo life. The Yazzies put more than "sentimental" value on the medicine bundles, and truly believe that even discussing the contents might diminish the power and protection they provide.

Lonnie explained that I had been permitted to view certain objects in Suzie's basket because they were used for common rituals that were not deemed as extremely sacred. These items symbolized things such as material wealth and included arrowheads and gems collected on the reservation. The objects Suzie showed me looked as if they should be exhibited behind museum glass, but for Suzie they served a purpose beyond aesthetic appreciation. Some were effectively chipped and beautifully shaped, some glossy and smooth to the touch. Not understanding the importance of these items, I began to play with the arrowheads. When Suzie gave me one particularly pretty projectile I pretended to be a deer, holding two fingers above my head to imitate horns. Suzie giggled as I aimed the arrowhead at my face, first dodging its point, then jabbing it to my neck as if a hunter had skewered me. We laughed at my silliness, but Suzie laughed at some of the questions I asked her as well, so I couldn't be sure if she thought I was funny or merely insane. Once we had a moment alone Lonnie informed me that I should not have played with any of the items. I felt myself blushing a million shades of crimson in my embarrassment, but at least I now knew to treat such information with more reverence.

Although Suzie did not completely open her most sacred of bundles, she fingered them constantly. It was clear that these parcels meant a great deal to her, and I found myself watching her long, worn fingers play upon each object. I wondered how many hours of weaving had made Suzie such a tactile person. She clearly seemed sensitive to everything she touched. Maybe this was a by-product of her hand-trembling gift. Over time I noticed that Lonnie and Effie habitually fingered things while they spoke, in the same manner as their mother. I began to call it "dancing hands" and I found the distracted, gentle way their fingers worked very peaceful to watch.

Suzie carefully re-wrapped the contents of her basket. Lonnie pointed out how a small opening was left so that corn pollen could be sprinkled within to ensure the potency of each item. Suzie placed the basket back on its high shelf and then reached for another that rested in the corner. Positioning it between us, she fingered through a collection of modest handcrafted items that included everything from earrings to dream catchers. Her hands settled upon a brightly beaded bracelet with a screw clasp. It was done in a traditional Navajo design, and its simplicity reminded me of the Indian jewelry that was so popular in my youth. Suzie motioned for my wrist, and placed the little band on me, carefully tightening the screw and giving it a final pat. Through Lonnie's translation she told me that it was her gift to me! I was very moved by this simple gesture, and as I thanked her I knew I would wear the little bracelet for the remainder of my visit.

The coffee pot bubbled and we sat in comfortable silence. I began to wonder about the differences between Anglo religious practices and those of the Navajo. I asked Lonnie if they actually thought of their faith as a "religion" or simply a way of life. "I guess we don't really consider our prayers and ceremonies as a religion the way you do," he answered, "it's a way to live that brings harmony. And we just wouldn't do it any other way. Some Anglos may forget to pray or may not go to church one week. But to us, the whole Valley is our church. We do our corn pollen prayers as a way of honoring that." I tried to grasp what my friend was saying, and I thought that perhaps the Navajo were on to something I hadn't figured out in all my years as a Christian. How much stronger would my faith be if I looked at it as a part of the very world in which I lived? I knew that I would have to turn that idea around in my head for a good while before it settled into my heart.

I was honored that Suzie had shown me her medicine bundle, but I could never hope to completely understand all that it symbolized to her and her family. Lonnie spoke of his own basket that he kept in much the same manner. He felt very strongly that his jeesh provided protection and harmony to his family. He explained that many baskets are passed on through each generation, but may also be created anew if a Medicine Man is available to bless the necessary items. The Yazzie tradition of keeping the medicine basket appears to have been passed on through Suzie. Clearly this was one element of Dine' culture that Suzie felt was important to maintain.

NAVAJO CEREMONY AND GENDER

"...When a child carried water for the home, an elder would give compliments, pretending to taste meat in water carried by a boy or berries in that of a girl..." – Mourning Dove: *Salish*

Because the Kinaalda ceremony was important to Suzie as a symbol of Navajo womanhood, I pressed her for more details concerning the ritual. She revealed the details of this puberty ceremony a little at a time, and I wondered if Suzie held back some information because it was sacred. On this particular day I asked her about the significance of the white clay that is used on a girl for the ritual. Suzie explained:

"Yes, white clay is used for the Kinaalda. The clay is applied to the girl from head to toe, when they tie the girl's hair. Many people don't have any of this clay, so relatives go from house to house asking if someone has any. My relative was looking for some recently, but I didn't have any around. Afterwards one woman came by to say she found some, and she gave me a little to keep around. It happens like that here, so we can keep ceremonies going."

Suzie asked me through her son if Anglos had puberty ceremonies as well. "When do your young people get a sing on them?" she asked. This question took me by surprise. I knew enough to decipher Suzie's use of the word "sing" to mean "ritual. But I was thrown by Suzie asking a question about my culture. Here I had spent hours with the Yazzie matriarch discussing every corner of her life, while offering only fragments of my own. Wasn't I the one who was supposed to be asking all the questions? And yet, why shouldn't Suzie be as curious about my life as I was about hers? I should have known by now that Suzie was a clever and inquisitive woman, and so naturally she must wonder about the differences between us.

I answered that, other than the Hispanic tradition of celebrating a girl's fifteenth birthday with a "*Quincenera*" and the Jewish Bat mitzvah, there were no ceremonies that I knew of that publicly recognized the transition from childhood to adulthood. I explained that oftentimes in the Anglo world a girl's menstruation can be an embarrassing topic that is approached in a delicate manner between mother and daughter. "It's not like that with us," laughed Effie, "But I've heard that girls that aren't Navajo do try and hide it. I heard that sometimes they even curse it!" Effie shook her head in disbelief, "Maybe that sort of rubbed off on me when I went to the White school. I didn't want anyone to know, but I told my mom later when I got home. I think it's kind of funny now, because when us Navajo girls start to menstruate the whole world around us knows and we have a big ceremony. People gather and eat. It's a pretty good time!" As I thought of my own daughters' upcoming adolescence, it seemed to me that the Dine' had a much healthier attitude toward the event.

There were other questions in my mind regarding Navajo religion. I wondered if certain religious responsibilities were allocated to different family members, and if they were designated according to gender. If a Navajo girl has the Kinaalda, then did a similar ceremony exist for young Navajo boys? All Suzie could remember was that every now and then a boy participated in a sweat lodge ritual. This was planned when his voice changed. She explained that, other than the puberty ceremony, daily rituals were the personal responsibility of every Navajo. "Each person has a song," Suzie mused, "and when you have one of these songs or prayers they are meant to keep your thoughts positive. That is what keeps us strong."

NAVAJO MEDICINE

"…*everything on the earth has a purpose, every disease an herb to cure it, and every person a mission. This is the Indian theory of existence.*" – Mourning Dove: Salis

"*There are many things to be shared with the Four Colors of humanity in our common destiny as one with our Mother the Earth. It is this sharing that must be considered with great care by the Elders and the medicine people who carry the Sacred Trusts, so that no harm may come to people through ignorance and misuse of these powerful forces.*" – Resolution of the Fifth Annual Meetings of the Traditional Elders Circle, 1980

From what I learned, Navajo religion and medicine occupied the same conscious space. Sensing this, I posed questions concerning both topics to Suzie simultaneously. I asked Suzie if she personally knew any medicine men, and she revealed that one member of her husband's family had practiced medicine. I then asked if there were any female Navajo practitioners. Lonnie told me that both men and women could practice the medicine, so long as they devoted the appropriate amount of time to learning a particular ceremony and the related songs from an elder. This involved shadowing one's mentor for some years. Since the number of Dine' ceremonies and songs were quite extensive and their structure elaborate, a practitioner could only hope to master a select few. In this way he or she would become known as a specialist in those rituals.

138

The novice learned every detail concerning how to perform a ceremony and what herbs to use to ensure success. Ritual and ceremony also serve as a way to unite with family and friends. Many Navajo live in isolated parts of the reservation, and a ceremony offers a welcome opportunity to reconvene with loved ones.

Over the years anthropologists came to recognize how ceremonies created balance among the Navajo. In his 1971 research anthropologist Chien Chiao stated that:

"Navajo ceremonies have both medical and social functions. One of the social functions of a major ceremony is that it provides an occasion for a social gathering, when people can meet friends and relatives and exchange news and gossip."

Chiao cited Kluckhohn and Leighton's findings that also indicated:

"The rite offers a chance to see and be seen, to talk and to listen. Enemy Way, better known as "Squaw Dance", and Night Chant, better known as "Yeibechi," more than the others, give the Navajos an occasion for socializing."[139]

I have been privy to some very personal moments in the Yazzie's lives. Yet, to this day I have yet to participate in any real Dine' ceremonies. I have no idea whether this is intentional on the Yazzie's part, or the result of my own subconscious insecurities that beg them to exclude me. I didn't know if non-Natives were invited to the seasonal Yeibechi ceremonies that took place throughout the reservation throughout the month of August, nor was I aware of any Anglos present during a "hand trembling" procedure. I assumed that few Anglos were invited to healing ceremonies in which sacred ritual was performed. What I learned for certain was that Suzie and her family took part in many ceremonies throughout the year for blessings, healing, and social contact. This aspect of traditional Navajo life was yet another example of the choices Suzie made to maintain her culture in the twenty-first century.

SUZIE AS HAND TREMBLER
"God gives us each a song." Ute

The gift of "hand trembling," a Navajo method of diagnosing illness and retrieving lost items, has served the Navajo people for generations. The origin and details of this ceremony, however, remain somewhat elusive to the outside world. Raymond Locke wrote:

"Very little study has been done in regard to extrasensory perception and mental telepathy as practiced by the Navajos. Many whites who have lived among The People are convinced that some, particularly older, Navajos are capable of accurately predicting future events and particularly their own deaths…"

Locke went on to state that hand trembling was most often performed to find people and lost articles. Within the Navajo community, a person possessing the ability to perform hand trembling is perceived as naturally gifted because, "in the Navajo

---

[139] Chiao, *Continuation of Tradition*, 51.

view, nature can be controlled to an extent."[140] The practice of going into trance and allowing one's hands to communicate information has also been used among the Navajo to diagnose illness that may then be healed by a Medicine Man. Suzie came from a long line of medicine men on her mother's side of the family, and the art of hand trembling was a capability that her family members were known to possess. She listed the long line of healers in her clan. "My late grandmother's brother was a Medicine Man," she began, "and on my mother's side, her dad was a hand trembler."

It was around the time of her Kinaalda that Suzie discovered she had inherited this particular gift:

"I was about fifteen or sixteen. It would start on its own. Repeatedly my arm would start to tremble. It would yank me around and I was afraid because it wouldn't stop. It attacked me constantly for a year. One of my younger sisters in Keyenta was also like that. My sister came to me and said, 'it's finally taken an effect on my body.' When she was a girl every place on her body was trembling once, even her legs. It was a while back in time when we were told that we were going to be hand tremblers, and that we had to be remade. I knew of some people in my community who were having the same problem, and they got help with a treatment. This treatment had to be done so I could learn to control it. One of the medicine men living around us did the ceremony on me. He put something on my arm and said, 'from here on it will stop unless you call upon it for service.' And then it was true. That made it stop coming up without my asking for it, and that made it better for me. I don't know if I'll pass it on to anyone, but it is in the family."

I asked Suzie if she still offered her gift as a diagnostic tool:

"Yes, just recently a boy came to me. His parents came with him and asked me to do a hand trembling on him for his problem. He is a little emotionally upset and they wanted to know how he can stop being like that. I decided he needed to do the Tobacco Way of prayers and songs. From there forth he should be fine, I told them. He is to smoke along with doing sacred songs and prayers. I knew him before he had any problems, and I told his parents that I sensed a ceremony would have to be done on him eventually, but I guess the ceremony never happened. When they later came for a visit again they said, "Maybe if the ceremony had been done like you asked, then he would not have gotten in trouble," I could feel he was using some kind of substance that's not good for him, and I told him the ceremony was important for his health. After the Tobacco Way ceremony he was fine."

I then asked Suzie what sort of payment, if any, she received for her services. Lonnie explained that Suzie usually negotiated payment depending on a person's economic situation. She confirmed this, saying:

"In the past some hand tremblers were very expensive. Now most people charge according to what the patient can afford. That is usually around ten or twenty dollars. I myself don't do it much anymore. I feel like it's not up to snuff as I get older. But if a person comes to me desperate I will still do it."

---

[140] Locke, 31.

According to Suzie, the art of hand trembling can only be performed under certain guidelines. Some family members should avoid being treated because it can lead to a fracture in relationships:

"They use to say that you never perform ceremonial ritual on your spouse. If you do, you split from him (giggles). That's what people use to say long ago. I guess I could have done hand trembling on my husband anyway, and it probably would not have hurt us. I almost did one time when he was sick, but it was obvious what he had. He was wheezing and couldn't breathe. However I knew this was because he was working in the uranium mine at that time."

The diagnostic talent that Suzie inherited was not a choice that she might have made. The onset of her gift was a frightening experience and it took time for her to become accustomed to using it to aid others. Still, Suzie chose to embrace her gift, and she seemed proud to carry on the Dine' healing tradition in her family.

Traditional healing methods continue to be in demand among the Navajo. The art of Dine' medicine is customarily passed through families that have had generations of healers; however distant clan member may also be allowed access to this knowledge. Each individual within a family of practitioners has the choice as to whether or not he or she will pursue the craft. Suzie became a student of Navajo medicine almost by accident. She explained to me that she only happened to pick it up because she was present during her husband's tutelage. As Tully's grandfather provided instruction to his pupil, Suzie not only tended to household chores, but also absorbed the grandfather's information regarding certain ceremonies and songs. In this way Suzie indirectly learned Dine' medicine from Lightweight Man, her grand father-in-law, as he attempted to instruct her husband:

"Yeah, he was very knowledgeable, my husband's maternal grandfather. He was my paternal grandfather by clan. My late father was born for Many Goats Clan, so my husband's maternal grandfather was my paternal grandfather. He did all kinds of ceremonies; all of them, even Blessingway Ceremony. My son's late father was learning, but I was just observing and listening (giggles). I paid better attention than he did, and sometimes I corrected my husband, saying, 'No, the song is suppose to be this way' or, 'This is where you made your mistake.' (giggles), I use to tell him that if he were not careful I would become a better student than him."

Suzie and her family were concerned over the decrease numbers of medicine men and their apprentices. This decrease was not for lack of need. Medicine men are in great demand throughout the reservation, and are still sought out to conduct ceremonies. Lonnie even proclaimed that the art of Dine' medicine was experiencing a sort of revival. Emily was not as hopeful as her husband, however, and she pointed out that finding a Medicine Man in their area was becoming increasingly difficult. Suzie echoed this concern over the limited number of Navajo medicine practitioners. I wondered out loud if a school offering this type of instruction could be founded, much like the demonstration school in Rough Rock that had been developed by Ruth Roessel. Mrs. Roessel had been a key figure since the early 1970s in bringing back Navajo tradition through classes available to young people living in and around Rough Rock. Lonnie could not be certain such a program would be proper however, since

141

learning Navajo medicine seemed to rely so much on family connections and how that family was respected within the community. We both agreed that something should be done soon to promote this sort of education, or the Navajo nation risked losing an important part of its culture and belief system.

WHO'S YOUR DADDY: The importance of Navajo kinship
"No river can return to its source, yet all rivers must have a beginning." — Tribe Unknown.

When Suzie referred to her "husband's maternal grandfather...my paternal grandfather..." I became confused about the relationship between family members. How could one man be both paternal and maternal grandfather to a married couple? In view of the Navajo taboo prohibiting the marriage within of one's own clan, this situation seemed quite impossible. An explanation might be found in the way the Navajo refer to relatives, both by blood and through marriage. To non-natives the Navajo present a picture of the family in which everything is not necessarily as it seems. "Mothers," "Aunts" and "Grandparents" may not follow the same definitions of blood relation as they do in the Anglo world. Instead, a number of family members may fulfill the roles implied by these kin terms. A variety of relations may "adopt" a Navajo child who suffers the loss of a parent. This may also occur if a parent is somehow unable to take on the responsibility of his or her offspring. A Navajo may refer to an aunt, grandmother, or any female on the mother's side as "mother" depending on who participated in raising that Navajo as a child.

The kin terms can be interchangeable where the needs of a child are concerned. In this rather subtle way the Navajo prioritize the child's needs for security and comfort. Noted anthropologist Gladys Reichard learned how the Navajo concept of kinship might be confusing when she observed Anglo livestock agents counting the number of sheep that were owned by a family. The agents determined that the mother and father had gone beyond the limit of livestock each family was allowed. Meanwhile, the family attempted to explain how the children helping to herd the animals were separate families unto themselves. The mother called these children "aunt" and "uncle." Ms. Reichard explained:

"The Navajo kin-terms were a handicap that the range men could never overcome. To the Navajo the speech was clear, for they knew every person and every animal individually. But as the interpreter proceeded the stockman became more and more bewildered. 'What do you mean your aunt and uncle?' asked the white man. There is no way [for Anglos] to understand these relationships. They just simply don't make sense."[141]

I had been confused over the kinship terms used by the Yazzies before. During one interview Suzie referred to "our older sister." Since I knew that Suzie was

---

[141] Reichard, *Dezba*, 12.

the eldest daughter this came as a surprise. I later learned that Suzie was speaking of a cousin whom she considered a "sister" by virtue of her close association with the family. I now struggled to dissect Suzie's relationship to her husband's grandfather. The only thing I knew for certain was that the man was knowledgeable and highly respected. Suzie's "grandfather" must also have felt a close connection to Suzie. Otherwise why would he reveal sacred information involving Dine' healing rituals? The Yazzie matriarch patiently attempted to clarify the clan structure and how it worked. "Manygoats clan is like my paternal grandfather or mother," she explained, "My late paternal grandmother use to be married to a Manygoats clan, so my late father was a Manygoats clan member."

"There can be more than two clans," her son chimed in, "The First Clan is your mother's clan, the Second is your father's First Clan." My head was swimming as Lonnie continued, "the Third Clan is your maternal grandfather's First Clan, and your Fourth is your paternal grandfather's First." All I could essentially grasp from this information was that Suzie's husband was distantly related to her own clan. Members of Tully's Manygoats clan and those of Suzie's Bitterwater clan often mixed because they resided nearby each other on the reservation.

Furthermore, knowing one's relationship with certain clans may be beneficial when times are hard. Lonnie told me that a traveling Navajo can seek out assistance from another clan member regardless of whether or not they have previously met. Suzie relayed a story of just such an occasion involving her and a girlfriend. The two young girls were heading home from Goulding's' trading post:

"We had no horses, so we went looking for some. You have to hunt for the horses first. Back then we just let go of them go loose; they were not tied up. But they always went home because they were tamed. This time my paternal grandmother had loaned some of her horses to us. But we got a late start because we still had to go looking for these horses. We went to Goulding's and were there almost until sunset. We bought some stuff and left just as the sun set. It got dark on us at Mitchell Mesa, and we said, 'let's just sleep here since it's too dark to go further.' Back then there were no houses down here where we could rest; not even on top of the Valley. There were only horse trails then, and a wagon trail near the butte. There was no one around, so we spent the night there, out in a meadow. We tied the horses up at the ankles so they were there the next morning. Then we saddled them up and rode near a wash by Mitchell Butte."

Suzie went on to explain her adventure:

"It was morning and we had no breakfast. My friend was saying that she was hungry and that her paternal relatives lived somewhere close around there. 'Shall we go over there,' she said, 'and ask to drink some of their coffee?' I said okay because even though I didn't know these relatives I figured she knew them well enough to suggest this. When we got there the family were cooking, and they had been butchering too! It was fresh meat and it smelled good, (giggles), but when you are around people cooking you just wait. After all, people don't always give you food just like that. My friend was a paternal granddaughter though, and she greeting this family as such. A lady was sitting there who was blind. To our way of thinking this woman was my friend's paternal

143

grandmother. My friend called this woman *shi nali'*(grandmother). 'Where are you from?' the blind woman asked my friend. My girlfriend said that we were from the Valley, and that's when she mentioned that her father was Red Beard. The lady said, 'Oh, now I know who you are.' She also wanted to know about my clan. In a way, this blind woman was probably my grandmother too, clan-wise, because she was of the Bitterwater. The blind woman did some figuring in her head too, because when she learned who I was she turned to her relatives and said, 'I think this other one is my cousin!"

"Because they all realized we were kin they gave us some meat and we ate. It was great because they had just boiled the mutton. There were some ribs too, but those were taken away to the mother-in-law (giggles). Back then the husband was never permitted to see his mother-in-law. It was taboo, and it kept harmony in the family. The family treated us well, and they even served us liver cut up between us. They put out the food for us along with some soup and bread. While we ate we told them how we had slept over by the Mesa because it had gotten dark after our shopping trip. We said, 'It was a good thing we decided to come over to see if we could get a meal over here!' After we ate we said our thanks and got up to go. We got home close to sunset and our bellies were still pretty full."

Upon hearing this story, I thought that everybody in the Valley must be related in some way. But how on earth did they determine their clan association, and why did it maintain importance among the Navajo? Perhaps it was the very isolation they enjoyed that made it necessary to depend on their extended kin from time to time. Suzie and her friend would have been forced to travel home with rumbling stomachs had it not been for the unspoken rule of helping one's clan member. Although the ways of Navajo kinship terms and relationships continue to baffle me, I find the nuances fascinating and unique.

SWEATLODGE
"Walk lightly in the spring; Mother Earth is pregnant." – Kiowa

In my conversations with the Yazzie family I discovered there were many different ways to treat an ailment using traditional medicine. Suzie spoke to me of personal rituals, such as sweat lodges, and how they were beneficial to the Navajo:

"When you have a cough or an ailment, you start the fire for the sweat lodge. When I was younger I got so sick my late father and other male relatives made one for me. They went in first, and after they finished my father told me to go it. Men and women never share a sweat lodge, so that's why I had to wait. When I was in there just the top shirt was off of me, and back then you had to drink an herb that makes you vomit in the sweat lodge. I did this, and then I inhaled the good air in the lodge because you are supposed to breathe deeply. You get to a point where you can breathe pretty good, and you get real sweaty. After you feel better you go out. Some people roll in the dirt for particular ceremonies, but I didn't when I was sick.[142] When you step out you drink more herbs and then rub some on your body. After this you may go in again. We did this whenever a cough wouldn't go away, and it always worked to make us feel right again."

I joked with Suzie that I should participate in a sweat lodge in order to relieve the aching all over from sitting cross-legged in the hogan. This led to a conversation regarding my own health. As a diagnostician Suzie was interested in the way my hands often appeared to be cold even under warm and pleasant conditions. I explained to her that since I was a teenager I had suffered from, Reynaud's Syndrome, a hereditary condition in which symptoms are brought on whenever I contracted even the slightest chill. For reasons unknown the chill restricts circulation in my fingers and toes, causing them to become white and numb. Suzie agreed that the sweat lodge would be helpful for this sort of ailment:

"It would help your hands. You just put rocks in the fire and when it gets heated up use a shovel to move the rocks into a corner of the lodge. The lodge looks just like a Fork-stick hogan and is wide at the bottom part that is buried. At the doorway you just lay a log to keep in the heat, and there's no fireplace hole. The lodge is built to be small, with a doorway that is real skinny. It is there where you crawl in. Even though it looks small, people can fit in there pretty good. About five or six people could be seated inside. I think this would work for your cold fingers and toes."

I hoped Suzie was serious about this endeavor. Not only would I benefit from such a cure, but the experience of engaging in a sweat lodge ceremony would be fascinating. I wanted to ask Suzie to perform a hand trembling on me as well, but felt this might be stepping over the line as an Anglo. If she that felt she must deny me the "treatment" of this ceremony because I was not Navajo it might put up an awkward barrier between us. There was no way I was going to jeopardize the relationship I'd so carefully built with Suzie. To this day I wonder what it would be like to witness this procedure, and Effie recently informed me that her mother rarely engages in hand trembling anymore. I try very hard not to feel regret over possibly missing the opportunity to actually take part in something so unique and spiritual.

At the time of our discussion it seemed important that I respect the limitations of my interaction with the Yazzies in sacred matters. I had access through the university library to volumes of material concerning Navajo rituals and healing ceremonies. Clearly there must have been some Natives in the past who were willing to pass on to anthropologists certain information that may be considered sacred to the Navajo. Perhaps the Dine' interviewed during this heyday of anthropological work in the Southwest (1920s to the 1970s) had not realized the information would be printed and distributed among non-Navajos. I was told by my friend, Ron Maldonado, that the restrictions under which I interviewed the Yazzies are the result of that work. Ron was my contact at the Navajo Nation's Historic Preservation Department in Window Rock, and he explained that once the Navajo realized their intellectual property was at stake

---

[142] Rolling in the sand outside a sweat lodge is one way in which the Dine' maintain contact with the earth and pay their respect to the spirits representing their homeland.

145

more care was taken to protect sacred material. It was disturbing to know that the legacy of past anthropological work had produced such a backlash. Because of this I felt I must respect the wishes of the Navajo people and do my best not to expose or exploit any sensitive piece of information. Like her ancestors, Suzie was exercising her choice of whether or not to reveal a ritual. Knowing this did not diminish the disappointment I felt when my hints for a demonstration of Navajo medicine were politely ignored.

I quickly moved on to more questions and asked whether Suzie had done a sweat lodge lately. "No," she laughed, "I probably wouldn't do one now, but I like remembering how it was done." I wondered if men and women still engaged in the ceremony, and Effie answered that it was unusual for women to perform the sweat lodge ritual at all. "I never did it," she stated, "my brothers usually do, and some cousins that are younger too." Through this statement I assumed that the sweat lodge ceremony was still maintained as a healing ritual among at least some of the Navajo.

Once again personal choice came into play regarding today's ceremonies and rituals. I had read that young Navajo men participated in a kind of puberty ceremony that involved the sweat lodge.[143] However Lonnie missed the opportunity to take part in this ceremony as a young man. "I never went in on my own when I was young because I was in school then," he explained. Although both Lonnie and Effie were not always able to practice their traditions in their younger years, they did take these ceremonies very seriously. And while a number of religious beliefs co-exist within the Yazzie family, traditional Navajo religion remains a particularly powerful and effective force in the lives of Suzie's adult children.

SKINWALKER: Navajo religion and the supernatural
"Every animal knows more than you do." – Nez Perce

For a number of Navajo, the traditional Dine' belief system includes not only a reverence for forces in nature that promote harmony, but also the recognition of negative forces that threaten to disrupt family and home. I first learned about "Skinwalkers" through Suzie's granddaughter, Elvina. Most of the Navajo I spoke with later preferred not to speak about these witch-like entities at all. I began to feel as if the only information I would obtain about the creatures would have to come from my library books. According to Navajo spiritual practitioner Joanne Teller[144], a *skinwalker* may be defined as:

---

[143] Kluckhon & Leighton, *Children*, 77-78

[144] Ron Maldonado later directed me toward Clyde Kluckhorn's "Navajo Witch Craft" as a more reliable source on this subject. He felt that Teller's work was geared more toward tourists that play up the skinwalker as a cartoon type character.

"...a person who comes out at night wearing an animal skin. When wearing the skin the person is able, through present spiritual ability and power, to mimic the abilities of the former owner of the skin. For example: a dog skin could give a mimic pattern of high running speed, a keen sense of smell, and acute hearing."[145]

According to the author, a skinwalker might inflict injury upon an enemy by using the power of the creature whose senses and skills it possesses. Only Yvonne would later clarify to me how some Navajo fear this power. It appeared to me that some Navajo were undecided about whether or not skinwalkers really existed, and it would have been simplistic to state that belief in the Navajo religion is automatically associated with a belief in skinwalkers. Not all Navajos believe in this phenomenon, and the subject of witchcraft is complicated by the tendency of some Navajo to speak ambiguously of it to a non-native. Lonnie explained to me that some Navajo who actually believe in skinwalkers may claim otherwise as a way of diminishing the creature's power over them. Teller did extensive study on witchcraft among her people, and in her work she treated skinwalking as a credible facet of her religion beyond the understanding of those who are not of Dine' culture. Her research provided a thoughtful explanation as to why some Navajo deny the existence of skinwalkers, or choose to avoid the subject entirely:

"The rule, reality is a majority belief function, holds true in this instance. If one were to visit the Navajo Reservation and ask a number of Navajo residents about skinwalker and witchcraft, a great many of them would give some type of acknowledgment of the subjects, if even with only a concerned denial or a no comment. The basis for the acknowledgments or lack of, lie in the fact that many Navajo have had indirect or direct experiences from the victim's position concerning skinwalker and witchcraft. Plus there are many other Navajo who possess the ability to see and be in the level that skinwalker and witchcraft exists... A majority of Navajos know of the existence of skinwalker and witchcraft; therefore, it is a reality to us."[146]

A Navajo interviewed in the mid-1950s explained that witches practicing on the reservation are very different from skinwalkers. His comments shed light on how a witch might do harm in a way that is different from the techniques used by skinwalkers:

"Witches cause sickness by all of these things: manos, metates, brushes, yucca, and the others. A witch might take a piece of an arrow feather, dirt from a feather...or similar things owned by a person, and bury it near ghosts or in a burial ground. If anything personal is taken from you, a witch can make you sick...Witches are people on the left side while most of the gods and people are on the right side by doing good and helping people."[147]

---

[145] Teller, Joanne & Norman Blackwater. The Navajo Skinwalker, Witchcraft, and Related Phenomena. Chinle: Infinity Horn Publishing, 1997, 17.

[146] Teller, Navajo Skinwalker, 19-20.

[147] Newcomb, Franc Johnson, Stanley Fishler & Mary C. Wheelwright. A Study of Navajo Symbolism. Cambridge: Harvard Museum Publishers, 1956, 60-A.

It was my discussion with Elvina that helped me to understand how witches and skinwalkers were a reality to some Navajo[148]. She gave little detail as to how this general consensus came about, and I didn't wish to press her for more information than she was prepared to give. She simply stated that specific people in Navajo society were feared because of their skills as a skinwalker. Elvina did not imply that these people were disliked exactly. But they were given a respectful distance "just in case." What became evident during our conversation was that the belief in skinwalkers, or any spiritual power related to the Dine' religion, was as genuine as the belief that many Anglos have concerning powerful supernatural entities within their own culture. Because I was speaking to someone I considered a friend, and because of her commitment to the belief system to which she had been exposed from an early age, I did not find it particularly difficult to accept what she was saying.

I tried hard to view this information as anything but superstitious, and I did not wish to regard her views as "exotic." I wanted to converse with her on the subject of witchcraft as one person to another, thus I had to relinquish the awe that one may have investigating a culture foreign to their own. Who was I to deny the existence of skinwalkers merely on the grounds that I had not seen one personally? After all, I'd had my own experiences involving "spiritual beings" that I kept to myself over the years.

Teller approached the conflict between Navajo and Anglo belief systems in her study as well:

"A denial by the dominant society surrounding the Navajo reservation, of the skinwalker and witchcraft does not make the subjects unreal. A denial just emphasizes society's spiritual blindspot in regards to the actual application of spiritual power and ability in everyday life. This deficiency is the reason no literature exists detailing the true workings of the subjects. Any writings would, in most likelihood, be produced by members of the dominant scientific community who rely on facts they observe in the physical world. I am not belittling scientific study; but in its present form, scientific methodology cannot qualify these subjects as they are not readily visible in the physical arena that present scientific understanding encompasses. In the outside dominant society the opinions of their scientific world are largely acknowledged as valid. Once again we come to the rule, reality is a majority function, and the outside dominant society has tremendous belief that seeing and feeling, (at their perception level), is believing. And if one cannot see it or feel it, then it does not exist. Skinwalker and witchcraft can be seen and felt, but only on the spiritual plane for that is where they originate."[149]

---

[148] Mr. Maldonado confirmed the very real problems the belief in skinwalkers present on the reservation. Some twenty years before my interview with Elvina two Navajo police officers were burned alive in their patrol vehicle. Ron explained that, in order to become a "witch", one must kill a relative. There was a trial currently underway in the court of the Pueblo of Zuni involving the murder of a man thought to be a witch.

[149] Teller, 20-21.

There was no way I could give myself up completely to the otherworldly aspects of Navajo beliefs. My own perceptions of Western religion had been engrained from a very early age. Ideas of Heaven and Hell, Christ and God, and even faith and science, would always hinder my ability to entertain the thought of embracing the Dine' belief system as my own. Instead I attempted to temporarily put aside my own religious concepts and listen with an open mind to the Yazzies speak of their faith.

I asked only a handful of the Yazzie family about their religious beliefs. I would never have the opportunity to speak with every family member, and the Navajo I met did not seem keen on openly discussing the subject of religion with outsiders. It seemed to me that they viewed the topic of religion highly personal and private. To be sure, members of the Yazzie family do have their separate beliefs from one another. Religion among the family is diverse, with some choosing Christianity, others practicing the Native American Peyote religion, and still others maintaining traditional Dine' religious practices that incorporate medicine men and corn pollen. A number of family members practice a mixture of two religions, calling, for example, upon elements of Christianity and Navajo ceremonies depending on need. I have determined that Suzie and most of her children are all content to practice their own particular brand of the Navajo religion. By this I mean that some of the Yazzies have maintained the more positive traditional beliefs, and disregarded a number of the negative concepts. Lonnie and his wife, for example, believe skinwalkers and others who practice witchcraft exercise power only over those who allow the magic to touch them. They personally choose to concentrate on those ceremonies and prayers that promote harmony and protection.

While this may appear to be an ambiguous stance to some Whites, Lonnie described to me how his beliefs kept him "in the right mind." He explained that his phrase referred to those Navajo people who have life figured out in a way that is peaceful and compatible with their culture. Suzie expressed the same feelings, and I felt that this was another example of how we must see the Navajo as individual agents as well as people operating within the parameters of common cultural beliefs. So, while some Navajo may fear witches, skinwalkers and bad omens, not all Navajo let these beliefs actually affect them.

When asked about her beliefs regarding the supernatural powers of skinwalkers Suzie claimed to have had no personal experience with any Navajo who embodied these powers, and she felt no fear of witches and skinwalkers:

"I don't know any skinwalkers. I don't believe in it. People talk about them still, but I don't care to listen to these stories. Up to this point I have never seen one; not with my own eyes. People have been with me and claimed a skinwalker has come and gone, but when I looked there were none. So, for me, there is no reason to believe in it."

These comments may indirectly validate Teller's statement that some believe in skinwalkers because of their own experience with these entities and witchcraft. It may also indicate, as Teller suggests, that Suzie simply avoided any negative effects of these creatures by denying any personal knowledge of them. Either way, Suzie has admitted to dealing with other supernatural aspects of her religion, such as the hand trembling she performs. However, she tends to regard phenomena like hand trembling not as supernatural, but rather as a natural ability that one may either nurture or ignore. Suzie's decision to pick and chose components from the Dine' belief system further illustrates how the Navajo operate within very flexible cultural boundaries. Suzie chose to maintain her own personal version of Navajo culture by selecting the more positive elements it offered.

SUZIE AND THE PLAIN'S INDIAN RELIGION

"We who are clay blended by the Master Potter, come from the kiln of Creation in many hues. How can people say one skin is colored, when each has its own coloration? What should it matter that one bowl is dark and the other pale, if each is of good design and serve its purpose well?" – Pokingaysi Qoyawayma, Hopi

I did manage to ask Suzie about her exposure to belief systems other than her own. She told me that a number of family members were part of the Native American Church. I later unearthed a study from the early 1950's on the Peyote religion practiced among the Navajo, and it revealed the differences between Navajo religion and the Native American Church. Partaking of the peyote plant was believed to be essential in understanding this Native American faith:

"Peyote songs are in languages unfamiliar to the Navaho or contain only meaningless vocables. Peyotists say that if you listen to the songs while you are taking peyote, you will find out what they mean. They always say that peyote "teaches you," and that a person cannot discover the meaning of the cult from instruction but only from experience…The peyote experience is one of an external and internal world of personal significance. And it is this which makes peyote religiously important."[150]

Suzie described to me her one and only participation in a ceremony practiced by church members involving the use of the peyote plant:

"When my husband died a family member wanted to have a funeral ceremony with the Native American Church. He was a member of this church, and they were having a peyote meeting after him. I really didn't want to, but we were told to go in. They were giving people peyote rolled up in a ball. I really didn't want it (giggles), but I went ahead and tried. It didn't taste too good, bitter tasting, and it didn't have much effect on me. I guess this was because I didn't eat very much, just a little piece of what they were giving out. These guys roll it up into a ball about the size of your fingernail. They actually gave a few of these balls to me, but I only put one in my mouth and the others I threw away (giggles)."

Suzie's daughter-in-law also attended a peyote ceremony at one time. Emily confirmed that the peyote was bitter and she recalled members making it "like corn mush." Just as Suzie had done, Emily ingested only a small amount of the

---

[150] Aberle, David Friend. The Peyote Religion among the Navajo. New York: Wenner-Gren Foundation for Anthropological Research, 1966, 7.

hallucinogen, and then quietly discarded the remaining portion. "You did what I did," she giggled to her mother-in-law, "I guess both of us were uninterested in knowing about that religion. I think we like our religion better."

The expression on my face must have indicated that I was unsure of why the ladies would hesitate in participating fully in the peyote ceremony. Emily attempted to explain that Suzie disliked taking any substance that alters her capacity to think clearly, and she felt the same way. In an effort to appease her family's wish to give her husband a Native American burial, Suzie agreed to attend this ceremony. By discreetly limiting her participation in the ceremony Suzie was able to maintain her own traditional beliefs while honoring her husband's religion.

I initially presumed that Suzie attended the peyote ceremony because she wished to participate in her husband's funeral. I later recalled, however, that Suzie once stated she preferred not to attend funerals because they "held little meaning" for her. Death, according to Suzie, was simply part of the cycle of life, and just as natural as birth, childhood, marriage or illness. When I asked her what she thought about birth and death, Suzie's answer was "This is part of life, the life cycle. It has always been like that. It seems okay to me and not something to be afraid of." Lonnie explained to me that this Navajo way of dealing with emotional situations helped his family many times over the years.

Emily told me that she learned long ago that Lonnie's family tended to mourn only briefly when loved ones passed on, or when tragedy stuck. They considered this loss as part of life's plan that would ultimately make a person stronger. I had to remember, however, that Emily came from a family that was more expressive about things such as death. She believed this was because they had been exposed to the outside world, including the Anglo custom of expressing sadness through crying when loved ones passed away. I thought it interesting how two families living on the rez could approach death differently; one in the manner of an Anglo like me, and one in the "Navajo way."

Lonnie cautioned me against seeing Suzie's practical view of life as coldness on her part. While eliciting a more overt emotional reaction to the death of a loved one might seem "normal" to others, Suzie's lack of emotion did not mean she wasn't moved by these events. Lonnie assured me this was not the case. Instead, Lonnie saw his mother's storytelling as a way for her to work through how she felt about the past. Clearly Suzie had been enriched or affected by the same things that we all confront in life. As she voluntarily told and retold many of these stories involving different experiences I could see her putting into place the landmarks of her life. She was proud of her link to Four-Horned Woman. She experienced profound loss with the death of her mother, and she loved her father in spite of his flaws as a parent. She was enormously proud of her children and grandchildren, and she spoke of her husband with a twinkle in her eye as well as a certain longing.

All the while Suzie displayed her own style of emoting how she felt about things. I came to recognize and appreciate her subtle nature. As tempting as it was to associate Suzie's manner with the tired stereotype of the "stoic" Indian, I learned that Suzie's way of dealing with life was a trademark of her own personality and not of the

Navajo per se. Like any of us, Suzie was influenced by her parents and her culture, but she also made choices throughout her life that allowed me to see her as an individual. Through these choices Suzie represented to me both a traditional Navajo and a woman of the twentieth century who is adapting to meet changing times.

The sun was not quite setting, but I felt my day with the Yazzies was done. The morning's adventure of searching for family members and an afternoon chock-full of spiritual information had worn me out. My head was spinning from all I had learned, and I wanted time to decipher, digest and organize what I'd been told about Navajo religion and its place in Suzie's life. As usual, Emily picked up on my feelings. "You look a little tired," she giggled. Yeah," I sighed, "I guess it's time to call it a day." Emily helped me gather my things, saying "Don't be overwhelmed, *Shay kiss*, not everybody gets to hear this stuff all at once. It affects you, but you're tough. Just go home and let things sink in." As I drove back to the lodge I wondered what "Shah kiss" meant, and if Emily was talking about Goulding's as my "home."

Photos

Suzie Yazzie and me in front
of the family hogan.

Suzie and daughter Effie in
front of the home Tully built.

153

Beautiful Monument Valley, Suzie Yazzie's "back yard".

Effie and daughter Earlene serving up mutton stew outside the Shade House.

Emily Yazzie teaching me how to make fry bread. All of my attempts ended up on the Shade House floor.

Lonnie, Suzie, Effie and me holding a Yei blanket woven by the Yazzie women.

Yvonne and
Earlene in front of
the old Shade
House. During one
of my first visits!

Lonnie Yazzie,
Suzie's son and
my guide,
standing by
some ruins in
Monument
Valley

Taking a Break
Susie Yazzie takes a break from weaving, closing her
eyes to feel the enjoyment of the warm noon sun.
Photo by Aiyana Studio of Photography - Bruce Rosco
Aiyanastudio@gmail.com

CHAPTER 8 – WORK IN THE VALLEY, BLESSING AND CURSE

"There is nothing as eloquent as a rattlesnake's tail." Navajo

HOLLYWOOD COMES CALLING

The next morning I awoke with my heart full of purpose. Lonnie had called me at Hill House the night before to warn me that he and Emily would be delayed in Chinle, so I planned to meet Effie at Suzie's as I had the day before. I quickly swallowed a bowl of cereal and pulled a sweater on to accompany my boots and khaki pants. Throwing my backpack in the back of my jeep I took off for the park under a promising clear sky. I arrived at the Yazzie's little valley in record time, and I reviewed the day's questions in my head as I rounded the bend to Suzie's home.

I saw, much to my dismay, a collection of RVs, vans and catering trucks hugging the rocks that surrounded Suzie's compound. A fleet of expensive sport cars were lined alongside the hogan and people with filming gear were everywhere. Lonnie told me that his mother often allowed people in the movie and advertising industry to use her land as a backdrop for their projects, but nobody in the Yazzie family had given me a head's up on this latest venture. Apparently, Suzie had given permission for a well-known car company to film their latest collection on her property. I sensed that it would be hours before I had Suzie to myself, and the commotion made by film crews, cars and helicopters buzzing overhead would be a constant distraction. I drove to the far side of Suzie's house where things were relatively quiet, parked my car, and contemplated how I would spend the remainder of the morning.

As I sat brewing and stewing over how unfair it all was, who should appear but Emily! I had looked up the name she called me yesterday, and learned that it meant "sister" in Navajo. How good it was to see my "sha kiss," but what on earth was she doing here? Hadn't she and Lonnie planned to spend the morning in Chinle? As usual, nothing went exactly as planned in the Valley, and Emily slid into the car seat next to me, giggling over my confused look. "Hey Sis," she chuckled, obviously pleased that she had surprised me, "bet ya' didn't expect to see me here!" I didn't know what to ask her first. Had Lonnie decided to drive back to Chinle himself? Had they known the film crew would be here, interrupting our work? If so, why hadn't they told me last night?

Emily anticipated one of my questions and launched into an explanation. "Suzie forgot to tell anybody until this morning that she'd signed a contract with these car people. She does that all the time. They get somebody besides family to translate for them, and she signs away her rights for next to nothing. She only got twenty dollars! We keep telling her not to sign anything unless we're around, but twenty dollars is a lot to her…so she just jumps on it."[151] I asked Emily if Lonnie had gone alone to Chinle. "Yeah," she confirmed, "but he'll be back later to help out with things. I think these people want to film him riding Beano."

Beano was Lonnie's horse; a rather wild pony who Lonnie could always bring to a cantor just by tickling his hind end. Beano was typical of the horses I'd seen on the Rez.' He was small, sturdy and a far cry from our pampered equines back home. I couldn't imagine how the film people thought they would work Lonnie and his horse into a shot with one of their zippy automobiles, and it bothered me that they'd low-balled Suzie, providing only minimum compensation for some spectacular scenery and completely upsetting the family routine in the process. I had to ask myself if I was only angry with these "industry" people because they had intruded on my time with the Yazzies.

One thing was certain; I was becoming more and more protective of my second family, and I couldn't deny how much it irritated me that strangers could take advantage of the matriarch. Clearly Suzie was vulnerable due to both her age and her inability to converse in English. "How long do you think they'll be working here?" I asked, dreading the inevitable answer.

"Oh I don't know," Emily shrugged, "I tried talking to the guy in charge. He's this big, white German and he seems like he's always in a hurry. Anyway, I guess you're stuck with me for a little while." I could think of worse ways to spend the morning, so I packed up my things and followed Emily into the house.

I needn't have worried about wasted time. Emily and I had only just sat down with our coffee when Suzie unexpectedly shuffled in, wearing her usual broad smile and

---

[151] Mr. Maldonado informed me that, as of 1960, all filming and non-native use of Monument Valley Tribal Park is regulated by the Navajo Nation Film Commission and Navajo Parks and Recreation. The producers do not deal with the families directly, and any fees are paid by the tribe to the family. In this instance, a few dollars may exchange hands as a good neighbor policy.

taking her place on the bed. Emily asked her something in Navajo and Suzie answered back "Ahoe," then plucked at her long skirt as if nothing out of the ordinary were occurring just outside her window. "I asked if they were all done filming her," Emily explained, "and she said they were. I actually think she's a little disappointed because she likes being where the action is."

"Well," I sighed as I got up and began fastening the microphone on Suzie's blouse, "let's see if we can liven things up here for her."

Since we were on the subject of visitors filming the Valley and its people, I opened with a question about when Suzie first began to work with the motion picture industry. The Navajo held the rather dubious honor of becoming one of the first tribes inaccurately depicted on celluloid. Trading posts that brought the Dine' into commercial contact with Anglos also attracted tourists from the fledgling Hollywood movie industry and ushered in a new phase of White and Navajo contact. The popular Western movies produced in this region reinforced stereotypical images of Native Americans initially brought about through dime store novels and Anglo-centric history.

When the dream-makers of Hollywood visited Monument Valley, Navajos like the Yazzies envisioned not stardom, but employment opportunities close to home. Director John Ford used many local Navajo as extras in the post-war Western films he made popular by the 1950s. Harry Goulding's biography gave detail of the trader's plan to convince Ford that the Valley was the perfect location for his films:

"This news came in over the radio that Hollywood was looking for a place away out somewhere, a good spot to make this Indian picture. United Artists it was. I had a friend out in California, that was associated with Hollywood, and he wrote me in his letter that they were looking for a location to film a western. Mike and I figured, "By golly, we're going to head for Hollywood and see if we can't do something about that picture."[152]

Goulding felt he could convince the people at United Artists to film in the Valley, "because we've got a lot of beautiful country and a lot of Indians to go with it."[153] Eagerly showing snapshots of the Valley to a location manager, he proclaimed, "We got Indians, just all kinds of Indians out there." United Artist's location manager initially balked at the idea of filming in the remote valley. Goulding persisted however, and convinced the film company that the Navajo were hard working and excited to begin. He raved about the perfect conditions Monument Valley offered, telling the movie executives:

"If you're looking for a place to make an Indian picture...And those Navajos, I know them all. They never went through the dole that we shoved out and ruined the rest of the Indians and got them lazy and worthless. The Navajos never took hold of that, so they're still alive."[154]

Like many Anglos of his time, John Ford chose to ignore the characteristics that made each Indian tribe distinct in his film-making ventures. A product of

---

[152] Moon, 144.
[153] Moon, 145.
[154] Ibid.

160

misinformation fed to the public about Indian culture, he presented a flat interpretation of Native American life. In *Hollywood's Indians*, author Ken Nolley pointed out that Ford tended to paint the Native Americans in a one-dimensional manner. While acknowledging Ford's well-meaning gesture in having his "Cheyenne" characters play an important role in his film "Cheyenne Autumn," Nolley also stated that, "because his actors were mainly Navajo, however, the language was not authentic."[155] "In this sense," Nolley further lamented, "Ford's films function as if they were historical texts, constructing a sense of American life on the frontier…and helping to construct much of what still stands for popular historical knowledge of American life."[156]

In addition to creating an image of the Hollywood Indian that was far from the truth, moviemakers disrupted Navajo life simply by maintaining a presence in the Valley. Trader Gladwell Richardson wrote of a film crew working near Monument Valley as early as 1925 who were "drunk all the time." Trader Gladwell Richardson wrote, "Even their technicians stayed looped on some of Flagstaff's finest bootleg." He claimed that accidents occurred with explosives because of the irresponsible atmosphere. [157] Negative elements of urban Anglo culture introduced into the area were ultimately detrimental to the Dine' community. For Suzie however, working with Ford and his team was an interesting, enjoyable and lucrative experience.

Members of the Yazzie family worked as extras in the films "Cheyenne Autumn," "The Searchers," "She Wore a Yellow Ribbon," and later in the 1970s the film "Legend of Billy Jack." Suzie claimed to have had very little contact with the major stars of each film. However, she remembered very well the experience of depicting the stereotypical Indian that lived in the imagination of the white, movie-going public. Suzie described how the Navajo were treated while filming took place:

"Not all Navajo got to be in the film, just some which lived around here. Sometimes it was just our family that was picked. People would gather at Goulding's asking to work in the film, but we were at Sand Springs with my daughter when Tall Sheep Man (Harry Goulding) and the movie director were there and they told us about the movie. We were on horseback when the director people met us, and they hired us right there, even the horse! They took pictures of us and then asked us whether we wanted to be part of it. We said yes, and we were told to go here and there to fill out some papers. Then we began to work. The film bosses treated us pretty fairly. We ate over there with them where they put up a big tent for us all to sleep in. This tent is even shown in the movie. My daughter was small at the time, but she worked with me. Some people kept trying to be involved with the movie because it was good money. They even asked us about getting them work too, but they were told by the movie people, 'This family are the only ones we need right now, but maybe we'll be able to use more of you in another part.' And later on some more people did get work."

[155] Rollins, Peter C. and John E. O'Conner, eds. <u>Hollywood's Indian</u>. Lexington: The University Press of Kentucky, 1998, 79.

[156] Rollins, *Hollywood's Indians*, 77.

[157] Richardson, *Navajo Trader*, 139.

I wondered whether the privilege that the Yazzies enjoyed as the most frequently employed extras caused dissention among their neighbors. There may have been feelings of jealousy within the community, however I never asked about this. For some reason I cannot explain, I just considered it bad manners to bring the question up. Anyway, Suzie never implied that her family's involvement with the film makers caused any ill will. I did learn that the additional income earned by the lucky few employed by film companies came as a relief during those years of hardship. The Navajo were thankful to benefit from the movie industry as the film makers returned again and again to create the popular Westerns.

The tape in my recorder clicked off, a signal for me to replace it with a blank one. I had learned to do this as quickly as possible so as not to miss any of the conversation between Suzie and whoever might be interpreting at the moment. I had been engrossed in Suzie's story however, and fumbled around for a fresh tape while Emily stood to stretch her legs. Gazing out the cracked window over Suzie's bed she turned and looked around the tiny room; smiling the closed-lip grin I now associated with her own brand of mischief. "What 'er we all doin' in here," she chastised us, "when they're out there serving up the food?!"

WHITE NAVAJO

"All birds, even those of the same species, are not alike, and it is the same with animals and with human beings. The reason WakanTanka does not make two birds, or animals, or human beings exactly alike is because each is placed here by WakanTanka to be an independent individuality and to rely upon itself." – Shooter Teton Sioux

Free food on the reservation was the equivalent of manna from heaven, and nobody missed an opportunity to enjoy the abundance and variety of the city folk's smorgasbord. I could not have posed another question to Emily and Suzie if my life depended on it. It was chow time! As far as the Yazzies were concerned, the current melee of visitors was especially tolerable if we were invited to sample the delicacies offered by the catering crew; the only trick being to extract an invitation. I had seen the Yazzies manage this before. The polite standing off to one side, the patient stance accompanied with a muted expression of expectation...all of this was done with diplomatic flair that I considered an art form. Unlike my children's playmates who heavy-handedly hinted at wishing to join us for a meal of my famous spaghetti, the Yazzies had a way of leading visitors to believe the invitation was entirely their own altruistic idea.

I collected my things with the idea that I would eat my own sack lunch in my rental car. Suzie began to follow her daughter-in-law out the door when Emily stopped and turned to look at me with a puzzled expression. "Aren't you coming?" she asked, as if my participation in the ceremony-of-the free lunch was a foregone conclusion.

"Oh, no, no Em," I stammered, "you guys go ahead. I don't think it would be right..."

But Emily cut me off with a tug at my sleeve. "It's okay," she assured me without the slightest hint in her voice that she was kidding me, "we'll just let them know you're

162

family." How Emily would convince the savvy film crew that I was part of the Yazzie clan was beyond my comprehension. She seemed assured of herself however, and so I allowed myself to be led toward the big catering tent flapping in the strong valley breeze.

We made our way to the back of the tent, and stood in the desert heat; one line of womanhood facing the crowd of Anglos just getting seated with trays holding mounds of food rarely seen on the reservation. This in itself was a strange experience for me, and one that somewhat illuminated what it might be like to exist as a Navajo dependent on "visitors." Emily whispered to me that an agreement was always made with film companies that, along with using their home as a backdrop to their work, the Yazzies should be offered lunch in the bargain. Still, I was surprised to learn that a certain amount of decorum was expected in this process. I do not know if these expectations came from Suzie or the film companies.

I stood there trying to recall if our horseback riding outfit had followed the same routine whenever meals were served in the Valley. I remembered that, as paying guests, we always served ourselves first, with the wranglers and finally Don and Shelly Donnelly taking up the end of the chow line. Now I could muster up the memory of Yazzie family members standing by somewhere out of the way beneath the mess tent, just as I was now. Back then it had been a little unnerving to see Suzie and two or three of her family waiting for us to sit down with full plates. I wondered then why they did not simply fall into line with the rest of us. There certainly was no shortage of food, and a few of the Yazzies were employed in cooking and serving the food up anyway. I just assumed this strange ritual was directed by the Donnelly outfit. Suzie was eventually escorted by a family member to the long tables of steaming chafing dishes. Then, smiling placidly, she would allow herself to be served any food she could eat without too much chewing, (at the age of eighty-two and no dental care she had lost a good amount of teeth). Suzie would then be given a seat of honor and begin to eat, saying little to those around her unless the conversation could be interpreted.

Now I stood with Suzie and her daughter-in-law, waiting for the expected invitation to share in the lavish lunch. It was at that very moment that I finally felt part of the Yazzie's world, even if it was just for the duration of lunch; And so we stood there, we two; me in my blue jeans and neutral colored T-shirt, and my Indian friend Emily, outfitted in her luscious red velveteen blouse and huge pieces of turquoise dangling from her ears. Suzie stood only slightly apart from us, a silent but irrefutable force. Observing my fellow Anglos with an expression that I hoped reflected a serene detachment, I suffered the curious looks of those already digging into their salads and hero sandwiches. The camera guy, the big shot boss, and the pretty script lady were resplendent in their tank tops, sunglasses and ball caps. They all cast glances our way, averting their gaze whenever our eyes met.

I could understand their interest in my Navajo sisters. In shiny, ruby red velveteen blouses, the ladies must have appeared both exotic and authentically Navajo. The large pieces of silver and turquoise jewelry rested naturally on their skin. But how could the film crew interpret my presence, a White woman standing next to these Native ladies in my khaki shorts and hiking boots? Under their scrutiny I only wished to retreat back into the safety of Suzie's house. But Emily gave me a look that indicated I was to stand my ground, and eventually I was to enjoy the meal alongside them. So there I trembled and twitched, waiting for the last crewmember in line to receive lunch. It was incredibly awkward, but I continued to follow my friends' lead and look idly around without directly meeting anyone's eyes.

Suzie and Emily appeared entirely comfortable with the procedure, and so I pretended the same. Meanwhile I was squirming inside. I shifted my weight from one foot to the other and felt as if I were holding my breath. Finally Emily turned to me and smiled. "Settle down," she giggled, "how hungry are you anyways?" More agonizing minutes passed, until a man that I suspect had some authority walked up to us and shook each of our hands. Without thinking I returned the man's strong grip with my weak one. Barely clasping his palm and keeping my fingers down, I gave him the same greeting as my Navajo friends. Before I could begin to explain that I was an imposter, and as such I really had no right to accept any food from his company, Emily stepped in. "This is Coco," she proclaimed in her lovely matter-of-fact manner, "She's family."

I nearly fainted. Even if she had been kidding around, I was elated to be introduced in such a way. It was hard not to burst out laughing as the man tried to hide the confused expression washing over his face. Blurting out a feeble invitation to join him at lunch he directed us to the tables laden with food. Without missing a beat Emily followed the man with Suzie and me following close behind. We queued up and the ladies filled their plates liberally, while I struggled to regain my appetite. Emily declined the man's offer to join his group at the middle table, opting instead to sit at an empty table in the back, away from the film crew now engrossed with their own meals and important conversations. I picked at my food and continued to feel out of place. Who was I in this surreal scene? What did I hope to accomplish by ingratiating myself into a family that needed so much more than the meager skills I provided to them as historian and biographer. As my thoughts tumbled over each other Emily turned to me with a knowing grin. "Now you see," she softly giggled, "now are you the White Navajo."

A feeling of pride swelled inside my chest. I remembered the day I'd asked Suzie for a Navajo name. The Yazzies had always referred to me by my nickname of "Coco," but Suzie frequently forgot who Coco was, and I had to reintroduce myself to her with every visit. Since Suzie had a name that described her appearance I suggested that a similar name might help her to remember me. After Effie translated this information Suzie looked at me in her usual shy manner. Glancing from under her lashes she gave a long "hmmmm," and her daughter translated back her response. "She wants a Navajo name? It should probably be "White Woman." I was devastated. After spending so much time with Suzie and her family I found it disappointing to be labeled with such a generic term. With fair hair and skin I certainly would never look like a Navajo, but I suppose I was hoping for something a little more Dine' friendly! "No," I protested to both Effie and her mother, "please don't call me that. There're already a lot of white women around here. You won't know which one I am! Suzie giggled while Effie looked at me in pity. "We'll think of something," she assured me. Now I was "White

Navajo," but this would not turn out to be my final "real" Navajo name.

DINNER AND A MOVIE

"The white people, who are trying to make us over into their image, they want us to be what they call 'assimilated,' bringing the Indians into the mainstream and destroying our own way of life and our own cultural patterns. They believe we should be contented like those whose concept of happiness is materialistic and greedy, which is very different from our way." – From the 1927 Grand Council of American Indians.

I was relieved when my friends finished eating and we all returned to our normal stations. The crew went about filming their fancy cars as they tore thorough Suzie's land, while the ladies and I shuffled back to the little house to work. We all plopped down once more as if we'd never left; the only difference being a full stomach. While fastening the microphone back onto Suzie's lapel, I asked Emily if Suzie had ever ventured far from home. She answered that, other than the occasional trip to Flagstaff, Suzie had done very little traveling away from the reservation. There had been only one time in her life in which she had ventured all the way to Los Angeles with her husband. According to Emily, that trip took place around the 1940s.

The purpose of this journey was to collect payment from John Ford's production company for their work as extras in one of his first cowboy movies filmed in the Valley. Emily translated back to me that Suzie had been largely unimpressed by the popular southern California destination. Her cryptic description of the ocean she viewed for the first and only time was "big." The golden city of Hollywood she deemed "crowded." Considering where she lived I suppose I could understand her lack of enthusiasm. But had the city of Hollywood, so exciting to fans of the cinema in the 1940s, really left such a lackluster impression on Suzie?

Emily provided some background to Suzie's story. "See," she explained, "Suzie had to go to Hollywood with Tully so that they could cash a check they received for working that summer. The check from United Artists was in both their names, and no local business would cash it. So they just took off to collect their money and to see the sights. Emily told me her mother-in-law called Los Angeles "The Hot Country," and I thought this was rather ironic considering the high temperatures she experienced within the Valley during the summer. Emily continued to translate Suzie's recollections about that land of fame and fortune. "It stinks," she flatly proclaimed, "I hear that now there are roads one on top of the other, but back then there were only two, and they were all somewhat stinky." Suzie went on to describe the adventure she took with Tully:

"It was a long time ago when my late husband and I went. When we left for the Hot Spot I didn't know what the name of the place really was. I just knew that we couldn't cash the checks they gave us in the Valley. We could only get paid way over there in California where the movie company lived. So we went all the way over there.

I think we spent about a month there, my daughter was about six or eight then, and she was away in school."

"I couldn't see too clearly there at the Hot Spot. It looked like it was cloudy but it was different, and it smelled like a bad fire. We were afraid of the roads because we didn't know them, so we rode buses and the train too, there and back. My husband spoke some English, just very little (giggles). He was getting good at traveling a lot to find work. I had no knowledge of movie stars, so I don't know if I saw any. It was crowded there in the big city, and we were just in a hurry all of the time. We rode from one vehicle and then into another, and then another. It felt strange somehow, but I was young so I didn't mind going. My husband was a good gambler, and he wanted to do some of that in the place they called Hollywood. I think he only wanted to go there to learn more about how to win at cards, and he was a very good card player. I thought it might be nice to get good sunlight; tan like one of the movie stars, (giggles, I believed Suzie was teasing here). I was also hoping to see a good sunrise; that was the thing I remember. The sun looked different, but it only went over the water in the evening. It was also in the Hot Spot where I got a tattoo. My husband thought that would be a good idea. He said, 'tattoo your English name on your arm, and then you'll know how to spell it if you need to, (giggles). It stings when they give you the tattoo."

"We paid for the trip with the money we received from doing the movie, but while we were there our money ran low. That was when we decided to leave. I don't remember how much we were paid, but it was probably a lot because it went a long way. We never really kept track of it, (more giggling)".

I learned firsthand that Suzie did find her tattoo useful on a number of occasions. I once presented a document for her to sign; the standard form required by my university that formally asks permission to interview a subject. While slowly signing the consent form Suzie continuously referred to her tattoo for the correct spelling of her name. With each letter successfully copied she would shyly glance up at me, then chuckle with satisfaction to herself. She liked using the pen I loaned her. It was from the Goulding's gift shop, and had a clear top filled with some sort of gel that allowed a tiny cactus to bob back and forth as she wrote. We were both delighted with the finished product, and Suzie laughed at my ridiculous pantomime indicating she keep the pen.

Was Suzie unimpressed by Hollywood because she had no real idea of what it meant to be a movie star? At a time when many Americans idolized those working in the film industry, Suzie was focusing on living as a Navajo woman, raising her children and managing her herd. The isolation in which she lived allowed her to carry on in much the same way as her ancestors had. This traditional lifestyle would continue to be important to Suzie even when aspects of the modern world eventually crept into the Valley. What remained a puzzle to me was how Suzie claimed to be unaffected by the entirely alien Hollywood culture and drastically different environment of California. Surely the sight of the big city must have been a shock to one who had lived all of her life in such a remote and peaceful location as Monument Valley. No matter how many times I asked Suzie about her initial reaction to the city, however, she always answered that it had meant very little to her. I expect that, given the choice, Suzie would have remained in the Valley simply because she regarded it as the best home in which she and her family could happily live.

The day had progressed in a choppy fashion. After the morning's confusion and the interruption of lunch with the film crew I felt less than pleased with the little we had accomplished. Now the sun was beginning to set and I had run out of blank tapes. The sound of slamming doors and folding chairs brought Emily to the window. "Well, they're packing up to leave," she informed Suzie and me, "guess it'll quiet down around here again." I sat there wondering how I could repair the disjointed events of the day. I thought of going back to the silence of Hill House and envisioned dinner it the big kitchen...alone. Suddenly it occurred to me. Why not have the family over for dinner and a movie! I presented the idea to Emily, and she wholeheartedly agreed that this would be a wonderful adventure for Suzie and her family. She promised to bring Suzie to Hill House that evening along with Lonnie and Effie. With this renewed purpose I said my goodbyes and left for Goulding's Market to purchase everything I would need for the evening. I then drove to the lodge itself to obtain the movie I'd heard so much about that day.

Goulding's Lodge offered many of the films Ford produced in the Valley for rent. But it was "Cheyenne Autumn" that I held my interest now that I had the inside scoop about how it was filmed. I wondered if viewing this movie with her family would allow Suzie to better recall her personal experiences during its production. I thought that at the very least it would be entertaining for all of us to relive her brush with Hollywood. Anyway, there was much to do before the family arrived. I sliced the few fresh vegetables available at the market and sautéed them with kalamata olives and mushrooms. Knowing the family's taste for pine nuts, I roasted a good amount for sprinkling on top of my masterpiece. Once I had the sauce simmering and the pasta cooked "al dente," Hill House was filled with the aroma of my famous dish. I heard the sound of wheels on gravel and headed to the door to greet my adopted family. Much to my surprise Suzie arrived with quite an entourage. Acting on the rumor that "Coco was cooking dinner," a hoard of Yazzie family members came piling out of the cars like circus clowns out of a tiny car. One after the other emerged until I wondered how they all managed to cram themselves into the vehicles in the first place. Emily led the long line of relatives, stopping at the doorstep to sniff the hint of what awaited them inside. "Mmmmm," she murmured with a smile, "smells different from fry bread, but just as good!"

I have a habit of making enough spaghetti to feed an army, and this usually resulted in a week of leftovers for me and my family. It seemed unimaginable to cut the recipe in half, even though I had to live with the shame of using dried herbs in place of my usual fresh ones. Now I was glad I'd made my feast in the usual gargantuan proportions. Emily and I set the table buffet-style while the rest of the family admired my accommodations, which were certainly luxurious compared to the Suzie's hogan and Effie's small home in Oljeto. Personally, I preferred both of those dwellings to the isolation of Hill House, but the location certainly afforded me the solitude I needed to work. How I loved this new atmosphere within my Valley home.

167

The warm chatter, the laughter, and the smell of a fine dinner waiting to be served to an appreciative audience, all made for a completely different vibe within the usually quite house. Suzie smiled broadly as I dished up her portion first. She nodded at my offer of pine nuts, even though we both knew she would have trouble chewing them. I gave equally generous portions to Emily, Lonnie, Effie and a number of other relatives who were introduced as in-laws, aunties, nieces and nephews. Last in line were three children ranging in age from five to nine. They sat on a couch facing the television screen, holding their plates of steaming spaghetti on their laps and giggling in anticipation. I gave Suzie the chair of honor directly in front of the screen, while I positioned myself to her right, with my tape recorder directed toward Effie sitting at her mother's left. She would be interpreting Suzie's reactions to the movie. The remaining adults pulled up chairs or found places on the floor, and with forks poised waited for me to push in the video. The adventure began...

Suzie remembered seeing a number of the major actors that were in the film on a daily basis around her homeland. She explained how her family first earned extra money by providing horses on the set:

"The blonde lady in the film (Carroll Baker) would be hauling Navajo kids around in that wagon all day long. They used our late pony to pull the wagon. The pony's mom was in the movie too; the mare. In one scene the Indians were acting like they stole that horse from the soldiers and were going to eat it, but the soldiers got it back. There were really three horses. One was red and one was painted. They painted the pony too, but I don't know if we got paid for him."

Suzie and her family participated in quite a few scenes within the movie, and she took delight in seeing on film the many locations where she played as a child. While viewing a scene, in which the "Cheyenne" were seeking shelter from the army in a cave, Suzie became quite animated:

"Yes, I knew some of them that they show in the movie. We were at the entrance of "Victory Cave," That's what the movie people called it, but we had another name long before. I was standing with my son's first wife, Harriet, and she was carrying her baby. She is the one I recognize the most in this scene with the cave, because she was standing ahead of everyone else at the front."

I remembered walking by this cave many times during my visits to the Yazzie compound. On warmer days when the latrine smelled particularly ripe I admit I sneaked over there to relieve myself. Close to the sheep coral and a good distance from Suzie's home, the cave area allowed an adequate amount of privacy and comfort, without the nuisance of having to hike any great distance from the compound. The family had Victory Cave filled to its opening with car parts and scraps that have been saved over the years. With no covered storage space available, and access to essential materials at least thirty miles away, the cave served as a garage of sorts for parts deemed too precious to haul out of the Valley. How strange to know that the cave once housed a bevy of actors and Navajo extras pretending to quiver in fear over approaching soldiers.

Suzie lived in a rural area, and so in true country style she had put this part of her land to practical use, even though many people would consider the cave a famous landmark of the Hollywood Western era. It certainly was an eerie-looking spot, and I wondered if the cave had once been a spiritual sanctuary of some sort. It looked as if it would make a good one, yet the Yazzies never indicated to me that had ever been the case. Now it seemed a shame that the cave was choking with debris that might never be put to good use or hauled away. I took the moment to remind Suzie of an idea Lonnie spoke to me about the cave. He felt it might be cleared out and presented as a tourist attraction to those visitors that were brought to the hogan. What a treat it would be for them to clamber from the tour buses into a real cave used in a classic Hollywood Western! Suzie agreed that the cave was in decline. "Now it's just a mess," she sighed, "My family keeps saying they want to clean it, but it hasn't happened yet." At that, the subject was temporarily laid to rest. Yet, I couldn't help wondering how much the family might benefit from the extra income such an attraction might generate.

PLAYING INDIAN

"When a white army battles Indians and wins, it is called a great victory, but if they lose, it is called a massacre." – Chiksika, Shawnee

Suzie went on to recall where she was placed in nearly every scene of "Cheyenne Autumn":

"Seeing this film brings back memories. During the Victory Cave filming I was in the back of the cave. In the background they were performing the Squaw Dance and the Round Dance. We also filmed some of this movie in the town of Moab. That's where the film company moved to when they left from here in the Valley. Only a few Navajos followed them out to work there. The late John Stanley went, with his brother. John Stanley was always there. He was *Kinyaa`a'anii*. [158] Everybody walked around a lot on foot, the women and everybody at Goulding's. The women spent a lot of time just hanging around over at Goulding's waiting to be called for a scene. In this scene where all the women are digging holes in the sand from where their men will shoot, we really used bowels like they show in the movie. We were filmed just as we began digging, but we just dug little holes (giggles). Then the men used shovels to dig further so it looked as if we did a lot of work! I guess they didn't want to wait around for us women to finish with the bowls, (giggles). Some White men helped, but mostly Navajo did the work. Then they were told to stand in the holes and wait for the soldiers' horses to come. Us women were then placed somewhere on the side near the rock ridges. The man in charge yelled something into a cone, and then the Indians and cowboys would start shooting!"

The make-believe aspect of movie making seemed to tickle Suzie and those family members who were present to watch the movie. When a Navajo was referred to as "Cheyenne" the room erupted in laughter. When a winter scene was filmed with artificial snow falling on the Navajo, the crowd made sure to tell me this was "fake."

The Hollywood actors who portrayed Indians provided the most amusement. The family collectively told me what the Navajo extras were saying throughout the film. Phrases such as "let's go" and "We have no food" were spoken in Dine' throughout the film and were translated to me verbatim. However, when Ricardo Montalbaun, the famous Spanish actor dressed as a Cheyenne warrior, began to speak, the entire family could hardly contain themselves. "He's just talking gibberish," Emily laughed, holding her sides, "He's just making words up as he goes along."

Because the Yazzies drew such pleasure from pointing out the false elements within the film I wondered if this were not a sort of release for them. It must have felt awkward and a bit insincere, after all, to "play Indian" when one is genuinely a native. I thought it might have been twice as difficult to conform to the ideals of 'Indian-ness'

---

[158] John Stanley was highly regarded among the Navajo as a Dine' actor of his time. Since he was of the Towering House clan he was related to Suzie from her father's side of the family. Her father was of the Folded Arms clan and her mother of the Bitterwater. Mr. Stanley was therefore Suzie's distant cousin.

170

expected by non-natives. By exposing the falsehoods in these depictions the Yazzies may have been subconsciously regaining their true Navajo identity. They may also have been diminishing the power exercised by the media to present an image of the Indian that, by today's standards, appear ludicrous. Then again, perhaps I was reading too much into their reactions. As Freud said, sometimes a cigar is just a cigar, and it could be that the Yazzies were simply enjoying an old Western film in which they took part. Stripping away the mystique of Hollywood's clumsy attempt to depict Indians might have merely been a source of entertainment to the Yazzies.

While we watched the movie, Suzie provided explanations for nearly every scene. She appeared to be continuously amazed by the way reality was set aside for the fictional world of Ford's Wild West promoted by Ford:

"The Navajo in this scene look like they're cooking, but I don't think they were really were at the time. One time we really did cook something. The film people said it was a cow, but I don't know if it really was. That would be a waste of a good cow...Here in this other scene you see the man acting like an Indian, but he was White. He was pretending to be dying and they hauled him around for awhile. He died lots of times (giggles). They pretended to put him in a rock grave, up on Flat Rocks. Even though he was a white man all the Navajo women were crying. They were saying in Dine' 'He's dead!' They hauled him around like he was dead here and there, then he just got up! I guess he was not quite dead (giggles). There was another man who got shot in the movie, but they are all just faking the blood...just faking. On the movie it looks real, but I know better. And you can tell who is Navajo and who is not. Our men were told to braid their hair on either side, but they kept braiding a long braid down the back or French braid (giggles). They kept it up even thought the movie people told them not to wear their hair that way. It was a good joke. My husband had a short haircut like a white man, so he had to wear a braided wig (giggles)."

I asked Suzie about her overall opinion of the movie industry and whether she remembered any other details about the experience. She responded in the same quiet fashion to which I had grown accustomed:

"We never really thought about how many people would see us when we were involved with the filming. It seemed like a waste of time because mostly we just sat around waiting. Sometimes we would be told to stand here and there, and that was it. But we were in a lot of movies and everywhere during each one. We were filmed near Sand Springs, Goulding's, and the airstrip, even down to Mexican Hat. When we were taken there we rode in big trucks. Then when we got out of the vehicles the people were all lined up. That's when you learned what you would be doing that day. I was in "Billy Jack" and "The Trial of Billy Jack," and I liked that. But sometimes the work was a little hard. We were on horseback for 'Cheyenne Autumn' and we were told to cross the river by Mexican Hat. I kept looking down at the water every time we crossed and I got sort of get dizzy. When you ride on horseback and stare at the river flowing downhill it can make you sick (giggles). I don't know how many times we rode those horses across the river. I liked working for the movie people most of the time. We all had work when they came, and it helped out a lot."

I never enjoyed watching an old Western more than when I viewed it with the Yazzie family, and I highly recommend viewing any old cowboy movie that depicts "Indians" with a genuine Native American. In a way, experiencing the movie through the Yazzie's eyes allowed me to put on their skin and discover what it might be like to work as an Indian...playing an Indian. The night's activities had been odd and wonderful at the same time.

By the end of the movie the children were asleep on the couch, and everyone was visibly tired. While the evening had been fun, the day had been long. We all stood up to stretch, and the ladies gently stirred the kids and led them to the cars waiting outside. I packaged up the few leftovers of my spaghetti dinner and handing them over to Effie. She gripped the plastic bag in one hand and supported her mother with the other. Suzie smiled at me and nodded her thanks. "My mom says you make really good spaghetti. She says you should come over again tomorrow." I stood at the door waving as the group drove away, and wondered how many other times Suzie had actually eaten spaghetti.

ONE LOST DAY
"If you see no reason for giving thanks, then don't give thanks." — Minquass

I left early the next morning determined to get a good amount of work in with Suzie. The faint smell of marinara sauce and garlic lingered in Hill House, but the air outside was fresh and clean. I drove up to the Yazzie compound feeling smugly confident that my family would be waiting inside and as anxious to begin as I was. I didn't bother to wait in my car, bound up to the door and knocked. Suzie answered with her usual smile, but she was alone. I faced yet another ineffective pantomime, or I could check the hogan for one of the English-speaking family members. I could feel last night's camaraderie slipping away as Suzie stood waiting for me to say something intelligent...preferably in Navajo. Instead I pointed to the hogan. "Effie?" I asked, and received a few Navajo words that might have meant Suzie's daughter could be found in the hogan...or not. The matriarch sauntered back into her home and shut the door. I had been dismissed. Feeling miserable about my inability to communicate I made my way to the earthen mound where a small plume of smoke above indicated that certainly somebody must be inside. I could hear muted conversation inside, and hoping that I wasn't interrupting some sort of ceremony, I tentatively knocked on the hogan door.

A large Navajo man answered, looking at me accusingly. "Is Effie here by any chance?" I asked, trying to be as polite as possible. He answered in a way that Emily sometimes did in answer to my broad questions... "I have no idea." I realized this man was a tour guide with a visiting tourist, and they were simply waiting for Suzie to return from whatever task she attended to in the house. He gave no indication that he even knew who Effie was and suggested that I "check in the residence." I apologized for intruding and made my way to my car as Suzie began to slowly walk to the hogan. "How can such a sparsely populated place contain people who don't know each other?" I complained to myself. As I pulled out I weakly waved to Suzie who looked at me in confusion. Hadn't she just told the stupid white woman that Effie wasn't there? I drove away feeling defeated and more like an Anglo than the "White Navajo" I hoped to be.

My only recourse was to try and catch Effie or Emily driving into the Valley. I returned to the Visitor's Center that was situated at the gateway to the park, and decided to bide my time investigating the "Hogan Village" that had recently been constructed at the end of the park lot. There was a male and a female hogan, a sweat lodge, (the first one I had ever seen intact because those I passed in the Valley have been left to disintegrate after use), and a shade house. There was a placard nearby listing detailed information regarding each structure. Every entrance was padlocked for the winter season, and I wondered if demonstrations ever took place inside. This could be very bad for Suzie's business.

I thought it would be helpful to have an English/Dine' dictionary and went looking for something of the kind in the gift store. I had visited this part of the center before, but somehow never got around to purchasing the language books available there. Turning the corner I received my second surprise of the day. The gift shop was drastically reduced to a small corner and counter where very little was sold in the way of souvenirs! I asked the woman behind the counter what had happened to the collection of Navajo blankets, sand paintings, jewelry and learning materials. The only explanation she offered was that they were liquidating everything. I purchased some cassette tapes of music and made my usual stop to look over the artifacts shown in long display cases. In spite of what seemed to be a slowing of business there was a sign taped to the door leading outside that advertised for positions available in the way of bookkeeper and maintenance. I left with even more questions in my head. What was going on around here? Why construct another attraction for tourists who don't appear to be coming, and why eliminate the souvenirs that they would spend their money on? The morning had been nothing but perplexing to me, and I decided to abandon my search for the Yazzies. Instead of taking the road back to Suzie's I drove down the long, straight road back to Goulding's. I was spending a long weekend in M.V. There would be plenty of time to conduct interviews. Maybe this was all a sign that I should work back at Hill House.

I passed the "Big Man" riding stables on the way and recalled a story told to me by Effie about her son hitting one of the horses owned by this operation. When she spoke of the "big man" I thought she meant it was a man of some standing in the community. I had to laugh when I realized the owner of the horse who destroyed the grill of Effie's truck was actually named Big Man. He had promised Effie that he would pay for the damage since his horse had been running free on the road, but payment had yet to arrive. Meanwhile Effie's truck limped along back and forth to Suzie's hogan.

Letting myself into the house I threw my unused back pack on the table. My intention had been to use the remainder of the morning to work, yet I felt restless and unable to focus. Perhaps a run would do the trick. I decided to take a different route and run opposite the road leading to Goulding's. My usual run went from Hill House down to the high school, almost to the line of souvenir sheds at the park's entrance, and back again. This road was shown in the film "Forrest Gump" and gives the runner a spectacular view as well as a great workout. I had grown tired of the constant line of cars that whizzed by me as well as the stares of curious tourists. The less-traveled road behind Hill House would be a relief. Having driven down the road once with Effie I knew it ended abruptly, becoming nothing but a gravel causeway leading to the back tiny settlement of Oljeto. But I liked the rock formations I passed along the way. They were different from what I usually saw in the Valley. These huge rocks had been swept by an unrelenting wind that created beautiful streaks within the rock that spiraled down each sloping monoliths. It seemed more peaceful there, a few locals passed by, but except for the occasional barking dog, I had the road to myself.

I went to the end of the pavement and back again, increasing my speed to a sprint until my lungs hurt from the cool desert air. Once back at the house I ran a well-deserved bath, and feeling refreshed drove to the main building to purchase a meal. While waiting for my take out I peeked into the Goulding's gift shop to once again try my luck on language instruction materials. There I found the Dine'/English dictionary I wanted. Unfortunately, it was alphabetized by Navajo word. How could I look up a word if I only knew it in English? Nothing was going to make any sense today. To make learning Dine' even more difficult, there didn't seem to be any one word that corresponded with another. They were more like phrases describing random actions. I decided to ask Lonnie to teach me one of the more simple Navajo songs. If I couldn't impress the family with my language skills, perhaps I could do so with my singing. That afternoon I watched too much television and therefore did very little work. Dinner consisted of a soggy sandwich left over from the lunch I'd packed that morning. I tried again to type up my notes, but lost all inspiration and went to bed in despair. All in all a disappointing beginning to what I'd hoped would be a day full of accomplishments.

ANOTHER TRY
"It's impossible to awaken a man who is pretending to be asleep." - Navajo

I slept fitfully that night. Hill House is rather isolated from the rest of the lodge and it could be a little creepy at night all by myself. I awoke to every creek and groan when the old house announced another gust of wind was buffeting its worn sides. By the early morning hours I had finally fallen into a deep sleep. Then the phone rang. Reaching for the phone I glanced at the alarm clock on my nightstand and was amazed to see I'd slept until eight o'clock! I thought the call might be from my husband back in California, but it was Emily. She and Lonnie were calling from the front desk. "What the heck are you doing Lady...sleeping?" I rubbed my eyes and told her I would join them at the restaurant right away. Throwing some jeans and a sweatshirt on and hopping into my boots I wondered how on earth I would ever get used to the Yazzie's schedule...or lack of one.

When my friends saw me enter the dining room they both came forward to offer hugs. Emily's sweater felt soft against my cheek, and Lonnie smelled of wood smoke.

It was wonderful to see them and they immediately began filling me in on why everyone had been absent the day before. Their car had once again failed them, and while they were repairing the old thing Suzie would have to do without the supplies they had promised to bring into the Valley. Hearing this Effie had decided to travel into Keyenta for the lard and flour needed to make fry bread for the camera crew that would be returning to the compound today. I was disappointed to hear our day would once more be disrupted by more filming. How long did it take to create a car commercial anyway? Emily told me they were also concerned about Suzie working too much with these visitors. Now in her mid-eighties, the matriarch became disoriented if she became overtired. I was astonished to learn that Suzie's health had been compromised the past month by what doctors determined was iron-poor blood. The resulting memory loss and physical decline was alleviated after a rejuvenating blood transfusion. Suzie continued treatment with special inoculations that increased her platelets, but the doctors warned her to take things easy.

As our breakfast arrived the conversation shifted to the Yazzie's financial concerns. I told Emily about some job offers I saw listed at the Tourist Center and suggested she apply there. Emily was a straight A student at the community college she attended in Chinle. Now that she was finishing up on her accounting courses she was very close to receiving her Associate's degree. A bookkeeping position at the Tourist Center would be good experience, and Emily expressed a desire to spend more time in the Valley. She was still caring for her teenage sons, Brooks and Sonny, but they planned on moving somewhere outside the rez after completing high school. Both Lonnie and Emily liked the idea of living closer to Suzie once they became "empty-nesters." Lonnie told me that the family was worried about the new "Hogan Village" located at the park's entrance. They had been told by the Center operators that it was meant only to provide a learning opportunity for the tourists. Nevertheless, the traffic to Suzie's hogan was dwindling, and I wondered if those in the community would consider working together so that all entrepreneurs could benefit from the tourist economy without hurting the business of one another.

Effie suddenly appeared at our table, having come to the restaurant to report for work. She looked at me with surprise, exclaiming, "Hey, where were you yesterday? My mom said you came by!" I explained my hopeless attempt to communicate with Suzie and Effie just laughed and plopped down to join us. "Yeah, she wondered what you were saying, but then you left and she figured you went looking for me. She's pretty good at figuring stuff out," she giggled. I asked Emily to write down for me certain phrases in Navajo that I could use the next time I saw Suzie. I felt more prepared now, and ready to begin work no matter what the circumstances. We all finished breakfast, and Emily agreed to drive with me to the Yazzie compound. At the top of the stairs outside we dispersed; Effie to prepare for a cookout...Lonnie to see a man about a saddle, and Emily and I to seek adventure in the Valley.

URANIUM – WEALTH AND POISON

"We know our lands have now become more valuable. The white people think we do not know their value; but we know that the land is everlasting, and the few goods we receive for it are soon worn out and gone." – Canassetego

Emily and I arrived at the Yazzie compound just in time to see a helicopter ascend in a swirl of desert sand. I assumed the cars would be filmed driving around the property as a way to show off their performance. I never thought this sort of advertising was particularly effective in selling cars, and I marveled at how much expense and energy went into them. We pulled up to the back of the house and ran in, trying to avoid the dirt and debris generated by the helicopter from blowing into our hair and clothes. Slamming the door behind us Emily called out for her mother-in-law, but the house was empty. I peered out the window to the hogan. Apparently Suzie had managed to hide from the film crew there, but she now slowly emerged like a creeping spirit. Emily hurried out the door to assist the old woman, while I arranged my tapes. I was determined to work today, and by the look on Suzie's face as she entered the house I sensed she was too.

After greeting each other and settling in I asked Emily to guide the interview toward Tully. I had heard from Lonnie that his father once sought employment with Kerr-McGee. This company operated a uranium mine from the middle 1940s to the 1980s. The Yazzies consider this one of the most intrusive episodes of white contact that took place within the Valley. Lonnie believed that while working in the mine his father developed respiratory problems due to contact with poisonous uranium. He claimed that, had his father not perished in an accidental fire, he surely would have died from the uranium dust he breathed while working for Kerr-McGee.

In an attempt to quell erosion within the Valley in the 1930s the United States government enforced a livestock reduction plan that left many Navajo destitute from the depletion of their herds. The Navajo believe that the disappearance of fertile topsoil was brought about because of natural reversals in the Four Corners region. Regardless of whether the stock reduction was necessary, many Dine' believed that livestock officials handled the reduction of Navajo livestock poorly. The random selection of herds earmarked for slaughter resulted in economic hardship for many Navajo families. Job opportunities presented by mining companies became one of the few methods of support for reservation families that were never effectively compensated for the decrease of their herds. [159]

The search for uranium in the Southwest took place after World War II, when the public was initially told that the extraction of vanadium, a mineral used in steel alloys, was the purpose of this mining. Trader Harry Goulding recalled finding uranium before the end of World War II:

"During the war we found uranium in here (Monument Valley). There had been some found here years ago, but all they used it for was the numbers on your watch, like

---

[159] Churchill, Ward. A Little Matter of Genocide. San Francisco: City Lights Books, 1997, 305.

radium, a little bit of stuff, and there was no market for it till after the war got to using it."[160]

Oddly enough, the author recording the Goulding biography made no mention regarding uranium poisoning among the Navajo mine workers. Perhaps Harry Goulding was unaware of the illness that many of his Navajo neighbors believed was caused by the uranium. This seems unlikely, however, since the trading post owner had always been very much attuned to the Navajo and their concerns. Likewise, it struck me as curious that the biographer, Samuel Moon had not touched upon this issue with his subject, particularly since the other interviews he printed throughout his book showed great attention to detail. This is not to imply that any sinister motive was behind Mr. Moon's failure to mention uranium poisoning among the Navajo. He may have omitted the subject for any number of practical reasons.

The extraction of uranium took place in the Valley by the mid 1950s. Kerr-McGee promised steady employment to the local Navajo, and the company set up their operation just outside the tiny town of Mexican Hat.

Most of the Navajo working in the mines later complained that they were not informed as to the hazards that existed in extracting the potent mineral from their land. Information supplied to the Atomic Energy Commission as early as 1946 was not made available to the Navajo mining crews, and these workers inhaled cancer-causing gasses such as Radon and Thoron emitted by uranium. In their zeal to provide funding and jobs, those in the Department of Labor's Small Business Administration who managed the endeavor failed to establish safe working conditions to the Navajo. No one bothered to ask why these employees had not been properly outfitted with equipment that could eradicate the dangerous gasses they encountered during digging procedures.[161]

Unlike their dealings with the trade economy and film industry, the uranium mining that occurred in Monument Valley had a negative effect on the Yazzie's lives. Environmental damage as well as ill health among the Navajo was the lasting result of mining. In spite of their complaints, companies such as Kerr-McGee continued to deny any responsibility for their former Navajo employees' illnesses. Tully, Suzie's husband was one of the more than five hundred Navajo who took advantage of the available work that allowed them to remain close to their families. To those Navajo men compelled to seek work out of state as railroad or agricultural laborers, work in the local mines was considered a real luxury. In addition to providing a steady income, mining allowed the men to return home each night. For men accustomed to spending long periods of time away from home this was a priceless opportunity to maintain relationships as husbands and fathers.

Ultimately however, many of the Navajo taking advantage of this employment opportunity suffered hardship owing to the risks of uranium mining.

---

[160] Moon, 175.

[161] Churchill, *Matter of Genocide*, 306.

Some workers met a premature death brought on by exposure to uranium and other lethal gases, depriving the widows they left behind of valuable income. These women then faced the struggle of supporting their children on a meager income derived from shepherding or craft manufacture and sale. Eventually some of the Navajo men who worked at uranium mining operations in the Red Rock area filed a claim for damages against Kerr-McGee in 1979. Although some damages were awarded, still others languished in the court system because the Navajo could not obtain adequate legal counsel. Suzie and her family have had difficulty claiming compensation from the Kerr-McGee Company for this very reason. Tully worked the mines for ten years until other opportunities for work became available to him. By the mid 1960s however he, like many of his co-workers, had contracted lung cancer. The Yazzies believe his illness was the result of inhalation of uranium gases.

Suzie stated to me that, after some weeks of steady work within the mine, her husband was informed by his superiors that the uranium he was helping to extract could pose a threat to a worker's health:

"Yes, he was told after a while that working the uranium mine might make him feel bad, and he did get sick from it while he was working there. He went to the hospital, and he was told at that time that his heart was affected. But he kept working there because the money was good, and I don't think he really knew what was happening inside his body."

According to Suzie, she and her children were in great need of reliable income during the time Tully worked in the mine, so it comes as no surprise that her husband would continue to work in the mine even after being informed of the danger to his health. When asked about whether she felt there should be compensation for the illness Tully suffered, Suzie expressed her frustration in the process of obtaining it:

"The uranium compensation? I haven't bothered with it again. I probably should go over to the agency again with my son. He would be better at speaking with the people who determine restitution. My son went over there to speak with them once before, but they offer very little money, so it seems to me like too much work. I do hope that maybe they'll close the mine the mine someday soon."

When Emily informed Suzie that the mine had already been closed for some years she expressed surprise. She said that children had been playing on the site of the abandoned mine for many years without being warned of the danger. She assumed that the Kerr-McGee company simply walked away without giving the mine another thought. At any rate, Suzie's children believe their mother has given up any hope of receiving any compensation for her husband's illness, and they wonder if future Navajo generations may also have been affected by the Uranium mining that took place in the Valley.

There is a possibility that even some of Suzie's children died from uranium poisoning. Two years before her husband left the Kerr-McGee mining operation, two of Suzie's children died in infancy. One child died only weeks after birth, and another after surviving only three months. Immediately after Tully left his job at the mine yet another child was born that did not survive past four months. This child had "learned how to sit up" according to Suzie, but perished soon afterwards. "Suddenly he

178

just...got sick." Suzie informed me, "He lived only one more day." Suzie went on to describe her children's' illnesses in detail:

"The child I had borned after my oldest son, Harvey, survived. And then my next son was born, and he survived too. This was before my husband found work at the mine. The child I carried after he went to work there died. Yes, he cried all night and then during early day he started moaning. Then towards sunset he finally died. That was when I had all my children at home in Little Monument Valley, behind that sitting rock. We use to have our winter home there. I had all my children there, but I took my sick baby to the hospital by Goulding's. That was a time when there were no records kept there, so I don't even remember his name. I just don't remember."

Suzie and her family have always wondered if these infant deaths were linked to their father's exposure to uranium. The Navajo Health Authority did, in fact, report that in 1981 there was "a twofold excess of miscarriages, infant deaths, congenital or genetic abnormalities, and learning disabilities among uranium-area families." [162] Unfortunately, the lack of medical records regarding these deaths makes it impossible to determine whether or not Suzie's babies died of any of these illnesses. The damage done to those Navajo employed at the uranium mines may never be fully revealed. According to research collected by Ward Churchill, statistics have shown that "of the approximately three hundred and fifty Dine who had worked in the mines before 1955, twenty-five were dead of lung cancer and at least forty-five more had been diagnosed with the disease by 1979.[163]

One Navajo employed at the age of nineteen in a Kerr-McGee mill reported "a haze of yellow dust flying around" that he and other workers inhaled. He continued in his position for some years because he was in desperate need of work. "I had a job," he explained, "and for poor people with low education, no skills, and high unemployment, that is the important thing." [164] According to Lonnie, most families that successfully filed suits against Kerr-McGee were rewarded around $100,000 each. So far the Yazzies have heard nothing back regarding their claim. After many years and no resources available to them to hire a lawyer, it is doubtful they ever will.

The uranium mining that took place on the Navajo reservation appeared to me to be an example of the double-edged sword presented to many Native American groups when they were offered a portion of profits gained by Anglo businesses on Indian land. The Navajo people's situation was unique because their exposure to deadly radioactive chemicals was a result of the demand created by the Cold War between the U.S. and the Soviet Union. In this way, the Navajo community felt the effects of international relations. Suzie and her Navajo neighbors lived in an isolated location far from Western politics, yet the far-reaching consequences of nuclear war were ultimately felt. The effects are present even today. At the time of my research Lonnie expressed concern over the abandoned mine that he feels was haphazardly "secured" by Kerr-McGee. Children continue to play in the area and Lonnie believed the mine remained a

---

[162] Ibid., 309.
[163] Churchill, 306.
[164] Ibid., 314.

hazard to families living just outside Mexican Hat. A feeling of sadness washed over me after learning the full story behind the effects of uranium mining to the Yazzies. Up to this time I believed that the isolation of Monument Valley provided a certain amount of protection for Suzie and her family. Now I knew that the outside world had a way of touching, and sometimes infecting, even the most remote communities.

CULTURAL CHANGE IN BURIAL

"A man who would not love his father's grave is worse than a wild animal." – Chief Joseph, Nez Perce

Suzie never learned what exactly had caused her infants' death, and she was unable to see that their burial adhered strictly to traditional ways. One infant was taken to the hospital for care and, as was the custom at the time, the white hospital staff interred this child as a service to the Navajo. The first child, however, passed away during a healing ceremony. This baby was buried within the surrounding rock crevices in the manner Suzie had earlier described to me. However, the child was not placed with the usual covering of rocks. I was confused by the discrepancies between the burials described in anthropological literature and the burial practices of the Yazzie family. I asked Emily why her people enlisted a number of different burial procedures. She explained that, although many Navajo had some burial practices in common, personal choice played a significant role in deciding how a loved one was put to rest. It was Suzie who decided that his particular child be placed in a crevice without any stones at all covering the body. Even Emily expressed surprise after hearing this. She too had only heard of instances in which the dead were placed among the rocks with boulders carefully covering the body. But Suzie explained that the body of her child had been left exposed so that the forces of nature might see to it that the loved one was returned to the earth from which it had been borne. By offering her child's remains to the elements and the creatures that inhabited the Valley, Suzie and her family avoided any future contact with the child's confused spirit.

In an effort to explain this unique burial procedure, Emily suggested I not think of the Navajo as a conservative ethnic group blindly following steadfast traditions without question. Each clan or family determined how it might navigate a situation based on both traditional methods observed over generations, and adaptations made to those traditions by the family to fit its needs. While one Navajo family might pursue a "traditional" burial as close as possible to nineteenth century customs, still another might decide to allow one who had no association to the family to tend to the burial. Some Navajo families today bury their loved ones according to Anglo custom because of legal complications that arise when a traditional burial is sought. Dine' families must now request permission from authorities to place the deceased in rock crevices or cremate the body within the hogan in which the loved one died. Depending on their faith, other Navajo prefer a Christian burial, or one that involves the Native American Church.

I came to realize that, just as there are a multitude of choices within Anglo rituals or ceremonies, so the same choices exist for the modern Navajo. It occurred to me that, while I had expected the Yazzies to conform to some preconceived notion of the "exotic" Native American, I had failed to see the obvious. Although every society has a set of rules and customs that dictate the norm, by no means are these standards written in stone. The individual within every society can either choose to follow those standards, or to deviate from those standards and even create one's own traditions.

I suggested to Suzie that I might research her children's deaths by examining any existing records of the hospital where they were taken. These children may have died for any number of reasons, including infection contracted during the birthing process, and Suzie agreed that it would be comforting to know exactly what had compromised their health. The chances of an infant dying in the first months of its life were great according to a number of studies done on the Navajo in the early twentieth century. [165] However, in light of the successful births of her other children, I felt there might be at least the possibility that these two children died as a result of fetal exposure to uranium.

According to the Yazzie family, the effect of uranium poisoning was evident in Suzie's husband even before he left his position at the mine to pursue other work opportunities in Idaho. Exactly how the chemical poisoning would have ultimately affected his health could never be determined because of his accidental death in 1974. I was not sure Suzie would feel comfortable discussing her husband's death with an outsider. We had broached the subject before, but Suzie usually redirected the conversation to other, happier events. I tried to understand Suzie's reluctance to relive what must have been a very painful memory. I knew that she preferred not to dwell on the negative aspects of her family history. This strategy may have allowed her to maintain a healthy mental attitude about the hardships that she and her family had endured over the years. Nonetheless, I pressed the matter so that I might better understand those hardships and how they shaped her personality.

Suzie had been deeply affected by the death of her husband and her two children. Yet, with five living children in need of care there was little time to dwell on her loss. Even when she spoke to me about this difficult period Suzie showed no outward emotion. Though her reaction to this loss may have seemed restrained or even cold, I was by now used to Suzie's quiet ways. With gentle prompting from Emily Suzie seemed willing to at last tell me the basic story behind her husband's death:

"It happened when he was looking for work. Over there somewhere near Salt Lake he died, not here. He was on his way to Idaho to look for a job, because he had worked over there before. The people who found him said it happened in a house fire. He did drink, and a lot. He was probably drinking then. He was with other people; one of them was his brother, Ford Yazzie. All of them except my husband were sitting in the vehicle outside the house. But my husband was inside where he probably passed out. I don't know this for sure, but I do remember how he use to always build a big fire at night to keep warm. I think this time the fire he built became too big while he slept."

---

[165] Just one example of anthropologists taking note of infant mortality among the Navajo is in Gladys Reichard's *Dezba, Woman of the Desert*, 48.

Suzie paused while Emily translated back to me the beginning of her story. The matriarch was becoming an old hand at working through the interview process. Looking up from her usual focus on her hands, she saw the expectation in my face and continued:

"Anyway, the house caught fire while the other men were sleeping in the vehicle. They were brought awake by the flames and then got out of the vehicle but couldn't get close to the house. It was too hot. They said my husband did at least make it out. They found him lying on the ground near the burning house. His clothes were all burned up and he was also burnt. That's the way he died. He was five years older than me, and at that time I was around forty-eight, so it must have been around 1968."

I had read that the Navajo "fear death" in a way quite different from that of Anglos.[166] Traditional Dine' religion does not recognize the concept of an afterlife in which the deceased are rewarded or punished for their actions in this life. Even by the late 1960s, when Tully died, many Navajo were requesting the help of others, particularly Anglos, to bury their dead. Anthropologist James Downs discussed how traders were often sought out to carry out this task.[167] The Yazzies told me that there are still Navajo who avoid the burial procedure as a way of minimizing family contact with the body of the deceased. They believe this makes the spirit of the deceased less likely to return and haunt the living. The Yazzies discussed with me the passing on of a family member without apparent concern. But because I thought they may still find the discussion of death uncomfortable, I put the topic of Tully's passing quickly to rest. Suzie seemed to prefer telling stories about the challenges, successes and adventures she shared with Tully.

I once asked Effie if her mother had ever considered remarrying. "No," she said laughing, "she never wanted to get involved with another man. She thinks it would be too much work!" Perhaps Suzie had never quite recovered from her husband's death, or it could be that she believed that, having been such a fine companion, Tully was irreplaceable. Gaining another partner might also have meant investing in yet another long-distance relationship. It could be that, after so many years learning to survive on her own, Suzie might have begun to value her independence, making remarriage that less appealing. Having become acquainted with her independent nature, I believe that Suzie simply enjoys living on her own terms, making her own decisions. At this stage of her life she seems satisfied with the ample companionship and comfort that her children, grandchildren and other family members supply. I asked Emily to thank Suzie for telling the story of her husband's passing. I was grateful to have heard it, because it allowed me insight into how she had once again adapted to a very difficult situation.

---

[166] Among many other texts, Kluckhohn and Leighton discuss the Navajos' concern with ghosts, undependable spirits of the Underworld, and other elements associated with death (*The Navajo*, 183-185). While these fears in no way hinder the Navajo from functioning on a daily basis, many prefer to avoid places of death even today.

[167] Downs noted that, "…the distasteful and dangerous job of burying the dead was often left to the trader." James Downs, *The Navajo*, 115.

Through Emily I told Suzie that I very much appreciated her candor. "Yes... I know," she responded with a smile. And with that she stood and stretched. I assumed Suzie was anxious to get back to the hogan, just in case there were visitors coming. She said something in Navajo, turned, and slowly made her way out of the little house.

It was only late afternoon, but it seemed like the logical time to end our work. I was a little tired, and I needed to pack for tomorrow's long trip home. As I gathered my things I thought of how content Suzie was, in spite of all the work her days required. Her years of middle-age had been difficult but fulfilling. Her children were healthy, her herds were large enough to support them, and she was free to live on her land much in the same way as her parents and grandparents had. Four-Horned Woman's great-granddaughter had acquired a life that women in her community would have deemed highly successful. Yes, there had been hardships along the way; times of want and uncertainty, but she seemed satisfied with how she had weathered the occasional storm. From what I could see Suzie did not fear or even think about growing older. The Navajo I encountered on the reservation seemed to truly respect their elders, and the Yazzies certainly valued their parents and grandparents. For Suzie, old age could be seen as the best time of life, though she spends it much as she always has. She tends to her livestock, weaves her rugs, and enjoys precious moments with her family. I didn't think anyone in my family had that kind of peace and satisfaction.

Emily helped me carry my gear out to the car, but after depositing her load in the passenger seat she hurried back into the house in search of something. I stood and stared at the little brown house and felt as if I were leaving "home." It had seemed a strange place to me at one time, but every visit reinforced the genuine connection I felt with Suzie and her family. I filled me with awe and gratitude. I was becoming a part of the beautiful Valley where my friends lived.

I absentmindedly plucked at my notes on the car seat. They were red with Valley sand, and as I shook them off Emily reappeared carrying something in her hand. "These are for you to remember me by," she said, and handed me a pair of beautiful turquoise loop earrings. "I know you usually wear small ones, but these match the ones I wear that my aunt gave me. You can put them on every time you come to the Valley so that you fit in," she giggled. We embraced, and I felt the hole in my heart that always grows when I leave the Valley grow bigger.

I hesitated by my car, not wanting to leave, but knowing I should. Suddenly, a jeep pulled up with a fair-skinned couple. A guide I'd seen in the park before helped a woman descend, while the man jumped easily from the vehicle and headed for Suzie who slowly walked toward the hogan. I stood watching with Emily. "He thinks you're another visitor who's just leaving," she whispered when the man dismissed me with a nod. After fumbling with his camera he looked to Emily and asked, "Could you take a photo of my wife and I with your mother?" I recognized the French accent from my years of studying the language in high school. "Oh, I don't know how to operate that thing," Emily lied while I made an effort not to smile. The man shifted his glance to me and asked, "Would you mind doing this for us before you go?"

"Oui," I answered. "You speak French?" the man asked in surprise, "Je parle un petit peu Francais," I responded to Emily's delight. I clicked the photo and handed back the camera to the man who then followed his wife and Suzie into the hogan. "I didn't know you spoke French?" Emily said as we made our way back to my car. "Just a little better than I speak Navajo," I countered.

I threw my things in the car and turned to Emily. "Well, I have a lot of writing to do," I sighed, "'hope I get it all down right."

"Oh you will *Sha Kiss*," Emily laughed, "that's why we picked you." I realized I still didn't know what that word meant, but the light was fading in the sky. We could no longer put off our goodbyes. I thanked Emily for the earrings, but she only shrugged in modesty, "Call me when you get back to California," she said with one last hug. It was hard to get back in my chiddy to go. I watched her wave as I turned the corner and drove out of the Valley that day with more tears than usual. With every visit it was becoming harder to leave, and I began to see why, in spite of the poverty and difficult conditions, so many Dine return. I knew that the Valley would call me again soon as well, and with my usual heavy heart I drove off under the vibrant blue sky.

CHAPTER 9 – LIVING WHITE, STAYING NAVAJO

"It is easy to be brave from a distance." – Omaha

A STRANGE GIRL IN A STRANGE LAND

I returned to Santa Barbara and concentrated on my family. I had little time to work on the Yazzie's story, but Suzie and her clan were always on my mind. I hated the nagging feeling of my beloved project being left undone. I read somewhere that the hardest part of writing is simply putting ass to chair, and it was true. I couldn't seem to find time to really sit down and embrace the huge task at hand. Part of my problem lay in the fact that my father had died quite suddenly.

My sisters and I had actually been in San Diego where my father lived. We planned to enjoy a rare "girl's weekend" together when my step-mother called in hysterics. My father had passed away during the night from, as it would turn out, cerebral meningitis. As a man obsessed with fitness, my dad seemed the last person on earth who could die in this way. Though emotionally distant as a father, I had always yearned for his approval. A former Navy pilot who had volunteered for three tours of duty in Vietnam, dad had always been the pristine picture of health. He was disciplined and mentally strong, if not warm and fuzzy. My father encouraged my love of history, and his curiosity about other cultures catalyzed my desire to study anthropology. He had expressed to me how proud he was about my writing, and I felt his influence every time I ventured into the Valley to work. Although unapproachable through my entire life, he was now gone…and all the approval I seemed to crave had gone with him. The emptiness I felt came as a real surprise.

Personal commitments also dogged me all year, and my husband's business travels meant that I was often left alone to care for my four young step-children. On the brighter side, I began to receive translations of my conversations with Suzie sent via Emily and Lonnie. Emily's work was particularly helpful in that it contained much more detail. Lonnie, like his mother, tended to be rather cryptic, and this showed in his translations. Emily's style was more like my own. She noted every passing remark and subtle joke, which allowed me to get a better sense of Suzie's innate personality. I still welcomed Lonnie's translations since it helped the work to proceed at a rapid pace. Because they both had been kind enough to help me, I overlooked the occasional gaps in Lonnie's stories, and relished the nuances found in Emily's work. And anyway, how could I explain to Lonnie that some random comment or passing remark in his mother's conversation might prove to be a gem to me?

I also had to remember that sacred information inadvertently brought up by Suzie was discreetly yet intentionally omitted by the family. I came to understand why my longing to just be that fly on the wall could never materialize. I wished I had learned to speak at least a little of the Navajo language. All of that time I listened to my instructional tapes only led to frustration. The Navajo share a complex language as subtle and evasive as they could sometimes be. My little flash card collection was a good start, but I would have to memorize a series of helpful phrases if I ever hoped to impress the Yazzies. I had to put aside all of the stops and starts, annoyances, personal issues and harsh self judgment. Letting these things go allowed me to return with a fresh outlook and an open heart.

My next trip out was during the intense heat of August. The rain came that summer as an answer to Dine' prayers, but the billowy clouds made my flight into Flagstaff bumpy and frightening. With my travel funds depleted I hadn't the option to take the comfortable train ride to "Flag," so I grudgingly boarded the plane swearing it would be my last venture into what I called "the tube of death." I survived the descent into Flagstaff, and the three-hour drive to Goulding's calmed me down. I had actually begun to enjoy the long, solitary ride into the Valley, and I greedily drank in scenery that I recognized and now called my own. I had no trouble marking certain landmarks along the way, such as the bridge that leads out of Cameron, and the two sandstone pillars that stand like sentries the next little town after that. I drove up the familiar steep driveway to Hill House, unpacked, and went for a run down the long road that took me past the lodge and the high school. Sucking in the dry air helped to clear my mind. I formulated a plan for this first evening in the Valley. As had become my custom, the first day was reserved for working alone to write and do research.

It was a pleasure to once again become settled in my little home behind the lodge. The two red rock walls that rose steeply on both sides welcomed me like old friends. Once again the wind whispered my name and caused bits of tumbleweed to dance through the little canyon. I loved how this place asked nothing of me, except the respect it deserved for providing such stark beauty. I wrote late into the night, and only gave myself up to sleep when my eyes became too heavy to work.

I expected Lonnie and Emily to meet me at the restaurant at nine the next morning. Assuming they meant nine in "Navajo Time" I was only just preparing my things to go at nine-fifteen and jumped at the telephone's piercing ring. It always startled me when the phone rang at Hill House. My family knew that on these trips I spent most of my days in the Valley, and that it was pointless to try and reach me at the lodge. "Where the heck are you?" Lonnie asked in a bemused tone when I picked up. Apparently they had been waiting thirty minutes for me to show up! I drove over to the restaurant in a hurry and found they had already begun their second cup of coffee. Both of my friends rose to hug me hello Anglo style. They looked healthy and happy, and once we had settled in and ordered breakfast we began our ritual of exchanging family gossip.

I was saddened to learn that one of the Yazzie brothers had been in a car accident and broken both of his legs. According to Lonnie, when the family went to visit his brother at the hospital they found he was still "alive and kicking." Emily rolled her eyes at the joke and filled in the story with her own information. Leonard was now staying with Suzie while he recuperated. The family had been worried about Suzie living out in the Valley alone at such an advanced age, so the accident seemed to them an indirect blessing. Even though her son could do little in the way of chores, at least now Suzie now had someone at the hogan to keep her company. When I told Emily about my struggles to learn the Navajo language she gave me a few simple phrases in Dine' for future study, including some words of greeting I could try out on Suzie.

The conversation then ambled over to stories about Lonnie's childhood in the Valley. I wanted to confirm a few points in the tale regarding an incident in which Lonnie hurt himself riding all day on the seat of the family wagon. "Was your tushy really that damaged from a simple wagon ride?" I teased Lonnie. "No, that must have been one of my other brothers, maybe Leonard or Harvey," Lonnie lied. But Emily would have none of it. "Oh no, it was you all right," she corrected her husband. She grinned at me, saying "he was hurting just like some of those visitors from Germany when they come on the Donnelley ride through the Valley." Lonnie laughed and nodded his head, "after a couple of day's ride I bet their butts look just like hamburger!" Emily and I giggled and Lonnie sipped his coffee, pleased to have directed the conversation away from himself. Later Emily told me that her husband was actually a pretty tough character and very strong for a man in his fifties. "He goes on a run sometimes two or three times a day," she marveled, "and he can run for an hour covering about five miles!" I asked her if he ran every day. "The only days he won't run are when he's called in to substitute teach," she informed me with a tone of pride in her voice. We both agreed that Lonnie would live to be a very old man because he was in such great shape. I secretly hoped that Suzie would also live many more years. In all the time I had known her she had remained physically active. She seemed so much happier when she could walk out to look at her sheep, and she was clearly keeping up her with her weaving in the hogan.

We finished our coffee and headed out to Suzie's to begin work. Lonnie went off on in his car to run errands while I drove with Emily to Suzie's. As we drove into the park we enjoyed our usual female conversation, bumping our way down the canyon and past the first visible monuments. When we reached the washboard road leading to John Ford's Point we came upon a dust devil. These little tornadoes of dirt are frequently seen throughout the Valley, and they were always amazing to watch. Emily told me a story while we let it pass in front of us. One day when she was a young girl she threw a rock into a dust devil and was severely scolded by her grandfather for doing so. "My grandfather was the strong silent type," Emily explained, "so I was really surprised that he got so mad at me for such a little thing."

Her grandfather warned that the little whirlwinds of dust were actually the spirits of the dead, and they should never be antagonized in any way. Furthermore, a person should never allow a dust devil to pass through them. These phenomena were to be respected and avoided at all costs. "He didn't have to tell me twice," laughed Emily. Thinking that it was better to be safe than sorry I made a silent promise to myself to heed the warning as well and avoid dust devils in the future. Following Dine' customs is always the safest bet whenever you find yourself in the Valley.

Continuing on our way, we happened upon Effie's daughters Erlene and Elvina. They were standing on the side of the road next to their mother's truck. The vehicle had stalled as they attempted driving up the hill to the Point. I was always surprised at how the family managed to eke out every drop of usefulness from this tired old relic. It was constantly in need of repair and only recently had Effie replaced the transmission. She saved money by doing it herself. "I know my way around a car," she told me. I thought that was a handy skill for someone living in the Valley. Unfortunately, after all her efforts she discovered that the truck refused to go into reverse, so all traveling had to be done in a forward motion. Now Effie's daughters could only wait by the car for a friend or relative to happen by and rescue them. As fate would have it we found them first, so we loaded up the girls and went on our way.

We arrived at Suzie's place to find Effie and one of Suzie's granddaughters. They all looked up at us in greeting when we entered, but Suzie was the only one who laughed as I struggled with "Yaa' t'eeh bah tah ishe' nana," the phrase of greeting I had rehearsed with Emily. I shook Suzie's hand loosely though I was certain she had once again forgotten who I was. Suzie resumed tying her hair into a "Tsiiyeel," the traditional knot worn by both men and women that is secured at the neck with yarn. Unsatisfied with her first attempt, she let her hair down and began again. I had never seen her with her hair untied, and I was stunned to see it stream halfway down her back in a long, gray wave. Fascinated, I watched her recoil the strands into a neat bun, then wrap yellow yarn around it over and over until it was nearly covered. With fingers that defied their visible arthritis, Suzie deftly secured her coif, smiling at me throughout the entire procedure. I smiled back, remembering our first meeting when she arranged my hair the same way using a weed brush called a "be'ezho'o'"

As we settled into work I pulled out a magazine I took from the America West airplane during my flight. Inside was an article that explained how the Navajo wrap their hair in traditional fashion. Suzie took great interest in the photographs, turning the pages until she came upon pictures of Navajo children participating in a rodeo. It was here that she came to an article describing how early in the twentieth century the Navajo engraved silver spoons as popular souvenirs. Suzie chattered on with Emily about the articles, pointing at various pictures and diagrams. I, of course, remained oblivious to the conversation and could only smile and nod, wondering what I was missing again!

I learned that Suzie would be leaving that afternoon for Keyenta in order to run an errand with her daughter. My hopes to conduct an interview were further dashed when I learned that Suzie already had visitors waiting for her in the shade house. I tried to hide my disappointment and went out to meet the nice Anglo couple visiting from the nearby town of Bluff. They had visited Suzie on numerous occasions, and ran a business called "Far Out Expeditions" that offered unique packages of travel to interested tourists. In their forties and very friendly, I found it difficult to remain angry over the intrusion on my day's work. The wife had been studying Navajo for two years and spoke it rather well. To make me even more jealous, I discovered that she was very good at making fry bread! All I could think of was my own poor attempts at forming the little cakes of bread. Unfortunately, Emily remembered the incident where I clumsily dropped the unformed dough in the dusty ground. She proceeded to tell everyone the story as I stood by trying not to look stupid. I suppose there was a bright side, as I did learn the Dine' word "dough" which is *"toss ne."* I also learned some helpful phrases such as *"k' ad da' ii da"* pronounced "kah dah ee dah" which means "now let's eat!"

This very kind couple turned out to be a real godsend. They taught me a lot. I learned that some Navajo children sometimes teach eager Anglo visitors profanity in Dine' as something of an inside joke. Should this occur, one is to reprimand the children, saying it is inappropriate to teach *"doh ah jah nee day"*, or "forbidden Navajo words." This couple was hosting a tour that day, and the small group of tourists began to file in for lunch. With little else to do I spoke to the guides who were making lunch in the shade house. One man by the name of Stuart Aitchenson told me about a book he wrote regarding plant life that grew in and around the Valley. In spite of my shyness the company was very pleasant. The fry bread smelled lovely, and they were made them into sandwiches of turkey, lettuce, mustard, ranch dressing and cheese. The company gave me a very kind invitation to join them, but not wishing to impose, I politely declined and slipped away. I was still coming to terms with the fact that life goes on at Suzie's place whether I show up with my tape recorder or not, and I stood by my rental car wondering what to do with myself.

Leaning against the car, I clicked my tape recorder on and off just for something to do. Nearby, one of Suzie's great granddaughters played in the dirt beside her cousins, who delighted in swinging a toy made of rope in front of the little four-year-old. I overheard the Anglo couple in the shade house asking if a photographer could take photos of Suzie and ask questions pertaining to her life in the Valley, and I experienced a strange sinking feeling when they commented that this photographer already had a company available to publish his work. I wondered in horror if I might have needlessly spent hours interviewing the Yazzies, not to mention all the expense of traveling out to the Valley! Could it be that the Yazzies might grow tired of waiting for my finished piece, and would perhaps find another interested party to tell their story?

And could I blame them if they decided to do so? Didn't Suzie need all the exposure she could get, along with the income that might come with it? Every bit of attention from outside the reservation could mean a small increase in the family income. The curiosity that came with it could bring in tourists interested in purchasing jewelry and rugs that could benefit the family. I knew the Yazzies struggled financially in order to remain in the Valley. Only this past year the owners of Goulding's had constructed a hogan by the airfield where rug weaving demonstrations took place along with the sale of crafts and jewelry. The convenience of visiting a hogan so close to the lodge lured tourists away from Suzie's place and cut into the livelihood once provided by her hogan business. I stood kicking dust off my shoes and watching the kids play nearby and realized I had no business pouting over any time kept short from the Yazzies. They were engaging in honest work, and I would just have to make the best of things.

After the tour people left and things had quieted down Emily and I sat down and chatted. She must have sensed how insecure I felt, and she assured me that I would be responsible for telling the family story. This brought me a sense of relief, but I suddenly felt out of place. The afternoon had come and gone and there now seemed to be no real reason for me to stay. I packed up my things and Emily walked with me to the rental. It was then that I discovered my keys were still inside the car behind doors that were securely locked! Once Emily calmed me down she put me in her car to seek out a ranger that might unlock my car with a slim Jim. The ride through the park gave me time to discuss with Emily my concerns about working with Suzie. Even if I spent every spare moment working on the project I still had my undergraduate work to complete and then possible graduate work to deal with in the years to come. When I finished the project who could say how it would be received? My writing skills had never been tested in such a way and I could not be certain that a publisher would be interested in the Yazzie story as I told it. Emily tried to quell my fears, quietly telling me that she and Lonnie felt that I was the right person to do the work and they had faith in me.

This made me feel a little better, and I turned the conversation to Emily and her own education. I knew that she wished to return to school and earn a degree, so I suggested that she seek out any loans and scholarships that might be available to her. What would be her major I wondered? Emily thought a while then said, "You know, I never really thought about what *I* would like to do for a career! I always just worked at what became available. I didn't mind the work, but it was never what I really wanted to do with my life." As with many women, raising a family and contributing to the family income had been her main priority. I respected her diligence, but told her that redirecting her focus would allow her to truly thrive in an academic environment. I encouraged her to pursue school and follow her heart to whatever life had in store.

We drove all the way to the tourist center to find a ranger, walked through the entrance to the information room, and Emily introduced me to Juanita. She easily tracked down a ranger willing to follow us back to Suzie's place. This man actually seemed to like the idea of taking the excursion and was able to open my car door in minutes with no damage done to the car. Judging by the expression on his face, he must have been a little surprised by the hug I gave him for saving my rental and me. I was finally able to drive out of the park and finish a very nonproductive day. I was hot, tired and a little depressed when I returned to my condo to work. Of course, I had to deal with my frustration, so I grabbed my old shoes and a hat to shade me from the still strong late afternoon sun and took a run.

I was invigorated by the afternoon exercise, and decided to use the rest of the day to do some serious writing. I showered, and walked to the spacious kitchen where I always enjoyed a spectacular view. I had no time to buy groceries yet, but I always liked the idea of making my own meals in Hill House. I knew it was time to make the drive down my street to the market, but I was lured to the patio to catch a breeze. Letting the warm air blow my hair around I reflected on how I would need to wrap up my interviews with Suzie.

So far we had covered her entire life memories, and now I needed to be more creative in my questioning. I wished to learn the finer details of Suzie's culture, and her personal take on current Navajo society. My questions would have to be presented in a broader, more open-ended manner. This could prove problematic, as Suzie has never been one for idle chatter. More than once I received a vague answer or no answer at all to a series of questions. This caused me to think of the two books that provided me with inspiration to work with Suzie in the first place.

"Translated Woman" by Ruth Behar, and "Nisa" written by Marjorie Shostak were both examples of the kind of work I wished to do with Suzie Yazzie. I already knew, however, that the subjects interviewed by Behar and Shostak were far more willing to participate in the endeavor of recording their lives. I yearned for the same kind of enthusiasm from Suzie, but it simply was not in her nature to open up her life for all to see. I didn't believe this was because she disliked me, or even that she had anything to hide. Overall, Suzie was a direct person and, while very hospitable, she simply liked her privacy. The problem of becoming more than a stranger in Suzie's eyes remained. Unfortunately, the long periods of time between my visits made it necessary to become reacquainted every time we sat down to work. Just as we began to understand each other I had to be on my way to resume a life very different from Suzie's. With every visit I re-established a rapport with her, only to watch it then disintegrate when I left the Valley.

Adding to my frustration were the constant interruptions brought about by those who visited Suzie. Warmer weather meant more tourists, and tourists meant income to Suzie. So often I had to stop our work together in order for her to concentrate on their needs. It was difficult to pick up where we left off, and the flow of any particular story was then lost because of the hogan business. Even friends and family who happened by could put an end to work, because these loved ones were a priority in Suzie's life. I tried to understand, but it slowed our progress and I found it hard not to be selfish about my short intervals with Suzie. I wondered if it would be better to interview Suzie in the evenings. Effie once told me that her mother was usually alone at night, so that time was sure to be quieter. I didn't expect an invitation to sleep in one of the hogans on Suzie's property however, and thinking of the long, dark ride back to Goulding's caused me to push the idea aside, at least for the moment. With all of this running around in my brain I threw my bag in the car and headed to the market. Perhaps a good meal would settle both my head and my stomach.

A FRESH LOOK AT TOURISM

"Traditional people of Indian nations have interpreted the two roads that face the light-skinned race as the road to technology and the road to spirituality. We feel that the road to technology.... has led modern society to a damaged and seared earth. Could it be that the road to technology represents a rush to destruction, and that the road to

spirituality represents the slower path that the traditional native people have traveled and are now seeking again? The earth is not scorched on this trail. The grass is still growing there." – William Commanda, Mamiwinini, Canada 1991

The next morning I drove myself to the Valley, intent on getting some real work done. Emily was there to meet me, and she seemed to be of the same mindset, because we both sat down immediately with Suzie in her little house and got going. During the course of past interviews Suzie had expressed concern over the future of her family and how the Dine' culture was evolving in the twenty-first century. We now discussed how tourism, exposure to Anglo culture and a lack of resources affected Navajo youth and their culture. I was interested in knowing how Suzie, as a Navajo woman, viewed the coming years. I knew her family had their own ideas about what the future held for themselves and their children. One thing was certain, the Yazzies had become very good about adapting to western influences while, at the same time, living "the Navajo way." As I spent more time with them in the capacity of a white student studying their culture, I began to recognize how I also influenced the Yazzies in subtle ways. It seemed inevitable that our relationship would change. What had begun as an opportunity to try my hand at ethnography now led to more intimate and complex interactions.

The tourist industry continues to play a role in Suzie's life both economically and culturally. Visitors are still invited into the hogan and encouraged to browse through her collection of the crafts available for purchase. This is offered as part of a package tour of Monument Valley provided by Navajo guides who ferry tourists in the open-air buses to view the picturesque monoliths and learn about the Navajo culture from natives. However, Suzie's relationship with the tourists who visit the family hogan business appears to have changed over the years. In the past many tourists arrived in the Valley with preconceived notions about how Indians should be. Visiting Anglos likely expected the Navajo to adhere to the stereotype presented in the media, such as in John Ford's Western films.

In some ways they were not disappointed. Most Navajo women continued to dress in the traditional velveteen blouse and full skirt until around the 1960s, and long hair was worn by both sexes in the customary yarn-wrapped fashion, though by this time many men kept their hair cut short. It was clear, however, that the Dine' were never the "Wild Indians" fabricated by whites in popular culture. Indeed, the Navajo enjoyed a rich and unique culture even during the assimilating years of the early and middle twentieth century, though few Anglos recognized the complexity of this culture at the time. It was only as anthropologists began to study Native Americans as a "disappearing people," that interest grew among the public regarding Navajo history and culture. The activism of the 1960s and 70s also inspired new ideas concerning ethnicity and race, and this in turn encouraged Native Americans such as the Navajo to see themselves as a culture separate from Anglo society.

A good number of tourists come from all over the world to see Suzie, and they bring with them different attitudes regarding her people. Some stereotypes regarding the Indian persist. There remain those visitors who expect to encounter the mythical "noble savage" or "lazy Injun." Yet today's visitor to Monument Valley is also more likely to have been exposed to new ideas concerning the Native American, and some of them exhibit a very sensitive and inquisitive outlook. Emily told me that, although Suzie speaks very little English, she does recognize certain phrases. Remarks made in her presence that imply the Navajo have a poor work ethic, or are prone to take advantage of government assistance, are not lost on her. On the whole, however, Suzie's experiences with non-Navajo visitors have been positive and enriching. She genuinely looks forward to the next arrival of tourists, not only because they support the hogan business, but also because they offer an occasional glimpse into the outside world. By making contact with these outsiders who speak of far away homelands, Suzie can become a "visitor" herself. In a slow and quiet way she asks through a family interpreter about her guests and the way they live. Most of these questions focus on topics that are important to her. Suzie will usually ask about a visitor's children, or about the environment of the country in which they live. She seems to enjoy learning about places that exist outside the reservation without leaving the safety and protection her home offers her.

From what I have learned about Suzie, she has never been interested in living anywhere but the Valley. A handful of relatives have instigated the few instances in which she ventured beyond the reservation. Throughout every experience she has remained unimpressed with places such as Hollywood and Salt Lake City, or "Sal Lay" as Suzie calls it. She once told me, "I never really went anywhere, just to Goulding's area. There's no place I want to go now. I like it here. Places like these different countries…there's nothing to see." It is not different places, but people that interest Suzie the most. She enjoys demonstrating the art of weaving to them while learning about their culture and how it compares to her own. Suzie has never given the impression that these tourists are an intrusion to her, though they certainly disrupt her daily life in many ways. And while Suzie has become accustomed to unannounced visits from strangers, I personally became irritated every time a truckload of them pulled up, bedecked in cameras and fanny packs. There were instances when Suzie and I were so immersed in one of her stories that we failed to hear the trucks approaching, and owing to these surprise interruptions, I would again lose one of those rare moments in which I had become her confidant.

Suzie's daughter told me that the hogan was officially opened as a business in 1975. The hogan business was Suzie's brainstorm after years in which she had sold her rugs, much as her mother had, at the trading post. Suzie's determination to make the best of the tourist economy evolved over time. It began when she posed for white visitors who had been brought into the Valley by Harry Goulding. As a child, Suzie modeled for photographs with her family during a period of time when automobiles were just beginning to make their way into the Valley. By charging fifty cents for every photograph, she and other Navajo were able to profit in some small way from the rare visit of an adventuresome motorist. Most tourists would pay the Navajo a few coins in order to photograph the natives at their weaving or sitting on a horse. Because of this early exposure to white tourists, Suzie grew up very much aware that her image had a value from which she could profit.

There is a small box in the hogan in which tourists are asked, by means of a hand-painted sign, to place one dollar for photographs. The Navajo tour guides usually remind their patrons of the fee required for photographs of Suzie and her family. I asked Suzie if she ever felt uncomfortable with tourists who wished to take her picture as well, but she never seemed to mind. It's okay," she responded in a good-natured way:

"I get some money out of them for doing it (giggles). Some of them don't pay very much, that's when I don't like it sometimes. But most of them do pay very good. Some are very nice when they come in, and some are not. They tell us that they don't understand the sign asking for payment because they come from across the Big Water (the Atlantic or Pacific oceans), but I ask anyway. It can be hard living here too."

Certain female family members will stand in for Suzie while she rests or has her noon meal. Those who take Suzie's place will usually wear the traditional clothing of velveteen blouse (or the now more accessible material of velour) and full skirt. One of Suzie's granddaughters seems to enjoy "modeling" for the tourists, and she has even earned her own money performing this service for visiting artists who are interested in capturing the image of an "authentic-looking" Navajo girl. The process of listening for vehicles and remaining prepared to do a weaving demonstration seemed to be an accepted responsibility that was just part of being a member of the Yazzie family.

It is important to the Yazzies that tourists be directed to Suzie's skill as a weaver and attracted to the handcrafted wares the family is selling. Most of the local guides are conscientious and keep visitors close to the hogan where weaving demonstrations take place. There have been occasions, however, when tourists were allowed to wander around the larger family residence or even peek into the shade house where the Yazzies were engaged in their noonday meal. The behavior of younger visitors also causes concern among the Yazzies, particularly when they roam the property unattended. I recall one day in particular when I witnessed a small boy racing around the hogan edges causing the earth supporting the structure to give way with every step of his Nike sneakers. Rainfall is required to repair the hogan so that the earth would be of a suitable packing consistency, yet no rain was expected for some time. Making this encounter even less productive was the female guide who failed to deliver the usual informative speech concerning Suzie and her work. "I was hoping she would bring more people," Suzie lamented to Emily.

"Yes," agreed her daughter-in-law, "and she just stood near the entrance (of the hogan) and didn't say much to her people (tourists)."

Lonnie laughed, adding, "That guide usually does that. She just stands there with her eyes wide open and stares."

Suzie giggled, adding, "She drives for the tour bus owner who's like that too."

Another cause for concern among the Yazzies is the rare event in which a guide bypasses the hogan entirely, in a rush to show his patrons more of the Valley. "Yes," Suzie confirmed when I asked her about the missed opportunity, "They just pass us by. We get dressed up and there is no visitor. This week we only modeled for one group. They just haul them (tourists) right by here. Sometimes the guides do that, but I hope next time they will bring more visitors." In spite of the occasional break in protocol, the guides usually work well with the Yazzies. Both parties recognize their mutual dependence on the tourist economy, and they do their best to provide a pleasant and educational experience. When the tourist season tapers off in the winter, everyone in the valley feels the effects. For the Yazzies, one week of slow or unsteady tourist traffic can mean the difference between having money to purchase feed for the sheep, and scrambling to keep them alive. On this particular day Emily told me that Suzie refused to go into town. "You have to have money to go over there," Suzie explained, "and I don't have any. Maybe if I stick around there will be a visitor, but so far no tourists came around…none all day."

I was also curious to know how Suzie felt about the tourists' disparaging remarks regarding the price of her hand woven rugs. Suzie always held fast to the original price of a rug, quietly refusing to barter; she was certain that the item would eventually fetch the listed price, and she refused to budge or barter. Suzie was proud of her work and confident in the quality of materials she used. "My rugs are expensive," she admitted:

"But I work very hard on it. Carding, then spinning, and washing the yarn more than once. It's very high quality and made of all natural material and a lot of natural dyes for color. I use plants from around here when I can. When the plants around here bloom they give you yellow, and that's when you use it to dye. You use the warp, and when you make a Yei for that it's a lot of work. This is why I charge the price I do."

I asked Suzie if she knew where her rugs ended up when they were sold to the tourists. "I don't know", she shrugged, "the visitors take them someplace away from here. I never see any of my rugs around here." She spoke of the demand created by returning customers who have collected her rugs over time. She took great delight in explaining the tourists' desire for her work, claiming:

"These people who have been here before, they come back sometimes, and they keep saying, 'I want another one… not for anyone else, but for me!' When I was younger people never ordered rugs to be made ahead of time. I use to do different kinds of patterns that I thought visitors might like. I tried a lot of different designs. I don't get bored doing the same designs. I am not like that, but some of my rugs would just end up different. On my latest one I thought the Yei would be too long, so I made the border wide. Things like that make each rug different, and I think visitors like that."

I asked Suzie if she believed the art of weaving was as important now to the Navajo economy as it had been in the past. "Yes," she answered, "but now it is different":

"There are still a few weavers around, but they don't weave as much. Now, in other places outside the Valley, even some of the younger girls don't weave. But I like to keep doing it. I like the tourists, and it's okay that they just come in unannounced. It's just the money that makes it important (giggles)."

I am uncertain whether Suzie would continue to weave if there were not a demand from the tourists for her rugs. Nevertheless, she seems to enjoy weaving and demonstrating her craft for visitors, and she is certainly highly skilled in this traditional art.

TWENTY-FIRST CENTURY NAVAJO FAITH

"You have noticed that everything an Indian does is in a circle, and that is because the Power of the World always works in circles, and everything tries to be round...The Sky is round, and I have heard that the earth is round like a ball, and so are all the stars. The wind, in its greatest power, whirls. Birds make their nest in circles, for theirs is the same religion as ours..." – Black Elk Ogala, Sioux Holy Man

It was during this trip to the valley that Suzie and I discussed the subject of faith at great length. She expressed some concern over the future of Navajo medicine and religion, yet she personally had great confidence in the practice of both. At this time she was still marking time in terms of the seasons, and she was able to gauge events according to what would be planted at a particular time of the year. She was very specific in explaining this way of thinking to me:

"June is the time of planting. And because planting is important we always know our directions; which way is east, which is north. You can tell when the weather is changing by the moon, for example if it is a quarter up that means it is time to plant a thing that goes along with that. I always notice when the moon is full, and I can tell when June is coming by the moon. March is called *Woozhch i'i'd,* May is *T'aatso'h,* and in July we start to see corn coming up. That means that school for the kids will soon start. After August, which is called *Binit'aats'osi'* comes the Early Harvest. Then we have a Big Harvest in September called *Binit'aats'oh.* There are a lot of fairs then, so that things may be sold. October is *Ghaaji.* It means "extended" or "an addition to." That is the end of harvest and the start of winter. I can tell things by the stars as much as I can with the moon. When it barely gets dark I can find The Seven Sisters, which you would call something else, but I don't know what that is. When the Seven Sisters begin to disappear it is time to plant again."

The fact that Suzie associated time with various seasons and celestial movements was further proof to me that she dutifully maintained these aspects of her culture as a personal choice. For some reason I took great delight in knowing that, while she had both a clock and a calendar in her home, she seemed more comfortable thinking of time in traditional Navajo terms.

I got the impression that older Navajo natives liked to do things according to tradition. However, not all Navajo chose to live in a traditional way, nor do all Navajo take part in important Dine' rituals. There are as many reasons for this as there are Navajo, once again because personal choice comes into play when one decides whether or not to embrace the native culture. Accepting the Kinaalda ritual as a symbol of womanhood, for example, may not be important to every Navajo girl. For some young ladies it may simply be too difficult to gather either the proper materials or the family support needed to conduct this ceremony. I asked Suzie how she felt about the declining interest among some of the younger Dine' in ceremonies such as the Kinaalda, and she was rather pragmatic in her answer:

"I think some girls don't want to do it because in some ways families are sometimes divided now. Sometimes their moms don't want to bother with it, and it is a lot of work (giggles). A girl and her mother need help to do this ceremony. To do it the right way the whole family must participate. Kinaalda is too hard to put together if it's just you and your mom. Some of my granddaughters got theirs done, but others have not because they lived too far away from family that would help out. I think some of them also were too shy about having it."

Suzie recognized how taking part in this ceremony might tax the family resources:

"It's hard sometimes, to put on ceremonies. It is hard to find a Medicine Man, and it is difficult to pay for everything. I can't afford much of it anymore. I don't work as much as I used to, and so there is less money. I hear that some of the old ways are starting to come back. There is more interest because the parents or kids themselves are pushing it. But a lot of the young people see the ceremonies as too much work, and that's why they don't get them done like they should. In the old days a young girl had two Kinaalda. We use to do the ceremony twice, with some months in between. Now some girls don't get the thing done at all, or they do a shorter version. They only run in the four directions and wash their hair. That is all, and there is no corn grinding or shaping of the girl."

Over time even more changes occurred within the Navajo religion. Certain actions that were once considered sacred or taboo no longer carry the same significance or concern among the Dine.' After reading some early literature concerning past Navajo taboos, I spoke to Suzie and was surprised to learn that there were quite a few of which she had no knowledge. This may be due in part to the passing of time, or perhaps knowledge of these taboos had never reached certain regions of the reservation. One important rule kept sacred among the Yazzies however was strict adherence of keeping one's Navajo name very private. When conversing with Suzie, I noticed that she avoided speaking her husband's English name, instead referring to him as "my late husband."

Some Navajo believe that speaking a Navajo's name in the presence of another Navajo is rude. I wondered if special care should be taken when speaking about family members who had passed on. Imagine my surprise then, when Suzie and I spoke of her Navajo name and she gave it willingly. "Isn't it wrong for me to hear Suzie's name in Dine'?" I asked her son. He seemed genuinely puzzled by this, and questioned his mother about the taboo.

"Yes," Suzie responded, "we didn't use to use them." When Lonnie asked why she simply stated, "I don't know. But it's not like that anymore." Lonnie went on to explain that Suzie had only given me her name of "Light-Skinned Woman" as it is pronounced in her own language. "She has another, more secret name that you haven't heard," he said with a smile. On another occasion I apologized for sitting cross-legged on the floor while conducting an interview. I had read that the Navajo do not consider this manner of sitting polite for a woman. Sitting Navajo-style was beyond my ability, however. The custom of maintaining the proper kneeling position caused my feet to fall asleep and my legs to cramp. "That's okay," Suzie reassured me, "lots of Navajo girls usually sit around like that." Suzie then let the topic drop, changing the subject to something more interesting to her. I knew the family well enough to realize they let me off the hook on a number of etiquette blunders. They were far too polite to call me out on any cultural faux pas, and like any visiting Anglo I was not expected to even know when I had made one. I was therefore lost in confusion over whether an action was taboo, or if had died out, or if I was misinterpreting a rule altogether. So much for my brilliant anthropological study!

While Suzie and her family discussed the future of Dine' religion, they pointed out to me the difference between Anglo and Navajo concepts regarding faith. Lonnie tried once again to explain what his traditional Navajo beliefs meant to him:

"White people call it Church. Catholics and people like that have a name for the place where they go to think things over. In Navajo we call it ceremony, in our own language. Even though we may refer to it in English as 'religion' or 'church', it's not thought of in the same way. We don't really have a word for what we feel about our faith. That's because our church is all of the land around us, and we practice our faith every day. Each day we sprinkle corn pollen for a blessing. In English, the white people go to church on Sunday. But for us, each day we use corn pollen and throw it to the wind is a sacred day."

"The sun, air, all the elements...we pray to each of them. Maybe that's why a lot of my family members don't use Christianity or go to a church very much. Maybe that's why we don't talk about these things. We pray all the time and we don't just set aside one day for church or praying. I know that white people pray outside of church too, but when we look around where we live, it just feels like we are surrounded by our place of worship. We do have certain things that we do in the hogan. Maybe a special ceremony day for certain illness is set aside, the Blessingway for instance. But the Christianity people talk about...well, we don't have that. There are a few people in our family that have become Christians, but my mother and myself and my kids, we are traditional in that way."

Suzie nodded in agreement as her son interpreted back what he'd said of their belief system. She relayed to me that her family felt much the same way about their faith when she was growing up:

"It was the same for us back then. A ceremony could take care of illness and anything else that caused you trouble. A Medicine Man would perform the ceremony and for one's self, you would pray on your own using corn pollen. You did this every day, early in the morning...at dawn. This is what they use to tell us to do to maintain harmony, and it is still important to me and my children."

While the Yazzies seemed comfortable in maintaining their native religion, it was clear that a certain amount of cultural change had occurred over the years. Of course, every society evolves, and no doubt Dine' society had been through a number of cultural shifts even before the appearance of the white man. By the time the United States acquired territory that included the Navajo nation, the Dine' had already adjusted from a society of hunters and gatherers to one concentrating on horticulture and shepherding. Environmental change in the 1930's brought about another shift among The People that leaned toward a tourist economy. Tourism became an especially important industry for those Navajo living in visually spectacular locations such as Monument Valley or Canyon de Chelly. It makes sense then, that these changes would alter the Navajo culture, although some of the changes were quite subtle. Through my conversations with Suzie I leaned how these were actually cultural adaptations her people chose as a way of surviving, and in some ways resisting, the Anglo society that was rapidly surrounding them.

I saw, for example, how Suzie had clearly made choices regarding the technology that slowly became available in the valley. To Suzie, there were certain advantages to owning a radio, but a television she could live without. And as she has grown older, she has changed her mind about what is and is not a necessity. I once asked her if she preferred her hogan to the stucco house in which she cooks, sleeps and stores most of her possessions. I expected her, as a traditional Navajo, to claim the hogan as a more acceptable structure. I myself certainly felt more comfortable in it. Suzie surprised me by stating that she preferred the house that stood some fifty yards apart from the traditional hogan:

"I like the house better (giggles). I still like the hogan a lot, but not as much now. I guess I would live in a hogan if there was one just for me, but now we use this one for other people as well, and for ceremonies. There is also a lot of dirt in the hogan (giggles), so if I had a real floor or even more rugs in there I would like it better. One thing that is different about it from the house is that the hogan is cooler in the summer and warm in the winter. I don't know why this is, but it works better in that way."

I never would have imagined that the dirt floor of Suzie's hogan would be a concern to her. After spending a good deal of time in the Valley I learned that the soft, red sand infiltrated every dwelling, be it tent, hogan or house. It was impossible to keep this insidious dirt from your home, your car, your clothes, and your life. I imagined that one simply got used to it and accepted the sand as part of the trade-off for living in such a beautiful and remote area. Yet, even for all the years Suzie tolerated the dirt, her standards of housekeeping were no different from my own. Her statement proved to me that her Navajo identity did not make her immune to seeing the valley sand as a nuisance in her home.

I asked Suzie what might make life in the valley more agreeable for her, and I expected her to make requests such as access to water, household goods or perhaps a vehicle for driving in and out of the park. I was surprised once again to hear that the changes most pleasing to Suzie would be aesthetic ones. "I would like everything nice looking," she decided, "like the sheep pen, even the house could be fixed up a little."

Her son agreed that these things would make Suzie truly satisfied. "She would like a real strong house so the wind doesn't push the sand in. Even the hogan could be built better, and maybe we should rebuild it soon." "The sheep pen, horse corral and cow corral could all be redone too," he explained, "but we need the supplies." Then Lonnie turned to his mother and said to her, "I told Coco that with a few repairs you would live happily here forever...no worries." "Yeah," Suzie giggled, "But everything is alright now anyway. I like it here the best."

SUZIE AND THE NAVAJO/ENGLISH LANGUAGE BARRIER

"How smooth must be the language of the whites, when they can make right look like wrong, and wrong like right." — Black Hawk, Sauk

Often when I spoke to Suzie our conversations would turn to the future of younger Dine' and the generations to come. Suzie seemed to realize that change was inevitable where young people were concerned. Exposure to Anglo schools and the media assured this, and Suzie rarely made any disparaging remarks about how such exposure had affected her grandchildren and great-grandchildren. However, she was saddened over the loss of certain elements within the Dine' culture. Suzie felt strongly, for example, about her family's ability to speak the language of their ancestors. When we were discussing how the Yazzie oral history had been passed on, she remarked that things had changed since she was a girl:

"I remember that the main storytellers use to be the grandfathers. My children's father's grandfather told us a lot of stories. Now some of the kids don't understand Navajo, and I don't understand English. *Dine' bizaad* (Navajo language) is usually learned through the mom. That's how we used to learn certain words for things. It was up to the mom to make sure their children understand Navajo. It isn't like that now everywhere, but my kids have been good about it."

Suzie's children were fluent in both English and their native tongue. Because they spent their young lives between boarding schools and the family hogan, a bilingual existence emerged out of necessity. Since her children provided the link Suzie needed between her world and that of the Anglos, it never became important that she learn English. I asked Suzie if there were any reason that she might wish to learn English now. "That's okay," she declined with a smile, "My kids all understand me, and I pick up a few English words here and there." This level of communication had been sufficient for Suzie in the past, and it seemed perfectly logical to her to speak only in her own language.

Emily took this opportunity to explain to her mother-in-law my desire to learn the Navajo language. She told Suzie that I knew other languages as well. "Hey, Coco knows how to talk Spanish," she bragged to Suzie.

"Oh," Suzie responded unimpressed, "is she a Mexican?" My translating friend giggled and said, "No, (laughter) she has always said she is a white woman." While I pouted over the implication that my identity was in question, Suzie went on to explain her thoughts about the white man's language:

"When people talk English I understand some. But I don't think I could learn it now. I don't know... (giggles). I'd like to learn more than the few words I know now, but I'm too busy, too many chores (giggles again). Anyway, English is a hard language to learn. I think that it is much harder than Navajo."

I was intensely curious about Suzie's feelings regarding communication between us. Was our connection destined to remain incomplete because I did not yet know the Navajo language? I imagined that my inability to grasp her language after a full year had created a wedge or a barrier between us. Any true exchange we might have was threatened by our mutual failure to grasp each other's language. I asked Suzie if learning her language would have made conversation between the two of us easier. "Yes," she answered:

"But I'm like that too. I think that I should learn English. It's just too hard for me now. Like you have said, it could take a long time to learn your language, and all the time I tried to learn English I would be thinking that the *Dine' Bizaad* is easier, (giggles). Some of us elderly people still use only Navajo, and we still do things our own way...the traditional way we were taught when we were young. I still point with my lips in the Navajo way, and things like that the young people don't do now. And now all the young people speak English too."

Knowing that Suzie struggled with my language as much as I did hers made me feel a little better. I will always wonder, however, if I could have forged a more meaningful relationship with Suzie if our interviews had taken place in the Navajo language. I feared that subtle meanings in Suzie's stories were often lost in translation. I knew that nuances that exist in most conversations that might have provided more clues about Suzie's life eluded me entirely. I went back to the lodge that day knowing that, in spite of the language barriers that existed between Suzie and me, we did have her story in common; my desire to know it, and her willingness to tell it to a stranger.

SETTING THINGS STRAIGHT – An Honest Conversation with Suzie
"You already possess everything you need to become great." – Crow

I had set my alarm for six in the morning in order to meet the sunrise. I was not disappointed by the event, and I quietly enjoyed the slow progress of the sun creeping into the Valley. The dawn broke to the left of my balcony where the park entrance gets the best of the sun. On my right the sky clouded over quite suddenly and a hard breeze picked up. To my surprise and delight a rainstorm passed over! It stirred up the comforting scent of wet dirt and warm rock. The sun soon returned and struck the buttes in a dramatic show of red hues. To complete the spectacle a rainbow appeared, arching from the rock formation across from my room to those behind me. I quietly padded down in my bare feet to get a better view, and standing directly under the rainbow I recalled the Dine' taboo against pointing to a rainbow. Lonnie had told me that angry gods creating the rainbow could climb from one's finger to the heart and wreak havoc. He explained that the Navajo do not generally point at anyone or anything. I had learned that old-timers like Suzie point with their lips, but I still wasn't sure if the idea of pointing with the finger is considered bad luck, or just considered a rude gesture. At any rate, I felt privileged to have witnessed such a display on the silent, freshly-washed road in the middle of my little neighborhood. It was almost as if the whole morning had put on a show especially for me, and it was a shame there was no one else there to share it.

I had a quick breakfast of cold cereal, and with a cup of coffee filling the remainder of my belly I threw my supplies into the jeep and headed for the Yazzies. I reached the hogan before Emily and Lonnie and brought in some fruit in for Suzie and her visiting granddaughter Lisa. Lisa had brought along her own daughter, little Myka. I gave the pretty girl with big brown eyes a candy bar, but then realized I should have waited. Now Myka was ignoring her morning meal of oatmeal, and instead concentrated on the chocolate. The day was already becoming warm, and my special treat to her went primarily around her mouth and cheeks. Throughout the exercise Myka still managed to look beautiful, and she shyly offered some of her chocolate to me. Suzie smiled her approval, and we three sat in comfortable silence enjoying the morning sun. Lisa told me that Suzie and other family members had been up late the night before talking about family business and telling stories. And I later learned from Lonnie that the family suffered from fatigue that morning because the corn pollen ceremony had not been done. He also felt very strongly that a Blessingway Ceremony should have been done for Lisa. The night's conversation had centered on her recent car accident, and Lonnie believed that a ceremony would put things back in harmony for her. They had reached an agreement during the night to have a ceremony that very week. How I would have loved to be present for it!

When Emily and Lonnie arrived we went directly to work. Emily put her skirt and blouse on and even dressed little Myka up for the tourists. The little girl was in her finest, and she began to stride boldly toward the hogan and the waiting strangers. Myka's skirt, a little too long and big in the waist, caused her to hitch it up every couple of steps as she made her way across the sand. The straight, black hair that had been all

202

askew that morning was now slicked back with water and combed away from her face. She was a delightful subject for the tourists' cameras, and I only hope she received her due pay for the trouble she took to clean up, not an easy thing for a four-year-old in the Valley.

I had practiced a little Navajo the night before, and I tried out a few phrases on Suzie. "*Nezhoon a nah nil sa*" I said with great difficulty, my mouth unable to form the words as they should have been. I meant to say "It's beautiful to see you again," but I actually ended up saying, "I'm beautiful to see you again." Suzie seemed very amused by my efforts. She laughed, but graciously accepted my greeting, nodding to say that she understood. Lonnie, Suzie and I moved to the shade house which was wonderfully cool and comfortable. It always surprised me how pleasant such a fragile-looking collection of branches could be. Lonnie discussed with me the family's developing case against Kerr-Mcgee. The family could not afford their own lawyer, so he wished to consult the company's representative about collecting the customary $100,000 offered to victims. Lonnie was hoping to increase the compensation to $200,000, but the family is in dire need of funds. They will most likely have to relent and accept the lesser amount in spite of the many health problems their father suffered because of his work in the mines.

Lonnie quickly moved to change our focus on work, and I began the interview with a hodge-podge of questions I had compiled through my readings of various books about the Navajo; some that had been recently published and some that were quite old. I wanted to learn how much of the Navajo culture had changed over time, and how well it had been recorded. I noticed once more how Lonnie asked Suzie's questions without looking directly at her, in the Navajo custom. She in turn did not meet his eyes. When translating back to me, however, Lonnie and I spoke eye to eye in the Western style. I observed as my friend practiced two cultures at once in an effort to be polite to both his mother and to me. I caught myself in the same dilemma. I could no longer speak with Suzie while looking her in the eye, and could only steal glances at her in the same manner in which she observed me. Did Suzie recognize my efforts to be respectful? I would never know, but I congratulated myself on my attempts to adapt and embrace the way things are done in the Valley.

I felt as if my time with Suzie was nearing its end, and it made me think of how I wanted to write out her story. My intent was not to glamorize Dine' life. Indeed, most Navajo living on the reservation face challenges that seem less than blissfully spiritual. After a peaceful and ancient corn pollen ceremony is performed in the morning, one still has to drive to the well for water, or look for sheep that may have wondered miles away in the cold or heat. The children still may have to travel far from home to attend school, while the rest of the family looks for work in an area that continues to grapple with economic depression.

It is no wonder then that some of the Navajo living here rely on their native faith. However, in spite of the hardships they endured, it seemed to me that the people living in the Valley had a terrific sense of who they were and what they believed in. While some skeptics may scoff over the "four-directions-honor Mother-earth" way that Native Americans are sometimes represented, the truth is that this way of thinking appeals to a rising number of non-natives. There is a good reason why the Indian's way of thinking has become popular beyond the boundaries of the reservation. There is a peaceful satisfaction among Navajos like Suzie and Lonnie who go through life with very little complaint. I do not mean to imply that the Yazzies are a complacent bunch. They have dreams and desires beyond their fledgling tourist business. But throughout each difficult day they truly appreciate the world around them. I envied their confidence that, no matter what, they could somehow make ends meet and continue to live as their ancestors had or at least as close to that as possible.

While all of this spun around in my head I sensed that Lonnie was having difficulty getting across one of my last questions to his mother. It was that age-old question so frequently asked by Anglos. I wanted to know what she had been told about the disappearance of the Anasazi. Scientific data that was available to me suggested that these people either left the area or were wiped out long before the appearance of the Navajo. Why, then, did Navajo legend, (according to Lonnie), suggest that these ancient peoples were actually an "old enemy" as the direct translation of the word Anasazi implied?[168] A mystery was always intriguing, and no one seemed to know where these people came from or what caused them to disappear. Had the Navajo encountered the remnants of the Anasazi population even as late as the seventeenth century, the approximate time of Navajo arrival into the area estimated by archeologists? I knew I would have little time to research this further, so in the meantime I asked Suzie about her view of the Anasazi legend. Suzie answered my tiresome little query in typical fashion; "I have no idea," she replied with a shrug. I had received this answer before, and I sensed that the phrase "I have no idea" was a well-used one in the Navajo lexicon. I certainly heard enough of it from them in English! I suppose I had it coming. Was I expecting some ancient Indian wisdom or timeless legend? I had to admit to myself how much I longed to discover some previously hidden knowledge or Navajo lore like a modern-day Indiana Jones. Instead I would have to be satisfied with the real-life stories Suzie gave me. They were interesting enough.

For the moment I went back to the question of religion. I felt as if we had not exhausted the topic and there was more to discover from Suzie about it. Lonnie tried once more to explain how Navajo corn pollen blessings and the performance of sacred ceremonies were simply considered a part of traditional Navajo life. He claimed that he carried out these spiritual actions without a second thought. Like living and breathing, the traditional Navajo practices prayer and rituals that have been passed on by their elders as a way to enhance their day and protect their own. I had never looked at religion in this way, though it seemed perfectly logical to Lonnie. I could tell by the look he was giving me that he found my questions a little silly. Why couldn't I just accept that his religion was different than mine, and just move on?

---

[168] According to Mr. Maldonado there is an on-going battle over this issue, but officially the Navajo Nation claims cultural affiliation to the Anasazi through oral tradition and ceremonial stories. Good references are "Wolf Killer" by Marietta Wetherill and "The Biography of John Holiday" by Bob McPherson.

Without waiting upon me, he turned to question Suzie in his usual rapid-fire manner. Before long I realized they were having a lovely conversation of which I was kept completely ignorant. I sat there pining for Emily's style of give and take translation that kept me abreast of the conversation's direction. Though I was denied the constant feedback I enjoyed from working with Emily, I did benefit from catching a few tidbits of information while mother and son conversed. It struck me that Suzie favored her father's side of the family over her mother's. I don't know why I assumed that in a matriarchal society the opposite would be true. Loyalty and alliance to one's family is based on many things, but Suzie simply felt her father's relatives cared for her more. By Suzie's account, her father's mother kept her and her siblings "better fed," and was considered "a real homemaker." Suzie spoke again of the occasions she was left with her maternal grandmother as unpleasant and rather unsatisfying. Her memories of time spent with that woman were only of hunger and a great deal of work.

She spoke of the days when her family lived by the Big Arches and raised corn, melon and other crops popular with her people that no longer grow in the area. I wondered how the Navajo acquired corn pollen today now that the crops had diminished to only the most fertile locations on the reservation. Lonnie told me that most Navajo had to purchase their pollen from these areas at the cost of five dollars for a very small vial. I made a note to look into collecting the pollen of corn that grew in abundance throughout the area of California where I lived.

Lonnie and Suzie now moved on to the topic of her grandfather, who had been a highly respected *Hataatii*, (a Navajo "medicine person" or "chanter.") He was the one who taught Suzie all the ceremonies necessary to raise her family. His granddaughter turned out to be a willing and adept apprentice and she was able to use this knowledge to her family's benefit throughout the years. Again Lonnie and Suzie became lost in their exchange with each other, and I was relieved to see Emily enter the shade house. Now the wooden structure virtually hummed with a mixture of English and Dine.' Swirling about in this soup of languages made my ears tickle, and it was difficult to separate the two while taking notes at the same time.

Lonnie turned and translated back to me his mother's recollections of her career in midwifery. I'd had no idea that Suzie delivered babies for her neighbors during her middle years. She explained how women came to her hogan for the procedure, using a "sash belt" tied from the roof. It offered support to the expectant mothers who would hold on while getting further assistance from Suzie. A "sing" occurred during the birth to take the woman's mind off the pain of childbirth, and a Medicine Man would fan the mother with an eagle feather to promote blessings. Meanwhile a "helper" such as Suzie would hold the woman from behind and help her to push the baby out. Songs and prayers for the mother and child occurred throughout the birthing, and Suzie explained that this helped to ensure the health and long life of both. Apparently blessings were given all throughout a woman's pregnancy, the actual birth culminating in the last of the prayers. She was unsure as to whether this type of childbirth still took place, but those present told me that it was doubtful and that most pregnant Navajo now went to the hospital to deliver.

It was the height of tourist season, and I could hear a tour truck rumbling into the compound once more. How many hours had passed while we talked away the afternoon in the Shade House? It had gone too quickly, but I sensed from my friends that our conversations would have to make way for the "visitors" arriving at the hogan. In true Navajo style I tried to keep my goodbyes brief and unemotional. I could now see the sense in this. Nobody likes to say goodbye to friends and family, so why say it at all? Lonnie and Suzie were already making their way toward the hogan, while I quietly packed my things to go. As I slowly pulled away from the compound it was only a solitary Emily who waved to me in her velvet blouse and long skirt. During the dusty drive home through the monuments I tried to imagine a middle-aged Suzie coaxing a new baby from its mother, and I suddenly realized the way I was telling her story had changed. It had evolved from a matter-of-fact record of Suzie's culture to something much more personal. I no longer felt the need to insert bits of historical reference that backed up Suzie's stories. There was very little I could find now that related to Suzie's thoughts on religion and culture. I was in uncharted territory now, relaying a history that was unique to Suzie and her family. Even at this time I didn't realize how much I was becoming part of the story.

CHAPTER 10 - SAYING GOODBYE

"Wisdom comes only when you stop looking for it and start living the life the Creator intended for you." – Hopi

SUZIE IN THE SPRING

Time marched on and I worked hard to complete my university program. I was done by spring break and was eager to once again resume what would be the last of my interviews with Suzie. With great anticipation I arranged yet another trip out to the Valley. I hoped to move on to interviewing Suzie's adult children, and finally one of her grandchildren, Elvina. I felt that getting a view of the past from the most present generation of Yazzies would give me a unique perspective. With this in mind I decided to also learn how they imagined the future for themselves and their families. With a renewed sense of purpose I ventured back to the peace and solitude of the Valley.

Lately I had felt the need to escape my house, with its responsibilities and teenager angst, even if it was for just a little while. I knew that if I had remained home I would have continued to put cleaning, cooking and caring for animals and children ahead of my writing. This would only make me irritable and not much fun to be around. My stepchildren had witnessed this restlessness in me before, and they urged me to take off for the Valley and work. They seemed equally pleased to have their dad all to themselves, so off I went in my desperate quest for a change of scenery and attitude.

I arrived in the Valley just in time to see the wildflowers in full bloom. Carpets of yellow and purple appeared as I drove onto the Rez.' It felt good to be back in the springtime. Something about the fresh air, the surprise of color and the occasional sighting of a little lamb made this trip "home" to the Valley fresh and new. When I finished unloading my provisions to Hill House I immediately got into the task of organizing the remaining questions I had for Suzie. It was hard to believe I was getting to the end of my long list! I wondered how many hours I had sat with the old woman and asked about her life. I had trouble recalling our first interview, and now we were nearing our last. The idea felt strange and satisfying at the same time. The afternoon was warm enough to work outside. I sat in my quiet little yard on an old log that overlooked the view of the familiar buttes and mesas. With only the chirping of the tiny native birds to entertain me, I sipped coffee and worked until the sun set.

The next morning I received a message from the front desk that Emily and Lonnie would meet me an hour later than planned. I used the time to shop for fruit, cheese, corn chips and the Hostess "Snowballs" Suzie so loved. One could never be certain how many relatives would be visiting, and I had no intention of showing up empty-handed. I closely examined the fruit section of Goulding's little market. Would Suzie like some bananas, and should I purchase oranges for any grandchildren who might be there? All of a sudden a pair of warm, brown arms enveloped me in a firm hug. I jumped and turned to see Emily grinning over my shoulder. She and Lonnie had recognized the New Mexican plates on my rental car and decided to sneak up on me. I graciously accepted the big hug from my Navajo sister and a fair amount of teasing from my Navajo brother.

Lonnie introduced me to a friend who worked at the market, and I shook his hand loosely in the traditional manner. The man glanced at Lonnie's baggy pants and said something in Navajo that made all three of them burst out laughing. Emily answered my curious look with the information that Lonnie's friend had just called him a "hommie" in Navajo. These people had a Navajo name for everything! After I paid for my groceries the Yazzies and their friend helped me carry everything to my car. From there we took off for our regular haunt of the Goulding's restaurant to plan our day.

Over coffee Lonnie announced that his mother had suffered a minor accident. I was alarmed to hear that Suzie had fainted by her home while out "looking for the sheeps." It broke my heart to think of the fragile old woman lying unconscious and helpless in the desert sun. Effie eventually found and revived her mother, then gave her a stern scolding about wandering out on her own. "The trouble," Emily explained, "is that Suzie doesn't think of herself as that old. I guess she thinks she'll never be too old to herd her own sheep. It's something she's been doing for years, and she doesn't like the idea of giving that up." Lonnie and I solemnly nodded our heads in agreement. It would take more than a fainting spell to take Suzie away from her sheep.

We quickly finished our breakfast and walked to the parking lot. Emily asked Lonnie to drive on ahead so "You girls could get caught up on your gossip." I did my best to keep his "chiddy" in sight as Emily told me about her concern for Sonny, her oldest boy. He had been violating his curfew, and was becoming more disrespectful of the house rules. At one point Emily tracked him down late in the evening and took him to the police station to "hand him over to the authorities." She was only trying to scare him into minding. My heart went out to Emily because I was so familiar with the antics of teenagers.

We arrived at the hogan just as a bus full of visitors was pulling up to park. Suzie strolled out to meet them, and I thought she looked pretty good for someone who had recently fainted in the desert. We sat in the car in the traditional way...respectfully waiting until the proper Navajo time had passed. Several minutes ticked by until Emily finally pulled open her car door. As we unpacked my things I caught sight of a face or two peeking out from the window. Cleary the people inside were getting curious. We entered the house where I was greeted with kindness and warmth. Leonard's daughter, Loretta, gave me a big smile and asked if I remembered her! I told her she was unforgettable and Emily and I exchanged handshakes with everyone in the room. Loretta went back to braiding her little daughter's hair and we all sat around to engage in the usual teasing that went on in this family. I didn't know if gently poking fun at one another was a custom specific to the Yazzies or a Navajo thing, but I was getting used to it. Judging by the laughter in the room I found I was also getting good at it! I took a moment to look around and noticed that the refrigerator and stove were gone from the main room. It made the living space around the wood stove much roomier, but I wondered what had become of Suzie's improvised kitchen. Emily explained to me that Leonard's presence in the house meant there were some changed in Suzie's set-up. Certain articles had been moved around a little to accommodate this son who was so tall he filled up a room no matter how quietly he entered.

Emily took me to the back rooms, which had been cleaned up very nicely as well. Gone was the collection of boxes and tools. Posters and pictures had been hung up and furniture rearranged. Even the floor had been swept, though the red sand was already starting to drift back in under the door. I glanced over at Lonnie and his older brother who were having a brotherly discussion. Leonard looked better than I had ever seen him. During my last visit he had been laid up from an auto accident with two broken legs. Now he gave me a smile which looked just like sweet Effie's, shook my hand and gently teased me in the Yazzie way. I felt as if Suzie's home was happier with the family filling it with their chatter and warmth. Unfortunately, with so much family present it also presented more commotion. How would I ever conduct a decent interview? Emily seemed to sense my concern, and she invited me to the hogan where I could work with Suzie once the visitors left.

This turned out to be an excellent suggestion. The tourists had finished their visit and were just starting to file out of the hogan. Emily and I watched the bus puff away down the dirt road, and then we retreated to the cool sanctuary of Suzie's traditional home. The hogan was definitely her favorite place, and she smiled a greeting to us before returning to her loom. She recognized me, and seemed enthusiastic about getting back to work. I rapidly set up for the interview. Once she saw my tape recorder Suzie abandoned her work and moved over to allow me to clip the microphone onto her collar. Emily seemed eager to begin as well, and she immediately began to translate my questions, giving Suzie time to think things through. I sat basking in the pleasure of working in the hogan. Like Suzie, this was the place I preferred but was too shy to ask outright about going in. The hogan always seemed too busy with family or paying visitors. At the moment it was quiet, and the sun streamed in from the stovepipe hole in the hogan's center. The singular shaft of light illuminated tiny bits of dust that danced in the lovely coolness of our earthen sanctuary.

During this interview I was delighted that Suzie talked up a storm. She enlisted that intriguing habit of pointing upward with her lips whenever she spoke of the past, and I enjoyed just watching her speak with Emily even though I had no idea what she was saying. I took the conversation in the direction of the Navajo tradition of burying their dead and how it had changed over time. I learned that not all Dine' placed rocks over the crevices where they buried their deceased loved ones. Suzie told me that when her little sister was buried in a rock shelter the body had intentionally been left exposed. It was hoped that animals would take the body away, thus returning the deceased back into nature from where it had come. Hearing this bit of information made me realize that I had once again made the same mistake of anthropologists who conducted the earliest studies of the Navajo. By believing there was only one way the Navajo performed burial I had pigeonholed all of them into neat cultural boxes. I had to remind myself that each family had its own traditions along with those passed on through their ancestors over the years. Although the Navajo were all members of a unique society, this society was made up of many different clans, families and personalities. I had wanted so desperately to see the Yazzies only as "Indian," that I failed to recognize their individuality!

Suzie and Emily went on to discuss various members of the family and the way they influenced Suzie as she grew up. I learned more about Suzie's relation to her aunt, Happy Cly. This woman's photograph appeared in many of the informational brochures and tourist books sold at Goulding's and the Visitor's Center. Emily explained that Willie Cly was Suzie's uncle on her father's side, and this made Suzie, Happy's cousin. Emily reminded me that Happy's name was ill-suited to the woman's demeanor. Happy was known to be quite abrupt and willful, or in the words of some family, "one mean lady." Suzie spoke once more about visits with her cousin where Happy "just tossed fry bread or mutton at the kids then told them to sit in the corner and be quiet." This struck Emily and Suzie as enormously funny, so I thought perhaps Happy was not really all that severe. If she was so unpleasant, how on earth did this woman get her name? "I guess she laughed when she was a baby," Emily answered.

I asked Suzie if she had felt closer to her mother because her father had been absent so much in his search for work. Suzie responded that she felt equally close to both parents, and she had loved her father very much. The only real flaw Suzie saw in his character was his unsuccessful gambling that taxed the family's resources. Just as I had looked past my own dad's shortcomings, Suzie forgave her father this weakness and remained loyal to him. Suzie giggled and said that her father was "a handsome man who had lots of new wives," after her mother died. Lonnie joined us in the hogan just in time to hear this information about his grandfather. "Yes, he was real good-looking," Lonnie said nodding, "and he would always have a woman even into his old age."

This made me wonder how Suzie felt about getting older, so I asked Lonnie if his mother had any concerns about losing her ability to herd or even weave. Lonnie answered that Suzie's generation did not view old age with any fear. "People in their right mind look forward to growing old because it is a time of wisdom," he explained, "People respect you more when you get older, and you spend time with your grandchildren in order to teach them the right way to do things." Lonnie had spoken to me before about being "in the right mind." He felt his mother had led a relatively peaceful and full life. The fact that she remained content with that life kept her in harmony, or in the "right mind." I wondered to myself how long it would take me to get my own mind "right."

However Lonnie shared many things that created anxiety for him and some of his family. The subject of Skinwalkers came up again. "Some of us know that witches and bad omens can have power, but only if an individual allows it can they be really hurt by these things." It seemed to me that a delicate balance existed between belief in the supernatural, and belief in one's own capability to resist any negative entity. Lonnie and his family were accustomed to maneuvering within the cultural constraints that promote both caution and self-confidence. While "witches," "Skinwalkers" or bad omens remain very real to them, it is up to the individual whether or not these forces have any effect. I told Lonnie that I read of other cultures in which witchcraft serves a practical purpose. When one member of a community accumulated a higher degree of wealth than his neighbor, for example, envy could manifest into an accusation of witchcraft. The wealthy neighbor's good fortune was attributed to something supernatural, allowing the less fortunate neighbors to save face. Lonnie agreed that gossip and envy could sometimes lead to trouble on the Rez.' "It's sad to sometimes hear this kind of thing still goes on around here," he lamented, "and it's been around us a long time."

The talk turned to maintaining the Navajo life style. It wasn't easy to keep it alive all of the time. "Lonnie and I are pretty traditional," Emily informed me, "but when we were younger we were introduced to other religions from white missionaries." She went on to remind me that it was the missionaries and white government workers who insisted every Navajo have a date of birth. "Remember when we told you about "birthdays?" Emily asked me with a giggle, "We didn't really go by that in the older days. We just knew what time of the season we were born in, so we had to make dates up." For the sake of recording the Yazzie history as accurately as possible I wrote down the "official" birth dates of Suzie's children. Still, it felt odd to know these dates had been randomly chosen by Suzie. No one, in fact, is really certain of Suzie's exact age or birth date. The date of April 15th had been chosen a long time ago, and her daughter could still only estimate the year of Suzie's birth to be "around 1920."

The Dine' faith appears to have held up well to the onslaught of missionaries and western education. While it is true that other religions exist alongside traditional Navajo beliefs, the synchronization of any religion with the Navajo faith cannot be said to have taken place because each religion is used in different ways. Some Navajo who consider themselves Christian may still seek out a Medicine Man or take part in a Navajo blessing ceremony. Even among the Yazzie's who do not consider themselves very "traditional," through their recognition of a taboo, or the utterance of a prayer out of habit, the Navajo faith remains a part of them. In her lifetime Suzie has witnessed a number of transitions within her culture, and she has expressed concern over the way some of the younger members of her family "don't have time for ceremonies." Lonnie told me that his mother recognizes how fragile traditions can become when people lose interest in maintaining them. To know that a tradition once held dear might disappear in the space of a lifetime is very disturbing both to Suzie and her son.

For my part, I was constantly asking Suzie about some taboo or tradition I had read about. It was confusing to study these things in some of the older literature I found on the Navajo, and then discover they no longer held any importance. I asked once again if it was acceptable to address Suzie by her name. Research dating from the 1940's maintained that speaking the name of any Navajo while in their presence was considered rude and dangerous. On this subject I had been partially right. Lonnie reminded me that the taboo did not pertain to one's English name, but to the "secret" name that was assigned at an early age. This name identified a person's spirit and gave one power. Anthropologists Kluckhohn and Leighton wrote in 1962 about these secret, or "war names:"

"Names are powers to The People. To use a name very often would wear it out, whereas if the name is kept fresh and full of strength, uttering it may get its owner out of a tight hole sometime."

Even by this time, however, the authors noted that:

"Although war names are still called 'secret' names by English-speaking Navajos, they are disclosed rather freely today, at any rate by girls and women."[169]

Suzie agreed that the younger generations had become lax about giving out their names:

"Yes, back when my great-grandmother ran away from the soldiers things were pretty sacred. That was how things were passed on, and our elders kept things up. They use to say we should keep our names to ourselves, and not to say each other's names. They use to keep a lot of things sacred. That was long ago, but things are different now. Anyway, you can say my name. There's nothing wrong with it to me. We have talked a lot together, so I don't mind."

Many of the older Navajo like Suzie, however, continue to respect certain taboos and traditions. Suzie follows the rules given to her in childhood:

"The Navajo way, that's all I use for most everything, even now. I still think of some things you have to watch out for. It's usually bad when a coyote crosses your path, and you say a prayer before crossing across where he was. Only after the prayer should you cross over anywhere he walked. There are a lot of things I'm careful about because that was what I was taught."

I learned that, for Suzie, some taboos make more sense than others. Lonnie explained that as a sheepherder his mother naturally saw the coyote as a threatening presence. To follow the rules that protected her from this creature's powers also meant to protect her property and any harm that might come to it.

Suzie spoke of how the Navajo religion has endured in spite of the introduction of other religions. She pointed to the fact that corn pollen, an important element in traditional prayers, continues to be in demand throughout the reservation. She worried that the climate of her homeland no longer favored those crops essential to following certain traditions. The once prolific corn fields have disappeared in many parts of the reservation, making traditional Navajos desperate to obtain corn pollen for prayer. "Especially now," Suzie lamented, "there's just never enough corn pollen. Some

---

[169] Kluckhohn & Leighton, *The Navajo*, 114.

people still sell it at the Swap Meets, but not too many." I offered to send Suzie some of my pollen the next time I put in a garden. Through Emily I explained to Suzie that that I had even grown a blue "Indian" corn. "She plants?" asked Suzie in surprise. Emily promised her this was true. "Why is she so surprised?" I asked my friend, "doesn't Suzie know that even white women who ask a lot of questions might know how to plant corn like the Navajo?" This brought on the usual laughter, but Lonnie grew serious when I suggested again that I might send them some pollen. He claimed this would be very helpful since pollen that is sold on the reservation often fetches five dollars per vial!

Dine' customs pertaining to burials were one of the traditions Suzie believed had gone completely out of practice. She saw this as a logical shift because burial services offered by white medical clinics served the Navajo well. For a people who preferred to limit physical contact with the deceased, it made sense to allow others to see to the burial:

"After a while people just always let the hospital workers bury the ones who passed on. A lot of us started going to the hospital to get better, but when someone died there the hospital workers handled the burial, and that seemed better for us. We could still bury the old way if we wanted, but after a while not many people wanted to. It's that way now. It's too hard to get rides to the rocks and places where a burial should be done. Back when I was younger, there were less people who could travel out here, so when someone died only their family who lived close by attended. Now when someone dies there are some families who have vehicles, so the burial is more crowded."

Suzie's daughter-in-law reminded me this was not the usual funeral rite for traditional Navajo. She explained that Suzie saw large memorial gatherings as something of an affront to Dine' culture stating, "That's the White man's way."

Over time Suzie has participated less in the Navajo practices she once performed, though she was well-known for her hand trembling and midwifery skills. In the art of hand trembling she felt less focused than during her younger years, and so refrains from providing this service to friends and family. As she grew older she also lost the strength to perform midwifery properly:

"No, I'm not helping women have babies anymore. The last I delivered was my sister's baby, my little niece. That was probably twenty years ago. That baby is probably twenty years old now! It takes a lot out of you to help with the birth. You need to be strong and help with the sash belt. I don't think many women have their babies here in the traditional way. This is something that they do at the hospital also."

Emily agreed with her mother-in-law. She had not heard of any women on the reservation giving birth in the traditional Navajo way because there were more clinics to assist new mothers throughout their pregnancy. Emily believed that Navajo women who received a white education were simply more likely to be attracted to western medicine. Increased access to white clinics caused Suzie to worry that Navajo medicine would die out completely. She believed that "white medicine" has diminished interest in traditional ceremonies among young Navajo. Suzie remembered a time when more faith was put in traditional medicine. She claimed that during her younger years the Navajo went to the Medicine Man first, only turning to white medical care as a sort of back-up measure:

"Yes, back then our people knew a lot more about how to find the best medicine. The first thing we did when you got sick back then, you would go to a Medicine Man. He would perform the ceremony, and then if you didn't get better you went to a white doctor. Right now many people go straight to the clinic, and so we are losing some of the ceremonies. It's like that because they are not learning the trade of Dine' medicine. I think this is probably because the people are going to white school now, and so they lose touch with the older ways of doing things."

Lonnie stated that he had more faith in the younger generation of Navajo. He had seen a resurgence of interest in Navajo medicine and religion among his children and their friends. "Nowadays," he offered, "there are young boys that are learning to be medicine men again, and that's what I see and observe. They are realizing it now how important our traditions are." Suzie seemed pleased to learn this.

"This is good to hear," she said, nodding in approval, "if the medicine is still there in people's minds then they probably will still practice it around here." Mother and son saw a glimmer of hope that the effectiveness of Navajo medicine would return. There seemed to be a strong "use it or lose it" mentality between them. Both Lonnie and Emily have done their best to expose their children to traditional Navajo ways, and Suzie believed that the future of her people rests with the younger generation. "But they have to practice it so that it can be done right," she warned, "Some Navajo regain their strength back by learning the older ways, and when they are strong the medicine still works."

HOW TO BE NAVAJO

"I will follow the white man's trail. I will make him my friend, but I will not bend my back to his burdens. I will be cunning as a coyote. I will ask him to help me understand his ways, then I will prepare the way for my children, and their children. The Great Spirit has shown me - a day will come when they will outrun the white man in his own shoes." — Many Horses

We could hear another tourist bus rumble up to the hogan, so I quickly threw my recorder and microphone into a backpack. Suzie understood what my actions meant and settled into her work at the loom once more. Emily and I retreated into the house to wait, but I found myself looking out the window to see when the visitors would leave. It still seemed strange to me how I had grown to resent their presence. I commented to Emily that even though I had once been the tourist tromping through Suzie's home haggling over the cost of jewelry and rugs trinkets, I now felt very protective of Suzie and the way visitors treated her. I knew that I had no right to be indignant. Hadn't I once been the "visitor" giving Suzie sideways glances? Even after I had started working with the Yazzies I had wanted Suzie to conform to the image I had of a Native American woman. Still, I couldn't help feeling that the tourists' presence was intrusive. When they failed to pay Suzie for a photograph it seemed wrong and disrespectful. And why didn't they ask Suzie more questions about her weaving? Why didn't they buy more of the beautiful work that the family worked so hard to produce? Didn't they know how much the Yazzies depended on the income generated from selling their work? Why were they allowing their children to climb along the bottom edge of the hogan? With the first rainfall the Yazzie's home would be eaten away where the little Nike footprints had left their mark.

Of course, not all of the visitors were as insensitive as I imagined them to be. Many of the tourists were quite respectful, kind and generous. But on this particular day I was literally on the inside looking out. Standing inside the Yazzie's house that I knew needed repairs, cupboards filled with less food than my own family ate in a day, I felt the urge to rush out to these visitors and explain how much the Yazzies relied on them. I knew these emotions were irrational, but I could not shake them. I had experienced just a tiny bit of what it was like to be the minority, the "other", or the Navajo, the conundrum being that I would never actually be Dine.'

The tourists finally left, and Emily and I tromped back out to join Suzie. I tried to put aside the notion that this was a silly ritual; rushing my White self out of the hogan so as not to diminish the tourists' experience with a true Navajo. It made me wonder how Suzie and her family felt about where they lived and how it defined them. Did Suzie and other Dine' look upon their reservation as something they truly owned? In a legal sense Suzie "owned" the grazing rights to a large chunk of the property surrounding the compound. But had she always seen the reservation as her home? Did it remain to her a sanctuary from the outside world? Were its boundaries seen as something that kept the Navajo in, or the Anglo world out? Through Emily I asked Suzie these question, and she came back with a poignant reply:

"This is my home, and I have always been happy here. My parents and their ancestors, they too were all happy to stay here. I have my sheep and other animals, and I want my daughter and other children to have it if they want to. I don't know what the younger people want. I know that white people are making plans out there [beyond the reservation], and they are the boss now. But this has always been the Navajos' home and it always will be."

Suzie went on to express concern over the young people who were forgetting the Navajo language and living urban, non-traditional lives. I listened to Emily's translation and asked her to explain my response as best as possible. "Maybe if you keep trying to encourage the young people to maintain their language, and the ways of their parents and grandparents, things will probably be okay," I said through my friend. I wanted Suzie to understand what I had been feeling for some time. "Some visitors come to see how you live because their lives are too complicated and they're looking for something else. We may be the bosses now, but that doesn't mean we're always making the right decisions. Our families are spending less time together and we have less time to do things we love."

Then I told Suzie why being with her and her family had become so important to me. "I don't really know my culture," I explained, "and even if I did I have no one to pass it on to. My stepchildren have never been interested in my religion or knowing about my ancestors. They have another mother, so they are not even entirely mine to love. I have few family stories, and none that date back to my great-grandparents," I continued to explain. Then I told her what had been bothering me for some time, "I cannot be part of your culture. It doesn't matter how much I learn about the Navajo, or how much time I spend with you. I will always be white and not Navajo. I like who I am, but I regret that I have few traditions, customs, or gods for my children." Emily translated while I thought over what I had said but had only just realized. Suzie nodded in agreement, and we three women sat in silence for awhile.

Luckily I didn't spend the entire day feeling sorry for myself. I snapped out of my melancholy, telling myself I probably wouldn't make a very good Navajo anyway. Suzie went on to discuss with her daughter-in-law how difficult it was to find a Medicine Man on the rez. Their numbers had declined due to a dearth of apprentices to whom they passed on sacred knowledge. This skill was always meant to be transferred from an older Medicine Man to his younger apprentice. It appears to rely on the connection to Navajo land and how the Medicine Man operates within the community. The trend among many young people leaving the reservation upsets the balance needed in the Navajo community, and decreases the number of prospective apprentices.

While we spoke I took note of how careful Emily worked to precisely convey my statements to Suzie. I could see that my friend had very good instincts as we worked together. She carefully thought through every question, and then decided the manner in which she would pose it to her mother-in-law. I believe this allowed me to gain a great deal of information in the most respectful manner. I could count on Emily to warn me when I was stepping over cultural lines and protocol. And yet, she always encouraged Suzie to supply the most complete answer.

Although Emily was as eager to provide me with information as I was to obtain it, she never pushed Suzie. The two of us became good at unspoken communication. She reminded me of questions I accidentally let slip by, and she explained why Suzie answered in a certain way or chose not to answer at all. Best of all, Emily translated according to what I have come to term "Suzie time." Nobody rushes the Yazzie matriarch, and Emily helped to quell my impatience as we waited through Suzie's long pauses. Emily taught me that when Suzie felt she had suitably answered one of my questions there was simply no way to get her to elaborate.

I cannot say how many times Emily and I gazed out to some invisible point waiting for Suzie to respond. Sometimes the answer came in the form of one sentence, and sometimes I waited through a very long explanation spoken in Dine' bizaad, the language of "The People." Though I could only guess what she was saying, I lived for Suzie's longer stories. When they came I found myself holding my breath, as if any movement on my part would break the magic of her storytelling.

One of the professors mentoring me while I wrote my thesis asked if I could reduce my block quotes of Suzie's responses to only the words that were pertinent to my question. "Do we really need to read the broken English?" he would ask me, "after all, it's not as if the form of her language really adds to what she basically means to say." I had to disagree however. I felt the way Suzie spoke actually enhanced the information she gave me. She was teaching me how to think like a Navajo, even though I could never be one. And anyway, I could not bring myself to eliminate any of Suzie's words that had been so hard won. If my professor had known how difficult it was to extract any response longer than a few sentences from Suzie, I think he would have allowed me those extra "I was told," and noted laughter I left in her narrative.

While I worked with the Yazzies they continue to teach me the proper way to behave in Navajo society. I tried to remember not to look directly at Suzie whenever we spoke, though I continued to catch her stealing amused glances at me. Sometimes I heard phrases repeated that I don't understand. One of the phrases that kept recurring was "it felt somewhat to me." I saw these words for the first time in one of Emily's initial translations, and I heard it again when Emily translated the phrase back to me verbatim from Suzie. I had asked Suzie about the stability of her culture as her once isolated world became more Westernized. All Suzie could say was that she recognized certain changes, and that now "everything's somewhat."

Emily immediately tried to bridge the language barrier that prevented me from understanding this phrase. She asked me, "How can a Navajo explain how the outside world feels? We can't really, and so we say things are 'somewhat,' meaning some things are good and some not so good. I've always felt that we are fifty years behind the rest of the world here," Emily continued, "And I'm not just talking about things like cell phones, but also for things like assistance for small businesses. We could really use programs that other people have in the cities, but they have been a long time coming." Emily went on to describe her mother-in-law's ambivalence, "When Suzie was young they needed assistance then too, but there was none so people starved. Now we need help managing the assistance we do get, and everything feels somewhat; somewhat strange, somewhat wrong, just everything sort of left undone."

This felt like a good place to stop our work. We were all tired, and my brain was over loaded with information I still had to process. Overall, we had enjoyed a very productive morning, so I made my preparations to leave and invited the family to my empty house for dinner. They had cooked mutton and fry bread for me so often that I felt the need to return the hospitality, let alone the need for companionship on my lonely little hill. We set a "Navajo time" for 5 p.m. and I hurried off to the market to purchase supplies.

I told Emily that I planned to make my special spaghetti dinner. "Oh anyone can make spaghetti," she teased, but I knew she would come to my house with an appetite. After racing to the little market and purchasing all the vegetables, garlic, pasta and ground beef I realized that I was running late. The Yazzies didn't seem to mind waiting however, because it gave them an opportunity to watch me cook. This can often be a spectacle in itself. As I danced around the kitchen furiously dicing and stirring food, the family laughed and pitched in when needed. Effie brought her mother into the kitchen and sat her down at the counter to watch. I offered her some grapefruit juice, but by the expression on her face I determined that Suzie didn't like it as much as her favorite orange juice. Suzie settled for tea instead. I felt her watching me very closely and later learned that she had asked her daughter and son if they were paying close enough attention to recreate the dish for her. My secret recipe was no longer safe.

Eventually the meal was ready and Effie went off to look for her mother who had wandered off during our kitchen conversation. Apparently she had become lost in the house after using the bathroom! I thought it very telling about how Suzie's immediate environment really had become her sole point of reference. Suzie knew her daughter's home and her own well enough, yet this house that had existed not twenty miles away in a place where few homes did exist, was alien to her. Perhaps I was reading too much into the situation, but it struck me nonetheless.

The Yazzies ate as much as they could stand; the ultimate compliment to a cook. We still had enough left over for Suzie to bring home and for Effie to feed her kids later that night. On this night it was just me and Em, Lonnie and Effie and Suzie. The five of us talked and laughed, reveling in each other's company and our full bellies. Lonnie turned the television on low, and in the background we could hear a rodeo taking place somewhere in New Mexico. It was so nice to entertain the Yazzies for a change, and I was sorry to see them rise as if on cue. It was getting late, and Effie wanted to take her mother to her house in Oljeto just ten miles away where she could enjoy a bath and the opportunity to visit her grandchildren.

We agreed to meet at the hogan in the late morning. Emily and Lonnie stayed a little while longer to watch the rest of the rodeo and sip tea, but they had to get back to the hogan where Leonard was staying alone. Emily helped me with the dishes first and I discovered she was as fastidious a housekeeper as I was. I even caught her scrubbing the burners on the stove until I shooed her away. "You still have to drive back into the Valley, and you know there will be chores in the morning." Emily agreed, no doubt contemplating how she would have to chop wood for the morning fire and help with the "sheeps." We all said our reluctant good-byes, and I before Lonnie had even driven down the hill I found myself falling into bed, completely exhausted.

A CHANGING ECONOMY
"Poverty is a noose that strangles humility and breeds disrespect for God and man." – Lakota

I worked in the morning, secure in the knowledge that Effie and Suzie wouldn't arrive at the hogan until 10:30 a.m. By the time I left for Suzie's it was nearly 10:15, and I was experiencing the Valley's own brand of rush hour. Stuck behind a tour bus I squinted through the dust it kicked up onto my little SUV as the larger vehicle slowly made its way down the steep incline toward the Mittens monument. It took some time for me to maneuver around and finally break free to the open dirt road. In my rear view mirror I could barely make out a big, green truck with Effie's smiling face at the wheel. We simultaneously arrived at the compound, and she parked right next me. With a deadpan expression I accused her of stalking me. She found this immensely funny, and I was welcomed into the compound once more to the sound of her laughter.

We agreed in would be best to work in the hogan again. Suzie led us to this favored place, and I adjusted my things in a manner that was now familiar to her. Once we settled in the interview flowed with ease. I liked the gentle way she spoke, and waited patiently for the translation of each answer. Suzie's voice hummed along like a warm summer day. She paused then resumed speaking in a rhythm so unique to the Dine' language. There were many different things a tongue were required to do when speaking Navajo, and hearing an eighty-year old Navajo woman was like listening to creek water falling over the rocks. Because of the time I spent with Suzie I could now sense what some of her responses would be, and when she would stop the conversation with "*doe-dah,*" Navajo for "I don't know." Sometimes I'd only receive a simple "*Aowh,*" for "yes." When I heard simple responses such as this I knew that the topic was generally closed. I sometimes pushed for more information, or I asked the same question in a different way. But as usual, if Suzie didn't wish to continue she simply changed the subject.

Emily stayed in the house, while Lonnie joined Effie and me in the hogan. Suzie chose this moment to bring out an artifact she had kept for years on her bedroom shelf. It was part of a bear claw that Effie said her mother had always cherished as a sort of talisman. Through Effie, Suzie told me that a white woman gave the object to her in appreciation for giving her information about the Yazzie's culture. I had heard from various family members that about thirty years ago a white woman before me had been to the valley to interview Suzie about Navajo life. I asked her about her previous contact with the woman I presumed was an anthropologist. She could recall very little of their association because it had occurred so long ago:

"I really don't know when the bear claw got here, but yes, the white woman had given it to me. She use to come over like you. What was the name of the place she was from? Was it Albuquerque? She's the one that gave me my sacred bear paw, with the claws still intact. I don't know where that lady went. Maybe she died of old age. She was just like you. She use to ask a lot of questions too. We would do things just like this...just talking back and forth. That was when my daughter was small, about eight years old. That woman use to visit my paternal uncle too. She asked lots of different stuff, like about our sheep and how we live, how a hogan was made and where the logs come from."

Lonnie remembered the woman fairly well. "Her name was Blanche or something," he recalled, "I remember we even went to her house all the way in Albuquerque when I was a kid." Although I never believed that I was the first person to learn of Suzie's life, I was surprised to hear that an anthropologist had paid Suzie a visit at a time when she was still living in relative isolation. Because I had discovered so much material on the Dine' dating back to the nineteenth century, it should have come as no surprise that academics were bumping around Navajo homesteads such as Suzie's. However, it was somehow disappointing to know that "whites asking questions" had pestered her and her family for so long. I asked Suzie if she ever tired of people like me delving into her life experiences. With her usual gracious attitude she answered, "No, I am not like that. I approve of what you're doing."

I wondered how much life had changed for the Yazzies since that anthropologist's visit some time back in the 1960's. Suzie and her family appeared to have adjusted well to economic changes that occurred in the Valley around that time. Like most families in the area they depended on agriculture and livestock, but sought out economic alternatives when these food sources became threatened. Suzie continued to maintain a healthy herd of sheep and goats for personal consumption. She keeps two horses for herding, along with a cow or two, depending on whether or not one is slaughtered. She also sees her ability to maintain livestock as part of her function as a Navajo woman, and she recalled a time when the herds were larger and absolutely necessary for survival:

"When I was young we use to slaughter sheep all the time. Back then we were always butchering. That was our only source of food. My paternal grandmother use to butcher sheep. She had lots of them and she kept everybody fed. The women usually did the butchering, and my daughter still does a good job at it. But we don't butcher as much nowadays. Now we only do it for special occasions like someone's birthday. People still have a taste for corn and mutton though. When the kids get together, they usually want sheep meat. I have about eighty sheep."

Lonnie agreed that keeping a herd was part of Navajo life when he was a child. He admitted that there were many times he craved the food that reminded him of home. "Yeah, sometimes you just get a taste for mutton," he reminisced. There was much discussion back and forth at this point. Recognizing I was getting left out of the conversation Effie answered my confused look. Suzie had been counting her sheep as they passed by the Shade House; carefully pointing each animal with her lips and adding the number in her head. This was a skill she had practiced for many years, and yet Lonnie disputed the number of his mother's herd. "I think you have ninety sheep now," he argued with his mother, "the sheep are 58 and lambs are over 30, so that's almost about 100." But Effie just shook her head and smiled at me saying, "I would bet my mom is right and Lonnie miscounted. My mom really knows her sheep. She's really good at math too."

In spite of the fact that Suzie had never attended school, she used those mathematical skills taught to her by her mother to keep close track of her herd. Lonnie agreed with his sister, explaining that Navajo women became even more adapt at figuring numbers since they were the ones doing business at the trading posts. Calculating basic math in one's head continued to be useful in Navajo families following traditional lifestyles. Lonnie went on to say that Suzie was religious about counting her livestock in particular because it kept her abreast of their condition. A lost or sick lamb might be saved once she noticed its absence. Lonnie was clearly very proud of Suzie's skills:

"My mom had a lot of early experience in trading that she uses now in the hogan business. She can add, subtract, multiply and divide in her head. A lot of Navajo women are good at geometry too. They think in patterns and shapes to use in their weaving. Moms teach their daughters how to do this so they can make rugs with nice designs. A lot of them are pretty complicated!"

Because Suzie still relied upon her sheep for weaving and food she was very good at identifying them. "My mom knows exactly which sheep are hers," Effie explained, "and she knows where they wander. She can track them down anywhere in the Valley." Even in her old age Suzie strongly believed that the welfare of her herd was one of her primary responsibilities, however she continued to struggle with the challenges shepherding brings:

"The coyotes steal from us, and that's why there were only a few sheep last year. When the sheep separate from each other, that's when the coyotes attack them. They go for the ones that are standing without a sheepdog. Sometimes the coyotes even cause the sheep to scatter and separate."

I asked Suzie how exactly she could tell one of her sheep from those in her neighbor's herd. She smiled as Effie translated my question:

"That's a good question, (giggles). We cut the sheep's tails to mark them in our own way. If a sheep goes into somebody else's flock you would know it's yours because of the way their tails look. We use to do their ears too, but we don't have as many to worry about, so now it's just their tails. My neighbors are good at knowing their sheep also."

Tourism is seasonal in the valley, and the Yazzies always experience lean months when the occasional meal of mutton and fry bread is essential for getting by. I sensed, however, that the sheep Suzie has kept all her life also provide an identity that is distinctly Navajo. Keeping her herd large and healthy gives her a great deal of satisfaction, and it is certainly one of the choices she made long ago about maintaining her culture.

KEEPING AND LOSING TRADITION

"If today I had a young mind to direct, to start on the journey of life, and I was faced with the duty of choosing between the natural way of my forefathers and that of the... present way of civilization, I would, for its welfare, unhesitatingly set that child's feet in the path of my forefathers. I would raise him to be an Indian!" Tom Brown, Jr., The Tracker

While I interviewed Suzie a Navajo man entered the hogan for a visit. I was surprised when he didn't follow the usual Dine' protocol of walking through the structure in a clockwise manner. Being Navajo I expected him to enter the hogan left and move toward the right as a symbolic gesture of respect for the sun's daily rising and setting in the sky. I had seen plenty of tourists come into the hogan to the right, but never had I witnessed a Navajo enter incorrectly according to tradition.[170] The man only made a brief visit and spoke mostly to Lonnie before he abruptly left. Once I heard him drive away I asked Suzie about this lapse in protocol. Her nod indicated she understood my question, and answered back that it wasn't unusual for a Navajo to ignore, or remain ignorant of certain traditions. "Not every person born Navajo knows how things should be done," she explained. Then with a giggle she said, "I think he was just in the dark. He doesn't know any better."

Suzie's son took the opportunity to tease me about the Navajo visitor. While in the hogan the man had asked about me, wanting to know if I were single. Apparently, he needed someone to take care of his home. "He asked her to take care of his house for him," laughed Suzie's son, "he'll do anything to get a woman to take care of him."

"He is a crazy one," Suzie agreed, "Remember, he's been married before.

"How many wives does he need?" asked Lonnie in mock surprise. Turning back to me he explained that the man probably thought I was a tourist, and that female visitors are the most fun to tease. "He probably says the same thing to all the German ladies," Lonnie warned while his mother giggled, "He just takes in women each day."

"He is nearly forty and too old to be flirting," advised Suzie, "maybe he should be fixed like a ram!" With this everyone in the hogan erupted in laughter.

All marriage proposals aside, I still wondered if traditions were disappearing among the Navajo. Effie told me that their friend actually knew more about his culture than some of the younger Navajo who reside in town. "A lot of Dine' children live like Anglo kids their age", she said. According to Effie, Navajo youngsters fall under the influence of the media in much the same way my own kids do. Popular images on the television or in rented videos determine their tastes in clothing and music. "The one thing that keeps us hopeful is hearing kids around here speaking Navajo again," Lonnie told me, "It's easier for them because instruction in the language has been offered in most of the schools. I've been seeing more young people attend ceremonies too," he

---

[170] Mr. Maldonado later told me that the traditional entry into a hogan to the right is only done during ceremonies. However, the Yazzies always made a point of entering the hogan in this manner.

went on, "I think they like being social in that way." Once again it was made clear to me that how much a Navajo practices traditional culture depends on each family and how they decide to live. The Navajo must continuously choose which parts of their native culture they wish to maintain, and which they decide to abandon.

Suzie has always felt more comfortable living much as her parents had. She even considered going back to wearing traditional velveteen blouses in place of the more popular and lighter valor. Velveteen material had ceased to be available in her area, so when she heard I could send her some from my city she became nostalgic:

"I like the velveteen better, it's thicker. Now there's hardly any in the Valley, but my mom and grandma wore it all the time. I just want to maybe look at it, and touch it. Women in my family use to sew coins on their blouses too. I still have the coins from that time. I put them away someplace. I know those buttons are stashed away. I'll put money on it"

Suzie said this with a giggle, and I wondered if it was an intentional pun. She continued to explain her preference in traditional clothing:

"I like wearing traditional clothes, but I understand why young people don't. I know some girls like jeans and T-shirts because they are more comfortable. Jeans were available to us through the white people when I was a girl, and now sometimes I wonder...why did my mom and grandma dress up in the Navajo way?" I still wear my jewelry, all of my silver and turquoise. A lot of us do, and we wear our hair in the traditional bun. I don't know why you would change it. Why would they cut their hair? I liked the bun better on men too. It looks better when their hairs were long."

Suzie then turned and gestured toward my hair. "You too," she noted, "you keep your hair long. You don't cut your hair either. You should let me put it up for you in the old way. I don't think you should ever cut it."

Suzie brought her children up to live the Navajo way, but makes no judgment on those who follow a different path. She encourages her grandchildren to speak the Navajo language and learn more about their culture. Yet, there has never been any pressure to strictly adhere to the customs and beliefs with which she was raised. Because Suzie was raised to be independent, she recognizes the value of allowing members of her family to decide for themselves what aspects of their culture are important to them.

Although she had faith in her children and grandchildren to remain strong individuals no matter what traditions they follow, Suzie also acknowledged that there are some things about their culture she thinks they missed. For example, she expressed regret that some traditions that would make her family stronger had fallen out of custom. The Navajo had a custom of encouraging their children from around the age of five to roll in the snow. This practice was thought to make a child hardy and able to withstand illness. [171] Suzie remembered this custom and commented on how the practice was dying out:

"It was good to make the kids roll in the snow when they were young, because it made them strong. We were told to go roll in it as many times as it snowed.

[171] Kluckhohn &Leighton, *Children of People*, 56-57.

If you did this you never felt the cold of winter, and even my grandkids did it. But now the younger kids don't make their babies do it, or they just have them sit in the snow for a few seconds, then run right back inside very quickly. They don't really roll in it like we use to. My kids had to. I made sure of it. I just told them to put some snow on their bodies and rub it around until they felt they had enough. But they were supposed to stay in it as long as they could. Then they could run inside and go around the fireplace."

Suzie seems resigned to the fact that the younger members of her family will be exposed to an entirely different world than the one in which she has lived. There came a time, for instance, when one of her grandchildren married someone outside their own tribe. I asked Suzie if marrying an Anglo or a person of any nationality other than Navajo, would cause any conflict in the Navajo community. I wanted to know if such an act would alter that person's standing in any way. She laughed and said:

"If I had married a white man back when I was young everyone would have teased me (giggles). Even now, if one of my grandkids marries someone who isn't Navajo we don't really like it. But we would never say anything about it. Nowadays kids meet their own mates, and there are no elders telling them who to be with. One of my granddaughters called from college in Nebraska, and she told us, "There's a black guy that is interested in me." She told her mom, my daughter, and her mom said it's probably not good. Because the man would probably want to live his way, how his people live, and not like a Navajo. I don't know if living that way would be easy after growing up here. Anyway, it worked out differently, because I guess now my granddaughter is going with a different guy. I think he is from the Ute tribe, but he seems okay."

Suzie saw patterns of behavior in younger Navajos that would have been unacceptable when she was a child. Like any parent she was disturbed by the careless waste many young people exhibit. Suzie was born and raised in an environment of scarcity and want. Nothing was wasted in a place where even the basics of food and water were hard to come by. One day Suzie and I were in the kitchen with other Yazzie women, when one of her grandchildren ran in for a snack. Suzie shook her head slightly and marveled at the haste with which this young girl discarded things that Suzie felt were valuable. "The kids just tear off a bunch of paper towels and throws them away," she sighed.

Nevertheless, Suzie seemed to understand that change was inevitable. Indeed, part of the resilience within Dine' culture lay in the way that it continued to evolve and adjust to the very forces that threatened it. Change had always been the one constant in Suzie's life. It was her love for the Navajo way sustained her throughout that change. When I asked her if she was ever bothered by the change she saw in her grandchildren, she simply stated:

"It happens. Kids use to be raised to only think about their home. But now things are different somehow. It's always the White man's language they use the most. And they don't think about the future like we did. We use to survive by making our own plans. If we wanted to eat we knew how to plan for the herd, and how to plan out a rug to weave and sell. Right now there are no plans and no goals. We are using the White man's plan instead. I guess young people think that way is easier."

I told Suzie that she and her family were still doing a good job of living the Navajo way, and that the "White man's plan" might never be appealing enough to completely change Dine' youth. I suggested she stick to her own "plan" of continuing her traditions and teaching them to the young people in her family. "Yes," she agreed:

"Some of them still have a grip on it, and they do a lot of things in the Navajo way. They like to have ceremonies on them, and they do speak Navajo when they are around here. I tell the Navajo creation stories to my grand kids and great-grand kids. They know their basic Navajo philosophy. I tell them about the old people and the oral history. I don't know…it seems as if some has been forgotten, because there are so many stories to pass on. I think a lot of it got lost along the way. It seems that way to me."

Suzie's son disputed this and reminded his mom that the Dine' culture was offered as a course in the reservation schools. His attitude regarding the survival of the Navajo way was more reassuring as he explained:

"For me, I think when I travel throughout the reservation; I think it was almost a good thing that our culture was almost lost. When I was younger they wouldn't let us speak Navajo in school, and it worried people. That was when we tried to speak it more at home, and that is why I teach it to my kids. Now I see a lot of people are learning it again. They are teaching the Navajo creation stories, some crafts and also the language in school. Some of the kids think a lot of it is cool, and they are begging to know about the culture and are re-learning it."

In addition to passing on knowledge of her culture, Suzie also must consider how to distribute among her family her wealth of livestock and family mementos. Suzie maintains a certain amount of flexibility when determining which of her children will receive portions of the family holdings. She has the last word regarding distribution of goods among them, and her decision is often based on an individual's need. While it is understood that her only daughter will inherit the hogan business and property, Lonnie and Emily will probably continue to take part in the hogan business as well. Effie has already taken over the management of some of the Yazzie property. Yet, she had told me that she prefers working at Goulding's and would like to attend college someday. Arrangements may ultimately be made to accommodate these and other wishes of individual family members. Most of Suzie's children take special pride in their plan to maintain the hogan business even after their mother's passing. Because they enjoy working with the tourists, and because the income is more or less dependable, they have assured their mother that the business she nurtured would continue to support the Yazzie family for generations. Lonnie explained to me how he and his mother spoke of this plan:

"I told her we could run it when she feels like she can't anymore. I told her we talk about it, all her kids. We all like the business. We say to our mom, 'hey, you started it, you should be proud. And after you pass on then keeping up the business will be the way we can remember you. We will always tell everyone that you started it from nothing.' So you can see that the hogan business is like a part of my mom. It is her legacy."

Suzie was very pleased with this plan, and she remembered her own decision to build the hogan business from her grandparent's and her parent's meager beginnings:

"Yeah," she smiled at the memory, "that is what happened back then. You learned how to run things from your elders. My late grandma and grandpa did things from the hogan too, with the tourists. They were good at making and selling rugs and jewelry. I mostly learned from my mom, and I did really well with it after that because more people came to visit. But this business, it's been passed on."

For the time being, Suzie remains capable of playing a major role in the hogan business, with her children taking turns in assisting her. A number of the Yazzie women weave, and the men usually make jewelry. They sell their work alongside Suzie's just as it has been for many years. In this way the Yazzie family works together in relative harmony while upholding Navajo tradition. I have no doubt that the sheep and other livestock will continue to be valued and maintained. It was comforting to know that some things in the Valley did not change.

As I once again packed away my things and prepared to leave, I wondered how long the Yazzies would be able to remain living in this beautiful place. Would this warm and cedar-scented hogan still be here for my own grandchildren to visit one sunny day? I wished with all my heart it would, and that generations of Yazzie children would be there to play as they had with my children during one of our horseback excursions. I could picture them even as I drove away, laughing and rolling down the steep hills of soft red dirt.

THE ANTHROPOLOGIST'S DILEMA
"If you raindance, you will get your teepee wet." — Unknown Tribe

I arrived back at Hill House just as the sun was threatening to set; just enough time for a quick run. I took the back road that stretched behind the lodge, and felt the wind push against my efforts and whipping the hair around my face. As I ran I thought of the words Lonnie had spoken about his own running habit. "I try to go farther each time because I feel Four-Horned Woman, who ran for hundreds of miles, looking down on me." I wondered if this ancestor was watching me as well. Half-way up the road I heard a truck approaching, and I jumped a little at the little honk the driver gave as he drove by. It was Emily and Lonnie! They must have been on their way to Effie's house in Oljeto. I could see Emily turn and wave, laughing over how they'd startled me. As I waved back I realized it had been a good day. I felt closer to my adopted family now that I understood a little better what it meant to them to truly be Navajo. I turned around at the end of the road; increasing my pace with the wind at my back. Yes, it had been a good day, and I felt the usual sadness sweep over my soul as I thought about leaving the Valley to return home.

That night the lodge restaurant was offering a Saint Patrick's Day meal of corned beef and cabbage. I had the ladies pack it up for me so I could eat and work back at the house. After dinner I called my husband to ask him about my laptop. I set it up for the first time since my arrival and was shocked to see it come alive with only two, broad vertical lines across its screen. This was what my daughter called "The Blue Screen of Sorrow." The call did not go particularly well. Maybe it was my disappointment that made the conversation with Ross so strained, but he didn't seem interested in talking and could offer no advice regarding the computer. I felt discouraged after hanging up, and only worked on some hand written notes for an hour before heading to bed. Maybe it was just as well to keep my phone calls back home to a minimum. I should concentrate on work when I'm in the Valley, and worrying about my family back home served no purpose.

The next day arrived bright and clear. I tried calling Ross just to let him know when I'd be leaving M.V., but no one picked up the phone back home. Out of curiosity I turned my computer on, and much to my delight received a fully functioning screen! Did my laptop just need a little nap? I didn't care how it had fixed itself. I only wished to make up for lost time, and I typed away at the little kitchen table as a warm beam of sun traveled along the floor. I was so involved with my morning writing that I lost track of the time. I was supposed to meet the Yazzies back at the compound by mid-morning. When I finally pulled myself from my laptop-induced stupor I realized there was just enough time to grab some crackers, cheese and candy bars; not the healthiest fare, but it would make do as lunch. I jumped in the jeep and made my way to the park.

Listening to some Navajo corn grinding songs on the CD player I thought of the work that awaited me back at school. Before this last trip I had spoken to my mentor, Ann Plane. She taught a course in Native American History at the university, and we discussed the way in which anthropologists were supposed to observe native cultures they were studying with the minimum amount of interaction. My anthropology mentor, Michael Glassow confirmed this, stating that a good anthropologist should never alter their subjects' lives by taking away something from the native's culture, or introducing anything from their own. No assistance should be offered because it was believed that doing so would alter the natural circumstances of the society under observation. Thinking back on these rules and how much the Yazzies' life now intertwined with my own, I had to laugh. Although these had seemed to be good standards to work by in the beginning of my project, I could see how they were now impossible to maintain with the Yazzies. After spending so much time talking about the past and each other, our hopes, dreams and disappointments, and sharing our concerns over family, fortune and failure, we simply had grown too close. How could remain distant under such circumstances. To do so would only show I had "empathic failure," a term I learned from a psychiatrist friend.

Perhaps even offering the few groceries I always brought to Suzie would be seen as unprofessional to my mentors. But I couldn't help myself. It was very difficult to see her bare cupboard and know that the person who offered me so much access to her life has nothing to eat. I could understand the reasoning behind these guidelines of anthropological or ethnographic work. It was a good idea to remain detached from the culture one is studying, but in my case an unrealistic one. I also thought it a bit unfair. Who were we, as academics, to consider ourselves invisible to those whose lives we undoubtedly affected by our presence? Did we really believe that the flesh and blood "subjects" we examined were unaware of our presence and our scrutiny?

I wondered how an anthropologist would feel if his subjects studied him, watched him struggle to survive, and offered no assistance so that he may remain "pure" within his Western culture. For that matter, what made the anthropologist believe she is *not*, in fact being studied by her subjects? It all seemed rather cold to me, and a little ridiculous. As I neared Suzie's compound I decided I would never be a very good anthropologist. When I joined them in Suzie's house I shamelessly offered my crackers and cheese with a clear conscience.

Lonnie helped himself to some crackers and announced that he was on his way to Goulding's market for evaporated milk. Apparently a stubborn little lamb was showing no interest in his mother or the nourishment she offered. Tucking the crackers into his denim jacket he tipped the dusty black cowboy hat he always wore and left us ladies to work. After Lonnie drove away the compound was quiet. Most of the relatives had left, and Leonard had gone to try out his healing legs by looking for the sheep. Emily and I gathered up some crackers and cheese and followed Suzie to her hogan.

Unfortunately, my time with Suzie was cut short when a guide entered with tourists bit failed to knock before entering the hogan. I had to scramble to unhook the microphone from Suzie's blouse. Flustered and a little put out, I gathered my notes and scampered out the door under the curious gazes of the tourists. I didn't know why I wanted to keep my work private. Maybe after working so closely with Suzie and her family I just wanted them all to myself. As I slunk back to the house I felt conflicted. I was disappointed that my work had been interrupted, yet I hated the idea that I might have ruined the effect for the tourists who, no doubt expected to see an authentic Navajo woman weaving in her hogan. Instead they were greeted by a suspicious-looking white woman who had the Navajo hooked up to twenty-first century gadgets!

I told myself it didn't matter. Nibbling on a cracker I realized that the majority of my questions for Suzie had already been answered. Perhaps Suzie and I had earned a break. Even Emily looked ready for a quiet day as she joined me in the little house that Tully built. I sensed that my friend had grown tired from translating all weekend long. We sat together drinking coffee and watching the late morning sun change the color of the rocks. I loved that beautiful, orangey glow. It made me feel as if the surrounding monoliths were embracing the house and protecting us.

SUZIE, SAGE AND FRAGILE
"Old age is not as honorable as death, but most people want it." – Crow

We heard the tourists drive away, signaling us to begin work once more. I had decided this would be my final interview with Suzie, and I asked Emily if she had it in her to translate this one last time. "Are you kidding?" she asked me with a grin, "I'm getting' so good at this stuff you're gonna want to hire me full time!" Suzie shot us both a quizzical look as we entered the hogan giggling. I asked Emily what her mother-in-law had said to the guide about my presence. "Oh she never said a word," Emily answered with an impish smile, "she wants him to wonder what the heck was going on here. Suzie likes being a woman of mystery!" We all laughed at that, even Suzie, who could only guess at what we were saying.

I began this last interview by asking Suzie how she felt about getting older. I hoped this question would not be considered rude, but I thought at the age of eighty-something Suzie must be beginning to realize that her independence would be somewhat challenged. Emily confirmed that physical limitations were starting to force her mother-in-law to alter the lifestyle she so loved. Just as any elderly person must rely on the help of others, so must Suzie be given support and assistance with certain tasks. I sensed that this new dependency on her children was a little irritating for Suzie. For years she had enjoyed the freedom to move about on her own and make every decision regarding her land and property. The new restrictions brought on by old age had to be frustrating. Suzie admitted that she experienced the challenges of growing older in a gradual way. She claimed to be prepared for these changes because she had seen how her own grandmother had struggled with the handicaps of growing older.

"My grandmother's name was eventually changed from "Light Skinned Woman" to "Deaf Woman" Suzie said with a laugh, "and I'm like her in that way. Hey, maybe that's why I sometimes don't know what's going on…I can't hear!" She and Emily giggled over this, and then Suzie paused and plucked at her skirt:

"I feel as though I don't move well on some paths now. I use to get around pretty good, even on the steep trails where some of the sheep like to go. It gets harder to walk now. I also don't see very well. A lot of times I feel as though I'm going to fall, and I did one time when I was out looking for my sheep. I got up alright, but now my kids tell me not to go out alone anymore."

Even household chores Suzie had done for years could now be a problem for her. Once, after a particularly long interview Suzie stood up to make coffee and staggered slightly. "Oh, whoa!" she exclaimed as she experienced a moment of dizziness. Luckily her daughter had been standing close by to offer her arm in support. Lonnie looked on with concern from the other side of the room. "It's probably because you got up too soon," Lonnie chided his mother, and I could tell that it worried him to see the fragile side of Suzie.

I asked Suzie about the day she'd passed out in the desert, and she explained that going to look for her sheep was second nature to her. At a very young age she had become accustomed to traveling for miles throughout her homeland helping to care for the family herd. She never once thought of herself as too old for the task. It was getting late. No family was around, and the sheep must come home. So off she went to look for her livestock as she had a thousand times before:

"I remembered I hadn't traveled far when I began to feel strangely. I don't remember anything after that until I woke up on the desert floor. I guess I got too hot or something. I got up and shook myself off. I don't know how long I was lying there, but I went back home and waited for my daughter. I never did find the sheep that day."

Once the family learned what had happened to Suzie they were very concerned. Effie chastised her mother and attempted to explain that it no longer made sense for her to go out alone looking for the sheep. Suzie, however, remained unconvinced, and the family had to keep a close eye out for the next time she decided to strike out on her own in the Valley she knew and loved. Suzie pointed with her lips toward the Fork stick hogan behind her house where Leonard now resides. She admitted that she enjoyed the company and appreciated her son's assistance. Yet, I sensed that, should Suzie have a mind to go herding once more that was exactly what she would do.

My next question to Suzie was difficult for me to formulate. I wanted to know if she was ever uncomfortable about the differences between herself and the tourists. Over the years Suzie had come into contact with all types of people of many different nationalities. I had seen busloads of German, Japanese and French visitors trample in and out of her hogan. I wondered if she had formulated an opinion on any one group, or if she viewed all visitors in the same way, myself included. Emily tried to explain how she believed Suzie felt by describing her own feelings on the subject. She stated that, for the Yazzie family, the most obvious difference between Navajo and "others" was the manner in which they viewed the world around them. "I don't know exactly how to word it," Emily mused:

"This Navajo belief, or Indian belief, is more of an inward thing. I think that compared to most Whites, we are more concerned about things that grow, like corn and sheep and horses. Things like that are at the top of our mind. We think about that kind of thing all the time, but the white people mostly think about owning things, not making them grow. They involve themselves in owning the land, and then they ruin it. All they seem to think about is how much they can pull around them, especially the new generation. I've seen White kids just throw perfectly good stuff away, and then they want more, only better. Everything is used up without any thought. Why do you think they're like that?"

I tried to explain to Suzie that it was how a lot of Anglo kids grew up. I used my own children as an example. They had access to nearly anything they desired, and yet that only led to the insatiable need for more. My son loved to play video games, but I believed the hours and hours we allowed him to indulge in those games gave him a sort of tunnel vision, along with a desire for instant gratification. I loved my kids, and I was very proud of how they excelled in school. They were made to do chores around the house, and they were always very giving to each other at Christmastime. Still, much like their friends who also came from wealthy families, the constant consumption of material goods seemed to lead only to waste and a constant feeling of dissatisfaction. I recognized this in myself as well, but it was difficult to explain to my Navajo friend, who had struggled all of her life for even the most basic things.

My voice trailed off as I realized there were some things I simply could not explain to Emily. Even though we had become as close as sisters, she had never been to my home as I had visited hers. I feared that if she did see how I lived in luxury compared to her, it might somehow ruin our relationship. The fact that our lives were so unequal would be glaringly obvious, and we would both be embarrassed. Emily simply stared out the hogan door that had been left open to allow the fresh air in. We sat in silence, listening to Suzie card wool and the occasional bleating of a lamb for his mama. I thought that as long as Anglos continued to be attracted to the beauty of Monument Valley, Suzie would graciously tolerate their presence. She seemed to genuinely look forward to the visitors, and Emily told me that her mother-in-law felt as if she learned something new every time a group of tourists came to see her. In spite of the occasional *faux pas* tourists committed by taking pictures without paying, or wandering her property without permission, Suzie found them to be pleasant and interesting.

THE MATRIARCH AND ME
"Be still and the earth will speak to you." — Navajo

This last interview felt different than all of the others. I wanted to get more personal and was also curious about my impact and impression on Suzie. I asked her pretty much directly what she thought of me initially, and she giggled in embarrassment for a moment. Blunt questions were not my forte with Suzie. But she soon collected herself and revealed what she had told her daughter after our first interview:

"That white lady is crazy. She asks a lot of questions. All the time she wants to know about how things were in the old days, and she also asks about the sheep and my weaving. She wants to sometimes know people's secrets."

I came to understand that the Navajo are not generally as open about their lives as Anglos. Many Navajo believe that telling one person everything about their past gives away power. They feel that when another person knows every aspect of your life they can then control you. Revealing your feelings, your name, or your past means you run the risk of losing your individual power. Maureen Schwarz wrote that:

"No Navajo will ever tell all that he or she knows about any one topic to any one individual. To do so is risky. To Navajo people, knowledge is a source of life-enriching and life-sustaining power because in the Navajo world an individual's knowledge can be used to exert power on reality."[172]

At first I shrugged off Suzie's comment. But later I realized that this Navajo idea made sense. Back home everyone lived in a world of "Facebook" and tabloid magazines. Nothing was sacred to a public hungry to give and receive the most intimate details of life. How refreshing it was to know that some people simply wished to keep their private lives private. As I sat there listening to Suzie and Emily chat I thought about how rude I must have seemed to Suzie with my constant questioning. She had been so gracious in revealing as much as she did, and yet I complained about how much she held back! I wondered how many other ways I had unwittingly made some cultural blunder. I suspected I had made quite a few. The Yazzies never brought these social errors to my attention however. I knew them well enough to see they

---

[172] Schwarz, 55.

231

would never wish to embarrass me. Some of my Anglo customs, in fact, rubbed off on my friends.

As I learned early on, the Navajo do not embrace upon meeting family or friends. They generally prefer a loose clasp of the hand as a greeting, and oftentimes they will leave without saying goodbye. Coming from a demonstrative family I never realized that my hugs and firm handshakes were an invasion of the Yazzies' space. When I read in one of my books about the Navajo that I had crossed this social boundary I was mortified. When I later asked Lonnie about it he tried to reassure me, recounting a story about the first time he met white people. He was still very young at the time, and he was surprised at the way they greeted one another. Laughing he told me:

"There were men that were so strong that when they shook my hand it hurt. They took my hand real hard, and now I tend to do that too. That's where I probably got it from. I remember we were told not long ago that we are never suppose to hug each other. When we were being brought up we were told only to talk to younger sisters and older sisters, not to touch them. With brothers you hugged them gently. Your uncles you would tease, and there's a kind of way to teach what is okay. Teasing is allowed with some people in your family, but not with others. When speaking to grandchildren you tease them in a way that sounds like you are jealous of them. You say to them 'who was that that came to see you, a boyfriend?' In this sense teaching of clanship goes on between different clan members. You respect each clan member. That means no touching, but it depends on a lot of different things."

"When you speak to your sister you can make hand gestures. You can marry into your clan, but it has to be the proper distance from a band of relatives of your grandfathers. Either paternal or maternal grandfather's clan is okay for marriage. But still, you were never supposed to go around hugging people all the time. Now it doesn't seem like that. We are doing more what the white man does when we greet each other. It use to be you only gave hugs when you love each other, like a wife and husband. Now even my mom lets people hug her. She didn't use to hug at all, only when we came back from school after being far away for months! We don't hug each other as much as Whites though. Around each other we still are careful."

Suzie nodded in agreement. She recalled how relatives teased one another to show affection. "Grandfathers would tease you about things like piercing your ears," she remembered, "anything at all would make them tease you. In this way you knew they were thinking of you." This teasing was acceptable as part of the relationship between Dine' family members, and could include sexual remarks. In one of his studies of the Navajo Clyde Kluckhohn noted, "The strongly institutionalized joking patterns between [certain relatives] are useful safety-valves...Sex is the subject of patterned jokes between certain classes of relatives..." [173] Suzie also confirmed her son's information regarding physical affection. "Yeah," she nodded, "some white people usually give you a very firm grip to shake, but Navajo relatives still do the loose handshakes." According to Kluckhohn and Leighton, confusion between Anglo and

---

[173] Kluckhohn & Leighton, *Children*, 88 & 101.

Navajo etiquette has come about ever since Dine' children began returning from boarding school. The anthropologists wrote:

"The returned schoolchild insists on aping white etiquette, this can prove most irritating to his elders. Navahos do not customarily say "good-by" when leaving an individual or a group; they simply walk off, even when departing for an absence of some duration. When they shake hands they do not exert pressure but keep the hand relatively limp – it is more a hand-clasp than a hand shake."[174]

Because of their contact with tourists, the Yazzies have somewhat altered their traditions concerning physical affection to accommodate white customs. Yet, the family continues to follow the Dine' way of greeting among themselves and other Navajo. Out of respect for them I also altered my style of saying "hello," but I still cannot bring myself to leave without saying goodbye.

We heard a rustling outside, and in a moment the figure of Lonnie shadowed the hogan door. "What's going on in here?" he asked with a smile, "Are you askin' a lot of questions again Coco?" As he settled in next to his mother I realized our interviews had not been one-sided. Over the course of our friendship the Yazzies asked me questions about my own family. Suzie was always curious about the lives of those living outside the reservation, and Emily filled her in on what she knew about me. Since Suzie knew that we were almost done working together I invited her questions and wanted to share what I could about myself. Emily asked Suzie what she wanted to know. The old woman admitted she was curious about the man who accompanied me from time to time on my visits. My husband never knew he had been the topic of Valley conversation. "The man has four of his own kids," Emily explained to her mother-in-law, "Coco tells me she didn't have any kids with him herself." One year Suzie actually saw me surrounded by my stepchildren. Ross and I brought them out for a horseback ride one year, and apparently she had expressed surprise to her family over how I cared for so many children, yet had none of my own.

"You mean that's not her kids, the ones she had with her?" Suzie asked in amazement.

"Yeah," Emily confirmed, "She is the stepmother." Suzie giggled and shook her head.

"She's not old. Why doesn't she want to get pregnant? Does she think the man's four is enough?" I don't believe I ever explained to Suzie that yes, four children by any means was certainly enough for me!

Now that we were wrapping things up I wanted to thank Suzie for allowing me to learn so much about her and her family. I hoped she didn't see my visits as a distraction from her hogan business. I asked Emily to explain how much I appreciated the time Suzie spent with me. "That's okay," Suzie smiled, "I like sitting here with you. Telling stories in front of my kids is a good idea. And I liked it when we worked in the hogan too." It felt wonderful to have made friends with Suzie and the rest of the Yazzies. They were a warm and caring family who treated me as one of them. Now they were all curious about the book I was writing and looked forward to seeing the

---

[174] Ibid., 74.

final product. Suzie was especially fascinated with the concept that her story would be written down in English. She saw this as the ideal way to share family history with her grandchildren:

"I see you writing, and you put it all down on paper. My grandkids will be able to read it now, and I want them to read the story back to me. I think it would be a pretty good story. Are you going to give me the book you make from the papers you wrote? Yes, that would be good. It would be good history for the kids. I thought it over, and I don't mind if other people read it. People should know how we used to live. And I like that it will be in a real book. That way I could hold a book with my picture on it."

Because Suzie was anxious to complete "the book" and enjoyed telling her stories, she often ignored the fatigue that came on after particularly long interview sessions. I cautioned her to take her time and rest between our conversations. "I'm probably going to get tired after this," she agreed, "that's why I'm going to lay sideways. That way we can work a little bit more." Watching Suzie adjust her skirts I wondered if she truly understood that we were offering others the opportunity to see the world through her eyes. She certainly seemed to enjoy our conversations, and Effie told me that whenever I left for home she would ask after me for days.

WHAT'S IN A NAME
"With all things and in all things, we are relatives." – Lakota

Since this was our last interview I asked Suzie if she would ever come to my house to walk on the beach, since she never actually set foot on the shore during her trip to Hollywood. She just giggled and said, "Is that where you came from? Do you take an airplane from over there?" I nodded and Suzie smiled, "Well, I would come. But I don't think I will come soon. I am like you, and scared of airplanes." I smiled back at my old friend, and we both knew she would never leave the Valley to see me in Santa Barbara.

Lonnie stood up and stretched. He had been a big help translating when Emily had to leave the hogan to see to some chore. However he already knew most of Suzie's stories so he had a habit of answering for his mother. He usually began his questions with "remember you told me…" and then launch into the story with his mother only adding occasional confirmation with a nod or "Ahoe." Emily told me that Lonnie had some wonderful stories of his own. I was curious to know about how he grew up in the Valley and experience with boarding school. I asked if he would agree to an interview along with his wife and sister. Lonnie liked the idea. "That way my kids will know more about what a bad kid I was," he laughed.

Suzie asked once more about my husband. Emily reminded her that Ross was the man she teased because of how much hair he had on his arms. Being of Scottish descent, poor Ross was indeed a hairy man. Suzie nodded that she remembered him:

"Oh yeah, he was handsome. We were saying he had a lot of hair though, (giggles), and maybe we should shear him in the spring. We could card his wool and make a rug! We could call him 'hastiin dibe' and tell him that means 'Sheep Man!'"

234

This brought about generous laughter all around, though I later learned Ross did not like this Navajo name. The next year the family would change it after seeing him work with their horses. My husband has a way with animals, and it took the family only one day of seeing their horses following him around to alter his name to *Chee Hastiin* or "Horse Man." My own name would go through one final alteration as well. Effie eventually let me know the family took to calling me *Asdzą'ni' na' id'di'shkid la'I' na' id'di'kid* "Woman Who Asks Many Questions."

I was having such a good time, but I needed to go back to Hill House and pack. Emily was surprised that I was leaving so soon. I usually stayed until just before dark. But I couldn't bear to prolong my goodbyes, and it depressed me to know my interviews with Suzie were over. I gave the old woman a hug, not caring that it was inappropriate. She smiled at me and quietly went back to her weaving as if I weren't going away for long. Emily sat quietly with me for awhile in my car, and then Lonnie came up to the window, and I gave his arm a warm squeeze. "Thank you so both so much for your time and companionship." It sounded so lame. They had opened their hearts and homes to me with no hesitation. They were a private people, and it could not have been easy for them to expose their lives. "Okay," Lonnie said with one final stretch before getting in the family truck, "I'm going to look for the sheeps." Emily gave me a knowing look and got out of my car. "Have a good trip back," she said and pointed to the sheep coming around the rocks. "He just likes to drive around," she explained with a laugh, "but I don't mind cos' he usually comes back." I drove away, this time without looking in my rear view mirror. I knew I would be back as well.

CHAPTER 11 - EMILY'S STORY

"If you chase two rabbits, you will lose them both." – Unknown Tribe

SPIDER WOMAN: Should I Stay or Should I Go?

I returned home and concentrated on my upcoming graduation. The first order of business was completing my honors thesis, and I spent the rest of the school year writing up Suzie's story so that I could submit my work as early as possible. With my mentors' help I accomplished my goals for graduate school as well. I wasn't really sure I wanted to continue my studies. It seemed unlikely that I would use a Master's Degree for anything other than a teaching position, and at the ripe age of thirty-nine I doubted I had the energy for such an endeavor. It was hard to resist my mentor's support and encouragement however, so I applied for the history program with the idea that if I didn't enjoy post graduate work I would simply pull out.

In the midst of all this activity I made time to call Lonnie and Emily. I wanted them to keep an eye out for the box of practically new clothing I sent that my kids had outgrown. Lonnie answered his phone in Chinle, and gave me the frightening news that Suzie has once again had an accident. After putting on an outfit that had been in her drawer all winter, Suzie was bit by a black widow spider hiding in the folds of her skirt! True to form, Suzie had not paid much attention to the pain and swelling in her leg, and went about her business at the hogan until it became difficult for her to move. When she finally mentioned something to Effie they drove to the clinic at Goulding's, only to discover that it was closed. The ladies had to make the hour drive into Keyenta where the "lady doctor," (Lonnie's words), did very little for Suzie. Over the telephone Lonnie became uncharacteristically irate; he complained of the poor care his mother received and she eventually ended up in the hospital.

I couldn't blame Lonnie. It could not have been easy for him to see his mother in pain. "All they gave her was some sort of pain reliever, "Lonnie explained, not bothering to mask his disgust, "they told us that the poison had already spread through her body and had to work its way out." Lonnie was concerned about how his mother's heart and lungs would be affected by the bite, and since there was so little done at the hospital, he took it upon himself to deliver Suzie to a local Navajo woman who knew the native cures for spider bites. "This woman gave my mom a remedy that has been used for as far back as anybody could remember," Lonnie told me. And over the phone I could sense the relief in his voice. He went on to say that after taking that remedy his mother's health greatly improved. "So now you can see," my friend explained, "our medicine worked better and faster than those pills the doctor gave Suzie in Keyenta." I had to agree with him. I had no health insurance, and therefore hardly ever went to the doctor myself, and I sort of wished we had our own type of "healers" in my town.

The family had still more challenges that year. Their business of taking visitors for horseback rides into the back country was now under tribal scrutiny. There had been grumbling by a rival operation that the Yazzies disrupted the environment and tourism overall with their riding excursions. I knew this was far from the truth. The Yazzies had always conducted the rides with great respect toward the environment and their neighbors. Nevertheless, the issue was undergoing a review and it was possible that year the family would be denied their permit. This was a real threat to the Yazzies, because the horseback rides not only provided income, they also allowed Suzie the opportunity to barter for some much-needed services. One year a group of riders pitched in to fix Suzie's hogan roof that was badly in need of repair. Other groups provided hay and essential provisions for the Yazzie's livestock. Out of desperation the family planned to present their case to the tribal council at Window Rock.

Emily then got on the phone to tell me she had graduated from Dine' Community College that spring. She and some other women wore traditional dress, and all of the students were photographed for the school's website. Emily's grand point average was so outstanding she won an award that included a laptop computer! There were also a number of computers donated to the school in her name. She had dreams of pursuing a Bachelor's degree, but was unsure about the cost. "I think I'll look into a scholarship," she said with excitement in her voice, "I want to see how far I can get."

I told Emily that I was planning to come out again to interview her. "Oh boy," she giggled, "now you're going to find out too much about me!" We set a date for that autumn, and as I hung up the phone I wondered how I would break this news to my husband. So far Ross had been gracious about my trips out to the Valley. Every time I scooted out to the Rez' he never once complained about our disrupted schedule. He always kept the kids focused on their schooling and maintained the house without complaint. I suppose he felt that my marrying a man with four kids was quite a challenge. It didn't matter how often I told him I willingly accepted his children as my own, and now it seemed unfair to be leaving them all yet again to travel out to the Four Corners. I wondered how long I could expect Ross to support my project with the Yazzies. And I didn't really know how many more trips I would need to gather information.

I called my sister Charlotte who had always been the reliable voice of reason. She listened to my concerns silently and then said, "Oh Coco, "the kids are in high school now. It's not as if they can't manage without you." But, I asked her, was it fair to put my little dream ahead of their needs? Was I being selfish in pursuing a writing project that may or may not get published? Char would have none of it. "Oh stop it," she finally said in exasperation, "If you drop the whole thing you'll end up resenting everybody. Get out there and finish the work or you'll feel a part of you is missing." I would be forty years old in one week, and decided to take her words to heart. Shaking my head I went downstairs to break the news to Ross.

A DIFFERENT SIDE

"There is no such thing as 'part Cherokee.' Either you're Cherokee or you're not. It isn't the quantity of Cherokee blood in your veins that is important, but the quality of it...your pride in it." — Jim Pell, Principal Chief of the North Alabama Cherokee Tribe

The summer came and went in a flash, and once again I found myself sitting at Hill House with tape recorder in hand. The room was warm with a gentle breeze slapping the venetian blinds against my open kitchen door. Sunshine filled the room but the air carried just a hint of September rain. Emily sat with me at the kitchen table in the little dining area just to the left of the huge picture window. I brought a supply of the Yazzie's favorite snack of sunflower seeds, and the sound of her breaking the seeds with her teeth combined with the Valley's gentle wind provided a symphony familiar and comforting to me.

She was here to tell me her story, and she would be the first of the Yazzies to divulge what it meant to grow up as a Navajo in "modern times," as she put it. We settled into the comfortable little home as two old friends bracing for a long talk. This interview with Emily was much different from what I had experienced with Suzie. No translation was necessary of course, so the conversation flowed with more ease, and by now Em and I were comfortable with one another. We had already shared stories that ranged from motherhood to life as older students attending college. Our bond had developed out of necessity, but grew stronger as we realized how much we had in common. So there we sat in sweet silence, eating sunflower seeds and staring out the big picture window at the Valley we both loved. Emily was a natural storyteller, so I had only to ask the occasional question to spur some memory. She knew me well enough not to anticipate my questions, and her life unfolded before me as if I were reading it from the pages of a book.

It was a nice change to interview someone who seemed born to narrate. Because my interviews with Emily flowed so easily, her testimony seemed to come out in one long, glorious story. The other Yazzie family members interviewed in much the same way, and it allowed me to present their lives in a format much different from that of Suzie's. Gone were the short, choppy paragraphs gleaned from constant questioning on my part. The Yazzies and I had the English language in common as well as a shared desire to learn more about each other. It was a nice change to record these fuller and richer tales from the Yazzies. They gave me clarity about what it had been like to grow up on the reservation. I started with Emily because she was the first one available for an interview. I began by asking if she knew her actual date of birth, and Emily took things from there.

EMILY SPEAKS:
"You cannot see the future with tears in your eyes." – Navajo

I was born September 8th, 1957. On the reservation it's kind of rare for Navajos my age to even know their real date of birth. Even as late as the fifties a lot of families still just went by the old ways of remembering what season a person was born in. But I have an actual date. I don't know why my mom remembered and wrote it down. Probably my earliest memory is when somebody hurt me. I think I was about four or five, and I was living in Chinle with my grandma. She was the one who primarily took care of me, although both sets of my grandparents lived close to each other, between Chinle and Many Farms. The only time we weren't there in Chinle was when we were in Idaho working out in the potato or beet fields. The whole family use to go; my grandparents, my aunts and uncles…everybody worked because we all needed the money. My mom, well I remember my mom was with us for a while then. My very earliest memory of her is when she slapped me (deep laughter). I think I was being bad, and she was trying to get my attention.

Yeah, at five years old I wasn't exactly working. My cousins and I were just in the way I think. We tried to stay out of trouble while the rest of the family worked in the potatoes, or in the fields of sugar beets, hoeing. That was what a lot of Navajo people were doing back in the fifties. We had to travel pretty far for work. We did that even when I was becoming a teenager. All the way up to 1972 or 1973 we did that kind of work. The money wasn't great, but it bought us clothes. And we needed clothes that fit for the school year, so we worked all summer. Us kids always told the employers that we were about sixteen, but by the time we were working as much as our folks we were really only twelve or thirteen. We would work with hoes in the fields together; my aunt who was about two years older than me, and then an uncle of mine who was about the same age as I was. We use to work along with the older adults. We hoed and we got our portion of pay. I *think* it was an equal portion of what my grandmother and those other guys were paid. We never questioned them about our cut. We just had to find a way to get through the school year, and boy that money helped a lot! We were able to purchase pretty good clothes with that money; pants that didn't have holes worn out from playing on the rez, and maybe even a skirt or dress.

It would take a long time to drive out there to Idaho from Chinle. We would leave close to noon, and sleep on the road at night when we got tired. I could never remember where we stopped to sleep, because we took off so early all us kids would just fall back asleep in the car. But when I tell you we used to sleep on the road, I mean we slept on the actual road, (giggles). We were camped out one time, (Emily giggled even harder), when I was about ten or eleven. There were three vehicles going to Idaho that time; my grandma's, and a couple of her cousins who had separate vehicles in their families. We used to work for a black guy and his family who were in the sugar beet business, and they used to ask us to come out every summer.

I remember pulling up on the side of the road, way off on the shoulder, and grandma along with the adults kicked back in the car to sleep. They told us to get our blankets out and we got out to our usual sleeping spots. When we were little we slept *under* the vehicles, because our folks figured that was the safest place for us, and it also made more room in the car for them. We were so little it was easy for us to just crawl right under the vehicles, (giggles) and it wasn't too hot. We put our bedding down and we all slept there. Early the next morning, I don't remember what time because it was still a little bit dark, a policeman drives up and says that we can't sleep there. We said, "That's okay, we've already slept" (giggles). We just got up and took off again.

We drove to Idaho with the back all filled up with belongings; utensils, food and everything that we needed for work…the hoes, hats. We had to bring all of our own stuff, but the pay was pretty good. We usually went to Idaho in the fall to pick the beets and potatoes and stuff like that. Kids used to work a lot harder back then. I think most of us around that time belonged to families that had to go off someplace doing seasonal work. Eventually we stopped doing that kind of work. I don't know why. We just never went back. Maybe it was because things got a little bit easier for us. The government started offering programs for us that allowed us to apply for food when money was tight. The state started helping out people that didn't have any income. That helped a lot of the older people who lost sheep during the reduction program. If those programs had never started I think most everybody would have left the reservation just to find work. We would have lost our entire culture. Instead the Navajo actually started coming back to the reservation, and a lot of folks figured out ways to make a little money. They would sell rugs and jewelry to the tourists. More visitors came during the warm months, and that helped a lot.

While I was very young my mom had an opportunity to get some schooling. She took nursing classes, and with that education she was able to find work in California someplace. I think it was in San Diego. Shortly after that she found work in Phoenix. It hurts me sometimes to think about how she just left me with my grandma. I guess she just didn't want to haul me around without a babysitter while she was trying to make a living for us. I don't know exactly how old I was when she gave me to my grandparents, but it's difficult for me to remember any of my childhood where she was around very much. I spent more time with her after I got older, but we never spoke of my younger years. I never really asked her about that time. Her and I don't really get along too well. We talk, but it's not like the discussions I have with my own daughter. My daughter and I can talk about anything. We can even argue and not let it faze us. We get things out of the way and then return to our normal selves; to each other again. I'm really proud of the relationship I have with her. My mom and I never really had a relationship like that. Even now when I get into an argument with my mom, she just totally ignores me.

Colette:

With this statement Emily took a long pause, lost in her own memories or perhaps saddened by them. At this time I offered to leave out the portions of our interviews pertaining to the more painful memories of her childhood. I told her that she had every right to simply choose not to discuss with me any details concerning certain family members in order to spare their feelings or maintain her own privacy. For Emily however, the idea of not speaking her mind seemed somehow dishonest. Was I not there to record the truth behind Navajo life? There could hardly be any point to our project if she hadn't spoken of what transpired in her youth, both the good and the bad memories. And while Emily did not appear to hold a grudge against her mother for abandoning her at such a young age, the experience certainly did shape who she would become as an adult.

Emily did not waste time feeling sorry for herself, nor did she seem to judge those who hurt her in her past. Instead she recognized the hurt, tried to understand the how and why of it, and placed it in its proper perspective. It was all very well and good to reflect on the past with me, but Emily lived in the present, and that was where she felt comfortable. I imagine such an outlook might save some Bilaga'ana a fortune in psychiatric bills. So it was decided that we would include any information regarding Emily's past. Emily explained her way of seeing the past as a lesson for her present life. She demonstrated the same pragmatic logic Suzie and other Yazzie family members enlisted as a tool for moving beyond those challenges that came with living on the reservation.

Emily:

My mom did what she had to in order to survive, and I understood that later. I think it's okay to talk about these things because they are true, and a lot of other Dine' families out there that had the same situation. And parents are still out there looking for work to support their families. The grandparents take care of the grandkids because their own kids are trying to make it out there in the world beyond the reservation. There just aren't any jobs here.

Colette:

This is a fact on the reservation. Unemployment has often peaked at seventy percent with relief only coming when temporary jobs become available during the tourist season.

Emily:

A lot of times the only option for young parents is to just give their kids to grandma. This is especially true for single mothers out here, and I realized what my mom did was in my best interest. In a sense it was good that she left me with my grandma. It took my mom awhile to wise up though, because she had another kid later on which she did the same thing to. That job went away pretty quickly though, and she kept my little brother with her as soon as she could handle it. My aunt took care of my little brother during that time. It's funny to think of it now, but when I was younger I just figured my mom was out goofin' off, and maybe she didn't love me enough to stick around. I didn't think about how she was working to provide for me.

Now I know better, and like I said, it's pretty common around here for relatives to watch over each other's kids. I raised my grandson while my daughter was trying to

241

finish school, and I've adopted my sister's daughter. Even the social workers around here know that if little ones are taken away from their original or biological parents, then the best alternative is either the grandparents or some other close relatives. There are so many that are willing to take on these kids as if it's their own kids. It has been a part of our culture for a long time.

Nowadays one of the main reasons kids are taken from their parents is because alcoholism has become a problem. Alcoholism can lead to abuse of the kids and then to neglect. Any time you have people around who don't have the opportunity to work you have problems with alcoholism. It's still a concern among our community. We always hope that things will get better but things are about the same because of the economy. We see the same young people with no work, roaming around out there or just hanging around at our local store. When there's nothing for them to do they get depressed, and that gets them in trouble sometimes. I had a couple of friends that passed on because of alcohol, close friends. They were about my age and they died pretty young, like around thirty, thirty-six years old. They are rehab centers that offer help, but usually the facility is outside of the reservation. Even if someone gets help, once they come back inside the reservation there are no maintenance programs; nothing like an outpatient thing. A recovering alcoholic looking for work usually can't travel to a program that is fifty or more miles away. That's just the way things are around here. Things can be tough.

So I grew up with my grandmother taking care of me. As for my father, well I never saw him. I never even met him. He was out of the picture soon after I was born. That never really bothered me since I always looked at my grandfather as my dad. He treated me so well. Because I stayed with my grandparents I never went to a boarding school like my aunts and my uncles did. They all got sent to Indian school, all the way down to my youngest aunt who is maybe about four years younger than I am. I think I was one of the few Navajo kids who didn't have to go to boarding school. Instead I went through a placement program in the few local schools that were around, and I did well there. Going back and forth among my mother's family was the only problem. I stayed at my grandparents' place a lot of the time, but also had a lot of uncles and aunts who filled in taking care of me. Sometimes they couldn't put me anywhere for one reason or another. I figured all this time that that my grandparents wanted me to be around them, (laughs) but later on I felt different. I thought to myself, 'wow, my grandmother must really love me if she's allowing me to stay here with her instead of getting sent off to boarding school like her other kids.'

I found out later that the whole reason I was staying with grandma was so she could collect welfare for me as her dependent. My grandparents had legal guardianship of me when I was about eight or nine. I know this because I remember standing in front of the judge at that age. This was when they started a program where if a child is put up, and given away, then the people caring for that child get funding. Apparently, my grandmother received what was called "Aid to dependent child." It's sort of like child support, but my grandmother had to let me go to a local school in order to be eligible for the money I brought in. And you know, she never even told me that. She never told me that she was getting money for taking care of me.

Mom came back for good when I was about fourteen, so I started living with her again. That's about the time I learned that my grandmother was afraid of missing the money I brought in, but I had to get out of that house. I told my mom about some problems with my uncle. He was abusing me, and I begged my mom to let me back to stay with her. I stayed with my mom, but all the while grandma was still getting help from the government. I guess nobody told the people in charge that I was with my mom. Anyway, it was good to get back with my mom and be a family. I had brothers and sisters by then. My youngest brother had been born. He passed away only recently.

My mom needed help taking care of the kids, and I liked doing it. After awhile I was staying home more to take care of my little brother and not going to school. At first I thought I would have more time to do my school work at my mom's, but it didn't turn out that way. I was pretty busy taking care of him especially, because he was still so young. I stayed with my mom during the school year, and only in the summer would I would go visit my grandma. By then it didn't feel right for me to be there anymore. It just wasn't the same. We all went back to Idaho that year for work, and we followed the same routine we had before. But when we got back to the house my grandmother really didn't have very much to say to me at all. It felt weird because once we got back home she made sure to be gone most of the time. She found a job working in a boarding school dormitory taking care of kids.

My mom had remarried by this time, and my stepdad was a bus driver. They did real well and had money for a change. Sometimes we could even afford a babysitter. They were doing okay, but they thought it would be better to put me on a placement program for Mormon educational assistance. That way the Mormons would take care of all the costs for my schooling. I was pretty surprised that all of a sudden my mom was telling me I was in a Mormon Church program that required me to move out of her home. Basically she put me in foster care, and I couldn't believe it. Maybe she did it because we didn't really get along. I never knew her, and she didn't want to know me. I came back later on to attend school while living with her again. After spending a little time back at the high school in Chinle I finished my senior year in Phoenix and graduated with my foster sister from the second Mormon family I lived with. The first time I lived with Mormons didn't work out as well.

KEEPING THE FAITH: Emily and the Failure of Evangelism
"If you take the Christian Bible and put it out in the wind and the rain, soon the paper on which the words are printed will disintegrate and words will be gone. Our Bible is the wind." — Unknown Tribe

Those evangelists intent on converting Native Americans probably did not consider the fact that their actions challenged and disrupted Indian culture.

Preservation of cultural traditions was not considered an issue of importance in Indian schools until the 1970s. When questioned about her childhood, Suzie's daughter-in-law spoke frankly of her introduction to Anglo religion and the effect it had upon her. Sent to live with a Mormon family to gain an education, Emily came to realize just how much more she identified more with her native religion. Many Navajo maintained an ambivalent attitude toward white religion. Some made use of the services these organizations provided, while quietly maintaining their traditional ways.

Mormons entered Navajo territory during the mid-1800s and eventually settled in Utah. They joined other Christian denominations in opening churches and schools on the Navajo reservation with the approval of the Indian Bureau, a federal government agency created at the time to assist Native Americans' assimilation. According to recent historical studies, missionaries acting within a number of Protestant and Catholic organizations were:

"…enabled to invade the reservation and force their beliefs on the Navajos by whatever means they chose to employ. Too often their stated purpose – educating the Navajos – was secondary to 'saving souls.'"[175]

While many Navajo children were diligent in rejecting the white man's religion, white educators often used tactics to discourage their practice of Navajo culture. Raymond Locke wrote that the children "were told that the songs and legends taught them by their parents were the work of the devil and had to be erased from their memory."[176]

The fact that many Navajo persevered in practicing a traditional belief system despite all efforts of white educators to the contrary speaks volumes about their tenacity and adaptability. Like other Indian nations, some Navajo chose to practice Christianity alongside their Navajo religion, further indicating that the attitude of Navajos like Emily toward Christianity can be characterized, as Locke stated, with "a shrug."[177]

Emily:

All during my Fifth, Sixth, Seventh grades I was in the placement program. The Fifth grade was the hardest; because that was the first year I was completely away from my family. I came in the middle of the school year, around February, and I felt pretty lost. I returned to Chinle that summer to stay with my mom, but in August I was back with a Mormon family for the next five months. I had a real problem with this Mormon family because of how they forced their religion on me. Before that time I had been raised in the Dine' faith and I was used to saying those prayers and using corn pollen. Heck, my great-grandfather was even a Medicine Man! When my brother and I were real little he would round us up in the hogan late at night and start telling us Navajo legends. It didn't matter to him if we fell asleep, because he felt just our presence would give us some understanding of the Dine' faith. He told us that even in our dreams we could remember the lessons and religious stories of our people, and he

---

[175] Locke, 415.

[176] Ibid., 417.

[177] Ibid., 415.

was right. I really didn't understand exactly what my grandfather was doing when he went out to visit people and perform his medicine. But I always saw him out praying in the morning, and he would get me up to pray too. I liked our Dine' faith and felt very secure in it.

I don't recall exactly how I ended up in the Mormon placement program. All I remember is that I was being passed on here and there, so I guess my family figured it was best for me to get into a family that could take care of me all through the school year. That first year was pretty hard. We met in the parking lot of the local Mormon Church, and all us students were put on the bus from Chinle. There were maybe three busloads of us that were taken all the way to Phoenix. All day we sat on those buses, and then when we arrived at the church in Phoenix we sat some more. Once the church people had us organized into groups they made us take showers. Then they gave us shots, I mean they cleaned us up real good, (giggles).

Then it was time to meet our families. Well, when everybody was picked up by their foster families...I didn't have one! I was there all by myself. Apparently, the family that was gonna take me never showed up. They never even bothered to let anyone know they had changed their minds about taking me. The church people didn't know what to do with me, so they dumped me on a family that had a bunch of little kids. The dad was important I guess; some kind of a bishop in the church. I think his wife was a little annoyed to find a Navajo girl living with them. I found this out at the very beginning. She told me so one of the first days I was there. For some reason she had decided to teach me how to play their piano, and she showed me how to practice. I worked on it for awhile and didn't hear her calling me to help with the kids. So this lady must have thought I was ignoring her, because she comes out she says, "You know, it's a lot of trouble having a Navajo girl around." She told me it was especially hard on her because there was an extra kid in the house that wasn't her own. I just looked at her thinking, 'Where the heck did this stuff come from?' It wasn't as if I'd asked them to take me in. Anyway, she kept on talking and making me feel bad. She told me, "We are trying to help you because we see through the eyes of Jesus Christ and the Lord. We do have our hearts open up for you to live with us, but this was unexpected. We only got you after a call late at night, and because my husband is a bishop we felt we had to take you." All this information made me feel weird and uncomfortable. After all, I was still just a young girl.

I don't remember this bishop's name, but I guess he was held to a higher standard or something. The wife made sure that I knew her husband was doing his duty by me. She said, "Being who he is, as a bishop, my husband couldn't say no to the request of taking you in. You are here whether I like it or not. If I had put up a fuss about you living with us it would have looked bad upon my husband...blah, blah, blah." That's when I kind of rebelled I guess. I told her, "Well, just go ahead and send me back." That's when the trouble started. The wife walked away from me all ticked off, and both her and her husband sort of got on my nerves after that. Sometimes in my frustration I would answer back to them in Navajo. I said things which probably I shouldn't have, because it made me feel better and they didn't understand any of it. That hurt their feelings I guess, (a little laugh), but at least then they knew how bad they were making me feel.

Colette:

As a Christian I felt concern that my own faith had been so poorly represented. Their heavy-handed attempt to introduce Emily to the idea of Christ never factored in her free will to choose their religion over her own. Knowing Emily as I did, however, I had to admit to myself that even a gentle approach to the Christian faith might have done nothing to swerve my Navajo friend from her Dine' beliefs. As it would turn out, her early experience with Christianity only increased her resolve to remain true to her grandfather's teachings. Just as I had come to understand and embrace the faith I had known as a child, Emily's Navajo faith had settled into her heart in a way that no other religion could. The prayers and spirit world of her people were a part of her, and they gave comfort when she needed it most. In spite of the negative experience she had with her first foster family, Emily did not hold a grudge against "religious people." She explained to me how she viewed my fellow Christians.

Emily:

Christians are nice people. I've only met a couple unpleasant ones, including my first Mormon foster parent. He was a pretty strict Mormon. But I have met nice Mormons and other kinds of Christian people. I just don't relate to 'don't do this or that because the Bible says so.' I think the idea of keeping harmony and respecting nature is a better way for me. Living with that first Mormon family was very different. They were real bossy, and I always thought 'why do they have to be so rigid about even the tiniest thing?' It was nothing like my own, traditional way of life on the reservation. With this Mormon family there was always an exact time to pray. Anyway, I didn't understand who it was we were praying to. I thought to myself, 'what am I doing here? What's the point of doing their prayers if I don't believe in them?'

At first I didn't have a problem practicing my own religion along with the Mormon one. My foster family didn't know I was keeping with my own traditional ways. I had corn pollen hidden that my grandfather gave to me for prayers. I remember how he gave me my own little bag of pollen the day I had to go back to Phoenix. He handed me this little bag and said "take this pollen and keep it with you all the time. If it runs out don't worry. Just find some corn meal for prayers until you see me again. It will still work for you." It felt good to have that pollen with me, but after awhile I stopped using it. I just kept it in my suitcase way in the back and never bothered with it. I'm not sure what had changed with me. Maybe it was too hard keeping it secret. Or maybe I was at that age where I thought, 'hmm, this praying with pollen is just old-timer stuff.'

Anyway, I didn't have a say with that other religion. In the Mormon Church they *forced* you to pray! It wasn't like the choice my grandfather gave me. The Mormons *insisted* that you be involved. There were different times throughout the day when they would look at you, and that made you think, 'oh, I guess it's my turn to pray now. They're all expecting it out of me.' Sometimes I got out of it. I told them I hadn't learned their prayers yet or some such thing. They eventually got the idea that I wasn't interested. I never did actually participate in the Mormon religious ceremonies. Maybe a couple of times I stood up and moved around like they did, but my heart wasn't in it.

As I said, the first foster family I stayed with was pretty strict. I took care of their kids, and they had four of them. I remember they had a little girl who was about seven, and another girl who was about five and a half. There was also a boy about three and then a baby. Because the father was a bishop at their church the parents were out almost every evening. Well, guess who the babysitter was? I think that's why they offered to take me in the first place. I was about twelve and taking care of all those kids. To be honest, they were kind of brats at first, but I didn't have any choice except to look after the whole bunch of them. I did the best I could, but I never felt like the parents appreciated it. Later on I found out they were so suspicious of how well I was taking care of their kids that they decided to spy on me! And you know what they did? They put a camera inside their house!

Colette:

Emily laughed over how ridiculous this was, but I was horrified. I had heard of "Nanny Cams," and other methods of checking up on babysitters, but I always thought these had been developed in the nineteen eighties as a way for Yuppie parents to keep an eye on those in charge of their children. I could see how hiding a video camera might ensure that a child was not mistreated, but this sort of surveillance seemed out of line in the case of Emily's foster family. The parents must have appeared to be a tangle of contradictions to the young Navajo girl. They were willing to take her in as God-fearing Mormons, but their behavior was anything but Christ like. They were more than happy to take advantage of Emily as an unpaid babysitter, but did not trust her enough to leave her with their children without the safeguard of a movie camera! I wondered what they expected to catch Emily doing that would have been so horrible. If there had been any doubt to her ability, why on earth did they leave her with their children in the first place? I sat staring in disbelief while my giggling friend continued her story.

Emily:

Well, I guess they were recording me all that time. It's kind of creepy now when I think about it. I don't know what kind of camera they used, but families were starting to use them a lot. It was one of those old kinds you just turned on and kept running somehow. What a waste of film! Anyway, I was called in to speak with these parents one day and they played this film for me. I had never really seen anything modern like that, and I thought that it was pretty cool to see myself on film. I was really enjoying it, until they let me know how mad they were with me. They acted like they caught me doing something wrong, but I had no idea what their problem was. It seemed so ridiculous that they didn't just ask how I was keeping their kids occupied.

See, I had the kids set up the only way I could watch them all in one spot, in the living room. The older two, they were pretty helpful. They liked it when I played with them, so they helped me keep the little babies in front where we could watch them and play at the same time. These two older kids and I put up all the sofa cushions like a fort. We moved the couches together, and I had them in their own little town just like that. One I would let walk around a little and the other one just crawled. This made it so that it wasn't too hard to watch the babies. When I had to go out to the other room for a second they were safe and happy. I only left them in their fort to go to the bathroom or make lunch for everybody. Well, these Mormon parents were mad when they found out what I was doing, but I don't know how they expected me to watch everybody without coming up with some kind of plan. I was actually proud I'd thought of it, but the parents got all worked up. I just ignored them and let them lecture me. In a way it was pretty funny, because they didn't know how to watch all those kids all at once either. Maybe they were mad because I'd thought of how to do it before they did (giggles).

I have to admit that I wasn't always good for them. I sometimes used their phone to call friends, but only because I was so lonely there. To tell the truth, I preferred being alone with the kids because I never really felt right with the mom and dad. I was always happy when they left for church. The kids and I had a good time playing, and I started feeling like a parent after a while. When one of the kids argued with the other I had to be patient and try to calm all of them down. That's when the Navajo words came in.

When these parents told me they had filmed me day after day without telling me I was really freaked. They kept screaming at me for stuff they saw on the film, but all I could see that the camera had captured was me acting silly; making the kids laugh and singing songs to keep them entertained. There was one time when the toddler stumbled and plopped back down on the carpet. It was off camera but you could see me going right to her and pick her up. She was whimpering a little, so I took her back to the sofa and sat her on my lap just talking to her in Navajo. For some reason this was the thing that bothered the parents the most!

I was told never to speak to the kids in my own language again. The dad who was bishop said he didn't like not knowing what I said to their daughter. I was only comforting her the way my grandmother did when I was a baby, and here they were worried that her mind might go nuts with my Navajo. They gave me all this trouble just because I was speaking Dine.' When they told me this I was pretty sure by then that they were the ones who were crazy. They told me that they didn't want me to speak my language even to myself, and that's when I knew I didn't belong there. I got mad at them, and so I started talking back in Navajo. I said some dirty words to them in Dine,' but I'm not sorry I did. They were acting nutty and I stood up for myself. I never said *anything* nasty to the kids in Navajo. I would never have done that, but those parents, well they deserved it.

I had never once given them a reason not to trust me, but I sure didn't have faith in them after that and they knew it. I didn't want to stay with them anymore, and I told them that I really wanted to go back home. They called my family and they traveled all the way out to Phoenix to get me. Grandma came with my aunt and uncle, and they were a little confused about what the problem was. I stood there begging for them to take me back, and I actually cried and hung onto my grandma until she said "okay, let's go."

I had my stuff packed and ready to go, and would you believe that was when those Mormon parents tried to convince me to stay! I guess they thought they were talking some sense into me, but I said, "no way!" I just left with my grandmother and my aunt and uncle. I never looked back. I told grandma later on how I was playing with the baby and just talking in Navajo. I explained to her how I was saying things like, "*e let e neh de bininah*, "what are you saying?" And I said "*Ah do cha*," "don't cry." At the same time I was crying with the baby, because I was so sad. Those parents filming me didn't even bother to ask why I was crying on their stupid camera. I remember that every time I watched their kids I felt sad and wondered what my purpose was there. I didn't like taking care of someone else's kids when my own little brother was at home without me. I guess that was one of the main reasons I wanted to go back to the reservation. I also knew that I would never get along with that Mormon bishop and his wife, no matter how long I stayed there. They would never treat me like their daughter, not even their foster daughter.

Colette:

Emily grew silent, and I sensed that the memory of living with this family, as well as being virtually abandoned by her own, was difficult to bear. I believe my friend always tried her best to leave painful memories in the past. I had always marveled at her ability to keep things in perspective, and she struck me as the kind of person who did not dwell on the negative aspects of life. Now I could see that it was not easy for her to relive those years. I had a hard enough time just hearing her relate her stories back to me! All I could see in my mind's eye was a sad and lonely little girl, uncertain of where she really belonged, or even who she was. This was even worse than picturing Suzie's childhood. So, there Emily and I sat, both of us struggling with emotions we'd rather not be feeling, and neither of us knowing what to say. Finally, Emily drew a deep breath, looked me in the eye, and smiled.

Emily:

Hey, the good news was I got the heck outta there! And I was able to finish the fifth grade in Chinle. I'll tell you one thing, no matter where I went for my schooling I always got good grades. At first I didn't even know if I liked school all that much. With all that moving around I didn't have time to form an opinion about it. But I always liked learning new things. Even now I take classes; mostly they're involving subjects I enjoy. I once even took a class about native plants. It was a ceremonial course, but I didn't learn as much as I thought I would. The teacher wouldn't let us ask any questions! I was hoping for more because he was a Navajo. But every time we tried to ask a question he would say "Oh, I'm going to get to that." But he never did. Then if we asked about something he'd already gone over he told us "Oh I already went over that. Didn't I, didn't I?" I could never like s teacher like that. You should be able to ask questions. That's how you learn.

A BETTER WAY

"We want freedom from the white man rather than to be integrated. We don't want any part of the establishment, we want to be free to raise our children in our religion, in our ways, to be able to hunt and fish and live in peace. We don't want power, we don't want to be congressmen, or bankers…we want to be ourselves. We want to have our heritage, because we are the owners of this land and because we belong here." – From the 1927 Grand Council of American Indians

So, to get back to my younger days…When I came back from that first foster family my grandfather got me back into the traditional ways that I preferred. Even while I spent part of the summer in the local Mormon program playing basketball, my grandfather would be sure to wake me up early to pray. Even if I was still half asleep he would push me out the door saying, "Let's go!" And every morning we stood outside our door praying. After that my grandfather would do his singing! I loved that, and now I wish I had been more awake to learn those songs. I was just standing there with my eyes closed most of the time, (giggles). But I really did like hearing him sing. If there had been a recorder around then and I would've taped him, cos' that man knew what he was doing! It sounded really cool.

Hanging around with my grandfather made me real happy I had come back home. I finished up sixth grade there in Chinle, and the very first day at school I found a friend. Her name was Kathy, and we really got along. She was Mormon of course, but she wasn't one of those real strict Mormons. Her family was much nicer to me. I was around twelve at that time, and I was supposed to start junior high that fall. Now, I should tell you that I did sort of like junior high. When I was ready to start the seventh grade one of those caseworkers comes up the second week of September, and she asks me whether I wanted to go back on the placement program. Well, I'd had enough of people giving me a hard time about being Navajo, so I said no to that lady. Even Grandma and my other relatives asked me to think it over, but still I said no. My grandfather told them, "She's already told you she's not interested in going off with the Mormons. Just go ahead and let her stay here."

But the rest of my family wouldn't let it go. My aunts and uncles were really pressuring me, saying, "Get outta here. Things will be easier for you with a different family." I didn't know what to do until I got the news that Kathy and her parents offered to have me live with them! That's when I agreed to go back into the placement program. Kathy's family moved to Phoenix over the summer, so my grandpa puts me on the bus, and I went all by myself to meet them there, (giggles). I went all the way to Phoenix by myself, and Kathy's family picked me up from the bus depot.

Living with this second family was very different from the first Mormon one. Kathy's parents made me feel welcome, and so I wanted to stay. They weren't very strict, and the kids were about my size, my age. They treated me as a normal human being. They could tell if something about their religion was confusing to me. If I asked for a soda, or wanted to do a certain thing that they had a taboo against, they would tell me right then and there, "We can't do that because of our faith." This family was straightforward, and they didn't beat around the bush. I also felt more comfortable with them because they were broke just the way my family had always been. They were always honest about the fact that they didn't have much money, but it didn't seem to bother them too much. I didn't mind either, because I had the basics. I had worked during that past summer, so I was able to buy school clothes, and Kathy's parents shared everything else with me. We all got along okay because together we were all just…normal.

250

They did insist on going to church, and I went with them so they could pray. But they never forced *me* to pray. They never pushed anything on me that they thought I couldn't handle. They just treated me like a member of their family, and because they were so good to me I did what I could to help them out. I didn't mind washing the dishes, and I helped at keeping the house clean. These were things that I had been taught as a little girl anyway. I was brought up to understand that if you're staying at somebody's house, and you're being taken care of, then you help out. Like in any family we sometimes argued, but afterwards we just stayed out of each other's way until we cooled off. The next minute everything was okay. It was like living with a regular family, and that's why I stayed with them. I never moved anywhere else, and even now I still visit them when I can.

I always knew that the one thing I could do for myself was to study and keep up my grades. Other than Kathy I didn't have any real friends. I knew some of the other kids at school, but we never really hung out. We weren't allowed to be friends with anyone other than Mormon kids, and all those kids did things together as a group. I wasn't invited to join them. Most all of the kids at school were white and not Mormons, and pretty much all of them knew that I couldn't be asked to their house because I was living with a Mormon family. So I stayed inside and studied.

Colette:

As I listened to Emily's stories about her foster experiences I believed I had somehow unlocked the mystery behind the reverence she now had for her Navajo traditions. At a tender age she had been placed in a family of a completely different culture and religion. Did Emily's early isolation from her people and her culture become the catalyst for her to resume her native traditions in later years? There certainly hadn't been any other young Navajo with whom the young Emily could commiserate. It didn't seem as if there had been any opportunity at all for Emily to practice her Navajo culture while she was living with either foster family. There seemed to be an underlying taboo even among Kathy's family against behaving as a Navajo. If Emily truly liked this family she might have put aside all thought of maintaining her cultural identity in order to please them. Had Emily actually felt free to maintain her Navajo identity she still would have stood out among her schoolmates as one who was different. I asked Emily if there had been anyone to whom she could speak in her language, and got quite a surprise when she answered.

Emily:

Oh, I wasn't the only Indian there, (giggles). My foster mother, Kathy's mom, she was part Hopi! Kathy's grandfather was full Hopi, so her parents went to visit family on the Hopi rez' all the time. I thought because of this I could try out a little Navajo on them, and they got a kick out of it. But they never came out and said it was okay to do my prayers or anything. I actually met the grandfather when he came for a visit, and he looked Hopi. He was dark, but they're not as dark as us Navajo, so it can be hard to tell. That's probably why none of the other Mormons figured out Kathy's mom was part Hopi. When I first met that grandfather I thought he was a little dark because he was a heavy smoker. Kathy told me he drank a lot, and the two tend to go hand and hand. So I just assumed his skin was a little bit dark because of that, (giggles). I was pretty surprised when I found out he was full-blooded!

After school was out that first year I went back to my grandparents' place, but I was just over there during the summer. I came home in June and left for Phoenix again in August. The summer was when I got a taste of traditional life again. My grandfather learned to be a Medicine Man from his father, and he kept practicing it at home. He was always singing, and he kept up his prayers outside, every single morning. When a family member decided to travel someplace grandfather would take the person in the morning for prayers outside. Then he would say special prayers to protect them until they got back. He did prayers and also traveling songs. I loved hearing those, and it felt good at that time to be home.

I ended up graduating with Kathy at her high school, and I thought about going to college. I applied and got accepted to BYU! (*Emily gave a wry little* laugh), but I didn't go...I don't remember why not. The scholarship offices would have paid for it, and my grades were very good. I had a three point something. I made mostly "A"s with only a couple of "B"s. Kathy's mom told me the people at the university didn't even have to think it over. I was accepted immediately. The caseworkers came over and filled out everything for me to attend BYU...and I just didn't go.

Maybe it was because I was tired of being away from home. I wanted to stay on the reservation and find a job. I wanted a family. Right around that time was when I got together with my first real boyfriend. I actually knew him from high school, but I didn't know he was gonna be my kid's future dad! I remember that I got a job in June or July...just after high school. It was a secretarial job for the local prosecutor, and that was considered pretty good pay. I had a truck that I bought with my own money. I was pretty quick about getting a vehicle and a job, with no help from anyone. Then all of a sudden I had a boyfriend, and I thought I was set, (*Emily laughed*). I thought I was doing okay.

Colette:

I told Emily that I heard from quite a few Navajo who had left to attend school that they always felt a strong desire to return to the reservation. It was hard for me to understand why they would want to come back, considering the high unemployment and difficult living conditions. I asked my friend if she had also felt the pull of her homeland. Didn't she ever wish to see the big city, or travel the world? What was it that drew people back to the rez'? Emily giggled and gave me a knowing smile.

Emily:

You know, if you've lived here most of your life here you learn to adapt to it. You get used to things and begin to appreciate the area. I never was completely comfortable staying with my foster family, even though they were good to me. Even just stepping outside was...really, really different from going outside here. Here on the rez' we have all this open space. I can go outside and look at the sheep and horses. I feel like I can really breathe! Living someplace else just isn't an option for me. And I think it's that way for a lot of people living here. Even though looking for work sometimes takes them out there someplace, a lot of people end up coming back.

My son, Max, is in his early twenties, and he doesn't have a job here even though he's a real hard worker. So he's probably going to have to leave for a while. He had a job helping to build some homes, but even then he had to drive pretty far to the construction sites. The work was in Tuba City, and from Chinle to Tuba that's a good three hour drive round trip. For now he's decided to go and live in Tempe and go to college. I'm a little worried about him though. Now he likes the night life. He goes to some clubs, he says that he dances, plays pool, goes bowling, goes to watch movies. I'm afraid he won't want to come back. He did say that someday he wanted to build his own home out here, have kids and raise some horses. We'll see.

When I was his age I was working all the time. I think that was about 1974. At first there wasn't any dating or romance for me. I was living with my mom at that time, and I walked to my job for a week until I got that old used truck. I got it real cheap, but boy was it ever a nice vehicle. It was a great first chiddy. I had to save up almost all my money from my job, and it took me about four months to pay that truck off (laughs). I couldn't buy anything else, and it was hard to get any groceries. But after paying for that truck I didn't have any bills. I was set!

EMILY'S DARK WALK
"Listening to a liar is like drinking warm water." – Unknown Tribe

It was around that time that I started going to the local dances with a girlfriend. We were regular Country and Western swingers, (giggles). My mom didn't seem to mind when I went to these dances. It was very safe because we knew everybody in town. We just went to see friends and hang out. I was never really dating and I never had anybody steady.

Eventually though, I met the father of my eldest children. I think I was about nineteen. It was during the Navajo Nation Fair, and my girlfriend introduced us. My truck had alternator problems that weekend, so we caught a ride with this guy. He and his friend were going to grab a bite first, and they offered to treat us. Well, my girlfriend said, "Let's go with them!" It was pretty unusual to get a free meal and we really appreciated that. There was going to be a dance at that fairground in Window Rock, and they asked if we wanted to go. The guy who sat next to me actually had attended my high school. That was my junior year when I came back to try it out. He said that back then he tried to get my attention, and I kind of remembered that he was on crutches. He was playing football and had apparently broke his leg. I saw this guy with crutches, and he came up and tried to make me laugh. He thought he was pretty smooth by *tripping* me with his crutch! I never paid no mind to him though. I just figured he was kinda weird. (laughs).

Well, he must have decided after that dance at the fairgrounds that he liked me, because he started coming around to the house. We got along okay, and would go out for walks. We would walk all the way down to his place and that's pretty far, but it was a chance to get to know each other. Eventually my mom didn't like it. She chased me out of her place, so I started staying with him. He was living with his sister. My first born, Max, came along until a year later, but I never married Max's dad.

When I was pregnant with Max I found out that my boyfriend had another kid...a little girl. This little one came running into the house crying and calling my boyfriend Daddy. That's when he started crying. He looks at me with tears in his eyes and said that he hadn't seen this kid for a long time. I don't know why he never told me, but once I knew about his daughter I never asked for details. I had my own problems, because after I had Max my boyfriend started to abuse me. I couldn't even look around a room without him hitting me. He really got total control of my emotions, and he decided who I could be with, who I cannot be with. He told me straight out that he was going to hit me if I did anything he didn't like. I left him so many times...but I never called the cops on him. And for some reason I always came back.

When Max was about a year old my boyfriend kicked me real hard, and I ended up in the hospital. It turned out that he had dislocated my back, and I guess it was a good thing that the cord was still attached to my spine. Another kick would've done it. The nurses tied me up to a real hard board, and I had to lie there for about two weeks. When my boyfriend came to visit me at the hospital I said to him, "I can't do this anymore. I can't live with you." But he and I both knew I was going to go back. I didn't have anywhere else to go, and I really liked his family. So I stuck around.

After that I had my little girl, Nina. She was still a baby when I found out my boyfriend was seeing somebody else. I kept finding all these red spots around his neck. What do you call them...hickys? (*Emily laughed long and hard over this*). I said to my boyfriend, "oh, somebody gave you a necklace huh?" He didn't even know what I was talking about! He only got it when he saw himself in the mirror and he said, "This is none of your business." I just let it go. You didn't ever want to talk back to this guy. He would throw you across the room! (*Emily sighed*), I sometimes wonder how I ever got away from him.

EMILY HAS ENOUGH
"Even a small mouse has anger."- Unknown Tribe

It all happened one day when I was going to work. I was still working for the prosecutor. Anyway, my boyfriend was driving me there, and all of a sudden he starts getting mad at me for no reason. At first I didn't get how mad he was. We were almost at my workplace, when he said, "Come here and sit closer to me." I got a bad feeling, and so I said, "na-ah, I'm fine over here." He started yelling at me for not scooting over closer to him, but I'd had enough of him treating me like dirt. I told him to shut up, and I made a move to get out. The vehicle was still moving, and it was just dirt road out there, but I didn't care. I opened the door to jump out, but he grabbed me and pulled me back in. I guess that's when he knew I was serious. I think he would have beaten me up that time, but I ran out of the truck as soon as we pulled up to my work. I was pretty upset, and my boss noticed.

That was when I finally told the prosecutor exactly what was going on with my life. He kind of knew anyway, because of the way I had been acting. He asked me whether I'd be willing to leave my boyfriend, and he offered to get me some help. I was afraid though.

When I went home that night he wasn't there. It was a Friday, and I wouldn't have to work the next day. So I packed up the kids and went back to my mom's place. I couldn't take my truck because it was broken. It slid off the road one time when I turned it too hard. Instead I took an old car that had been sitting at my boyfriend's place. Well, the next morning we didn't have any milk for the babies, and this old car wouldn't start, so my sister and I decided to walk all the way back to my boyfriend's place to get the milk I'd left there. My mom watched the kids, and we eventually got to my boyfriend's house. We knocked on the door, but nobody answered. I didn't have a choice but to go inside. I needed the milk, so I went in while my sister waited outside for me. She was about fifteen at the time.

Well, I went inside and there was my kids' dad and another woman. She was totally naked! They were both sort of out of it, and I guess they had been drinking. When my boyfriend saw me he went nuts. He came after me screaming, "See? This is what you did to me!" He actually blamed me for the fact that he was drunk and sleeping with another woman. Then that woman woke up, and she started bitching at me too! All I wanted was to get my things, so I told her, "Hey, I'm not your problem and you're not mine. I already know he sleeps around, so keep out of my face. I just came here to get some stuff for my babies." I went to gather my things, and up comes my boyfriend behind me. He jerked me around and drew back his hand to hit me, but I stood my ground. I thought, 'if he wants to hit me let him go ahead and try."

I guess I sort of surprised him, or maybe it was the look in my eye, but for once he didn't clobber me! I took advantage of that and went for the door with my stuff, but that other woman kept screaming at me and stood in my way by the door (giggles). That made me mad, so I grabbed her hair, threw her out the back door and locked her out. I ran out the front door and locked it behind me. By the time I ran out my sister-in-law was driving up to the house wondering what the heck was going on. There I was standing in the yard with my sister, holding all my stuff while a naked lady was banging on the back door screaming! (*Huge laughter at this*). I ran up to my sister-in-law and asked her for a ride, and she never said a word to us the whole way back to my mom's.

I stayed with my mom after that, and eventually I decided to go back to school. I attended Navajo Community College, and I started jogging in my spare time. I was just running for exercise, and it helped to clear my head. The prosecutor closed down the Chinle office where I worked, so I found a job at the Kentucky Fried Chicken. My mom and step-dad took care of the kids while I was working and going to school. After awhile I moved back to my grandma's house, because I knew my boyfriend would eventually come looking for me at my mom's. And I knew I would probably go back to him if he ever came by saying, "I'm sorry...blah, blah, blah." Grandma lived just outside of the town of Many Farms, so every day I would take the kids on the transit bus that ran from Window Rock to Keyenta. I took my daughter to daycare and my son to his school in Chinle. Then my mom would pick Max and my daughter up after school, and she'd stay with them until I got off work. We'd hop on the bus and head back to grandma's house for the night. It was a little complicated, but it worked out okay.

I was running and running more every day, and I went to school. The kids and I only went to visit their dad once, and he was still with that girl I'd thrown out. After that we didn't see him for a long time. I heard later that he got thrown in jail a couple of times for DUI. I thought it was better for my kids if we stayed completely away from him while he was drinking. About four years of abuse was enough for all of us. Later on he came to see Max and Nina, and we were on good terms after that. I never regretted leaving him though. I never once cried, and after I left I never felt lonely. I had my kids and I had my grandma. I was working and going to school so life was real good for me. My boyfriend got together with a few other women, but he never tried to hurt me again. Sometimes when he came to pick the kids up I'd even tease him, saying, "How's the new lady going?" (Giggles). One time he saw me with another guy, and I could tell he hadn't changed. He made it clear he didn't like me being with someone else. He was with his girlfriend in town, and he just kept *staring* at us! Finally the guy I was with asked who that angry dude was, and I said, "That's my kids' dad." I guess that kind of scared him, because he never came back to see me, (giggles).

Colette:
I sat and looked at my friend in amazement. She had been through so much with this man who abused her. Yet, she had found the strength to defy and leave him. Emily got back on her feet, cared for her children, worked and went to school, all seemingly without missing a beat. In spite of all the time we'd spent together, there were so many things about Emily that I'd never known. I didn't even know that she loved to run like I did, and I wondered how much more about my friend there was to discover.

A SAD END. A FRESH START
"Many have fallen with the bottle in their hand." – Lakota

Colette:
Much like Suzie, Emily told a sometimes tragic story in a matter-of-fact way punctuated with laughter. Although her young life had been incredibly sad, the entire sage flowed out of her with ease. I loved listening to the rise and fall of her voice as she carried me along with her story. Emily could reveal the most disturbing tale in a way that was almost calming. Her laughter trickled out like creek water falling over the rocks, and at the end of it all I found my sides ached from giggling along with her. She paused to pensively crack open another sunflower seed, and chucked the shell out the open door. I waited to see where the rest of her story would take us.

Emily:
Then Lonnie came along…that's a different story. I met him at a song and dance, and I guess I was the one pursuing him, (*Emily gave a throaty laugh*). I was about twenty-five, and it was right before my kids' dad passed away. It was my second year at Dine'

College, and my old boyfriend was still sometimes coming around. First he came to ask if he could claim the kids as dependents when he filed his income tax. I said, "no way. I'm the one who's been supporting them." He reminded me that he bought the kids clothes whenever he came into some money, but that kind of thing wasn't very consistent. His girlfriend at that time was working, so they were getting by. I have to admit, he loved his kids very much; I can say that much for the guy. He supported the kids whenever he could, just by giving a little here and a little there. But it was pretty hit and miss, and I had to work hard as a single mom. He did the best he could, but he was struggling.

When I first met Lonnie I told him about the kids' father. It put Lonnie off at first. He seemed to care for me, and we talked about my situation. But he was unsure about things, and so he kept his distance. I didn't mind, I mean I just figured that guys are guys and it's going to happen again. A guy would like me, but when it came to my kids and all, well that would be the deal breaker, (*Emily laughed*). Then the day before Thanksgiving came around. You know, the day when Indians celebrate how they saved the White man, (*we both giggled furiously over this statement*). I think maybe it must have been about eight o'clock in the evening, and the kids' dad comes over to say, "We're having our Thanksgiving dinner tomorrow. Why don't you come over and join us?"

It's funny, but I could tell that he had been drinking that night. He even offered me some beer. I told him no thanks. He asked me at that time, "Don't you take liquor anymore?" I said to him, "I try not to." He was in a good mood, and he was doing his best to convince me I should have just one drink. But I said no. We were standing outside, and I didn't dare let him into the house. The kids were inside; it was late for them and they were already asleep. Besides, it was never a good idea to have their dad around after he'd been drinking. Would you believe he had a beer right there in his back pocket? He opened it up and gave it to me, but when I took it from him I poured it out. That ticked him off, and he says, "Don't do that; it's a big waste!" I told him we might as well pour it out because I wasn't going to drink it. Well, guess what…he pulled out another one! I did the same thing to it. I just poured it out in front of him. I guess he thought this was kind of cute, and he started laughing and began to chase me around his truck! He was yelling for me to come back, but I kept telling him I wasn't going with him anywhere.

I didn't want to get his hopes up. I knew we were no good together, so I tried to put a stop to all this. I got real serious with him and told him he should leave, but he began to speak to me in Navajo. He said a phrase that means "you really look terrific!" I knew I looked better than I had in a long time. All of that running, and going to school and working…well, it had been good for me. But being with this man would have been a mistake, and I told him once more, "I ain't going back!" I went to his truck then, and I collected all his beer. I think he must have had a six-pack, and I just dragged it all out. There was a wall right between my house and the one next door, and I smashed those beers against it, one by one. When I was done he looked at me like I was crazy, and I said, "Seems to me you've had enough beer." He rubbed his head and told me "Well, looks like I'm not drinking any right now."

He asked to see the kids at that point, and I felt like I couldn't say no. My mom and step-dad were still awake, so I told them to go ahead and let him in. But as he walked into the house I whispered to my mom, "Can you guys sit in the front room with me, just in case this guy gets mad?" Normally my ex-boyfriend wouldn't hit me in front of family, but I figured there's a first time for everything. So I sat in the front room with my mom and step-dad while my kids' dad went in to kiss them goodnight. When he came back out he had tears in his eyes. He told me how much he missed his kids, but I just thought he was just a little drunk, and maybe pretending to be hurt as a way of getting me to feel sorry for him. I kind of did feel bad for him, but he knew he shouldn't be drinking and I wasn't going to wake up the kids so they could see him like that.

All of a sudden, my ex-boyfriend looked at his watch. I guess he noticed then that his band was falling apart. So he slams his watch against the wall, and I thought, "Uh-oh, it's starting now, he's getting mad." I was just standing at the doorway, and he said, "Shit, I guess it's time. It's my time to go now." It was a real uncomfortable moment, and he said something else that struck me as strange. He said, "Take care of my kids for me. I won't ever come back this way if you're not ever going to want to be with me." It was as if he knew he was never coming back again to see his kids. Then he walked out of that house for the last time. I went to the window that looked out to the driveway just in time to see him back his car in front of it. As I was looking out I saw him put a cassette tape in, and with his window down he turned it up so I could hear it play. He looked at me then, and the last words he said to me were, "Remember me by this song, you bitch!" He was yelling at me with so much anger, and I'll never know where that anger came from. It always came when you didn't expect it. (*Emily shook her head in disbelief*). And I had to wonder, after all that time, why was he still mad at me? It's not as if I ever hit *him*! Whatever brought all that anger up it really did seem aimed at me, but we were done and over with long ago. I don't get it. Why stay mad at me when he didn't really want me in the first place? I guess he always wanted what he couldn't have. Anyway it was easier to be angry with me than to try and figure himself out.

My kids were sort of awake when their dad went in to kiss them goodbye, so at least they got to see him one last time. When he left I settled them back down, and it must have been about one o'clock when finally left I tried to go to sleep. But I was too upset, so instead I stayed up and studied. At that time I was doing a little bit of volunteer work for the fire department, and I had a scanner in the house to track accidents, just in case the rescue guys needed my help with anything. Mostly my job was to help direct traffic. I never really looked at who was involved in any of the accidents. I didn't want to see people in pain, and I only assisted if the medics needed bandages. I would just deliver that sort of help to the emergency crew members, and then let them to take it over. At that time I felt it was a way for me to stay busy, and I really liked listening to the scanner to see if the crew needed me.

Well, on this particular night I heard emergency sirens coming through town so I listened more closely to the scanner. I knew the general direction my ex-boyfriend was going in, and as I was studying I heard over the scanner that there had been an accident in that area. I called in at that time to see if they needed help, but they told me to stay put because I didn't have a ride to the accident site. Besides that, I didn't want to leave my kids. So I just stayed behind thinking it would be better if I didn't go.

But for some reason I kept wondering about it. I tried to convince myself that I was over reacting over the weird evening I'd had with my ex-boyfriend, but deep-down I knew it was him. Sure enough, the next morning at around five o'clock my sister-in-law came over. She told me the kids' dad had been in an accident and he had died. I thought she was talking about her dad because he and her brother had the same name. I just looked at her in confusion and I said, "I thought your dad already died a couple years back." She looked at me like I was crazy, and she said, "No, not that one! It's the kids' dad!" She told me he had made it all the way to the hospital, but very soon after he passed away.

Boy that was a shock! I just walked away and went into the restroom to take a shower. I felt like I had to wash the whole thing away from me. I couldn't even shed any tears, because I didn't really believe he was gone. I was in a daze until my aunt came over to say she was sorry. My mom wasn't much help at the time. She didn't know what to say, and she wasn't good at comforting me because we had never been close. As for me, well I just walked around most of the time thinking, 'What in the heck has just happened? That guy was here last night! How can he be dead when I just told him to fuck off?' Even though I hadn't wanted to be with him I felt bad for my kids. Now they really didn't have a dad anymore.

You know, I went to that guy's funeral. He was the father of my children and I wanted to pay my respects. I saw his current girlfriend there, and I felt sorry for her. She was standing all alone, so I went over and gave her a hug. What else could I do? I think she was a little surprised, like I was supposed to be jealous of her or something, but I had no hard feelings. I mean he chose her to live with; they chose each other. And there she was all alone. Anyway, she seemed to appreciate the hug, because all the other people there were just ignoring her. It wasn't really fair because the car accident hadn't been her fault.

I sat there wondering why everyone was snubbing this lady. Nobody should be treated that way, and you could tell she cared for this person who had died. I found out later he used to hit her around too. I still see her around sometimes, and she's got kids from left to right. She must have about ten kids now. It's funny; at the funeral she asked me if it would be all right to bury my ex with something of hers. It was a silver cross with turquoise. It was really nice, and I told her I had no problem with it, but I thought she should ask the immediate family. It was up to his mom and his sisters how to bury him. What was kind of sad was they said no to her about giving my ex the cross. I went over to them to try and change their minds. I said, "Hey, he chose to be with this lady and he cared about her. Why not just let her give him the cross to be buried with? There's really nothing wrong with it."

I couldn't understand what the big deal was, because it was a Christian burial. Understand, he wasn't really a Christian, but all the burials were done through the church system. His family went to church every now and then, but even if they hadn't been attending the church would have helped them out. These were the days when

Navajo began to ask Anglos for help in burying their loved ones. Navajo don't like to handle those things if they can avoid it.

Finding a Medicine Man to perform the ceremony was always difficult, and it's the same way today. Most medicine men even now prefer not to be involved with burials, because it's a complicated procedure. All that extra work hinders them in their other duties. They need extra protection, like a prayer from another Medicine Man. It's a really big deal to cleanse yourself from a burial. I had a grandfather who never even went to his own son's ceremony. He just said he couldn't risk going to those things. He was a Blessingway Medicine Man, and so he had to keep himself clean to perform that ceremony. That's just the way we are about these things.

In the old days, if you couldn't find a Medicine Man you just asked a couple of people to put away the body, and then those two people would be set aside separately for a cleansing. Nowadays nobody wants to go to the trouble. If you ask you can still bury at your home site, and you don't have to have a Christian funeral. But you need permission from the chapter level and from the tribe. You just can't bury people here and there anymore. We asked Suzie if she wanted a Medicine Man to do her service, but she said not to go to the trouble. She said, "We all pray for the same thing, it's the same spirits and white people just have different names for them." So she said it would be okay to have Christians help us.

Anyway, life went on for me and my kids, until one day I saw Mr. Yazzie at a dance. I found out later that he had been married before, but his marriage didn't work out. He and his ex are on good speaking terms now, and he has two daughters by her that he loves a lot. But he and his first wife, they didn't love together well. I met him when I was about twenty-five. Man! I guess I've been with him a long time! I'm forty-three now, so I think that means I'm old.

Colette:

I explained to Emily that I would be forty that very year, and also felt as if I were getting older. She only laughed at this and said I was still "a youngster." I didn't understand how forty was that much younger than her forty-three years of age...but she insisted I was still "a baby" and waved away my protests about aging.

Emily:

Oh Lady, I've got a lot more years on you, (giggles), just because of everything I've been through. Yeah, I feel older than even forty-three, but I had a better life once I met Lonnie. He just started taking care of us right away, bringing us food when we needed it, and firewood. I really appreciated his help, but we didn't start living together until a year later I think. Before that we went out all the time and he paid a lot of attention to me. Now he doesn't. (*Emily smiled*) I guess that's how it goes with the married life. Anyway, those first few dates we had I knew right away how I felt about Lonnie. It was nice...we were good. The only thing I regret about those days is that we were out all the time. Max and Nina were left with their grandparents, (giggles).

We mostly went to song and dance things. Or we'd go to town for something to eat and drive around. It was nice just to be out. Eventually we moved in together, and I became pregnant with my first son with Lonnie. When Sonny was born we just decided to get a marriage license. I think that was around 1986. It wasn't like Lonnie dropped on one knee and said, "Emily, will you marry me?" That's just not his style...no, not Lonnie. (*Emily gave me a wry* smile), I should have forced him to do something like that. (giggles) He probably would have, if he thought it was important to me. I was real happy with Mr. Yazzie though. If I think about anything else happening to me, as if I hadn't met him...life wouldn't have been the same. The whole meaning of me would be different. I can't even imagine life without my kids and Lonnie. I think I would never have been happy; not like I am now anyway.

Lonnie was always a great dad, even to my other kids. Maybe he understood how important it was to love them, because he had kids from a former marriage too. He must have done it right, because he recently got a Valentine's Day card from my daughter that was pretty neat. She wrote in the card that she really appreciated how he was always there, especially since she hadn't really known her real dad. She told him how she considered him a dad, and when he read that he just started crying. He had tears in his eyes just like mine now.

Colette:

Emily paused, and looked down at her hands. I could tell she was letting the feelings wash over her. I was getting used to the way my friend expressed those things that meant the most to her. There were some matters that even Emily could not shrug or giggle away. I admired the way she handled her emotions, though it was completely different from how I had been taught to express myself. My family was gregarious and demonstrative almost to a fault. Sitting in the sun-washed room with only the sound of the wind coming through the cracks of Hill House, I watched Emily collect herself. The gentle manner in which emotion played upon her face seemed powerful beyond mere words.

EMILY'S DREAM

"I am a red man. If the Great Spirit had desired me to be a white man he would have made me so in the first place...Each man is good in his sight. It is not necessary for Eagles to be Crows. We are poor...but we are free. No white man controls our footsteps." - Cherokee

Colette:

Emily and I sat in silence once again. A pile of sunflower seeds lay uneaten in her hand, and a tiny desert finch flew into the yard. It perched on the old wagon wheel that rested on the fence, and then hopped onto the porch step; cocking its head in expectation of a wayward seed that might be thrown his way. "Are you going to eat all of those?" the little bird seemed to ask, with a curious glance at Emily, then back at the seeds in her hand. My friend laughed and tossed a seed to the bird that, in one eager movement pounced upon the seed, jammed the entire thing in its beak and flew away. The light returned to Emily's eyes, and she began to tell me her dreams for the future.

Emily:

Sometimes I wonder what it would be like to move into Monument Valley for good. If I lived here right now I'd probably be weaving all the time and it would feel as if I had a real job. Back where we live in Chinle I'm just cooped up in one house all the time. I would rather be outside doing something interesting. That's why I went back to school. I don't have to go to college, but I don't want to be closed in anymore. The problem with me is that I know you have to work in order to earn a good living, but the words "have to" bother me. I think you've got to enjoy something in order to deal with the "have to" part, (giggles). It's confusing.

It's like the time when I was weaving in my spare time, just for enjoyment. I loved it! But it got to a point where I was taking orders to make rugs for more and more people, and I knew I could do it. I *wanted* to take the orders, but at the same time I didn't like how it made my weaving like a chore. I really took up weaving to enjoy it. It's different when you're making a living at it. If I lived down here full time I would weave more, and then I could make a living out of it too. I just think living here would allow me to weave my own pace.

If Lonnie and I moved out here I'd like a nice home with real windows. Maybe we could have a big window looking out like you have here at Hill House. I'd put up a big loom and a sewing machine; the kind you can work with a foot pedal. Then I wouldn't even need electricity. Maybe we could get a generator just to watch dirty movies on T.V. (*Emily and I laughed long and hard at* this). Nah, I'm just kidding. I don't think we'd even need electricity. I for sure would want some sheep though. It would be nice to have things like that we could call our own. Most everything we do now contributes to Suzie and the whole family. That's okay. It works out for everybody, but it would be nice to have my own sheep.

Colette:

I thought that it must be hard on Emily to be so dependent on her husband's family. The Navajo system of ownership leans toward the matriarchal line. This means that most of the family property is "owned" by the women. Emily's situation was unique in that she was not close to her mother, and therefore relied on her husband and his family. Emily clearly felt comfortable with these relatives, but the dynamics of operating within that family as an in-law must have been awkward for her. My friend sighed and popped another sunflower seed in her mouth. She swirled it around in her mouth then cracked the softened shell in her teeth. Pulling the empty shell out and flicking it towards the yard she resumed her daydream.

Emily:

Yeah, I'd like to have a job and keep trying to get my degree. I'm going to be Superwoman you know (giggles). I'll do it all! But if you asked me what I think of as "perfect world" it would be to live down here and just sew and then weave. When I got tired of weaving I would be sewing. Lonnie could take people out on rides, and I would help him with that too. I once asked him what he thought about that plan. I asked if I should just go ahead and continue my schooling, or hold off for the big dream. He just said, "It's up to you." I told him we could live and work here in the Valley if we got it together real quick, but he said, "No, we still have a lot of time." I tried to explain to him that we didn't have a lot of time. We only have about fifteen good years of work left in us!" (*Emily laughed at this*), but he wouldn't listen. That man won't listen to a word I say.

I think Suzie would let us build a place right there in the campsite. I think she'd appreciate the extra help. It's funny; when I first met Lonnie we were always in the Valley. He taught me how to find my way around here, and I felt so comfortable I went back into weaving I learned as a youngster. As a kid I never really knew how to weave that well, but my grandma taught me all she knew about it. I put it aside for a long time, and only really got into it when I started coming here. Weaving is a good and honest way to make money down here, and it's also good to carry on the tradition. I think it really needs to be taught to the young people. I'm trying to show my own granddaughter, but she's still just a baby, (giggles).

Colette:

I told Emily this was how traditions became lost over time. The younger generations either don't make the time or have any interest in what their grandparents wish to teach them. My friend was fighting the familiar battle that pits loyalty to one's culture against the allure of modern life. Emily nodded her head in agreement.

Emily:

Yeah, that's why I keep on my granddaughter about her weaving, even when she doesn't seem that interested. She's got a rug started on her loom that's been there for over six months. She has a ways to go on it, and she's pretty busy with school. My niece, Ramera, is getting into it, and I even taught my son, Brooks, how to weave. He's a modern man, (*Emily giggled once more*). Suzie has been a big influence on me in that way. She's always teaching her grandkids stuff. I care a lot for her, and I feel sorry for her sometimes. There are people who take advantage of her kindness and then give her nothing in return.

A few family members have been helping her out, but she's going through some rough times. We have people come down and stay with her, like Lonnie's brother or Effie. They all take turns keeping an eye on the sheep and helping their mom. Lonnie was alone with her all last week because I had exams. He got some friends down here from Colorado, and they got the roofing fixed on her house. These are white friends of ours who we've worked for. One time I made a rug to trade with them, and they brought down some hay for our animals. Lonnie wanted to pay for their help in fixing up the roof, so Effie paid them again with another rug. Their home's gonna be full of rugs! (*Laughter*) Oh well, I guess you can never have enough rugs.

So yeah...if I could combine the convenience of living in Chinle with the peacefulness of the Valley, that would be ideal. I would give up television and all that stuff without a second thought. I really love the quiet of this place. How can I explain it? It's just more open; not like how we live now in Chinle.

Colette:

I had been to Emily's home in Chinle. Indian housing in that area is affordable for the locals, but far from inspiring. The little condominiums are situated close together in a mundane line of gray and brown. The residents have access to more goods and services, but the drab government development could never offer the majestic view or connection to the earth so prevalent within Monument Valley. I asked Emily why she and Lonnie didn't just take the plunge and move out to valley right away. She sighed and shook her head in resignation.

Emily:

We don't have any choice right now. There's really no permanent place to stay around Suzie's house. When we come down here we mostly live out of our car. I leave everything in there and it's sort of like camping. I don't want to cramp Suzie or move into anyplace that her other relatives might need when they visit. If it's warm outside we can sleep in the Shade House, and we sleep in the hogan sometimes but I'm scared of spiders and mices. I don't know if there's any in there but I'm sort of a city girl about those things! (*Emily chuckled at the thought*).

Anyway, I'm trying to plan for the future. One of the reasons I went back to school is so I could eventually get a better job; maybe buy into a really good retirement plan. I just don't know if that's possible at my age. I asked Lonnie what he wanted to do when he got too old to take guests out on horseback rides. He just looked at me like I was crazy and said, "I'm going to raise my sheep and stay in the Valley." (Giggles) I said, "Well, once you're about sixty-five I guess you can start living over there amongst the sheep!" (*Emily found this idea tremendously funny*). So I guess we'll just wing it. I'm pretty flexible about how things go when I'm old. I just want to be able to visit my grandkids…and maybe have a car that works.

Colette:

Hearing Emily mention old age made me think about what she must have been like as a girl. I asked her if she had done her Kinaalda, and she nodded her head.

Emily:

Um, hmm, I did it when I was thirteen. I told my mom right away that I'd started my menstruation, and she told my grandma. They both went and got this one old lady to help them with my ceremony. This lady showed them how to tie my hair back, and she did all the stretching on me. They wanted her to help because she was a real tough lady. She had a strong character that would rub off on me when she did the stretching. She also knew how to weave, and I think that rubbed off on me too. She died just recently, about two years ago. Her mind was good all the way up to then though. She could still recognize people and at ninety-something years old! She still had her black hair with only a little bit of white, but she had gotten thin. I went with my mom to visit her when they put her in the hospital. Here my ceremony had been about thirty years ago, and she remembered me! I thought that was pretty cool.

When I had the ceremony done on me I just did the one. In the old days they said you should do two of them; the second a couple of months after the first one. Instead my mom had me do one, but it lasted four days. Girls were starting to do that then because the school schedule kept them away from home a lot. I made the corn meal myself with hardly any help, and that's a lot of work. You have to ground the meal with a stone grinder. I guess that way you're saying something to the gods that you put effort in. I put the cake in the ground…the whole thing.

I ran mostly towards the south, but I couldn't go in all four directions as I would have liked. According to the Medicine Man working with us there was a river in the way. A real hard rainstorm came through and I couldn't run through the wash. That would have been east, the way I was supposed to go first, because that's how the sun rises. The first day you run a bit, and then each day your distance goes a little bit further. I actually ran twice each day. That's just what the Medicine Man told me to do. I didn't even know you had to go in four directions until Suzie told me! (*Emily giggled*), the kids that were up for the ceremony ran with me, and my late uncle ran after me too. He persuaded me to go faster, and he was on a motorbike! (*More laughter*). That's not fair you know! He just kept after me on that motorbike yelling, "Go! Go!" I don't know how many miles I went, but I should check one of these days because I know it had to have been a lot. I went as fast as I could because I wanted to get back to the hogan early. But by the end of it the sky was pitch dark! I think that's why my uncle had that bike to accompany me. He should have been running too, but we cheated a little bit. It was in the summertime and I was in full dress. It got pretty hot out there, but I was young and skinny. When you're in shape things like that don't bother you.

I'm not sure it felt like a life-changing thing. No, I just thought it was fun, (*big laughter*). I liked having all that attention then, you know? I feel badly that I didn't have my daughter's Kinaalda. It was impossible because we didn't have much family to help out. My grandma was willing to help, but my aunt didn't want us to use the property. She told us, "No, I want that corner of land to do the ceremony for my own daughter." I was pretty disappointed, because my grandma was real willing, and I was willing to buy all the corn and everything. (*Emily sighed heavily*), the other grandma, my daughter's *nahlee* (paternal grandmother), didn't want to help out, and there so was no place else to go. Later on I told that to one of my grandma's cousins, and those old ladies said, "You should have just came to our house, we would have loved to have done something like that." And I should have! My niece, Ramera is going to have hers soon. We got everything ready. The corn is all cooked. Now we just have to set the time for it.

Colette:

I told Emily that one of my youngest stepdaughters had gotten her period the past fall. She pulled me aside to let me know and ask for help; however she refused to tell her own mother who lived only twenty miles away. All of my stepdaughters were incredibly shy about their bodies, and none of them would discuss puberty with me. The mere mention of the subject caused them to turn red from embarrassment and run from the room. I felt this was a shame, since I could have told any of my girls what to expect as they approached adolescence. At the very least an open discussion might have made the transition from childhood to young adult easier for them. But sadly, it was not to be. Emily thought that the Kinaalda ceremony allowed a young girl to feel special and cared for.

Emily:

I think you should have brought your girl out here. You could have had us do the ceremony done for her too, (giggles). You know what we've always said about it? Over here…everybody knows that you got your period, (laughter), the whole town! I guess if I were raising my kids in a completely traditional way I would have raised them more like Suzie. Being quiet and patient is important…no yelling, things like that. I think it's best to set examples for your kids, work hard with weaving, and make no gripes about being tired. That was possible for Suzie. She somehow managed to do that. That's more the tradition I wish I could have followed. But back in Chinle I do yell, and I'm tired all the time so I sometimes bark orders at my kids. It's a different world there, with a lot more distractions for kids. You really have to push them.

I tell them that when they grow up it's important to find someone you really care about and who cares about you; someone who will really help out. Family is important because you depend on them and they depending on you. Most people don't really need too much, just love and some kind of support. That's all anyone wants.

Colette:

Emily rose from the table and went to stand at the back kitchen door. Turning her face to the warm breeze she looked out over the valley below. Taking a break sounded like a very good idea to me, and I joined my friend at the door to watch the sun begin it's slow decent behind the monuments. My bones ached from sitting for too long, so just for the sake of moving them I stepped out to the dirt yard. Like a cat I stretched my arms to the sun and took a deep breath of clean, dry air. As I let out a dramatic sigh Emily quietly came behind me to and gazed at the road below. A lone and dusty car chugged its way toward us in a slow deliberate way. Recognizing the driver inside, Emily giggled softly.

Emily:

It looks like Mr. Yazzie's coming back! (*She peered at the car as it drew closer*). No, it can't be. He's not that quick at getting stuff done. He's always an hour later than he says he'll be.

Colette:

Defying Emily's logic the car turned at our driveway and crawled up toward Hill House. Emily shook her head and giggled.

Emily:

Sonofagun that *is* him! Man, he really made good time!

Hey Shah kiss, you should ask Mr. Yazzie about his life next. I'm tired of talkin' anyway.

Colette:

With that my friend opened the front door and walked out to greet her husband. I sighed and walked back to the little dinette table. An entire unwrapped package of blank cassettes waited to be filled with stories. It didn't feel to me as if Emily had really told me everything about her life. But maybe the Navajo were right. Maybe I didn't need to know absolutely every secret my sister, my "shah kiss," held in her heart. I pulled out the tape that had been running in my tape recorder and labeled it with my black pen. "Emily: Autumn 2000" I wrote. I glanced out the front door and spotted Lonnie as he stepped out of his chiddy and remove his cherished black cowboy hat. He smacked it against his black Levi jeans to clear off the dust. I smiled and went out to join the Yazzies. If Lonnie was as keen on telling his story as his wife was it was going to be a long night.

CHAPTER 12 – LONNIE'S STORY

"Beware of the man who does not talk, and the dog that does not bark." – Cheyenne

COYOTE, THE TRICKSTER

"Yah tah hey, Coco!" Lonnie jubilantly came toward me with arms outstretched for an embrace uncommon among the Navajo. Going in for my hug I buried my face in his worn jeans jacket, heavy with the smell of juniper smoke. It was a scent I associated with Lonnie, and its familiarity brought back memories of the rides and adventures we'd shared over the years. We headed to the house with Emily following behind carrying Lonnie's black cowboy hat and giggling at the both of us. "Hey old man," she teased, "how come you never greet me like that?"

Lonnie turned and smiled back at his wife. "You don't make spaspetti for me like she does!" I had to smile at the way he mispronounced the Italian dish just as his sister did. The Yazzies were particularly fond of my trade mark meal, but I hadn't planned on having the family for a big spaghetti dinner during this trip. I wondered if I could appease Lonnie with the few snacks I had waiting inside Hill House.

The three of us stumbled into the entryway and I shut the door against a gust of wind. Lonnie took a look around the living room where Emily and I had been working. "Are you guys done yet?" he asked. "Yeah, she's got me all figured out," Emily answered for me, "now she wants to interrogate you." Lonnie smiled, his white teeth shining from under his salt and pepper mustache, "good, cos' I got plenty to say!"

"That's what we were afraid of," his wife countered, "why don't you wash up and we'll sit here waitin' on you." Lonnie obediently headed for the closest bathroom while I popped a new tape in my little recorder. Emily moved the bag of sunflower seeds from where she'd been sitting and took a position in a chair to the right of me. Cracking another seed in her teeth she turned pensive:

Emily:

He's gonna tell you a lot about growing up here. He wants to move away from our place in Chinle. I don't blame him. It's so pretty here, and Lonnie has always considered Monument Valley his real home. It's also the place where his family meets up. His sister and his nieces and nephews look up to him. They rely on him to keep an eye on things. When Lonnie goes out to his mom's place things tend to get done. The repairs are kept up and supplies come in. His mom likes having him around and he likes spending time with her. The whole family benefits when Suzie's place is kept ship-shape. We all expect that Effie will take over the role of caring for the hogan business, since she's the only daughter. The Navajo still keep things along the mother's line, so she'll have a lot of say-so about how things are done, but she gets advice from her brothers on the best way to do things. It all works out pretty well.

Colette:

I set out more refreshments for Lonnie; string cheese and crackers and a good strong cup of coffee. Mr. Yazzie could drink a whole pot of coffee all by himself. Lonnie emerged from the bathroom just as I began to settle into my own creaky dining room chair. Em stood up and sauntered into the living room to plop down on the sofa. Tucking her feet beneath her she cuddled up with a book I'd brought with me of collected testimonies about the Long Walk. She'd heard all of Lonnie's stories before, and was content to ignore us both while she disappeared into the tales of her ancestors.

Lonnie had a different style of storytelling than his wife. His speech was slow and deliberate, like his mother's, and filled with long pauses as he thought of just the right way to say things and to recall events long past. I had become accustomed to the way he spoke, so I let him take his time knowing it would be worth the wait. I held back on my tendency to interrupt or interject. He reminded me of my stepfather, a Cherokee man who taught me patience, because he certainly took his sweet time telling a story. Conversations with Byron Cline, or "Papa" as I knew him, often involved periods of silence that lasted as long as ten or fifteen minutes. Once I became used to them I began to trust these pauses would yield golden jewels of advice and family history. So I sat back, listened and changed out tapes as quickly as I could so as not to miss any part of his story.

Before sitting down Lonnie snatched the bag of sunflower seeds from his wife's hands. "You're misbehaving," he chastised Emily and returned with them to his seat next to me. He plunged his hand into the bag and gave me a Cheshire cat grin, "You gotta save the seeds for the guy telling the stories!"

LONNIE'S SPEAKS

"A wee child toddling in a wonder world, I prefer to their dogma my excursions into the natural gardens where the voice of the Great Spirit is heard in the twittering of birds, the rippling of mighty waters, and the sweet breathing of flowers. If this is Paganism, then at present, at least, I am a Pagan." – Zitkala-Sa

Lonnie:

I was born in 1949, I think. March 5th was my given birthday, and maybe it was sometime in March, but it was just an assumption back then. We didn't really keep track of things like that. People would just say, "Oh, I think you were born around harvest time," (*Lonnie laughed*). We didn't really need to know our date of birth until somebody finally had to take us to the hospital for something. The nurses would ask mom and dad about our birthdays, and my folks told them, "oh, let's just say March 5th." Back then you always heard people describe things by saying, "it happened in the early spring," or "that was fifteen or five years ago." Exact time just didn't matter as much as the story behind what happened. So just like that I was given the birth date of March 5th, 1949. All of our birthdays are like that. I think Effie's birth date is the closest to being exact.

Anyway, I remember my mom saying I was born when spring was just around the corner. She told me she was pretty sure she got pregnant with me when they were working up at Salt Lake. She was cooking for the railroad crew at that time, but they came back to the Valley for me to get born. I remember quite a bit about my mom during those days. There isn't anything else to do, (laughter), except keep those memories. The earliest one I have is when I went up to the west end of the canyon where all the farms were. I remember sittin' on my mom's lap on a horse. We were trucking right along, looking around at all the corn fields. My next memory is of how we used to lay under a tent in the middle of the summer. We'd see all these flashes of lightning and the rain coming down. It lighted up the whole Valley, and we'd see so many waterfalls that were not there before. I could hear the rain pounding hard on the tent and it just put me to sleep. It was one of my favorite times of the year.

I loved playing in that corn. Nobody has fields like that around here anymore. My sister tried to plant some. We all tried after the weather changed. Before he died, I went with my dad to Sand Springs to haul in water for the fields, because the rain stopped coming. We got a bucket or so each day to grow that corn. But it only grew to about a foot high. That was it. We got none of those five footers any more that our ancestors had. The wind came and blew all the fertile soil away until the things we used to plant just wouldn't grow anymore. As I grew up it got drier and drier and drier. When I was a kid we used to plant in places where we could be certain of runoff, like over by Sand Springs. There was always more moisture in places like that because they were flat. But even that didn't help us after the weather changed. Eventually the soil only grew desert plants. We keep our hopes up though, that things will change back. Some of the smaller plants are coming back. It just depends on the climate that year.

I guess I was about four or five years old when I started herding sheep. I went out with my older brothers, and we'd kind of hang out together. My eldest would hang out by himself. He was real ornery, (laughter). I did other stuff to help out too, like chopping woods. Sometimes we had to haul in that wood for the old folks. Us little kids would just gather all the small firewood and the bigger guys threw in the big logs. We did a lot of walking back then. That was about the only thing we did until my dad's horses started multiplying. That's when I got into riding. We had horses and donkeys before, but they got into some of the wilder groups of strays so they were too hard to corral and ride. If we could get them to stick around home they were calmer. Most of the folks then had horses for travel, with a wagon to take the family to the store. My grandpa used to run a lot of sheep wool back and forth that way. Back then people had thousands of sheep, and after we sheared them in the spring we'd have these big tubes of wool, maybe seven or eight at a time. Before Goulding's my family would haul wool all the way to Tuba City for trade.

Nowadays it takes a little over an hour to get to Tuba City by car. But back then it took about a week. You had to take an extra team of horses or mules. If you had eight or more tubes of wool in the wagon you would need four sets of mules with some more tied on the sides for switching off. It was just too hard on the animals. Back then the road were rough and sometimes just washed out.

But as a kid my big job was to herd the sheeps. My brothers and I were told just to keep an eye on them, so we figured we had time to play (laughter). At first I asked myself, 'Well, how do I watch sheep?' My brothers showed me that you just start following them around. When the animals settled into a spot we would play in the rocks. We could still see the sheep from up there, and when they moved we would too. There was always another spot to play. We got to know their pattern and knew when those sheep got itchin' to move. Well…there were a couple times we were so involved in our playing we forgot about the sheep! (giggles). Then my brothers would cry, but I would say, "Ah don't worry about it, we'll find them tomorrow."

(*I gave Lonnie a look of surprise and he burst out laughing.*) Yeah, I know I was being bad. But I wanted to go home then, because it was dark. We got in big trouble though. Oh yeah, the worst tongue-lashing you've ever seen. My parents were pretty strict, but not too bad. We only got spanked every now and then, and usually it was because of losing the sheep. We sure liked to play though. We climbed the rocks as high as we could. We got to the highest part of a slope and made sleds out of the smaller rocks. Then we would slide on that piece of flat rock all the way down. It was a great way to go for a ride. Nobody ever killed themselves.

Colette:

I had seen some of the younger Yazzie grandchildren playing on these rocks in much the same way. It made me hold my breath and close my eyes. I told Lonnie I could never have been his mom. I would have been worried about him every time he went out to play. My friend just smiled.

Lonnie:

I guess it was a little crazy, but we grew up around those rocks, so we were never afraid. A lot of times when we were herding we just didn't feel like coming down to the sheep. That much walking could get kind of monotonous, so instead we would climb along the top of the butte. At one point we were walking like that, toward the Arches, and we all decided to change clothes. My younger brother was three years old, I was five and my older brother was seven. We were just bored, so my younger brother, who was kind of tiny, got into my older brother's clothes. He was pretty darned tall, so you can imagine the difference. (*Here Lonnie enjoyed lots of laughter*). My older brother had on pants that came way up to his knees, and little Key was tripping all over the pants he had on. I had on his really small shirt, and we just rolled around in the dirt there and laughed our heads off!

Sometimes we would have to climb on top of the buttes to look for goats. The sheep weren't too hard to keep track of, but when the goats came along it was tougher. Goats really like to climb. One day we went out with about fifty goats, and we were pretty tired from all the climbing. Now in those days the weather was almost always pretty. Days were warm and clear, so we could look around and see for miles. I remember during the rainy season it could storm sometimes for days at a time, and that's when we mostly stayed in. When it turned windy it was harder to herd. The sand blew right into your eyes. You couldn't see from one mesa to the other because it was pitch red from the wind. There was nothing you could cover your face with if it came on all of a sudden. One day me and my mom were way over by Rooster Rock. I must have been about three years old and the sheep had kind of drifted and moved until they disappeared. My mom had me along to help find them, but she was pretty good at this all by herself. Anyway, we would get along the edge of the herd and sit behind the brush away from the wind. To keep me occupied my mom gathered up some little sticks, and we turned them into people. We built them a little hogan, a summer shade home...it kind of ticked the time away. We watched the sheep from our playground until they disappeared again. Then we'd gather up our stick family, find the herd and a new play spot and start playing all over again.

I have to admit, as a little kid I wasn't too interested in keeping clean. One winter we had a little problem with lice. I don't know how I got them...I guess from not taking a bath. We spent the whole winter staying at our place just the other side of Little Monument Valley, and we couldn't get our hair cut because we didn't have any clippers there. I liked to wear my hair long anyway, so I didn't care. Well, one day we started scratching ourselves all over. I guess my folks could see us kids all scratching our heads and they knew we got lice. They tried cutting our hair with the sheep shears, but those lice weren't going anywhere but closer to our head.

There wasn't a lot of water to waste that winter, so the final solution was to melt some snow and wash everything. My parents built a big fire and boiled up snow in a thirty -gallon washtub. We used that thing for washing all the time, or sometimes we used a barrel cut in half. My mom would just throw a lot of clothes in there to soak all day long. She ended up using kerosene on our heads to kill the lice. It didn't hurt too bad, but we sure did stink! Normally she would have used yucca plants to cure us, but I'm allergic to them. (*I asked what kind of Navajo is allergic to yucca plants, and he thought that was hilarious!*) Yeah, I guess I'm not a real Navajo, because every time I tried to wash with yucca I started itching. My mom told me yucca doesn't work for some people. I guess if she had clippers we would have had our heads shaved. That might have been easier. You know we had lice on every part of our bodies, in the seams of our pants and everything. So that was one nightmare of a winter, (*Lonnie laughed some more, shaking his head*). We just walked around smelling like kerosene. It was a good thing nobody lit a match!

Back then it seemed like we never had enough food to eat. We were a good-sized family, so we wolfed down whatever Mom cooked for us. Sometimes we traded for food in Keyenta or go up to Goulding's, but that was kind of later on in life when we'd gotten to our elementary and junior high ages. Before that we spent some nights all by ourselves with no food. My dad would be gone looking for work, and my mom might be trading rugs at Goulding's or helping a woman have a baby, so in two or three days we would run out of food. That was when we'd look for the flour and lard to make fry or dry bread. My mom always kept those two things around so we'd have something to fill our stomachs.

When she got back from trading we'd have food again. Mainly we ate potatoes, usually fried, and anything with gravy. Sometimes there wasn't anything to eat except a barrel of onions. We'd cook up a big onion soup and put a lot of salt in it. In the wintertime we went rabbit hunting. We'd go for looking for *gah*. One jack rabbit was a prize catch! Around here there's mainly cottontail, you see very few jackrabbits. If we caught one that meant we could have a feast, because you only needed one to make a good stew. Us kids were sort of scrawny and skinny, so that little bit of stew could tide us over for a while. We got vegetables mainly from our farm. Back then we grew things in the summertime like squash, corn, melon and cantaloupe. We also got a lot of fruit from our peach groves.

As I got a little older Harry Goulding started to bring out visitors who were sightseeing in the Valley. Every time he saw us out there herding the sheep he'd stop by with his group and ask, "Would you like something to eat?" We'd say, "heck yeah!" and he would open up a can of tomatoes and a tube of crackers. Boy! The visitors would take some snapshots of us and then we'd take the food behind some rocks. Once we saw those crackers and tomatoes it was "See ya later!" We loved that stuff. Every now and then I get canned tomatoes and saltines to snack on. They remind me of my struggle-for-survival days, (laughter).

Harry Goulding was the only one that would truck some people in there. Other than that people would ride through there on a horse, and there was never too many white people going through there until Mr. Goulding started taking them in. After a while he got to taking maybe two or three groups a week. That was during the Navajo summer dry spell. Some kids could sell arrowheads to visitors for a quarter apiece. We'd collect them all year, and by the summer we'd have a big pile saved up, but we never sold them. We didn't have anything to put them in so we'd use a rag and tie the ends together (laughter). There aren't as many arrowheads out there now as we saw growing up. I heard some people get five bucks a head for them now, but I don't believe it.[178]

INDIAN SCHOOL
"Seek wisdom, not knowledge. Knowledge is of the past, wisdom is of the future." - *Lumbee*

I was about six when the people from Bureau of Indian Affairs started coming around looking for me. They suggested to my mom that I go away to school, but she was putting it off. Me and my brothers were usually up by Totem Rock herding sheep, and every time we came back home we'd peak over that little sand dune up by the Totem Pole to see if there was any of those BIA guys there. I didn't want to leave my mom or my family to go to school. I never really knew what school was about, but I knew I was having too many fun times at home. Then one day I was trapped.

Nobody was around that day, so we thought it was cool to hang around the hogan. My brothers and I were playing on the rocks when we saw a vehicle making a trail of

---

[178] The collection and sale of artifacts are actually prohibited by both federal and tribal law for all people.

dust toward our place. We paid attention to that, because we rarely had any visitors in those days. There were only a couple Navajos that had a truck, and you could see Goulding's vehicle from a mile away. We were going to keep playing anyway, but I asked my brother, "are you sure that's not a government vehicle?" Back then the BIA people drove a car we used to call "gold bucket," or "golden panel," and this car coming up had that gold lettering on it. There I was outside and I thought, "Oh shoot! I should've been way up behind the sand dunes by now." I left my brothers and slipped back into the house.

This was when my dad worked for the uranium mine and we were doing pretty good with keeping up the place, so the government gave us a real house to live in. The hogan was about fifty feet away, with a summer shade home in the middle. I got in the house and wondered, 'Hmmm, where should I hide?" There were two beds in one room, and I went under the second one just as I heard the vehicle driving up to the house. I could hear the BIA guys outside asking about me, and my mom said, "Oh, he's inside." So they knew where to find me. Two of the guys went in and said, "Okay, we know you're here. It's time to go to school." He said it in English, but there was an interpreter with him talking to me in Navajo.

After a while they peeked under the bed and said, "There you are! Come on out. You're going to come with us one way or the other." I looked at the interpreter and screamed, "Don't let them catch me! Don't let them take me!" But they just lifted up the bed and dragged me out (*Lonnie laughed*). I didn't want to go with them, so I kept yelling, "*doh da*" (*the Navajo word for "no."*). But they told me I didn't have any choice and got me dressed. They had brought me a pair of brand new pants and some shoes, the kind that lace up. I was squirming around so much they could only get one shoe on, so they carried me to the vehicle like that and kind of threw the other shoe in after me before closing and locking the door.

I had never worn shoes before that time. That's just how we grew up. We didn't really need them until we got older and had to travel around more. The shoes the BIA guys gave me were just an assumption of what my feet size were. They just carried a bunch of them in the vehicle and guessed what would fit a kid. It wasn't like you got to try them on. Well, these shoes were too tight, and my toes were crushed against my feet. Since I never even knew what having shoes was like I just figured having my feet crushed was a normal part of wearing shoes. The pants they put on me were kind of baggy, but I guess they didn't have any other kind. I liked my old pants that had holes in the back of the cheek, (laughter), but they took those from me in the vehicle and threw the new ones at me to put on. Then they just drove me away while I looked out the back at my brothers hiding in the rocks. My younger brother Kee was under age, and considered too young to start school back then. Leonard, my older brother, got taken to school later on. But I was alone that day. They drove me all the way to Keyenta.

Back then the little town of Keyenta was a bare place, with not much there except the BIA school. There were separate dormitories for the girls and the boys, a cafeteria, the main school building and an old trading post next to the tribal chapter house. I went to that Indian school from when I was six all the way through fourth grade. I started the fifth grade at a different school located even further away in Tuba City. Kids attended there for a five year "special education." After you finished that they got you oriented towards learning a trade or a vocation. That program was like a technical school. Most people took drafting or auto mechanics, bakery classes, stuff like that. From there they went straight off to work in different cities, right after they graduated.

When I first got to that first school in Keyenta I didn't know anything about living in a building, so I was pretty confused. They got registered and took me to the dormitory. All I could see was this long building, and I began to wonder where a kid could go to the bathroom. I looked around on the other side of the buildings at the bushes and the rocks and thought, 'well, should I just take a dump here?' At home I used the brushes and the rocks. I figured I'd just hold it for a while until I got this mystery straightened out. Walking beyond the dormitory I found a sort of lobby where a bunch of kids were lining up for their supper. They all came out of their rooms, and suddenly there were a bunch of beady eyes staring at me. I thought they looked pretty funny, because they all had bald heads, (giggles). I probably looked like a wild savage to them, because my hair was really long, the traditional way. In another line, a couple hundred feet away, was all the girls. At that time they sometimes let the girls keep their hair in braids, but if it was dirty or had lice the BIA folks would just whack those braids off.

While everybody was staring at me I recognized one of my friends! I went up to him all wide-eyed, and asked him, "Hey, where do you guys take a dump here? I went outside and I didn't see any place."

He told me they had a different place to go inside. It was called a "restroom." I thought that was real peculiar. At first I didn't believe him. I said, "You guys go in the house here? That's kind of strange. At home I usually go out behind the dunes." He said he'd show me where it was, and he took me to my first restroom. It was full of stalls, but I didn't know what those separate rooms were for. I looked at the sink and asked him, "Well, how do you use this thing?" He said, "You don't use that. That's a sink where you wash your hands and face. If you have to pee and stuff you go in those little holes." He opened the door to one of the stalls and I thought, "Ah-ha!" So that was my first introduction to indoor plumbing (laughs). I think that guy even had to tell me what to do with the toilet paper.

Boarding school days were pretty tough, and at first there was a lot about it that confused me. For instance, that first pair of shoes the BIA guys put on me. I didn't really understand what they were for. In the warmer months back home I went barefoot, and in the winter I wore real comfortable shoes like moccasins. Well, when they crammed those real shoes on me it was kind of awkward. My toes were all squished up inside and pushed toward the front of the shoe. I thought that was how shoes were supposed to feel so I wore them without complaining even though they really hurt. Some years after I started school they came out with a uniform, but until then we just got by with whatever we had or whatever used clothing they gave us. Later in the day they shaved all my hair off, my entire head. My hair was past my shoulders, but they shaved me bald. They said it was for hygiene purposes, and they showed me where to shower too. It didn't bother me. Living out in the Valley we didn't get to shower much. When it was warm we could wash up in the river, and when it rained we'd run under a waterfall that came off the rocks. If there wasn't any rain for a while people could get some juniper or yucca and use that to shampoo their hair. It was maybe a once a month deal.

At first I thought living in an enclosed area was kind of fun. We got to shower every other day. There was a process to it though. The folks in charge would run us through the showers and then inspect us when we were done. They made sure we cleaned everything we were supposed to, (laughs). So I was taught how to shower. There were always these different personnel lecturing you. The majority of them were pretty harsh, even the teachers. Some of the teachers had pointers or rulers, and if you made a mistake they gave you a good whack with it. I didn't think that was very cool. I thought, 'hmmm, I don't know about staying here.'

They were only willing to talk to us in English. That was the other thing that took some getting used to. They had some Navajo workers who interpreted things to us at first, but sometimes they weren't around to help. That didn't stop the BIA folks though. Even if we didn't understand them they'd still talk and talk and talk. We just stood there and listened. Another thing they wanted us to do was to march. We would march after school, and early in the mornings. Then we'd march again on the weekends. In the mornings they woke us up at about five in the morning, when it was still dark outside. We would have a certain amount of time then to fix all our beds army-style. The people in charge wanted our beds made real tight, so that they could bounce a penny off it. By six o'clock we'd march to breakfast in the cafeteria.

It wouldn't be long before one of us did something to get everyone else in trouble. A kid would get distracted or start goofing off. Maybe somebody would have stepped out of line at the cafeteria. That's when we'd all get it once we got back to the dorm. We'd have to line up again to get walloped with the dust brush. You'd have maybe seventy or eighty kids waiting in the lobby just to get smacked for what one kid did. This brush was about a quarter inch thick and two feet long, and the guy in charge would say, "Okay, everybody line up....first row, we'll start with you." We'd get a little lecture, and then he'd smack us one after the other, wham! Wham! Each of us usually got two really good hits on the butt. Some of smacks were hard enough to make you cry. Most of us did cry actually. Some of the kids would giggle then cry after that (laughter). I was one of those kids that kind of giggled and cried at the same time. I don't think it really taught us anything. It was ridiculous that all us had to pay for one kid messing up.

Most of us kids were pretty hyper. We were used to running around the desert with the sheep. We were accustomed to getting along on our own because we had been raised to be pretty independent. There were times when the staff woke us up in the middle of the night because they caught some kid running around instead of staying in bed. If that happened they made us sit along the hallway until about twelve o'clock, just to tire us out. Sometimes we'd all stand in the hallway and be told to touch our toes. That would go on for an hour or so. Sometimes they just made us run two or three miles around the school.

Eventually they would tell us to go back to bed, and by then we were ready for it. The classroom was the same way. You would march to class and try to be quiet, because the teachers all carried around these long pointers or rulers. If you missed a problem or couldn't answer a question correctly you got a whack in the back or on the hands. So we were on our guard all the time. This went on from the beginning of kindergarten all the way through my first year.

On Saturdays they'd wake us up at five o'clock again, so that we could clean. We'd have to start sweeping one portion of the dorm, and then move to the other. Each dorm had maybe thirty or forty beds for about eighty kids. They were all sort of double bunk beds, and they filled up half the dorm. We'd push all those beds to one side and scrub the floor with a hard brush, then wash it down with a string mop and some towels. Then we moved everything again and did the other side. With eighty of us it didn't take too long because everybody did their part. After washing the floor we'd have to wax it so it would shine. The whole process took about half a day. At noon they'd lecture us some more, then we'd march into the cafeteria. After lunch we'd march again, all eighty of us. We must have looked like one long centipede, but boy we got good at marching. It was just like the military, and nobody stepped out of line. In the afternoon they'd give us an hour or thirty minutes to ourselves. They'd say to us, "Okay, go ahead and play."

Around three o'clock they'd call us back inside and lecture us again. Then we'd go march off to supper. After supper there was one last lecture. I was never really sure what they were lecturing us about (laughs)! We'd just nod and say, "Yeah, okay...uh-huh." In the warmer months it would still be light out at seven o'clock when they made us go to bed. We'd laugh at each other and say, "Hey, the sun's way up there in the sky, what 'er we doing in bed?" It was hard to fall asleep, but once we did we slept hard because we were pretty tired from all the scrubbing. In addition to doing the floors we all had separate chores. There were a couple of us who had to clean out the restroom and stuff like that. Then we'd rotate after a week. There was a kitchen staff that did the cooking and the dishes so we didn't have to do that. Most of the motel personnel from the area were seasonal, and they didn't know what to do with themselves in the winter. That was when BIA promised them jobs working at the schools.

There were a mixture of Navajo and black and white people working at the schools. Overall there were more whites than Indian or blacks. The people working in the cafeteria were mostly black. I never had any complaints about the food because I was just glad to be getting three meals a day! When I was a kid there was usually no food at home, so school was like a paradise or heaven for us in that way. Once I adapted to the dorm way of life it got easier. As long as you did as you were told things went okay. Unfortunately, not all the kids caught on to that idea. There was always somebody getting into trouble and we'd all get a whippin' for whatever dumb thing he did. I got used to it after the first couple of years. I just figured it was a harsh life, but at least I was eating. And in the summer it was a nice place to leave. Yeah, we all had that to look forward to...leaving the BIA school.

Colette:

276

I couldn't imagine what it would have been like to be forced into a school environment as Lonnie had endured, but I could understand the fear he must have felt as a young child thrust into a new and alien environment. As a Navy brat I had struggled with the unsettling experience of changing schools nearly every year. Each time my father gained a new assignment he was stationed to a different base where we would have to move and settle all over again. I attended kindergarten in San Diego while dad was at Miramar Naval Base. During my first and second grades we lived in Ohio close to Wright-Patterson Air Force Base, and by the third grade we had moved to Florida where dad flew from a carrier ship at Mayport Naval Station. We moved to New York when dad retired as a Navy pilot and started working for Grumman Aerospace. I spent fifth and sixth grade back in San Diego until dad's work took us to the exotic Middle East. Change was the only constant in my childhood. Yet at the time it seemed to be endless adventure. I could never compare my experience with the brutality and confusion Lonnie went through during his schooling. Typical to the rest of the Yazzies I had spoken with, Lonnie took the misery of his past with a grain of salt.

Lonnie:

Like I said, I never wanted to go to school in the first place, but I don't think my parents would have let me stay home. They didn't want us to struggle like they had to, looking for the next meal and traveling around for a job. They wanted us to have an education so we might find a better way to make a living. I asked my mom one time, "What did you think about us going off to school?" She said, "Yeah, I didn't want you to go. I missed you guys. But I figured this was the best thing to do, was to get you guys educated." My dad never talked much about it, but in his own way he wanted that for us to. He wanted us to have a more secure life than he did.

That first year we were told we could go home for Christmas, for a week or two. Well, there were no real roads in the Valley at the time, and my dad couldn't find a way to get to Keyenta. It was pretty tough for him to travel the dirt roads because they weren't kept up. I figured he couldn't get a vehicle or a horse to come get me, so that Christmas nothing happened, nobody came for me. I wasn't the only kid who kind of expected their parents to come and was disappointed. So that Christmas we all had to stay at school. The second year at Christmas everybody had the mumps, and that's a pretty contagious deal. They didn't want anybody to go home, so eighty of us were stuck in the dormitory the whole time, eating soup and oatmeal. It wasn't like we actually celebrated Christmas. Back then Christmas didn't have a lot of spirit to anybody. The white people would pass out little presents, and I guess that's when they brainwashed us that Christmas was when you gave gifts out. But back home we never knew what Christmas was. We didn't celebrate Thanksgiving either.

So we didn't really know what we were missing, other than missing our parents. The BIA folks didn't allow us to go home until the summertime. The second year when I was in first grade, once again hardly anyone went home because so few of the parents were able to show up. To be at school and away from home for nine months out of the year really affected us. We felt sort of disconnected from our home. The three months of summer when we were finally at home felt like time spent in Paradise!

277

LONNIE'S LONG WALK

"We walk in our moccasins upon the Earth and beneath the sky. As we travel on life's path of beauty, we will live a good life and reach old age." — *Navajo Blessing*

Once I started school in Tuba City they began to put paved roads in, that was sometime in the 1960s. After the Tuba City school I was sent to school in Brigham City, Utah, and that was the biggest school ever. At that school there was a lot more freedom for us kids, and we kind of went nuts up there because of it. We used to raid the farms that surrounded the school, and we loaded up on watermelon and peaches and apples. It felt so good to have more freedom to roam! I was about sixteen then, and feeling old enough to get home on my own instead of waiting for my dad to come all that way to get me. I didn't even wait for them to excuse us for Christmas. I just left that school in November and hitchhiked from Brigham City, Utah all the way back to my home in Monument Valley. I got rides pretty consistently up until Flagstaff, Arizona. Then I had to stay in the Flagstaff bus station for two or three nights. I had called people who knew my folks, asking them to pick me up from there, but somehow they didn't receive the message. I spent my days walking around downtown just looking into shop windows.

Sleeping in the bus station had sort of lost its appeal by the third day. I figured then that nobody was going to show up, so I just started walking. I only had about seventy-five cents to my name. Back then doughnuts were about ten cents and coffee fifteen cents, so that was my meal for one day; three or four doughnuts and a cup of coffee. That tided me over for a couple of days, and I walked all the way out of Flag' until about three or four o'clock in the afternoon. Finally, some people who worked for the government picked me up and gave me a ride to Tuba City. They told me to check into the dormitory at the school there, but I wasn't about to do that. I wanted to get home. When the government people dropped me off by the school I made like I was heading over there, but as soon as they got out of sight I turned back to the road and headed for M.V. I got another ride that took me as far as Cow Springs, but they forgot I was in the back of the truck and nearly took me all the way to their home! I had to knock on the back window to get their attention before they finally pulled over and dropped me off, (laughter). I started walking down the highway again until it started getting dark.

There wasn't a lot of action on the roads back then. Every now and then a diesel truck would roll by, but other than that it was pretty quiet. I came up on an old bus stop as night was falling. They had these wooden structures back then where you could wait for the bus with a little roof and a bench to sit on. It was getting colder, so I decided to make a fire with some wood I scrounged up. I knew that I'd be on the road for awhile, so I had picked up a book of matches at the café where I bought my doughnuts. I was really glad that I had them with me and I think I would have froze otherwise. As the night wore on the fire dimmed and I had to go searching for more wood. I had a little fire at first, but by midnight I got it blazing. I began to feel drowsy, so I got as close to the fire as I could and fell asleep. I stayed in that little bus shelter all night.

By early dawn the fire had gone out and I woke up shaking. I made one more fire because it seemed like morning was taking a long time to come. I was really looking forward to the sun coming up! Once it did I put out my fire and took off down the road again. The whole night I'd been in that little shack with only had a thin coat and a hat, so for the entire night I had been sort of rolling around by that fire trying to get as close as I could. I ended up getting a little dusty, but I had no idea that my face was black with soot. I just tasted something funny when I licked my lips. Of course, I didn't have a mirror with me, so I didn't know that I looked like a black guy! After walking about five miles I realized I was thirsty. I saw a house a mile toward the closest mountain, so I figured I could find some water there. It was about ten in the morning, so I was hoping people would be up and around. Sure enough I found a hogan with a barrel full of water next to it. I didn't see any people, but there was a little yellow container I could use for drinking, so I filled it up and headed back for the main road.

Eventually a family stopped to give me a ride. It was a man and woman with a couple of kids. I hopped in the back of their truck and was taken all the way to Keyenta. The whole time those kids were staring at me, and I couldn't figure out what the big attraction was. I was just glad to have a ride the rest of the way. Once I got to Keyenta I stopped into an old café to get some food. I still had thirty cents to my name, so I ordered coffee and one last doughnut. While I sat at the counter waiting for my stuff people kept staring at me sort of funny. I thought it was because I was a little dusty and looked like a hobo. Everyone was smiling at me just like the guy who gave me a ride. I figured they were all just really friendly! I took a sip of my coffee, and then went to use the restroom. That's when I saw myself in the mirror. I almost scared myself! My face was completely black with soot, and all you could see was my eyes. I looked like an owl! My lips were all licked around the edges to just this one brown spot. It was my only shiny spot.

Well, the joke was on me, and I washed my face so that I wouldn't scare people anymore. I sat at the café for a little while until by the afternoon I was ready to start walking again. I headed toward Monument Valley, but just as I got to the bridge here comes my aunt with her husband. She was married to a Ute man, and they came truckin' through and asked me what the heck I was doing there. I told them that I was ready to go home. I'd had enough adventure for awhile. They took me back to where they were living at Three Sisters monument. From there I took the horse trails to my mom's hogan which was situated a little further in the Valley. When I saw my mom I didn't know what to tell her at first. We just stared at each other, (laughter). I finally explained, "The people at school told me to go home, so I did. It took me awhile, but here I am." Of course, I would be suspended for leaving early, and she knew that. I didn't know how to act because I didn't know if she would be mad at me. But she didn't let on like she was angry. She just took me into the hogan and said, "Well, I think my son's hungry." She started taking out pots and pans and she cooked me something to eat. That was the best meal I'd had in a long time. I was glad to be home, but getting here had been quite an experience. I don't think I'd want my own boys to survive on the road like that.

After I got out of school I spent most of my time at home helping out my mom. She always made sure we knew how important it was for us to take care of each other. That was the main thing. Now she needs all the care she can get, so it's our turn to look after her. When I got older and found work in Keyenta I still went to my mom's place to check on her. I brought her groceries and hay for the animals, and I would chop wood and bring it in. Then I would cart in some water. That stuff goes on around here. It's a never-ending cycle in most families. Even now when I'm home I try to patch up the hogan and look after the livestock, and my brothers do the same. It's a responsibility we just accept.

My mom always took care of us kids pretty well, and my dad did his best too. Growing up we all felt he did his best to provide for us. In a lot of ways we were better off than some people because dad had a couple mules and a wagon. With that he could always haul woods and water. He was the one who taught us how to farm. When I was a kid we had some real nice crops. Back then we had lots of rain and we could raise corn, squash, watermelon and peaches. And of course we always had sheep. When it rained we had a little tent we put up to stay dry, and it was so neat to just sit in that tent and watch the rain come pouring down. We always saw waterfalls forming over the rocks and lightning on the horizon. It was really pretty, but it stopped raining like that as I grew up. The corn stopped growing tall when I was around six years old, right about the time they dragged me to school.

I don't agree with some of those government people who said that we had too many sheep grazing causing the topsoil to blow away. That's when they began slaughtering our sheep against our will. But a lot of us knew that it wasn't the sheep's fault. Our climate changed like it has over the centuries, and we just got stuck in that cycle. The weather pattern out here has always decided how we live. Our ancestors used to hunt a lot, but when settlers came we started farming more. When the weather changed we switched from farming to having livestock. Now we depend mostly on the tourist trade to survive. I think it's going to stay that way until the weather pattern changes again.

Colette:

Once again I found myself in awe of how one of the Yazzies breezed in and out of what could have been a disastrous situation. A thousand "what ifs" swirled through my head as I listened to him tell of his exodus from the Indian School that cold autumn day. As a mother I could only imagine the many ways in which the young Lonnie might have become lost, hurt or perished altogether. What had Suzie really thought when she saw her boy walking toward her...tired, hungry and no doubt a ragged mess? I know that I would have become slightly hysterical and bombarded my errant child with questions about his dangerous trek. Then I suppose I would have chided him for taking such a risky trip on his own. Luckily for Lonnie his mother was nothing like me. Anyway what good would it have done to squawk at a kid who had managed to make it home after all?

LONNIE'S FAITH

"If a man is as wise as a serpent, he can afford to be as harmless as a dove." - Cheyenne

Lonnie:

Church-wise all us kids went to church in town. The school had us going to Catholic, Baptist, and Presbyterian services. Whatever was there in town, we'd all have to attend. Eventually we were all baptized in each of the churches. We started with Presbyterian and worked our way through to the Catholic, then ending up with Latter Day Saints. LDS kind of faded in and out.

There were a lot of missionaries from LDS, and they were trying to push their way into each hogan way out there in the boonies. The Navajo would just let them in and hear the missionaries say, "We'd like to talk to you about this and that." The Navajo would just say, "um-hum...okay," and let them have their talk. Later on in life I asked myself, 'well, what's the purpose of religion?' I sat there and looked at each church that I'd been though and figured they were all basically the same. Then I thought a lot about my own faith. That's when I finally figured out it would be best to keep my own religion. I learned it through my mom's teaching a long time ago. This was back when we didn't have television. During the cold winter nights she would tell stories about the Long Walk or the time of emergence. That kind of stayed in my heart through all the years. Maybe that's how I remained so stable. I sort of grew up with my faith always in the back of my mind. I began to pick it up more, and I practiced stuff my dad, my mom and my grandpa did. I preferred doing things the same way as my ancestors. I think the basic philosophy of all religions is the same as ours. The main thing was that you never take the life of another human being, and you treat yourself and other people with respect. We also respect nature. That's always been understood through time.

My mom taught me that remembering our history was a way of keeping our religion. After the Western Expansion our ancestors were kind of like savages, they would wipe out anything that came close to the Navajo. But that wasn't their usual way of thinking. To them every life was precious. They went through that period of warring with others who they felt were threatening their way of life. Some were fierce warriors and excellent in their fighting techniques. I think there was one or two of them who could have wiped out a whole troop of soldiers. There were several who always had conflicts with Mexicans or Spaniards and other tribes because these people picked on the Navajo. These particular warriors wouldn't stand for it, and they always retaliated. They chased some Spaniards all the way back to Mexico, and they chased the Cheyenne back to the plains. They decided to do the same things the Spaniards were doing, and took prisoners as slaves and stole horses, sheep and cows. That was their way of getting revenge and scaring off settlers. It was a way to pester the Whites. For the most part though, our ancestors valued life and only wanted to maintain harmony. Because of this some of my ancestors never really picked up arms to protect themselves.

The earliest memory of learning about my Navajo faith is being in a ceremony. I was getting prayer done on me. I had to follow the Medicine Man exactly in the way he did the prayer. That was one of the most technical things I ever did, just following him along. It was like taking dictation. I didn't really know what he was saying. I just said it along with him and the rest of the people at the ceremony. That was one of the toughest things I ever did...keeping up with the Medicine Man. I would lose him...space out a little bit, and have to do it again. It's like a repetition where there are always four sets of different prayers or songs. I remember another ceremony they did when my sister was being born. Mom was in the hogan using the sash belt, and there were a couple of ladies who used a shawl to keep her pride. That was the best way to keep her privacy, because there was a bunch of folks there singing along. She was on her knees and the ladies put blankets around her and the sash belt. I must have been about five years old. My sister is about five, six, seven years younger than I am.

I thought she was kind of cute as a kid. We were taught to respect certain relationships a lot growing up together. You were supposed to treat your sister as well as your mom or brother. There were certain relatives or siblings that you can tease about their genitals. It was just the subject matter you used to tease them. I could do that to my mom's brothers. It would acceptable to get a little nasty with those guys, whereas you wouldn't do that with your own brother or sister. The purpose of this teasing was to get an education in sex without overstepping boundaries. That way you wouldn't be showing off your genitals as a kid to the wrong person. The sweat lodge worked like that in a sense also.

The sweat lodge is another very important part of our religion. It's like...how would you say it? It's like an endurance-builder. I was taught that the sweat lodge came in to being because at one point the Navajo were on the verge of giving up on the struggle for survival. The people were saying, "We can't do this anymore. Life is just too hard." That was when the spirits told them to build a sweat lodge. They were told to how, and after they built it and were instructed in how to use it. They sweated the heck out of themselves and finally saw the light. They said to each other, "Oh yeah! We'll do things this way, and we'll do things that way." It brought them more of a positive sense, without any negative feeling.

This is really just a tiny hogan with no chimney; just a little doorway that you block off with a bunch of blankets. Then you build a fire outside to heat up the rocks. You build a little hole inside the hogan where you throw in all the rocks about the size of your hand. It takes about eight to ten pretty good-sized chunks of rocks. You do the whole puppy like that until it's about a foot or more deep. You keep the rocks under the heat for about an hour or so, until they turn fiery red. Then you stoke it with little sticks with piles of rocks and put those in there. You find some fresh sage and lay it on the floor, but the best thing is to throw wet sage inside so that you get more steam. You don't need to pour water on the rocks. It gets so hot the way we do it that if you used water it would be too much. Boy, it smells good! It cleans out your whole system. You just kind of sweat it out.

I had the worst time with my first sweat. This would be my puberty ceremony when my dad went in with me. I wondered then why I had to do it. They didn't explain it to me that it was the male's puberty rite. I had to figure that out myself. You sit in there and your elders tell stories, sing some mountain songs, and do a little Navajo prayer. After a while of being in there, you come out and you roll around in the dirt. Once it dries you brush it off and jump back in there again. We went in around four times. At the beginning I didn't last but five to ten minutes. I just wasn't used to it at first, but the more you do it the easier it gets. Nowadays I can go for about thirty minutes at a time. The afternoon is the best time to do a sweat, all the way up to March or so. You usually want to do one after the first snowstorm. You stay inside as long as you can, then jump out and roll around in that snow.

We could fit five or six skinny Navajos in there, but sometimes there were some big, big lugs! (Laughter) We did it on the other side of where the airstrip is now; right off toward the canyon where my uncle used to live. I can still do a sweat there if I want to. Whenever I want I just take some woods over in that place and get it done. I still like to clean things out of my body and get positive reinforcement that way. When you think you're kind of negative about life or struggling with something you can do it two or three times a week. While you're in there, solutions just kind of come to you. Life is good after you do the sweat lodge.

That's the way you usually feel when you get out of the sweat lodge. You say, "Oh, I can conquer the world!" You have more clarity. At times we used it as Ex-Lax, that's what we used to call it. It'll clean you out in all different ways, (laughter). It's a spiritual healing, and it builds endurance to the harsh world that we have always lived in. Around here it's cold in the winter and frying hot in the summer. But if you do the sweat lodge you can't even feel the heat, because you're aware that you can take something hotter. You're so clean that the air just kind of penetrates your skin making you feel cool even though you're out in the hot heat. That's probably another secret to adaptation of the Navajo. All of my siblings were interested in our native faith, especially Leonard, Kee and I because we always kind of hung out together. We all feel sort of the same way about things. My eldest brother was kind of a rebel on his own. He got into more of the Native American Church thing, and I think maybe it was good for him. He had been trying out some destructive things until he turned to the Prairie religion. It's a faith different from ours, but it's allowed him to focus on his job. He went through a rough time trying to adjust to life, and I guess the Prairie religion put him back on track.

Some folks, even other Indians, get on their high horse and look down on their own people's culture. That's the trip they take you on, forcing their way of doing things on everyone else. When my eldest brother got into the Native American religion he wanted us all to be in it. But I had to say, "Hmmm, I don't think so." I didn't want to say no to an elderly brother, but as time went by I thought, "I got my own religion. I don't need anything else." It was the same with my sister. She was kind of stretched out in all different directions from her family. Her eldest son is really into his Christian religion, and he says to her, "why can't you be saved?" But we stuck to our own traditional ways, and everybody's settled down now and let things be.

Our kids have their own system and it's kind of rough to figure out where you belong, (laughs). Some of them are Christian and some are practicing other things. My kids are mostly still praying with the corn pollen. I tried to stress that as they grew up. I'd have them take the corn pollen every chance they get. But it took a long time for it to sink into me, so I don't expect them to get it right away. You know, the older you get the more you think about these things. You get a little bit wiser. I think not understanding our prayers causes a lot of young ones to move away from our tradition. If you're taught young to pray but with no explanation you take your traditions for granted.

Colette:

In my mind I compared Lonnie's religious experience to my own. I had been baptized and raised as a Lutheran and along with my siblings sat with my mother in church. She was the driving force in our spiritual education, and after a few explorations into other religions I came back to my Protestant roots. I have always felt at peace as a Christian, though I could see how different faith systems work for others. My father went from disgruntled Catholic to professed Atheist, and my eldest sister converted to Judaism. Over time I came to understand that religion is, above all, a very personal thing. As I sat there mulling over this idea Lonnie began again:

Lonnie:

So yeah, I respected my elder brothers. I was one of the middle kids, so I didn't tell my younger siblings what to do. I didn't really feel the need to boss them around. We always hung together, even though we fought most of the time, (laughs). But the eldest in our family…you didn't give any lip to him. That was his version of being the oldest anyway. His track record didn't always instill that. I guess like a lot of guys growing up as the oldest he thought, "I got what it takes and I've been through more, so I think my younger brothers should listen to me." When we were kids he'd try to throw his weight around a couple times, but we just threw it back, (laughter). He was a pretty good brother though. As for my sister, I think she's still making her mind up about living a traditional life. Maybe she's thinking it ain't her bag, but her daughters are both very traditional. One of her sons is different and says being a Christian is better than following Dine' traditions. That's how things are different nowadays. Kids decide for themselves and there are a lot of other influences than I had growing up.

Anyway, when I was growing up part of our tradition involved doing certain chores. Most chores were all "not my favorite," (laughter). I was like every kid I guess. I didn't want to work. But chores had to be done in order to survive, so we didn't have any choice. The Dine' philosophy through the story of emergence tells us what the traditional responsibilities of a Navajo man are. All the stories are attached to a particular event or animal through time. In the emergence stories we learn how marriage between men and women marriages were attacked at that time. The women and the men decided that liberation from specific tasks didn't work out for anybody. Just like in the modern times when women or men say, "Oh, we don't need the other sex for anything." We can do it all ourselves," people realized that was silly. A real good Medicine Man will tell you these things. Somebody may ask why we're different, or wonder how we should live, and a Medicine Man will tell you a story along those lines. If you ask, "How come I split up with my wife?" Or, "How come we have so many problems?" A Medicine Man will tell you the separation of the genders story, and what happened a long time ago. The men thought they could do everything by themselves, and the women thought they could too. They each went to live on different sides of a river, but a lot of folks realized it couldn't work, and they died trying to swim back to one another. That's where a lesson is taught that it doesn't work being liberated. Is that what Whites call it? Where the guy tries to do everything a woman does and vice-versa? Yeah, it can really mess things up. That's why women do certain things better than men and the other way around. I know a little bit about weaving, but that's not one of my chores. I'm better at other things so that's what I do to help out.

LONNIE'S DREAM
"The strong man walks in virtue." - Zuni

Colette:

I wondered if Lonnie aspired to the same things his wife, Emily did. What would ultimately make him feel content and successful? Had he already achieved that goal? Emily shared her feeling that living a traditional life would bring her the most joy. I was fairly certain that Lonnie had the same desire, but how did de define living as a traditional Navajo? I asked him what life would be like for him if he were living his dream.

Lonnie:

The perfect life for me as a Navajo man would be just soaking everything in around me. I would love to just ride my horse every morning and mind my livestock. I used to wonder why my grandpa and some of those old folks went that way, but after a while I saw how they had gotten secure in their world. They just followed their sheep and took care of their animals. I've figured out lately that it's real simple. It's good to be just a normal person, a human being trying to survive on earth. Once you accomplish that you get a peace of mind and just keep driving your herd of sheep, (laughter).

Even while I was at school, well...my whole mind was here in the Valley. And I had a lot of friends in Keyenta. My dad offered to get me a job where he worked at the uranium mine. He asked one of the technicians, or engineers about it. He said, "Hey, I've got a guy that'll work real hard for you." So I worked there for a while, but not for long. I preferred taking care of things in the Valley. When my dad died my mom and my sister were on their own here, and I knew that I had a big responsibility. A man was needed, so I just started working more. We weren't real worried about our sheep, horses, and the cow because they were grazing on the vegetation. But mom and my sister needed groceries from time to time. I actually finished high school in Keyenta. After that I worked for the tour operator for the summer. I tried some community college around 1972, but I didn't really know what I wanted to do for a living. I didn't finish junior college, or vocational school.

My brother and his wife moved to Keyenta, and that's where I met my first wife. She lived a couple blocks down and I got to know her. We just got closer and closer, and eventually we got married, but never got around to actually getting a marriage license. We actually started our family in Keyenta, and I traveled into the Valley to help my mom out. Our first little baby girl we named Ronnie, and then we had Tiffany, the youngest. I also have daughters named Missy and Norma. Ronnie came back here to the Valley, and she went a little wild because that's how it goes sometimes when you're young and living on the Rez, (laughter). For three years she worked and saved enough money to buy herself a truck. She and her friends just went nuts with it, and eventually they rolled it way down there by the Sand Springs. That's when she got chewed out, and we sent her back to school in Arizona. She got work at Arizona State University and is doing pretty well there now.

My other daughter, Tiffany is doing great too. She switched from studying aerodynamics to becoming a mechanical engineer. I have another daughter, Rachel, from when I wasn't married. She's twenty now and doing well also. She finished high school and college. Now she's trying to get her Master's degree. She and her husband bought a house and it's pretty big…two stories. She's got three kids now! Missy is next in line, then Norma, she's my stepdaughter. She and Missy are almost the same age.

All of these kids are from my first marriage. I didn't get married traditionally back then. My first wife and I just met in the middle of rush hour, (laugher). Just kidding…we don't really have a "rush hour" in Keyenta. Back then I was just struggling to put my life together as a new dad. Everything came at me all at once…marriage and working full time. I was about twenty-one or two when I got married that first time. I hadn't been dating or anything. Then the ship started rocking. My first daughter was born very early on in the relationship.

When I broke up with my first wife I ended up back in the Valley, and then I got together with Emily. We met in Window Rock. She said she saw me across the room at a dance, and I kind of remember that. I might've taken a glance at her too. She came over and asked me to dance, and I said to myself, 'Hmm, this lady is interested in me. 'Guess I'm kind of interested too!' We were too busy with our own lives for about a year, but after that I ran into her again and asked if we could go out sometime. She said, "You've got to ask my grandma." So I tracked that lady down and said to her grandma, "I want to take your grandchild out." Well, she looked at me kind of surprised and said, "Why the heck are you asking me?" (Laughter), I guess it was kind of a set up to see how serious I was.

Emily and I took a lot of walks after that. We started thinking about getting married, and I knew she needed help with her children. I might not have thought about getting married again, but when it looked like we were going to have our own baby I knew that was where I belonged.

LONNIE AND THE GAME OF LIFE
"Man has responsibility, not power." - Cherokee

Married life was exciting, and I really enjoyed it. I just always figured, 'This is what a man is supposed to do...what a man's got to do.' How's that saying go? "A man's gotta do what a man's gotta do," (laughter), yeah...that's how I felt. That was my whole outlook on that, and it worked out real good. At first I had trouble staying in a job though. I guess time took its toll and little things started cropping up as an excuse to get into an argument with whoever my boss was at the time. I think working with the Public Health Service for twelve years was a real good job, one of the best jobs I ever had. I worked with the PHS as an engineer. We built water and sewer lines for individual homes or whole communities. I did about fifteen major projects including some in Mexican Hat, Keyenta, Dennehetso, Black Mesa, Shonto and all the places going toward Navajo Mountain.

I'd like my kids from this marriage to grow up doing different work than what I did though. I'd like them to do the same thing as my girls are doing. I think during their teen years, when they're getting out of school most of them just like to hang out in the towns or cities. That's a good experience for them as they're growing up, but pretty soon they always get fed up with those places. Usually a Navajo kid will say, 'hmm, I get the feeling I need to go home.' We like to go back to where our roots are. That's instilled in most of our young ones. So I wouldn't mind if my boys went through that city life thing to figure out what they want. I encourage them to hang on to their traditional stuff. My stepdaughter, Nina is only twenty years old, and she's already on a mission to carry on the Dine' traditions. She speaks Navajo fluently and can read and write it as well.

A lot of people look at the negative side of our lives. They say, "We're losing our language! We're losing our traditions!" It seems like they're constantly afraid our kids aren't learning about our culture. But I say that's not gonna happen while I'm around. I'm one person who's going to carry through and teach it. I know there's some kids out there who will eventually suck it in and say, "Oh yeah, I guess I'm willing to be taught this Navajo stuff." Even though they don't know their own language, a lot of them are willing to carry forth their traditions and relearn their language. I've been bugging my stepdaughter about teaching it to her son. He's still a baby, but I tell her this is the best time to teach it. Little kids are such fast learners. They are like little computers and they constantly want you to feed them information.

We also have a big demand out here for medicine men. Folks still like to have ceremonies done on them, so the future of this is on the youngsters who are interested in learning this medicine. I've seen a few of these kids go to ceremonies just to watch and observe. A lot of them are the kids or grandkids of medicine men, and it's good to see them at least try to carry on the tradition. Even though they kind of live in their Anglicized surroundings they're willing. Us older folks were worried there for awhile, because interest seemed to faded out during our generation. There were no jobs here in the Valley and in other parts of the reservation, so the youngsters kind of gave up. Now I see a lot of young people where I'd never seen them before. They're at the ceremonies kind of pushing for instruction in traditional medicine and things like that. I think it's a turn for the better.

LONNIE'S WAY
"When a man moves away from nature his heart becomes hard." - *Lakota*

Our economy is getting a little better, but it's mainly based on tourism. It would be nice if sheep herding could come back again as a way to make a living, but I don't think it will. We all think it's good to have it around however, because it teaches our youngsters to have that connection. There are a lot of Dine' creation stories that involve animals, and I think working with animals helps people function better in life. I feel like I'm connected with my surroundings because of the livestock. One time I read a story about this guy who didn't have a clue about herding or farming. He could only make his way by bartering for things. His friend started out with less money, but he knew a lot about animals and the earth, so he ended up coming out ahead! He respected and understood about nature more than the other guy who was just reckless and going through life trying in desperation. This was a modern story I read, but it sounded a lot like "The Tortoise and the Hare." The point is one guy had a lot more common sense than the other guy. Just looking around here I can see that it's absolutely true. Staying connected to the land and nature really does bring you more common sense. You see what really matters.

I still feel the same about tourists as I did growing up. It helps to have them come for visits, and we like to show them around. I just wish we had extra time to create more of our artwork. They seem to appreciate that the most, and selling our crafts helps us get through the slower, colder months. My mom weaves and my sister makes jewelry, but that doesn't satisfy me. I like to meet new people who come into the Valley. It gives me an opportunity to get my message across of what we're about and how we struggle to survive out here. We like to share our traditions and customs with people from the outside. I can sense when someone's just here for the scenery, and I'll kind of shy away from those types.

Now there are some real forward-thinking visitors who question how their ancestors behaved in the old days. They sometimes ask, "Why did we, as whites, do things to hurt your people?" They want to know how we feel about the past and events like the Long Walk. I always say, "Well, maybe our ancestors just didn't understand each other." There was a time when our land was looked upon as free to the whites, and it was that grabbing for land that changed things. Now I see tourists think twice about how their actions affect us. They ask, "How do you live? What was here before? What's your religion?" I think that by writing down our stories, like we're doing here, it will help others to know us better.

Colette:

I admitted to Lonnie that sometimes I hoped the information about his family would not get published. I secretly wanted the Yazzies all to myself. I didn't want more people to visit "my" Valley and disturb this perfect world. I knew this was a selfish attitude. More visitors meant a better life for the Yazzies; food for their sheep and other livestock and more of the basic essentials they needed just to exist in this beautiful place. Still, I didn't want to share my Navajo family, and give up the peace

288

and quiet of Suzie's compound. In the back of my mind I worried over the exposure I was giving the Yazzies and how it might affect them. Lonnie nodded in understanding...

Lonnie:

Yeah, I get it. It's like what they call a "double-edged sword." We want people to come visit us, but not to disrupt our lives. My hope for the future is to do the same things we've been doing down here for years; take people on tours, raise sheep and teach people. I want to keep an eye on my mom and help her as much as I can. After she passes on we'll continue on with things. I asked her one time where she wants to be buried, if she wants to be buried in the Valley.

CARING FOR SUZIE
"Cherish youth, but trust old age." - Pueblo

Colette:

I told Lonnie about my conversation with his wife and how we both wondered if Suzie really wanted a Christian burial.

Lonnie:

Nah, I can't see that she would really want that. She just doesn't want to be any trouble to anyone. Anyway, it's up to us how we would deal with her passing, because it's our grazing land. My younger brother buried a couple of his grandchildren down here. We built our own boxes and everything. I told him that I didn't see very much difference in going and spending thousands of dollars on a casket when a box we make ourselves does the same thing and has more meaning. I think we'll probably do a traditional burial for Suzie. We would bury her then go ahead and build a hogan on top of that spot. She was an important lady growing up here, and she might just be the oldest lady in the Valley nowadays. A lot of people respect her, and she's has friends all over the world. The way she brought us up has shown me that she's one of the sweetest and the gentlest ladies I've ever known. I've known quite a few sweet ladies, (giggles) but she's special. I think people from outside the Valley would like to come to her own private burial. My brother and I would take care of it. Tradition says that you don't wash for four days before dealing with a burial and then for the four days after that you clean up. You still mingle with people, we don't go off on our own anymore like they used to. If you didn't have much else to do I guess that would be okay, (laughter). But now we have to adjust.

Suzie's still pretty strong though. I'm really proud of her. Boy, she couldn't even remember anything last fall. She'd come to the door and look at you like you were a stranger. She wouldn't smile and she had a mean old look on her face. Sometimes she just lay down and slept all day. When she woke up to go to the restroom she'd walk halfway outside to the latrine in the rocks then have to sit down to rest a while. Then coming back she'd have to sit down halfway again. She fainted a couple of times when she went looking for the sheep, and when we were talking I'd have to repeat things.

After awhile I stopped talking to her. We'd just glance at each other and say, "Yah ta hey, have some coffee." (laughter). By October I was with her every day and night. In November when the tourist season started slowing down, I talked to my sister about it. We took her into the clinic in Keyenta and they told us, "This woman don't have no more blood!" (Lonnie laughs), that's when we found out mom needed a blood transfusion.

The doctors were amazed at how my mom survived all that time. They said she should have died or else had permanent brain damage. We don't know how she lost the blood, but it was just a little bit at a time. I think it was through her urine, because it's really dark at times. I said to her, "hmm, why is your urine coming out so dark?" She said that she didn't know, but there was no place else she could have lost it. Somewhere along the line the doctors suggested that Suzie should have a bone biopsy to check stuff out. But then I heard that a bone biopsy was one of the most painful surgeries you could have, so I told them, "I don't think my mom would want that." I thought we would just have to play along with these doctor guys and see what else they came up with. For awhile my mom continued to struggle. She was all down and out all the time, but after that transfusion settled in she got back on her feet. When we finally got her home she was running around all over the place. Those transfusions just made her a little cuckoo that way.

Mom looked really good by around Christmas. Oh, she was the happiest woman! I said to her, "Hey, you were flip-flopping the last time I saw you." (Lonnie laughed) I don't think she remembers much but I told her, "You were pretty out of it! You used to be cold all the time and heat your house like an oven." She just laughed and said she didn't remember any of that. We were all glad to see her get better. She doesn't seem to be any the worse for wear.

Colette:

I shifted the conversation to a more spiritual topic. I told Lonnie that many Anglos I spoke to believed that the Navajo look at the Anasazi as their ancestors. Yet, I read in one of my Navajo books that this culture that mysteriously disappeared from Navajoland is actually looked upon by the Dine' as an intrusive group. In fact, the name "Anasazi" literally means "old enemy" in the Navajo language. I asked Lonnie for clarity on this subject.

Lonnie:

We don't call them "enemy" really. It translates more like "person of the past."[179] I guess it was believed that the Anasazi left behind some artifacts on our land, and we found them when we came back from our journeys. I always wonder how the Anasazi could live here if we were here first. When people ask us "Where were you guys when the Anasazi were here?" I think they don't understand our history. Sometimes they say, "You Navajo are not originated from here." But I remind them of our legends. Anyway, the oral history stories tell about the Emergence, (the "Emergence" is the Navajo explanation of their origin). This is part of our religion, just like your Bible. It

---

[179] Mr. Maldonado explained to me that Anasazi does not literally mean "old enemy," but translates more as "old ones" or "one who came before us/past relative."

tells us Dine' were made here. We emerged from this land and were intentionally placed in this area. That is what we know about our history. As far as the Anasazi's story…well, we don't know much about them.

Some say that the Anasazi came onto our land while we were making our final journeys to the North, many hundreds of years ago. It was said that they lived here for around one thousand years, while our people were gone exploring. There's a land where it is cold; you call it the Bering Strait. That was where the land connected up North. It was said that we traveled around while the Bering Strait was a land bridge. Then we came back here, and in that way the Anasazi story is linked to ours. My mother remembers this history, and we heard it from her. The story of Emergence tells how man was made, and in our language it is still being told.

Colette:

The Navajo believe that the original Dine' evolved from a number of spirits who emerged from deep within the earth. While passing through each world, these spirits learned lessons that they would pass on to the Navajo when The Emergence into the present world took place. The Air-Spirit People, the Swallow People, the Grasshopper People, Changing Woman, First Man and First Woman were, among other entities, important in the Navajo creation legends that the Dine' hold sacred.[180] Complex and rich with meaning, the Navajo religion has been part of Dine' identity throughout their oral and written history. Because of this, many Navajo take offense at the tendency of some non-natives to refer to their stories of origin as fiction. Suzie's son corrected me when I asked him about the Navajo creation "myths," explaining why it was important for others to recognize the legitimacy of their belief system. "A white person would never refer to the Bible as a lot of myths," he pointed out, "even if he wasn't a Christian he would respect that. We know our legends are based on things that really happened, and so to the Dine,' that is reality."

To Lonnie, the story of his people's origin transcends time and space. Although Lonnie refers to a period of time that would not correspond with Western scientific thought, it will remain, in his mind, a tangible thing. The Bering Strait to which he refers when speaking of his ancestors' prehistoric travels was scientifically determined to be a land bridge for migrating peoples around 13,000 BC, well before the time that Suzie's son states in his account.[181] Lonnie may have been drawing from historical information that points to the period of time when the Navajo are believed to have entered the Four Corners region. Ron Maldonado later explained to me that the notion that the Navajo migrated into the Southwest is a false idea once spread in schools throughout the reservation. Ceremonial history states that the Navajo were created within the four sacred mountains, and Mr. Maldonado felt very strongly the notion of migration should be corrected.

---

[180] Paul G. Zolbrod *Dine' banane', The Navajo Creation Story*, (Albuquerque: University of New Mexico Press, 1995), 35-55.

[181] Brian M. Fagan discussed the Bering Land Bridge and its function at length in *People of the Earth*, (New York: Longman Inc., 1998), particularly on pages 124, 152 and 177.

The term "one thousand years ago" may also have been passed on with the legend through generations of Navajo, meant to signify only that a great deal of time had passed since the event. What concerned Suzie's son more than the exact period of time in which his story took place, was the fact that his people had accomplished a journey that took them beyond their homeland and had successfully returned. The essence of this Navajo legend was the actions of important ancestors. The way in which Lonnie dealt with time was, once again, something that I needed to reconsider from the Yazzie's point of view. Ethno historians have come to realize that Native American concepts of time and events are quite different from that of whites. In *The Cambridge History of the Native Peoples of the Americas,* historian Bruce Trigger quoted fellow historian Calvin Martin's recognition of these differences. Martin stated that:

"The most extreme subjectivist view maintains that a historical consciousness is totally alien to North American Indians, who have always conceived of their relationship to the cosmos very differently from the anthropocentric one that dominates Western thinking."[182]

Calvin Martin denies that ethno historians can legitimately write about societies that were not "conceived in history," and therefore could not willingly launch themselves into a historical trajectory. Recognizing how Anglo and Native American perspectives of historical time differ can offer those who study this brand of oral history a better understanding of them.

Frederick Hoxie takes exception to Martin's insistence on the impossibility of Westerners completely grasping Native American views:

"Martin is correct when he cautions scholars not to assume that Indian behavior is understandable in Western European terms; scholars need to acknowledge—even celebrate—the distinctiveness and complexity of tribal traditions. On the other hand, it is fatuous to think historians can or should cast off "time" and turn their back on the notion of rational inquiry. A great deal can be accomplished with a more modest approach; historians of Indian life should invent approaches that utilize all the sources, illuminate the meaning of events, and prod their colleagues into unfamiliar perspectives."[183]

Throughout my interviews with the Yazzies I confronted the issue of time and the way it is treated by the family. Was the way in which this family regarded historical time a Navajo view, or a view unique to the individuals of this family? How were Dine' concepts of time reflected in their religion? These would be recurring questions during my analysis of the information provided by the Yazzies. Presenting their views precisely as the Yazzies stated them would be respecting their voice and the integrity of their perceptions. However, I also considered it part of my analytical task to also attempt to translate the Yazzie, or Navajo, sense of time in a way that would be

---

[182]Trigger, Bruce G.& Wilcomb E. Washburn (ed.s) *The Cambridge History of the Native Peoples of the Americas,* Vol. I, Part I; p. 105 Calvin Martin (ed.), *The American Indian and the Problem of History* Oxford, 1987.

[183] Frederick E. Hoxie, *The Problems of Indian History* (The Social Science Journal, Vol. 25, No. 4, 1988), 389-399.

coherent to the Anglo historian. I struggled with the issue of "Navajo time" while Lonnie and his mother chatted. To this mother and son time must have seemed in ample supply, and sitting here listening to their legends gave me the same feeling.

Lonnie paused and sat back in his chair with a sigh. It seemed we had finally reached the point where he was all talked out. I looked to my right and saw the tall stack of cassette tapes I would have to transcribe when I returned home. My back and neck were sore, and I desperately had to use the bathroom. Emily looked up from her book. "Are you two quitting already?" she joked. We all agreed it was a good time to put off work for the day. Lonnie suggested we all drive down to Suzie's to see who might be there with his mother, but I begged off. I needed time to process all I'd heard from my two Navajo buddies. Though I loved them both and enjoyed their company I knew I had to be alone for awhile. I wanted to stare at the sunset and appreciate the silence of Monument Valley.

Lonnie and Emily took the last of my sunflower seeds and headed for their car. They seemed to understand my desire to be alone, and perhaps they too needed time together as a couple. We said our goodbyes and I promised to come back out to interview Effie and maybe her daughter Yvonne. They drove off waving, and I hurried to the back yard to watch their car disappear down the road and head to Suzie's. Sitting on the step just outside the kitchen door I let the warm breeze caress my skin. The occasional vehicle ambled by below me carrying the usual ice chests, water tanks and grinning Navajo kids. One truck stopped for a roadrunner to cross the street. It was the largest bird I had ever seen in the Valley.

A delicious shiver ran through my body as the sundowners increased. Gusts of wind caused the leaves on a nearby tree to shimmer. I leaned back and let each breeze pull the kitchen door away and against its hinges in a rhythmic tap-tap-tap. I thought of how I had come to love the Valley, and I remembered how I had not started out as much of a fan. I thought the climate irritatingly dry, and I secretly scoffed at those who raved about the area. "Turquoise-wearing hippie tourists," was my first thought when I encountered them on my first trip out to the Valley. Now I was visiting on a yearly basis, sometimes twice a year. My Navajo jewelry collection was larger than I deserved. I felt lucky to have happened upon the Yazzie's story. It had taken on a life of its own and burrowed a place in my heart like a kitten curled up in a sweater. I could never let it go, and I was thankful now to be a part of it.

The sun began to sink lower, turning the rocks that familiar, warm red against azure sky. The shade shifted, causing the wooden porch slats to change its geometric pattern. As I turned to go back inside for the night I heard an eerie yelping from the rocks to my left. Could it be "Coyote the Trickster" wishing me sweet dreams? A couple of Navajo parked at the clinic below Hill House hollered back and forth to a truck full of friends passing by. The magic of a valley sunset was once again a happy memory.

CHAPTER 13 – EFFIE'S STORY

WHITE SHELL WOMAN: A Navajo Summer
"Our first teacher is our own heart." – *Cheyenne*

I always saw my next step in graduating from the university was to pursue a Master's degree. I thought I might like to teach, specifically history at the community college level. Then one day, not long after I'd begun my post-graduate studies I changed my mind. I was watching my twin step-daughters that afternoon as they played with the chickens we had raised for fresh eggs. The two girls ran after the clucking birds laughing and yelling for me to watch them. The beautiful autumn sun was shining on their hair and fair skin, and I wondered how many moments like this I'd missed with my nose buried in a book. I suddenly realized it wasn't worth it to miss any more, and decided then and there to drop out of the Master's program.

Ultimately I believed this was the best move, but without the work of a school year to anticipate I felt a little lost. As I continued writing up the Yazzie's story I asked myself over and over again, "What am I doing? What purpose did the hours of study and attending classes serve?" I truly believed that my education inspired me to follow a line of inquiry and curiosity which ultimately led me to the Yazzies. Certainly my education had provided me the skills I needed to collect their story. For now, that would have to satisfy. By now I was wrapping up my interviews with the family, but the thought of actually completing this long, heartfelt work seemed strange. I knew my intimate time with this family would soon diminish to fewer visits and less frequent phone conversations. Yet I had to admit I was proud of myself for successfully documenting their amazing narrative. I looked forward to gifting the Yazzies a record of their personal history, and they were excited about getting a chance to see what I had been up to all of these years.

Before my next trip I wanted to type out the interviews from my last visit out to the Valley. I worked furiously away in the Santa Ana heat. Sometimes the Santa

Barbara coastal fog blissfully rolled in, replacing the stifling air with a wonderful coolness that crept over the bougainvillea and across my balcony. Unlike many of the locals in my town, I liked the fog. It was a nice change from our usual warm weather and it gave the surrounding trees and hills a mysterious look. Happy at home, I confess that with every word I typed I felt the gentle pull of the reservation. I was always surprised at how such a high desert could feel peaceful and vibrant at the same time. The place and the people of the Valley were constantly on my mind and in my soul, and soon I was packing my bags to travel there once more.

Stepping over the threshold of Hill House felt like slipping into a favorite pair of blue jeans. I settled in and worked on my writing until I was too exhausted to continue. The bed felt wonderful, and I was almost in a dream state when I heard "the noise." It started as a low groan and seemed to be coming up from the floor of my bedroom! I lay there staring into the darkness wondering if Hill House was either haunted or inhabited by squatters. It was only nine-thirty, so I called the front desk under the guise of checking to see if my phone was working properly. The pleasant voice of a Navajo woman answered my call.

I spoke briefly with "Wanita" about the phone…then hesitated, wondering if she would laugh over my silly fears. I thought she was psychic when she said, "On nights like this the wind travels right up through the floor of that place. Are you hearing a noise in the house?" I told her that I had, and what it sounded like. Only half-joking I said to Wanita, "I'm afraid it might be a Skinwalker!" We both giggled, but she was genuinely surprised at my comment. "You know about them?" she asked. "Yeah," I said, "but I guess it's just ridiculous to put thoughts like that into my head right at bedtime." We were both were making light of the subject, but Wanita made no attempt to discount the fact that such creatures existed on the reservation. "Well," she assured me in an authoritative tone, "A Skinwalker wouldn't bother you because you're not Navajo. It's not their way, so probably they would avoid you." It should have felt strange to be discussing such a thing with a near stranger over the phone, but I had come to expect the unexpected in the Valley. I told Wanita that it was nice to know there were some advantages to being "*bilaga'ana*," or "white." Wanita chuckled softly, "Yeah, you don't have to worry, but I'll send a security man up to look around. Albert's just sittin' here with me anyway."

Albert drove up and introduced himself as Wanita's husband. With some chagrin I informed him that I had located the source of the creepy noise. The wind was blowing a loose screen door against the back wall. Once secured, the noise went away, leaving me looking like a hysterical female. Albert had promised his wife he would look around however, and he poked around the outside of Hill House just to be sure. As is the way of things in M.V. he actually seemed to relish the opportunity to visit for awhile. I mentioned Effie and Lonnie, and his face lit up in recognition. "Oh yeah, I know them!" Albert proclaimed. He spoke of the welcome rain that the Valley had recently received, and I commented on how a Yeibechi ceremony must have worked to do the trick. "That's the best way to bring in the rain," Albert agreed, "but sometimes you have to do a lot of them." He left with a promise to keep an eye out around my place, and I headed back to bed. I snuggled into the blankets on my bed thinking what it would be like to see a Squaw dance, and fell instantly to sleep.

The next morning I awoke to a room bright with sun. Glancing at the clock on my nightstand I discovered I'd slept until seven o'clock! I was used to automatically waking up at sunrise whenever I came to the Valley. In spite of the full night's rest I couldn't shake off the bleariness in my eyes until my second cup of coffee. I sipped the magical brew and called the number for Effie's place in Oljeto. She and her daughter were the last family members I planned to interview, and I wanted to be certain they would be available. Effie answered on the first ring with a "where the heck are you!" and told me that Lonnie and Emily were at Suzie's asking about me. It made me feel like family, and I promised to meet up with Effie later that morning so we could drive into the park together. I didn't mention my experiences of the previous night.

Before spending time with the Yazzies I might have regarded the Navajo as a superstitious group. Now that I'd stayed out in the Valley on my own I could understand their feelings. The monoliths and canyons really seem to possess their own personalities. During my afternoon runs, or while taking the long drive from Suzie's place back to Goulding's, I never sensed the presence of any malevolent spirits. But I confess to a very strong feeling of being carefully watched by some unseen entity. Perhaps I was protected by my status as an Anglo, but a certain amount of respect for my surroundings seemed warranted. Now in the light of day it was easier to shake off the heebie-jeebies, and I flipped open my computer and launched into work.

Effie arrived mid-morning, toting two new rugs she had made of Yeibechi design. We loaded up some fruit, herbal tea and water to share with Suzie and took off for the Tribal Park. On the way Effie told me about a recent fall she'd taken from a horse. For some reason my fifty-two year old friend started to cantor on her very fresh horse wearing only sandals and cut-off shorts! The ride went along reasonably well until the mare spotted a rabbit darting from the brush. "That horse tucked her head down and bucked so hard I just flew," laughed Effie, "I must have flipped up pretty high, because I remember seeing sky before hitting the ground!" While Effie's horse raced home without her, she lay in the summer heat wondering what to do. "I was up by that concrete well close to Sand Springs," she explained, "and I couldn't move without it hurting. The pain was so bad that I blacked out a couple of times." After a half-hour of shooing ants from her leg and trying to forget her thirst, Effie's son arrived to help. The riderless horse had made its way back home, and Timmy hopped back on the miserable beast to search for his mother. Eventually the family truck was brought around, and Effie was carted to the clinic for care. Unfortunately, the trip took an extra hour because the boys had to dig out their "*chiddy*" when it became mired in the soft sand.

"That drive to the clinic hurt pretty bad," Effie said, shaking her head, "I yelled a lot when we went over that washboard part of the road." At the clinic the doctors were amazed to discover Effie's bones had only been badly bruised. Nevertheless, it took weeks for her to move without searing pain. "As soon as I'm feeling a hundred percent I'm getting back on that horse," Effie sniffed in indignation, "she's already come up and nuzzled me to apologize."

I stepped out of the car and into a bear hug from Lonnie. Emily stood behind him waiting her turn. "Mister Yazzie," my voice was muffled against the flannel of his shirt, "how the hell are you?" We caught up on gossip while I unloaded Suzie's groceries into Lonnie's waiting arms, then the three of us headed into Suzie's little house. Suzie looked up from her usual place on the bed, and beamed at the bags of groceries her son dumped onto the old kitchen table. Effie reminded her mother of who I was, and the old woman nodded her hello. She spoke something back to her daughter who then turned to me, announcing with some surprise, "Hey, she remembers you!" I was delighted to hear this, because Suzie's short term memory had suffered during the last five years. There had been other occasions when, even though my visits had not been spaced so far apart, she had to be reminded of my identity. "Are you sure?" I asked Effie. "Yes," my friend confirmed, "she remembers the tape recorder you used." I motioned with my hand to Suzie's lapel and she nodded again. I couldn't help but feel pleased.

Effie had a few chores to attend to at her mother's request, so Emily offered to take me on a short hike to the nearby rocks behind the family's horse corral. It sounded like a nice adventure, so we marched one behind the other past the latrine in the direction of the rocks. My white Keds became red with sand, and the sun bore down my bare shoulders. Nothing could be heard around us but the sound of our footsteps and our labored breathing. Eventually we reached a point where we could view Suzie's compound and the surrounding area for miles around. Emily and I stood in mutual silence until we could catch our breath, and then poked around in the shade created by the monolith. Just behind a nearby Juniper tree we discovered a weather-beaten horse corral. "They should fix this up and use it again," Emily said softly, "It would keep the sheeps cool, and there might be water run-off from the rock when it rains." I picked some yellow plants growing at the base of the rock and showed them to Emily, who confirmed they could be used for dying wool.

Other than some rhubarb growing wild we found nothing else of interest in the dunes and made our way back to the house. Effie met us on her way to the latrine. She happily took the yellow flowers from me and rubbed together the tender yellow blooms. I sucked the blood from where a yucca plant had pricked my thumb while she inspected the plants. "These smaller ones are horse weed," she finally proclaimed, "We can use it for making yellow dye. I thought it wasn't growing around here anymore. Where did you find it?" I pointed to the spot where Emily and I had been. "Yeah," she confirmed, "I'll have to go up there and get some."

EFFIE SPEAKS

"Ask questions from your heart and you will be answered from the heart." – Omaha

Effie was in her early fifties at the time of our interview. She had long divorced the husband that had given her four children who were now grown and starting families of their own. When she wasn't working for Goulding's as a cook-out chef or taking tourists out on horse-back tours, she spent time at Suzie's hogan, helping her mother run the business and caring for the animals. She had recently taken up weaving again, and found that she enjoyed the craft more than she had as a younger woman. "I'm even selling some of my rugs!" she proudly informed me. From time to time Effie would take her mother to the little house in Oljeto for a shower and to spend some time with her granddaughter Elvina. As Suzie approached her nineties however, Effie found herself spending more and more time at the family compound. I had a feeling she would be taking over her mother's business one day soon.

Emily offered to sit with Suzie in the hogan while I worked with her sister-in-law. Effie and I settled into the house but left the door slightly open to catch the occasional breeze. A gust blew Effie's bangs lightly across her eyes. She brushed her hair aside and sat waiting while I fumbled with my recorder. "Man you take too long getting that tape recorder ready," she teased, "I'll be asleep by the time you start asking questions!" Embarrassed, I finally managed to arrange the microphone onto Effie's shirt. As I gathered my list of questions in from of me I remarked to Effie that I'd seen a picture of her as a baby. It was in one of the tourist books sold at Goulding's. In the photo Effie was perched on her own horse beside her mother, who sat astride a Pinto with John Ford's Point in the background. Suzie had her arms around a younger child; "a cousin" I was told. The rock formation was called "Wind's Ear," and a herd of sheep surrounded the young family. Since Lonnie could remember herding sheep by the age of five, I wondered if Effie could recall how young she was when she began to help her mother with chores.

Effie:

I guess I can remember being maybe about four or five when I started getting up to things. Back then it always seemed like my younger brother, Kee and I were the ones that were herding the sheep. I remember when I was little we had a house out by Three Sisters. My dad's sister lived nearby, and my grandfather lived on the other side of us in his hogan. My aunt had a lot of kids, and her oldest girl was a year older than me. My mom always warned me to stay away from them because they'd misbehave, but you can't tell a kid that, and my cousin and I ran around wherever we could. My oldest brother and my uncle's son hung around too, and those two guys got into a lot of trouble. Both of them were the same. One day we were playing with water and got into trouble. We were all sitting under a tree in the mud by a barrel, we suddenly my brother got pissed off at me about something, *(giggles)*, so he just hauled off and hit me! I ran home, but he followed me. He caught me by a rock and shook me up until I cried. I think that's why I used to hate boys when I was young. They were always doing something like that.

Another time we were playing behind the rocks with my cousin. She had her dolls and I had an old spindle. Kee had shown me how to use a rubber band on it to make tires, so I learned how to make a little car from the whole thing. I was showing my cousin this car I made, when all of a sudden her brother came and dropped something on the spindle and crushed it. He laughed about it in a really wicked way, and my oldest brother was sitting in a nearby tree eating berries and laughing with him. They told us, "You girls better get the heck out of here or we'll tie you to the tree!" We got scared and took off. We left all of our toys behind. That's just the kind of life we had. We got used to it, and it made us sort of tough.

I don't really remember my other brother, Leonard, hanging around much. I asked my mom about it once, and she told me my aunt was taking care of him a lot back then. Ever since he was a baby until he turned twelve she cared for him. It was only after that when he came back to us. I think my mom was just overwhelmed, and my aunt needed help around the house. My middle brother, Lonnie, was helping out my aunt a lot too. So mostly it was just my two brothers, Harvey and Kee, along with me, herding sheep and helping my mom.

Before long my older brothers were off at school. It was just Kee and me. My parents got us up every morning to herd, but Kee would always try to play with me a bit. When he got older he sometimes had to attend school as well, and he would tell what was going on at the school he went to. He told me these things when we were out herding sheep when he was home during Christmas or Thanksgiving. One day we were just lying on our backs on the ground with the sheep all around us. We were looking at the sky when suddenly a plane flew by. It was a big jet plane with these little smoke trails behind it. I had never seen one up close, and I said out loud, "I wonder how big that airplane really is?" I was asking Kee things like this.

Well, my brother said, "it's really, really, really big!" I had a hard time imagining it.

So I asked him, "what kinds of things are in there?"

He said, (giggles), "Oh, they carry all kinds of animals in there. There's...there's giraffes, and elephants and lions in those planes!" (*Effie and I both laughed*) Then I asked my wise brother, "How in the world do those giraffes with the long necks fit in there?" I had seen pictures of giraffes, and I knew they were supposed to be pretty big. Kee looked me straight in the eye and said, "Oh they have holes in the top of those airplanes, so they fly around with their heads sticking out!" (*Effie giggled some more*) He just kind of made all of it up as he went along, but I didn't have any idea he was telling me stories. I just lay there trying to picture these giraffes flying around with their long necks hanging out of the plane. Kee pointed to the one in the sky, and he told me, "If you look real hard you could probably see their heads!"

I was pretty young and only knew life in the Valley, so for the longest time I kept thinking about those planes full of animals. Every time I saw an airplane in the sky I thought, "Oh that's probably carrying a giraffe or maybe even an elephant!" I didn't really know anything about how elephants looked. Kee would have to describe them to me. He said, "They're really big and have a long nose." We didn't have a picture or anything like that, so he would draw a picture in the sand of an elephant. He was a little older than I was so I listened to him.

I was the youngest and Kee was five years older than I am. Our oldest brother is Harvey, then Leonard, then Lonnie, then Kee. I'm the baby I guess. My mom and I were talking about the past just a while ago, and she figured she was about forty-five when I was born. I was kind of a mama's girl, (laughter), but I loved doing what the boys did. When they went out to watch the sheep they spent time playing cards and going hiking. They could climb around on the rocks or chase the horses all day long, and so I liked being among them. One day my dad got me a doll. Well, I didn't know what to do with it! I just left it laying around because I didn't like it! (*giggles*) I never touched that thing. It could say, "Mama", and if you tilted it back it could blink its eyes. It was just too scary looking.

Instead I spent most of my time playing with Kee. He used to have a whole bunch of little cars…you know, those "Matchbox" things. I think they were called "Hot Wheels." He had the big ones too, the Tonka trucks. Back then those little cars used to be made out of rubber. I remember one looked like a fire truck, and then there was one like a pickup. He would always carry the whole bunch of little ones collected in a bag. I loved playing with Kee and those cars of his, but then I started collecting plastic horses. Every time we'd go out herding sheep I would play with my horses, and my brother played with his little chiddies. That was a lot of fun.

Colette

I reminded Effie about the stories her mother told about playing with clay figures of animals when she was a girl. I remarked how clever children can be when they have time on their hands and the world at their feet. Effie shook her head in amazement:

Effie

Oh yeah, I almost forgot about that story. It's funny how my mom was just like us. I guess most kids want to play when they're stuck with some chore. I hear a lot of other people talk about how they played when they got stuck herding. You can still find some of those clay toys around if you look for them. Kids used to make them all the time. Maybe they still do! Kee sure liked those little cars though, and I loved my model horses. But then, I don't know…I just think we both kind of grew up. One day he went out and hid all his toy chiddies in the Valley somewhere, and I did the same thing with my horses. Even today I don't know why we did that. I just remember that when I got a bit older, ten or eleven.

See, by the time Kee was sent off to school I was by myself all the time. I usually herded the sheep way past Totem Pole, by a place called Sitting Hen. One day, I was way underneath the rocks there, watching the sheeps and playing with my toy horses. All of a sudden I had the feeling somebody was watching me. I looked to see who it was, and there was a guy nearby who had some horses…real ones! He looked about the age of a teenager, and he was just staring at me. Well, heck…I felt so embarrassed! I wondered what he thought of me, and I guess I thought he was saying to himself, "isn't she too old to be playing with toy horses?" I didn't like the way it made me feel, so all of a sudden I packed up all of my horses and ran away. I found a sand dune and buried all of them then and there. That was the last I ever played with toys like a kid, but as I got older I spent a lot more time with real horses. I got good at riding.

Colette:

I remarked to Effie that one day some archaeologist might be digging around in the sand and unearth her horses or her brother's car collection. We laughed as we pictured these scientists wondering what ancient culture had a ritual that involved the burial of such strange artifacts! Mimicking the archeologist's I'd met at university, I solemnly pronounced my findings. "This must have been a very complex society." This set Effie to laughing, and she screamed, "Don't touch them! Don't disturb these important relics!" This caused us both to fall into fits of giggling, and it took some time for us to regain our composure.

Effie:

Around five years ago some kids playing around here did find just one of my brother's old rubber trucks. I couldn't believe they actually brought that thing back. I think it's still in the family for the kids to play with. Anyway, there wasn't a lot of time to play with my brothers all away. When I wasn't doing other chores my mom started to teach me how to weave. She used to show me while she was at her loom. She'd say, "This is how you make rugs and you should start learning." Every now and then she'd turn to me and say, "You're a little girl, so start learning to weave." But I had no interest in it at all. I'd just look at her and say, "Nah, I don't like doing girl stuff. I don't even like to cook. I don't like to do housework. I just like being out in the opening!" (I smiled at Effie's alteration of "out in the open." She also had the habit of saying "all of a suddenly" which I thought was charming.)

My poor mom…I think she was kind of disappointed when she heard me say that. Sometimes she found me just laying around looking at a magazine or a comic book, and she'd try to get me interested in weaving again. But I wouldn't budge. Comic books were my favorite. I had a collection of them. Back then they used to cost something like fifteen cents. Now they're two dollars! I used to read Archie and Superman and Spiderman. I remember my dad brought them home for me. He knew what I really liked, and he liked seeing me giggling in a corner with a comic book. I guess that wasn't much help to mom, because she just couldn't get my attention away from comic books. That's what I did with my free time (giggles).

EFFIE FIGHTS BACK
"The way of the troublemaker is thorny." – Umpqua

I don't remember exactly when I started school, but it was around this time. I don't even remember how I ended up in boarding school, but I kind of remember my first year there. Lonnie says he remembers the first day they brought him in and from that day on. But for me there's no hard memory of it. I just remember thinking, "okay, so this is how life is now." Once they put me in I only came home on Christmas and Thanksgiving. Once in a great while my dad would come by and bring me candy and things like that. I remember him saying, "Give some candy to your brother when you see him." But I never saw Kee, (giggles). I kind of made sure I didn't see him when I had candy. Anyway, the girls' dormitory was pretty separate from the boys,' so we didn't really have an opportunity to hang out.

I didn't really form an opinion about school until my second year there. That's when I decided I really didn't like it because they treated everybody so mean. They made us all to do the things that I hated...like cleaning, (laughter). At least by the time I was in they didn't make us march around like they did with my brothers. But they used to line us up boy-girl-boy-girl. I'd be standing there minding my own business and the boys standing next to me would pull on my braids. The girls also had to wear a dress all the time! I hated that, because the boys would put their feet up your dress to lift the skirt up! It got to be that I hated those boys, and I decided I wasn't going to put up with it, so I fought with them all the time. Sometimes we'd all be just sitting in the classroom and one of the boys would start picking on me. This always made me real mad, and I'd turn around and say to them, "Get your hands off me." At first they all thought they were tougher than me, because I was a girl, but I showed them where they were wrong.

Once we got out of class and were walking back to the dormitory I ran to whatever guy had been teasing me, and I would tackle him! We'd roll around until I beat him up. One time I beat up a kid until he was crying. He yelled that he was going to tell his friends on me. He said, "They're going to beat you up!" But I could take care of myself. All during the next three years I was an enemy to those boys. They didn't like me at all, because some of the other girls started fighting back as well. One day I was hanging around with my friend Evelyn, who has been my friend for a long time. She lives in Oljeto now, sort of by my place, and she changed her name to something she liked better. But back then her name used to be Ellen, and she had the same last name as me! We thought that was cool, and we used to pretend we were sisters. Her brother's name was Tommy, and he was the same age as my brother, Kee. So Kee and Tommy would hang around like brothers too. Everybody was fooled.

Well, one day those boys who were my enemies beat Evelyn up. She had a black eye and a big swollen cheek, and she had to go to the clinic. There were three of those boys who ganged up on her, and that made me so mad, so I went looking for them and found one kid by himself. I beat him up until he was crying, but then the two others came along and ganged up on me. I was so mad I fought all three of them off, but from that day on they really hated me. I think they still do. I was working the night shift at the hospital only ten or fifteen years ago, when all of a sudden I ran into one of the guys who I beat up. I remembered his name was Samuel, and he remembered me too. He came up to me and asked, "Are you Effie?" I told him that yes, I was Effie, and he shook my hand! He said, "I never like you as a little girl. I always wanted to come back and find you so I could beat you up." I said to him, "Well, would you like to fight with me now?" But we both just laughed. He was visiting the clinic for some illness. He was really sick, so I said, "Nah, you're too ill to fight with now!" It's funny how he looked so old, and he had white hair. He had gotten thin and didn't look healthy at all. I hadn't seen him since 1961 when I beat him up for hurting my "sister." All this time he'd been thinking about finding me for revenge, (giggles), but he never got the chance for it.

The whole time I was in grammar school I didn't like boys. I thought they were all like the ones who beat me up. As I got older I moved closer in school to my brothers, so if one of the boys ever made me cry I'd go to them. They took care of everything so I wouldn't have to fight. I just told Lonnie, or Kee, or one of the others what happened, and they'd say, "Okay, we'll talk to that guy," and then the kid who was bugging me would back off. My brothers took care of me that way. I remember back when they were teenagers how funny it was to hear girls say, "Oh, your brothers are so cute! (Giggles), they all wanted to be my sister-in-law! Just because my brothers were good-looking the other girls would treat me like a queen. I was pretty popular because my brothers were cute.

Mostly it was Kee, the youngest, who got the attention. I would sometimes stare at him and say, "Hmm, let me take a good look at what the fuss is all about." But I never thought he was that handsome. He had hair almost golden from the sun, and you know, back then the boys wore their hair like Elvis Presley. Kee's hair was all nice and wavy, and his complexion was practically white. It almost looked like yours! Both Kee and I were fair, like my mother. I once asked my mom why we had that light complexion in our family, and she told me it came from her grandfather, her mother's father, who was from Red Mesa. That man's father was a Mexican with some Spanish blood, and that's probably why we have fair skin. I also asked my mom why were so tall, at least for Navajo we are; my brothers especially. It had to have come from my mom's side, because my dad was kind of short. I used to wonder if that tallness would trickle down to my kids, and boy did it ever, on my two boys. Both of them are pretty tall. Their dad and uncle are both short, so it must come from the ladies' side of the family. One of my mom's nephews broke the record. My cousin is six-four!

Anyway, my good-looking brothers and I stayed in boarding school for a while. I only went for five years when they began to make that movie out here in M.V. I think I was about to enter fourth grade, but I was home for the summer, and that's when they were making this movie called "The Searchers." My dad and mom decided to keep me out of school to be in that movie, and it was good work for all of us. Our whole family got into that movie as extras. I remember there were a lot of movie people living out here while they were making the film. The movie stars stayed at Goulding's, but every morning they'd show up with a bus, and we'd get on to go wherever they wanted to haul us that day. They'd drop my mom off somewhere, and then drop us kids off in Sand Springs or somewhere else. On a couple of days they were filming some lady with blonde hair. She just kept hauling some of us kids around in a wagon, but I don't remember why. For one scene we were in this old building, (giggles), pretending it was a classroom, and that white lady was pretending to be teaching us. They would film that for awhile, and then all of a sudden they would yell, "Start running for the door!" We did as we were told, but once we got outside they had us stop and do it all over again. I remember thinking that those folks making the movie were pretty nutty. I saw that film once and I looked for myself, but I couldn't make out where I was. Anyway, they weren't really showing the Indians. We were just background.

Colette:

As I sat listening to Effie I noticed how her sense of humor slipped into every story. Like her brother Lonnie, she had a slow and regulated style of speaking. Her expressions were all her own, however. The rise and fall of her speech was very different from that of Lonnie's, and her stories meandered in a different way. Phrases were connected like so many train cars, separate little vignettes became part of a whole experience related in one flowing trail of thought. Effie's life unfolded before me, interrupted only by the occasional "emmmm...." as she recalled part of a tale, or a giggle when the story tickled her. She reminded me of her mother.

Effie:

So yeah...we were having a good time filming with the movie people, but just when it was getting good somebody from the government showed up and took me back to school. There was one particular woman who worked out there, and I hated her. I remember walking into the dormitory and she said, "Where the hell have you been? You know that you have to attend school! What were you doing out there?" She made it sound like I did something bad. I didn't say anything back to her because I was scared, but she kept yelling at me. She said, "Look at your hair! You look like a raggedy, wild woman! Get into the shower!" She screamed at me and pushed me until I fell down. Then she grabbed my hair and pulled me up by it. It was only she and I in that room and I remember thinking she might not get away with this if someone else were around...but who knows. I kept wondering, "What did I do to this lady that she hates me so much?" I was crying as I walked to the showers, and she kicked me right in the butt. I fell down again and she grabbed my hair again.

She yelled, "What are you crying for?" She said it in Navajo. She said to me, "Are you crying for your husband?" That's just something people used to say in Navajo to be mean. I couldn't understand how I deserved to be treated this way, and I kept crying all the way through my shower.

At one point she threw a scrub brush at me. It was the kind of brush you use to scrub the shower walls! She threw that at me hard so it hit me, and then she said, "Scrub yourself with that! You're filthy!" I tried not to rub too hard on my skin because it hurt. But she grabbed the brush from me and scrubbed me herself...really hard. She said, "You're supposed to scrub like this, because you probably brought all that lice and tics back with you from out there!" I had no idea what lice and tics were (giggles). You know those little bugs that get in your hair? There were a lot of kids who brought that in, but I never got it. Anyway, she wasn't making any sense to me at the time. She just kept screaming, "Those bugs are probably crawling all under your skin! Scrub hard with this brush all over your body!"

Oh, it hurt so bad. I don't know what was wrong with her that she treated me so bad that day, and it's weird because she was a Navajo lady! I still see her around. She was still at the school when my kids went! I told my girls about it, and they said that she had that same attitude when they went to school. She's pretty short though, and I think I could take her now. I would make her pay for how she treated me, but you don't throw yourself at the elderly. I'll always remember her though. It all happened when I was about seven or so, and I stayed at the school another two or three years. I wasn't really interested in school after what she did to me. When I went back home to visit I would beg my mom to let me stay. I told her that I didn't want to go back to a person in charge who was treating me so mean. But my mom never really said anything about it. She's like that about a lot of things.

Colette:

Effie paused and I sat in dumbfounded silence. How could a woman looking after small children behave so badly? Abuse happens even today of course. I had experienced it in my own family at the hand of my father. Still, I could not get the picture of that woman beating Effie out of my head. I had come to expect hearing stories like this involving whites looking after the natives, but why had this Navajo woman mistreated what was virtually one of her own? Effie tried to shrug off my questions, but I could tell it continued to affect her.

Effie:

Gosh, I'm pretty tired now. I guess it's because I stayed up until eleven playing video games with my daughter. We just got this hand-held thing that's fun to play with. We love those things. We're addicted. We had a great time, but I had to yell at her this morning to get her up! Now where was I? Oh yeah, so my mom didn't say anything about the lady who beat me. Maybe she wanted me to continue my education. It was my dad's idea to get me out of school. I remember him saying to me, "I only went to fourth grade, and that was plenty of education. Just look at me! I'm working and supporting the family. I'm just as good as all the white people who have lots of schooling!" I thought that sounded pretty sensible, so I started begging my dad not to send me back. He agreed that I had a point. He said, "You can stay here and start learning how to be a woman." By then I didn't care if I had to learn to cook and weave. I just wanted to get out of that school and away from that nasty woman.

That was the year they began hiding me. I remember my dad saying, "Try not to stay at home too much. Go climb around on the rocks or something." So I was always out riding the horse way, way out there in the Valley. I went out herding the sheep and taking care of the horses. I usually ended up at my grandfather's place. I liked hanging around him. Sometime he would always say, "Granddaughter, let's go out to those rocks and get some water." And then we would carry buckets and a barrel to the wagon. He would drive us a little ways until we got right up to the rock where he thought some water was hiding, and then both of us would climb to a big water hole on top. Sometimes he would take me to where he grew corn and had planted peach trees. He taught me how to gather all the corn and fallen peaches.

Every now and then he would say to me, "Go chase my horses." He had a whole bunch of them that needed looking after. He had twenty-five over here, and fifteen over there, and maybe ten more a little further on. They were untrained horses that you couldn't ride! They were wild, but they were his. I remember him saying, "I see my horses going down around the rocks. Be a good granddaughter and go chase them back." He used to let me use one of his horses that he always rode. I loved doing that! Grandfather would warn me, "Try not to let my horse run. Once that horse starts running he'll never stop." I did what he told me while I was within sight, but as soon as we got over the hill I would take off (giggles)! He was afraid I would have a hard time getting his horse to stop, but I ran with that horse anyway. I was a good rider by then, and I could control the horses. I didn't care if there was any danger. I just loved riding.

I still do. Anyway, that's how I spent most of my time, hanging around my grandfather's place.

When Kee came home to visit he would tell me about school. We would do stuff together and catch up on the gossip. I don't know if they were missing me at school. I never really asked. Sometimes my mom would tell me, "Oh the people from the government came by. They were looking for you, but I just told them you were out climbing rocks and if they wanted to find you they could go climb around after you." (*This made both Effie and I laugh*). My mom knew by then I was never going back to that place. Did you know that if you even tried to speak Navajo at that school they'd smack you?! They always told us, "Even if you don't know any English, you are not to talk Navajo!" We would try so hard to speak English, but it was hard at first. If they caught you speaking Navajo, even just once, they would punish you. They would tell us to go wash out our mouth with soap! You had to do it while they stood over you. They gave you a toothbrush with soap on it and made you scrub (laughter).

They also told us to learn how to braid our hair if we wanted to keep it long. We had to wear one braid down the back, or two on either side. They said, "If you don't braid your hair, and brush it the way we want you to, you'll lose it." If a girl didn't do it perfectly they got their hair cut! We were all pretty miserable in that school, and when I left I felt bad for my friends. Thank goodness I didn't start my period there. Luckily I didn't start that until I was sixteen! They wouldn't prepare you for that at school anyway. They may have started teaching that later, I don't know.

So the BIA people finally got tired of trying and they stopped coming around. Maybe they thought I was a lost cause, (giggles). That's when I got the taste for comic books. And because I was doing my chores my mom kind of let me do whatever I wanted in my free time. She never really bossed me around like that...only my dad did that kind of thing. Sometimes I think my mom just didn't know how to talk to me. She wasn't really the disciplinarian in our family. I think she cut me some slack because when she was growing up she had to do everything. She knew what it was to have all that responsibility, so maybe she was giving me a break. If she saw me doing something wrong she would just say, "You're not supposed to do this or that." For instance she would tell me that you're not supposed to hang around with your brothers. You know, we were warned not to do that when we were growing up. It's against our customs. I never understood why I couldn't just hang out with them. They were a lot of fun, and I would ask my mom, "Why? Why can't I just do stuff with them? What happens to you when you're around your brothers?" She just said, "You want to be sure nothing inappropriate happens." But I had no idea what she meant by that.

I guess I had a feeling it had something to do with my becoming a woman, so I was kind of scared when I got my period. I hid it from my mom, (giggles). I guess that sounds silly know, and I don't know why I didn't just come out one day and tell her. I remember her telling me, "When you become a woman we have to have a ceremony for you." But I said, "Oh, I don't want to do all that! Can I not have that done?" It all sounded like too much work. You have to do everything yourself; grind all the corn and serve it up. I hated anything to do with fixing up food and kitchen work. I wanted nothing to do with it. I tried to convince my mom a Kinaalda ceremony would be a bad idea for me. "I don't even know how to make fry bread or cook," I told her, "It's going to be really embarrassing!" She must have thought this was kind of true, because she didn't push it. She must have been thinking, "My only daughter knows nothing!" (Lots of laughter), that's probably what my poor mom thought. She must have been crying to herself, "My precious daughter...my only one! How can she not have a ceremony?!" In the end I knew she really wanted me to have a Kinaalda, so we just had a small ceremony. She said, "If you don't want a big ceremony all you have to do is have your hair tied." I didn't do the official run because, hey, I was always running around anyway! I didn't have to make the corn cake either.

When it came time for my daughter, Elvina to have the ceremony I said to her, "It's getting to the point when you to reach womanhood. Do you want to have a Kinaalda done on you?" She said, "Noooo!" She begged me not to make her do it. I told her we could get her a lot of help, but she said, "no way." She's always been kind of shy, and she didn't want to do that with all those people. Then my other daughter, Erlene, said, "I *want* to have a Kinaalda! I want to have it no matter what. I don't care if I have to do all the work." When she got her period we went ahead and had one for her, and she had a lot of fun. I remember when we had all these people pulling on her, they said, "You're going to grow about seven feet!" (Laugher), it was so funny!

As I became a teenager I kept riding horses because I loved it so much. By this time my dad was away working a lot. First he worked in Phoenix, then in California. In between that my uncle's kids who lived by Totem Pole started visiting. I had a lot of girl cousins from my dad's side of the family, and we kept each other company. We would dig into my comic book selection and just lay around reading. It was around this time that I met a guy who became my friend. He was in the tour business when he met my mom, and he brought visitors to see her. It was tough to make money around here though, so he went away to find other work. We missed seeing each other, so we started writing letters. I was already about fourteen years old, but my handwriting was awful. My letters looked like a little kid wrote them! In his letters my friend would ask what I wanted from whatever place he was visiting. I always wanted writing paper, pencils and pens. Even now it's kind of hard to get those things around here. If you want the good stuff you have to go clear to Keyenta.

He sent me a nice camera too, so I took pictures and sent the film back to him. I took lots of photographs of my horses... so many that he wrote back saying, "Wow, you must really like horses!" I also told him that I wanted some records and a record player. I don't know why I asked him about that, because nobody I knew had a player. I just had this feeling that it'd be fun to have one. My friend came through for me, but he really didn't know my taste! He sent me records that were popular in those days. It was 1966 or 67, so he was sending me the Beatles and the Beaches... I mean the Beach Boys. He also sent me some Elvis Presley. I guess I liked the Beatles okay, but mostly I liked that group called "The Monkees."

Colette:

I told Effie that I had loved The Monkees when I was a girl, and that I still had a few of their albums. I had a huge crush on the band's singer, Davy Jones, and I watched their television program religiously every Saturday morning. I explained how my sister and I pretended to be part of the group, holding hairbrushes as make-believe microphones as we sang along with the band. Effie just laughed and nodded.

Effie:

Yeah, they were my favorite too! We were all so in love with this one guy in the group named Mike, (*big, big giggles!*) I told all my girlfriends, "I love him!" But he was so ugly! Anyway, we used to play records all the time, and this guy gave me extra batteries to work this record player. It was pretty small, but it was my treasure. My cousins and I would just sit there and listen to records and look at my comic books. After a while my mom didn't like it! She began to say, "Hey, where's the sheep? You guys are supposed to be out watching them and you're just lying around being lazy!" She began to really get after me to help out more, so off we'd go herding the sheep. But we took our comic books with us.

And you know, we did get our exercise. We'd climb the rocks and go all over the Valley looking for those sheeps. If there was a mesa we hadn't climbed then we'd all take it on. We'd come across some rocks and say, "Hey, we never climbed these. Let's try it!" After a day of climbing we forgot all about the sheep. Sometimes we came home in the evening without them. My mom would look at me and my cousins like we were crazy, and she would say, "Where have you been? The sheep came home by themselves hours ago!" I think our behavior must have really upset her, because she eventually told my dad. He went to his brother and told him to keep his girls home because they were going wild with me, (giggles). A couple days later they got picked up by their dad in a van and got taken home. We secretly planned to meet up at the Sand Springs whenever we could. So just about every afternoon I told my mom, "I'm going to take the sheep to the Sand Springs." I took my sheep and my cousins brought their horses. We'd have a wild time all afternoon just racing around. We'd say to each other, "My horse can outrun your horse," and then we'd race them. We climbed the sand dunes and rolled around until we put holes in our clothes. We had a great time together.

Well, my cousins were really becoming teenagers, and they began to convince me to go back to school. They said, "Oh, there's this boy who is so cute! He goes to our school and you'd like him." My cousins asked me if I'd ever seen a guy.

"Yeah, sure," I answered, but I didn't know what they meant at first. Up to this point I had been pretty sheltered.

They told me, "You ought to see a guy. You should start dating. Come back to school and you'll get to meet boys." I was way behind everybody else in my schooling, so I was nervous about returning. After spending that whole summer with my cousins they went back to school, and I went back to my usual ways. I was at home herding the sheep, chasing the horses, reading my comic books and listening to my music... all alone. I got pretty lonely, and eventually I got the feeling that I wanted to go back to school.

I started to write to my cousin going to school in Keyenta. By then my brothers were at boarding school in the mountains in Salt Lake, and I wrote to them too. The more I heard about school the more I wanted to go. My dad was looking for work off the reservation, so I went to my mom and asked her if I could go back to school and learn more. I told her that I didn't feel like I had enough education. My mom said, "Yeah, that's what I want for you too. I would like for you to get more schooling. It's probably good for you."

My aunt and uncle lived by Three Sisters, and we visited them a lot. I got to know my cousin Opal really well, and my mom and hers were really close friends. When they were both young moms they traveled around together and hauled us along with them. One day my mom was talking to Opal's mom about how bad boarding school was for me. My mom said that was why they hadn't made me go back. My aunt Virginia said, "You should put your daughter in Mission School. It's nice, and not like boarding school at all." She said that "Mission School" was run by Christians in Winslow, Arizona. I sure as heck didn't want to go back to the other place. All my enemies were there! (Laughter),

So I said okay, and got put into Mission School. I was worried about my mom though. I said to her, "What are you going to do for help? You're going to end up all by yourself!" In knew my dad would be concerned about me leaving mom alone. I asked her, "What are you going to tell my dad?"

But she just shook her head and said, "Ah, I'll think of something." So she lived by herself and took care of the sheep and everything. I left in August and had so much fun. I liked my new school and I learned a lot. At first they asked what my last grade was that I had attended, and I had to tell them I'd only completed the fifth grade. Well, I was too old to be with those kids, so they put me in the combined classes of seventh and eighth grade kids. They told me it would be hard to learn stuff all at once, but that things would eventually get easier. They seemed pretty certain things would work out for me, so I just studied hard to catch up. I was just happy to be with kids my own age, and so it really didn't seem that hard. Now that I'm older I don't think I would want to try that now. But back then I was willing to learn everything. I asked a lot of questions.

There were no Navajo teachers, just people from the Mission church who were all white. But there were all kinds of students. There were Apache, Hopi, Ute, Sioux, and Blackfoot...all kinds. We had about three hundred and fifty girls there. Including the boys it came to about seven hundred. There were more Navajo there than anything. The Hopi reservation was nearby, so we had a lot of them too. The town of Show Low was also pretty close, and that's where a lot of Apache came from. I just got along with everybody and had a great time. What I loved best about this school was all the traveling we did. Every weekend we went somewhere different. Once we went to Hopi land, and another time we went to Apache land. We'd go and sing to them and then we'd talk to people about what God does for you. It was mostly like that. I didn't even miss my home.

Around September my mom had Opal's mom write a letter to me. She would tell my aunt what to write and she said, "Everything's okay, don't worry about me. I went and wrote to your dad, and I told him that you're doing good with all the sheep and helping me a lot. I don't want to tell him you're back in school." I felt so guilty. My mom told me to write a letter to my dad, and then send it back to her. She would send it from our home in the Valley. She told me to write about what I was doing with the sheep and stuff like that. So I guess the two of us were kind of telling a fib, but my dad never did find out I'd gone back to school. He died that year in the house fire, and I'd been at school that whole year. I was there until May, but I came home for break right before he returned from working in California. That summer I stayed with my mom until it was time to go back to school in August. Dad found work in Idaho right before then. That's the place where he died. The fire happened in October, while I was in school.

I remember I had a good friend in class named Elizabeth. She was older than me, around eighteen years old. We also hung around with another girl who was Apache, and I thought those two were perfect teenagers. They were very Christian and would never do anything stupid, but one day something got into them. I usually worked in the kitchen, and I was coming back from there to my room. They walked up to me and Elizabeth said, "There's this guy who would like to talk to you. He's a senior." This guy was eighteen, and I was only something like fifteen.

I couldn't believe it, so I said, "Me? What am I going to do with him?"

They just started laughing and said, "Hey, believe it. Johnny likes you!"

"I don't think so," I told them, and started walking away. I guess I was a little embarrassed.

They were pretty sure about it though, and they said to me, "You know what we're going to do tonight? We're going to sneak out the back door by unlocking the window from the outside after school. We can sneak out that way and meet Johnny and his friends. Do you want to come along?"

I didn't think that was a good idea. I said, "No, why would we do that? What would we do once we met up with them?" (*Effie gave a big laugh*).

They said, "Oh come on. Don't' be shy. You could at least talk to this guy." I was scared, but they convinced me to come along. They said that it would be fun.

That night I went to bed early because I was pretty tired. Elizabeth told me to pretend to dress in my pajamas, but to sleep with my pants on, but I did it backwards. I actually had my pajamas on underneath, and slipped my pants on once I was in bed, (giggles). I didn't really think they would pull it off, so I fell asleep. I don't know what time it was when they came sneaking into my room, but they woke me up and said, "Effie, let's go!" So I went with them into the restroom, and we opened the window and climbed out. We sneaked around behind the dormitory where there's a big building called "Administration." Behind that was a shop where they had classes in metal work and stuff like that. We waited there until we heard the boys whistling for us. We whistled back and they came over. Lizzie and this guy hooked up and went off one way and the Apache girl went off another way with the other guy. I ended up just standing at the wall with this guy who claimed he wanted to meet me.

He said, "So, um…your name is so and so…" blah, blah.

I didn't know what to say, so I just mumbled, "Um-hum." I was still kind of scared. I wondered what he was going to do next, and what was I supposed to do?

He told me, "I liked you the first day you came to school. I was asking all the girls about you, and they said you weren't always in school. Were you in school last year?"

I said, "Uh-huh," you know, keepin' it short and sweet.

Then he asked me, "Who did you like last year?"

I told him, "I don't know," because I had a lot of friends from different tribes who were boys. I was thinking he could be like that...just a friend to me. But this boy was kind of different. I think he wanted to be more than friends.

He kept coming up to me closer and closer. He stood there by me and sort of tried to hold my hand. I kept pulling away, so he grabbed me and said, "I can see that you've never been touched before."

I said, "What kind of touching?" (*Again, big laughter*), my heart was just pounding and my body was shaking.

He asked me, "Are you cold?"

"No," I told him.

Then he asked me, "Are you nervous?"

And I said, "Yessss."

He said, "I can calm you down. You have never let a boy put his arm around you or hold your hand?"

I said, "Nah-uh...no way."

Then he said, "Do you want me to try that? It'll calm you down." He put his arm around me and I got *really* scared! (*giggles*)

I said, "No I don't feel that comfortable. I don't think so!" I kind of pushed him away and turned my back to him.

He said, "God, you're scary!"

That's what's so funny! Here I was scared to death of him, and he says something like that! "I've never been with a boy," I explained to him, "and I don't know how it feels to like one. Usually I don't like boys like that." He said that was okay, so we just talked instead...no more funny stuff. He said he lived close by, somewhere around Holbrook. He told me about what he did around home, to help his family out. He told me there was a Christian school where he was going to continue called Thunderbird Academy in Phoenix. I found out he was half Navajo and half Apache. He was really light complected, like me. (*This is how the Yazzies explain someone who has a light complexion.*) He kind of looked like my brother, Kee, but not as handsome. I decided I didn't want him, (*laughter*). I was still too shy. He wasn't shy about anything, and there I was being a scardy-cat. I kept looking around for my friends saying, "Where are they?"

He said, "Don't worry about them. They can take care of themselves."

I finally got mad and said, "I'm going back! I'm scared I'll get in trouble and I don't want that." I was just kind of thinking that way, so I took off. I only stood there talking with him about thirty minutes or so, but for all I knew it could've been an hour. I went to the dorm and crawled back into the window and went right back to sleep. The next day the girls laughed at me and said, "Oh, you're a chicken!" But I thought they were the ones being stupid. I told them I didn't know why they even talked to guys. They never had anything to say.

Colette:

I found it charming that my friend had been so innocent. I joked with her that she'd been out too long with the sheep and horses! Effie laughed long and hard over that.

Effie:

Yeah, I didn't know nothing about boys. Anyway, I saw that guy the next day. We were in the classroom working on something. That day somebody came over the intercom and said, "Miss Effie Yazzie, can you please come to the principal's office?" I thought, 'Oh no! They found out and now I'm in trouble!' I started shaking, and I wondered, 'what can I do? What can I say?' I was really scared when I walked into that office.

The principal said, "Have a seat. You don't want to be standing up."

I just looked at him and said, "What did I do? What's going on?" Goodness, I was so scared. That was when they said, "We got a call from home. They said your dad passed away."

I forgot all about the last night. I just thought, "Okay…this is not what I expected." I don't remember what went on after that. I don't recall what I did. I do remember that I started crying, and everybody started telling me they were sorry. I told them, "Just leave me alone," and I started walking. I walked away from the school to a hill behind the buildings. I wanted to get away from everybody, and up on that hill I could be by myself. I was out there crying my eyes out for I don't know how long. It was probably for two hours until I couldn't cry anymore. I just sat there alone. Even though everybody had tried to comfort me I just wanted be by myself.

Then, for some reason they all had to tell that guy I met last night to come after me! Why him? I don't know. The next thing I knew he was standing right in front of me, saying, "Effie, are you okay? I can try to comfort you." To be honest, he acted more mature in that moment than anyone else I knew up to then. He was more like a man than any other guy there. I still wondered, "Why is this guy here?" But he said, "I can talk to you if you feel like it. You know, things like this happen. I've been through it. My dad died. My sister died, and my brother died. I know how it feels." He talked to me a long time. Then after awhile he must have figured I'd had enough talking. That was when he told me, "Let's just go back now. I think they're going to take you back on the plane. You're going back to the Monument Valley with the airplane, so you better pack up if you want to go back home" So I said okay, and we walked back down. I felt more relaxed with him after that. He told me, "At a time like this you need somebody to comfort you. That's why I just felt like I had to do this for you."

He kidded with me saying, "You thought you had girlfriends who cared for you, and here I was the only one to comfort you. I just met you last night!" (*Effie giggled for a long time*), so he walked with me all the way back. He had his arm around me the whole time, but it was no biggie. It felt nice. We got to the dormitory and I went to pack up, even though I didn't really know what to take. I went to the office after that to get a whole bunch of paperwork done. The office staff said to me, "We'll give you a week or two to deal with things. Then you'll come back." I said okay, and the airplane came to take me home.

Mr. Rose, who was a teacher there, came to help me. That was my first time on an airplane, but I didn't even think about it. I was too busy thinking of my dad and my mom. It was like being in darkness a long time. People would speak to me, but even they wondered if I was listening to them. I have to admit, I barely remembered what any of them said. I went onto the plane, and even though it was my first time it didn't bother me. I looked down on the tiny little places as we were flying over, and I couldn't believe how short a time it took to get home. It felt like only twenty minutes! We parked at the airstrip where my mom and Virginia were waiting, and I thought how that airstrip had always been there, for as long as I can remember.

When I got home I found that all my brothers were there. They talked a lot about what they were going to do; now that dad was gone. All of this was going on, but I only felt guilty because we never told my dad I went back to school. I felt real bad about it. I thought that I should have written and told him. But at the same time I thought, "What would he have said to me anyway?" All of this was going through my mind. I felt so guilty and ashamed thinking it was too late to make everything alright.

We had a Christian funeral for him here in the Valley. They had to use a closed casket because he had been burned really bad. He was... how do you say it? He was unrecognizable. He's buried right here behind the lodge. There's a cemetery there that not many people know about. After it was all over my mom asked me if I was going to go back to school, but I told her, "I don't think so." That guy who put me on the airplane, Mr. Rose; he and his wife told me I could go to school there by Goulding's in order to be closer to my mom. I remember him saying, "We could provide a sleeping area for you there at the lodge." See, at that time it was still considered a ways from home. I told my mom about that arrangement, and she said, "That sounds alright. As long as you're closer to me I won't feel so lonely." They had a school in that old building right by where you're staying here at Hill House, so I went to school there.

Every other day my mom would come by. My brother, Kee was working as a teacher's aide in Oljeto back then, and every time he came to work he'd pick me up from my mom's to take me to school. If he was gone somewhere, and I had no place to go, I would stay with Mr. and Mrs. Rose who had a place nearby. Kee was the only one driving back then. We had a truck for the whole family to use, but now that I think about it, it seems like we always had some kind of a vehicle when I was a kid. My mom said that before I was born all we had were horses and a wagon, and I kind of remember using wagons to go to Sand Springs and Hidden Arches to get water. I just remember that as a kid we were always hauling water in the wagon.

Now, at the Mission School they didn't really force you to become a Christian. They never said, "In order to be a Christian you have to do this, or you have to do that." It was just like a regular school. They would sometimes read to you a little prescription; (*Effie means scripture here*). They sometimes asked you to memorize Bible verses, and they'd warn us we might be asked a question about it the next day. But I never got a beating like at the first school. The only problem was that you couldn't

313

wear pants. You had to wear a dress all of the time. I never liked that. Anyway, the way it worked was, when I was at home we'd do traditional religion, and when we were at school we sort of went along with the Christian thing in a quiet way. When I was real little my dad used to tell me stories about the past…about our history. I always wanted to rehear the same old story, so he would begin, "…this story is about an old Mexican named Belo." He always used to tell me that story over and over because I loved to hear it. Every evening I would curl up on his lap when he was playing cards, and I'd say, "*shisi ahh a*, tell me the Belo story!" He would play with his cards as he told it again.

It's kind of like a legend to us. It's about a Mexican man who liked to steal and make problems for everybody. He sounded a lot like Coyote, (giggles) The Trickster. It's a really interesting story. Other times I would be laying with my mom, and she would tell me creation stories…about how things were in the beginning. Back in the old days there were no humans, and she would tell how our people grew up through the First World. I used to ask her for the creation story all the time. Then I'd ask her questions about it, but she'd always say, "Ask your dad." When I went to him with my questions he would always tell jokes to go along with the stories. Or he'd say, "It's not time for that kind of story. You have to wait until winter." I'd remember asking him, "Why can't you tell me them? It doesn't matter…isat?" (*This is a common phrase used among the Navajo. It's a loose translation of the term "Is that right?" But it may be used in a variety of ways to imply agreement, and can include "Don't you think?" or "Isn't that so?"*) My dad would always say that it did matter. He told me that if he told the story at the wrong time, "Well, the lizards will laugh at us." Or he'd say, "A spider will come to you at night and put a web all over your mouth and your body. You'll be tired up until next winter." It's the same with those strings you play with between your fingers. You're not supposed to mess with games like that, because the spider woman will come tie you up. All of these simple little sayings that tell you what not to do got into our brains, until we would be convinced. We wouldn't even mention some little things because we were afraid the lizards would laugh at us.

Even before my dad passed I was close to my brother Kee. Unfortunately I didn't see him or my other brothers much as I got older.

When I got back from school and started living in the Valley I started taking care of my mom. I thought about college, and I missed my schooling. At the same time I thought, "What am I going to do with college?" I didn't really know what I wanted to do. I knew I didn't want to be a secretary or something like that. Instead I wanted to be more like my mom. I wanted to work around the home, but I still don't know how to cook. The funny thing is, now I have a job cooking for Goulding's! I couldn't decide what to do, so I just kept going to the school here in the Valley. It was okay, because they didn't care if we spoke Navajo, but they did tell us not to believe in our traditional religion. They'd say things like, "our prayer is stronger than yours."

You know, it kind of hurts when people say that to you. You wonder, 'Well, who can I believe?' Back at the Mission school they told us that as long as we prayed, good things would happen for us. They said it didn't matter if we thought we were Christians or not, it was still praying so it would help. My teacher, principal and foster parents at the new place though… they all put more pressure on me. My foster dad would sometimes preach at the church. So we went there every Wednesday night and every Saturday morning. They were Seventh Day Adventists, so he told us not to work on Saturday. He would say, "Saturday is your holy day. You should not work or swear…speak no dirty words." He said on Saturday you couldn't even think anything dirty. Eventually he told us that Friday evening was strict as well. You were not to do anything sinful all the way up to Saturday at sunset. Then you could swear as much as you wanted (*laughter*). Anyway, that's what I remember my foster dad telling us.

He was the guy at school who acted like our dad. But when I went back home I always joined my mom in her corn pollen prayers. The whole thing didn't even bother me. That was my religion, and the other stuff didn't matter. I was just living my life, (giggles). Anyway, I was glad to have my own religion after my dad died. I finished school by Goulding's. I went one full year there and then I went to high school in Keyenta. That's where I started the tenth grade.

A CHANGE IN PLANS
"Tell the truth always, even if it is bitter to taste." — *Unknown Tribe*

Once I got to tenth grade I had to stop. I got myself in trouble, (giggles). We used to have a prayer meeting down at the church every Wednesday night. All us local kids would go down there after supper, because we were told we had to. Then the white LDS folks would talk and talk from the Bible. My foster sister and my foster brother used to go with me, but my foster sister and I would just sit there and giggle. The rest of the students who sat up front had to listen. But my sister and I liked to sit in the back and talk about girl things. I guess we were pretty wild. They sometimes let us out thirty minutes ahead of time, so we'd run back up to the trailer where we were living to hang out. That trailer is still there, just up the road from Goulding's. My foster brother was twelve or eleven at the time. He was an adopted child and he was *really* wild! That boy never did what you told him. As soon as he got to the trailer, right away he'd turn the radio to a rock station. Then he would dance his butt off. His older sister always yelled at him, "Turn that thing off or I'm gonna tell on you!"

But he'd just say, "You can't tell me what to do. You're not my mom!" I just sat there and watched the whole thing unfold. Sometimes I'd have to go outside and sit on the porch until things eventually quieted down.

Every now and then I got invited to one of my friend's house. I had one friend named Sandra, and she lived right behind Goulding's close to us. Her sister's name was Marie, and they lived with a lady named Joanne, but her real name was Janaye. Sometimes they would say to me, "Hey, let's go up to our house," and off we went. They were funny to me because they always talked about boys. There were some in one family they really liked, so when they saw these guys they flipped out. They'd tell me to come over because, "The Holiday boys are here!" They thought these guys were so handsome, and they just went on and on. They always managed to find those boys too. They knew if they were at Goulding's or at the hospital. "Ooooo," they would say, "those good-looking Holliday's are around! Let's go see 'em!" They were distantly related through an uncle. One kid was a cousin by the name of Wilson, and another was called Denny. But there were actually five of them, and they always hung around each other.

The girls' foster parents were not as strict as mine were. If Sandra and Marie said, "Mom, dad, can we take a walk? We're just going up to the canyon…" their parents would always say, "Yeah, sure. Just make sure you're home before ten because it's a school night." Then we would take off walking up the road as if we were little girls going to play. When we figured the parents weren't watching we'd turn back around and head for the clinic. We ended up in the hospital lobby where all these Holiday boys were always hanging out. They just hung out there in the lobby with the rest of the teenagers because there was nowhere else to go.

I did think one of the Holiday boys was sort of cute. My son Timmy looks a lot like him. Sometimes when I see Timmy I'm reminded of his dad. Anyway, everybody would hang around and talk, but I was still sort of a shy type. The Holliday boys would pick on me and say, "Hey, how come this one isn't talking?" Because I was only fifteen all I could think of to say was, "Oh don't bother me." One day Sandra said, "That Holliday boy, Tom…he really likes you." I didn't believe it, but Tom eventually told my brothers the same thing. He asked them to see how I felt about him, so I told my brothers that I thought Tom was okay-looking." After that we were in class one day and Sandra said that she had written a note that said, "Hi Tom…remember me? I'm the girl you like from around here…" and so and so. She had written, "I think I like you too. So if you want to go somewhere and hang out with me I wouldn't mind doing that." Then she signed my name! I couldn't believe she wrote that as if it came from me! I said, "Don't you dare give that to him!" But she gave that note to Tom.

A couple of days later my foster parents and I were working on something in the hospital, I don't remember what. I went over there with them and helped them until it started getting a little dark. My foster mom told me, "Well, you better get ready for school tomorrow. You still haven't done your chores." So I started to leave, and when I turned the corner around the hospital, there was Tom standing there. I think he was kind of drinking. He made that noise we sometimes do to get people's attention, like a whistle. (*I have actually heard this whistle a few times from Lonnie when he wanted to get my attention*) I looked over and saw Tom hiding behind the wall. He stepped out and said hello, and we talked for a while. I asked him where the other boys were, since they were always together. He said he wanted to see me alone, and I guess I wasn't too shy of him anymore. Then he showed me that note that my friend had written. He said, "Thanks for writing to me." I'd kind of forgotten about what Sandra had done, and I thought to myself, 'where did he get that note? Who wrote it?'

I snatched the note away from him and read it, but I didn't let him know it hadn't come from me. He handed me another piece of paper, but I didn't read it them. I just put it in my pocket and said, "Well, I gotta get back home and do some stuff." He must have wondered what the heck was going on, (giggles). That was our big romantic night. I went back to my place and read a note he wrote back to me. First I locked myself in the bathroom. Then I saw he had written, "I like you too. You're so cute and I'm glad you're thinking of me, because all this time I've been keeping an eye on you. I thought it was only me, but it's good to know that you have that same feeling." I thought to myself, 'Oh no! Now what do I do?' I went to my friend and said to her, "How dare you give that note to Tom Holiday!" My foster brother was there and he said, "What note?" He wasn't Navajo but he was like a brother to me, and I guess he was looking out for me. He said to Sandra, "that's not right that you did that." Then my foster brother went and talked to all of the parents! One of the daughters we hung out with got in trouble too. All five of us got busted. We were told not to go out at night anymore because they thought we would be up to no good with these Holiday boys, (big giggles). My foster dad said, "It's not right that you hang out with these boys at night." Boy did I ever get it.

After that Tom Holiday only kind of said "hi" to me in passing. But I saw him around all the time. I began to think he was around all the time just to look at me, (laughs). I eventually got chances to talk to him from time to time. He started giving me small notes again. Sometimes they said, "I miss you," and sometimes they said, "Why didn't I see you at school today." He gave the notes to one of the students that I walked to school with to hand off to me. I was too scared to write back to him. I didn't know what I should say! It just went on like that for a while. At the end of the school year we had some kind of a school party, and he was there. I couldn't talk to Tom though, because I had to run back to our trailer to get something, I don't remember what. The place was pretty quiet because my foster sister was off to college at some academy. My foster parents weren't home, and my younger foster brother was at the party. Back then everybody knew where everybody else was. I had to get back to the party in a hurry, because I was supposed to keep an eye on my brother. But on the way back there was Tom again!

I almost bumped into him because he was drinking. He had told me he wasn't drinking anymore, so I said, "What are you trying to do to yourself these days?" He told me he was drunk. He said, "I can't help it. My friends make me drink." I said he shouldn't be doing that kind of stuff, and that's when he let everything pour loose. He asked me, "How come you never write me a note saying that you like me? You never say how you feel! How do you feel about me?" I was embarrassed, so I just laughed and said, "I don't know! I don't even really know you!" See, I thought that we were just really close friends. I didn't know anything about love. I said, "I don't know what to say to you, but before you pass out you'd better head home."

I don't know what he did after that conversation because I just walked back to the party. I knew that he was starting to get serious about me, and I didn't really know how to feel about it. Finally school got out and I didn't see him all summer. That fall I went to high school in Keyenta where he was a senior. I was only a freshman. All of a sudden he turned shy on me! He wouldn't talk to me like he used to. He acted like he didn't even know me. I decided I didn't care, because I was having fun hanging around with my girlfriends. One of my cousin's was in my class, and I hung out with her and her friend. She and her friend were different because one was Christian and the other was of the Navajo religion. At that time Lonnie lived and worked in Keyenta, so I stayed with him. I kept up my grades and was pretty good all year. Tom was into sports and so he was really popular.

We didn't really speak until the next summer when I went home to M.V. Tom drove his parent's truck to my mom's place, and asked if I wanted to go for a ride. So that summer that's what we did. We would drive around, and climb the rocks, and do crazy stuff like that together until school started again. By the time I was halfway through the fall semester I knew I had gotten myself into trouble. I found out that I was pregnant! (*Effie gave a deep, long chuckle*).

You know, I really liked Tom. He was a nice guy. He didn't talk much but he would do anything for you. When we got close I knew what was going on, but I didn't really know how to handle it. I'd heard a lot from my girlfriends and my cousins. They would say, "When you do this and this with a guy you have all these feelings!" (*Giggles*) But I guess it's not always like that. Anyway, I was sixteen and pregnant and I didn't know what to do. I gave birth to little Tomas by the time I was seventeen. (*Chuckles*) I was so scarred! At first I didn't even know I was pregnant. I was eating breakfast and all of a sudden I threw up everything. I guess my mom kind of noticed that I was doing that, and she asked me, "Are you pregnant?"

My eyes popped out and I said, "Huh?! What's that?!" By this time I was spending the whole summer with my mom, and she kept an eye on me. I said to my mom, "Pregnant…. I don't think so! How do you know?"

She said, "You've been throwing up a lot."

I told her, "Oh it's probably just a common cold or something." But my mom looked at me as if to say, 'Yeah, sure.'

Then she asked me when was my last period and I said, "I don't know. I don't remember."

She asked me, "Well have you had one lately?" That's when I started to think about things. I thought, 'Hmmm, I did have sex, so it's possible I am pregnant like my mom says.' I kept hoping I wasn't though. I didn't want to get married. I wanted to go to school and finish. I finally talked it over with my mom, and she said, "Well, you have to discuss this with the boy you were with, and see what he wants to do." I asked my mom what she thought about it all, and she said, "*Ha la.*" That means she doesn't know. I really didn't want to see Tom any more. I kind of hated him for what he did to me, (*laughter*).

About four months after talking to my mom I finally got the courage to talk to the father of my child. He said, "What?! I'm a dad?!" He didn't know what to do either, so he told his parents, and they talked to us about it.

Everyone from my family said we should have a wedding. I thought to myself, 'I'm not going to have a wedding. I'm not gonna go through with it!' They said, "we can plan a wedding in the next two or three months. We'll do it the traditional way." I thought, 'Oh no! I'm going to be six or seven months by then!' I didn't even think about abortion. I don't think I would've wanted to do that. That's kind of against our religion because we cherish life so much. I had a relative who got a little wild and doing crazy stuff when she was young. She got pregnant twice and had two abortions. She went somewhere in New Mexico, and then Arizona to do it. When I heard about that I wondered how she could do it. I thought that was a crazy thing to do. When I told her about my pregnancy said that I should have found out earlier. She said, "You could have had an abortion. Now you're too far along so it's too late." But I just said, "Nah, I'm not going to kill a human being. It's part of my life now."

(*Effie laughed*), I was just so surprised that people sometimes did that. Anyway, my son was eventually borned and he was big! He weighed eight pounds and I was in terrible pain. Every time I felt a contraction I yelled, "I hate this!" (*Laughter*), I was in labor for twelve hours! I couldn't wait for that kid to get out. I was hanging on to my mom yelling, "Mom, don't leave me! You have to stay here with me!" Every time I felt a labor pain I screamed like a baby. I was terrible; not tough at all. By the time my son stuck his head out I was yelling at him, (*giggles*). I said to him, "get out of here, I'm sick of this!"

Tom and I did have a traditional wedding. I was about six months along, but I wasn't really showing. Nobody knew I was pregnant! Three months later when I had my son everybody was so confused. They said, "Hey! Didn't you just get married?" It was pretty funny to see them scratching their heads. We never got married legally; just the traditional way. We took his mom up to Tuba with us to check out how to make it legal, but the official folks just said, "Come back after you get a blood test." And we never did. We never got a license. We were living with my mom down in the Valley. We lived in the shed where they keep the hay now.

I think everything went downhill after that. That's when I really started to struggle. I needed money for food, and a vehicle to take my kid around. My husband worked, but he was starting to drink more. I didn't think my husband was going to provide, so I looked around for a better job. My cousin, Opal, was working at the hospital at the time, and she said, "You should come over here to find work. They really need to hire some girls now." She said, "I don't like the night shift, so you should go out there with me and see if you could take it. Come and see how it feels." So she dragged me into the hospital to fill out all the papers to get a job there. Then Opal told me, "You do this," and, "You do that." All through the night she just dragged me around. We had something like fifteen patients in that little hospital, and she showed me how to check up on them. She showed me how to wash all of the instruments, clean the operating room and all this and that, whatever keeps you awake in the middle of the night.

For two nights I was in training. I knew nothing about taking care of patients, so Opal showed me how to take their pulse and check on things called "vital signs." She said to me, "You just take their blood pressure, their pulse and their temperature. Those three things are the most important. Do it at midnight and around four o'clock in the morning." I did everything she told me, and I learned how to figure the math that goes with it all. The third night I was by myself and for every night after that. I had to learn everything pretty fast, but I got the hang of it. I've been working there off and on ever since then, for twenty years!

After awhile I had two little daughters. My mom delivered both of them at home. I wasn't sure about having babies in the hogan, but it was okay. They just came so fast. One day I had a tummy ache and the next I just felt like pushing. I said,

"Mom, I don't think we're going to make it to the hospital." But she was real calm, and she said, "Okay. I know how to do it." She helped me have first daughter all by herself, in the middle of the night. I was at home with my boy and my mom was herding the sheep. Little Tommy was following me around, wanting this and that. Around six or seven o'clock that night I felt like I had to go to the bathroom. I said to my son, "Come on honey, mommy has to go to the restroom." He just talked to me in baby talk and we went out to the outhouse. I was sitting there feeling funny and suddenly I thought, 'I wonder if it's close to my due date.' I couldn't really remember when it was, but I thought, 'Nah, I can't be due yet.'

I guess it's a good thing I didn't have the baby there in the outhouse! (*Laughter*), I finally went back to the house and cooked something for my boy. The sun was going down and I thought, 'I wonder where my mom is.' I was starting to think I really might be in labor by then. Just then both of my son's *nallys* , his grandparents, came by. They wanted to know if I'd seen Tom. I told them, "I have no idea where he is. He disappears back behind the canyon and doesn't come back for a week or two."

They asked me, "Why does he do all these crazy things when his wife is pregnant?"

I just shrugged and said, "I don't know. He's your son." (*Effie laughed again*), I was going to tell them that I felt like I might be in labor, but I was too embarrassed. I just let it go, and they left looking for their son. That was when I wished I had said something. My husband had the truck, so I was pretty much stuck there. There I was with no vehicle, and no way out of the Valley except for horses. I waited and waited for my mom. I knew soon enough that I really was in labor. I could feel the pain coming on more often.

It's pretty light in the summertime, so I thought she was out herding pretty late. I walked around crying, "Mother, please... where are you?" You get comfort from walking around when you're in labor, and I was pulling my boy around by the hand. He was crying because he wanted me to carry him. I said, "Sorry... I can't even pick you up!" I walked back and forth until finally I saw my mom walking back from my aunt's hogan! That's where she had been all the time! It was after nine o'clock in the evening before she came back. I told her, "I think I'm in labor mom." She said there were no vehicles at my aunt's hogan, and nobody there that could help...just the elderlies. She said, "I used to do this before, when you were young. I delivered babies a lot, and I think I remember how to go about it. Don't worry. I know what I'm doing." She told me, "we have to boil some water to clean the string and we need to boil the knife to cut the cord too." That way the umbilical cord doesn't get infected. Then she said that we needed to set up some towels for me. I just said okay to everything because I had to have that baby.

I yelled at that baby too! I said, "Hurry up! I'm dying here. I'm tired of waiting!" I was having more and more labor pains but we still had to wait until around midnight for my baby girl to come. The next day somebody finally came by, and we took her to the hospital. They asked my mom how the head looked when she came out, and how did she pull my baby out. My mom said, "I don't know. I wasn't looking.

The baby just came out." Apparently she checked out okay though, and so we just took my daughter back home.

The same thing happened with my other girl. We didn't even have time to boil water with her! I was asleep at my mom's place, and all of a sudden my stomach started hurting. I thought I just had a stomachache, so I went outside, walked around, and went to the bathroom like last time. All of a sudden I felt a sharp pain. I knew the baby was coming and I said, "Aw shoot!" I tried to hurry back to the house to get help, but it was about two or three o'clock in the morning and everyone was asleep. Just as I was reaching the door I realized I couldn't go any further. I couldn't even make it to the cement stoop, and I felt the baby right there ready to come. Here I was fully clothed in my jogging pants and I couldn't move. I yelled, "Mom!" She must have heard me, because she came out running, and I told her the baby was coming. I was on my hands and knees at the doorway, and I could feel the baby's head coming out. My older brother was there and my nieces too, so my mom told my brother to go start up the car. I told her, "I don't think I'm gonna make it anywhere... the baby's coming now!" She said, "Then why do you have your coat on?" I yelled back, "What do you want me to do, run around naked?"

It was a pretty crazy scene, (*giggles*). There was no pain at all though. I barely felt a thing. I just felt the water break. I still had my hand between my legs just holding the baby, and I yelled to my mom, "Put something here to hold the head!" I was screaming and yelling, "I don't have time to wait for you to start the *chiddy*. Just help me have this baby!" Well, my mom threw a mattress down right there. I couldn't crawl any further than just inside by the stove. My brother turned on a light and my mom threw me a sheet. I pulled it around me and took my pants off. My mom took one look and said, "Oh yeah, that baby is coming! The head's halfway out!" I was just hanging on for dear life. I couldn't walk anymore. I pushed along a little longer, and that little girl came out screaming her head off. My mom just laughed and said, "Look at her! She doesn't have any hair!" She had nothing on the top of that head! (*We all giggle away*), it was like your hand Coco; just soft and smooth. That's what her head looked like. The hair on top of her head was so golden you couldn't see it. That's how fair she was then.

Finally, I had my youngest, another boy, in the hospital. I was about twenty-two years old by the time I'd had all my kids. My mom took care of the kids while I worked, and during the day I had kids crawling all over me. I would lay down with them while my mom was out herding the sheep. I put a whole bunch of cushions and blankets all the way around me. I put all the kids in there with me like a playpen. I usually asked my mom to take my oldest boy with her to herd the sheep. He was always sort of the rowdy one. He liked to pick up his sisters and carry them around, so when he was about five or so we figured he was old enough to go herding. When I started to work at the hospital my husband and I weren't doing very well. He only saw one of our babies get borned, our second son. We got into an argument about that once. I said to him, "You're not even around when your kids come into the world! You never comforted me when I need it, and you never cared for me all these years. You're always out drinking and you're just a bad father."

He said, "Well the first time I tried to be with you when our first son was born, but every time I tried to stick my head in the door you just told me to get out." (*Effie laughed*). He had a point. I didn't want him hanging around that first time because I was so young. Anyway, it seemed like as soon as all the kids were born we were always in an argument. I would tell him, "You never bring money or clothes for the children!"

It was true. I had the hardest time making ends meet. I had no money and no way to get clothes for my kids. I started to sew as much as I could to make them clothes myself. I bought patterns and material that I could get pretty cheap, and I made really pretty outfits for them. It was actually kind of fun. I saved money in other ways too. I never went to the Laundromat. I washed everything at the house. I had cloth diapers and washed everything by hand. We hauled water all the time. Meanwhile my kids were growing up. My eldest boy was a fast learner, and he started walking at ten months! In a year he was out of diapers, already toilet trained. I started breast-feeding him but my nipple got sore. It hurt so bad I couldn't stand it. Finally a doctor gave me some pills to dry it up and I switched my boy to formula. He was only on the bottle for six months. That was it. He grew up fast.

My oldest girl didn't start walking until she was about thirteen months, and my boy was always so good with his oldest sister. They took her toys outside so she could watch him herd the sheep way out in the hills there. He would pick really pretty yellow flowers, the tiny ones that grow around here, and he would bring them to her. By the time they got back she would have flowers all over her head! I would ask her, "Where did you get those?" And my boy just smiled. He was really good with the girls, but he got in a lot of fights with his brother. I remember he always used to make his younger brother cry. I would tell him, "Be nice to that boy! You don't have a bag full of brothers! That's your only one." But you know how boys are. They're just rough.

When my oldest boy was born I didn't have a cradleboard right away, so his *nally* went to find some of his own wood and made one for him. My mom still has it, and all of my kids used it. The tourists used to take pictures of my kids all the time. My mom would dress them up in traditional clothes, and the visitors would just snap away with their cameras. So not only was I working, but they were earning money too! (*Laughter*). My mom saved every dollar they made. She waited until they were thirteen, then by the time school came along that year they would have all kinds of money. We would take them to Farmington or even as far as Flagstaff, and they could buy whatever they wanted. They would buy five sets of clothes!

EFFIE STANDS ALONE

"I grew up knowing it's wrong to have more than you need. It means you're not taking care of your people." - Navajo

So that's how they used to survive. Just like me, they made money during the summer in the Valley, and then went to school. Seeing them made me remember how I posed for tourists when I was a kid. Money was nothing to me then. I didn't even know what to do with it. Visitors would give me a quarter or ten cents, and I would just look at it. I always gave it to my mom. When I was a little kid I didn't need school clothes because I wasn't going to school. Then later I never felt the need for a lot of clothes like teenagers nowadays do. I never knew where my clothes came from, and I didn't care. But my mom was always happy to see the tourists. She used to say to me, "Now that they've shown up we can make a little money and not go hungry." I loved how my dad came home from working, and he usually brought us stuff from the trading post. He treated us with candy and pop, sometimes some popcorn. Once in a great while we would get that stuff, and it was good to have him home too.

Thinking about the old days made me feel bad for my kids. Their dad wasn't around much. I started getting a clue, and I split up with my husband when the youngest was about seven or eight years old. We were only officially together for six years. After we split he kept begging for me to come back. At first I would agree, as long as he could control his life. But it really turned me off when he kept drinking. I thought maybe we just needed to be alone, so we bought a trailer up by Goulding's. I told my mom, "I really need to be closer to where I'm working. That way I can get there even if I don't have a vehicle." I said, "Maybe if we have a place of our own, and I'm working close by my husband will understand what living really is. Maybe he'll try to live separately with me, if I'm not living under you."

My mom helped me to buy the trailer, and a local man sold it to us at a good price. I told him what the problem was and he understood. I went to talk to my husband's parents, and they said to go ahead and set it up on a little bit of their grazing land by Goulding's. By this time most of my kids were in boarding school, but I wanted them closer to home. I felt bad about them being gone. During this time I just had my youngest boy with me. He was only in preschool, and I always dropped him off right over by the hospital. That way I could go home to sleep a little. I was still working the night shift, so I would sleep a little and go pick him up in the afternoon. That's when he said, "Mom, put the battery in the TV so I can watch cartoons!" I would connect the battery from the vehicle to the television, and that's how he kept himself busy so I could get sleep a little more. He would just play around until I woke up for work.

One day we were driving in the truck, and I told Timmy that he was probably going to spend the weekend in the Valley with his grandma. The other kids were coming home too, so they were all going to stay there at my mom's. He said, "Mom, can I ask you a question?" He was really serious for just a kid.

I said, "Yeah, sure...go ahead."

He said, "Who is my mom for real?"

Well, I had no idea what he was talking about, so I said to him, "I am your mom!"

He said, "But, I'm always staying with grandma. Is she my really mother or are you my really mother. It seems like my grandma is the one who takes care of me...so who's really my mom?"

That made me feel really bad, and I told him, "Hey, I'm your real mom. She's my mom, and so she loves you, but she's your grandmother!" I could tell this was a really hard question for him, so we just talked and talked about it. He always had questions for me when he was growing up. I thought he was going to stay like that, but now that he's grown up you can't really get anything out of him. Maybe I answered all his questions.

As for Tom...well, the kids' father, that never really worked out. When we were all living up here by Goulding's all he ever did was drink. When he found work he always got fired from it because he was going in drunk all the time. He could never really hold onto a job. I kept working at night and sleeping part of the day so I could go back to work the next night without being really tired. Well, the kids needed looking after when they came home from school, and especially on the weekends. I'd be dog-tired and bring the kids home from school, and here was my husband all passed-out with two or three of his friends. I would think to myself, 'I have two little girls at home with these guys I don't even know. What if something happened to them?' That was the last straw. I told my husband, "I don't ever want you bringing men home that we don't know. What if they did something to harm our girls?" He said he didn't think they would do anything. But I told him, "You never know. You just meet these guys when you're out drinking. You don't know anything about them and I'm not taking any chances!"

Colette:

I thought of how strong my friend was to take on raising four children on her own. She was very much like Suzie; practical and resourceful. I remembered the last time I'd seen Suzie. We were sitting in her Shade House trying to escape the summer heat. It was late afternoon, and time for the sheep to return from their distant grazing area in the box canyon by the Three Sisters monument. Suzie's head turned when she heard the barking of sheep dogs and the clanking of the bells some of the sheep wore around their necks. As the herd trotted briskly by I saw Suzie's lips move in some silent litany. "She's counting the sheep," Effie had told me that day, "most of us Navajo ladies are pretty good at math. My mom could tell you exactly how many sheeps she has...right down to the youngest lamb!" Now that I was learning about Effie's years as a young single mother, I wondered if that would be her job once she took over for her mother. Would Effie one day be sitting in the Shade House, counting sheep? My "sister" pulled me back from dreaming and went on to explain her argument with Tom Holiday.

Effie:

Anyway, I told my husband, "I'm saying these things because I love all my kids. If you loved us you would listen to me." He would agree with me, then turn around and bring strangers home again! So finally, finally on the weekends I started bringing my kids down to the Valley. We wouldn't even go back to the trailer. I let him drink away a little longer, until I finally told him, "You think this is your home, but it's not yours to bring your drunk buddies in with no thought for the kids." We got into an argument about whose home it was, and I said, "Who paid fifteen-hundred dollars for this trailer? It didn't come out of your pocket. It came out of my mom's purse and you haven't even paid her back!"

He said to me, "I'll straighten out. I'll fix things." But I knew things would never change with him.

We began to argue more and more, even when my kids were around. One day we got into a fistfight in front of the kids. He had been drinking and he started hitting me around. Well, you know me...no man was ever going to beat me up. I fought back and started to beat him up. My eldest boy was standing there crying. He said, "Mom, don't kill him!" He was only eleven back then, and I guess he was worried. If your kids are telling you to stop you don't want to do anything to make things worse. So I just kind of went to lay down and be calm. I lay there thinking that I'd had enough, and so I got up and I gathered all of our things. I said to the kids, "Let's go." Once more we took off back down to the Valley, and we didn't come back for a long time. I left the kids there when I had to work, and just went back and forth from work to my mom's. Tom left us alone for a month, and then he came looking for us. He said, "How come you guys aren't showing up at the trailer no more?"

I said to him, "You knew what we both need to do for our kids to make them grow up right, but you wouldn't even try. I don't ever want to fight in front of our kids again. I don't want them growing up thinking that's what parents do. If you can't stop drinking then I guess it's better if I raise the kids myself. I can handle it."

I told him, "I have a good job and my own vehicle. I won't go back to the way things were. I've tried and tried so hard to make things work. Now I'm just going to stay here with my mom and you do what you want."

He said, "Okay, I'll stop drinking."

But I told him, "You always want another chance. Just leave us alone. If you want the trailer take it." Oh, I got so tired of it. I thought, 'I never wanted to live this way, and I'm going to change things.' That's what I did. I left for good, and I think that trailer is still up there.

EFFIE'S DREAM

"Only when the last tree has withered, the last fish has been caught, and the last river has been poisoned, will you realize you cannot eat money." - Cree

After that my kids grew up with just me and my mom raising them. They all finished school and some of them went on to college. My eldest daughter was going to school in Nebraska, but she met a Ute man that she liked and they ended up having a little boy of their own. He's in the military and fighting in Iraq, but he's coming home soon. She lives over there in Nebraska, but I think sometimes she misses her family. His family is real nice and they like her, and they're almost like our family because they have traditional beliefs. Their traditions go way back just like ours, passed on from generations. My daughter told me that one day she was brushing her hair when her husband's mother came in. My daughter pulled her hair out of the brush and threw it in the trash, but his mom stepped into the restroom and grabbed the hair. She said, "Don't throw your hair away! The boogieman will take your hair and give it to the body of ghosts! You'll be hunted by them for the rest of your life!" I think in that particular tribe they have taboos like we do. She put the hair in my daughter's pocket and told her, "You'd better send your hair home or take it with you."

So it's good that some of their beliefs are like ours. We have certain taboos about how to deal with the dead. We don't like to have a lot of contact with that. We used to be careful about what we did with hair and nails because it was believed that a skinwalker could use it to perform misfortune on you. My mom still doesn't throw hair in the trash can. She throws it in the fire instead. She saves little pieces in her pocket when she's at my place, then when she gets back to the Valley she throws it in the fire. That's what you're supposed to do I think.

Colette:

I smiled at this statement from Effie, recalling that during one of our interviews Suzie claimed not to believe in Skinwalkers. At that time Effie explained that verbally admitting to the existence of Skinwalkers was believed to give these entities power over a person. I couldn't be sure one way or the other if Suzie truly feared these legendary creatures. Here, it seemed, was proof of the sometimes nebulous nature of Dine' belief system. What may appear perfectly clear to my Navajo family continued to leave me wondering what was "real" and what was "unreal." What I did know by now was that over the years Effie and her mother had grown to understand each other better. Raising children can really make a daughter see her own mother in a different light, and it was clear to me that Effie admired her mother for the strength and love she exhibited while caring for such a large family with minimal resources.

Effie:

Yeah, my mom always wanted the best for me, and I have high hopes for my kids... my dreams for them. I guess I'm still holding onto them like they're my babies. I'm hoping they'll end up with happy lives. At least they didn't get married off like I did, so early in life. I know it's tough to have kids when you're young. Somehow everything worked out for me. They turned out okay, but I want them to finish their education and find decent jobs. I want them to find a nice guy or a nice girl to settle down with. My eldest son already is married to a nice girl. He was twenty-six when he got married, but my daughter-in-law was only nineteen. They don't have any kids yet. My son wants his wife to go on to college, because she always dreamed of becoming an attorney. That's her dream, and my son encourages her to do that first. I want all my kids to have marriages where the family works together. That's what I always dreamed they would have.

The dream I have for myself is a little different. When I get older maybe I could retire and go on a "senior vacation." (*Effie laughs*), I want to see the world! I would love to travel to Hawaii. I don't know why, I just always said that one of these days I would go over there. I have kind of an idea of what it would be like. My youngest daughter always talks about going to Alaska. I told her, "I don't want to go over there. It's too cold!" But any traveling would be nice. Other than that I don't mind staying home. I really love it here. If I had my dream home it would be in the Valley next to my mom's place. I'd like to be known as a good woman like my mom is. I would live down there and take over the hogan and the sheep. I wouldn't mind that when I get older.

For me it would be a lot easier because lately I've been driving until I can't see anymore! I drive my mom around all the time. I tried to teach her how to drive once, but she just screamed, "I don't want to, I don't want to!" I guess she was kind of afraid of it. I did make her drive once when we were going after the sheep. They were way out in the bushes over by Totem Pole Rock, and I put her in the driver's seat, (*giggles*). I said, "Just drive to there where the sheep are. It's easy!" My truck is an automatic, so I figured she could handle it. And guess what…she did it! She kind of went all over the place, and she drove pretty slow, but don't let her fool you. She sort of knows what to do in a car now. I said to her, "One of these days you'll be driving all around the reservation like the other, elder ladies." She just laughed though. I don't think she really wants to ever drive again.

She can be so funny when she's sharing her memories with me. She once told me that she used to dance with this one guy a lot when she was younger. It was before she met my dad, and she met this boy at a Squaw Dance. They would have them at the local school, and everybody went to these dances to meet up. I guess my mom and this kid were sort of regular partners. She told me, "I always used to tease my partner," and she meant this in a Navajo way. We do that a lot with certain people. She said, "One day I was just dancing away with him and he got really close. I didn't know what to make of it!" (*Laughter*) My mom told me that when they were dancing that day this guy told her, "I'm not going to be able to see you anymore. They told me that they have a girl for me, and I guess I'm supposed to marry her." It was kind of sad, because my mom and this guy had become close friends. Mom described their relationship as kind of like a boyfriend and girlfriend. Anyway, this guy told mom that he was going to have his family chase the horses to this other girl's place. That's what they used to do in order to get married. It was an arranged marriage, and this girl he didn't even know was younger than him… only fourteen or fifteen. He was about five years older than her, and closer to my mom's age.

When mom told me about that guy I told her she'd better brush up on her driving. Because that guy she used to dance with? Well, his wife is the only elderly lady around here that drives a car! She's close to eighty now, but she learned how to drive. Her husband never learned. He never drove a truck or any vehicle at all. Both of them are still alive, so I tell my mom she'd better watch out (*giggles*)

My mom and I talk a lot now, and she's told me she wants to stay in her home. I hope she can just stay where she prefers, but we need to have somebody with her all the time now, in case she falls again. It's probably going to be me who stays with her most of the time. I know it's going to be hard, but I want to take care of her. It's just a lot of driving to go back and forth between her place and my place in Oljeto. I can't complain because I don't know how much longer mom will be with us. I'm glad we're writing down all of the family history, because it will be like she's always with us. She tells a really good story, and I think when you get finished all of our history will be interesting to other people too. One of my friends already told me that she would read it!

I hope people read everything you've written down, and then they'll say, "So that's how it is to grow up as Navajo. Now we know what life is like for them." Maybe it will bring interest to some of the problems we have here on the reservation. Maybe we could earn money to build more health clinics, or even a place where we could be together more as women. We don't really have a place to socialize together, and that's important in our culture. The traditional Dine' ways for women have changed because we're more isolated. I wonder sometimes what will happen to women here on the reservation. Sometimes it seems as if things were better back in my mom's day. Women were always working hard and spending time with the sheep. They could get a lot of exercise, and they ate the right kind of food like corn, squash and peaches. People worked all the time back so they could grow that good food and raise a lot of animals. Back in my mom's day, as soon as the spring came people started working on their cornfields. Then they would put in the rest of their vegetables, and in two weeks had corn. People were very involved in their fields, just pulling weeds and making sure everything got watered. They were always interested in planting. It was part of our culture, and so our ancestors were continually working for the whole year on the land.

Sometimes I wonder what life would be like if we still had that. If only we didn't have so many stores. Nowadays we just say, "Oh, I'm out of food. Let's go to the store." We have vehicles that always need gas. Sometimes I think we'd be better off using horses and wagons again. It's easier to feed a horse and live off the land if the soil is good. Nowadays everybody depends too much on a paycheck, and sometimes we buy things we don't really need. I bet if we didn't have so many "conveniences" we'd be happier. My eldest son Thomas told me that he and his wife would probably stay out here in Monument Valley if we had cornfields to keep, and maybe his own sheep. I would love to live like a family that way.

I think maybe that's why having you write this book is a good idea Coco. It might help people understand the Navajo better, and it's a good way to preserve our history. I know of other families that tell stories similar to ours about Four-Horned Woman. It could be that somebody heard the story from relatives we used to have in Gallup. Retelling the story helps it get around to young people, but it's not like having it printed in a book.

Colette:

The sound of an approaching vehicle interrupted Effie's dream. We both turned to see if a busload of tourists had come to visit Suzie, but Effie smiled when she recognized instead a dusty carload of relatives. "Oh that's my cousin Loretta," she laughed, "she can help out Suzie for a while. I want to show you something before you go." The invitation threw me off a little. As Effie led me from the Shade House back to her mother's brown stucco home I wondered what could possibly be stored away in some mysterious nook. I couldn't imagine what Effie had in mind, but I was always up for some new discovery.

I followed my friend into the house and quickly closed the door to keep the red sand from blowing in; a hopeless gesture, since the floor had already received a light dusting from the morning's activities. Effie brought me into the back room where I rarely ventured. This was the private sanctuary of visiting family members, and the temporary home of Suzie's son Leonard. Effie reached into a makeshift closet, and pushing aside an old horse blanket brought out a shoebox yellowed with age. She brought me back into the main room, and together we sat on Suzie's bed where Effie placed the box between us. Lifting the flimsy lid and gently pulling out the contents Effie revealed a stack of old photographs that looked as old as the box in which they lived. Additional photos had been glued into an old scrapbook Effie explained she kept as a teenager.

There were the usual doodles and drawings on now-limp construction paper. She had embellished some of the photos of herself and friends with penned on make-up, or the occasional set of horns. I felt as if I was traveling back in time as I gazed at pictures of Effie and her siblings. Matching the family stories I'd gathered to the smiling young faces made the Yazzie history much more tangible. There was a grinning teenaged Effie standing next to a very strong and healthy Suzie. Their outfits varied between the styles of the 1960s and traditional dress, yet Suzie was always adorned in Navajo skirt and velveteen blouse with turquoise jewelry around her neck and wrist. We laughed at the hairstyles and at fat baby pictures. I now understood why all of the local girls had crushes on the Yazzie boys. Lonnie and Kee struck their best James Dean poses. Dressed in their slim, tapered pants and sporting thick pompadours the boys looked lean and muscular.

The door opened, and with a gust of wind Suzie entered the house wearing a quizzical expression. "She must have wondered what the heck we were doing in here," Effie laughed. She said something to her mother in Navaho, and Suzie slowly lowered herself to sit next to her daughter on the bed. She smiled and pointed to one of the photos Effie held in her hand. It showed Suzie with a young white man learning to weave. I giggled and teased Suzie, asking through Effie, "Is that your boyfriend?" Suzie giggled and shook her head, but gave no further explanation to the mysterious picture. Instead she pawed through the other photos with Effie, pointing out various family members and giving their names.

Rummaging through the box Effie presented a small snapshot of her father. All of the Yazzies were very good-looking in the photos, but Tully's picture took me by surprise. He was downright handsome with olive, smooth skin and a strong chin. This was the only real photo that the family had of Tully, and I felt honored to finally see the man who had captured Suzie's heart. We stared at the little photograph in silence, and then Effie gently handed it to me. "Can you put that in the book?" she asked me. I looked up at her with surprise. Effie was entrusting me with the only lasting image of her deceased father. I pushed aside the fear that it might come to some harm or even become lost while in my care. Instead I thought of how I could preserve it. "Yeah, this is cool Effie," I stammered, "maybe I could have it blown up and even have copies made for the rest of your family." Effie smiled and nodded while I carefully placed the old, creased photo in a plastic baggie. She giggled when I promised to protect the photo with my life, but we both knew that if anything happened to it there would be nothing left of Tully but a memory.

A sunbeam slowly moved across the cracked window behind us, changing the light within Suzie's home from gold to auburn. The day had been long, and I reluctantly began to pack my things to head back to the lodge. Suzie sat watching me, by now knowing this routine indicated my imminent departure. Slinging my back pack over my shoulder I glanced around the room. Effie stood to accompany out to my car, but first I wanted to say my goodbyes. The traditional way of leaving would mean a discrete exit with perhaps only a nod to Suzie. But I still found it difficult to follow this Navajo protocol, and instead took Suzie's hand in mine and uttered a timid *"Hah go neh"* as my goodbye.

The old woman smiled, and gently wrapped her long fingers around mine in an unconventionally warm farewell. The small calluses Suzie earned from years of carding her own wool brushed against my own smooth palm. Even so, I thought she had the most elegant hands I'd ever seen. Suzie looked toward the bags of fruit and tea I'd delivered that day, and said a big *"ah heh heh"* or "thank you" for all of the supplies. Through Effie I explained that I would return later in the year to see how she was doing. Suzie nodded and said something to Effie that caused her daughter to giggle. "She wants to know how you can keep coming out here alone. She doesn't understand how your husband would allow it!" I never thought to explain to Suzie how I a woman like me could feel free to be gallivanting around the Valley unaccompanied by a man, and I found myself blushing and speechless. Effie just shook her head and giggled again. "Don't worry *Shah kiss*, she laughed and patted my shoulder, "I'll tell my mom that you're a modern woman!" We left Suzie standing in the doorway, and Effie helped me load my jeep with the remaining water and my leftover lunch bag. "One day you gotta let me drive your rental," she said with a sly smile, "it looks like a lot more fun than my one-eyed Ford." Effie's truck sat forlorn and dirty next to my shiny, new jeep. One headlight remained broken from a previous encounter with a cow, giving it the standard Navajo name of such a wounded vehicle. I smiled in agreement and we shared an embrace. As I drove away I stole one last look in the rear view mirror. Effie turned and walked back to the hogan, but Suzie stood in her doorway and waved at the trail of dust I left behind.

CHAPTER 14 – ELVINA, CHANGING WOMAN

"Don't let yesterday use up too much of today." - *Cherokee*

THE LAST BIG ADVENTURE

A full two years passed before I could get out to the Valley once more. Autumn came, and with it the usual rush to prepare my kids for a new school year. Only my twin daughters remained at home now, and soon they would be off to attend a university out of state. My eldest daughter was now married, and my son living and working in a town two hours away. Everything seemed to be changing so quickly. My kids growing up, becoming an empty-nester and finishing my work with the Yazzies…all of it loomed ahead and I didn't feel at all ready for it. And yet, I'd let so much time pass since my last visit out to the Rez.' How could life go by so fast?

With a mixture of sadness and anticipation I made plans for one last trip out to the Valley. I wanted to record the story Effie's youngest daughter, Elvina. She came from one of the youngest generation of Yazzies, and I hoped to get a fresh perspective of life on the reservation. I had spent time with Elvina before, and we got along fairly well. She had the wonderful sense of humor so typical of the Yazzie's, and a certain energy that was contagious when I hung out with her.

My wise and patient husband didn't complain when I informed him I would be traveling out to the Valley yet again. He merely sighed, leaned back in his desk chair and studied me for a moment in silence. "It's the last time Ross," I promised. This was met with a dubious arch of one eyebrow. "No, really," I went on in what I hoped was a convincing manner, "I only have one last interview to do." Ross sighed and shook his head. "Oh I believe it's your last interview," he said with the smile I loved so much. That smile meant he was putting up with me, and I had come to appreciate it. "But I don't believe for a minute that it's your last trip out there," he said softly, turning back to his work.

I thought about Ross and the kids during most of the train ride to Flagstaff. Looking out at the familiar landscape rushing by I realized I was a lucky woman. In a sense I was blessed with two families, and the only problem seemed to be leaving one to spend time with the other! Some of my favorite memories involved the opportunities we could all get together. The whole Waddell clan went on one of the rides led by Don Donnelly through the Valley. Some of the Yazzie kids, now young adults, still remembered sliding down the sand dunes my son and the twins. My kids cherished the memory of experiencing their first snow fall. A picture of the twins running through the yard at Hill House, attempting to catch snowflakes on their tongues, would be forever in my mind. These reunions had given our families a chance to bond, but like all my adventures in the Valley, they ended all too soon.

A WHITE GIRL AT THE SQUAW DANCE
"When the Earth is sick, the animals will begin to disappear; when that happens, The Warriors of the Rainbow will come to save them." — Chief Seattle

I heard a knock at my door just as the afternoon light was dimming. "Would you like to come with us to a Squaw Dance?" she asked, as if it was the most common of invitations. Of course, I had never been asked by my friends to any type of ceremony, though I kept hoping the invitation would someday come. I had read up on the squaw dance a little, but not knowing this Emily explained its purpose. The squaw dance, or *Nda*, was performed for those among the Navajo who felt the need to cleanse themselves of a negative experience, such as a recent encounter with an enemy. "That's really the closest I can come to a definition of it," Emily said, obviously in a hurry to be off. I later received clarification from Ron Maldonado regarding this event. He informed me that the Blessing Way and the Enemy Way were very different and never to be confused. The Blessing Way does not have dances associated with it. By the description I gave him of the event I attended, Ron believed I was at an Enemy Way, also known as *Nda* in the Navajo language.

I told Emily I would love to come, but wondered if it would be appropriate for me to attend, since I was not Navajo. My friend assured me that, so long as I stayed with her and Lonnie, there would be no problem. We agreed to take my car, since it could handle the rough terrain the Yazzies expected to encounter. "These things are always off the beaten path," Lonnie said with a grin. We drove past the park entrance about a mile or so, and then pulled off to a dirt driveway heading into the eastern side of the Valley. Driving and driving down the increasingly rough road I wondered if we were lost, until suddenly we came to a creek surrounded by willows. I was thankful for my little four-wheel drive vehicle as we slogged through the mud and finally made our way to a clearing where about fifty or more people gathered around a huge wood pile. Old Ford trucks and cars in various stages of decay were parked in a large circle. Navajo attendees milled around enjoying picnic meals and conversation. Singers and drummers provided the music for two long lines of dancers, one facing the other. In the middle of the circle, the pyre of logs and brush stood ready for torching later that night. Most of those standing by the cars were women, patiently observing the dance while keeping an eye on the occasional roaming child.

After pulling up to an empty space Emily, Lonnie and I sat in the car for a while and discussed the event that was taking place before us. Sometimes called the "Blessingway" or "Enemyway," this ceremony would last all night and into the next morning. One young woman in the long line of dancers was in attendance there because she had been dating a white man. "It's not unheard of to date someone white," Emily explained, "it's just…different to us, you know? I remember when I was a young woman and sitting with my girlfriends. One of them said that she was having a *Nda* done for her." Emily went on, "We asked her why, and she said it was because she had slept with a white man. My other girlfriend was really surprised and said 'is that all?'" Emily laughed and shook her head, "See, to some people a thing like that is a big deal, and to others it's not. Anyway, I always stuck to dating Navajo guys. They know our traditions and that makes life easier."

Emily reminded me of her courtship with Lonnie in which her suitor made his intentions known by bringing gifts. "He showed up at my door with groceries and firewood for my daughter and me," giggled Emily, "and I was pretty impressed by that." Lonnie grinned at me in the rear view mirror, "Yeah," he said with a laugh "I knew the way to her heart." He went on to tell me the various reasons a Navajo might attend a Squaw Dance. "War veterans come to these dances quite a bit. To our people the taking of a life is a serious act of disharmony. A person might also want to do the Enemyway ceremony if they entered a grave site or an Anasazi ruin," he explained.

After observing for some minutes, the Yazzies told me that it was time to join the group, but they reminded me to be respectful and as inconspicuous as possible. I wondered how I could manage this when I was clearly the only white person attending the dance. The Yazzies slowly guided me along the circle of trucks where I felt the curious stares of everyone I passed. I hadn't dared to take a camera, but now I was wishing that I had at least brought a pen and paper to record something of my experience.

I needn't have worried; the unforgettable evening soaked into my skin and memory. The smell of barbecued mutton tickled my nose, and I realized that I was hungry. But I couldn't muster up the courage to ask anyone for a nibble. Eventually, the crowd seemed to accept my presence, and the focus turned back to the dance. We watched the two lines of Navajo, young and old, dancing toward each other in time, then stepping back again to create a distance between them. I stood transfixed by the way the dancers followed the rhythm of drums and song. I almost failed to hear Emily ask if I would like to join the line! Before I could answer each of them an arm and gently pulled me in.

We easily melded into the group of dancers, some of them grinning at me and the look of utter surprise on my face. As we stepped toward the line of people facing us, I came eye-to-eye with the young woman the Yazzies spoke of when we arrived. She glanced at me beneath long lashes, and then averted her gaze to some far-off point beyond me. A little girl with big, brown eyes appeared in the line to her right, and shyly smiled. I was so delighted to be part of the dance that I didn't notice the sky turning darker. Emily and Lonnie pulled me from the line as easily as they had brought me into it. No one seemed to notice as we stepped up into the truck. As we drove away I saw the light of the bonfire in my mirror. The flames reached for the sky just as we turned into the willows and crossed the river.

On the way back to the Valley we were treated to a magical lightning show. The air was warm and it smelled slightly of rain. I pulled up to Hill House and thanked the Yazzies for the wonderful, new experience. I asked if I would see them the next day, and they promised to come in the morning to join me for breakfast. We said our goodbyes, and as they headed back to Chinle I let myself into the house with the night's events still playing in my head.

THE NEXT GENERATION

"We do not inherit the land from our ancestors; we borrow it from our children. Duty on us to return it to them in the absolute situation." — Unknown Tribe.

I woke up early and bustled around Hill House silently wondering how long it would be before I returned. Maybe it would be to deliver the final manuscript to my second family. In anticipation of my guests arriving I had coffee waiting, when Effie came instead. "I don't know what happened to Lonnie and Emily," she said after giving me a warm hug, "we didn't hear from them, so I figured I'd come and check you out." Accompanying her was Paco, the little dog she'd adopted some time ago and now kept as a constant companion. Paco sniffed at the porch with suspicion, and then curled up in a ball to snoozed in the sunshine. Effie and I sat and sipped our coffee, all the while making plans on how I might get some time to interview her daughter, Elvina. Lonnie and Em were still at home in Chinle, but would be coming up the next day. I'd only planned on two full days for this stay. It didn't leave me much wiggle-room. We finished our coffee and I followed Effie's truck into the park. The morning was clear and warm, so I drove with my window open, allowing the October sun to kiss my face.

As we drove up to Suzie's compound I could already see a small group of Navajo sitting in the Shade House. They peered out between the roughly hewn Juniper branches to see who was approaching. Once they determined we weren't "visitors" they turned back to their conversation. It wouldn't be like the Yazzies to rush out in a mass greeting, and I now preferred this more subdued form of protocol. Sauntering into the Shade House with Effie seemed somehow more genteel. Suzie sat in the corner in an old padded chair. She smiled a greeting and loosely shook the hand I offered. Two small children played with Paco in the sand; too shy to acknowledge me. Leonard nodded his hello, and then slowly made his way back toward the house. I had no way of knowing if he had finished his conversation with Suzie, or if I'd interrupted it, but it didn't really matter. As usual, everyone acted as if I'd only been gone for a day instead of several months. I was used to it now. I stood while Effie spoke with her mother, and watched how the sun pouring through the Shade House branches made sharp designs on the sand floor, only occasionally disturbed by the children and Effie's little dog, Paco.

Effie turned to me and smiled. "We're in luck," she said, grabbing my arm and pulling me from the Shade House to follow Leonard, "My daughter is inside having breakfast." Sure enough, Elvina was enjoying a bowl of cereal and reading a magazine. She looked up and smiled. "Hey stranger," she laughed, "where ya' been?" She looked about the same age as my eldest daughter, Raven, and I wondered how long it would be before she too became a bride. Effie had told me that her daughter had no desire to wed any time soon, and wasn't seeing anyone anyway. "She's been too busy working," was her only explanation. I asked Elvina if she was open to doing an interview. "Oh yeah, I'm the last one, huh?" Elvina laughed. "Okay, but give me a minute to finish my chores."

Effie and I carried the groceries I'd brought to the back of the house, where a new kitchen of sorts was set up to replace the one in the front room. Leonard sat at the table playing solitaire. Since he had always been a man of few words, I was surprised when he smiled at me and asked how I was. This was the first time he'd ever addressed me directly, and Effie explained later that her brother was incredibly shy. After Effie and I piled Suzie's goodies into her pantry I left in search of the new latrine I'd heard Lonnie had constructed the previous week. Sadly, the beautiful new structure had blown over in the windstorm, a testament to nature's power over man's desire to tame her. At a loss for something to do, it seemed a better idea to see if Elvina needed help with her chores. I walked down to the sheep pen situated against the sheer rock monument just next to "Victory Cave." The little lambs remained penned in away from harm, while the sheep had been put out to graze.

Playing amongst the lambs was a number of puppies that I assumed were the offspring of all the sheep dogs out guarding the rest of the herd. Elvina explained that the family allowed these pups to grow up with the lambs in order to encourage their instinct to protect them. Fluffy in their winter coats, they played a spirited game of tag with the lambs and each other. One particularly determined puppy held tight to the head of a lamb that refused to play. Another pup was stretched out in the sun sound asleep amidst the melee. Oblivious to the chaos around him, he kicked his little paws in a dream. Two lambs huddled for warmth under their larger friend, who stood gazing out of the fence. Another two focused their energies on a salt lick.

Elvina and I just watched and laughed at the scene. She pointed out one lamb that had been born blind and stood alone. Since it was rejected by the others, she wasn't sure this lamb would survive. My heart broke for the little guy as it trotted around, baaing over and over as if asking a perpetual question. As Elvina continued her chores I realized there wasn't much I could do to help her. The young lady knew exactly what she was doing and I merely got in the way. She worked at filling large bins used for watering the animals. The barrels in the truck were higher than the storage containers by the sheep pen, so gravity allowed water to flow through a hose from one to the other. Elvina tipped the water barrel to catch the last of the precious liquid, and then saved the small leftovers for Suzie's wash basin back at the house. She told me that during the summer months people could wait in line for water at the well for up to two hours or more. Elvina left early in the morning in order to obtain her share without the wait. The longer days meant that she could return to the well as late as eight in the evening. "I won't go there after that though," she said, shaking her head, "Strange things happen there when it gets dark."

As we walked back to the hogan Elvina told me she and her mother planned to work the next day cooking fry bread for a large group of visitors. "I need to help my mom," she said, "but maybe later on I could come to your place and we could go for a run." I happily accepted her offer, and hoped I'd be able to keep up with the girl who was ten years my junior. Paco had been trailing behind us, so I made a little practice run with him while Elvina slowly followed us in the truck back to the house. We both arrived back at Suzie's laughing and I struggled to breathe in the thin air. After stomping the red dirt off of our shoes we entered to find Suzie sitting in front of the crackling wood stove, nibbling on one of the cheese sticks I brought her. She had moved her bed closer to the fire, which allowed more space for her numerous piles of yarn, fabric pieces, finished rugs and knick-knacks. Elvina settled in with her grandmother, and she allowed me to clip the microphone onto her collar. Suzie smiled and nodded at the familiar routine.

I knew that the microphone could intimidate people. So far I had been successful in getting the Yazzies to forget about the little device, but I sensed Elvina was not altogether comfortable with it. According to Effie, Elvina was hesitant to do the interview, feeling that she had little to say. When we first met I did notice that Effie's daughter tended to clam up in conversations that were one-on-one. We had become closer over these few years however. I was confident my young friend would be happy to provide, not only her own story, but a fresh outlook on Navajo life. As the latest generation of Yazzies her opinion and thoughts about the future were vital to the family story, so I did my best to put Elvina at ease.

The family called her "Yvonne" at times, leading to a lot of confusion on my part. I was initially introduced to "Elvina," then after many months heard her called Yvonne and wondered if I'd met her twin! Making matters even more confusing, I tended to mix her up with her sister, Erlene. "Why can't you people just stick with one name?" I once yelled to Effie. It was just like their language; no hard, fast rules and many different meanings. Effie only laughed at me. "You white people are easily confused!" she teased.

Now I gathered up the few notes of questions I hoped would get her young daughter talking. Initially, Elvina comes across as a shy person, but I'd spent enough time with her to know she felt very strongly about certain things. Once I got to know her she was easy to talk to, and there were times when I was working with Suzie when she seemed perfectly comfortable just watching and listening. Elvina struck me as a very bright and kind person who cared very much for Suzie, her mother, and the rest of her family. At the time of her interview she was in her late twenties, but looked much younger. She had the same light skin of her mother and grandmother, and her long dark hair was pulled into a careless ponytail. Tucking some rebellious strands back into place, she began her story.

ELVINA SPEAKS: Growing up Dine'
"We are all one child spinning through Mother Sky." — Shawnee

Elvina:
My real name is Elvina Jean Holiday. I guess that's what you would call my full name. My mom named me Elvina, but I never liked it. When I was younger a friend of mine teased me about it. She said to me, "Is that a hippie name? Was your mom a

hippie?" She laughed when she said this, but I didn't think it was very funny. I asked my mom if Elvina was a hippie name, but she said, just looked at me like I was crazy and said she didn't think so. Anyway my grandma, Suzie couldn't say "Elvina," so she's the one that started to call me Yvonne. I like that name better. I was born May 23rd, 1975. I'm twenty-eight now, but people always think I'm a lot younger. My dad, Tom Holiday, was with us up until I was ten years old. I loved him, but I thought it was a good thing when he left. He was drinking all the time and I never really thought he was much of a father. When he left for good I just told him, "Adios!" (*Elvina laughed*), I thought of my uncles as my real fathers. I'm closest to the youngest uncle, Kee. He was the one that was always there for me.

I remembered my dad leaving when I was ten, but my earliest memory is when I was about eight years old. I used to spend the summers with my grandma, Suzie, and I think those were the best years. It was sort of like a job for me to help her out, but we made it fun. We dressed up for the tourists, and that's how we made money. Us kids would go up to the hogan in traditional dress and sit by grandma, and people would take our pictures. We thought it was kind of cool, and we made pretty good money. That was a good thing too, because we didn't have much for clothes and things like that. Back then there was a lot of "*bilaga'ana*" or "white people." They came over to see us every summer, and during a good season we could make up to one hundred dollars each! Nowadays there are a lot fewer tourists, and you can really see the difference in how much people have to spend. I think the economy is bad here and around the nation because of the war, but even before that things were getting bad. One problem is that other Navajo are building hogans and offering weaving demonstrations like Suzie does. Suzie's way out here in the middle of nowhere, and sometimes the tour guys don't bring visitors by her place.

Also, people's attitudes have changed. When I was little, pretty much everyone living here got along. Now it's kind of weird. Some of the locals don't want the tour business or horseback riding groups coming in any more. A few people think that it's destroying the environment here in the Valley. They think the amount of traffic hurts the trees and bushes and the plants that the sheep depend on. When I look around at people living here I notice that a lot of things have changed. It's really sad.

I liked the old days when I could put on a skirt and a velveteen blouse and hang around the hogan. I was comfortable with it because I had seen my grandmother dressed like that. To me it seemed like a very natural way to dress. I guess as a kid I was really playing dress up, but it still felt like a normal thing to do. Suzie always used to tell us to sit nicely when the tourists came. She would say, "Be polite, and don't pull your skirt up!" (*Elvina giggled*). She disciplined us if we didn't behave ourselves.

Out of all the visitors we had there was one guy who really stuck in my mind. When the tourists came in I always looked at their shoes, never at their faces. There was just something about the different kinds of shoes they wore that fascinated me. The soles made different kinds of tracks on the sandy floor of the hogan. I used to imagine things in the art that they made with their shoes. But one guy I looked at really surprised me. When I finally looked at his face I noticed that he had no eyes! No eyes at all were there, just skin. I was staring I guess, and when I realized I was being rude I looked down again. I think he sensed that I had been staring, and he said, "Do you want to feel my eyes?" He took my hands and let me touch his face. It was weird. It felt like smooth skin. He said that he was born like that. That was one of the things I liked about staying with my grandma. I met a lot of people that had something really different about them.

I was talking to a friend recently about how my family used to make money. Not all kids on the reservation grew up like that. My friend thought it was the most interesting thing she'd ever heard. Most kids went out to the Valley just to have fun, but at a young age I already had responsibilities. I enjoyed it, but it was a job. I really didn't know what I was going to do with that money, so I just saved it. The job and saving the money became sort of like a habit. At the end of the summer we took our money and went shopping for school clothes. That was nice.

I eventually went to boarding school like my mom and her brothers, but by then most of the faculty were Navajo. When you're surrounded by the same kind of people it's interesting to meet somebody different. I think that's why working with my grandma during the summer was good for me. I got to see what other people looked like. I didn't know much about other languages because we all spoke Navajo. That's just how we all communicated. I didn't want to even learn English until I started to work at Suzie's hogan. I guess that's real different from how my mom and uncles grew up. They were forced to speak English in school.

A PROUD HERITAGE

"We, the great mass of the people, think only of the love we have for our land. We do love the land where we were brought up. We will never let our hold to this land go. It would be like throwing away our mother that gave us birth." — Letter from Aitooweyah to John Ross, Principal Chief of the Cherokees.

I grew up just like my mom and uncles. We took care of the sheep for my grandma. We had a lot more sheep and goats back then than we do now. During the summer there were always some lambs that had come during the spring, and we had to watch out for them. Some of the lambs lost their mothers or for some reason the mother had disowned the lamb, so we had to feed them with a bottle of milk. It was hard to take care of them as babies and then watch them get butchered later on. I never could bear to watch it. When the meat was cooked though, we all ate it. It smelled so good and we were usually pretty hungry. Eventually we started to learn from my mom how to butcher. She would have us hold a part that she was cutting off just so we would get used to it. She would explain that this was our food and we shouldn't be squeamish about it. My mom has really strong hands, and she can butcher a sheep without any problem even now. When I was a kid it was our job to carry the stomach sack far away from the hogan. It could be sort of smelly, and eventually the wild animals would haul it away. Anyway, we got used to it. It was all part of the chore of putting a meal together.

Every morning during the summer we had to wake up early and let the sheep out. Then we had to run back to the house to feed the dogs so that they could go after the sheep and keep an eye on them. After they went on their way we could eat some breakfast. If the sheep didn't come back at the end of the day we had to go out looking for them. We walked past the first hill and sometimes they would be right there on their way back. They usually knew when it was time to come home. If they were far away we had to hike way out there in the sand and chase them back to the corral. I was about seven when I started riding horses, and I still ride sometimes. I still like it.

At night my grandma would tell a lot of stories. Usually Suzie would tell us about this crazy old Mexican guy who wandered around stealing people's crops. He looked for money and food to steal, but in the end he always wound up with nothing. I think this was a legend that she used to teach us that you can't get something for nothing; that you have to work for things. She had so many stories about our ancestors, and she still tells those stories. A lot of times I didn't pay attention. My mind would wander because I was so young and daydreaming about something else. Just the other day she told me about the time that she met my grandfather. I said to her, "You never told me that!" She said, "Oh yes I did! You just weren't listening all the time. You remember what I told you here and there, but you always got the whole story." My *Nah lee* can't tell all the old stories anymore though. She complained to me about it recently. She said, "Now I'm just like a kid, and that's how I remember things; just a little at a time."

I lived in the Valley all of my young life; up until I was nine years old and went to boarding school. School was about thirty miles away, but at least it was closer than when my mom and uncles went. My school in Keyenta is called Community School now, and it's still a boarding school. I guess I was pretty young when I started there. I was only six and I still don't know why they started us so young in those days. I began in a sort of kindergarten, but I liked staying at my grandma's place better. When I was living in the Valley with Suzie we had bunk beds in the room where my uncle Leonard is now. Just like today, there was no running water or electricity. If we wanted to bathe we used this round, silver tub. My mom would heat up the water for us on the stove and pour some cold in to make it warm. I liked taking a bath. My mom said we weren't stubborn as kids and whatever had to be done we just got it over with. So taking a bath was no big deal and it actually felt good.

My mom was pretty laid back and didn't really get mad at us most of the time. She wasn't around much because she had to work to support us. It was really my grandmother that raised us kids. She loved us, but she was strict so we did what she asked us. It wasn't too bad because there was always time in between chores to play and climb rocks. I think that's pretty much how my mom lived too, when she was growing up. I'll tell you one thing; playing on those rocks will destroy a kid's clothes. We would slide down the rocks and tear holes in our pants every time, (*giggles*). It sure was fun though.

Sometimes we liked to take our toy chiddies, the little cars that were called "Matchbox," and make roads for them to go on in the sand. We would create little towns and play in the sand all day. I was never really into dolls; sort of like my mom I guess. We had Barbie dolls, and we played with them for a little while. But pretty soon we'd get bored and throw them aside to get the chiddies out. My dad was still around at this time, but it's weird how I don't really remember him. My mom always used to tell me, "Yeah, he was there all the time when you were a little kid," but I don't remember him being there. I do remember he worked a little bit as a tour guide. He would introduce the *bilaga'anas* to us, so they could get a photograph of us in our clothes. But half the time I don't think that he was really there like a real dad.

I do remember watching the sheep a lot though. When we went out we never got lost. It's sort of surprising because we were really young and we wandered far away to find the sheep. I was never scared being out there on my own, but we did believe in a sort of "Big Foot" creature that was said to be around. (*Elvina laughed*), we would use our imaginations and find "Big Foot" tracks in the sand. My grandma Suzie would say, "You kids are full of baloney. There aren't any tracks out there." We knew better though, because she was the one who told us about Skinwalkers. We believed her, and I wanted to see one but I never did.

There was this one time when a lot of us were staying at my grandma's house, and I'm pretty sure I saw something. My cousin Loretta was about seventeen then and she was staying with us. It was almost dark, and all us kids were outside playing when all of a sudden we saw a light-blue thing coming out from behind the Big Wheel Mesa. It was a light that shone all the way across the mesa in a big, blue stream. We said to each other, "What is that?" And Loretta said, "It might be something like a U.F.O." We'd heard a couple of things about those kinds of things, so we looked at this light real closely and waited for something to happen. I don't even remember how long it was there exactly, but the whole time it just shined away. All of a sudden it just disappeared! That was mysterious, and we were scared from it. We ran into the house after that, and kept looking out the window. It was scary because my mom and grandma weren't there. We were all by ourselves, so we stayed in that house.

If there had been any trouble there was no way to really defend ourselves. But the grown-ups sometimes had to leave, and we were so isolated they figured there was nothing that could bother us I guess.

Colette:

I could not help thinking of what a coward I had been the other night. There I was, shivering in bed over every creak and groan of the old Hill House, when really I had nothing to fear. If Suzie and her grandchildren could face the mysteries of the Valley then why couldn't I at least handle staying at the lodge like a brave *bilaga'ana*? I pictured Elvina giggling at how I'd overreacted, and decided that would not share the story of that particular night with her.

THE VALLEY HAS SECRETS
"After dark, all cats are leopards." - Zuni

Most of the time we felt safe, but out there a lot of strange stuff would happen. We figured there would always be things we couldn't explain, just because it was the Valley and so mysterious. I remember one time when my sister came back from a walk that she and her friend were taking out in the same area where we always played. It was June or July and really hot. They went walking where the dam used to be, and they had been gone for quite a while. All of a sudden, they came racing back to the house where the rest of us were hanging out. We said to them, "Wow, you must have run back fast!" We could tell by their expressions that they had seen something, so we asked them what had happened. They said, "It's a good thing we climbed up on the highest rocks out there." We asked why, and they said, "That way we could see this weird thing from a safe distance."

That's when they told us they had seen creatures that looked like panthers! They were big and catlike. My sister described them as all black, and they were wandering around the shady areas. They were minding their own business in a pack of five. She said it was as if they were just looking for a place to rest, then they just took off. They went over the sand dunes and walked away. My sister and her friend figured they should get out of there, so they ran for home. I asked her over and over, "Are you making it up?" She would always say, "No. We really saw something!" Even now I believe her. This happened in broad daylight too, which is twice as freaky. If it were the nighttime you might think that the light was playing tricks on you. But this was right in the middle of the day.

It's really beautiful out here, and we're all used to how quiet it gets, but sometimes I think my grandma gets scared when she's staying all by herself. By the time she turned seventy she started to think about it more. Before that we used to leave her out here by herself all the time, and it didn't bother her. She always said, "Yeah, go ahead and take off. I'm fine here by myself," and we'd go to Goulding's or wherever. But when she got older she started to think about what could happen if there was an emergency. Just today she said to me, "You better get back before dark. I don't want to be here alone." I know that she gets especially nervous at night. When she was younger she was alone out here all the time, but I guess that was different. I don't blame her. I spent the night alone out here recently, by accident. I thought Suzie was out there alone so I went to be with her. I got there just before dark, but she was gone! Somebody had already come by and taken her into town. I had been dropped off, and I thought mom was coming back to get me, but she never showed up.

I was so tired, but I was too scared to fall asleep. The house wasn't even open. The whole place was locked up. I tried to open the windows, but it was all closed up tight. As a last resort I went into the Shade House and tried to sleep on the little bed with some blankets that were always there. I couldn't believe I was sleeping out there alone. I covered my head with the blankets and just hid. I kept hearing weird sounds, and I jumped at every little thing. The hogan would have been much more comfortable. There are no windows in there, so it seems safer. I finally did fall asleep, but it wasn't comfortable. I don't think I'd ever sleep out there alone again.

Colette:

It seemed like such a personal thing to hear Elvina speak about the strange occurrences she witnessed in the Valley. I thought back to the day we drove together to Suzie's and the conversation turned to the Skinwalker legend. Elvina explained to me then about even admitting to a belief in these creatures might give them power over you. Even then she struck me as a person who hovered between two worlds, the Western and the Navajo. Elvina managed to balance between those worlds very well, and I admired her commitment to both her culture and her family. Just like her mother and grandmother, Elvina loved the Valley, and she was always excited to discuss the various changes and improvements that took place at the Yazzie compound.

Elvina:

Now they're talking about moving the old Shade House because the *Bilaga'ana* keep wandering over from the hogan to look in. The new Shade House is going to be further away to discourage that. It's our private space, and Suzie doesn't like how people sometimes poke around there. She's put up with it for a long time. There's a difference between the time Suzie demonstrates her weaving and the time she sits to rest for lunch and time with her family. Other than that one scary night I always loved the Shade House. I played there a lot when I was a kid.

Back then I also hung out with my sister a lot of the time. My oldest brother played a little too rough, so we let my younger brother hang out with us too. We felt bad for him, because Thomas was always making him cry. We protected him and told my older brother to go do something else on his own. Back then my mom tried to spend time with us as much as she could. She was always there when she didn't have to work. That's when she taught me how to weave, but my grandma was the one who really encouraged me. If I decided all of a sudden I didn't want to weave my grandma stepped in.

She set up a loom for me and encouraged me to keep it up. It was hard at first. I didn't even want to touch the loom because I thought it wasn't right for me, but my mom said it had been made especially for me. She told me this was why I had to finish a rug on it. She bought me all these different colored yarns and told me to start of just making lines. So that's what I did. My first attempt was crooked and funny looking, but I was proud of it, (*she laughs*). My grandma Suzie still has that rug. I was only about eleven when I did it, but after that I started to do more of them. I really wanted to do a good job the next time, so I started to learn how to do the "Mittens" monument really well. My mom or grandma would just talk me through it and say, "String this piece of yarn, then this one and that one…" That's how I learned to do it right.

I've even sold some of them. So far I've made about five rugs, and I just finished one last week. I'm trying to make another one for my sister. She's going to come out to see us this summer and I want to have it for her then. I was about fifteen when I sold my first rug. It was pretty small, but it felt good to get paid for my work. I kept thinking to myself, 'that rug of mine could be somewhere in Germany, in someone's home far away.' We probably have rugs all over the world by now. People like to decorate their places with our arts and crafts. I see wedding baskets hung up on the walls all over the place, but you're not really supposed to do that. They're supposed to stay flat, but they're not Navajo so it's okay. Even my mom has fake ones on her wall for decoration.

ELVINA'S SCHOOLING: Same story, different ending

"In age, talk; in childhood, tears." — Hopi

I got used to doing things around my grandma's place, and I really liked it out there, but then I got the news I had to go to school. When my mom first told me about boarding school I thought it would be pretty cool. I thought it might be good to try something different, but then I heard the dorm maids were really strict. I was worried about that, and when my mom took me to the school it was scary. I cried and hung onto my mom. I even hung onto the door so they wouldn't take me from the hogan. That's how scared I was. It's funny to think about it now, but as a kid it felt pretty bad to leave everything I loved. The first week I hated it. I was counting the days until Friday.

I found out the dorm maids really were mean ladies. They were all in their forties, and I was afraid of them. If you ran down the hall, one of them just popped out and pulled on your hair to stop you. If you forgot to clean your teeth they would make you brush with soap so that you wouldn't forget again. I couldn't understand how they could be so mean when they were all Navajo too. When we first got there they would baby us because we were so homesick. They tried to comfort us, but after a while when they got tired of it. That's when they started to mistreat us. One time I came back late from a weekend at my grandma's place, and I didn't have time to shower or clean up much before I left the hogan. My mom had to just drop me off, and I thought I was going to go straight to bed, so I was putting on my nightgown. All of a sudden here comes the dorm maid yelling at me, "Get into the shower!"

She put on cold water and threw me in. She got this big toilet brush and told me to scrub with it. She hit me so hard in the face with it I almost passed out. While I was trying to recover she began to shake me and screamed, "Get busy and clean up!" When I thought I was through she came over and pulled on my hair, and yelled at me some more. She said, "Wait a minute. I have to look through your hair for lice." Then she said something that I'll never forget. She told me, "You're just like your mom." She said it like it was a bad thing to be like my mom. My mom was tough as a kid, and she got beat up a lot. I thought it was very strong of her to keep her head up no matter what. Back then people were talking behind her back, saying her father was a *yahna slachi*, a skinwalker. He wasn't, that's just what they said. Rumors go around like that sometimes. Anyway, when that lady started to insult my mom I remembered something that she told me before I left for my first week at school. My mom said, "No matter how mean the dorm maids are to you, don't cry in front of them. Never let them see that they got to you." I just glared at that lady and she backed down. She just said, "Don't give me that look," but she knew I wasn't going to take it. I learned from a lot of other people that school was always like that in the beginning.

The food they gave you was terrible. I hated the meat they served. They told us it was ham, but I'm not sure what it really was. Some days they had good tasting food like burritos and Spanish rice. They were trying to mix it up a little I guess. But most days they just threw anything at us. We used to drink all of our milk, and then stuff the grossest food into the carton. We never did get caught, but we had to do it fast, because they checked our trays to make sure we finished everything. They would only let us go if our trays were clean. The few good things we got were vegetables, like green beans, and fruit. Sometimes we got peaches, and most of it was canned, but we liked it. You sort of got used to canned stuff, because out here was too expensive to get fresh food. Kids still go crazy over oranges around here.

I looked forward to the weekends and tried to hang on until then. One girl never went home on Friday, and I felt so sorry for her. She always wanted to go but her parents never came for her. One weekend my mom checked her out with us, as a favor for the girl's parents. It turned out they just never had a vehicle to go get her! These days it's easier. If a kid is still at school after everyone else has left they just put him in a van and take him home themselves. Some of my relatives' kids still go to that school, but now there are also day schools available. The only thing that hasn't changed is the bus rides. They're still real long. After I became a teenager I was lucky to attend high school in Monument Valley, and I graduated in 1993.

While I was at boarding school my brothers and my sister attended too. The boys were in a separate dorm, but my sister made me feel more comfortable. I started making friends and things got better after that. We all had the same ideas about the dorm maids, and we made up names about them like "Darth Vadar." The other girls told me, "You don't have to be scared of those ladies. If you make fun of them then they're not so bad." As school continued I began to like it more. We had basic classes like math and English, but my favorite class was P.E. I liked to play basketball, and cross-country, but never volleyball. It hurt my wrists to hit the ball. In cross-country we ran all over Keyenta. There was a four-mile trail that we did in three laps. When we competed I always came in third or fourth place, but I didn't care because I was having fun. I don't remember what my fastest mile was, but it was under twenty something minutes, and my coach was really proud of me.

Colette:

I was delighted to learn of yet another interest that Elvina and I had in common. I ran in the cross-country team when I returned to college in my thirties. I loved the feeling of pushing myself and improving my time. I especially enjoyed learning to use the terrain to my advantage, and I shared with Elvina how fun it was to overtake my competition on the uphill. Now it seemed even more important that we take that run together through the Valley, though I risked certain defeat from my younger advisory. I asked Elvina if she ever saw her father around the Valley.

Elvina:

Well, whenever I came home from school I went to Suzie's place, and we stayed there until I was about eleven years old. That year my mom got a trailer, and she moved it by my father's parents' place over near the high school. It's still there, way up by the hills. It's a red trailer and my dad lives in it now. I sometimes see my dad, but he doesn't ask about me. At first, when I was younger he would say hi to me, and "How are you doing?" Now he acts as though he doesn't know us. He'll sometimes talk to my brother, but that's about it. He remarried to another lady who has kids of her own. Anyway, while we were living in that trailer we would visit Suzie almost every weekend.

345

My uncle Leonard was usually there with her to help out, so it was never a problem for us to come by because he could watch us.

So things just kind of went along like that while I went to boarding school. By the time I was in the fourth grade my teachers started to suggest I advance a grade up. They told me that I really belonged in an upper level where I would be more challenged. I ended up skipping sixth grade and went on to seventh. When I was twelve years old I was able to switch transfer to the local school here in M.V. I liked that it was so close to my family, but it felt weird to be so much younger than the rest of the kids. Luckily I knew most of them pretty well, and I was good at making friends. My favorite subject in school was still sports, but after that I liked English the best. I remember they used to show those old films…you remember them? You had to thread the film around the projector, and sometimes it sounded like they were talking underwater. They had us study the Navajo language with those films. They were teaching it in the schools by then, and they even had films in our language that taught the Creation story. I used to love watching those.

I joined the Indian Club then too. They called it that because we learned things about our culture when we went to meetings. We would perform in these little talent shows, to do whatever we did best. You could tell a poem or sing or whatever you wanted to do. I had long hair, so they liked to put me in front of people to perform. Most of the other girls had bangs like Briget Fonda. That was a really popular look back then. But I always kept my hair long and they thought that worked better when doing traditional stuff. I didn't really want to be in front, but they would tell me, "You look really pretty with your long hair. Get up there and do something with yourself."

It makes me laugh now, but they made me sing. I made all kinds of excuses to get out of it. I told them that I was sick or whatever worked. But most of the time they forced me to get up there and sing. I hated it for a very long time. It took me a while to eventually appreciate Corn Grinding Songs and stuff like that. Those were the kinds of songs they made me sing, and I was shy about it. Especially when they put me up there with a guy! They told me, "This boy will escort you up to the stage, and then you'll sing with him." It was so embarrassing. I was tormented and tortured in this way.

Colette:

It was fascinating to learn how much the curriculum had changed in the Navajo schools by the time Elvina attended. It seemed that the transition occurred just as Effie's daughter transferred to her local school. Elvina's story at first mirrored that of her mother's; complete with the separation from home and a shower beating from the woman assigned to look after her. What a pleasing twist of fate that Elvina could break the pattern of abuse so common in the boarding school system, and finally enjoy the benefits of a more traditional day school. I was curious to know if there were any other similarities between Effie's girlhood experiences and those of her daughter. I asked her if she had ever had a crush on a boy at school.

Elvina:

I don't remember having a boyfriend even as I got older. I wasn't really into guys when I was younger. I did have encounters with them every now and then. There was one guy I recognized from school just recently. He works as an EMT in Keyenta now.

346

I saw him there and wondered why this guy kept looking at me. All of a sudden, one of the nurses called him by his name, Gayland Tracy. That's when I recognized him! I thought, 'That's the guy we used to beat up in school!" He and I got into a fight one time. I was only about eight or nine years old, so it was when I was still staying at boarding school. This Gayland kid was pulling my hair and flicking spit wads at me. I couldn't understand why he was pestering me, and I didn't like it one bit.

Finally, one of my friends told me, "The reason he does those things to you is because he likes you." We were in line for lunch one day and he patted my butt! I got so mad, and I turned around to take care of business. I hit him really hard in the stomach, and he couldn't breathe for a long time. I was so mad at him that I didn't care. All of his friends were so surprised. They asked me, "What did you do that for?" I said, "Well, he asked for it!" He was rolling on the floor holding onto his stomach. I said to him, "That's what you get for bugging me!" I got in so much trouble. They told me not to eat lunch and to go back to the dorm, but I didn't care. I was happy that I did that to him because I was sticking up for myself.

The next day, believe it or not, it happened again! (*Giggles*), I guess he was pretty persistent. This time he just jumped on me. He started to beat on me like a real fight, just like I was a guy! I remember I was on the ground, and I got a hold of a whole big handful of sand. I threw it in his eyes and he fell down away from me. He was crying because I guess his eyes were burning from it. I kicked him once, while I could, and that was the end of it. I didn't want to get in trouble again, so I just walked away. Anyway, when I saw this guy in Keyenta I guess he recognized me. I didn't know what to do, so I just said, "Hi Gayland." He looked at me and said, "Don't I know you?" I didn't really want to say how he knew me, so I just said, "Well back in boarding school we kind of knew each other."

His eyes popped open, and he said, "That was you?!" We both sat there and laughed, and then we started talking and catching up. He told me that he was married, and I was thinking, 'Oh my God, this is the guy I used to hate!' He was such a nice guy, and I felt a little guilty for punching him that one time, and for throwing the sand in his face. And hey, it's not like all the guys teased us. They had dances every now and then, where you could meet other kids your age. There were some pretty cool guys there, but mostly I hung out with my friends. It was always just us girls hanging out. Most of the time I didn't understand what happens between a guy and a girl. My mom was working so much that she didn't have time to talk to me about that kind of thing. We never had "The Big Talk" you're supposed to have.

I was sort of confused about how to act around guys because of that. I relied on my friends to explain to me what was going on. They would tell me why a guy was acting weird, or treating me differently. They taught me a lot of those things, but it was the dorm maid told us what would happen when we got our periods. She told us what would happen and about womanhood...all that stuff. My mom did tell me about *Kinaalda*.' In a way, I wanted one, and in another way I didn't. I was kind of shy, and I didn't want all that celebration over something that was personal to me. My mom told me how it would go about, and she said, "People are going to be watching you, and of course they'll know that you have your period." I really didn't want to go through with it because of that. My sister had hers though. I think she was more secure about it.

Now that I think back on it, I wish that I'd had it done, just because it would have been appropriate to recognize my mom and my grandmother at that time. It's a lot of work to get all the supplies together, and then the ceremony takes two or three days. You have to try and stay awake all night, and then you do your run early in the morning. Back in the old days they wore less jewelry, so they could run pretty far. Nowadays the girls wear more silver and turquoise, plus they're probably not used to running around as much, so they don't go as far. They still tie the girl's hair back in a simple pony tail, and when you're running it sometimes falls out. My sister ran as far as the really big mesa by Suzie's, then back again. She also went east as far as she could. When I decided not to have the ceremony done I thought that it would hurt my grandmother the most, but she said it was okay. It would have been difficult, because my mom was working so much at the time, and Suzie was attending to the sheep. She was still pretty healthy back then, but she had a lot of responsibility. I know that my grandmother wanted me to have it done, but she understood why I didn't want to. She just told me that it was my decision.

As I got closer to finishing school I thought about going to college. One of my counselors encouraged me to take a summer job made available through the school. The job lasted from May to July, so anyone who was interested could fill out an application from the front office. I wanted to work and earn some money, so I signed up and got accepted that summer to work at the Oljeto Chapter House. Mostly I swept and mopped the floors, picked up trash around the Chapter House, watered the trees, and stuff like that. I also got to do some administrative things, like help the secretary to answer phones and type up papers. As I was growing up I always wanted to be a nurse like my mom. I wanted to follow in her footsteps. But now I think of doing other things. I would still like to work in a clinic. But I also found out that I like to work with kids. Maybe I could teach school like my Uncle Lonnie and Aunt Emily. I would like to do something like that. Even my Uncle Kee taught school at one time.

I went to NAU in Flagstaff first, but then I realized that it was too far away. I really wanted to be closer to home, so I came back to stick around my family more. One of my teachers talked to me about my options, and she said I could go to Dine' College in Tuba City, or to Blanding, which isn't as far away. So I went to the College of Eastern Utah in Blanding, and I graduated with my Associates Degree in 1997. Now I'm trying to go for my Bachelor's Degree. I'd like to go back to Fort Lewis, but I'm looking into an extension program that you can do as an independent study right here in the Valley. I checked on some classes recently, but I got distracted. If I went back I would work on getting my teaching credentials.

While I was going to college in Blanding I visited with my family as much as I could. I spent time with my grandma a lot, and just hung out with my brothers and sister. There are four of us kids in the family. My brother Thomas is the oldest, then me, then my sister Erlene, then my younger brother Tim. Thomas is married to Rene and Erlene just had a baby. My sister Erlene was always a little different from me. She didn't really know what to do with her life after she graduated. I think whatever she put her mind to she could accomplish, and she did try different things to see what she'd like. One of her friends suggested they go to school in Nebraska, and they stayed for a year. I thought Erlene's friend would end up staying there, but it was the other way around!

She's twenty-six, a year younger than I am, and she's getting married this year. The last time I went over to Nebraska to see her she looked older than me. When she was going to school out there she met the man she's going to marry. He's the father of her baby and stationed in Iraq now. We're all real happy he'll be coming home soon. Now that my sister is raising a child she's much more responsible. When I visit her she looks different to me. She used to be really slender, but now she has a fuller face. You can tell she's a mother. When I was in grade school we were asked what we wanted to do when we grew up, and it never occurred to me to be a mother. Not right away anyway. At that time I told my mom and my teacher that I wanted to wait until I was thirty to get married and have a family

I think that if I did get married I would do it the traditional way. Most girls around here like a modern wedding, but not me. One of my brothers is a Christian, so he got married in a church. My sister is Seventh Day Adventist, but I think she's still planning to have a traditional wedding, and she'll probably do it in Suzie's hogan.

ELVINA'S DREAM

"In our every deliberation we must consider the impact of our decisions on the next seven generations." – Form the Great Law of the Iroquois Confederacy.

Staying home, staying true

I think people come back here to the reservation to be with their family. Even my sister's friend came back from Nebraska because her mom got sick, and she was the only one who could help. It seems like most people come back here eventually. They prefer living here where their ancestors lived. One of my friends got her PhD, and both of her parents raised her sort of like an Anglo. They told her that it would be best to find work outside the reservation, because here there's nothing. There's no way to support yourself. So now she's up in Tucson, but I think she'd rather be here.

I grew up in a very traditional way, so this place really pulls at me. It's weird, but I notice that most of the kids living here now don't want to go elsewhere. It's kind of sad though, because there are less young people here on the reservation than when I was growing up. They have to leave and search for jobs. I don't think they want to go, but they have to in order to survive. For now, I work at the high school here in M.V., and I hear things from the students. Two of them came back here during Spring Break and actually tried to find work in the area. But it was just too hard. Most people work at places like Goulding's Lodge. It used to be that the students could find work there, but now businesses don't want to hire the young people. There are too many older residents who want to work, and they're here year round if work is available.

So if you're young, where do you get the money to pay for a house? When kids realize there's no way then they start packing up for Phoenix or Salt Lake. The cities always have opportunities for work, but when the young people go to the cities their culture disappears. I see that a lot. There's no way to have a ceremony or speak Dine.' There's nobody to encourage you to keep up with the songs and prayers. There were other things to distract a person from Dine' culture when I was growing up. People made the choice to practice other religions that have come to the rez. Now everyone is worried about losing different parts of our culture. The topic of listening to your elders didn't used to come up much, but you see it in the local press and on bulletin boards all over the place now.

It's like the parents now realize that their kids are growing apart from them. Parents are now encouraged to read to their kids in Navajo, and kids are told to respect their elders. We used to take better care of our mothers, but now with all the kids living elsewhere it's too difficult. I see it a lot, and teenagers do what they want now. They don't stick around home as much. They hang around their friends more, and they don't help around the house. When I talk to my cousins I hear about how their relationships with their moms are not as good as it could be. Nowadays kids question their elders more. They have access to television, and that influences them a lot. I hear more now about teenage pregnancy, and it seems so sad to see girls having to give up school.

I try to encourage girls I know at the school to be careful, but they sometimes get pregnant anyway. Then they have to find any old job to support their baby. Maybe the elders should be more forceful in teaching these kids how to grow up, or maybe the young people think they can handle having a family when they're seventeen or eighteen or nineteen years old. It's a problem now because they have to work harder than our mothers and grandmothers did to get by. These girls don't have the family infrastructure that used to exist. Eventually they have to find work off the rez, and that puts their family even further away.

I see a decrease in traditional ceremonies as well. It's been a big issue here and I think others see it too. I heard on the local station KTNN that most of the medicine on the rez now is incomplete. A lot of ceremonies, prayers and songs have been forgotten. The very religious ceremonies that can heal people are disappearing. The sons and grandsons of medicine men don't usually want to learn the traditional ways. They also want to find work outside the reservation because it pays better. None of that stuff for ceremonies is written down you know. It has to be passed down from one person to the other. Even if you did want to have a ceremony, there's less medicine men that could do it properly.

There have been quite a few Squaw Dances this past summer though. Many times a *Nda* is done because a Navajo woman had relations with a man not of their tribe or with an Anglo. The dance is done for other reasons too, to put things back in harmony, or if family members keep getting sick. But I hear a lot about how young girls want one done for the other reason. They still feel kind of weird about being with a boy who's not of their people. I think maybe it's one of the most important reasons they have Squaw Dances now. I know of one incident when a tour guide brought some *bilaga'ana* to these dances. I don't even know if the guide got permission. They were supposed to just observe, but the white people took pictures and everything. I only saw it the one time, so I don't know if it happens a lot. To bring people to watch like that is usually considered impolite. Nowadays of course anything can happen. You never know what to expect.

Colette:

I had listened to Elvina describe the Squaw Dance with my eyes seemingly focused on my notes, but inwardly I cringed. Hadn't I been the lone White woman at yesterday's "Nda" ceremony? I never thought my presence would be an insult to the participants, but now I replayed the night's events, imagining disdain in the face of every Navajo who loosely shook my hand and smiled a greeting. My God, I'd even danced with them! I should have at least asked, but I'd been swept away in the moment. I would ask Emily about the whole mess later, but there was no way I was going to confess to Elvina I'd been the "pushy Anglo" stupidly participating in a Squaw Dance, blithely unaware my presence went against protocol. I pretended to scribble some notes, while Elvina continued to relay her concerns about the Dine' culture.

Elvina:

My grandmother Suzie has also noticed that things have gotten pretty bad. We were talking about it recently, and she said that things used to be much stricter. The Medicine Man was much respected because of his ability to heal, and they used to have medicine men for all different ceremonies. Also, there was no way an Anglo would ever show up for any kind of dance. Now I see things that really surprise me at ceremonies and dances. I see drunks that show up just for the fun of it and they destroy everything. It takes away the power of the event. It's not supposed to be a show. It's an important religious act. A lot of times I don't even feel safe at these dances anymore. By the time it gets dark I'm always in the car with the doors locked. That's how scary it can be now. I heard of one incident in which a little girl was sleeping in the back of a truck, and she got raped. People get drunk and don't think about what they're doing, and it really needs to stop. Compared to a lot of other Native American cultures ours is still pretty strong, but there are these things threatening it.

I still like living here though, even with the difficulties. You have to adjust to things. For instance, if you get yourself hurt you're miles and miles from a hospital. The lack of job opportunities is the other challenge. There are also very few recreational activities for people now. It used to be that people could play basketball and volleyball up there by Goulding's, but they closed it off to that kind of recreation. They wanted to use the area for cooking for tourists. It is also very hard to get any supplies here. You can't buy a radio or a washer and dryer, nothing like that. You have to drive three hours to Flag.

So, you can see that it's cool that we're so out of the way, but it's also a problem if you need anything. Just living through the seasons can be pretty hard here sometimes. For the past couple of weeks it's been really windy. It blows sand under the doors, and that gets into your clothes and food. My mom and I thought of going somewhere just to get out of the wind. Out past Chinle it's not as bad, but you need a vehicle to get away. I don't know why we get so much wind here in the Valley. It's prettier here so I think it's worth it, but the elements can be severe. There aren't many social activities here either, but the way I am I don't really mind it. I'm comfortable being by myself or with my family. I don't pay much attention to my surroundings when I go into town. I just get what I need and leave. I used to have insecurities if a guy came up to me just to flirt or whatever. I used to get uncomfortable with that, but it seems like I can take care of myself now. I'm more prepared and know what to say. I'm nice about it, but mostly I walk away from things like that. I'm more interested in finishing school, then after that I want somebody with me. I want to have a family when I'm ready.

I would like to explore other parts of the world as well. I want to find out what else is out there without thinking that I have responsibilities at home. It would be kind of nice to feel free to move around by myself for awhile. But for now I'll continue working at the high school. I control the media to each classroom, the TVs and microphones they use for things. I hand out exams and homework assignments, and I help out the students with their English or their Math. They have a program that offers schooling by television to students in Blanding or Bryce, and I help with keeping the students focused. I guess I could call myself a teacher's aide, or an audio visual aid. I will go back to school, but in the meantime I'm happy here.

It would be hard for me to leave the Valley, if the opportunity came up. There's so much peace here. It's so calm and quiet, and you can really breathe. I like to go running out in the Valley where my grandmother lives. I can wear whatever I like and run around the mesas. I just love that feeling of open space. It's beautiful to me, and I feel as if I can do whatever I want. If I went someplace off the reservation it would probably be culture shock for me. It might take me some time to get used to the commotion and stuff. Sometimes I think I could travel just a little, like to a different state, but I would always come back to the Valley.

Maybe I'll get together with a nice guy some day, but there aren't many guys my age out here. My sister is visiting here now, and the other day and I said to her, "There are no cute guys out here. Let's go look around in Nebraska." (*Elvina giggles*). Most of the guys out here are related to me anyway, so that's no good. Every time I meet someone I ask, "What's your clan?" Most of the time they say, "Bitterwater," and then I have to say, "Oh, you're my brother or my uncle." It's so hard. I knew one guy who was half *bilaga'ana* and half Navajo. He was nice, and I was seeing him for awhile. Because he was half white it wouldn't have mattered what his clan was anyway. But I found out he was from Folded Arm People. That made it appropriate for me to be with him. He was very good-looking, and I still have a picture of him. But for now I'm on my own, and I feel like I'm doing pretty good for the time being.

Colette:

Effie entered the little house, breaking the trance Elvina and I had been lulled into by her storytelling. "Hey, what's going on in here?" Effie laughed, throwing a bag of supplies on the table and taking a seat in front of the wood stove. "Ah, you missed it," her daughter teased, "I just told Coco about my entire life!" Even Suzie laughed at this, which made me wonder just how much English she really understood.

Effie and I chatted about when I would be leaving the Valley, while Elvina looked through the pile of books I always had with me. She happened upon my Navajo language study tools; flash cards I'd made up myself, and the dictionary I'd purchased at Goulding's long ago. Elvina became engrossed in these materials, and it was strange to hear her quietly sounding out the phonetic table as if she'd never spoken a word of Navajo. Like the rest of her family, I knew that she was fluent in her native language. And yet she closely examined every card, saying the word first in Navajo, then flipping it around to see if it matched the English translation. The words sounded better on her tongue, and I wondered if she would be willing to teach me a little "Dine' bizaad."

I tried to concentrate on what Effie was saying, but the wind was becoming fierce outside, causing the tree outside Suzie's window to make an eerie scratching sound. The view from the window was obscured by swirling dust, and I wondered out loud what had happened to Em and Lonnie. Effie suggested they might be waiting for us at Hill House, so we decided it was a good time to pack up and go. Effie would follow us in her car with Suzie, but only as far as the turn-off for Oljeto. Suzie was looking forward to a proper shower at her daughter's house, and this would give Elvina and I time to wrap things up.

She and I listened to the Dine' station on my car radio, and Elvina sang along to some of the songs. We spoke a little bit about our families, and discovered we both struggled with keeping them together. "It seems as if White people leave each other for good when they separate," Elvina softly said, "maybe that so they don't have to see them around all the time." I agreed that many divorced couples I knew back home were able to disappear from each other's lives quite easily. Maybe this was because there were so many people and so many cities and towns in which to escape. "We don't really have that around here," Elvina explained, "once you live someplace you usually stay there, especially if there's work for you. And we see our ex's around all the time, sometimes with their new partners, which can make it pretty uncomfortable."

We reached Hill House and found Lonnie and Em waiting in their dusty car. Stepping out to greet us I learned that they had been through a terrible ordeal. While making the long drive home the previous night Emily fell asleep at the wheel and had driven into a ditch! Lonnie was asleep beside her, and the two of them awoke to find the car tilting to one side in the sandy trench. I thought of Elvina's comment earlier that day about how common it was to have this type of accident on the rez, and we exchanged knowing glances. The reservation roads are long, straight highways that can lull you into a kind of mesmerized stupor. These roads can be twice as dangerous at night, when the driver's eyes can only focus on the white, dashed line in the middle. Towns are sometimes hours apart, and if one is not well rested the act of driving can begin to feel like an exhausting video game. Lonnie and Emily were both accustomed to late-night driving in the area, but apparently even they were vulnerable to the conditions from time to time. Several members of the family have injured themselves and their vehicles while driving late at night.

Emily told me that her husband had offered to take over if she became sleepy, but knowing he was tired from a long day of work, she let him sleep. She listened to the radio and even sprayed her face with a misting bottle when she began to feel particularly drowsy. "We were almost to Chinle," Emily explained, "and I thought, 'heck...why wake up Lonnie when we're so close?" The next thing Emily recalled was the jolt of her car going off the road. After she had fallen asleep at the wheel, her car wandered onto the road's edge, then tumbled into the side ditch. "We were actually pretty fortunate," Emily said with a shudder, "because if I'd driven a little further where the edge drops off we wouldn't have had that soft dirt to save us!" Luckily Em and Lonnie suffered only a few cuts and bruises. However, their "chiddy" was smashed in front and would need expensive repair.

I had never seen Emily really cry. I had seen her tear up on occasion, but most of even our deepest conversations had been accompanied by laughter. Now, as she surveyed the damage done to her car, I saw my friend wipe her eyes and rummage in her purse for a tissue. It was hard to know what to say, and my heart went out to her because I knew she blamed herself for the car's condition. It felt strange to see this side of Emily. I always had the advantage of placing the work of ethnography between us. Yet, she had been a shoulder for me to cry on when I shared my own problems. Didn't that make us family? I wanted to return the compassion she had shown me, so I listened and tried to give advice. Emily's body was still sore and aching from the crash, so I told her there was no need to do anything until she rested up from her injuries. It took some time to stop her from running the event over and over in her mind. "I just don't remember feeling sleepy," she fretted, "gosh, I could have really hurt us!" Elvina and I helped her into the house with Lonnie following closely behind. I decide my workday was over, and made us all a cup of tea.

After drinking her tea Emily appeared to bounce back, and she shooed away my suggestion she and Lonnie stay the night. "Nah, she said with a wave of her hand, "You gotta leave in the morning. Don't worry *Shah kiss*, we'll just head home." They offered to take Elvina back to her mother's place in Oljeto, and I embraced each of them as they got into the sad little car. As I watched them drive away I tried to think of where I really fit into their family. Was I really helping with my infrequent phone calls and Pollyanna advice? I had spent years with the Yazzies, but was it presumptuous of me to think of them as family at all? The idea nagged me as I walked back inside the house, and the noise of the Yazzie's car clambering up the street grew dim.

CHAPTER 15 – FULL CIRCLE

"What is life? It is the flash of a firefly in the night. It is the breath of a buffalo in the wintertime. It is the little shadow which runs across the grass and loses itself in the sunset." – Crowfoot, Blackfoot Warrior and Orator

THE DREAM INTERRUPTED

In May of 2007 I began to put together all of the transcribed material from the Yazzies and to create some kind of coherent story. I had compiled multiple binders of notes and pages of dialogue that weighed in at about two pounds. Just gathering research material and interviews had taken well over five years. I was ready to begin the final task of making all my work into the fascinating story I knew it could be. It was a beautiful spring morning and I was deeply immersed in my notes when the phone rang. It was Effie, and she cried so hard I couldn't make out at first what she tried to say. Between her sobs, and much to my surprise and horror, I finally understood --- Lonnie had died in a car accident late the previous night.

Lonnie perished in a way not uncommon on the Rez.' Getting from one small town to the next often required long hours of driving on monotonously straight roads, and there were many who fell asleep at the wheel. On the few occasions I'd been unlucky enough to travel to Goulding's in the dark I had been lured into a dangerous half-conscious state. I felt completely engulfed by the pitch dark of desert night. The broken yellow line hypnotically teased my eyes into closing until I finally had to sing along with the radio in order to stay awake. Both Lonnie and Emily had recanted episodes in which one or the other awoke to find they had drifted off to sleep and ran their car into a roadside ditch. Apparently, this was what occurred when Lonnie drove from the Valley to Keyenta, however on this occasion it led to his demise.

According to Effie, Lonnie was heading home some time before midnight after a full day's work in the Valley. I suppose his intention was to spend the night in Keyenta just thirty miles away. There had been one or two other cars on the road at the half-way point, one traveling behind him and another passing him on the way to Goulding's. The drivers of both vehicles reported seeing Lonnie's truck continuing

356

straight as the road made a gradual curve. Lonnie must have awakened just then and, realizing his mistake, jerked the truck back toward the road causing it to spin out of control and topple into the deep sand. According to the witnesses, his vehicle flipped and ended up on its side.

They ran to help just as Lonnie attempted to crawl out of his window, but he lost strength and collapsed. Those who had pulled over to help managed to drag him out of his truck and lay him in the sand. Because cellular telephone access is unreliable in the Valley it took the ambulance from Keyenta a full hour to arrive. By then Lonnie had no vital signs, and he was officially pronounced dead of internal injuries at the hospital the next day, May 20th.

Effie was inconsolable, and I desperately wanted to leave for the Valley to comfort her and to check on Emily. I wondered if anyone had notified Lonnie's teenage sons, Sonny and Brookes? Then I thought of Lonnie's two grown daughters, Veronica and Tiffany. Who would tell them? Effie had not been able to reach the boys, and she was in no shape to do much more than try to grasp what had happened. She asked if I could try contacting them, and I promised to try. However, I knew I would feel terrible being the one to break the news.

I gave Effie what solace I could over the phone, and then told her to try and rest while I attempted to pull things together.

Apparently, I was the first person Effie called, and I felt I should try to make things as easy as possible for her and the family. It was Lonnie who ran all of the riding excursions, some that had been booked for the remainder of the summer as well as this fall. This was the Yazzie's main source of income. Who would take the groups of tourists out now, and how could they manage the other tasks Lonnie had taken on when everyone was already stretched thin with work? I didn't know what sort of memorial service Lonnie would want or even if such things had been discussed by the family. Knowing how they tended to live in the moment I doubted anything had been planned. My head was spinning as I went downstairs to break the news to Ross.

I burst into tears before I got the words out, but eventually my husband learned his old riding buddy would no longer be accompanying him on those long Valley excursions. We held each other and felt a huge part of our lives fall away. We couldn't grasp the idea that we would never again be privy to one of Lonnie's bad jokes or hear his songs echoing in the canyons. Surely if we drove out to the Valley now we could somehow back up time and erase what had happened. Lonnie would walk up to us with his wry mustachioed smile, black dusty cowboy hat and bowlegged, dusty jeans. He would laugh as if the whole terrible thing had been a practical joke on the White People.

SPREADING THE WORD
"The soul would have no rainbow if the eyes had no tears." — Unknown Tribe

I reached Brookes by telephone only moments after he had been told by another family member that his father died. I was not accustomed to hearing any of the Yazzies

357

cry. Even after my tearful discussions with Effie I was not prepared for Brookes' grief. He had only recently turned seventeen, and he sounded incredibly vulnerable over the telephone, trying not very successfully to contain himself. Brookes had been forced to grow up so quickly. Even before his father's passing he and his brother Sonny had taken on the task of caring for their mother, Emily. Without Lonnie checking in on them from the Valley they were truly on their own. Speaking with Sonny was no easier. Always a man of few words he did what he could to express his sorrow, but he was clearly in shock and would need time to heal from this terrible loss. I knew things were desperate when Brookes said goodbye. "I love you Coco," he mumbled; words he had never spoken out loud to me. Though I knew he and Sonny cared for me because of the friendship I shared with their mother, it was strange to hear so much emotion from them and agonizing not to rush out and care for them all.

For her part, Emily was trying to be tough but failing miserably. She and Lonnie had been separated for over a year, but she had never really stopped loving him. The last words spoken between them were full of anger and hurt. Now Emily would never know closure and I was concerned that she might fail to muster the strength to resume her life as a single mother. They had no gas money to drive out to the Valley, so I sent a check to her and the boys.

I could not wrap my mind around the concept of sitting in the Shade House without Lonnie sitting next to me munching on sunflower seeds and telling me stories. Now I would never have the pleasure of handing him the completed family history. It was Lonnie who first suggested I write the Yazzie story. What would it mean to carry on the work without him? It seemed so pointless, but Ross would hear none of this sort of talk. "It's even more important now that you finish," he told me as we clung to each other. But the only thing on my mind was getting back to the Valley.

The airlines informed me that booking a flight at such short notice would cost over $2000. I would then have to rent a car and drive to Keyenta where the only room available would cost another $150 per day. Ross and I were at a point in our lives when cash flow was poor, and we were still assisting our children financially while they transitioned into the real world. Still uncertain as to what I would do, I called Effie the next day to learn what sort of service would take place for Lonnie.

"We're doing sort of a church service because we don't really know what else to do," she informed me. 'But Lonnie is not a Christian,' I thought to myself, envisioning him at practice with his corn pollen prayers. I wondered why a Dine' ceremony had not been considered, but now was not the time to have a discussion about Navajo culture. "We're going to have a procession into the Valley," Effie continued, "after that so we can bury Lonnie behind my mom's place. Frank said he would help." I thought of Frank Amther and his wife Pat. Like us, they had forged a long-lasting friendship with the Yazzies after participating in a horseback riding trip. One year, when Lonnie and Emily were in desperate financial need, they found employment on the Amther's property up in Cortez. Frank had always come through for the family, using his carpentry skills to create the latest edition to the Yazzie compound; the sturdy and handsome new Shade House. I remembered a couple of very entertaining barbecues in that very structure getting to know Frank and Pat. They were good people.

358

I telephoned the Amthers and was let in on their plans. With his usual genius and generosity of spirit Frank had somehow managed to commandeer a backhoe tractor with which to cut a road around "The Dragon" rock formation to Lonnie's final resting place. Family had been buried there in the past under piles of rocks; however the backhoe would ensure a more substantial grave for our old friend. Pat would travel with him to offer emotional support to the Yazzies. "You're welcome to stay in our trailer if you want to Coco," Frank offered, and I knew Pat would appreciate another woman out there to help. I thanked Frank and told him to give my love to Pat. I knew that I couldn't afford to fly out to them, but I was determined to contribute in some way.

Two days before the funeral I made my decision and placed another call to Effie. The Yazzies were short of funds to pay for expenses such as the simple pine box in which Lonnie would be buried. I suggested to Effie that my money would be better spent toward helping them with these necessities rather than giving it up to the airlines. Ross and I would have to pay our respects to Lonnie at a later date. In the meantime the Yazzies needed financial help and we felt Lonnie would appreciate our caring for his family in this way. It was a terrible decision to make, but it seemed practical and Lonnie had been a practical man. Effie agreed, and she thanked me for the donation with relief in her voice. Still, that night I had a pain in my gut thinking how I wouldn't be present when the family said their goodbyes to Lonnie.

The next day I felt so useless, and I called Effie once more, just to see how she was holding up. "They wanted me to pull out photographs of Lonnie for the service," she said with a long sigh, "but after looking at a few of them I just lost it. I wish my girls were here with me," she said of Elvina and Earlene, "I want them to hurry up and come." I asked if Suzie had been told about her son's passing. "I tried," Effie explained, "but she just looked at me as if she didn't understand. I felt terrible trying to tell her and I just wanted someone to hold me. My nephew, Harvey's son, came home and he calmed me down." I later learned that Suzie did not truly come to understand Lonnie had died for days after the service. "Kee is the bravest one," Effie told me as she spoke of her youngest brother, "He knew mom didn't understand when we were at the funeral and she saw everybody there. She asked 'who's looking after the hogan?' When Kee was finally able to get her to listen she got real quiet. Then she said 'Just leave me in peace,' and that was it. We haven't really talked about it since then."

I believed that the entire family could have benefited from sitting down together and letting their feelings out about their loss. But then I realized that this was purely an Anglo way of looking at things. The Yazzies handled things differently and I would have to support whatever method they chose that would allow them to heal. Emily later told me she felt awkward at Lonnie's service, and I longed for the way things used to be; when harmony and peace was so prevalent among my Navajo family. I loved them all, and silently said many *sodizan,* or prayers, for their healing.

THE FAREWELL TRIP
"Don't be afraid to cry. It will free your mind from sorrowful thoughts." - Hopi

A full year passed before I could make my next trip out to Monument Valley. So much had occurred to both my Navajo family and my own. My eldest daughter, Raven married her boyfriend, Ethan. Shortly thereafter I became a grandmother to their son, Atlas. My son, Casey became an apprentice electrician and grew up to be a kind, (and if I may say so), a very handsome young man. The twins, Rhianna and Carly moved to Seattle, Washington. After one year of attending the university there they decided to take a year off to work and re-think their lives. All of the struggles and heartbreak that came with raising four teenaged step-children were behind me. The crazy teenagers were now responsible adults, each unique and wonderful in their own way. I should have felt relief when the last of our little birds flew the nest. Instead I was a little lost. I didn't miss the drama behind our efforts to become a cohesive family, but the house was too clean and too quiet.

Ross and I rattled around in our big house in Carpinteria. We had to put down one of our aging horses, and we gave the other away to keep it from becoming lonely. We now felt compelled to lead a simpler life, and I longed to move where the four seasons marked the time and people were not as concerned with material things. With this in mind, we remodeled our home so that it would sell better, and while awaiting a buyer spent our days in the bliss of a sort of second honeymoon. We had more time to ourselves than we ever had when the children were young. Gone also were the late night arguments over how to care for them. I never really thought the day would come, but Ross and I were finally in a place in which our decisions were based solely on our own personal needs. Unfortunately, Ross' mother was beginning to show signs of dementia and we feared the onset of Alzheimer's, a disease that afflicted her father before he died. She would have to accompany us wherever we decided to move, and so it seemed that life was destined to be at least a little complicated for us.

Now that things were relatively settled at home I was anxious to get out to the Valley. Ross supported my plans, but because of ongoing business dealings he could not accompany me. He wanted to visit the Yazzies as much as I, and like me he felt a need to pay his respects at Lonnie's final resting place. I offered to wait so that we could go together, but Ross just shook his head. "No," he said before putting his arms around me, "this is something you need to do, and the sooner the better." He was right of course, but as I watched him wave at me from the train platform I couldn't help but feel just a little bit selfish.

I made my connection at Union Station in Los Angeles, and as the train chugged dutifully toward San Bernardino and beyond I could see great billows of smoke on the horizon. The horrific fires that had been ripping through the region for several days were turning the sunset a mean orange color. My sister in San Diego was evacuated from her home. Caroline cried to me over the phone about the almost certain demise of the little cabin she and her husband own in the San Bernardino Mountains. I thought of the weekends she spent fixing the place up that year; on her knees replacing tile, painting and refinishing every room. The idea of that little cabin burning to the

360

ground broke my heart. The fires only strengthened my resolve to move up north, away from the oppressive heat of California.

My train pulled into Flagstaff on time for a change. It was so early that I had to sleep in my rental car until six o'clock when the grocery store opened and I could buy supplies. The drive into M.V. was glorious, and I watched a rising October sun change the colors of the reservation. I arrived at Goulding's just before noon, and was met at the registration desk by one of the owners, Julie LaFond, and her assistant Bessie. I was warmly welcomed like a returning family member. I think Julie always remembers me because her husband hails from Santa Paula, a town close to where I live in Santa Barbara. "We were wondering when you would get here," Julie said with a smile, "and hey, you cut your hair!" It was true. While the kids were growing up I had always worn my hair long, usually just throwing it up in a ponytail to save time. Lately I had grown tired of my shoulder length mane and decided that with all the change occurring in my life I may as well alter my hairstyle as well. It was now very short and took only minutes to dry. That morning I had only to run my fingers through to consider myself properly coifed. What had I been waiting for?

I noticed a few changes that had seeped into the Valley, the first being that a clear radio station that now came in from Tuba City. They played a fairly decent selection of pop music that was a nice change from the scratchy Navajo station I always listened to on AM. Later I became nostalgic for the simplicity of that fuzzy 660 AM with the constant chatter in Dine.' The ride onto the rez was more entertaining with the modern music, but the Valley seems less isolated and unique now. At Goulding's they switched from playing the constant Native American music over the speakers to this new pop station. I liked the Native music better, but the staff had to have grown weary of it. Julie also put new carpet in Hill House, and a new table in the dining room along with a nice black patio set outside on the hill. All of these improvements made the place seem quite plush, and I wished more than ever that I could live in Hill House forever. Well…perhaps for part of the year.

I caught up on all the Valley news with Julie before collecting my key, then drove straight to my little house on the hill to begin work. My intention was to begin editing my manuscript and prepare it for submission to a reputable publishing company by the end of the year. I'd created my own little publishing company and took on the entire cost of producing my first book, "Through the Eyes of a Survivor. My life had been enriched by working with my friend Nina Morecki, a Holocaust survivor and amazing woman, and I was proud of how I told her story. But the cost was substantial and had bled TopCat Press dry. Now I wanted only to return to my first love, the tale of life in the Valley and how my Navajo friends changed mine. I hoped that handing the Yazzies the completed manuscript might in some way honor Lonnie.

Though just as beautiful as I remembered it, the Valley seemed a little emptier without him. Lonnie and I had laughed, cried and wondered over many things over the course of a decade. Now, for the first time, I was looking out at the beautiful horizon of monuments knowing he wasn't out there somewhere riding his horse. I thought of how he had gone much like his father, Tully had; dying way before his time in a terrible accident. It made me wonder how Effie was doing, and since I owed her a call anyway I gave her a ring.

Her machine answered, and I guessed she was out with the last group of riders Lonnie scheduled before his accident. I left a message confirming that I would make my traditional "spaspetti" dinner, (Effie's words). I didn't mention what was foremost in my mind; visiting Lonnie's grave and paying my respects. With little else to do I sat down to work at the table by the kitchen. I planned to use the setting of Monument Valley to reconnect with the muse that had guided me to this place from the beginning. I'd let the Yazzie's interviews and my diary entries languish during the past year, and I hoped the time alone would ignite my desire to write again. This last entry was to be an epilogue, though I had no doubts that the Yazzies would continue to live with as much energy and enthusiasm as I had been illustrated in the pages of their book. I worked the rest of the day, and had not heard from Effie even as the sun went down behind the rocks standing sentry over Hill House.

IN THE ARMS OF FAMILY

"Even the seasons form a great circle in their changing, and always come back again to where they were. The life of a man is a circle from childhood to childhood, and so it is in everything where the power moves." – Black Elk Ogala, Sioux Holy Man

I called Effie's house again the next morning and caught Elvina just as she was going out the door to work at the local high school. It was so good to hear her voice, and while the two of us giggled over the telephone I had a hard time imagining her as anything but the young girl I met years ago. Now she was about the same age as I was when I first came to the Valley. Elvina confirmed that her mom was indeed working at Suzie's place with a group of riders, but "the guests" would be leaving today. She promised to remind her mom to call me about who would be coming to spaghetti dinner that night. I was truly looking forward to it as the hours of complete solitude at Hill House had left me feeling restless.

I ventured into the gift shop to kill time and make some purchases, finding some music and a book about local medicinal plants. I couldn't help noticing a big fake spider hanging over the ladies who worked behind the counter. Apparently they were prepared for Halloween, and I asked them if they were planning on killing the big spider above them. Without looking up from her work one of the younger ladies said, "That's our pet. His name is Xavier...Xavier Goulding." This produced giggles all the way around, and I wondered how many others had asked about the spider before me.

The day wore on and I ticked off many of the items on my "To Do" list. I went for a run on my favorite road behind Goulding's, and for lunch I enjoyed a "Navajo Taco" made with the fry bread I missed so much. I watched the sun rise and set, changing the colors of the rocks surrounding me, all the while missing Lonnie and thinking how I would complete the Yazzie story. I would not see Emily during this

362

trip, but hoped to return with my Ross sometime in the spring for a Canyon de Chelley visit. I want to see how Emily is doing and check up on her boys Sonny and Brookes. From what I could tell the family was still somewhat fractured, and I wished more than ever for their hearts to mend so we could all be together again.

Effie finally called and we arranged a meeting at the Goulding's grocery store. I gathered my tape recorder, (because you never know), and took off down the road, thankful for a break in my work. Waving from the driver's side of the truck was Lonnie's daughter from his first marriage, Tiffany. She looked all grown up from the last time I saw her and her sister, giggling over soft handshakes years ago. She and Effie emerged from the truck and we hugged Anglo-style all the way 'round. Effie had another little dog to keep her company. Though Paco could never be replaced, "Sheila" was a delightful little pug with plenty of charm. I fell instantly in love with her. We three women stood in the parking lot and caught up on the last few months' events. I apologized to Tiffany for not attending her father's funeral, but she was more than understanding and promised to take me to his grave site the next morning before I left for Flagstaff.

She and her Auntie were heading to Keyenta to do laundry and a multitude of other chores brought about from hosting the last of their riding guests. Tiffany was exhausted from a night ride she led the night before, and I knew her father would have been proud of her efforts. When I asked if Kee was the other guide they both laughed and Effie proclaimed, "You want to know who led most of the rides? It's me!" For a woman in her fifties she was awfully tough, and she had apparently led the rides with no trouble. Both she and her niece were sore however, and Tiffany suggested they purchase "those new cushioned girdles that give you a bigger butt," for the next ride.

Tiffany had been in touch with her half-brothers, and was able to convince Brookes to stop working and return to college. This caused me some relief; however I still worried about Emily and her eldest Sonny. Effie lamented the fact that Tiffany would have to follow her into Keyenta in her car, since the truck once again was on its last leg. This time Effie hoped to repair a broken fuel pump but the cost would be dear. We spoke about the book and the possibility of having it published, and I promised them that if we ever saw any profit I would make certain they always had running vehicles. We dreamed over that possibility for a few blessed moments and then it was time to say goodbye. We all hugged again and agreed to try and squeeze in dinner at Goulding's restaurant some time during my stay.

THE LAST SUNSET
"We are made from Mother Earth and we go back to Mother Earth." - Shenandoah

The next morning my mother called to say that my sister's cabin had been spared! Although many of the homes around their little place had been reduced to rubble, Caroline and her husband Randy were lucky. Their cabin had miraculously stood firm.

This news felt like a little ray of light that lit up my day. My next call was from Effie telling me she was held up on business in Keyenta. She suggested I call Tiffany to see what she was up to. Telephone call number three got me Tiffany who asked if I could "hang out" with her while she finished her laundry. "Everything I brought to the Valley smells like a horse!" She exclaimed.

I drove past the market and turned into the hub that offered just about everything a tourist would need. Next to a car wash was the gas station, mini-mart and laundry mat, all in one building. I pulled up to the little playground situated just behind the building and stepped out of my dusty rental. The mournful squeaking of a rusty swing set filled the air, as a group of Navajo kids pumped furiously away on the hot rubber seats. One little girl waiting her turn on the swings stared at me as I made my way to the laundry mat door. When I walked into the hot room jammed with whirring machines I was met by a host of even more curious gazes. For a millisecond every Navajo woman in the place stopped folding their clothes to look me over. Then I saw the familiar face of Lonnie's daughter and made my way toward her. "Hey Coco," she greeted me with a smile. The rest of the women, deciding I was no longer of interest, went back to their folding.

Poor Tiffany stood over piles of blankets, towels and blue jeans that she had used during her stint as a guide. I helped her fold while we talked about her dad. Tiffany told me that she and her sister Veronica spent many summers with Suzie when they were very young girls. "I didn't speak very good Navajo," Tiffany explained, "but I could sure understand what grandma was saying to us. Ronnie and I loved that place, and Ronnie has talked before about going out there to live if they ever needed her."

I asked Tiffany what she had been doing before being called back for her father's funeral. "I was going to school to get my Bachelor's degree in Criminal Psychology," she explained, "I did my internship in Washington, D.C. and then did another in Chicago. My focus was learning how to counsel Native Americans in the area, but Indians are much different in the city. They didn't even know what mutton was!" We both gasped in mock surprise, and then I asked her if she had visited her dad much before he died. "Not really," she sighed, "not as much as I would have liked. My dad asked me to come to this big event that was sort of like a Pow wow. It draws a lot of people to the Valley every year, and he kept pestering me to come out and see it with him." Tiffany managed a little smile, "He had even purchased tickets for Ronnie and me. I wanted to come, because I had been missing the place. I had just got home from that trip to Chicago when I heard about my dad's accident."

We each grabbed a corner of a large and battered blanket, and then walked toward each other to make the ends meet. "So you came back and never left?" I asked as she took my corners and completed the task of folding the blanket. I wondered what had prompted this well-spoken and bright young woman to stay in the Valley when she had so much opportunity waiting for her in the Big City? "My auntie needed me," Tiffany answered with a shrug, "and I wanted to help with the rides as a way of reconnecting with my culture. I'm going to stay another year and learn some stories and songs, then maybe Ronnie can take over, or maybe Brookes and Sonny." Tiffany went on to say that she had convinced her younger half-brother to return to college, while Sonny made the decision to help his mother at home in Chinle.

The clothes were folded, so we sat in plastic bucket chairs and waited for her last load to dry. "Oh hey," I exclaimed, and reached inside my backpack, "I almost forgot what I brought you." I pulled out a copy of the book I had published a few years before and, placing it on Tiffany's lap; I explained that I would try to create the same kind of book containing her own family's life history. My new friend's eyes grew wider, and she flipped through the pages. "As big as this?" Tiffany asked shaking her head. "Well yeah...sure," I answered, "after all we're telling a pretty big story." We smiled goofily at each other, and then both leaned over to look at the photographs in my book, our heads nearly touching as I explained some of the captions.

We talked until it grew dark outside, and because Tiffany was "starving" we piled the rest of the still damp laundry into her car just in time to see Effie arrive with her brother Kee. They had both already eaten but accompanied us to Goulding's for desert. There the conversation naturally turned to Lonnie, and Tiffany pulled out a small, yellowed photograph of her father taken some time during the 1950s. His black hair was set almost in a pompadour, but the picture revealed the familiar slender build and bowlegged stance. Lonnie was even sporting the black jeans he favored so much.

We all agreed he had been a handsome man, and glancing across the table at Kee I realized how much he looked like Lonnie. It was somewhat unnerving when I first saw him walking in with Effie, because it was almost like seeing Lonnie. Even their voices and manner of speech were similar. I had only met Kee a handful of times, and because he was rather shy his eyes seemed always to be examining the floor and very little conversation took place. He appeared to be comfortable with me now, however, and he spoke earnestly of his brother's love for the Valley. He revealed how he would like to honor Lonnie by spending more time in the Valley, and as he spoke I was astounded at how much he resembled Lonnie, particularly when speaking of the home they both cared so much about. A kind and quiet man, Kee now was intent on assisting Effie and Tiffany with the rides. He was not a carbon copy of his brother however. It had been difficult for Kee to overcome his shyness and perform songs for the guests as Lonnie had.

"I used to be that way when I spoke to strangers too," Kee explained, "I was real nervous about speaking English to people. I only finished high school and I don't know a lot of those big words people say. I can speak Navajo so much better, and I was embarrassed to ask people to explain what their words meant. But I got over it, and now you can't shut me up!" We all giggled at Kee and continued our lovely meal. Tiffany and I gobbled down dinner until we could barely move. The sun was getting ready to go down and everyone was tired. Effie agreed to meet me in the morning to take me to Lonnie's grave, and I gave both Kee and Tiffany a hearty *bilaga'ana* hug. Tiffany promised to read the book I gave her, and Kee asked me to send him a copy as well. I smiled and waved at him as he shuffled off to his truck. I finished saying goodnight to the ladies, then and headed back up to Hill House for my last night's sleep. It felt good to have been surrounded by Yazzie smiles once again, and when I reached the house I made my way out to the yard on the little mesa to watch the sun and let the warmth in my heart settle into my bones.

This would be my last sunset before I had to leave the Valley. Tomorrow I would make the drive to Flagstaff and onward to California to carry on with life. The sun felt warm on my back as I took one long last look at the rocks surrounding the house. By now I regarded them as old friends. The monoliths stared back at me, quietly witnessed the passing of time as they always have. As well as any ancient cathedral, the massive rock formations had protected the Navajo for many years. The way they endured while at the same time slowly eroding away seemed like such a mysterious contradiction to me. There in the Valley dirt roads eventually became paved. Trading posts were replaced by proper markets and hogans were traded for government housing. Goulding's now even have internet access, much to my dismay.

Meanwhile, the windblown mesas and jutting boulders looked on. They knew they were the one constant here in the Valley. I imagined Lonnie riding with his father Tully and the rest of his ancestors through his homeland; the place that changed my life forever. Somehow this thought comforted me.

A SACRED PLACE
"Life is not separate from death. It only looks that way." - *Blackfoot*

Effie knocked on my door just as I had completed packing. I let her in and handed her the bag of food left over from last night's dinner. It would make a fine meal for her hungry and hard-working sheep dogs. After I checked out of Goulding's she left her car in the parking lot and joined me in my rental car. Making our way down into the Valley Effie spoke with pride about Tiffany. Effie believed that her niece had a beautiful voice. With obvious pleasure she explained how Lonnie's daughter was memorizing some traditional Navajo songs to perform for visitors. "She had forgotten a lot of our language, but just before Lonnie asked her to come out last spring she heard a Navajo song in her dream," Effie went on wistfully, "She sang it for me after Lonnie died, and it was so pretty."

I felt my skin tingle at the thought of Tiffany singing her dream song. "Now she and I are trying to memorize more songs together, "Effie went on, "like the lullaby Lonnie used to sing to her when she was a little girl." I told Effie how sorry I was that we never recorded Lonnie singing, but Effie smiled at me and patted my hand on the steering wheel. "Hey, didn't anyone ever tell you? We had an Anglo friend of ours tape Lonnie singing a lot of his hits! We got him doing "Pretty Red Wine" and "Indian School!" She promised to look for the tape and send it to me. Wouldn't it be lovely, I asked, if we could include Lonnie's and Tiffany's songs with the book?

Effie and I shared our ideas for the book as we bumped along the old familiar road to Suzie's place. When we drove up to the compound it felt like coming home all over again. How I loved the ramshackle structures, the jerry-rigged but sturdy horse corrals, the loyal outhouse and the weathered boards and branches of the Shade House. I thought of all the hours I spent there, hearing stories. I remembered all the winter days huddled around a cedar-scented fire in the hogan or mud-brown house, drinking endless cups of coffee. The memories came flooding back and enveloped me like a favorite sweater. We brought the food Effie had purchased from the store into the back room of Suzie's house, and there we found Leonard puzzling over an old hand-held computer game. I thought he looked funny; a grown man playing with a Game Boy. He looked up when he heard me giggle, and gave me a welcoming smile. "Coco," he said in surprise, "when did you get here?" Tossing the game aside on a chair he rose and clasped my hand in an uncustomary strong grip. "Hey," I teased, "what kind of Dine' handshake is that? You're becoming *Bilaga'ana* like me!" Leonard just chuckled and said, "That's a workin' man's handshake!" Certainly Leonard had been pulling his weight during this year's rides, and was just as tired as the rest of the family, (but twice as strong as I remembered him!).

I looked around to see that Effie had disappeared back into the main room, and I ventured in after her to see that Suzie had returned from a weaving demonstration. Now Effie and Suzie sat with a spinning wheel that I'd never seen before between them. I gave the old woman a warm smile and sat next to the two ladies while Effie explained once again who I was. Suzie hadn't a clue until her daughter made the motion of someone placing a microphone on her collar. Then the old woman giggled and nodded. She even remembered my husband, *dibe' hastiin*, or "Sheep Man." This memory produced still more giggles.

Suzie looked very good. Her conversation was animated and her skin glowed. "That's the vegetables we're making her eat," Effie explained, "Mom eats meat if it's cooked soft, and we try to keep her healthy with the greens. But she gets pretty mean if you take away her sugar. We're trying to get her to cut back." I remembered the Hostess "Snow Balls" I used to bring as a gift to Suzie. "Yeah," Effie laughed when I reminded her of her mother's favorite treat, "I caught her with a pop, and I made her cry when I took it away. I felt awful but she just can't keep having that stuff." As her mother fiddled with the spinning wheel, Effie showed me a collage of photos one of their Anglo friends had created for the funeral service. Lonnie was in the center, singing with his drum, and surrounding him were photos of my old friend sitting and even standing on his horse! I told Suzie I would always remember her son a certain way, and mimicked his bow-legged walk. My imitation brought peals of laughter and when I placed a feather above my upper lip to produce a Lonnie "mustache" both ladies clapped and rocked in delight.

Looking around I noticed that Suzie's home looked different. The walls had recently received a fresh coat of white paint, and the crowded shelves of souvenirs, knick-knacks and numerous family photos had all but disappeared. "We never got around to putting them back up after painting," Effie explained. Still more changes in the Valley. We stayed long enough to take a photo of me with Suzie in front of her house, and then with a heavy heart I accompanied Effie back to my rental car for the short trip out to Lonnie's grave. I didn't want to leave Suzie. I longed to stand outside the hogan listening to the wind. I wanted to close my eyes and hear Suzie and Effie speaking in Navajo, and feel the wind play around my face, tousling my hair.[184] But Effie had to be back at Goulding's by noon, and I had a train to catch. We made our way down the road, made dusty from last spring's big rain. Suzie smiled and waved from her doorway.

---

[184] After reviewing my work, my wonderful advisor, Ron Maldonado, told me that my references to the wind held special meaning. In Navajo belief, the wind is a living being, and when the wind surrounds you He is "getting to know you." Many of the older Navajo say they cannot leave an area where they were born, for the wind would not know them.

ANOTHER DAY, ANOTHER WORLD
"There is no death, only a change of worlds." — Duwanish

Lonnie's resting place was just beyond where Don Donnelly's group always stayed, past the "Dragon" campground to the "Little Dragon" rock formation. I saw the big, red sand dune where my twin step-daughters played with the Yazzie kids years ago. They had tumbled down the steep soft sand one after the other, plopping down in a pile, filthy and laughing, and then climbed the hill once more to repeat the whole routine. All of those kids were grown up now. Many had children of their own. The hill had become covered with brush, neglected by the latest generation of children who must have had better things to do. We passed the big juniper tree where Effie told me Suzie was born. At that time it was only a temporary encampment until a final spot for a hogan could be decided upon. "They liked to move around the Valley a lot," Effie explained.

She continued to point the way while I struggled to keep my car moving in the sand. I tried to remember what Lonnie once told me about driving in the Valley; too fast and we would spin out, too slow and we most certainly get stuck. I began to contemplate exactly how I would explain to the rental company why I left their car in a foot of sand, when Effie pointed to a small mound and said, "That's it."

Now I was standing in silence with my Navajo sister, finally gazing at Lonnie's new home, and trying to sort out my feelings. His grave was nicely kept just under the huge ledge jutting out from the "Dragon." The plot was surrounded by a neat little fence, with a mound of sand in the middle that both disturbed and delighted me. Bits of memorabilia and bunches of dusty silk flowers stuck out of the sand at crazy angles over the grave. A plastic toy horse rode eternally up the mound, and the sunglasses Lonnie always wore lay broken and partially buried by the sand. A strong sun hit the black glass of the lens, causing them to gleam through the dust.

Just above a plaque etched with Lonnie's name hung a small dream catcher. A breeze pushed at the little souvenir so that it made a tap-tap-tapping noise against the pole upon which it was tied. I felt badly that I brought nothing for my friend, and I made a silent promise to have some offering when I returned with Ross. Perhaps we would make it out as soon as the coming winter.

"This is where I think all of us will be buried now," said Effie, breaking the silence. It seemed strange to me that Suzie would be joining her son there in the sand. It was out of order and unfair that yet another of her children preceded her in death. I asked Effie why a traditional ceremony had not taken place since, after all Lonnie was not a Christian, and had been very committed to his Dine' faith. "It just wasn't practical," Effie said quietly, "his cousin was a preacher and he wanted to do a service for my brother. So many people wanted to come pay their respects, and if we had done it Navajo-style very few people could have anything to do with it. They would have to have had a long cleansing ceremony, and nobody has the heart to do it that way anymore. This way was better."

Memories of my Navajo friend drifted through my mind, bumping into each other and slipping away; incomplete like a dream and leaving me hungry for more. Couldn't

369

we have just one last ride? Would it have been so hard to come out more often just to hear him sing, or let him take my husband on one more dangerous adventure so that they could laugh over it later as brothers? I thought of my own time with Lonnie. We had giggled, cried and wondered about many things over the course of a decade. Now he was gone, and our beloved Valley seemed just a little too empty for me to bear.

It is strange how life sometimes repeats itself. Lonnie went much like his father, Tully; in a freak accident and really not an old man at all. Pushing the thought from my head I sighed and looked at Effie. "I'm so sorry I couldn't be here for the funeral," I murmured. I was embarrassed by my own lame apology. It sounded insufficient and felt awkward.

"Yeah," Effie murmured without a hint of blame in her voice, "you would have liked it...it was really nice. There were a lot of people here and everyone helped out a lot." Effie and I became lost in our thoughts once more. The warm mid-morning sun burned our shoulders, and a gust of the ever-present wind began to throw our hair across our eyes. We stood there, two sad and silent friends in the middle of the desert, in the middle of our lives...waiting.

Suddenly, a piercing cry struck the late summer air. Effie and I looked up to see a huge bird circling directly overhead. Its massive wings outlined against the Valley's famous azure sky. "It's an eagle!" Effie gasped.

"But that's impossible," I whispered back, even though I could clearly see Effie was right, "There aren't any birds like that in the Valley anymore. I even asked your mom once if she remembered seeing any, and she told me she hadn't even seen a hawk in over fifteen years!" Meanwhile the eagle blithely rode the wind, floating almost motionless on a current of the strong Valley wind. Effie and I stood in awe as he glared down at us in defiance. It circled twice more; then with a final and victorious cry the beautiful and mysterious bird disappeared behind "Little Dragon," leaving only the sound of the tapping dream catcher behind.

For possibly the first time since we'd met, I had nothing to say to Effie. I stood next to her, still examining the sky where the eagle had been only a moment before, refusing even to breathe for fear it would break the spell. Had we really seen an eagle? What was it doing here, and how strange that it should appear now, while Effie and I stood in mourning? My Navajo sister didn't appear the least bit confused or in doubt of what she saw.

"It was Lonnie," Effie stated frankly with her usual calm, "he came to see you, and to let us know he's okay. He must have known you were here, and he wanted to say goodbye." We both marveled at the idea, and I did my best to blink back tears of wonder and joy.

"Yeah, you must be right," I said to Effie, trying hard not to cry, and the admission brought a sense of relief and a sense of completion.

We pulled our gaze away from the sky. There was nothing more to see, or to say. We only smiled at each other and instinctively knew it was time to go. Heading back to the car I sent a prayer up to Lonnie, thanking him for the poetic send-off he had given. Just like the owl that had guided Four-Horned Woman's journey back home, Lonnie had come to say all was well, and to prove that he was free. We returned to the car, and

I turned to look back one more time at the little grave site. "That was just so cool Effie," I gushed, no longer able to hold my excitement, "it was just like Lonnie to turn up with style and to impress us."

Effie stopped and laughed, resting her arm on the open car door "Yeah, my brother was a character," she agreed, "He liked to show off like that." We both ducked into the car, and I pulled away without even thinking of how I would manage to drive through the soft sand of the Valley floor. I knew we would get home safely.

EPILOGE: Living, loving and letting go
"There is a big difference between having knowledge, and knowing wisdom." —
Nancy Fresilli, spiritual Counselor

When we returned to Goulding's Elvina was waiting in her car to give me a hug and to tell me good-bye. We explained to her about the eagle and the three of us stood in silence, wondering about it. "You have to come back," Elvina instructed me, "you should bring your husband." I agreed! I now knew that nothing would stop me from returning to the Valley that winter. There would never be a "last trip." This place and its people were a part of me now.

After hugging the ladies goodbye I headed for Keyenta and went by the turn where Lonnie had perished. I always cried a little whenever I left the Valley, but this time felt different. I thought of the eagle, and promised my friend Lonnie that I would finish writing the story of his family, and I would find a way of publishing it somehow. The Valley was my home, and his family had become mine. This had become my story as well as the Yazzies, and I silently swore to Lonnie on that long road to Keyenta that I would do it right. I knew that I would do everything I could to make the Yazzie's life and legends come alive to anyone who read them.

Looking back at the long process of collecting and writing out the Yazzie narrative I can see that I came away from it all with more than an interesting slice of history. I inherited a loving and intriguing family, and with a new respect for a way of life so different from my own. Surprisingly, typing out the last words of the Yazzie story did not bring about the feeling of "what now" I expected. I felt as if their story would continue to unfold before me, as long as I took the time to travel out to the Valley to see them.

Ross and I did indeed make it out to the Valley that winter, and while my husband stood at Lonnie's grave missing his old friend, I told him about the eagle. Every time we come out to see the family we go by Lonnie's final resting place, but I know his spirit isn't there. Lonnie has moved on to some other grand adventure.

I've become closer to Kee and his wife Opal. When I completed the manuscript of his family's life story I brought it out to the Valley, and Kee poured over it. He finished reading it in two days, and told me, "This is really interesting. There are things in here about my family I didn't even know!" We've been out riding the Valley with Effie. She took us through the box canyons where her ancestors lived, and up to the Three Sisters and past John Ford's Point. Ross has always had a way with horses, and after the

Yazzie's herd followed him around for a couple of days he received his new Navajo name. "Sheep Man" is now known as "Horse Man," much to his relief. Suzie is still "alive and kicking" according to Effie, but she's pushing ninety-something and we're preparing ourselves for when she goes. We'll be driving a new generator up to her place sometime soon. She'll finally have electricity at the compound, though what she and her family will do with it remains to be seen. Perhaps she will run the old refrigerator that stood empty in her kitchen for many years.

I know that ending my project with the Yazzies means that, in a way, the journey is over. I will see them less, and I'll miss their warm smiles and good conversation. I will miss the Valley, especially the little things that make it so endearing to me; the scratchy sounds of Navajo radio station AM 660, the taste of the Valley's fine grit in my mouth and the fine layer it leaves on my skin. But I've come to understand that Monument Valley, and the people living there, will somehow lure me back. It is a timeless place, and I like the way the passing of the years don't seem to matter much when I'm there. Life goes on in the Valley, and it is a very good life.

Hogone, Colette Waddell

"We are now about to take our leave and kind farewell to our native land, the country the Great Spirit gave our Fathers. We are on the eve of leaving that country that gave us birth. It is with sorrow we are forced by the white man to quit the scenes of our childhood...we bid farewell to it and all we hold dear." – Charles Hicks, Tsalagi (Cherokee) Vice Chief speaking of The Tail of Tears. November 4, 1838

"Listen to the wind my friend, and hear the sounds of the Valley...for it will find you." Ron Maldonado

Appendix

"Studies serve for delight, for ornament, and for ability." Francis Bacon, *Essays: Of Studies*

When I was a student at UCSB, I took a number of courses from Dr. Brian Fagan. He was my favorite anthropology professor and an amazing teacher. Many of us considered him "old school" because of the way he lectured; without notes, expounding on theories and reciting from memory the anthropological adventures he'd had during the bygone days when there were still cultures left to be discovered. Dr. Fagan taught me an effective way of looking at how one may collect and organize research information. He called "How to Cut the Cat." Whenever he assigned us into groups of study he took the time to help us map out exactly how we would gather, analyze and present out work. This he did on three wide chalkboards placed one after the other, and by the time he'd finished they were all full of horizontal and diagonal lines leading to the culmination of what would become our masterpiece. It was wonderful, and it helped tremendously to break down our tasks in a way that made sense. Fagan's method made our projects much less daunting, and so I never minded that cutting up a cat was an uncomfortably graphic way of presenting this method.

I thought, therefore, that it might be a good idea to explain how I managed to "cut the cat" while pulling together the Yazzie's story. Not everyone who picks up this book will be a student, (at least I hope it appeals to a broader audience), so I've placed this information at the end of my book, so as not to distract from the Yazzie's story. For those interested in the various challenges I encountered while working on "Shade House" and the solutions I chose, this information might offer some perspective on how tricky ethnography can be.

I wanted to share the Yazzie's fascinating story with others, but I also wanted to respect the protocols for any piece based on a culture and its history. This required me to enlist my personal take on the content as well as include academic reference points, both anthropological as well as historical. Fortunately, this approach has become much more accepted among professionals in both disciplines. In his article *Culture Theory in*

Contemporary Ethnohistory, William S. Simmons described the benefits of joining history and anthropology. He wrote:

"Modern historians [have] replaced such mythconceptions (produced by colonial thought) in part through having familiarized themselves with the anthropological point of view. While historians replaced myth with anthropology, anthropologists struggled to reconcile their own myth of timeless primitive with history. One can't do this without taking account both of local-level social and cultural environments that affected that history and the larger-scale social and cultural environments that affected that history. This kind of holistic, diachronic approach is most rewarding when it can be joined to the memories and voices of living people."[185]

I followed the methods introduced by other historians and ethnographers to present a coherent treatment of the Yazzie's life both as Navajos and as individuals choosing to follow or not follow a traditionally Dine' lifestyle.

In much of western culture, older adults live as an untapped resource linking us to our heritage. There are some societies, however, in which elders such as Suzie are regarded as vital members of the community, and caring for them is considered an honor. Unfortunately, this way of thinking has been abandoned in many parts of America. Seniors are often reduced to a troublesome duty at best, or worse, a neglected minority. Yet the grandparents we often warehouse in retirement homes can be treasure chests of information concerning our past. For many Navajo, the elderly remain an asset to the family, both as sources of family history, and as teachers who impart knowledge to their children and grandchildren. This in turn allows the more mature members of the Navajo community to feel useful and enhances the quality of their lives.

To supplement my interviews, I examined both primary literature (in the form of collected Navajo narrative) and secondary sources. This gave me a way of cross-checking and supporting Suzie's information. It also allowed me to confirm dates and events to some extent. The primary literature became particularly important because it permitted me to compare the Yazzie experience to that of others within the Navajo community. I found few Navajo primary sources dating back to the 1800s; however a number of narratives concerning that period were recorded in the early twentieth century. Although some of these testimonials fell under white interpretation, they nonetheless proved invaluable to my work.

My secondary sources included accounts of Anglos from the nineteenth and early twentieth centuries; some of which would be considered quite biased by today's standards. I also used the writings of later historians who demonstrated a more even-handed, or revisionist style. Primary accounts by Anglo-Americans regarding contact with the Navajo helped to contextualize events from Suzie's youth. These sources shed light on the effects of white intrusion into Navajo lands, and comparison between the

---

[185] William S. Simmons, "Culture Theory in Contemporary Ethnohistory." Presidential Address at the 1987 annual conference of the American Society for Ethnohistory, Berkeley, California, Saturday, November 7 *Ethnohistory* 35: I (Winter 1988). 1.

written and oral accounts illuminated differences that existed between Native American and Anglo views.

Storytelling seems a healthy answer to the depression and isolation experienced among the elderly in white culture. So long as our seniors continue to hold memories that are clear, and their hearts are willing, why should we not enlist their assistance in teaching us about our past and sharing their wisdom as well? No textbook could do the job of a living ancestor who witnessed the goings on of our country before we were even a thought. In addition to firsthand accounts, a great deal can be learned by reading outdated historical literature. Indeed, the very bias that caused early historians to paint their own picture of the past may reveal how perceptions of other cultures have evolved over time. Using these two resources together, coupling primary and secondary information can provide a more comprehensive picture not only of life as it was in the past, but also how it was perceived.

Halfway through my interviews with Suzie I hit something of a plateau in my work. I simply did not feel the usual enthusiasm for a process that had finally become comfortable to me. That particular school year began without the usual sense of anticipation I had for my studies. Like climbing the rungs of a ladder I always approached each September as another step closer to my graduation and the degree that would proclaim the huge amounts of obscure historical and anthropological information I had successfully crammed into my head. Yet, this year there were none of the familiar rites to perform that heralded a new school year. I had completed all of the courses required for both of my majors. There were no books to purchase and nothing to read during the summer. This tactic had become necessary when I entered a university operating under the cruel quarter system. With a mere ten weeks in which to absorb volumes of textbooks, I realized that reading the material before the class even started could be a huge advantage.

Now I was somewhat at a loss. I felt strangely unproductive with only my thesis to focus upon. There wasn't even the joy of becoming acquainted with new professors and the courses they taught; no lecture styles to adore or criticize, and no suffering peers with whom I could commiserate. I even decided to forgo the usual purchases of school supplies. I missed the smell of freshly sharpened pencils, and it hardly seemed possible that, at the ripe age of thirty-eight, I had finally reached a point in my academic life where the end of study was near. This little funk lasted a good four weeks before I finally willed myself to put ass to chair and get some work done. I met with my mentors, checked out mountains of books on my subject, and rented a locker for five bucks that was close to the library in which to store them. I then booked a trip to the Valley, and prepared the last of my questions to Suzie. I suppose everyone has these moments of self-doubt, and they can be exasperating. What I learned, however, was the value of trudging through those moments until I opened that one book, or transcribed a past interview that gave me the traction I needed to once more come to enjoy the work. It was a case of ignoring my doubt until it went away on its own.

In order to focus I was forced to consider my project as a task that had to be completed in spite of my feelings of inadequacy. The romance of recording the life history of a Navajo family dwindled, particularly as I discovered how the Navajo nation had become affected by white culture. To me, the initial appeal of studying a different society had always been the way it contrasted my own. When I first met Suzie and the rest of the Yazzies I had never been on an Indian reservation, and I had certainly never known a Native American personally. Our initial encounter seemed magical; their environment and culture unique and somehow mysterious. The very difference in their way of life pulled at me and produced within me a desire to learn more about the Navajo. I quickly came to see, however, that this was not a society completely isolated from western ideals. Indeed, few of the so-called "primitive" societies remain hidden away, waiting to be studied by doe-eyed anthropology students. Native American societies were examined long before I'd stumbled onto the reservation. Some tribes had died out altogether from disease or outright extermination. The Indian societies that had survived were already well chronicled in my history and anthropology books. I had to find a different way of looking at the Navajo.

I decided to allow the Yazzies the chance to review all of my work so that they could ultimately determine what information should be left out and what to let stand. I would steer the interviews away from issues of alcoholism or abuse unless the family chose to speak of them. These topics did, in fact, come up on occasion. I was obliged to discuss with each interviewee whether that segment of our discussion should remain in the record. Information of a sacred nature never came up, so I didn't have to fret over how to eliminate this type of data. The youngest family member I interviewed was in her twenties, so I decided there were no underage issues to contend with. I made very clear to the Yazzies that all information was their own "intellectual property" to the point that I think I became a little tiresome. All things considered, it was the Yazzie's idea that I record their family history in the first place, so I felt confident that I had not broken any major rules on the reservation. I only hoped that my depiction of the family could remain honest, while at the same time show them in a positive light. These people represented to me just one of the many stories of survival that many other Navajo families share and Navajo survival was the ultimate message that emerged during my interviews.

Bibliography

Standard Western American History
Primary Sources:
Aberle, David Friend. <u>The Peyote Religion among the Navajo</u>. New York: Wenner-Gren Foundation for Anthropological Research, 1966.

Adams, William Yewdale. Shonto: <u>A Study of the Role of the Trader in a Modern Navajo community.</u> Washington, U.S.: Government Printing Office, 1963.

Blanchard, Kendall A. <u>The Economics of Sainthood; religious change among the Rimrock Navajos.</u> Rutherford, N.J.: Fairleigh Dickonson University Press, 1977.

Chiao, Chien. <u>Continuation of Tradition in Navajo Society.</u> Nankang, Taiwan: Academia Sinica, Institute of Ethnology, 1971.

Downs, James F. <u>Animal Husbandry in Navajo Society and Culture.</u> Berkeley and Los Angeles: University of California Press, 1964.

Downs, James F. <u>The Navajo.</u> New York: Holt, Rinehart & Winston, 1972.

Gwyther, G. "Navajo Indian Reservation." *Overland Monthly* 10 (1873): 123.

Kelly, Lawrence C. <u>Navajo Roundup: Selected Correspondence of Kit Carson's Expedition Against the Navajo, 1863-1865.</u> Boulder: The Pruett Publishing Company, 1970.

Moon, Samuel. <u>Tall Sheep: Harry Goulding Monument Valley Trader.</u> Norman: University of Oklahoma Press, 1992.

Newcomb, Franc Johnson, Stanley Fishler and Mary C. Wheelwright. <u>A Study of Navajo Symbolism.</u> Cambridge: Harvard Museum Publishers, 1956.

Richardson, Gladwell. <u>Navajo Trader.</u> Tucson: The University of Arizona Press, 1986.

Roberts, John M. <u>Three Navajo Households; a comparative study in small group culture.</u> Cambridge: Peabody Museum Publishers, 1951.

Simmons, William S. "Culture Theory in Contemporary Ethnohistory." Presidential Address at the 1987 annual conference of the American Society for Ethnohistory. Berkeley, California. Saturday, November 7 (*Ethnohistory* 35: I Winter 1988).

Wagner, Sallie. Wide Ruins, Memories from a Navajo Trading Post. Albuquerque: University of New Mexico Press, 1997.

Vogt, Evon Zartman. Navajo Veterans: a study of changing values. Cambridge: Peabody Museum Publishers, 1951.

Additional Research Material – Not Referenced.

Reichard, Gladys. Spider Women, A Story of Navajo Weavers and Chanters. Glorieta: The Rio Grande Press, 1934.

Primary: Government Documents

Lake Mohonk Indian Conference, First Session. October 8, 1890. Twenty-Second Annual Report of the Board of Indian Commissioners for the Year 1890. Washington, D.C.: GPO, 1891.

Additional Research Material – Not Referenced

Jenkins, Myra Ellen and Ward Alan Minge. Navajo Indians II: Navajo Activities Affecting the Acoma-Laguna Area, 1746-1910. New York: Garland Publishing Inc., 1974.

Native American

Primary Sources:

Chee, Patty et al. (Staff of Lake Valley Title Project.) Oral Stories of the Long Walk. Crownpoint: Lake Valley Navajo School, 1994.

Crapanzano, Vincent. The Fifth World of Forster Bennett. New York: The Viking Press, 1972.

Johnson, Broderick H. ed. Navajo Stories of the Long Walk Period. Tsaile, Navajo Nation: Navajo Community College Press, 1973.

Kelly & Francis. Navajo Sacred Places. Bloomington: Indiana University Press, 1994.

Reichard, Gladys. Dezba, Woman of the Desert. Glorieta: The Rio Grande Press, 1971.

Roberts, David. "The Long Walk to Bosque Redondo." *Smithsonian* 28, no.9 (December 1997): 46.

Sapir, Edward. Navajo Texts. New York. Iowa City: AMS Press, Inc., 1942.

Stewart, Irene. A Voice in her Tribe, A Navajo woman's own story. Socorro: Ballena Press, 1980.

Teller, Joanne and Norman Blackwater. The Navajo Skinwalker, Wichcraft, and Related Phenomena. Chinle: Infinity Horn Publishing, 1997.

Zolbrod, Paul G. Dine bahane' The Navajo Creation Story. Albuquerque: University or New Mexico Press, 1984.

Secondary Sources:
Behar. Ruth. Translated Woman. Boston: Beacon Press, 1993.

Bulow, Ernie. Navajo Taboos. Gallup: Buffalo Medicine Books, 1991.

Churchhill, Ward. A Little Matter of Genocide: Holocaust and denial in the Americas 1492 to the present. San Francisco: City Lights Books, 1997.

Fagan, Brian M. People of the Earth. New York: Longman, Inc., 1998.

Green, Rayna. "Native American Women." Chicago: The University of Chicago, *Journal of Women in Culture and Society*, 1980, vol. 6, no. 21.

Hoxie, Frederick E. and Peter Iverson, eds. Indians in American History: An Introduction. Illinois: Harlan Davidson, Inc., 1998.

Hoxie, Frederick E. "The Problems of Indian History." *The Social Science Journal*, vol.25, no. 4, 1998.

Kluckhohn, Clyde and Dorthea Leighton. Children of the People. Cambridge: Harvard University Press, 1948.

Kluckhohn, Clyde and Dorothea Leighton. The Navajo. Garden City: Anchor Books, 1962.

Kluckhohn, Clyde, W.W. Hill and Lucy Wales Kluckhohn. Navajo Material Culture. Cambridge: Harvard University Press, 1971.

Locke, Raymond Friday. The Book of the Navajo. Los Angeles: Mankind Publishing Company, 1992.

Moore, William Haas. Chiefs, Agents and Soldiers. Albuquerque: University of New Mexico Press, 1994.

Reichard, Gladys. Navajo Religion. New York: Bollingen Foundation, 1950.

Rollins, Peter C. and John E. O'Conner. Hollywood's Indians. Lexington: The University Press of Kentucky, 1998.

Roessel, Ruth. Navajo Studies of the Long Walk Period. Tsaile (Navajo Nation): Navajo Community College Press, 1973.

Roessel, Ruth. Women in Navajo Society. Rough Rock: Navajo Resource Center, 1981.

Schwarz, Maureen Trudelle. Molded in the Image of Changing Woman, Navajo views on the human body and personhood. Tucson: University of Arizona Press. 1997.

Scott, James C. Domination and the Arts of Resistance, Hidden Transcripts. London: Yale University Press, 1990.

Thompson, Gerald. The Army and the Navajo. Tucson: The University of Arizona Press, 1986.

Trafzer, Clifford E. The Kit Carson Campaign: The Last Great Navajo War. Norman: University of Oklahoma Press, 1982.

Trahant, Lenora Begay. The Success of the Navajo Arts and Crafts Enterprise. New York: Walker and Company, 1996.

Trigger, Bruce and Wilcomb Washburn. Cambridge History of the Native Peoples of the Americas. Cambridge: Cambridge University Press, 1989.

Young, Robert W. The Role of the Navajo in the Southwestern Drama. Gallup: The Gallup Independent, 1968.

Additional Resource Material – Not Referenced

Baily, Garrick & Roberta Glenn Baily. A History of the Navajos: The reservation years. Santa Fe: School of American Research Press, 1986.

Roessel, Ruth. <u>Navajo Studies at Navajo Community College.</u> Many Farms: Navajo Community College Press, 1974.

Made in the USA
San Bernardino, CA
28 July 2020